COMPENDIUM
OF THE
WORLD'S
LANGUAGES

BY

GEORGE L. CAMPBELL

ROUTLEDGE

LONDON AND NEW YORK

First published 1991
by Routledge
11 New Fetter Lane, London EC4P 4EE

Simultaneously published in the USA and Canada
by Routledge
a division of Routledge, Chapman and Hall, Inc.
29 West 35th Street, New York, NY 10001

© George Campbell 1991

Typeset by Computype Limited, Horton Parade, Horton Road,
West Drayton, Middlesex UB7 8EP

Printed in England by Clays Ltd, St Ives plc

British Library Cataloguing in Publication Data
Campbell, George L.
Compendium of the world's languages.
1. Languages. Dictionaries
I. Title
413

ISBN 0-415-02937-6 (set)
ISBN 0-415-06978-5 (Volume I)
ISBN 0-415-06979-3 (Volume II)

Library of Congress Cataloging-in-Publication Data
Campbell, George L.
Compendium of the world's languages / George L. Campbell.
p. cm.
Includes bibliographical references.
1. Language and languages.   I. Title.
P371.C36 1990   90-35827
401'.2—dc20   CIP

CONTENTS

COMPENDIUM
OF THE
WORLD'S
LANGUAGES

——

VOLUME II
MAASAI TO ZUNI

MAASAI

INTRODUCTION

This member of the Nilo-Saharan family is the language of about 3,000 to 4,000 pastoral nomads in Kenya and Tanzania. Some educational material in written Maasai has been produced in Kenya in the last few decades.

SCRIPT

Roman; the script does not reflect the distinction between open and closed vowels, nor does it show tone.

PHONOLOGY

Consonants

plosives: p, t, k
implosives: 6, ɗ, ɟ
affricate: tʃ: the voiced correlative is implosive: ɗʒ
fricatives: s, ʃ, j, w
nasals: m, n, ɲ, ŋ
lateral and flap: l, r, rr

The plosives are softened after a nasal, giving [mb, nd, ng], and the implosives are usually pre-nasalized: [mɓ, nɗ, nɟ]. There is therefore an important distinction between plosive /mb/ and implosive /mɓ/. In medial position, /p, t, k/ are realized as [v/w, dh, γ].

Vowels

long and short: i/ɪ, e/ɛ, a/ɑ, o/ɔ, u/ʊ

The distinction here is phonemic, and extends to the diphthongs; e.g. /ei/ eɪ/ /ɛɪ/. In this article /ɪ/, /ɛ/, /ɔ/ are marked by subscript dot: i̦, e̦, o̦, but note that the distinction between the pairs of phonemes is not made in the orthography.

Tone

There are three tonal levels: mid, high, and low, plus a high-to-low glide. Tonal sandhi takes place at junctures. Tone in Maasai is of crucial phonemic importance; cf. *kĩdǫ́l nĩnyę́* 'we see him'; *kĩdǫl nĩnyę̀* 'he sees you'; *ędǫl entĩto* 'he sees the girl'; *ędǫl entĩtó* 'the girl sees him'.

MORPHOLOGY AND SYNTAX

Noun

Maasai nouns are masculine or feminine. Gender is marked in both singular and plural by coded prefix:

Masculine		Feminine	
Singular	*Plural*	*Singular*	*Plural*
ol/ǫl	il/ĩl	en/ęn	in/ĩn

The *-l* of the masculine prefix is elided before *s, l, j*; e.g. *o.soit* 'stone', plural *i.soito*. Similarly, *-n* of the feminine prefix is elided before a nasal or *s, j, w, r, l*.

NUMBER
A plural form is made by various affixes, by modulation of vocalic final, by tonal change or by suppletion: e.g. *ol.dia* 'dog', plural *il.die.in*; *ǫl.tungani* 'person', plural *ĩl.tungan.a*; *ǫl.cani* 'tree' plural *ĩl.keek*.

GENITIVE RELATIONSHIP
This is expressed by means of a particle coded for both terms: e.g.

> masculine object possessed by masculine: *lǫ*;
> masculine object possessed by feminine: *lę*;
> masculine object possessed by plural: *lǫǫ*;
> feminine object possessed by masculine: *ę*;
> feminine object possessed by feminine: *ę*;
> feminine object possessed by plural: *ǫǫ*.

Examples: *ǫl cǫrę lǫ layioni* 'the friend of the boy'; *ǫl cǫre lǫǫ layiok* 'the friend of the boys'; *ĩl cǫręia lǫǫ layiok* 'the friends of the boys'.

Adjective

The adjective follows the noun as attribute, precedes it as predicate and takes plural forms: e.g. *olosowuan tǫrrǫnǫ* 'bad buffalo'; *tǫrrǫnǫ olosowuan* 'the buffalo is bad'.

Pronoun

The independent forms are: singular: 1 *nanu*, 2 *iyie*, 3 *nĩnyę*; plural: 1 *iyiook*, 2 *ĩntaĩ*, 3 *nĩncę*. These are seldom used, as the verbal forms are equipped with personal prefixes (see below).

POSSESSIVE ADJECTIVES
These follow the noun, with gender and number concord: e.g. the masculine forms *lai* 'my', *lino* 'your' *lęnyę* 'his/her/its'; the equivalent feminine forms drop

the *l*-: *ai*, *ino*, *ẹnyẹ*: e.g. *osikiria lẹnyẹ ẹldẹ* 'that is his donkey'

DEMONSTRATIVES
Also coded for gender and number, for immediacy of topic, and for degree of spatial removal: masc. *ẹle*, fem. *ẹna*, pl. *kulọ*, *kuna* 'this, these'; masc. *ẹldẹ*, fem. *ẹnda*, pl. *kuldọ*, *kunda* 'that, those'.

INTERROGATIVE PRONOUN
Masc. *(aị)ngaị* 'who?' pl. *lọọngaị*; *(k)alo* 'what?' pl. *(k)akua*.

RELATIVE PRONOUN
The relative particle is marked for gender, person, and number. The third person forms are:

	Singular	Plural
masculine	o-/ọ-	oo-
feminine	na-	naa-

Examples: *ọl.tungani o.gol* 'a man who is strong'; *ọl.ọ kuẹțita* 'he who is running'.
   When the antecedent is first or second person, the relative particle is masc. *l(ị)*, fem. *n(ị)*, pl. *n(ị)*: e.g. *ọl.tungani l.a.lam* 'the man whom I avoid'; *ọl.tungani lị.kị.lam* 'the man whom we avoid'; *ọl.tungani l.aa.lam* 'the man who avoids me'.
   The form is negated by -*m*-: e.g. *ọl.tungani lẹ.m.ẹ.lam* 'the man whom he does not avoid' or 'the man who does not avoid him'. Tone is the deciding factor.

Numerals

The system is decimal. The forms for 1, 2, 3, 4, 7, 9 are marked for gender, and may have a locative referential form: e.g. for 1, masc. *obo*, fem. *nabo*, loc. *nebo*.
   The masculine forms for the numerals 1 to 10 are: *obo*, *aare*, *okuni*, *oonguan*, *imiet*, *ịlẹ*, *oopishana*, *isiet*, *oondo*, *tọmọn*. 11–19 = ten + 1 etc., *tọmọn ọ obo*; 20 is *titikam*; 30 *tọmọni uni*; 40 *artam*; 60 *ntọmọni ịlẹ*; 100 is *iip*.

Verb

Two classes are distinguished: stem verbs, and verbs with *i*- prefix.

CONJUGATION
The formula for the present tense is personal marker – stem (invariable) – ending (second person plural only): e.g. from *rany* 'to sing':

	Singular	Plural
1	**a**.rany	**kị**.rany
2	**ị**.rany	**ị**.ranyịranya
3	**ẹ**.rany	**ẹ**.rany

To form the continuous tense, -*ịta* is added: e.g. *a.rany.ịta* 'I am (going on) singing'.

PAST TENSE

The formula is personal marker + *-ta-* + stem + *-a*: e.g. *a.ta.rany.a* 'I sang'. There are subjunctive and imperative moods; also a sequential tense.

NEGATIVE

m-/mi- precedes the personal marker in the present tense: e.g. ***m**.a.rany* 'I do not sing'; *mị.kị.rany.ịta* 'we are not singing'. The past tense negative marker is *eịtụ*: e.g. *eịtụ a.rany* 'I didn't sing' (i.e. the *present* tense form negated by *eịtụ*).

PRONOMINAL OBJECT

A third person pronominal object is not overtly marked; first and second person objects are marked by *aa-* and *ki-* respectively: cf. *a.dọl* 'I see him/her/it/them'. *A.dọl ninyẹ* limits the referent to the singular. Plural referents are added from the independent pronominal series: e.g. *ẹ.dọl iyiook* 'he sees us'.

In cases like *kị.dọl* 'we see him', etc. or 'he/she sees you', a difficulty arises which can only be settled by tone.

PASSIVE

Marked by an *-ị* suffix: e.g. *e.ịnọs.ị* 'is eaten'; *m.e.ịnọs.ị* 'is not eaten'.

Inchoative, reiterative, potential aspects of an action are generated by means of auxiliary verbs: e.g. *a.ịdịp* 'to finish doing something'; *a.ịdịm* 'to be able to do something'. These auxiliaries are followed by the subjunctive in *pee-*: e.g. *pee.a.rany* 'that I may/might sing'.

Some irregular verbs have different stems for plural number and past tense: e.g. *a.lo* 'to go', plural base *puo*; past tense *shomo*.

Prepositions

These are noun stems minus the gender prefix; invariable.

Word order

Noun, S or O, follows verb, and O follows S where both occur; i.e. VSO is normal. Intonation helps to clarify meaning. O may precede V for emphasis.

1 TE 'ngiterunoto etii ororei, ore ele 'rorei
naa tenebo eng'Ai, na eng'Ai ele 'rorei.
2 Neija eitu engiterunoto tenebo eng'Ai.
3 Neitobirake 'ndokitin poki te ninye; na
teneme ninye anata metii endoki nabo naito-
birake. 4 Atwa ninye etii engishon; naa
ore engishon na ewañgan oltoñgana. 5 Ne-
wañgu ewañgan ti atwa enaimin; kake eito
etum enaimin. 6 Nelotu oltoñgani oiriwake
oiñgwaa eng'Ai, oji engarna Johana. 7 Nee-
wo ele aako shakeni, pe etum ataa shakeni
le 'wañgan, pe etum iltoñgana airuko enga-
rake ninye. 8 Neme ewañgan ninye, kake
keriwake metaa shakeni le'wañgan.

MACASSARESE

INTRODUCTION

Macassarese belongs to the Malayo-Polynesian branch of the Austronesian family, and is spoken in South Sulawesi by about half a million people. It is fairly close to Buginese (*see* **Buginese**) and has a literature.

SCRIPT

The Buginese-Macassarese syllabary is used. Macassarese lacks the neutral vowel /ə/ found in Buginese, and accordingly the diacritic ', which denotes /ə/ in Buginese, is used in Macassarese to indicate that a nasal consonant follows a vowel so marked.

PHONOLOGY

As in Buginese, minus /ə/ as mentioned above. The vowels are /i, e, a, o, u/, short and long, where *i* represents both /i/ and /ɪ/. In his grammar of the language, Matthes (1858) makes a distinction between 'soft' and 'sharp' articulation of the vowels; the 'sharp' being produced by sudden suspension of the air stream, akin to glottalization. The sharp vowels may be accompanied by nasalization or by gemination of the following consonant. The distinction is phonemic, e.g. in the pronominal marker system: 2nd person *ki*, for example, is 'sharp' to distinguish it from 3rd person -(*k*)*i*: cf. *ki.lampa* 'you go' (with sharp vowel in *ki*); *kebo.k.i* 'he is white'.

MORPHOLOGY AND SYNTAX

Noun

As in many Malayo-Polynesian languages, derivatory nouns are formed in Macassarese by adding prefixes and/or suffixes to stem or stems: cf.

lukka 'to steal'	pa.lukka 'thief'
sare 'to give'	pa.sare 'gift'
ranu 'to hope'	pa.ranu.w.ang 'hope'
lompo 'big'	ka.lompo.w.ang 'bigness'
koki 'bad'	ka.kodi.y.ang 'evil'

GENDER

In so far as human beings are concerned, gender may be indicated by the addition of *buranne* for male, *bainne* for female referents: e.g. with *ana* 'child': *ana buranne* 'son'; *ana bainne* 'daughter'. There are similarly coded words for animals.

The affixed definite article, corresponding to Buginese *-e*, is *-a*; e.g. *djarang* 'horse', *djarang.a* 'the horse'; *tupanrita* 'scholar', *tupanritaya* 'the scholar', where *-y-* is inserted as euphonic linking element. Similarly *-w-* is used in *ta(w)u.w.a* 'the man', from ta(*w*)*a* 'man'. /k/ appears as a linking element after a sharp vowel: *balla* 'house', *balla.k.a* 'the house'.

Plurality can be expressed by such modifiers as *djai* 'many', *sikamma* 'all'; these take the definite article: e.g. *ta(w)u djai.y.a* 'the many men'. The prefix *si-* emphasizes singularity: e.g. *si-ta(w)u* 'one man'.

There is no form of declension. As object, a noun usually follows the verb: e.g. *na.sare.yang.a anjdjo kongkonga* 'he gives me this/that dog'. (Where *sare* is the verb root to give, *na-* is the third person subject marker, *-yang-* is a relating element, and *-a* is the first person marker). For emphasis, the noun object may precede: *anjdjo kongkonga nasareyanga*.

A dative is made with the preposition *ri-*: *akutanang ri.karaenga* 'to ask the prince'. *See also* **Preposition**, below.

A definite genitival relationship can be expressed by means of the nasal link element; the order is possessed – possessor: e.g. *balla karaeng* 'a prince's house'; *balla.na karaeng.a* 'the house of the prince'; *tuwa.ng patanna* 'belonging to you (Sir, Mr)'.

Adjective

The adjective follows the noun: e.g. *balla lompo* 'big house', *ta(w)u badji* 'good man' and takes the definite article: *ta(w)u kodi.y.a* 'the bad man', *balla badji.k.a* 'the good house'.

Ma- + adjective stem is a stative verb: e.g. *ma.lompo* 'to be big', *ma.djai* 'to be many'.

A comparative is made by means of the suffix *-ang*, with euphonic sandhi at junctures: e.g. *labu* 'long', – *labuwang* 'longer'; *kebo* 'white' – *kebo.k.ang* 'whiter'. The prefix *pa-* also makes a comparative: e.g. from *tinggi* 'high', *lompo* 'big': *pa.tinggi = tinggi.y.ang* 'higher'; *pa.lompo = lompo.w.ang* 'bigger'.

Pronoun

The pronoun in Macassarese has full (independent) and bound forms:

		Full		*Bound*
singular	1	(*i*)*nakke*		*a* (sharp vowel), *ku*
	2	(*i*)*kau*, (*i*)*katte*		*nu, ko, ta, ki*
	3		*iya, i, na*	
plural	1	(*i*)*katte*, (*i*)*kambe*		*ki, ta, kang, mang*
	2	(*i*)*katte*, (*i*)*kau*		*nu, ko, ta, ki*
	3		*iya, i, na*	

Socio-linguistic considerations play a part here. Thus, in the second person forms, (*i*)*katte* + *ta*/*ki* is more formal than (*i*)*kau* + *nu*/*ko*.

The bound forms provide the subject and object pronominal forms affixed to verbs, and also function as possessive markers: e.g. *lompo.w.i* 'he/she/it is big'; *battu.w.i* 'he/she/it comes'; *nu.tjini* 'you see'; *nu.lampa* 'you depart'; *ku.tjini.ko* 'I see you'; *ta.ku.w.asseng.a.i* 'I don't know it' (where *ta...a* is negating circumfix); *na.buntuli.ki* 'he calls you'.

POSSESSIVE

ka.badji.kang.ku 'my welfare'; *ka.badji.kang.ta* 'your welfare'.

DEMONSTRATIVE PRONOUN

-*a* and -*i* are affixed to nouns; *anne* corresponds to Indonesian *ini*; *antu*/*anjdjo* seems to refer to more distant objects.

INTERROGATIVE PRONOUN

(*i*)*nai* 'who?'; *apa* 'what?'; *kereyang* 'which?': e.g. *ta*(*w*)*u apa* 'which man?'; *balla kereyanga ki.pamantangi* 'in which house do you live?'

RELATIVE PRONOUN

None; relative clauses are formed by apposition: e.g. *bili.na.katinro.wi.ya* 'the room (in which) he sleeps in it'.

Numerals

1–10: *sere, ruwa, tallu, appa, lima, annang, tudju, sagantudju, salapang, sampulo*; 11 *sampulo assere*; 12 *sampulo anruwa*; 13 *sampulo antallu*; 20 *ruwampulo*; 30 *tallumpulo*; 100 *si.bilangang*.

Sandhi is observed at junctures: e.g. in 20, -*m*- links *ruwa* and *pulo*. In *djarang ruwa.ng.kayu* 'two horses', the link element is -*ng*-. Similarly, *lima.n.ta*(*w*)*ung* 'five years'.

Verb

Macassarese has root verbs and derivatives: e.g. *a*- forms verbs from nouns: *djarang* 'horse' – *a.djarang* 'to ride a horse'.

> *A*- + homorganic nasal is an active/transitive formant (in general, non-nasal initial is associated with stative verbs, though there are exceptions): e.g. *tjini* 'see' – *anj.tjini.ki* 'to see him'; *polong* 'a cut' – (*a*)*molong* 'to cut something'; *koko* 'a bite' – (*a*)*ngoko* 'to bite something'.

> *Ni*- is a passive formant: e.g. *buno* 'to die' – *ni.buno* 'to be killed'. This formant may also be added to nouns and adjectives: e.g. *edja* 'red': *ni.y.edja* 'to become red, to redden'; *giring.giring* 'a kind of bell' – *ni.giring.giring* 'be fitted with bells'.

> *Ta*- is also a passive formant: *sungke* 'open' – *ta.sungke* 'opened, be opened'.

> *Pa*- and *i*- are causatives: e.g. *tallu* 'three' – *tallu.w.i* 'divide into three';

labu 'long': *labu.w.i* 'lengthen'.

Si- is the reflexive/reciprocal formant: *tjini* 'to see' – *si.tjini* 'to see each other'.

There is no conjugation. Personal pronouns must be used, either full or bound forms: e.g. *inakke asare = kusare* 'I give'; *inakke nisare = kunisare* 'I am given'.

Specification of tense is optional: *ta-* may indicate past, *ka* future: e.g. *sungke* 'open' – *ta.sungke* 'opened'. Various temporal particles are also available for this purpose: e.g. *leba* (past), *sallang* (future): *inakke leba ni.sare* 'I have been given'; *inakke asare sallang* 'I shall give' (or, *kusare sallang*).

NEGATION

ta (bound form of *taena*): e.g. *takuwassengako* 'I don't know you' (*ku* 'I'; *-ko* 'you'; *ta...a* = negative).

Prepositions

Ri is an all-purpose preposition, meaning 'in, on, at, to', etc.: e.g. *amanta.yi ri.Djumpandang* 'he lives in Macassar'; *battu.wi.i ri.Djumpandang* 'he comes from M.'; *mange ri.Djumpandang* 'he goes to M.'

Word order

SVO is basic in active construction, but OSV is possible.

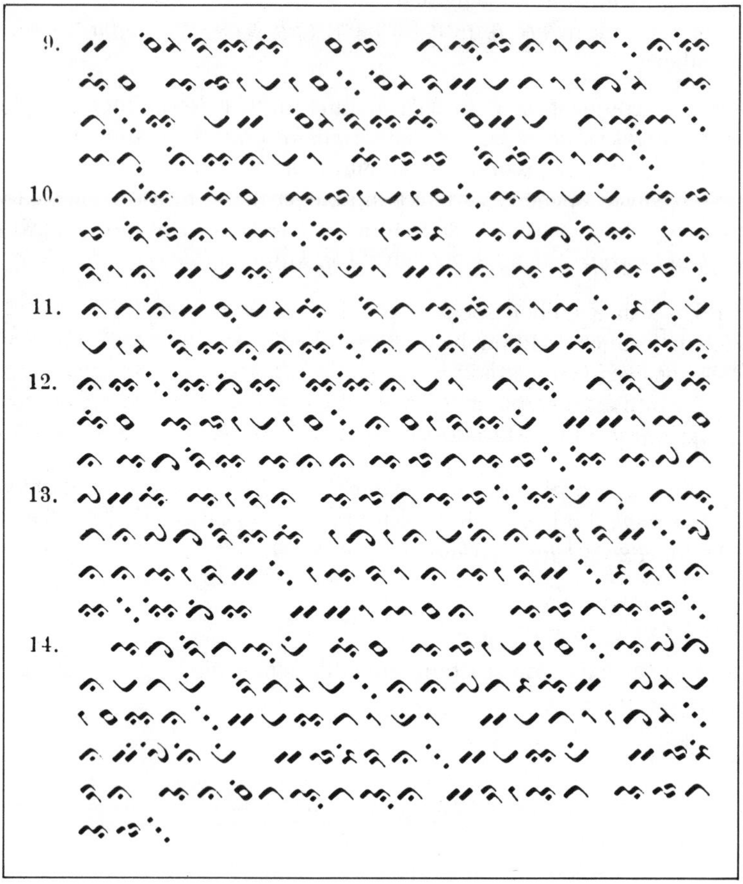

9. [Macassarese script]

10. [Macassarese script]

11. [Macassarese script]

12. [Macassarese script]

13. [Macassarese script]

14. [Macassarese script]

(Matt. 6: 9–15)

MACEDONIAN

INTRODUCTION

There are about a million speakers of this South Slavonic language in the Macedonian National Republic of Yugoslavia; an estimated half-million Macedonians live in Greece and Bulgaria. The literary language dates from the early nineteenth century, but it was not until after the First World War that any organized movement for Macedonian cultural expression got under way.

SCRIPT

Cyrillic with certain extra and modified letters: these are, with their phonetic values:

Ѓ = /d'/, Ј = /j/, Љ = /l/, Њ = /n/, Ќ = /t'/, Џ = /dʒ/, Ѕ = /dz/

PHONOLOGY

Consonants

    stops: p, b, t, d, k, g; ǩ and v́ are mid-palatal plosives, which approximate to palatalized: t', d'
    affricates: ts, dz, tʃ, dʒ
    fricatives: f, v, s, z, ʃ, ʒ, j, x
    nasals: m, n, ɲ, (ŋ)
    laterals and flap: l, ł, ʎ, r

Vowels

    i, ε, a, ɔ, u

All short – Macedonian has no long vowels. All vowels retain their full value in unstressed position (i.e. there is no reduction as in Russian). Vocalic *r* occurs: e.g. *smrt* 'death'.

Stress

On antepenult in words of three or more syllables, on first syllable of disyllable: e.g. *plánina* 'mountain': *planínata* 'the mountain', i.e. the stress shifts when a syllable is added to three-syllable word.

Both the first and second palatalizations are observed in Macedonian:

first: e.g. *rekov* 'I said' – *reče* 'he said'
second: e.g. *volk* 'wolf' – pl. *volci*

MORPHOLOGY AND SYNTAX

Three genders: masculine, feminine, and neuter. The case system has been almost entirely lost: a trace is found in nouns denoting male kin, which end in a consonant: these have an accusative form in *-a*, often followed by a dative enclitic pronoun: e.g. *brata mi* 'my brother (acc.)'. Syntactic relations in general are established with the help of prepositions, e.g. genitive with *od*, *na*, dative with *do*, *pri*, instrumental with *so*, locative with *v(o)*, *na*, *pri* (*see* **Preposition**, below).

Masculine plural forms are: *-ovci*, *-i*, *-ce*, *-ovi*, *-ni*: e.g. *grad* 'town' – *gradovi*; *prst* 'finger' – *prsti*. Feminine nouns in *-a* or a consonant make a plural in *-i*: *žena* 'woman' – *ženi*. Neuter nouns change *-o* to *-a*; *-e* to *-in'a*: e.g. *pole* 'field' – *polin'a*.

Macedonian has three postfixed definite articles:

(a) masc. *-ot*, fem. *-ta*, neut. *-to*; pl. masc./fem. *-te*, neut. *-ta*. This article is neutral, used when degree of removal need not be specified: e.g. *grad.ot* 'the town'; *žena.ta* 'the woman'.

(b) *-ov*, *-va*, *-vo*; pl. *-ve*, *-va*: used to emphasize proximate locus: 'this here'.

(c) *-on*, *-na*, *-no*: pl. *-ne*, *-na*: the distal correlative: 'that there'.

Adjective

Marked for gender in the singular; one common plural form; e.g. *crven* – *crvena* – *crveno*; pl. *crveni* 'red'. The attributive adjective precedes the noun and can take the article: e.g. *arna.ta kniga* 'the good book' (*aren* 'good'). For the comparative grade, *po-* is prefixed to the positive: e.g. *ubav* 'beautiful' – *po.ubav*; *golem* 'big' – *po.golem*.

Pronoun

PERSONAL

The personal pronouns have indirect and direct objective forms:

	Singular				*Plural*		
	1	2	3 masc.	3. fem.	1	2	3
nominative	jas	ti	toj	taa	nie	vie	tie
indirect	mene/mi	tebe/ti	nemu/mu	nejze/i	nam/ni	vam/vi	nim/im
direct	mene/me	tebe/te	nego/go	nea/ja	nas/ne	vas/ve	niv/gi

The neuter third person pronoun *to(v)a* has the same indirect and direct forms as the masculine.

Full and shortened forms of the objective pronouns are often used together: e.g. *tebe te vide* 'he saw you (sing.)'.

POSSESSIVE PRONOUN
moj, moja, moe; pl. *moi*; similarly, *tvoj, naš, vaš*. The third person forms are: masc. *negov -a/-o/-i*; fem. *nejzin -a/-o/-i*; pl. *nivni -a/-o/-i*. These forms are often used with the postfixed article and a linking element *-i-* where necessary: e.g. *negov.i.ot* 'his' (masc. referent).

DEMONSTRATIVE PRONOUN/ADJECTIVE
ovoj 'this'; *toj/onoj* 'that'; these are marked for gender, and have plural forms *ovie, tie*.

INTERROGATIVE PRONOUN
koj 'who?'; *što* 'what?'. *Koj* has acc. *kogo*, dat. *komu*.

RELATIVE PRONOUN
koj/što.

Numerals

1 *eden/edna/edno*; 2 masc. *dva*, fem./neut. *dve*; 3–10 *tri, četiri, pet, šest, sedum, osum, devet, deset*; 11 *edinaeset* = /edinajse/; 12 *dvanaeset* = /dvanajse/; 20 *dvaeset*; 30 *trieset*; 40 *četirieset*; 100 *sto*.

Verb

A notable feature of Macedonian is the presence of a perfect tense, constructed, as in the Romance languages, by means of an auxiliary and a past participle: thus, the auxiliary *imam* 'I have', plus the neuter past participle passive: *imam raboteno* 'I have worked'.

The passive participle of an intransitive verb is used with *sum* 'I am': e.g. *jas sum dojden* 'I have come'; participle shows concord with subject.

TENSE STRUCTURE
The aorist and the imperfect are both present. *-am* has been generalized as the first person singular ending of the present tense of all verbs.

Present tense: the endings are: *-am, -š, -Ø*; pl. *-me, -te, -(a)t*: e.g. *vidam* 'I see', *vidiš, vidi*; pl. *vidime, vidite, vidat*.

Aorist: is formed from perfective verbs, and expresses completed action vouched for by speaker: e.g. *dojdov* 'I (start to) come, I came': *dojdov, dojdeš, dojde*; pl. *dojdovme, dojdovte, dojdoa*.

Imperfect: progressive action in the past, vouched for by speaker: the endings are the same as those of the aorist except in second and third person singular: e.g. *idev* 'I was going', *ideše, ideše*.

Future: the present tense can be formed from verbs of either aspect, but the perfective form does not have a future meaning. A future tense is made by prefixing the particle *ḱe* to the present of either aspect: e.g. *ḱe idam* 'I shall go': *ḱe pokažam* 'I shall show'. This future is negated by the formula *nema da* + present: e.g. *nema da idam* 'I shan't go'.

Imperative: *-i, -ete* for consonant stems; *-j, -jte* for vowel stems: e.g. *idi, idite*; *stoj, stojte*.

A gerund is formed from imperfective verbs; it is invariable: e.g. *idejḱi* 'going'; *begajḱi* 'running'.

PARTICIPLES
Past participle active: *-l, -la, -lo*; common pl. *-le*; past participle passive: *-t, -ta, -to*; common pl. *-ti*; or, *-n, -na, -no*; pl. *-ni*.

As noted above, compound tenses are made by using these participles with the auxiliaries *imam* and *sum*. In the compound form with *sum*, the auxiliary itself can be dropped in the third person singular or plural: e.g. *sum begal* 'I have been running': *begal* 'he has been running'; *begale* 'they have been running'.

Prekažanost: the inferential form corresponding to *preizkazano naklonenie* in Bulgarian (*see* **Bulgarian**) is used in the second and third persons in Macedonian: e.g. *toj rabotel* (= compound past minus auxiliary) *cel den* '(they tell me) he worked all day'.

A pluperfect is made with the imperfect form of *sum* + the active past participle of either aspect: *bev/beše* (etc.) *storil* 'I/you (etc.) had done'.

Conditional: invariable particle *bi* + past participle active: *toj bi došol* 'he would come'.

Prepositions

All Macedonian prepositions govern the nominative base form, even if an oblique form is available.

1. Во почетокот беше Словото, и Словото беше во Бога, и Бог беше Словото.

2. Тоа во почетокот беше во Бога.

3. Сé постана преку Него и без Него ништо не стана, што постана.

4. Во Него имаше живот и животот им беше светлина на луѓето.

5. И светлината во темнината свети, и мракот не ја опфати.

6. Имаше еден човек по име Јован, пратен од Бога;

7. тој дојде за сведочанство, да сведочи за Светлината, та сите да поверуваат преку него.

8. Тој не беше светлина, туку да сведочи за Светлината.

MACRO-ALGONQUIAN LANGUAGES

Geographically, this is the most widely distributed family of North American Indian languages. Its territory stretches from Hudson Bay in the north to the Gulf of Mexico, and from the Salishan-Wakashan area in the west to the Atlantic coast. Several Algonquian languages, e.g. Natchez, Tunica, Tonkawa, have been extinct for some years, and several more, e.g. Mohican, Menomini, Potawatomi, Shawnee, Delaware, Yurok, are spoken by very small numbers of people.

Numerically the largest of the Algonquian languages still spoken are Cree and Ojibwa, the former with 40,000 to 50,000 speakers in eastern and central Canada, and the latter with about the same number in Ontario. Three languages have between three and five thousand speakers: Cheyenne in Montana and Oklahoma, Blackfoot in Montana and Alberta, and Micmac in the Maritime Provinces.

An important sub-division of the Macro-Algonquian family is the Muskogean group, whose main representative, Choctaw, is spoken by about 12,000 people in Mississippi. Another Muskogean language, known variously as Creek, Seminole, or Muskogee, is spoken by over 10,000 in Georgia.

See **Arapaho, Blackfoot, Choctaw, Cree, Menomini**.

MACRO-SIOUAN LANGUAGES

In his 1929 *Encylopaedia Britannica* article on the Indian languages of North America, Edward Sapir listed Hokan-Siouan as one of his six super-stocks. It was sub-divided as follows:

1. Hokan;
2. Yuki;
3. Keres;
4. Tunican;
5. Iroquois-Caddoan;
6. Eastern (Sioux).

Part of this schema was reclassified in 1965 (Voegelin and Voegelin) as a separate Hokan phylum, and a Macro-Siouan phylum was postulated, comprising more than twenty languages divided into three groups:

(a) The Siouan group, containing Dakota (Sioux), Crow, Hidatsa, Winnebago, and Osage. This group lies to the west of the Great Lakes, and centres on the Missouri–Mississippi river system. The culturally advanced Mandan tribe, a member of the Missouri sub-group, is now extinct.

(b) The Iroquois group follows the Appalachian Mountains in a broad band extending from the St Lawrence estuary down to the Carolinas. The main members are Cherokee, Seneca, Mohawk, and Oneida. The last three named, together with the Onondaga and the Cayuga, formed the Iroquois League, which played a military, political, and economic role of considerable importance in American colonial history of the seventeenth and eighteenth centuries.

(c) Caddoan, in Arkansas and Kansas; Caddo, Wichita, and Pawnee are all close to extinction.

Two further Macro-Siouan groupings, now extinct, were Catawba in the Carolinas, and Yuchi in the southern Appalachians.
    The number of Macro-Siouan speakers is estimated at between 35,000 and 40,000, with Cherokee and Dakota accounting for about 80 per cent of this total. Crow and Seneca each have between 3,000 and 4,000 speakers.

See **Cherokee, Crow, Dakota, Seneca**.

MADURESE

INTRODUCTION

A member of the Malayo-Polynesian group of Austronesian, Madurese is spoken by between 7 and 10 million people in the island of Madura, in eastern Java, and in several smaller islands. Four socio-linguistic levels of speech are distinguished, ranging from *basa tenggi*, corresponding to high Krama in Javanese, to *basa enja'iya*, corresponding to Ngoko. (*See* **Javanese**.)

SCRIPT

Formerly written in a variety of Javanese script; now romanized.

PHONOLOGY

Consonants

The stops appear in triple series: unvoiced stop – voiced stop – aspirated voiced stop, e.g. /p, b, bh/; the dental series, /t, d, dh/, is paralleled by an interdental series, /t̪, d̪, d̪h̪/. The affricate series is /tʃ, dʒ/. The nasals are /m, n, ɲ, ŋ/; the glottal stop is present, /r, l, s/; the semi-vowel /j/; /h/ and /w/ appear only in loan-words.

Vowels

    front: i, e, ɛ
    central: ə, ʌ, a
    back: ɔ, o, u

MORPHOLOGY AND SYNTAX

Noun

Nouns are primary, e.g. *mata* 'eye', *aeng* 'water', *api* 'fire', *ojan* 'rain', or derived, much as in Bahasa Indonesia: e.g. from *tedhung* 'to sleep', *katedhungan* 'bedroom'; *angko* 'to take away' – *parangkoan* 'removal'. Gender may be indicated by such words as *lake* 'male', *bine* 'female'. There is no plural form: reduplication of non-initial syllable may be used: e.g. *pal.kapal* 'ships'; *reng-oreng* 'people'; *na'kana* 'children'. *Bannya'* 'many' (BI *banyak*) is also used.

POSSESSION

Various linking syllables join two nouns in genitive relationship: e.g. *jaran.a oreng madura* 'the Madurese man's horse'; *jaran.a sapa?* 'whose horse?'.

Adjective

As attribute, adjective follows noun: e.g. *olar raja* 'big snake'; *bako alos* 'finely-cut tobacco'; *pamerinta pusat* 'central government'.

COMPARISON

A comparative can be made by adding *-an*: *lebar* 'wide', *lebaran* 'wider.'

Pronoun

PERSONAL SERIES

There are no third person singular or plural forms. In the first and second personal forms, a high/low distinction is preserved: i.e. first person high *kaula*, low *sengko'*; second person high *sampeyan*, low *ba'na*. For 'we' a phrase like *sengko' mosso ba'na* is used. The missing third person forms are supplied from the demonstrative series.

A Ngoko possessive form is made with *tang*: e.g. *tang jaran* 'my horse'. The Krama equivalent puts the personal pronoun after the possessed object: *jaran kaula*.

DEMONSTRATIVE PRONOUN/ADJECTIVE

Theoretically there are two series, a *tenggi* set based on *neka – aneka, paneka, gapaneka* – and an *enja'iya* set based on *reya – areya, jareya*. Other forms also occur, e.g. *rowa, enggaruwa*, etc. Gradation is three-fold: proximate and two degrees of distal.

The demonstratives follow the noun: *panoguna songay reya* 'the guardian (spirit) of this river'.

The high/low distinction is also present in the interrogative pronouns: cf. *enja'iya, apa* 'what?'; *tenggi, ponapa*. Similarly, *sapa* 'who?' = *tenggi pasera*.

RELATIVE PRONOUN

se, e.g. *areya se entar.a* 'he (is the one who) will go'.

Numerals

1–10: *settong, dhu(wa'), tello', empa', lema', ennem, petto', ballu', sanga', sapolo*. 20 *dhu polo*; 40 *pa' polo*; 100 *saratos*. Plain forms without the final glottal stop are also used, and the forms given above can be reduplicated. There are also enclitic forms.

Verb

Derived verbs are made from primary bases (nominal and verbal) by means of prefixes, suffixes, and circumfixes as in Indonesian; *see* Bahasa Indonesia and

Javanese for detail. As in these languages, initial consonants in Madurese verbs are subjet to assimilation when affixes are added, e.g. from base *bukka'* 'open' is formed *mukka'* 'to open, be opened'.

The *ma-* prefix is subject-focused, the subject acquiring or performing the quality or action indicated by the base: e.g. *bannya'* 'much, many' – *mabannya'* 'to increase'; *lancar* 'fast' – *malancar* 'to speed up'; *maju* 'to progress' – *mamaju* 'to advance' – (secondary derivative) *kemajuwan* 'progress' (noun); *kanca* 'friend' – *makanca* 'to make friends'. The prefix *pa-* denotes the agent: e.g. *togu* 'to wait' – *panogu* 'guardian' (note change of initial *t-* to *n-*).

A perfective marker is made from *pongkor* 'back' – *tapongkor*: e.g. *e bakto se tapongkor* 'in the past (over and done with)' (*bakto* = Arabic *waqt*).

A general past marker is *ampon* = BI *sudah* 'already': e.g. *Sampeyan ampon oneng polo Madura* 'You have already seen (= been in) Madura'. The future may be marked by final *-a*: e.g. *areya se entar.a* 'he will go'; *Laggu' sengko' lako.a* 'Tomorrow, I'll work.'

Prepositions

Examples: *dhari* = BI *dari*; *dha'* = BI *kepada* 'to(wards), on to'; *kaangguy* = BI *untuk* 'for'; *e* = BI *di-*; *pada* 'in'.

The negative marker is *ta'* = BI *tidak*.

Word order

SVO.

1 ꧋ꦲꦸꦤ꧀ꦠ...

2 ...

3 ...

4 ...

5 ...

6 ...

7 ...

8 ...

MALAGASY

INTRODUCTION

Malagasy is a Western Austronesian outlier, most closely connected to Indonesian. Separation between the two seems to have taken place about 2,000 years ago. At present, Malagasy is spoken by around 9 million people in Madagascar (of which it is the official language), the Comoro Islands, and the Seychelles. There are several mutually intelligible dialects; the literary language is based on the dominant Central dialect known as Merino.

LITERATURE

Until the mid-nineteenth century Arabic script was used to notate Malagasy. This *ajami* writing, which dates from the fifteenth century, consists mainly of astrological works and genealogies. In 1823 King Ramada I opted for the Roman alphabet, and during the remaining five years of his reign a start was made on producing religious literature in Malagasy under the auspices of the London Missionary Society. Under Ramada's successor, Queen Ranavalona I, these activities were suppressed, and translation was not resumed until the 1860s. The second half of the nineteenth century saw a remarkable growth of literacy in Madagascar. In 1896 the island became a French colony, and the resultant proliferation of operettas in both French and Malagasy was very much in line with the native tradition of the *mpilalao*, the theatrical competition. During the twentieth century many talented writers have emerged, working in both languages. The rich oral folklore should also be mentioned.

   The language has many loan-words from Arabic, Iranian, Bantu, French, and English.

SCRIPT

The original Roman alphabet included *ñ* = /ɲ/ and *ṅ* = /ŋ/. Both phonemes are now written as n. The digraphs *tr* and *dr* are pronounced as /tr̺/, /dr̺/, i.e. as retroflex sounds; *j* = /dz/. /ɔ/ is notated as *ao*; /u/ as *o*, and /ə/ as *a* final: e.g. *laoranjy* /lɔrandzi/; *fotsy* /futsi/; *ala* /alə/.

PHONOLOGY

Consonants

The stops /b, p; d, t; g, k/ are accompanied by the nasals /m, n, ŋ/ and sibilants /s, z/, the fricatives /f, v/, and affricates /ts, dz/, and the liquids /l, r/. There are two retroflex sounds /ʈ, ɖ/ and the glottal /h/.

The sibilants and /l/ are slightly palatalized: [s', z', l'].

Vowels

i, e = [ε], a, o = [ɔ], u, ə
diphthongs: ei, au.

Stress

Stress, which is phonemic, is on the penultimate, moving to antepenultimate before certain endings. Assimilation is a major factor (*see* **Word formation**, below).

MORPHOLOGY AND SYNTAX

Noun

In the absence of grammatical gender, number (but *see* **Demonstrative pronoun**, below), person, and case, nominals, and verbals are indistinguishable. Indeed, most basic roots can function as either, and as adjectives. Roots used as nominals are mostly di- or trisyllabic: e.g. *trano* 'house'; *hazo* 'tree'; *sofina* 'ear'. There are also monosyllabic roots: e.g. *ra* 'blood', *fo* 'heart'.

To specify gender, *lahy* 'male', *vavy* 'female' may be added: e.g. *zazalahy* 'boy'; *zazavavy* 'girl'.

ARTICLES
ny preceding the noun is a general definite article: e.g. *ny trano* 'the house'. *Ilay* is used with nouns denoting persons; *ra* and *i* are used with proper names: e.g. *fahaleovantenan' i Madagasikara* 'the independence of M.'.

POSSESSION
Possessed precedes possessor. The suffixed personal markers are -*ko*, -*nao*, -*ny*; pl. -(*n*)*tsika*, -(*n*)*area*, -*ny*: *ny masoko* 'my eye(s)'; *zazany* 'his/her/their children'

Adjective

As attribute, adjective follows noun: e.g. *teny malagasy* 'the M. language'; *ny rano lalina* 'the deep river'. The adjective may, however, precede the noun to form a stable compound: e.g. *tsara* 'beautiful' + *tarehy* 'face': *ny vehivavy tsaratarehy* 'the beautiful woman'. In predicate position, the adjective is marked for tense: e.g. *mafana* 'is hot'; *nafana* 'was hot'; *hafana* 'will be hot'.

COMPARISON
A comparative is made with *kokoa* 'more' (+ *noho* 'than'): e.g. *tanora kokoa hianao noho aho* 'you (*hianao*) are young (*tanora*) more than I.'

Pronoun

Basic personal forms (all cited forms have variants):

	Singular			Plural		
	Subject	*Object*	*Enclitic*	*Subject*	*Object*	*Enclitic*
1	(iz)aho	ahy, ahiko	-ko	isika, izahay	antsika	-ntsika
2	hianao	anao	-(n)ao	hianareo	anareo	-nareo
3	izy	azy	-ny	izy(ireo)	azy(ireo)	-ny

The enclitics are used as personal markers (*see* **Possessive**, above). Use of full objective forms: cf. *faly aho mahita anao* 'glad I to-see you'; *nanao 'veloma' azy izy* 'he greeted him' (lit. 'he said – "greetings" – to him – he').

Second person singular *hianao* is neutral polite form. Variants are coded for status of addressee; i.e. a form of respect language, as in Javanese, etc.

DEMONSTRATIVE PRONOUN

There are two series: (a) based on *itý* for relatively proximate field of visible objects; (b) based on *izatý* for more distant field. Here, Malagasy makes a distinction in gender and number: cf. *ilay ity* 'this' (male), *ilay ireto* 'these' (male); *ikala ity* 'this' (female), *ikala ireto* 'these' (female).

INTERROGATIVE PRONOUN

iza 'who?'; *inona* 'what?'.

RELATIVE PRONOUN

izay 'who?'; *ilay* 'which?': e.g. *ny vola izay nomeny ahiko* 'the money which he gave me'. *See* **Verb**, below, relative/contingent form.

Numerals

1–10: *irai/isa, roa, telo, efatra, dimy, enina, fito, valo, sivy, folo*. 11 *iraika ambin' ny folo* (*ambin'* < *amby* 'surplus'); 12 *roa ambin' ny folo*; 20 *roapolo*; 30 *telopolo*; 100 *zato*.

Verb

Almost any Malagasy word can be modulated by appropriate prefixes to provide a verbal base; cf. *asa* 'work' – *miasa* 'to work'; *folo* 'ten' – *mifolo* 'to split into ten'.

There are various classifications of Malagasy verbs into groups, based on such criteria as transitivity, potentiality, reciprocity, and so on. Each group has its specific prefixed marker. Transitive verbs, for example, have the following prefixes: *man-, mam-, manka-, (mi-)* with consonantal assimilation at juncture with stem: thus, *n, t, s, ts,* are discarded when *man-* is prefixed to a verbal base beginning with any of these: e.g. *-soratra* 'to write' – *manoratra* '(I) write'. Similarly stem-initial *l* becomes *d*: *-leha* 'to go' – *mandeha* '(I) go'. Other examples: *r* > *dr*: e.g. *-roso* 'to go in' – *mandroso* '(I) go in'. The *-n* of *man-* assimilates with labial initial: e.g. *-fana* 'to warm up' – *mamana* '(I) warm'. Other prefixes are: *maha-* (potential), *mampan-* (causative), *mifan-* (reciprocal), etc.

These forms have been illustrated here with *m-* initial, which marks the tense as present. This initial changes to *n-* for the past, and to *h-* for the future. Thus, *miteny* '(I) speak'; *niteny* '(I) spoke'; *hiteny* '(I) shall speak'.

The particle *efa* combines with the present tense to indicate continuous action; with the past tense to indicate completed action, and with the future tense to mark the future perfective.

The passive participle is formed with the suffixes *-ina*, *-ana*, *-ena*: e.g. *soa* 'good' – *soavina* 'improved'; *vono* 'to kill' – *vonoina* 'killed'. *no-* is prefixed to these forms for past tense, *ho-* for future.

A series of verbal bases, corresponding formally to the passive participle – i.e. without the formative prefixes – take pronominal enclitics to express grammatical subject, and the construction is passive: e.g. *tia* 'liked', *inona no tianao?* 'what is-liked-by-you?' = 'what do you like?'; *hita* 'seen'; *hitako* 'seen by me' = 'I see'. *Efa* is prefixed to make a past tense: *efa hitako izy* 'I saw him'; and *ho* to make a future: *ho hitako izy* 'I shall see him'.

The negative particle is *tsy*: e.g. *Tsy fotsy ny vary* 'The rice is not white' (*fotsy* 'white').

THE RELATIVE OR CONTINGENT FORM

This is made by adding the circumfix *a(n)-/i(n)- ...(a)na* to the stem: e.g. *mi.asa* 'to work' – rel. form, *iasana/anasana*. This form takes the pronominal enclitics as possessive markers denoting the logical agent; it also takes tense markers: Ø for present, *n-* for past, and *h-* for future: e.g. *Omaly no nahitako ny zazalahy* 'I saw the boy yesterday.' Here, the temporal factor is focused: it was *yesterday* that I (*-ko*) saw the boy. Other contingent factors may be focused, e.g. place: *Aiza no nipetranao?* 'Where (it is that) you (did) live?'; means or instrument: *Ny fangady no iasanareo ny tanimbary* 'With the spade (is it that) you till the ricefield?' The form may also focus target, cause, or value, and express a benefactive or partitive sense.

IMPERATIVE

In general, the stress moves to the final vowel: e.g. *miláza* 'speak' – imper. *milazá*; *tsára* 'good' – *tsará* 'May you fare well!'

Prepositions

Prepositions are both simple and compound; e.g. *ambony* 'on': *ambony latabatra* 'on the table' (note that the French article figures as part of the Malagasy borrowing); *am-badika* 'beyond': *am-badika ny tendrombohitre* 'beyond the mountain'.

Word formation

Compounding is a prolific source of lexical items. In this process, assimilation and truncation play a major role; cf.:

tany 'land' + *ny* (article) + *vary* 'rice': *tanimbary* 'rice field';
lay 'sail' + *ny* + *sambo* 'boat': *laintsambo* 'sailing boat';
vohitra 'hill' + *be* 'big': *vohibe* 'big mountain'.

In derivation, prefixes, suffixes, infixes, and circumfixes are used: e.g.

fan- + root: *lainga* 'to tell lies' – *fandainga* 'liar';
maha- + root: *soratra* 'to write' – *mahasoratra* 'to be able to write';
mpan- + *fi* + root: *anatra* 'to teach' – *mpampianatra* 'teacher';
mi- + *fan* + *fi* + root: *mifampianatra* 'to instruct each other';
faha- + root + *-ana*: *vita* 'finished' – *fahavitana* 'the end';
infix in root: *hehy* 'laughter' – *homehy* 'person who laughs'.

Word order

VOS is normal.

---

1 TAMY ny taloha ny Teny, ary ny Teny tamy n'Andriamanitra, ary Andriamanitra ny Teny.

2 Izy tamy n'Andriamanitra tamy ny taloha.

3 Izy nanava'ny ny zavatra rehetra; ary raha tsy izy, tsy nisy nanaova'ny izay efa natao ny.

4 Tao amy ny ny fiainana; ary ny fiainana no nahazava ny olona.

5 Ary ny mazava mahazava ao amy ny maizina; fa ny maizina tsy nahasarona azy.

6 Nisy lehilahy nirahin'Andriamanitra, i Jaony no anara'ny.

7 Izy avy 'mba ho fanambarana hanambara ny Mazava, 'mba hampinoa'ny ny olona rehetra,

8 Tsy izy izany Mazava izany, fa nirahi'ny 'mba hanambara ny Mazava.

MALAYALAM

INTRODUCTION

This South Dravidian language is spoken by about 24 million people in Kerala, and is one of the officially recognized state languages of India. Lexically, Malayalam is close to Tamil from which it seems to have diverged in comparatively very recent times, perhaps during the thirteenth century AD. The earliest literary monument in Malayalam is a *Rāmacarita* in a recension dating from the fourteenth century, though the work itself may be older.

There are two main points of difference between Tamil and Malayalam: the personal endings of the verb, present in Tamil, have been lost in Malayalam; and, second, the extent of borrowing from Sanskrit is considerably greater in Malayalam. From the nineteenth century onwards, there has been a gradual tendency for the colloquial language to replace the heavily Sanskritized literary style.

The outstanding figure in the history of Malayalam literature is that of Tuñcatt' Eẓuttacchan (sixteenth century), to whom we also owe the modern Malayalam script.

SCRIPT

The syllabary is in order and content an exact copy of the Devanagari grid. There are numerous ligatures, including graphs for geminated consonants.

PHONOLOGY

Consonants

> stops: p, t, ṭ, k; with aspirated and voiced/voiced aspirate values: e.g. /p, ph, b, bh/
> affricates: tʃ, dʒ; with aspirated values
> fricatives: j, v, s, ṣ, ʃ, h
> nasals: m, n, ɲ, ŋ, ṇ
> laterals and flaps: l, ḷ, r, ṛ, ṭ

/ṛ/ tends towards dental [t]. Retroflex phonemes are notated here with a subscript dot, e.g. ṛ.

Vowels

short and long: i, e, a, o, u
diphthongs: ai, au

Sandhi based on homogeneous assimilation is very extensive; glides /j/ and /w/ are used at vocalic junctures. The distinction between single and geminated consonants is phonemic.

Stress

Slight; on first syllable.

MORPHOLOGY AND SYNTAX

Noun

Three genders – masculine, feminine, and neuter – are distinguished, and certain endings are gender-specific, e.g. masc. *-an*, *-kāran*; fem. *-i*, *-tti*, *-kāri*. Sanskrit words retain their original gender; cf. *kumāran* 'son'; *kumāri* 'daughter'; *mīnkāran* 'fisherman'; *mīnkāri* 'fisher-woman'. Lexical gender: e.g. *āṇpakṣi* 'male bird'; *peṇpakṣi* 'female bird'.

NUMBER
The plural is formed in three ways:

(a) with *-kaḷ*: e.g. *vīṭu* 'house', pl. *vīṭukaḷ*. Juncture with *-kaḷ* is subject to sandhi: *maram* 'tree', pl. *maramkal*;
(b) masculine nouns in *-an* change this ending to *-ar*: e.g. *manuṣyan* 'man' – *manuṣyar*;
(c) honorific plural in *-mār*: e.g. *amma* 'mother' – *ammamār*.

CASE SYSTEM
There are seven cases. As specimen, declension of *manuṣyan* (masc.) 'man':

nominative	manuṣyan	instrumental	manuṣyanāl
accusative	manuṣyane	genitive	manuṣyante
comitative	manuṣyanōṭu	locative	manuṣyanil
dative	manuṣyannu		

Plural is *manuṣyanmār*, to which the same endings as set out above are added.

The base for the oblique cases often varies from the nominative. For example, *maram* 'tree', adds the oblique endings to the base *maratt-*: e.g. *maratt.in.ōṭu*. Similarly, *malayāḷattil* 'in Malayalam'.

Adjective

Malayalam has very few true adjectives. As attribute, the adjective precedes the noun: *nalla* 'good', *periya* 'big'. *nalla veḷḷam* 'good water'.

Adjectives may be nominalized: e.g. *nallaval* 'a good woman' (cf. third person feminine pronoun).

Pronoun

The basic personal forms are:

		Singular		Plural
1		ñān	incl.	nām/nammaḷ, excl. ñaṅṅaḷ
2		nī		niṅṅaḷ
3	masc.	avan/addēham		avar(kaḷ)
	fem.	avaḷ		
	nt.	atu		ava, atukaḷ

These are declined in all cases. The oblique base of *ñān* is *en-*: thus, *enne, ennōṭu, enikku, ennāl, ende, ennil.*

DEMONSTRATIVE PRONOUN
The three genders are distinguished in the singular: *ivan – ivaḷ – itu* 'this'; *avan – avaḷ – atu* 'that'. In the plural, *ivan* and *ivaḷ* combine to give plural *ivar*, in opposition to neuter plural *iva*. Similarly, *avar* (masc./fem. pl.) – *ava* (neuter).

INTERROGATIVE PRONOUN
ēvan, ēvaḷ (sing. masc., fem.) 'who?', pl. *ār/ēvar*; *ētu* (neuter) 'what?', pl. *ēva*.

RELATIVE PRONOUN
See **Participle**, below.

Numerals

1–10: *oru/onnu* (this is not a gender distinction), *raṇṭu, mūnnu, nālu, añju, āṟu, ēṟu, eṭṭu, onpatu, pattu*; 11 *patinonnu*; 12 *pantraṇṭu*; 13 *patimūnnu*; 20 *irupatu*; 30 *mūppatu*; 40 *nālpatu*; 100 *nūṟu*.

The noun following a numeral is in the singular if it is neuter, plural if masculine/feminine: e.g. *mūnnu kutira* 'three horses'; but *raṇṭu peṇkaḷ* 'two sisters'.

Verb

Thanks to the elimination of person and number (except in the imperative), the verbal system in Malayalam is considerably simpler than that of the other Dravidian languages. All verbal forms are built on the basis of the root, which takes such endings as -(*k*)*kuka*, -*yuka* to express the infinitive. Verbs in -*kkuka* are strong; verbs with any other infinitive ending are weak.

There are four moods: indicative, imperative, conditional, and necessitative.

Indicative mood: tense formation:

Present: -(*k*)*kunnu* is added to the root, e.g. *ñān vāyikkunnu* 'I read'; *niṅṅaḷ vāyikkunnu* 'you (pl.) read'.

Present progressive: *-uṇṭu* or *-kontirikkunnu* is added to present form, e.g. *ñān naṭakkunnuṇṭu* 'I am walking'; *avar samsariccu.koṇṭirikkunnu* 'they keep on talking'.

Past: formation here is much more heterogeneous and irregular: the marker is *-tu* or *-i*, with extensive stem modulation and sandhi: e.g.

	Past tense
čeyyuka 'to do'	čeytu
snēhi.kkuka 'to love'	snēhičču
varuka 'to come'	vannu
paṟayuka 'to speak, say'	paṟaññu
vīṟuka 'to fall'	vīṇu

Future: two forms are possible: (a) *-um* added to present minus *-unnu*, e.g. *avan čeyyum* 'he will do/make'; (b) in *-u/ū*, usually with link consonant, e.g. *varū* 'will come'; *koṭuppu* 'will give'.

Imperative mood: the second person singular is provided by the root: e.g. *pō* 'go!'. For the second person plural *-in* is added: e.g. *pōvin!* This mood has first and third person forms in *-ṭṭe*, and a polite form in *-ālum*: e.g. *tannālum* 'please give'.

Conditional mood: the marker is *-āl* or *-eṅkil*: e.g. *čeyt.āl* 'if ... does/do/did'.

Necessitative mood: has three tense forms: cf. *paṟayēṇḍunnu* 'has to say'; *paṟayēṇḍi* 'had to say'; *paṟayēṇḍum* 'will have to say'.

NEGATIVE CONJUGATION
The characteristic marker is *-ā-*: e.g. *paṟa.y.ā.yka* 'not to speak'. Present, past, and future negative tenses can be formed either by *-ā-* + tense ending, or by affixation of the particle *-illa*: e.g. *paṟa.y.ā.yunnu* = *paṟa.y.unn.illa* 'don't/doesn't speak'.

FORMATION OF RELATIVE CLAUSES
The participial form is neutral as to voice: cf. *pustakam vāyičča strī* 'the woman who read(s) the book'; *strī vāyičča pustakam* 'the book read by the woman'.

Malayalam has about 20 auxiliaries, which express perfect/imperfective aspect, and modality (benefactive, inceptive, terminative, etc.).

Postpositions

Examples: following nouns in genitive case: *nāṭuvē/naṭuvil* 'between, among'; *vīṭukaḷute naṭuvil* 'between/among the houses'; *mukaḷ* 'on': *marattin mukaḷ* 'on the tree'; *kīṟē* 'under, beneath'; *vrikshattin kīṟē* 'beneath the tree'. In these two examples, *maram*, genitive, *marattin(te)* is the native Dravidian word for 'tree'; *vriksha* is a Sanskrit loan-word. *čuṟṟum* 'round': *sūryante chuṟṟum* 'round the sun'; *mutal ... ōḷam* 'from ... to'; *janičča divasam mutal maraṇattōḷam* 'from day of birth to death'.

With locative case: e.g. *ūṭē* 'through': *nagarattilūṭē* 'through the town'.

Word order

SOV.

ആദിയിൽ വചനം ഉണ്ടായിരുന്ന ആ വചനം ദൈവ
ത്തോട്ട കൂട ആയിരുന്ന ആ വചനം ദൈവവും ആയിരുന്ന *
ആയത ആദിയിൽ ദൈവത്തോട്ട കൂട ആയിരുന്ന * സക
ലവും അവനാൽ ഉണ്ടാക്കപ്പെട്ട ഉണ്ടാക്കപ്പെട്ടതൊന്നും അവ
നെ കൂടാതെ ഉണ്ടാക്കപ്പെട്ടതുമില്ല * അവനിൽ ജീവൻ ഉണ്ടാ
യിരുന്ന ആ ജീവൻ മനുഷ്യരുടെ വെളിച്ചം ആയിരുന്ന * വി
ശേഷിച്ചും ആ വെളിച്ചം ഇരുളിൽ പ്രകാശിക്കുന്ന എങ്കിലും ഇ
രുൾ അതിനെ പരിഗ്രഹിച്ചില്ല *

ഒരു മനുഷ്യൻ ദൈവത്തിൽനിന്ന അയക്കപ്പെട്ടിരുന്ന അ
വൻറ നാമം യോഹന്നാൻ എന്നായിരുന്ന * ആയവൻ
താൻ മൂലം എല്ലാവരും വിശ്വസിക്കേണ്ടുന്നതിന ആ വെളിച്ച
ത്തെ കുറിച്ച സാക്ഷിപ്പെട്ടത്തുവാനായിട്ട സാക്ഷിയായി വ
ന്നു * അവൻ ആ വെളിച്ചം ആയിരുന്നില്ല ആ വെളിച്ചത്തെ
കുറിച്ച സാക്ഷിപ്പെട്ടത്തുവാനായിട്ട (അയക്കപ്പെട്ടവൻ) അ
ത്രെ *

859

MALTESE

INTRODUCTION

Maltese belongs to the Semito-Hamitic family. Following Roman and Vandal occupation, the Arabs conquered the islands in the late ninth century, bringing with them a form of Arabic akin to that spoken in Algeria and Tunis. The Romance influence on Maltese begins in the late eleventh century, when the Arabs were ousted by Norman forces from Sicily. Angevin, Spanish, and French invasions followed over the next 600 years. The British presence in Malta dates from 1800. It is probable that the language contains a Phoenician substratum.

Maltese has been a written language since the seventeenth century. Since 1934 Maltese and English have been joint official languages of Malta.

SCRIPT

Devised by the Maltese Writers' Union in the 1920s; Roman alphabet + dotted and barred letters. Thus, $\dot{g}$ = /dʒ/, $\dot{c}$ = /tʃ/, $\dot{z}$ = /z/; ħ = /ħ/; *għ* is phonetically /γ/ but is not pronounced; *x* = /ʃ/, *z* = /ts/. Both ħ and *għ*, themselves silent, lengthen preceding and following vowels: cf. *deher* /deːr/, 'he appeared'; *għerf* /ʔeːrf/, 'wisdom'; *bogħod* /boːt/, 'distance'. The Arabic roots corresponding to these three words are: *zahara, 'arafa, ba'uda*.

PHONOLOGY

Consonants

    stops: p, b, t, d, k, g, ʔ
    affricates: ts, tʃ, dʒ
    fricatives: f, v, s, ʃ, z, h
    nasals: m, n
    lateral and flap: l, r
    semi-vowels: w, j

ASSIMILATION

The *l-* of the definite article fuses with the so-called 'sun letters': $\dot{c}$, *d, n, r, s, t, x, $\dot{z}$, z* (*see* **Arabic**). A prosthetic vowel is added: e.g. *l-dar* /id.daar/, 'the house'.

Vowels

> short: ɪ, ɛ, a, ɔ, u
> long: i, e, a, ɔ, u

A specific Maltese sound is /iə/ representing Arabic /ɛː/; it is always stressed: e.g. *bierek* /biərek/, 'he blessed', Arabic *bāraka* /bɛːraka/.

MORPHOLOGY AND SYNTAX

Noun

The definite article is *l-/il-*: e.g. *il-qamar* 'the moon'; *id-dar* 'the house'.

GENDER
Masculine/feminine following natural gender; other nouns are masculine or feminine by virtue of grammatical ending. Broadly speaking, nouns and adjectives ending in a consonant are masculine. Typical feminine endings are *-a*, *-ti*, *-i* (the latter two endings are characteristic of Italian loan-words).

NUMBER
A dual exists (*-(t)e/ajn*) but is used only for parts of the body which occur in pairs: e.g. *idejn* 'the hands', and for certain measurements of time e.g. *sentejn* 'two years'. Plurals are either sound or broken. Sound plural endings are, e.g., *-n*, *-at*, *-ijiet*, *-iet*, all of them stressed.

Broken plural: there are two or three dozen models, most of them coupled with internal flection: e.g. *ktieb* 'book', pl. *kotba*; *bint* 'daughter', pl. *bniet*; and with prosthetic vowel: *baħar* 'sea', pl. *ibħra* (*see* **Arabic**).

POSSESSION
The construct formula (*see* **Arabic**) is the authentic Maltese way of expressing the possessive relationship, e.g. *bieb id-dar* 'the door of the house', *bieb dar is-sultan* 'the door of the Sultan's house'; but it is often replaced by an analytic formula with the preposition *ta'*: e.g. *il-belt qadima ta' Malta* 'the old city of Malta'. *Ta'* is preferred where, as in this example, the presence of an adjective would complicate the construct formula.

The Semitic feminine ending *-t* may reappear in the construct formula: e.g. *mara* 'woman', but *mart it-tabib* 'the doctor's wife'

Adjective

The attributive adjective follows the noun, and is in concord with it for gender and number. If the noun is definite, the article is recapitulated: e.g. *il-ktieb il-ġdid* 'the new book'. Failing recapitulation of the article, the phrase would mean 'the book is new', as Maltese has no copula.

THE COMPARATIVE MODEL
$VC_1C_2VC_3$ is the same as that for the masculine form of adjectives of colour: cf. *kbir* 'great', comp. *akbar*; *twil* 'long', comp. *itwal*; masculine adjectives of

colour: *aħmar* 'red'; *iswed* 'black', *abjad* 'white'; the corresponding feminine forms being: *ħamra, sewda, bajda*.

Pronoun

The base independent forms with object enclitics and possessive markers are:

		Singular			Plural		
		Base	Object enclitic	Possessive	Base	Object enclitic	Possessive
1		jien	-ni	-i/-ja	aħna	-na	-na
2		int(i)	-o/-ek	-ek/-ok	intom	-kom	-kom
3	masc.	hu(wa)	-h/-u	-u/-h	huma	-hom	-hom
	fem.	hi(ja)	-ha	-ha			

That is, the gender distinction in the third person singular is not carried into the plural.

DEMONSTRATIVE PRONOUN
Masc. *dan(a)*, fem. *din(a)*, pl. *dawn(a)* 'this', these'; masc. *dak(a)*, fem. *dik(a)*, pl. *dawk(a)* 'that, those'.

INTERROGATIVE PRONOUN
min 'who?'; *xi/x* 'what?'.

RELATIVE PRONOUN
li/illi is used for both genders and numbers, and can be followed by preposition + personal suffix: e.g. *it-tabib li miegħu tkellimt* 'the doctor with whom you spoke' (*ma'* 'with' – *miegħu* 'with him' = Arabic *ma'ahu*).

Numerals

1–10: basically, the Arabic forms in Maltese spelling: e.g. *wieħed/waħda, tnejn, tlieta, erbgħa, ħamsa*. These are the forms used in counting without reference to objects; when objects are enumerated, a second set is used for 2–10 inclusive: e.g. *żewġ, tliet, erba', ħames, sitt*. Thus, *tlieta* 3, but *tlitt soldi* 'threepence'.

From 2 to 10, nouns enumerated are in the plural; from 11 to 101 in the singular, though concord may be plural.

Verb

As in Arabic, the citation form of a verb is the 3rd person singular perfective: *KiTeB* 'he wrote: to write'; *QaRa(J)* 'he read'; *KaŻBaR* 'he reviled' are examples of Maltese triliterals, biliterals, and quadriliterals. The capital letters indicate radicals.

Stems are classified as (a) sound, e.g. *KiTeB*; (b) weak, e.g. *QaRaJ* 'he read' (where Q is the glottal stop, and J is quiescent); (c) hollow, e.g. *GHaX* 'he lived'; (d) doubled, e.g. *RaDD* 'he restored'.

The tense structure is essentially aspectual, perfective contrasting with imperfective, the latter covering present and future. There is an imperative mood. A typical set of forms is: *KiTeB* 'he wrote'; *jiKTeB* 'he writes/will write'; *iKTeB* 'write!'.

The personal endings of the perfective form are, 3rd masc. *-Ø*, fem. *-et*; 2nd *-t*; 1st *-t*; pl. 3rd masc./fem. *-u*; 2nd *-tu*; 1st *-na*. The imperfective has the following prefixes: 3rd masc. *j/i-*, fem. *t-*; 2nd *t-*; 1st *(i)n-*; pl. 3rd *j/i-*; 2nd *t-*; 1st *(i)n*. The suffix *-u* is added to all plural forms of the imperfective: e.g. *huma jiKTBu* 'they write'; *aħna niKTBu* 'we write'. The object enclitics are added to these forms: e.g. *QaTLu.h* 'they killed him'; *Alla jBieRKe.k* 'God blesses you'. *-l* + personal marker expresses the indirect object: e.g. *KiTBit.il.na* 'she wrote to us' (change in vocalization is due to stress shift).

THE DERIVED STEMS

As in Arabic (*see* **Arabic**); e.g. II geminated second radical, *KiSSeR* 'he smashed'; III first vowel lengthened, *SieFeR* 'he emigrated', etc. IV appears to have fallen into disuse in Maltese.

NEGATION

In the indicative *ma/m'* precedes verb + suffixed *-x*: e.g. *hu ma jiKoL.x* 'he doesn't eat'. Imperative *la...x*: e.g. *la tikoL.x* 'do not eat'.

Prepositions

As in Arabic: e.g. *fid-dar* 'in the house'; *bil-lejl* 'at night'. *Għand* is used to express notion of 'to have': e.g. *għandi* 'I have'; *ma għandi.x* 'I haven't'.

Word order

SVO is normal.

1 Fil-bidu kienet il-Kelma, u l-Kelma kienet ma' Alla, u l-Kelma kienet Alla. 2 Din kienet fil-bidu ma' Alla. 3 Kollox sar biha; u xejn ma sar mingħajrha milli sar. 4 Fiha kienet il-ħajja; u l-ħajja kienet id-dawl tal-bnedmin. 5 U d-dawl jiddi fid-dlamijiet; u d-dlamijiet ma fehmuhx.

6 Kien hemm bniedem mibgħut minn Alla, li kien jismu Ġwanni. 7 Dan ġie bħala xiehed, biex jixhed għad-Dawl, biex il-bnedmin kollha jemmnu bih. 8 Hu ma kienx dak id-Dawl, iżda nbagħat biex jixhed għal dak id-Dawl.

MAM

INTRODUCTION

This Eastern Mayan language, belonging to the Penutian family, is spoken by something approaching half a million people in north-west Guatemala. It is the third-largest Mayan language, after Quiché and Cakchiquel.

PHONOLOGY

Consonants

    stops: p, t, k, q, ʔ; palatalized k'; ejectives: b'/ɓ, t'/ɗ, k', q'; palatalized k''
    affricates: ts, tʃ, tʂ; ejectives: ts', tʃ', tʂ'
    fricatives: s, ʃ, ʂ, x
    nasals: m, n
    lateral and flap: l, r
    semi-vowels: j, w

In the transcription used by England (1983), and here, the ejectives are notated as *b'*, *t'* etc.; the palatalized values as *ky*, *k'y*; the retroflex fricative /ʂ/ as *x*, the velar fricative /x/ as *j*. England uses 7 for the glottal stop: here '. The affricates are notated as *tz*, *ch*, *tx*: ejectives add '. /ʃ/ is notated as *xh*.

Vowels

    short and long: i, e, a, o, u

MORPHOLOGY AND SYNTAX

Noun

A noun is assumed to be definite if the indefinite marker *jun* is absent. Nouns may be marked for plurality by the particle *qa*: e.g. *xu'j* '(the) woman'; *qa-xu'j* '(the) women'.

    Number is normally inferred from the concord signalled by personal markers on verbs. *See* **Pronoun**, below.

    Case relations are expressed by means of a series of relational nouns derived from primary nouns; e.g. for the locative *t-witz* 'on', derived from *witz-b'aj*

864

'face'; similarly *t-uj* 'in', *t-jaq'* 'below': *t-uj jun a'* 'in some water'; *t-jaq' tx'otx'* 'below the earth'.

Possession is expressed by circumfix, marked for person: e.g. *n-jaa-ya* 'my house', *t-jaa-ya* 'your house', *t-jaa-ø* 'his/her house'. Not all nouns can take possessive markers; e.g. nouns denoting natural phenomena never do. On the other hand, nouns denoting parts of the body are invariably accompanied by the possessive marker *b'aj*, which is elided when a personal marker is added: e.g. *qam-b'aj* 'foot' but *n-qan-a* 'my foot'.

Adjective

The adjective is treated as a nominal. Attributively, it may (a) follow or (b) precede the noun qualified, depending on (a) the presence or (b) the absence of another modifier. Thus *matiij tx'yaan* 'big dog' but *kab' tx'yaan matiij* 'some big dogs', where *tx'yaan* denotes 'dog', and *kab'* (basically the numeral 'two') is used to indicate plurality.

Pronoun

PERSONAL

There are no free forms. Mam has two sets of bound personal pronominal markers: (a) an ergative set, functioning as the agent markers with transitive verbs; and (b) a non-ergative set, providing subject forms for intransitive verbs, object forms for transitives. Each set has enclitic forms.

England (1983: 62) gives a complete paradigm for the root *tzeeq'a-* 'to hit'. Three examples are given here:

> *ma ø-n-tzeeq'a-ya* 'I hit it' (recent past marked by **ma**)
> *ma ø-t-tzeeq'a-ya* 'you (sing.) hit it'
> *ma ø-q-tzeeq'a-ya* 'we (exclusive) hit it'

Cf.

> *ma tz'-ok n-tzeeq'an-a* '1st p. sing. hit 2nd/3rd p. sing.'
> *ma **chin** ok t-tzeeq'an-a* '2nd p. sing. hit 1st p. sing.'

where *tz'-* and *chin* are personal absolutive markers indicating patient of ergative verb; *ok* is a directional prefix meaning 'in(to)'; *ma* is the verbal aspect marker for events taking place in the recent past.

CLASSIFIERS

The nominal referent of a third person pronominal form can be at least partially identified from the classifier accompanying the verbal complex: e.g. a third person form plus *txin* identifies the referent as a young woman; *xhyaa'* added to the same pronominal forms signals an old woman.

DEMONSTRATIVE PRONOUN AND ADJECTIVE

Singular *aj*, plural *ajaj/aqaj* for both proximate and distal: e.g. *aj kab' samaan* 'these two weeks'.

alkyee 'who?'; *al* 'who, what?'.

RELATIVE PRONOUN
The demonstrative *aj* also functions as a relative pronoun preceding the head word: e.g. *aj xjaal ...* 'the person who ...'.

Numerals

1–10: *juun, kab', oox, jwe', qaq, wuuq, wajxaq, b'elaj, laaj*. 11–19: *junlaaj, kab'laaj, oxlaaj*, etc. 20 is *wiinqan*. For numerals above 20 the old Mayan terms have now been replaced in Mam by Spanish loan-words.

Verb

Mam is an ergative language; verbs are transitive or intransitive. Roots are agglutinatively marked for person (*see* **Pronoun**, above). First person plural is inclusive or exclusive, the distinction being marked by change in enclitic: e.g. *ma qo b'eet* 'we walked (incl.)'; *ma qo b'eet-a* 'we walked (excl.)'.

Aspectual markers identify the action expressed by the verbal complex in a principal clause as past (*o*), recent past (*ma*), future or potential (*ok*), in progress (*n-*). Secondary markers function for the expression of past time, general or recent, in subordinate clauses. There is an imperative mood.

The order of components in a typical Mam transitive verbal complex is: aspect marker – patient marker (always explicit, may be zero) – directional – agent marker – root – enclitic person marker.

DIRECTIONALS
As in German and Georgian, directed or vector motion is indicated by a series of particles known as directionals: e.g. *ul* 'hither' (cf. German *her*, Georgian *mo-*); *pon* 'thither' (cf. German *hin*, Georgian *mi-*): e.g. *ma tz-ul w-ii-'n-a* 'I brought it here'; *ma Ø-pon w-ii-'n-a* 'I took it there' (root *ii-* 'to take, bring').

POSITIONALS
These roots combine the descriptive properties of adjectives with (a) locus and (b) verbal action. England (1983) gives several examples of these roots, mostly of the type CCVC(C): e.g. *slinky-* descriptive of actions performed by someone who is naked; *(x)lank-* used with reference to someone without shoes; *(ch)jenky-* someone, something fat is doing something somewhere. Specific suffixes transform positional stems into transitive or intransitive verbs.

NEGATION
There are several negating particles, each with a specific function. All precede the item to be negated. Thus, *miyaa'* negates stative verbs and the markers introducing transitive verbal complexes: e.g. *saq* (it's) white' – *miyaa' saq* '(it's) not white'; *miyaa' t-u'n X xhi tzaj t-Y-'n Z* 'it wasn't X who did Y to Z', where *t-u'n* is a third person singular relational noun denoting agency: 'by'; *xhi* is the

dependent aspect marker for the recent past; and *tzaj* is a directional: 'toward'.

Mii'n negates verbs in the imperative or potential mood; existential verbs are negated by *miti'*/*nti'*.

The regular passive formant is *-eet*: e.g. *ma chi ku'x t-noj-sa-'n Mal saaku* 'Maria filled the sack(s)' (where *chi* is the third person agent marker; *ku'x* is a directional meaning 'down toward'; *noj* is the root meaning 'full'; and *sa(a)* is the causative formant); *ma chi noj-s-eet saaku t-u'n Mal* 'the sacks were filled by Maria'.

Other passive formants are *-njtz* and *-j*, which suggest accidental, involuntary passivity.

A transitive stem can be detransitivized by the addition of *-n* to the stem, and the replacement of ergative with non-ergative markers; i.e. the transitive/ ergative construction is restructured as an intransitive/nominative one. The resultant form is known as the anti-passive. Two examples from England (1983: 212) will clarify the restructuring: *ma Ø-tzaj t-tzyu-'n* X Y; *ma Ø-tzyuu.n* X *t-i'j* Y. Both sentences mean 'X grabbed Y'. The first is transitive: *tzaj* = third person singular absolutive marker (Ø) + directional *tzaj* 'toward'; the stem *tzyu* 'grab' has the third person ergative marker *t-* and a directional suffix *'n*. The second sentence is anti-passive: the stem is now prefixed by the third person singular absolutive marker (Ø), and followed by the anti-passive marker *-n*; X is followed by the patient relational noun *t-i'j*. In each sentence, *ma* is the recent-time tense marker.

The anti-passive is used in Mayan languages in certain specific situations: see England (1983: 209–22) for a full discussion of this interesting feature.

Word order

VSO is basic indicative order; OVS and SVO occur.

> **1** [1] T-xe' tnejel attok ju Yol; ex ju Yol attok tuc'il Dios, ex ju Yol ax Dios te. [2] Ate jlu' attok tuc'il Dios atxix t-xe tnejel. [3] Nok tu'n o bant jnic'ju tcyakil; ex tcyakilju o bant, miwtloti o bant nokwit mya ate binchante. [4] Attok chwinklal tuc'il, ex aju chwinklal at tuc'il atzunju spic'un cye xjal. [5] Aju spic'un lu' in koptz'aj tuj klolj, ex minti in yupj ju spic'un tu'n klolj.
> [6] Ul jun xjal Juan tbi, tzaj sama'n tu'n Dios. [7] Ate jlu' ul tu'n toc te testiw tu'n ttzaj ttx'olba'n ti'j ju spic'un, tu'ntzun cyocslan cycyakil xjal nok tu'nju tyol. [8] Mya ate Juan spic'un; nok o'cx ul tu'n ttzaj ttx'olba'n ti'j ju spic'un.

MANCHU

INTRODUCTION

Manchu is the most important member of the Tungus-Manchu branch of Altaic. It was, with Chinese, the joint official language of the Qing Dynasty of China (1644–1911). By the late eighteenth century Manchu had ceased to be a spoken language in the Manchu court and administration, but it continued to be written for another century at least. It is now virtually extinct except for the Xibo dialect, spoken in Xinjiang by about 18,000 people, the descendants of Manchu frontier troops posted to the area in the middle of the eighteenth century. Classical Manchu literature consists mainly of translations of the Chinese classics.

SCRIPT

In 1599, Nurhaci, the founder of the Qing Dynasty, commissioned his chief interpreter, Erdeni, to provide a script for the hitherto unwritten Manchu language. Erdeni was able to adapt the Mongol script to Manchu requirements, a fairly straightforward process, as the two languages are phonologically close to each other. This initial Manchu script was systematized in 1632 by another outstanding linguist, Dahai, who also introduced a method of using diacritical points to distinguish between homographs. Thus, in the earlier script ⟋| could be read as *n*, *a*, or *e*. Dahai restricted ⟋| to *a*, adding a point at the left for *n*: ⟋| and a point at the right for *e*: ⟋|.

PHONOLOGY

Consonants

    stops: p, b, t, d, k, g, q
    affricates: tʃ, dʒ
    fricatives: f, v, s, ʃ, j, γ, h
    nasals: m, n, ɲ, ŋ
    lateral and flap: l, r

[g/γ] and [k/q] are non-phonemic allophones. As in Mandarin Chinese, only /-n/-ŋ/ can be a consonantal final in Manchu words. /r/ cannot be initial.

Vowels

    i, e, a, o, u

The nature of a sixth vowel, variously notated as *û* or *ô*, has not been exactly determined.

In Manchu, *a, o, ô* were hard, *e* was soft, and *i, u* were neutral. The opposition was not strictly observed, however, and many affixes have one single form only, which is attached to stems regardless of stem vowel (cf. an analogous development in **Uzbek**). There is, on the other hand, a specific relationship between the vowel system and the male/female dichotomy, *a* being associated with the male principle (yang), *e* with the female principle (yin). Thus, *haha* 'man', *hehe* 'woman'; *ama* 'father', *eme* 'mother'; *amila* 'cock', *emile* 'hen'.

MORPHOLOGY AND SYNTAX

Noun

No grammatical gender, but natural gender is, as noted above, linked to the *a/e* vocalic alternation. The paired opposites *haha/hehe* and *amila/emile* can be added to other nouns if sex has to be distinguished: e.g. *amila temen* 'male camel', *emile temen* 'she-camel'.

Number is marked only for nouns denoting humans and human relationships. There are several endings, which show vowel harmony: e.g. *-sa/-se/-so, -ta/-te*: e.g. *sakda* 'old man', pl. *sakdasa*; *mongo* 'Mongolian', pl. *mongoso*; *eme* 'mother', pl. *emete*. A collective may be made by adding *gemu* 'all': e.g. *irgen gemu* 'people'.

There is only one set of case markers for all declinable nominals in Manchu.

Specimen declension, *ama* 'father':

	Singular	*Plural*
nominative	ama	amata
genitive	ama **i**	amata **i**
dative, locative	ama **de**	} endings as in singular
accusative	ama **be**	
elative/ablative	ama **či**	

Examples: *i bo **be** weilembi* 'he builds a house'; *ere niyalma **de** bumbi* '(I) give to this man'.

Adjective

Treated as a nominal; if used independently takes all case endings. Attributively, adjective precedes noun, and is invariable, as it is when used as predicate: e.g. *sain niyalma* 'good man'; *sain niyalma i gisun* 'the word of a good man'.

A comparative is made with the ablative case: *i min či ahun* 'he is older than I am'

Pronoun

	Singular	Plural
1	bi	be (excl.), muse (incl.)
2	si	suwe
3	i	če

These are declined with the usual case endings – added in the first and second persons singular and plural to a suppletive base, e.g. *bi*: gen. *mini*, dat. *min de*, acc. *mim be*. A common circumlocution for the personal pronouns is made with the noun *beye* 'body': *min i beye* 'my body' = 'I myself'.

DEMONSTRATIVE PRONOUN
ere 'this', pl. *ese*; *tere* 'that', pl. *tese*.

INTERROGATIVE PRONOUN
we(i) 'who?' (with reference to persons only); *ai* 'what, who?' (unrestricted).

RELATIVE PRONOUN
None. For relative constructions *see* **Verb**, below.

Numerals

1–10: *emu, juwe, ilan, duin, sunja, ninggun, nadan, jakon, uyun, juwan*; 11 *juwan emu*; 12 *juwan juwe*; 20 *orin*; 30 *gusin*; 40 *dehi*; 50 *susai*; 100 *tangu* (*tanggô*).

Verb

Derivative stems are formed from primary stems by various affixes, e.g. *-l-, -r-, -d/t-, -s-*, plus harmonic vowel: *aba* 'hunt' – *aba.la.mbi* 'to go hunting'; *gisun* 'word' – *gisu.re.mbi* 'to talk'.

The Manchu verb is nowhere marked for person, number, or gender. Voice, mood, and tense/aspect are expressed by affixes.

VOICE
Passive and causative share the same formant *-(m)bu*, but cannot be confused, as the two constructions differ. The agent in a passive construction is in the dative: e.g. *bi in.de gelebuhe* 'I was frightened by him'. Haenisch (1961) gives the example: *Nikasa manjusa de gidabuha* 'The Chinese were defeated by the Manchus'.

There are also co-operative and reciprocal forms in *-n/č-* and *-ndu-*: e.g. *omičambi* 'to drink together'; *afandumbi* 'to fight each other'.

MOOD
The citation form in *-mbi* is used as an aorist ending in the indicative: e.g. *alambi* 'speak(s)'; *tembi* 'sit(s)'. The time frame is divided aspectually: imperfective marked by *-ra/ro/re*; perfective marked by *-ha/he/ho*: e.g. *alara* 'is/was/will

be speaking'; *alaha* 'spoke, has spoken'. These forms are negated by *-akô* (= Chinese *méiyŏu* 'there isn't'): e.g. *genembi* 'go(es)': *generakô* 'doesn't go' (i.e. *-akô* and *-ra* marker coalesce); *si dahambio daharakôn?* 'are you coming or not?'. There is a second negative form *waka* (= Chinese *búshì* 'is not').

Imperative: there are five forms, graded for respect, starting from the impolite bare stem. Negated by *ume*: e.g. *ume fonjire* 'do not ask'.

Optative: the sense-verb has the marker *-ki*, followed by the auxiliary *sembi*: e.g. *alaki sembi* 'wish(es) to speak'.

An apprehensive mood is formed with the affix *-rahu*: *alarahu sembi* 'I'm afraid he will say'.

NON-FINITE FORMS
The inventory is not as extensive as the similar system in Mongolian. As in Mongolian, the participial/gerundial forms are used in the syntactic linking of clauses, and with auxiliaries, in the formation of compound analytical tenses. The base forms are: imperfective *-me*, e.g. *alame* 'speaking'; perfective *-fi*, e.g. *alafi* 'having spoken'.

Other markers:

-   *-mbime* indicates concomitant action in the past, e.g. *alambime* 'while speaking';
-   *-či* marks hypothetical mood, e.g. *alači* 'if … speaks/spoke';
-   *-čibe* marks concessive mood, e.g. *alačibe* 'although … says/said'.

AUXILIARY VERBS
Examples: *bimbi*, *ombi*, *sembi*; these are used in the formation of analytical verbal forms, e.g. an indefinite future is provided by the imperfective participle plus the optative of *bimbi*: *genere biki* 'will go (at some future time)'.

RELATIVE CLAUSE
Participial constructions are used, e.g. *lamai yaluha morin* 'the horse the lama rode' (*i*-genitive of *lama*; *yaluha* 'he rode', used attributively); *sini gisurenge umesi inu* 'that which you say is good' (the ending *-nge* substantivizes the possessive pronominal forms: cf. *miningge* 'mine'); *bi sinde yanduha baita* 'the matter which I entrusted to you'.

Postpostitions

Postpositions may follow the base case, the genitive, dative, or ablative: e.g. *džalin* 'for', *emgi* 'with', *sidende* 'between' take genitive; *isitala* 'as far as' takes dative.

Word order

SOV is basic.

MANSI

INTRODUCTION

Formerly known as Vogul, Mansi belongs to the Ob'-Ugric sub-division of Finno-Ugric. It is spoken by about 5,000 people in the Khanty-Mansi National Area, which lies between the Urals and the Ob. The Gospels were translated into Mansi in the middle of the nineteenth century, but writing in the language dates only from the 1930s. The literary standard is based on a northern dialect, and contains many Russian and Tatar loan-words. It is used in primary education, and to some extent in the media.

SCRIPT

Since 1937, Cyrillic + ӈ. /γ/ is notated as *g*.

PHONOLOGY

Consonants

stops: p, t, k
fricatives: s, ʃ', x, γ
nasals: m, n, ɲ, ŋ
laterals and flap: l, ʎ, r
semi-vowels: w, j

Voiced stops, plus several fricatives and affricates, are found in loan-words. Palatalized /t'/ occurs.

Vowels

front: i, e
middle: ɪ
back: a, o, u

All, except ɪ, occur both short and long. Length difference is not notated in the script. Short /ɪ/ → [ə]. There is no vowel harmony.

Stress

Stress is on the first syllable.

MORPHOLOGY AND SYNTAX

Noun

No gender. The noun has number and case, takes possessive affixes, and is definite or indefinite. The definite article or topicalizer is *-an'*, used of a known referent or one that has already been identified in discourse. The indefinite article is *akv* /akᵒ/, much used in folk-tales.

The noun has three numbers. The dual marker is based on /ɣ/, i.e. *-g/-gɪg/-ig*: e.g. *ne* 'woman', dual *negɪg* 'two women'; *sali* 'reindeer', *saliyig* 'two reindeer'. The plural marker is based on *-t*: *yiv* 'tree', pl. *yivɪt*.

There are six cases; the nominative/accusative opposition is lacking, and there is no genitive. Specimen declension of *kol* 'house', singular: nom. *kol*; adit. *koln*; loc. *kolɪt*; abl. *kolnɪl*; instr. *kolɪl*; translative *kolɪg*.

The possessive affixes for singular possessed object are:

	1st person	*2nd person*	*3rd person*
singular possessor	-um	-n;	-e, -te
dual possessor	-men	-ɪn	-en, -ten
plural possessor	-(y)uv	-ɪn	-(a)nɪl, -yanɪl

Where two objects are possessed, the marker *-ag-* is inserted before the personal ending; where more than two objects are possessed, *-an* or *-n-* is inserted. Thus: *kolum* 'my house'; *kolagum* 'my two houses'; *kolanum* 'my houses' *kolaganɪl* 'their two houses'.

Adjective

The adjective is not differentiated from the noun: e.g. *yiv* 'tree, wood, wooden'. As attribute, adjective precedes noun and is invariable; as predicate, it agrees with the subject in number.

Pronoun

Independent personal: singular, dual, and plural first, second, third persons: *am – naŋ – tav*; *men – nen – ten*; *man – nan – tan*. These are declined in five cases (no translative), giving 45 possible forms, including an accusative: e.g. *anum* is accusative case of *am*; cf. *men.(a)menɪn* 'to us two', *man.an.ɪltɪl* 'by them (pl.)'.

DEMONSTRATIVE PRONOUN
ti 'this', *ta* 'that'; declined in three numbers, six cases.

INTERROGATIVE PRONOUN
xoŋxa 'who?' (general); *xot.yut* 'who? which?' (of specific number); *manɪr* 'what?'. These also act as relative pronouns, declined for case and number.

Numerals

1–10: *akw* (giving indefinite article), *katɪg*, *xurum*, *nila*, *at*, *xot*, *sat*, *nyololov*, *ontolov*, *lov*; 11 *akw.xuypu.lov*; 20 *xus*; 30 *vat*: 21 **vat.nupɪl** *akw* (where *nupɪl* is a postposition meaning 'to'). 40 *naliman*; 50 *atpan*; 100 (*yanɪg*)*sat*: 90 *ontɪr.sat*.

Katɪg 2 has an attributive form, *kit* (cf. **Hungarian**): e.g. *kit negɪg* 'two women'.

Verb

As in Hungarian, there are definite and indefinite conjugations, active and passive voices, with five moods – indicative, subjunctive, imperative, conditional, and inferential. The indicative has two tenses, present–future and past. All finite forms are marked for three persons and three numbers.

INDEFINITE CONJUGATION
Example of present tense of *tot-* 'carry':

	Singular	Dual	Plural
1	tot.**eg**.um	tot.**i**.men	tot.**e**.v
2	tot.**eg**.n	tot.**eg**.ɪn	tot.**eg**.ɪn
3	tot.**i**	tot.**eg**	tot.**eg**.ɪt

The past-tense marker is *-s-*: e.g. *mina.s.um* 'I went'; *mina.s.uv* 'we (pl.) went'.

DEFINITE CONJUGATION
The markers *-l-* (sing.), *-yag-* (dual), *-yan-* (pl.) are inserted between the tense marker and the personal ending: e.g. *tel.g.l.um* 'I eat it' (def.); *var.i.l.uv* 'we saw it' (def.).

> passive: *-(a)ve* + tense marker + personal ending, e.g. *tot.ve.s.um* 'I was brought';
> imperative: the marker is *-n*;
> subjunctive: *-nuv*, with variants, e.g. *tot.nuv.l.um* 'I'd take/have taken him/it' (def.)'
> conditional: the affix is *-ke*: e.g. *totsɪn ke* 'if you bring/brought';
> inferential: *-ne-*, e.g. *tot.ne.n* 'it seems that you are bringing'.

Further markers provide inceptive, semelfactive, reiterative, durative, habitual forms. The causative marker is *-t/l-* (with geminated, *-tt-*, or combined, *-lt-*, variants). The negating particle is *at*: e.g. *am at vislum* 'I didn't take it'.

PARTICIPLES
-n (general), *-m* (action in the past); a temporal relative clause can be made with *-ke-...t*: e.g. *min.ke.m.t* 'when I go'.

Postpositions

Examples: *ont.sɪl* 'near by', e.g. *vor ont.sɪl* 'near the forest'; *porat* 'during', e.g. *tuyt porat* 'while it was snowing'.

Word order

SOV, OSV.

MANX

INTRODUCTION

Manx belongs to the Goidelic group (Q-Celtic) of the Celtic branch of Indo-European. There seems to be a British (Brythonic) substratum in Manx, dating from pre-Roman times; but the main component in the language is Eastern Irish, brought to the Isle of Man by settlers from Ireland. The island was Christianized in the fifth/sixth century. No attempt was made to write Manx till the early seventeenth century when Bishop John Phillips (a Welshman) translated the Book of Common Prayer into Manx (c. 1610). In the absence of any etymological or historically justifiable orthography, Phillips used a phonetic transcription in terms of the English alphabet. This same notation was used for the translation of the Bible (1770s) and became standard. Manx ceased to be taught in schools in mid-nineteenth century. Thereafter, the decline into disuse was steep. The 1901 census showed a little over 4,000 speakers, almost none of them monoglot. By 1950 only a couple of dozen Manx speakers were left. The language is now extinct, though efforts to resuscitate it continue. Societies for the preservation of Manx were established in 1858 and 1899. Until recently, Tynewald legislation was promulgated in both English and Manx.

SCRIPT

English alphabet minus x, z; the cedilla is used, e.g. *çh* = /tʃ/.

PHONOLOGY

Consonants

    stops: p, b, t, d, k, g; palatalized t', d'
    affricates: tʃ, dʒ
    fricatives: f, v, s, z, ð, ʃ, ʒ, x, γ, h
    nasals: m, n, ɲ, ŋ
    laterals and flaps: l, ł, ʎ, r, r'
    semi-vowel: j

In the vicinity of /a, o, ɔ, u/, /d/ tends to become retroflex or emphatic [ɖ]; in some words, /d/ → [ð]: e.g. *moddey* /mɔːðə/, 'dog'.

    A final nasal tends to be pronounced with the corresponding voiced consonant: e.g. *kione* [k'oːdn], 'head'. Similarly with /rl/ and /rn/: e.g. *Baarl* [bɛrdl] 'English'.

Vowels

front: ɪ, iː, e, ɛ, ɛː, y, yː
central: a, ə, ʌ, ɑː
back: ɔ, ɔː, o, u, uː, œ, œː

There are fourteen diphthongs, most of which are glides to -i/-u: e.g. /ai, ɔi, ɛi/.

Mutation

The mutation system in Manx is rather close to that in Scottish Gaelic (*see* **Scottish Gaelic** for a fuller description). Some examples of standard mutation will be found (marked by bold face) in the Morphology section, below.

MORPHOLOGY AND SYNTAX

Definite article

Singular nominal masculine *yn*; feminine *yn*; common plural *ny*. The masculine and common plural forms do duty for all cases; the feminine has a specific genitive form in *ny*. Before a consonant initial, *yn* /ən/ may become *y* /ə/.

Noun

GENDER
Some nominal endings are coded for gender; e.g. *-an*, *-ys* are masculine, disyllables in *-ag*, *-aght* are feminine. A gender distinction can be made by using *fer* 'man', *ben* 'woman': e.g. *fer-obbee* /ferɔvi/ 'wizard'; *ben-obbee* 'witch'; *jee* 'god'; *ben-jee* 'goddess'; *ben-varrey* 'mermaid' (*mooir* 'sea' (fem.), genitive, *marrey*).

PLURAL
Most Manx nouns make their plural in *-yn* (= Gaelic *-an*): e.g. *creg* 'rock', pl. *creggyn*; *awin* 'river', pl. *awinyn*; *coo* 'dog', pl. *coyin*. Mutation occurs: *fer* 'man', pl. *fir*. In *cabbil* 'horses', slender *l* replaces the broad *l* of *cabbyl* 'horse'.

DECLENSION
A few singular genitive forms survived, and there are some irregularities, but essentially Manx had lost the old case system. *Ben* 'woman', may be given as an example of a highly irregular paradigm:

	Singular	Plural
nominative	ben	mraane (also acc.)
genitive	mrieh	ben
dative	ben (also acc.)	mraane
vocative	ven	vraane

POSSESSIVE
Construct formula with ellipsis of article of possessor: e.g. *mac yn dooinney* /dun'ə/ 'the man's son'; *rehollys vooar ny gabbyl* 'the great moonlight of the horses' (entry in the *Cregeen Dictionary*, 1866).

Adjective

Invariable, apart from plural ending which is often added to monosyllables. The attributive adjective follows the noun, with mutation: e.g. *lioar vooar* 'big book'. A few adjectives, e.g. *jeih* 'good', *drogh* 'bad', *ard* 'high', precede and coalesce with the noun: *ard-ree* 'a high king'; *drogh.spyrryd* 'an evil spirit'. A comparative was made with the formula *ny s'...na*: e.g. *ny s'baney na* 'whiter than'. Manx has the usual suppletive formations: *olk – messy* 'bad – worse'; *beg – loo* 'small – smaller'. Cf. *ta'n wooa vooar doo* 'the big cow is black'; *ta'n wooa ghoo mooar* 'the black cow is big'.

Pronoun

Personal independent, with emphatic forms:

		Singular		*Plural*	
1		mee	mish	shin	shinym
2		oo	uss	shiu	shiuish
3	masc.	eh	eshyn	ad	adsyn
	fem.	ee	ish		

Several prepositions combine with the personal pronouns: e.g. *at* 'with': sing. *aym, ayd, echey/eck*; pl. *ain, eu, oc*; *er* 'on': e.g. *orrym, ort, er* + emphatic forms; *hug* 'towards': e.g. *hym, hood, huggey*.

POSSESSIVE PRONOUNS
my/m', dty/dt', e 'his' + aspiration; *e* 'her' (no aspiration); plural first, second, third *nyn*. For example, with *thie* 'house': emphatic forms:

		Singular	*Plural*
1		my **hie's**	
2		dty **hie's**	nyn **dhiesyn**
3	masc.	e **hiesyn**	
	fem.	e **thieish**	

DEMONSTRATIVE PRONOUN/ADJECTIVE
Three degrees: *shoh* 'this' – *shen* 'that' – *shid* 'that (yonder)'.

INTERROGATIVE PRONOUN
quoi 'who?'; *cred, ke* 'what?'.

RELATIVE PRONOUN
ny, with negative form *nagh*: e.g. *yn dooinney ny chadlys* 'the man who is sleeping'; *ny dooinney nagh vel g'obbragh* 'the man who is not working'.

Relative with *ta*: cf. *ta'n dooinney g'obbragh* 'the man is working'; *yn dooinney ta g'obbragh* 'the man who is working'; *yn dooinney ta cabbyl echey* 'the man who has a horse' (lit. 'who – a horse – is at him'). *Ny* and *ta* are interchangeable.

Numerals

1–10: *nane, jees, tree, kiare, queig, shey, shiaght, hoght, nuy, jeih*; 11 *nane...jeig*; 12 *ghaa...yeig*; 13 *three...jeig*; 20 *feed*; 30 *jeih as feed*; 40 *daeed*; 50 *jeih as daeed*; 100 *keead*.

Examples: *kiare cabbil* 'four horses' (noun in plural); *kiare cabbil jeig* 'fourteen horses'.

'One' and 'two' – *nane, jees* – have alternative forms, *un, daa*, used with nouns.

Verb

The Manx verb behaves very much as its counterpart in Scottish Gaelic. There are indicative and imperative (second person only) moods, and conditional and relative forms. There are two conjugations: consonant-initial and vowel-initial.

The substantive verb *ve* 'to be' plays an essential part in conjugation. Its principal forms, with negatives, are:

> Present tense: sing. 1 *ta mee*, 2 *t'ou*, 3 *t'eh*, fem. *t'ee*; pl. 1 *ta shin*, 2 *ta shiu*, 3 *t'ad*.
> Negative: *cha nel/vel mee, cha nel ou*, etc.
> Future tense: sing. 1 *bee'm*, 2 *bee oo*, 3 *bee eh*, fem. *ee*; pl. 1 *beemayd*, 2 *bee shiu*, 3 *bee ad*. Negative: *cha bee'm*, etc.
> Conditional: *veign, veagh oo, veagh eh*, etc. Negative: *cha beign*, etc.
> Preterite: sing. *va mee, v'ou, v'eh*; pl. *va shin, va shiu, v'ad*. Negative: *cha row mee, cha row oo* ...

These forms are used in analytic compound tenses with verbal noun: e.g. *ta mee breh* 'I am carrying'; *va mee breh* 'I was carrying'. In the future and conditional, first person singular and plural retain synthetic forms, while second and third are analytic: e.g. *moyllym* 'I shall, would praise', *moyllmayd* 'we shall praise'; but, *moyllee oo, eh, ee; moyllee shiu, ad*.

The preterite shows aspiration as in Scottish Gaelic: *voyll mee, oo*, etc. Negative: *cha voyll mee*, etc.

Passive with *va*:

ta mee caillit	'I am lost'
va mee caillit	'I was lost'
bee'm caillit	'I shall be lost'
veign caillit	'I would be lost'

Prepositions

(*See* also **Personal Pronouns**, above). In Old Manx the prepositions governed the dative or accusative case, + mutation. The mutation remains: e.g. *yn mullagh* 'the top': *er y vullagh* 'at the top'; *yn cabbyl* 'the horse': *lesh y chabbyl* 'with the horse'.

Word order

VSO is normal in principal clause.

1 AYNS y toshiaght va'n Goo, as va'n Goo marish Jee, as va'n Goo Jee.

2 Va'n Goo cheddin ayns y toshiaght marish Jee.

3 Liorishyn va dy chooilley nhee er ny yannoo; as n'egooish cha row nhee erbee jeant va er ny yannoo;

4 Aynsyn va bea, as va'n vea soilshey deiney.

5 As ren y soilshey soilshean ayns y dorraghys, as cha ren y dorraghys goaill-rish.

6 ¶ Va dooinney er ny choyrt veih Jee va enmyssit Ean.

7 Haink eh shoh son feanish, dy ymmyrkey feanish jeh'n toilshey, liorishyn dy voddagh dy chooilley ghooinney credjal.

8 Cha nee eh va'n soilshey shen, agh v'eh er ny choyrt dy ymmyrkey feanish jeh'n toilshey shen.

MAORI

INTRODUCTION

Maori belongs to the East Polynesian branch of the Austronesian family, of which it is the most southerly member. When Cook discovered New Zealand in the eighteenth century the Maori population numbered about 300,000, and had been in the islands for over 500 years. At present, Maori is spoken by around 100,000, which makes it in terms of numbers the leading Polynesian language. English has had a considerable effect on the vocabulary of Maori, and some effect on the syntax. Dialect forms vary mainly in phonological detail and in the lexicon. The first Maori grammar appeared in 1815 (Kendall).

SCRIPT

In the 1820s a phonetic script for Maori was devised in Cambridge. Bible translation soon followed.

PHONOLOGY

With ten consonants and five vowels Maori has the richest phonological inventory of any East Polynesian language.

Consonants

The stops are /p, t, k/ with their associated nasals /m, n, ŋ/; /f/ and /w/ are present, and an alveolar /r/ close to /l/. The glottal /h/ tends to [ʔ] in one dialect. /f/ is written as *wh*: e.g. *whare* = /farɛ/.

Vowels

long or short: i, e = [ɛ], a, o = [ɔ], u

Long vowels are notated either by doubling or by macron.

Stress

Stress is on the first long vowel or diphthong; if neither is present, then on the first syllable.

MORPHOLOGY AND SYNTAX

For a general note on Polynesian structure *see* **Polynesian Languages**. The parts of speech in Maori may be broadly divided into two categories: bases and particles. Nominal bases are compatible with preposited nominal particles; verbal bases are compatible with pre- and postposited process particles. Internal flection is limited to certain plural formations occurring in a very few nouns, e.g. *tangata* 'person', pl. *tāgata*; *wahine* 'woman', pl. *wāhine*. Plurality is normally established by the article, by pronominal concord, or by the presence of a numeral: e.g. *te kōtiro* 'the girl', *ngā kōtiro* 'the girls'.

Nominal particles

1. Indefinite article: *he*, e.g. *he kōtiro* '(a) girl/girls'.

2. Definite article: *te*, pl. *ngā*, e.g. *te rākau* 'the tree', *ngā rākau* 'the trees'.

3. Article with proper nouns: *ko/a*. *Ko* is used if a name is the first word in the sentence: e.g. *Ko Tiare te māhito* 'Charles is the teacher'; *Kei Ākarana a Tiare* 'Charles is in Auckland'.

4. Demonstratives: *tēnei* 'this', proximate to first person, pl. *ēnei*; *tēnā* 'that', proximate to second person, pl. *ēna*; *tērā* 'that', removed from both, pl. *ērā*. Examples: *ēnā māhita* 'those teachers (near you)'; *tēnei whare roa* 'this long house'. Demonstrative pronoun follows predicate: e.g. *he whare tēnei* 'this is a house'. The sentence is introduced by *ko* if the noun is definite: e.g. *Ko te māmā tēnā* 'That is the mother.'

5. Object, target marker: *i*, e.g. *E mātakitaki ana ngā tamariki i te hōiho* 'The children are watching the horse' (for *e...ana*, *see* **Process particles**, below).

6. Possessive markers: *o* and *a* series. *See* **Polynesian Languages** for general note on alienable/inalienable possession in Polynesian. The Maori taxonomy is not entirely clear. The *a* series includes kin (spouse, child), animals (unless used in transport), articles of food, various disposable items, etc. The *o* series includes immovable property, relatives not in the *a* category, articles of clothing, etc. Cf. *te wahine a Hohepa* 'Joseph's wife'; *te matua o Hohepa* 'Joseph's father'. Similarly, *na/no* are used for 'belonging to', with reference to these two categories: e.g. *he potae no te mahita* 'a hat belonging to the teacher'.

7. Agentive markers: *e/ki*, e.g. *I matakitia te kēmu e ngā tamariki* 'The game was watched by the children' (for passive verb form, see below; *tamariki* is irregular plural formation from *tamaiti* 'child').

8. Locative markers: *kei/kei* + noun → preposition, e.g.

(a) *kei Ākarana a Tiare* 'Charles is in Auckland';
(b) *kei runga i* 'on top of, on'; *kei raro i* 'under'; *kei roto i* 'in', etc.: e.g. *Kei runga i te tēpu te pukapuka* 'The book is on the table'; *Kei tawhiti te maunga* 'the mountain is far away.'

The pronominal system

PERSONAL PRONOUNS

	Singular	Dual	Plural
1	ahau/au	tāua (2nd + 1st p.)	tātou (2nd + 1st p.)
		māua (3rd + 1st p.)	mātou (3rd + 1st p.)
2	koe	kōrua	koutou
3	ia	rāua	rātou

POSSESSIVE PRONOUNS

These are closely related to the above listed pronominal forms. In the first person plural, both dual and plural subject have inclusive and exclusive forms, the former in *t-*, the latter in *m-*. All possessive forms are marked with *tā* or *tō*, plural *ā/ō*, with reference to the possessive markers described in 6 above. Thus *tā tāua* denotes singular *a*-category object belonging to us two; *ō rātou* denotes a plurality of *o*-category objects belonging to them (several); *ō tāua tamariki* 'our children' (dual inclusive); *ā māua tamariki* 'our children' (dual exclusive).

Process/verbal particles

These generate tenses:

1. Simple past: *i*, e.g. *i haere a Hohepa* 'Joseph went'.
2. Present continuous: *kei te* + verb, e.g. *kei te mahi rātou* 'they are working'.
3. Continuous action, neutral as to tense: *e* + verb + *ana*, e.g. *e tākaro **ana** ngā tamariki* 'the children are/were/will be playing'; *e mahi **ana** ngā tāngata* 'the men are/were/will be working'.
4. Past continuous: *i te* + verb, e.g. *i te mahi a Hohepa* 'Joseph was working'.
5. Perfective: *kua*, e.g. **kua** *tae mai te rangatira* 'the chief has arrived'.
6. Onset of action in narrative: *ka*, e.g. *ka haere te pahi* 'the bus left'.
7. Agent-focus in future: *ma* + agent + *e* + verb, e.g. **Ma** *Hohepa e hanga te whare* 'It's Joseph who will build the house'.
8. Agent-focus in past: *na* + agent + *i* + verb, e.g. *Na rātou i waiata nga waiata Māori* 'It was you (pl.) who sang the Maori songs.' *Ma/na* may indicate future/past even where no verb is present: e.g. *na rātou nga waiata Māori*.
9. Imperative: *e* + verb/*me* + verb.
10. *kāhore/ekore* negates verb: e.g. *kei te mahi a Hohepa* 'Joseph is working'; *kāhore a Hohepa i te mahi* 'Joseph is not working' (*kei* is not compatible with *kāhore*).
11. Supplementary particles: e.g. *tonu*, stresses continuation of action; *pea* marks potentiality, feasibility; *rawa* intensifier; *nē*, *nēra* interrogative.

PASSIVE

A variety of endings turn active verbs into passives, e.g *-a*, *-ai*, *-tia*: *I matakitia te kēmu* 'The game was watched.' The passive endings are also used to make a polite imperative: e.g. *Whakamāoritia* 'Please translate into Maori'. Here, *whaka-* is the causative prefix.

A verbal noun is made in *-anga*: e.g. *kōrero* 'to speak' – *kōrerotanga* 'speaking'.

RELATIVE CLAUSES

There are several constructions, e.g. *Ko ia te tangata i haere mai inapō* 'He is the man who came yesterday'; *Ko as te tangata i kite ai au inapō* 'He is the man I saw yesterday' (*haere mai* 'to come'; *kite* 'to see'; *ai* used if subject changes).

Agent-focus in relative clause: cf. *te tangata nāna nei i hanga te whare* 'the man who built the house'; *te tangata māna e hanga te whare* 'the man who will build the house'.

Numerals

1–10: *(ko)tahi, rua, toru, whā, rima, ono, whitu, waru, iwa, tekau.* 11 *tekau mā tahi*; 12 *tekau mā rua*; 20 *rua tekau*; 100 *kotahi rau*.

Word order

VSO is basic and normal (V is a verbal complex).

I TE timatanga te Kupu, i te Atua ano te Kupu, ko te Kupu ano te Atua.

2 I te Atua ano tenei *Kupu* i te timatanga.

3 Nana nga mea katoa i hanga; a kahore tetahi *mea* kihai hanga e ia *o nga mea* i hanga.

4 I a ia te oranga; a ko te oranga te maramatanga mo nga tangata.

5 E witi ana te maramatanga i roto i te pouritanga; a kihai tangohia e te pouritanga.

6 ¶ He tangata ano i tonoa mai i te Atua, ko Hoani tona ingoa.

7 I haere mai ia hei kai korero, kia korero ai ia ki te Maramatanga, kia wakapono ai *nga tangata* katoa i a ia.

8 Ehara ia i taua Maramatanga, na, *i tonoa mai ia* kia korero ki taua Maramatanga.

MAPUDUNGU

INTRODUCTION

Mapudungu, also known as Mapuche or Araucanian, is classified by some authorities as a Penutian language, as an outlier, that is, of a North American Indian stock. Others allocate it to the Andean-Equatorial family. When the Spaniards arrived in Chile they found three groups of Araucanians, one of which – the Pikumche (*piku* 'north', *che* 'people') – was speedily conquered. By the eighteenth century the southern group too had lost its specific identity. The central group, however, the Mapuche (*mapu* 'land', *che* 'people') has maintained its identity as a socially compact and self-aware indigenous grouping, and, as such, takes second place only to the Quechua-Aymara and the Guaraní. They number about a 250,000 in Chile, with a further 100,000 in Argentina. The Mapuche call their language Mapudungu (*mapu* 'land', *dəŋun* 'to speak').

SCRIPT

If written, Mapudungu is notated in the Roman alphabet. Félix (1916) uses the additional letters, *ə, ü, ŋ, ñ*, plus *tr* for the emphatic ejective /tṣ/.

PHONOLOGY

Consonants

    stops: p, t, d, k; q (*see* **Vowels**, below)
    affricates: tʃ, tṣ
    fricatives: f, s, ʒ
    nasals: m, n, ɲ, ŋ
    lateral and flap: l, ʎ, r
    semi-vowels: j, w

Félix distinguishes allophones of /t, n, l/, which he notates as *t·, n·, l·*. In this article, these allophones are not marked. *d* tends to [ð]; *sh* = [ʒ].

Vowels

    i, e, a, o, u, ə

Félix uses *ü* to denote a very guttural [ɪ] sound, uttered with the lips in position for [e]. In some descriptions of the language, the sound is compared to the

Guarani *y*. In certain positions, e.g. as initial followed by *i*, *ü* acquires a consonantal value between [g] and [q]; e.g. *üi* 'man': [qɪ].

/ə/ in Mapudungu has several values, depending on consonantal environment; e.g. preceding /f/ → /œ/.

Stress

On the penultimate syllable for vocalic finals; on final for consonantal. There are exceptions; e.g. first person plural forms ending in the semi-vowel /j/ are stressed on the final syllable.

MORPHOLOGY AND SYNTAX

Noun

Mapudungu has no grammatical gender. Natural gender is indicated by lexical means: e.g. *wentru che* 'man-person'; *domo che* 'woman-person'. *Wentru* and *domo* are also used to differentiate grade: e.g. *wentru kal* 'coarse wool'; *domo kal* 'fine wool'.

An animate/inanimate opposition is reflected in the use of *pu* as a plural marker for nouns denoting animate; some authorities give *yuka* as an equivalent marker for inanimate nouns: *Chi* may be used as a definite article: e.g. *chi wentru* 'the man'; *pu wentru* '(the) men'.

The numeral *kiñe* 'one', functions as indefinite article: e.g. *kiñe wesha ad niei ñi kawellu* 'my horse has a nasty habit' (*wesha* 'bad'; *ad* 'custom'; *niei* 'has'; *ñi* 'my').

A collective plural for animates is made with *wen*: e.g. *fotəmwen* 'father and son', where *fotəm* denotes 'son' (with reference to father). Similarly *pəñeñwen* 'mother and child' (male or female).

A partitive plural is made with *ke*: e.g. *alü ke che* 'many people' (*alü* 'many'). *Ke* is placed between the attributive adjective and the noun: *küme ke kawellu* 'good horses'.

Infixed *-ume-* and *-ye-* also act as pluralizing formants: e.g. *pofreŋe.**ume**.lu* 'those who are poor' (*-lu* is the participial form used to form relative clauses); *aku.**ye**.i fentren che* 'many people arrived' (*akun* 'to arrive'; *fentren* 'many').

Compounding is frequent in Mapudungu: e.g. *küdau* 'work' – *küdau.fe* 'worker' – *küdau.we* 'place of work'; *piku.m.che* 'people of the north' – *piku.kürəf* 'north wind'.

Syntactic relations are expressed by particles: *ñi* (gen.), *meu* (loc., abl., etc.). Prepositions help to clarify the situation. These are often derived from nouns, e.g. *furi* 'shoulders' comes to means 'behind': *furi ruka meu* 'behind the house' (*ruka); fei ni furi meu* 'behind him' (*fei* 'he, him'); *pərəmfiñ ñi pəchü fotəm kawellu meu* 'I accustomed my little son to the horse' (use of *fotəm* shows that the father is speaking; *pəchü* 'small'; *pərəmn* 'to accustom, train').

-tu is the formant for an instrumental sense: e.g. *namu.tu* 'by foot'; *kawellu.tu* 'by horse'.

Adjective

The adjective is invariable, and, as attribute, precedes the noun: e.g. with the noun *lafken* 'stretch of water': *fücha lafken* 'the sea'; *pəchü lafken* 'a lake'. Cf. *nieiñ wesha antü* 'we're having (*nieiñ*) a bad (*wesha*) day' (not getting much).

The adjective can take the plural marker: *pu fücha* 'the old (people).' A comparative is made with *doy(el)*: e.g. *iñche doyel mai wesha loŋko ŋen* 'my headache is really (*mai*) getting worse' (*loŋko* 'headache'; *ŋen* 'I have').

Pronoun

The personal forms are:

	Singular	Dual	Plural
1	iñche	iñchiu	iñchiñ
2	eimi	eymu	eymn
3	fei	feyeŋu	feyeŋn

Truncated forms of these serve as possessives. *Ñi* functions both as 1st person singular possessive and as a general marker: *ñi chau* 'my father', *ñi chau eŋu* 'their (dual) father', *mi chau* 'your father', *ñi ruka* (*y*)*eŋn* 'their (plural) house' and as oblique forms: *elueyeu eŋn pətrem* 'he gave them tobacco' (*pətrem*).

DEMONSTRATIVE ADJECTIVE/PRONOUN
təfa, *təfei* (masculine/feminine; singular/plural): e.g. *təfa.chi pu mapuche* 'these Mapuche'; *təfei.chi küdau meu* 'in this work'; *iñche fei kim.la.n* 'I don't know this' (*kimn* 'to know'; *-la-* negative marker).

INTERROGATIVE PRONOUN
inei 'who?'; *chem* 'what?'.
Mapudungu has interrogative verbs, e.g. *chemn* 'What to do?'; *chum.a.imi* 'What will you do?'; *chum.ke.imi* 'What are you doing?'

RELATIVE PRONOUN
None; the participle in *-lu* is used, if necessary with the adjectival formant *chi*: *elu.lu* 'he/she who gives'; *ñi elu.ŋen.chi weshakelu* 'the thing which they gave me'; *wadkü.le.chi ko* 'water which boils'.
Chi may be added to nouns or verbs in gerundial form: e.g. *ipeyüm.chi ruka* 'house in which one gets something to eat' (*ipeyüm* 'eating utensils').

Numerals

1–10: *kine, epu, küla, meli, kechu, kayu, relqe/reqle, pura, ailla, mari*; 20 *epu mari*; 30 *küla mari*; 100 *pataka*. *Meli semana* 'four weeks'; *küla rupa* 'three times'.

Verb

The infinitive ending is *-n*, which can be added to other parts of speech to form verbs: e.g. *küme* 'good' – *kümn* 'to be good'.

Many Mapudungu verbs are semantically dense information-packs, the root meaning being extended by modal, circumstantial, affective overtones, all of which would be expressed adverbially in Indo-European languages: for example, cf.

> *pinamalkan* (root *pin* 'to say'): 'to denigrate someone who is, along with others, without confronting him/her directly';
> *inakonkəlen* (root *konkəlen* 'be inside something'): 'to be in a region, house or family where one was not born; i.e. is a stranger'.

Verbs are transitive (primary or derived) neutral or impersonal. They are fully conjugated in three persons and three numbers. The personal endings are reduced reflexes of the personal pronouns. There are active and passive voices and four moods: indicative, imperative, optative, subjunctive. In the indicative, the following tenses are distinguished: present (null marker), imperfect (marker *-fu/i*), future (marker *-a-*) and perfect (marker *-uye-*).

POLYPERSONAL VERBS

As Félix (1916) emphasizes in his *Diccionario*, it is misleading to illustrate the Mapudungu verb by setting out such forms as *elun* 'I give', *eluymi* 'thou givest', *eluy* 'he/she gives' (from *elun* 'to give'). These are deficient in that one must give something to someone: i.e. the transitive verb form must be polypersonal:

> *elufiñ* 'I gave it to him';
> *elu.la.qeneu* 'he didn't give it to me' (*-la-* is the negative infix);
> *elueyeu* 'he gave it to them';
> *elune.a.imi* 'they'll give it to you'.

Such forms, coded for both subject and direct and/or indirect object, can be further generated from simple transitive roots by the addition of such formants as *(e)l*, *lel*, *(n)ma* to the root: e.g. from *küpaln* 'to bring, draw something', are formed *küpal.el.n/küpa.ma.n* 'to bring, draw something to someone'; *küpa.lel.fi.ñ manshana* 'I brought him/her apples'.

Further examples of polypersonal verbs in Mapudungu:

> *ŋillan* 'to buy': *ŋillaleneu* 'he bought it for me', *ñi chau ŋillaleneu təfachi kawellu* 'my father bought me this horse';
> *akuln* 'to bring, carry': *akul.el.eneu ñi chumpiru* 'he brought me my hat';
> *puwəln* 'cause to arrive somewhere else': *iñche fei puwəl.el.a.qeyu* 'I'll get it to your house for you';
> *anümn* 'to plant': *anüm.el.ye.a.qeyu mi manshana* 'I'll plant your apple trees for you'.

DERIVED STEMS

The following formants (among many others) are used to generate aspectual and modal meanings:

> *(ma)ke*, customary/habitual action: e.g. *weñei* 'he steals' – *weñe.ke.i* 'he's always stealing';
> *ŋilla*, causative: e.g. *ŋilla.faln* 'to have made, order to be made';

küpa, desiderative: e.g. *küpa.amu.la.i* 'he doesn't want to go';

mәñal, inceptive with future tense, completive with past tense: e.g. *mәñal.pra.kawelln, akui witran* 'I had just mounted the horse when a stranger arrived';

pepi, potential: e.g. *pepi.amu.la.ian* 'I shan't be able to go', *tәfachi ruka pepi.mәlen ŋelai* 'one may not enter this house';

(ә)rke, continuative: e.g. *fei weñeñ.ma.rke.eneu ñi kawellu* 'so then he goes and steals my horse';

rupa(n), terminative, perfective: e.g. *rupan.küdau.fu.iñ* 'we had finished working';

(ә)rpu marks intermediate stage in action: e.g. *nütram.әrpu.i = pi.rpu.i* 'he said' (while something else was going on), *la.rpu.i Temuco* 'he died in Temuco' (on journey from Valdivia to Santiago), *aŋkan.tu fele.rpu.i* 'as time went on, he became blind';

pu, perfective infix: e.g. *trann* 'to fall' – *tran.pu.i* 'he fell', *küdau.pu.an* 'I'll go and do a day's work (and finish it)', *mәle.pu.an hospital meu* 'I'll go to hospital (and be cured there)';

tu marks return to original state or condition: cf. *küpai* 'he came' (of a stranger), *küpa.tu.i* 'he came' (return of a native), *amu.tu.i* 'he went away' (from where he did not belong).

PASSIVE

ŋen is added to transitive stems: e.g. *ñi elu.ŋen* 'I am given'.

VERBAL PREFIXES

Examples:

fente-, terminative, 'as far as': e.g. *fente.dәŋun* 'to fall silent, having been talking', *fente.kәnun* 'to stop doing something';

wәño- indicates reversal, return: e.g. *wәño.kintun mapu* 'to return to see the land' (i.e. escape death), *wәñonmatuimi mi kure?* 'Has your wife returned to your side?'

NEGATION

The general negating infix is *-la-*: e.g. with root *femn* 'to do something specific' – *fem.la.n* 'I did no such thing'; *koilatun* 'to tell lies' – *koilatu.la.n* 'I'm not lying'. *-la-* may be reinforced by *newe*; e.g. with root *adtun* 'to find something pleasing': *iñche newe adtu.ke.la.fiñ chi dәŋu* 'I do not find this matter (*dәŋu*) at all pleasing' (for the ending *-fiñ*, indicating first person → third person deixis, *see* **Polypersonal Verbs**, above).

-keno-/-ki-, negates the imperative: e.g. *küpa.keno.pe* 'he is not to come'.

Prepositions

Examples:

aŋka (basic meaning, 'stomach') 'in the middle of': *aŋka n.amun nien ñi kutran* lit. 'in the middle of the leg I have my pain', i.e. 'my leg hurts in the middle';

inau/inafel + *meu* 'close to': *iñche ñi inau meu* 'close to me';
minche 'below': *minche ruka meu* 'below the house';
wente 'upon': *wente mesa* 'on the table'.

Many verbs carry specific spatial information, rendering pre- or postpositions superfluous; cf. *takunaqkəlen* 'to be below and covered by something': *piuke takunaqkəlei ponon meu* 'The heart is below the lungs (*ponon*) and covered by them'. *Meu* is an all-purpose locative postposition, exemplified several times in this article.

Word order

As described above, if V is a transitive verbal complex, it is coded for S and O. Where nominals are present, order is rather free: SOV, OVS, and SVO are all possible.

---

1. Llitun meu deu felefui ta Dungun, ka feichi Dungun Ngünechen engu felefui, ka feichi Dungun, Ngünechen nga tfei.
2. Fei tfa rüf llitun meu Ngünechen engu felefui.
3. Kom küfchi dungu, fei ta ñi deumel ta tfei, ka ngenofule fei chem no rume ñi deumyel, ngelayafui.
4. Fei meu mlefui ta mongen, ka tfeichi mongen, ta che ñi pelom ta tfei.
5. Ka ta pelom, pu dumiñ meu llemllemi ka ta pu dumiñ yerpulaeyeu.
6. Mlefui mai kiñe wentru Ngünechen ñi werküel, fei mai Juan pingefui.
7. Fei mai küpai pifalngealu, ka ñi wülpayafiem pi falchi dungu ñi felen kai feichi pelom, ñi feyentuam kom che fei meu.
8. Fei ta pelom no fel, re ta ñi pifalpatiem ñi felen tfeichi pelom.

MARATHI

INTRODUCTION

As one of the official state languages of India, Marathi is spoken by about 50 million people in Maharāshtra, with some degree of spread into adjacent territories. There are also outlier groups of Marathi speakers in Dravidian country. There are three main dialects: dēsī, the base for the modern standard literary language; kōṅkaṇi /kokni/ the dialect spoken in Goa; and Eastern Marathi, which shades gradually into Oriya and Eastern Hindi.

The Mahārāṣṭrī Prakrit (*see* **Prakrit**) from which Marathi derives differed markedly from the Śauraseni and Māgadhī Prakrits underlying most of the other New Indo-Aryan languages, and this difference continues today to mark Marathi off from its congeners. Dravidian influences seems also to have played a part in the formation of Marathi, particularly in the structure of the verbal system.

Writing in Marathi dates from the thirteenth century, when Jñāneśvar wrote his commentary on the *Bhagavadgītā*. Jñāneśvar is also the first of the poet–saints, the long line of Marathi poets who wrote hymns in honour of the god Viṭhobā of Paṇḍharpūr. The most celebrated of the poet–saints are Nāmdev (fourteenth century) and Tukārām (seventeenth century). Under Western influence, the novel and the short story figure very prominently in modern Marathi writing. Hari Nārāyaṇ Āpṭe (1864–1919) was the first Marathi novelist to deal candidly with social issues in his fiction.

SCRIPT

The Bal Bodh ('understood by children') version of the Devanagari script is used for Marathi. Vocalic /ṛ/ and /ḷ/, short and long, are missing.

PHONOLOGY

Consonants

stops: p, b, t, d, ṭ, ḍ, k, g
affricates: ts, dz, tʃ, dʒ
fricatives: v/f, s, ṣ, ʃ, h
nasals: m, mh, n, nh, ṇ
lateral and flap: l, lh, ḷ, r, rh
semi-vowel: j

All of the stops and affricates have aspirated correlatives, except /ts/: /ph, bh/, etc. Retroflex sounds are notated in the following text with dots, e.g. /d/ = ḍ.

Vowels

> short: i, a, u (where a = [ʌ] or [ə])
> long: iː, eː, aiː = [əi], auː = [əʊ], aː, oː, uː

In the script, length is marked (here by a macron) but is not phonemic; nasalization is neither marked nor phonemic, and seems to have acquired an optional or spontaneous character except in the first person endings of the indicative mood.

The pronunciation of consonantal clusters is assisted by an epenthetic vowel; e.g. *gar^{a}mī* 'hot'; *jang^{a}lāt* 'in the jungle'.

VOWEL REDUCTION
/a/ tends to be full in a first syllable, reduced in final and in a syllable preceding a full vowel.

MORPHOLOGY AND SYNTAX

Noun

With Gujarati, Marathi shares a three-gender system of masculine, feminine, and neuter. Words in *-ā* are typically masculine, in *-ī* feminine. Neuter endings were typically nasalized, but this feature has been lost in modern Marathi.

NUMBER
Broadly speaking, most plural direct forms are identical with their singular direct forms, or simply add thereto a long vowel: e.g.

	Singular direct	*Plural direct*
masculine	hāt 'hand'	hāt
	bājū 'side'	bājū
feminine	bhint 'wall'	bhintī
	šāḷā 'school'	šāḷā
neuter	ghar 'house'	gharẽ
	ḍokē 'head'	ḍokī̃

CASE
Direct and oblique forms: the oblique form is incomplete without one or another of the agglutinative case affixes, or a postposition. Thus, the genitive case is provided by the oblique base plus the affix *cā/cī/cē* (i.e. marked for gender).

The dative/aditive marker is *lā*, which is also the objective marker for an animate object: e.g. *Tyānē āp^{a}lyā mitrālā pāhilē* 'He saw his friend.' The instrumental/agentive marker (illustrated in the last example) is *-nē*.

These case affixes have plural forms: e.g. for the genitive, *-ce*, *-cyā*, *-cī*; agentive pl. *-nī*.

An ablative case is made with -(*h*)*ūn/tūn*: e.g. *gharūn* 'out of the house'; *khiḍ*ᵃ*kĭtūn pāh*ᵃ*ṇē* 'to look out of the window'.

Comitative: the affix is *śī*: e.g. *dus*ᵃ*ryā desānśī sah*ᵃ*kāry*ᵃ 'collaboration with other countries'.

Adjective

Variable or invariable; the former are marked for gender and number, and take -*yā* in the oblique for all three genders and both numbers: e.g. *cāng*ᵃ*lā mul*ᵃ*gā* 'good son': *čang*ᵃ*lyā mulālā* 'to the good son'.

Pronoun

PERSONAL INDEPENDENT

	Singular	Plural
1	mī	āmhī
2	tŭ	tumhī

These are declined in all cases; e.g. for the first person singular: aditive/dative, *malā*; agentive, *mī̃/myã̄*; comitative, *mājhāśī̃*; ablative, *mājhāhūn*.

The third person forms are supplied by the demonstrative series: *to* (masc.), *tī* (fem.), *te* (neut.), with plural forms: *te*, *tya*, *t̃ī*.

POSSESSIVE ADJECTIVES
mājhā 'my', *ām*ᵃ*cā* 'our', etc.

INTERROGATIVE PRONOUN
koṇ 'who?'; *kāy* 'what?'

RELATIVE PRONOUN
jo.

Verb

In broad outline, the Marathi verbal system is similar to those of its New Indo-Aryan congeners. At many points, however, it is much more complicated, and this complication is due to several factors:

1. the retention of certain archaic Indo-Aryan features, e.g. the endings of the subjunctive and the imperative moods;
2. the concomitant growth of secondary forms, both synthetic and analytic;
3. the wide expansion of participial constructions of a Dravidian rather than a New Indo-Aryan type: e.g. material which would figure as a verbal dependent clause in other languages becomes a nominal member of the principal clause in Marathi;
4. the presence of an ergative construction with specific conditions for object–predicate agreement;
5. an elaborate system of personal endings with many archaic variants.

infinitive: in *-ŭ*: e.g. *karŭ* 'to do'

supine: *-āyā/-āvᵃyā*: takes certain case endings, e.g. with aditive, *bheṭāyᵃlā yēṇē* 'to come to see someone'.

participles: imperfective with characteristic *-t-*, long and short forms: e.g. *karīt(ā)* 'doing'; shortened form: *karat*; perfective with characteristic *-(i)l/-(i)lel* + gender marking: i.e. *kelā* 'having done' (irregular formation from *karŭ* 'to do'); future participles: in *-ṇār* (invariable).

gerunds: imperfective: *-(i)tā/-(i)tāṅnā*; perfective: *-ūn*.

Examples: supine: *lihāyᵃcā kāgad* 'writing paper'; *pyāyᵃcē pāṇī* 'drinking water'; imperfective participle: *tī hasat mhaṇālī* 'laughing, she said'; perfective participle: *tyaṅnī lihililī nāṭᵃkē* 'plays written by him'; gerund: *Tī māṇᵃsē jivant asᵃtā mṛtā-samān* 'These people, though alive, are as good as dead.'

CONJUGATION

Synthetic forms:

(a) primary: simple past indicative, simple future, imperative;
(b) secondary: simple present formed from imperfective participle, simple past formed from perfective participle. Analytic forms: provided by participles plus auxiliary verb.

There are two conjugations:

(a) intransitive verbs: characteristic is *-a/e-*;
(b) transitive verbs: characteristic is *-i/ī-*.

NEGATION

na precedes certain verbal forms (future, optative, infinitive, etc.); *nā* follows inflected forms. *Nāhī* is the negative copula.

PERSONAL ENDINGS

		Past	Future	Imperative	Simple present		
					Masc.	Fem.	Neut.
Singular	1	-ē/-ī	-en/-in	-ū	-to	-te	-te
	2	-es/-is	-(i)šil	Ø	-tos	-tes	-tes
	3	-e/-i	-el/-il	-o	-to	-te	-te
Plural	1	-ū	-ū	-ū	-to		
	2	-ā	-al	-a	-ta		
	3	-at/-it	-(i)til	-ot	-tat		

In the paradigm, all vowels are long; all first person forms are nasalized in both singular and plural; and past and simple present forms for the second person plural are also nasalized. The nasalization here is a stable feature inherited from southern Apabhraṁśa (*see* **Prakrit**).

COMPOUND FORMS

The perfective participle is marked for person; the imperfective participle appears in the shortened form (e.g. *karat*) and is invariable.

Some examples of tenses in the indicative mood:

> general present: e.g. *Vāgh jaṅgᵃlắt rāhᵃtāt* 'Tigers live in the jungle'
> present continuous: e.g. *Āj phār garᵃmī hot āhe* 'Today is (being) very hot.'
>   In the colloquial the participle and the auxiliary tend to fuse: e.g. *karᵃto ahe → karᵃtoyʰ* = is doing
> past habitual: e.g. *Te darᵃroj kāmālā jāt asat* 'They went every day to work'
> future (presumptive): e.g. *To vidyārthī hoṇār* 'He's going to be a student'
> passive: the locative case of the gerund of the sense-verb may be used + *yēṇē* 'to come' (Katenina (1963) compares the Sanskrit: *māraṇaṁ yāti*): *Tyālā ispitᵃlắt neṇyāt āle* 'He was taken to hospital.'

ERGATIVE

If the perfective participle or a related form appears in the predicate, this predicate agrees with the object which is in the direct state, while the logical subject is in the agentive: e.g. *mī don bāyᵃkā pāhilyā* 'I saw two women' (lit. 'by-me were seen …').

A neutral construction is also possible in certain conditions, e.g. if no direct object is expressed: e.g. *putrānē mhaṭᵃlē* 'the son said'.

Double concord is also possible but only if the agent is second person singular pronoun: the predicate then agrees with the object in gender and number, but with the subject in person: cf. *tū hē kām kelēs* 'you did this work'; but *mī hē kām kelē∅* 'I did this work'.

Postpositions

There is some duplication between case affixes and postpositions: e.g. *mumbaĩt* (locative case) = *mumbaī madhye* 'in Bombay'.

Word order

SOV is basic in nominal construction.

पर्व ॥ १ ॥ प्रारंभीं शब्द होता आणि तो शब्द ईश्वरज
२ वळ होता आणि तो शब्द ईश्वर होता ॥ तोच प्रारंभीं ईश्वरज
३ वळ होता ॥ त्याने सर्व उत्पन्न केलीं आणि जें जालें तें त्याज
४ बांकून कांहीं उत्पन्न जालें नाहीं ॥ त्यामध्यें जीवन होतें आ
५ णि तें जीवन माणसांचा प्रकाश होता ॥ आणि तो प्रकाश अं
धारांत प्रकाशला आणि अंधाराने त्यास धरिलें नाहीं ॥

६ ईश्वरापासून पाठविला असा येक माणूस होता त्याचें नाम
७ येहान्न ॥ तोच साक्षणाकरून अवघ्यानीं विश्वास करावा ह्मणोन
८ त्या प्रकाशाविषयीं साक्ष द्यावयास साक्षीकरितां आला ॥ आप
ण तोच प्रकाश नव्हता परंतु त्या प्रकाशाविषयीं साक्षी देण्यास
९ [आला] ॥

MARGI

INTRODUCTION

Margi belongs to the Bura-Margi group of the Niger-Kordofanian family, and is spoken in Adamawa and south-eastern Bornu by between 100,000 and 200,000 people. Westermann and Bryan (1952) allocate Margi to the Chadic languages.

The description by Carl Hoffman (1963), which is followed here, is of *Màrgyí bàbál* 'the Margi of the open plain', the form on which the literary language is based.

SCRIPT

An extended and modified Roman alphabet is in use. A main defect is the absence of a sign for the very common vowel sound /ə/.

PHONOLOGY

The phonological inventory of Margi is extremely rich; indeed, in numbers of phonemes, it may be rivalled only by the Khoisan languages of the Kalahari (*see* **!Kung**). As described by Hoffmann (1963) the inventory includes the following.

Consonants

stops: p, b, t, d, k, g, ʔ with palatalized k', g'
voiced implosive stops: 6, ɗ
labialized stops: p°, b°, 6°, t°, k°, g°
labio-alveolar stops: db, bɗ, pt
pre-nasalized plosives: mb, mp, md, mt, nd, nt, ŋg, ŋk, ŋg', ŋk'
affricates: ts, dz, tʃ, dʒ
labio-alveolar affricates: bdz, pts
pre-nasalized affricates: mts, mdz, mdʒ, mtʃ, nts, ndz, ndʒ, ntʃ
fricatives: f, v, s, ʃ, z, ʒ, ç, x, γ; labialized: f°, v°, s°, x°, γ°
labio-alveolar fricatives: bz, ps
labio-palatals: bj → vj, pç → fç
laterals and flap: l, ɬ, lʒ, blʒ, r
nasals: m, n, ɲ, ŋ, m° (see also pre-nasalized plosives)
semi-vowels: j, w, with glottalized values, notated by Hoffmann as 'y, 'w

Vowels

Notated as *i, e, a, o, u. i* includes /i/ and /ɪ/; *e* = /ɛ/; *a* = /a/ and /ɑ/; *o* /ɔ/ with allophone [œ]; *u* tends towards allophone [y] in certain positions. The ubiquitous vowel /ə/ is usually notated as *i* or *u*, and has an allophone in final position tending towards [əu], which Hoffmann notates as ʉ.
    Vowel length is not phonemic.
    Reduction of vowels in non-final position is regular: e.g. *sʉ̀* 'thing', pl. *sə̀'yàr*.

Tones

High ´, low `, up-glide ˇ. Tone is phonemic.

MORPHOLOGY AND SYNTAX

Noun

No gender; no noun classes; no form of declension.
There is a definite form: e.g. *sál* 'man' – *śalárì* 'the man (known, referred to . . .)'; *ŋú* 'mountain' – *nwárì*.

PLURAL

In -*'yar*, or suppletive (often + -*'yar*). The -*'yar* suffix subsumes sense complex, e.g. construct phrase: *ndə̀r.gə́.Íjʉ́.'yàr kú* 'these words (*ndə̀r*) of (*gə́*) God (*Íjú*).

GENITIVE RELATIONSHIP

Qualified noun precedes qualifier, e.g. *mbwá kúzə́gʉ́* 'house of medicine' = 'hospital'. -*á* is genitive marker for inalienable possession: e.g. *shúwá hyà* 'the dog's tail' (*shú* 'tail'). Otherwise *gə́* is used: e.g. *ndə̀r.gə́.Íjʉ́* 'the word of God'. -*r* is the formant for a genitive of purpose: e.g. *sʉ́* 'thing' + *sə́m* 'to eat': *sə̀r.sə́m* 'food'.
    Pronominal genitive construction: -*nyá* (only with qualified noun).

Adjective

As attribute, adjective follows noun, which is in non-final form. It may reduplicate for plural, e.g. *ŋú dzə̀gàm* '(a) high mountain'; *nú dzə̀dzə̀gàm* 'high mountains'.

COMPARISON

A comparative is made with preposition *àrá*; e.g. with *də̀gàl* 'great, old': X *də̀gàl àrá* Y 'X is older than Y.' *Mdiá* 'to surpass', may also be used + *də* 'with', + adjective: e.g. X *àmdiá* Y *də̀ də̀gàl*.

Pronoun

Absolute and subject:

	Singular	Dual			Plural
1	nàyự̀, niyự̀, nì	(no excl.)	excl.		nà'yà
		nàmà	incl.		nàmə̀r
2	ǹagự̀				ǹanyì
3	ǹajà				ǹandà

Suffixed subject and object forms:

	Singular				Plural	
	Subject	Object			Subject	Object
1	yự́ (yí)	ɗaỳa	excl.		'ya	'yà
			incl.		mər	mə̀r
2	gự́	ŋu/-ŋ			nyi	nỳi
3	já	nyi			nda	ndà

There is a dual inclusive form: *ma* (both subject and object).

The suffixed object forms are basically direct objects; they may be used for indirect object but this is usually introduced by *ànự́* 'to, for'.

All object pronoun suffixes are attached to the stem, preceding past-tense marker and subject pronoun suffix.

POSSESSIVE SUFFIXES
-*á* + subject pronoun suffix; -*r* + object pronoun suffix: e.g. *kɔ́r* 'head' – *kɔ́rá.yừ* 'my head'; *mwál* 'friend' – *mwálɗa* 'my friend'. There is also a possessive construction with *gə*: *fà* 'farm' – *fà gɔ́yà* 'my farm'.

DEMONSTRATIVE PRONOUN
Three-term series graduated by relative distance: e.g. *kừ* 'this', *ta* 'that', *na* 'that' (not visible). Tone varies. These follow the plural marker: e.g. *kákádə̀'yàr kừ* 'these books'. Pronounced with high tone, these are demonstrative pronouns: *kừ́, tá, ná*.

INTERROGATIVE PRONOUN
wà 'who?'; *mì* 'what?'. Final interrogative particles: *yà, ra*.

RELATIVE PRONOUN
kừ, na, ŋừ́ if referent is subject of sentence; *də* if referent is object.

Numerals

1–10: 1 *tàŋ* (used in counting) *pátlự́*; 2 *s̀ə̀dàŋ* (used in counting) *mə̀tlừ̀*; 3 *makə̀r*; 4 *fòɗừ̀*; 5 *ntə̀fù*; 6 *ŋkwà*; 7 *mə́ɗə́fừ̀*; 8 *ntsìsừ̀*; 9 *ɔ́mdlừ̀*; 10 *kúmự́*; 11 *kúm gà sɔ́r taŋ*; 12 *kúm gà pwá mə́tlự́*; 20 *mɔ́tlkùmì*; 30 *ḿarkùmì*; 40 *fóɗukùmì*; 100 *ghàrú*.

Verb

Stems are simple or derived. Aspectual system rather than tense. Stems are in principle neutral, and become transitive or intransitive according to valencies generated in given situation: e.g. *ŋkyừ* 'to pay', 'to be paid' if object is present.

Some verbs retain basic tone throughout conjugation; others change tone. Most stems are consonant-initial and disyllabic: e.g. *pìdà* 'to lie down'. Some are monosyllabic: e.g. *bà* 'to go out'; or polysyllabic *tlàdlàɓừ* 'to learn/teach'.

Suffixes are added to stems to make derivative verbs. Reduplication is used for reiteratives and intensives.

Where the subject is overtly expressed by anything other than a pronoun, resumption by pronoun is not necessary. Subjects other than personal pronouns precede verbal complex (subjunctive is an exception). Personal pronoun as subject may precede the verb: then in base form (unless it follows certain particles): cf. (with *ə́vər* = progressive tense marker) *ni vər wì* = *ə́vər wì yừ* 'I'm running'.

NARRATIVE TENSE

gà precedes stem, e.g. *nì gà wì* 'I ran'; negative past: *nì ndà wì mài* 'I didn't run'.

Present: *a-* prefixed to stem, e.g. *ni áwì* 'I run'; negative *nì áwì mài*.

Past: *a-* prefix on stem + *-(ə)rì* suffix, e.g. *nì áwìrì* = *áwìr yừ* 'I ran'.

The particle *ská*, preceding or following stem, indicates non-performance or exclusion of action.

AUXILIARIES

Examples: *bə́rá* + verb indicates repetition of action of main verb; *dzùgwà* + verb marks subsequent action.

Prepositions

Simple or compound; compound prepositions are simple prepositions in genitive construction with noun: e.g. *àgá* 'with', *ànừ* 'for', *ár* 'on, at, in', *də* 'with'.

Word order

SVO. Indirect object follows direct object unless former is expressed by direct object pronoun.

1 Wu baditsini ndang Ndir ai. Ndir ku ai aga Iju. Ndir ku jangu Iju. 2 Naja ai aga Iju wu baditsini ndang. 3 Ar ja di su caca ga irkir. Wu su yer ku caca ga miliakir kwo tituku nda na kula naja akwa mai. 4 Ara ja mpi ai, di mpi ku ngu parakur mji. 5 Di paraku ivir mbil wu kwuthlu, amma kwuthlu ai mdia ngyi mai.

6 Mdu ai ku di Iju ga hyanba ngyi di thlim ngyi Yohanna. 7 Naja ga shili gadabar sagida, abur ki ja aiu sagida arkira paraku na, gadabar ki mji ahungguri jiri gadabar ngyi. 8 Ai naja ngu paraku na mai, amma naja ga shili ga iu sagida arkira paraku na.

MARI

INTRODUCTION

Formerly known as Cheremis, Mari belongs to the Finno-Volgaic group of Finno-Ugric. It is spoken by about half a million people in two main forms: Meadow-Eastern Mari and Hill Mari. Most Mari live in the Mari Autonomous Soviet Socialist Republic (established in 1936), others are scattered through the Bashkir ASSR, the Tatar ASSR, and elsewhere. The lexicon contains a considerable number of Turkic and Chuvash words (e.g. from Chuvash: *oksa* 'money', *kalasaš* 'to speak', etc.) bearing witness to long-established Mari settlement on the Middle Volga.

The earliest translations of liturgical texts into Mari date from the late eighteenth century; in 1827 appeared a New Testament in Hill Mari. There is a flourishing modern literature in both literary standards.

The difference between the two forms is mainly phonological and lexical. Here, Meadow-Eastern forms are described.

SCRIPT

Cyrillic, with hooked *n* for /ŋ/ plus *ö* and *ÿ*. Hill Mari adds *ä*.

PHONOLOGY

Consonants

    stops: p, b, t, k; /b/ occurs following /m/
    affricates: ts, tʃ'
    fricatives: ß, f, s, z, ʃ, ʒ, ð, j, x, γ
    nasals: m, n, ɲ, ŋ
    laterals and flap: l, l', r

Vowels

    front: i, e, œ, y
    central: a
    back: ɪ/ə, o, u

VOWEL HARMONY

The normal Finno-Ugric correlation of back with back, front with front vowels is present, but not rigorously observed. A curious kind of harmonic echo at several removes is found with the locative affix -*što*[3], where the index 3 indicates three possible variants *olıkıšto* 'in the meadow'; *kindıšte* 'in the bread'; but here too there are variants, e.g. *č'odrašte* 'in the forest'.

Stress

Associated with vowel length in any syllable. Vowels in unstressed syllables tend to be qualitatively and quantitatively reduced.

MORPHOLOGY AND SYNTAX

Noun

No grammatical gender, no articles. The noun has two numbers. The plural marker is -*vlak*. There are seven cases, only four of which (nominative, genitive, dative, accusative) apply to persons: e.g. *pasu* 'field':

nominative	pasu	locative	pasušto
genitive	pasun	aditive	pasuško
dative	pasulan	adverbial	pasuıš
accusative	pasum		

The possessive markers are: sing. 1 -*m*, 2 -*t*, 3 -*žV*; pl. 1 -*na*, 2 -*da*, 3 -*št*. This marker precedes the case ending in the first four cases, follows it in the others: thus, *kniga.m* 'my book', *kniga.m.(vlak).ın* 'of my book(s)'; but *kniga.(vlak).(ı)šte.m* 'in my book(s)' (*kniga* is a Russian loan-word).

Adjective

Some have two forms, a short form used as attribute, a full form as predicate: e.g. *šem pıl* 'black cloud'; *pıl šeme* 'the cloud is black'.

COMPARATIVE
In -*rak*, e.g. *ošo* 'white', *ošərak* 'whiter'.

Pronoun

	Singular	Plural
1	mıy	me
2	tıy	te
3	tudo	nuno

These are declined for genitive, dative, and accusative: e.g. *mıyın*, *mılanem*, *mıyım*.

DEMONSTRATIVE PRONOUN
tide/tı 'this'; *sade/sede* 'that'; *nine* 'these'.

INTERROGATIVE PRONOUN
kö 'who?'; *mo* 'what?'. Also used as relative pronouns.

Numerals

1–10: *ikte, koktɪt, kumɪt, nɪlɪt, vizɪt, kudɪt, šɪmɪt, kandaše, indeše, lu*; 11 *latikte*; 12 *latkoktɪt*; 20 *kolo*; 30 *kumlo*; 40 *nɪlle*; 100 *šÿdö*.

Verb

Marked for voice, mood, tense, person, and number. The indicative mood has a present–future and six past tenses, two simple and four compound. There are two conjugations, each with positive and negative versions. As specimen, the present–future and first past tense of *užaš* 'to see', positive and negative:

		Singular		Plural	
		Positive	*Negative*	*Positive*	*Negative*
Present future	1	užam	om už	užɪna	ogɪna už
	2	užat	ot už	užɪda	ogɪda už
	3	užeš	ogeš už	užɪt	ogɪt už
First past	1	užɪm	šɪm už	užna	ɪšna už
	2	užɪč	šɪč už	užda	ɪšda už
	3	užo	ɪš už	užɪč	ɪšt už

A past continuous is formed from the present–future tense + auxiliary *ɪe* 'was': e.g. *užam ɪle* 'I was seeing'; neg. *om už ɪle*.

IMPERATIVE
Examples: from *ludaš* 'read', sing. *lud*, pl. *ludsa* 'read!'; neg. *it/ida lud*.

OPTATIVE
The marker is *-ne* added to stem, e.g. *užnem* 'I'd like to see'.

PARTICIPLES
The inventory includes active, *ludšo* 'reading'; passive *ludmo* 'being read'; negative *luddɪmo* 'not reading, not being read'; and future *ludšaš kniga* 'a book which is to be read'.

Gerundial forms provide, for example, temporal frames, e.g. *ludšemla* 'while I was reading', *ludšetla* 'while you were reading'.

To express aspect, specific converbs are used, e.g. *pɪtaraš* 'to finish' (perfective).

Postpositions

Postpositions follow nominative case: e.g. *deke* 'to', *gɪč* 'from', *dene* 'during, because of', etc. They may take the personal affixes: *mɪy denem* 'with me'.

Word order

SOV.

Пертаріöкъ шамáкъ ы́лэнъ, шамакáтъ ы́лэнъ 1
Юманъ дорáнъ, и Юма ы́лэнъ шамáкъ. Сéда 2
пертаріöкъ ы́лэнъ Юманъ дорáнъ. Цылá ты́- 3
да дóно йиштэма лíйнъ, и ты́да-гы́цъ пасна́
нимáптъ лíйтэ, мā йиштэма лíйнъ. Ты́данъ кӱр- 4
гышта ильшáйшлукъ ы́лэнъ, ильшайшлукáтъ
сóта эдэ́мвлялaнъ. Сотажáтъ пицкэ́мешта 5
сотэмя́лтэшъ, пицкэ́мешъ варā ты́дамъ эль-
тáленъ-кýчедэ. Ы́ля эдэ́мъ Юма-гы́цъ кóлтэма, 6
лю́мъ ты́данъ Іоáнъ. Ты́да тóлэнъ видѣ́те- 7
лешъ, видѣтельсвовáяшъ сóта вéрецeнъ, ты́-
да гáчь цылáпъ иня́нэжтъ. Ты́да шкè сóта 8
агáлъ ы́ля, а кóлтэма ы́ля варā сóта вéрецeнъ
видѣтельсвовáяшъ.

MAYA

INTRODUCTION

Maya belongs to the Yucatec branch of the Mayan stock; other branches of this linguistic complex are Western Maya (including Tzotzil and Chontal): Eastern Maya (including Cakchiquel, Mam, and Quiché); Huastec. The area of Mayan speech stretches through the Petén region of Guatemala, and the Campeche region of Mexico, northwards into Belize and Yucatan. The Classical Maya language was centred on Yucatan. The differences between it and modern spoken Yucatec are not great. The number of present-day speakers is put at around half a million.

Classical Mayan literature was very extensive, covering many fields in literature and the arts, religion, astronomy, and history. Almost all of it was destroyed after the Conquest, by the Spanish ecclesiastical authorities. Three codices survived, and are now held in Dresden, Madrid, and Paris. An extensive post-Conquest literature, in the Roman script provided by the Spanish missionaries, includes the prophetic 'Books of Chilam Balam' (cf. the *Popol Vuh* book in Quiché).

SCRIPT

For some 1,500 years, the outlandish and visceral Mayan script was used for inscriptions on stone, and for written manuscripts. The bulk of the epigraphic record dates from the Classical period of Mayan culture, which lasted from the third to the tenth century AD. The main sites are Tikal in Guatemala, and Copan in Honduras. About a thousand individual glyphs have been identified and catalogued. Until recently, however, few could be interpreted, apart from consistently recurrent glyphs denoting dates, numbers, cardinal directions, names of months and place markers (H. Berlin's 'Emblem Glyphs'). Common nouns and verbs are now being added to this basic repertory.

An 'alphabet' of 29 glyphs, ostensibly with phonetic values, was provided by Bishop Diego de Landa of Merida (1524-79), but proved to be useless in practice (*see* **Appendix of Scripts**). In the 1950s the Russian linguist Y. Knorosov showed that the Landa 'alphabet' was in fact a syllabary, yielding phonetic equivalents of the type Cv: when combined, two such syllables $C_1v_1 + C_2v_2$ give a Maya word: $C_1v_1C_2(v_2)$, where v_1 and v_2 show vowel harmony, though v_2 is usually elided. Mayan scribes seem to have written words either with the syllabary alone, or with the syllabary plus logograms or determinants. The complete series of syllabic glyphs Cv where C = b, ch, ch', h, k, k', l, m, n, and v = a, has been identified.

For v = e/i/o/u, about half of the possible grid is known. Many phonetic syllables have multiple representation, and, conversely, many glyphs have more than one reading. Structurally, glyphs usually occur in compounds or in tightly packed clusters, where the central position is occupied by the focused theme, surrounded by various aspectual and spatio-temporal markers. The complex is read from left to right, and from top to bottom.

As regards language, glyphs of the Classical period are either in old Yucatec Mayan or in Cholan. No plural forms are attested, nor are forms for first or second person. An ergative marker in -u marks the subject of a transitive verb in the present tense. Word order is V (O) S.

From the late sixteenth century onwards, Spanish scholars used an amended Roman alphabet to notate Maya. By far the most important of these early studies, and a prime source for the Classical language, is the so-called 'Motul Dictionary', dating from c. 1580/90, which was finally printed and published in Mérida in 1929. It is in two parts, Maya–Spanish and Spanish–Maya, covers about 10,000 lexical items, and gives many examples of usage.

This article is largely based on Tozzer (1921).

PHONOLOGY

Consonants

/p, t, ts, tʃ, k/ have glottalized counterparts: /p', t'/, etc. The only sonant appears to be the labial /b/. Some authorities note a glottal stop. Vowel initials appear to be initiated by hamza onset. Other sounds: /m, w; l, r, n; s, ʃ, j/; /x/ is notated as *h*; /ʃ/ as *x*.

Vowels

a, e, i, o, u = [a, ɛ, i, ɔ, u]
diphthongs: ai

A high tone is marked by an acute sign.

MORPHOLOGY AND SYNTAX

Noun

No gender. In the older language, (*i*)*š* marks the feminine of rational beings, contrasted with *ah* for masculine: e.g. *ah cambezah* 'the male teacher', *iš cambezah*. The usual definite article is *le*: e.g. *le winik* 'the man'.

Plural is in -*ob*: e.g. *winikob* 'men'; *šipal* 'boy', pl. *šipalob*.

Genitive relationship is formed by means of possessive marker (*see* **Pronoun**, below) and appositional: e.g. *u yatan in zucum* 'my brother's wife'; *u yatan a zucum* 'your brother's wife'; *u yatanob in zucumob* 'my brothers' wives'.

Other cases – locational, directional, etc. – are expressed by means of prepositions. *See* **Prepositions**, below.

Adjective

As attribute, adjective precedes noun: e.g. *noxoč kaš* 'big village', *noxoč polob* 'big heads'.

COMPARATIVE
Made with -V*l* + vowel harmony: e.g. *tibil* 'good'; *tibilil* 'better'.

Pronoun

The independent personal forms are: sing. 1 *ten*, 2 *teč*, 3 *lay/leti*; pl. 1 *toon*, 2 *teeš*, 3 *loob/letiob*

PRONOMINAL AFFIXES
(a) nominal series: (b) verbal series:

	Singular	Plural			Singular	Plural
1	in/w	k(a)...Ø		1	en	oon(eeš)
2	a/aw	aw...eeš		2	eč	eeš
3	u/y	a/y...oob		3	Ø	oob

The verbal series provides the objective pronominal infixes; in the verbal complex they precede the subject pronominal suffixes. The nominal series provides the possessive pronominal prefixes: e.g. *inyun* 'my father'; *kayum* 'our father'; *ayumeeš* 'your (pl.) father'. The attributive marker -*il* is used mainly with inanimate referents: e.g. *u muul.il oliboob* 'the Mount of Olives'

DEMONSTRATIVE PRONOUN
The article *le* combines with a vocalic series *a – o – e* graduated for relative distance: e.g. *le winik.a* 'this man here'; *le winik.o* 'that man there'.

INTERROGATIVE PRONOUN
maš 'who?', pl. *mašob*: e.g. *Maš in naa...mašob in zucunob?* 'Who is my mother...who are my brothers?' (Mark 33.3).

RELATIVE PRONOUN
See **Verb**, below.

Numerals

The numerical system is vigesimal, with unit terms introduced for each multiple of 20. Thus, in Classical Maya, 20 units formed 1 *qal*; 20 *qal* = 1 *baq*; 20 *baq* = 1 *pik*, and so on. In this way very large numbers were expressed, e.g. 20 *qintšil* = 1 *alaw* = 64,000,000.

In present-day Maya, the numbers 1–10 are: *hun, ka, ǒs, kan, ho, wak, wuk, wašak, bolon, la hun*; 11 *buluk*; 12 *la ka-*; 20 *hun qal-*; 40 *kakal-*; 60 *oškal-*. That is, the base *kal* is used for numeration up to 1×20. Thereafter, *hunbaq* = 20×20 takes over; *pik* = 20^3, etc.

There are many numerical classifiers in the Classical language. In modern Maya they tend to be reduced to two; *tul* for animates, *p'el* for inanimates.

Verb

The difference between transitive and intransitive verbs in Maya is formal, and does not correspond to the distinction made in Indo-European. Similarly, the active/passive dichotomy is conceived and expressed in ways alien to Indo-European.

Stems denoting action or state take the suffix *-Vl*, where V is any of the five vowels. Choice of vowel depends on vowel harmony: e.g. *lub.ul* 'fall'; *het.el* 'open'. These forms are often equivalent to passives, as the subject is felt to be the patient of, or affected by, the action expressed in the verb.

By changing *-Vl* to *-ik*, a form is made which relates the base meaning of the verb to an object: e.g. *(tin) het.ik* '(I am) opening something (specified)'. The personal pronoun used here is also the possessive pronoun (see table above): thus, *tin het.ik* means literally 'my-opening-at-present something'.

Transitive/causative sense is further stabilized by certain infixes: *-s-*, e.g. *tin kim.s.ik* 'I am causing-to-die someone', i.e. 'killing'; or *-be-*, often *-be + s-*, e.g. *tin kam.be.s.ik* 'I am causing-to-make-learn someone'.

A durative or habitual sense is added to the root by the suffix *-tal*: e.g. *tin kuš.tal* 'my being-heart-endowed' = 'I am alive'; similarly, *tan kuš.tal* 'your being heart-endowed' = 'you are alive'; *tun kuš tal* 'his/her being heart-endowed' = 'he/she is alive' (For explanation of *tin, tan, tun, see* **Tense**, below).

Many verbs are made from nouns: e.g. *nai* 'dream' – *tin nai* 'my dreaming' = 'I am dreaming'. Several denominal formants exist; e.g. *-ankil: al* 'weight' – *tun al.ankil* 'she is giving birth'.

TENSE

Intransitive forms make their present tense by means of the present tense marker *tan* as modified by coalescence with the personal pronoun nominal series + stem + *-Vl/tal*: *tan + in → tin*; *tan + a → tan*; *tan + u → tun*: e.g. *tin het.el* 'I am opening'.

Indefinite future: marker *bin* + truncated stem + *-ak-* + verbal pronoun: e.g. *bin kim.ak.en* 'I am going to die'. Similarly, *bin.kim.ak.eč, bin.kim.ak.Ø*, etc.

Past: here the stem is compounded with the verbal pronoun: e.g. *lub.en* 'I fell'; *lub.eč*, etc. Verbs in *-tal* have a past tense marker in *-ah*.

Transitive verbs: As noted above, Mayan object-related verbs have *-ik* in the present tense: e.g. *tun kim.s.ik* 'he is causing-to-die something specific'.

Future: future marker *he-* + nominal pronoun + present stem in *-ik* + *e*: e.g. *hen kim.s.ik.e* 'I shall cause-to-die (something specific)'; or, *bin* + bare nominal pronoun + stem minus *-ik* + *e*: e.g. *bin in het.e* 'I shall open (something specific)'.

Past: particle *t-* or *tşok* + nominal pronoun, with or without *-ah* suffix: e.g. *t.in šul.ah* 'I finished something specific'.

Several stems are used in conjugation with sense-verbs to provide various modal and aspectual shades of meaning, e.g. *pat.al* 'to be able': *u pat in binel* 'I can go' (lit. 'it's-being-able – my-going'); *qabet* 'to have to': *qabet in binel* 'I have to go'.

A potential meaning is provided by the *k-* marker + nominal pronoun: e.g. *k.in ṭṣon.*(*e*) 'I may shoot'. Desiderative/optative: *tak*(*tel*)/*qat*, e.g. *takal in wen.el* = *in qat wen*(*el*) 'I want to sleep'. The imperative is in *-en*: *nak.en* 'climb!'

THE COPULA

yan 'to be ' (see independent personal pronoun in the chart above): e.g. *winik.en* 'I am a man'; *teč in mehen* 'thou art my son'; *batab.h.en* 'I was a chief'; *batab.h.eč* 'thou wast a chief'.

NEGATIVE

The markers are *ma*, *matan*, or *mawil*: e.g. *ma utz yokol Pedro* = 'Pedro is not well'; *tin bin* 'I go'; *ma.in bin* 'I don't go'.

THE VERB COMPLEX

Left-hand adjuncts – stem(s) – right-hand adjuncts. Left-hand adjuncts include certain temporal and modal markers, some auxiliaries; right-hand adjuncts include transitive/intransitive markers, voice, mood, aspect markers (if any); object pronoun, subject pronoun. The object pronouns in an object-related verb complex precede the subject pronoun: cf. *u.xaṭṣ.en.oob.e* 'they hit me' (*-en-* is obj. pron.: verbal series *u...oob* is sbj. pron. nominal series).

RELATIVE PARTICLE

lik(*il*) 'that which': e.g. *likil in mey.a* 'that with which I work'.

Prepositions

Some Mayan prepositions take the suffixed verbal pronoun: e.g. *yetel.en* 'with me', *yetel.eč* 'with you'. Others take the prefixed nominal pronoun: e.g. *in.tial* 'for me', *atial* 'for you'. *Ti* is an all-purpose directional preposition: e.g. *cat nac ti le muul* 'and he went up the mountain'; *cat talob ti leti* 'and they came to him'; *ti le na* 'into the house'; *ti le winik* 'from/out of the man'.

Word formation

A noun may be inserted as an integral part of a verb complex: Tozzer's (1926) example is *šot.tše.n.ah.en* 'I cut (past) wood' (*šot* 'cut'; *tše* 'wood'). From the Mayan point of view, such a verb is intransitive.

Abstract nouns are made with *-il*: e.g. *kohan* 'sick', *kohanil* 'illness'.

Direct compounding: e.g. *ahcananbaalba* 'farm, estate supervisor' (*ah* masc. marker; *canan* 'keeper'; *baalba* 'estate').

TU yaxchun leti cach le Tħan, le Tħan ti yan cach icnal Dios, yetel le Tħan leti cach Dios.

2 Letilela yan cach tu yaxchun icnal Dios.

3 Tulacal le balob mentabob tumen leti, xma leti ma t' mentab mixbal ti le bax mentab.

4 Ti leti yan cach le cuxtal, le cuxtal leti cach le u zazil ti le uinicob.

5 Le zazil cu zaziltal ti ekhocħenil, hebac le ekhocħenil ma tu natahob.

6 YANHI huntul uinic tuchitahan tumen Dios, Juan cach u kaba.

7 Letilela tal hebix ah hahiltħan, utial u ɔaic u hahil-tħan ti le zazil, utial ca yoceztuyolob tulacal tioklal leti.

8 Leti ma leti cach le zazil, uama tal utial u ɔaic u hahiltħan ti le zazil.

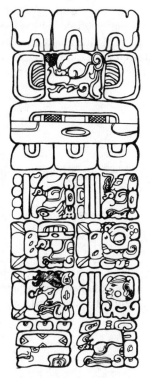

Initial Series date inscription

MENDE

INTRODUCTION

This language belongs to the Mende branch of the Niger-Congo family. It is spoken by around 1 million people in eastern and southern Sierra Leone.

SCRIPT

A Mende syllabary was devised by Kisimi Kamara in 1921, but this was rejected first by the Protectorate Literature Bureau in the 1940s, and then by the Vernacular Literature Bureau, both opting for romanization in their mass literacy compaigns. There is some literature in Mende.

The Latin alphabet as used in Mende is extended by the following letters: ɛ, ɔ, ŋ. The acute, the inverted circumflex, and the circumflex are used to mark tone in pedagogical literature, but not in ordinary Mende usage. *See* **Tone**, below.

PHONOLOGY

Consonants

>stops: p, t, k; b, d, g; mb, nd, ng, nb; kp, gb; ngb
>affricates: dʒ, ndʒ
>fricatives: f, v, s, h
>nasals: m, n ɲ, ŋ
>lateral: l
>semi-vowels: j, w

/p, t, k/ are non-aspirates. The digraphs /mb/ etc. represent single sounds; thus /kp/, for example, represents simultaneous velar and labial closure; /gb/ is the same sound voiced. /r/ is absent. /dʒ/ is notated as *j*.

Vowels

>i, e, ɛ, a, ɔ, o, u

These have long and short values, and are written double when long. All occur nasalized.

Final *ŋ* marks nasalization of the preceding vowel: e.g. *lóŋ* 'quiet' = /ló/.

Tone

Mende has high and low tones, with two glide tones (rising and falling). Stress is evenly distributed over the syllables of an utterance. In connected utterance, words may retain their citation-form tone, or they may react to the tonal pattern set by preceding syllables by changing tone. The situations in which such tonal change occurs are governed by rules.

A key factor in Mende structure is provided by the system of initial-consonant mutation, which is as follows:

p → w, t → l, k → g, kp → gb, f → v, s → j, mb → b, nd → l, nj → y;

ng → *w* before *o*, *u*; → *y* before all other vowels.

Briefly, the mutated form replaces the citation initial of a word when that word follows another: e.g.

fandeí 'cotton' – *Mεndé vándeí* 'Mende cotton';
sɔngɔ 'price' – *gbέ jɔngɔ* 'what's the price?';
fula 'village' – *Mεnde vula* 'a Mende village';
ndopô 'child' – *sukúlu lopoísia* 'school children'.

MORPHOLOGY AND SYNTAX

No gender. Formally, Mende words are homogeneous, i.e. there is no formal difference between 'nouns', 'verbs', 'adjectives', etc. These categories can be distinguished by two criteria: (a) the positions they can occupy in sentences; and (b) the specific affixes they can accept.

There are no articles, but nouns can be made definite by addition of -*í*. All stems ending in -*a* change this vowel to -*ε* before -*i*: e.g. *mahá* 'chief' – *mahεí* 'the chief'.

The indefinite plural marker is -*nga* added to the indefinite stem; the definite pl. marker is -*sia* added to the definite stem. In the case of some animates the two endings may be combined with -*í* as a link vowel: e.g. *mahá* 'chief' – *mahángεísia* 'the (specific) chiefs'.

GENITIVE

Possessor noun or pronoun precedes possessed; both nouns may be definite: e.g. *mahεí nyahεí* 'the chief's wife'; *nyá nyahεí* 'my wife'. In genitival constructions of this type, where alienable possession is concerned, the tone of the second component is regulated by that of the first. This is not the case where inalienable possession is concerned, e.g. kinship terms, words denoting parts of the body, and so on. Kinship terms must be preceded by personal pronouns, even when a nominal subject is present: e.g. *ndopói ngí nje* 'the child (its) mother'; *nguí* 'head' – *nyá wuí* 'my head'.

Adjectives

There is no separate class. A neutral form, normally functioning as a verbal or a nominal, can be construed as an adjective when it occurs as the second element in a binary compound: e.g. *lɛlí* 'to be black' – *númú léli* 'a black person'.

Pronoun

In the following table the first item in each row is the personal subjective pronoun, the second is the disjunctive, the third the possessive pronoun:

	Singular			Plural		
1	ngí	nyá	nyá (wó)	mú	muá	mu (wó)
2	bí	bíá	bí (wó)	wú	wuá	wu (wó)
3	i	tá	ngi (wó)	tí	tiá	ti (wó)

Disjunctive pronouns are used in such sentences as *Nyá mia* 'It's me'; *Tá lɔ mbéí/ táa mbéí*, 'He is here'.

In addition to their usage in genitival constructions (*ngi bowɛí* 'his knife', citation form *mbowɛi*), the possessive pronouns function with the copula -*ng*: e.g. *ngí nyámúngɔ* 'he is bad' (lit. 'his be-bad is'). In the negative of this construction, the possessive pronoun is replaced by the subjective + the particle *ii* (pronoun and *ii* fuse; *ngɔ* → -*ni*): e.g. *ti wóvángɔ* 'they are old'; neg. *tíi wovani* 'they are not old'. Note change of tone.

The possessive series also provides the objective pronouns. For a third person object, the verb form alone suffices without mutation: e.g. *nyáa paáma* 'I'm killing it'; *nyáa ngí waáma* 'I'm killing him/her'.

DEMONSTRATIVE PRONOUN/ADJECTIVE
ji 'this', pl. *jísia*; *ná* 'that', pl. *násia*. These forms follow the noun, which is always singular definite. Tone is fixed. Example: *ngílɛí ná* 'that dog'; *ngílɛí násia* 'those dogs'.

INTERROGATIVE PRONOUN
yɛ̌ 'who?', pl. *yɛ̌ni*; *gbɛ̂* 'what?', pl. *gbɛ́ga*.

RELATIVE PRONOUN
None. The antecedent is made definite by means of a demonstrative pronoun, and the relative clause follows on.

Numerals

1–10: *yilá, felé, sawá, nááni, lɔ́ɔlu, wɔ́ita, wɔ́fela, wáyákpá, táálú, pǔ*; 11 *pǔ mahú yilá*; 12 *pǔ mahú felé*; 20 *nú gbɔyɔ́ngɔ* (= 'person finished'); 40 *nú felé gbɔyɔ́ngɔ* (= 'two persons finished'); 60 *nú sawá gbɔyɔ́ngɔ*; 100 *hɔ́ndɔ yilá*.

In an enumeration like 'five X' the Mende order is X – numeral, where X is indefinite singular; the initial of the numeral does not mutate, and citation form is retained: e.g. *ngíla sawá jísia* 'these three dogs'.

Verb

While there are Mende nouns which cannot function as verbs, there are very few Mende verbs which cannot function as nouns. As noted above, the class of verb/

nouns also includes a sub-class of words which would be defined in other languages as 'adjectives'. For example, the root *nyandé* can mean, depending on position in sentence and on syntax, 'to be pretty', 'pretty', 'prettiness'.

A key role in the tense structure – i.e. in the system of affixation, as the stem itself does not change – is played by the pronominal series. Pronouns are essential, as verbal forms are not marked for person. Three sets of pronouns are used:

(a) the subject pronouns: in past and perfect tenses, and in the subjunctive mood;
(b) the disjunctive pronouns: in the present continuous (*-ma* and *-ngɔ* forms);
(c) a specific set, sing. *ngá, bá, a*; pl. *má, wá, tá*, is used in the future tense, and to express habitual action.

CONTRACTED FORMS
The disjunctive pronouns combine with the identifying particle *lɔ* as follows: *nyá lɔ → nyáa*; *bíá lɔ → bíáa*; similarly, *táa, muáa, wuáa, tiáa*.

In the negative conjugation, the disjunctive pronouns are replaced by the subjective set, and the negative particle *ii* combines with these to form the series: *ngíi, bíi, ii*; pl. *múi, wúi, tíi*.

PRESENT CONTINUOUS
Stem + *-ma* marker: *táa píé.ma* 'he is doing it'; *ii píé.ni* 'he is not doing it'. The tone of *-ma* is correlated with the presence or absence of consonant mutation.

PAST
The marker is *-ni* or *ni lɔ>(i)lɔ*: e.g. *i píé.ilɔ* 'he did it'; *ii píé.ni* 'he didn't do it'; *ngí kɔ́líí lɔ́ilɔ* 'I saw a leopard'.

PERFECT
The marker is *-ngá*; the subject pronoun series is used in both affirmative and negative versions: e.g. *ngí píé.ngá = ngí píéá* 'I have done it'; *ngíi ya píéni* 'I have not done it'.

FUTURE
The positive marker is *lɔ*; the negative marker is ∅. Specific pronoun series: e.g. *a píé.lɔ* 'he'll do it'; *a + ii → ɛɛ píéɵ* 'he won't do it'.

SUBJUNCTIVE
Stem + subject pronoun: *ngí píé* 'let me do it'.

IMPERATIVE
(*a*) + stem + (*o*); *a* is a pluralizer; *o* renders the verb less peremptory.

Postpositions

Consonants liable to mutation do so following a noun or pronoun (the possessive series is used): thus, e.g. with *kulɔ́* 'in front of': *táa nyá gulɔ́* 'he is in front of me', *péɛ́í gulɔ́* 'in front of the house'; *ngumbá* 'on top of', e.g. *péɛ́í wumbá* 'on the roof of the house'; *ma* 'on, at', e.g. *ndɔlé lɔ nyá má* 'hunger is on me' = 'I am hungry'.

Word order

SOV is frequent.

Itātǫmẹ́i Njiẹ́i iyẹ na lo, kẹ Njiẹ́i ta Ngẹ́wǫ yẹlẹ̄, kẹ Njiẹ́i Ngẹ́wǫ yẹlẹ̄.

2 *Na sẹ̄ lo iyẹ itātǫmẹ́i a Ngẹ́wǫ.*

3 *Ta lo i hānísia gbi gbātẹni; kẹ ngi wǫma hāni gbi īyẹ gbātẹni, na iyẹ gbātẹni.*

4 *Ngi hũ lo Ndẹ̄vu iyẹ na; kẹ Ndẹ̄vui na lo i wẹni a nūnga, i ti vǫvǫ.*

5 *Kẹ Hẹ̄mui i vǫa kpindi hũ; kẹ kpindi ī hũgǫni.*

6 *Hindǭ yẹ̄la lo iyẹ na Ngẹ́wǫ tẹ̄wẹni, ngi bijẹ́i lo a Johani.*

7 *Ta sẹ̄ lo i wāni sẹli va; sẹli hǭu va Hẹ̄mui ma, ta lo nūmui gbi a hǭu a tǫnya ngi jā hũ.*

8 *Ta ī lẹ̄ Hẹ̄mui na a wẹ a ngiẹ̄, kẹ tiyẹ ngi dẹwẹ̄ lo, sẹli hǭu va Hẹ̄mui na ma.*

MENOMINI

INTRODUCTION

Menomini is a member of the Central-Eastern division of the Algonquian family. Spoken by a few thousand people in the late nineteenth–early twentieth century, it is now extinct or very nearly so. The Menomini were settled in Wisconsin.

PHONOLOGY

Consonants

> stops: k, p, t, ʔ
> fricatives: s, h
> affricate: tʃ
> nasals: m, n
> semi-vowels: w, j

The glottal stop is notated by Bloomfield (1962) as *q*.

Vowels

> long and short: i, ε, e, a, o, u

Long *e* = /eː/, short *e* = /ɪ/. /ɛ/ is here notated as *ä*; long vowels are notated with macrons, e.g. *ē*.
Diphthongs: ia, ua.

Stress

Stress is on a long vowel or diphthong, followed by short.

MORPHOLOGY AND SYNTAX

Noun

Nouns are animate or inanimate, singular or plural: e.g. animate sing. *enäniw* 'man', pl. *enäniwak*; inanimate sing. *wēkewam* 'wigwam'; pl. *wēkewaman*. The animate/inanimate categories naturally reflect an Algonquian, not an Indo-European, taxonomy of the environment.

This distinction is also present in the demonstrative series; e.g. *ayom* 'this' (anim.), *yōm* 'this' (inanim.), and in such verbal forms with object as *neniak* 'he sees me'; *neniakom* 'it sees me'. (*See* **Verb**, below).

PERSON
Normally marked by prefix; three persons in the singular and plural (the latter with additional suffixed marker), plus an obviative singular; the first person plural makes the inclusive/exclusive distinction. The forms are:

	Singular		*Plural*
1	nä-	excl.	nä...enaw
		incl.	kä...enaw
2	kä-		kä...owāw
3	o-/w-		o...owāw
4	mä-		—

Nouns are divided into alienable and inalienable possession categories. An inalienable item which is not specifically marked for first, second, or third person possession, obligatorily carries the fourth person (obviative) marker: e.g. *mäsēt* '(a, the) foot, i.e. someone's foot'. In the nominal system, the obviative marker is *-an*: e.g. *mätämohs-* 'woman'; pl. *mätämohsak*; obv. *mätämohsan*. Obviative forms are not marked for number.

Verb

Predicative and non-predicative modes: the indicative, inferential, interrogative, present tense, and preterite tense are predicative; the negative, the imperative, and conjunctive are not.

Personal and demonstrative pronouns can be marked for predicative modes: cf. *nenah* 'I' (non-predicative form); *nenäq* 'it is I who ...' (predicative form): e.g. *nenäq kähkenaman* 'I (am the one who) know(s) (it)'. The personal prefixes are used in the non-predicative modes: e.g. *kan näpōsenan* 'I do not embark' (*kan* is negative particle); *kan käpōsenan* 'you do not embark'.

INTRANSITIVE VERBS
Animate or inanimate (many impersonal): e.g. *pāpähčen* 'he falls'; *pāpänen* 'it falls'; *käqsiw* 'it is cold'; *päqnan* 'it is snowing'.

TRANSITIVE VERBS
Agent is of either gender: e.g. *nekōqnek* 'he fears me', *nekōqnekom* 'it fears me'; *neniak* 'he sees me', *neniakom* 'it sees me'. These forms are coded for first person object. Where both agent and object are third person, the forms are, for example, *näwäw* (proximate agent), *niak* (obviative agent) 'sees'. Examples:

> *Näwäw enoh enäniw anenoh metämohsan* 'The man (prox.) sees the woman (obv.)';
> *Niak enoh enäniw anenoh metämohsan* 'The woman (obv. agent) sees the man (prox. obj.)';
> *Näwäw enoh metämoh anenoh enäniwan* 'The woman (prox. agent) sees the man (obv. obj.)';

Niak enoh metämoh anenoh enäniwan 'The man (obv. agent) sees the woman (prox. obj.)'.

The proximate/obviative distinction is ignored in the possessive marking of nouns: e.g. *owiahkwan* 'his (prox. or obv.) hat'; and also in the transitive verb if the object is first or second person: cf. prox. *neniak enoh enäniw* 'that man sees me'; obv. *neniak anenoh ōhnan* 'his father (obv.) sees me'. Equally, the distinction is ignored if the agent is first or second person: *nenäwāw enoh enäniw* 'I see that man'; *nenäwāw enenoh ōhnan* 'I see his father'.

MEROITIC

INTRODUCTION

Meroitic was spoken and written between the sixth century BC and the fourth century AD in what is now Nubia (divided between Egypt and the Sudan). The ethnonym was Kuš; the main city was *mr'*, transcribed as Meroe.

No connection with any other language has been conclusively demonstrated. Recent research goes to suggest that Meroitic may be related to the Koma languages belonging to the Chari-Nile group.

SCRIPT

The Meroitic script was first deciphered by F.LL. Griffith in the early twentieth century. As in the case of Etruscan, the absence of a major digloss means that the language cannot be understood, apart from a few standard formulae and some isolated words. There are two alphabetic systems: (a) a series of 23 phonetic signs borrowed from Egyptian hieroglyphic script, often in adapted form; (b) the same signs in cursive. The language was written from right to left, rarely vertically. The presence of vowel signs in the Meroitic script was taken by some authorities as proof of Greek influence; others disagree, pointing out that if Greek were indeed the source, consonants would also have been borrowed, as in the case of Coptic. An innovation in the script is the presence of markers to separate words. It seems likely that the script is, in part at least, a syllabary; i.e. some consonants have an inherent vowel, e.g. tə, tu.

PHONOLOGY

Consonants

Zavadovskij and Katsnel'son (1980) give the following inventory:

labial: b, p, m, w
dental: t, s, n
palatalized: d', n', š', j
velar: k, ẖ = /x/
uvular: q, ḥ = /χ/

plus /l, r/, and ʔ (Arabic hamza) notated as ;.

Vowels

The four vowels identified by Griffith are *i, e, ê, a*, whose phonetic values are only approximately known: possibly /i, ə, u, a/. /ə/ is notated as ∃.

Many words are written in the Meroitic script without vowels, e.g. *MK* 'god', *LḪ* 'big', *QBŃ* 'star', *MŠ'* 'sun-god'; others are vowelled in more than one way.

MORPHOLOGY AND SYNTAX

Noun

There is no trace of gender markers, which suggests that Meroitic was not a Semito-Hamitic language. *Qure*, for example, means both 'emperor' and 'empress'. Words for 'man' – ;*BR* = /ʔbr/ – and 'woman' – *KZI* = /kd'i/ – are known. These two words may be used to specify gender: e.g. *MK∃Z∃* /mak-(k)əd'ə/, 'goddess'. (In this connection, Zavadovskij and Katsnel'son (1980) compare the Bantu (Zulu) suffix -*kazi*, in compounds like *inkosi.kazi* 'she-chief'.) ;P = /ʔpa/ 'father', and *ŠTə* /ʃtə/, 'mother' are also known.

NUMBER
Apparently unmarked. Some researchers have suggested that the demonstrative pronoun-affix -*L* + the suffix -*B* may be a plural marker meaning 'these'; thus ;*BRLB* /ʔabr.ləb/, '(these) men'; *ŠŠLB* /ʃəʃ.ləb/, '(these) children)'.(?) The -*B* affix also appears in verbal plural endings and in some pronominal forms.

There is no case system; suffixes seem to be used to indicate genitive, locative, etc.

NOUN CLASSES

(a) Names of gods (local and Egyptian), e.g. ;*ŠUR* /ʕaʃurə/, 'Osiris'; *MŠ* /maʃ/, 'the Meroitic sun-god'.
(b) Proper names of persons: often with suffix *Y∃*: e.g. *WY∃T∃Y∃* /wayətə.yə/, is a masculine name, *M∃T∃Y∃* /mətə.yə/, a feminine.
(c) Place-names: e.g. *B∃Z∃WI* = /bəd'əwi/ 'Meroe'; ;*RUM* /ʔarum/, 'Rome'; *Q∃Š* /qəʃ/, 'Kuš'.

Adjective

Qualitative adjectives seem to have short forms attached to nouns: e.g. -*LḪ* 'big'; -*MḪ∃* /mhə/, 'copious, rich in ...'; e.g. *MKLḪ* /mak.laḫ/, 'great god'; ;*TuMḪ∃* /ʔatu.mhə/, 'well-watered'.
Zavadovskij and Katsnel'son (1980) point out that these forms may well be verbal forms used attributively: 'he who is great', 'which is rich in water'.

Pronoun

The demonstrative pronominal affix -*L* (sing.) and -*LƎB* (pl.) have been tentatively identified: e.g. *'abr.l* 'this man'; *br.ləb* 'these men'. -*TZ* seems to be an objective pronominal affix: e.g. *ƎKƎZ.TZ* /əkəd'.tad'/, 'killed them(?)'.

-*NL* and -*Tə* seem to be locative affixes: *BƎZƎWI.Tə* 'in Meroe'. -*S* is a genitive marker, apparently for third person.

Numerals

The numerals are not known, apart from a tentative identification of -*tbu* as 'two'.

Verb

Number is marked: the -*B* affix is sometimes inserted between the stem and other endings. Only one triliteral is known: *D'TD'*, a form which underlines the non-Semitic nature of the language, already implicit in the paucity of triliterals.

Prefixes may indicate aspect or tense.

MIAO-YAO LANGUAGES

Miao and Yao are spoken by up to 5 million people, who live in small rural communities scattered over virtually the whole of south-east China. The two languages, which are close to each other, though not in general mutually intelligible, are allocated by some authorites to the Sino-Tibetan grouping, by others to the typologically closer Tai languages. (*See* **Tai Languages**). Both are extensively fragmented into many dialects.

Phonologically, Miao is remarkable for its extensive system of pre-nasalization. This affects the labial, dental, palatal, velar, and uvular stops, and the dental, retroflex, and palatal affricates. In each series, surd and aspirate (both voiceless) occur with homorganic pre-nasalization: e.g. /p, p^{c}, ^{m}p, ^{m}p^{c}; k, k^{c}, ^{ŋ}k, ^{ŋ}k^{c}; ç, ç^{c}, ^{n}ç°, ^{n}ç^{c}/. Also present in the Miao inventory are the fricatives /f, v, s, z, ʃ, ʒ/; the nasals /m, n, ŋ/, and the lateral /l/. The nasals and the lateral have voiceless counterparts: /m–m̥, l–l̥/.

Miao has five basic vowels: /i, e, a, o, u/, plus several diphthongs. Miao words are typically vowel-final, whereas Yao shares /p, t, (k)/ endings with the contiguous Yue language (*see* **Yue**).

Eight tones are characteristic of Miao.

Numerical classifiers are widely used, as in all Sinitic and South-East Asian languages. Interestingly, the Miao classifiers undergo tonal/vocalic modulation to contrast definiteness of referent versus indefiniteness, or to introduce an augmentative or diminutive nuance.

Word order is SVO.

1. Chivkeeb huamyuaj puag thaum ub 1
los txojlus ntawd twb muaj nyob lawm.
Txojlus ntawd yeejlos nrog Vajtswv Saub
nyob. Txojlus ntawd yog Vajtswv Saub.
Chivkeeb huamyuaj puag thaum ub nws 2
yeejlos nrog Vajtswv Saub nyob. Txhia 3
yam huvsi puavleej yog nws tsim. Huvsi
uas tsim los lawd tsis muaj ib yam dabtsi
uas nws tsis tau tsim li.   Nyob hauv 4
nws thiaj muaj txojsiav. Txojsiav ntawd
ua tibneeg li txojkev kaj. Txojkev kaj 5
txeem kiag tuaj rau hauv txojkev tsaus
ntuj.   Mas txojkev tsaus ntuj kuj kov
tsis yeej txojkev kaj ntawd kiag li.

Muaj ib tug txivneej uas Vajtswv 6
Saub twb txib tuaj lawm. Nws lub npe
hu ua Yauha. Nws tuaj ua tus timkhawv. 7
Yauha ua txojkev kaj tus timkhawv kom
xwv tibneeg sawvdaws thiaj li ntseeg.
Yauha tsis yog txojkev kaj. Tiamsis nws 8
tuaj thiaj li ua txojkev kaj tus timkhawv
xwb.

Miao

924

MIN

INTRODUCTION

Belonging to the Sinitic family, Min languages are spoken by around 40–50 million people in Fujian, along the south-west China seaboard, and in Taiwan. The Amoy dialect is perhaps the best known of the mainland forms.

The Amoy consonantal inventory shows the surd – aspirate surd – voiced stop sequence for the labial, dental, and velar series, as in Wu, but /d/ is missing, and /dz/ is present. Apart from /j/, the entire palatal series, present in Wu, is also lacking in Min, which is one of the most archaic forms of Sinitic.

Northern and southern forms of Min differ on a number of points, e.g. in retention or loss of initial /m, n/; in the Amoy dialect, these have become /b, l/. There are six vowels (/o/ and /ɔ/ are distinguished), which can be nasalized.

The Amoy dialect has seven tones, which undergo extensive sandhi in connected speech.

MINANGKABAU

INTRODUCTION

This Malayo-Polynesian language is spoken by about 5 million people in west Sumatra, and it is estimated that a further 3 million use it elsewhere in Indonesia, especially in the large cities. The Padang dialect has gradually emerged as a supra-dialectal medium of communication between various regions of Minangkabau speech, and hence as the basis of a literary standard. Apart from the rich folk-literature, there is a considerable amount of writing in modern Minangkabau (see Moussay 1981: 316–21). It must also be remembered that many writers using Malay/Indonesian come in fact from the Minangkabau social background, and often deal with its specific and distinctive issues – e.g. the conflict between the matrilineal and matrilocal system, characteristic of Minangkabau society, and Islamic law: e.g. Marah Rusli (*Sitti Nurbaja*, 1922) and the works of Nur Sutan Iskandar, whose language shows Minangkabau influence.

SCRIPT

Originally Arabo-Malay; romanization dates from the 1870s.

PHONOLOGY

Consonants

    stops: p, t, k, b, d, g, ʔ
    affricates: tʃ, dʒ
    fricatives: s, h
    nasals: m, n ɲ, ŋ
    lateral and flap: l, r
    semi-vowels: w, j

Vowels

    i, e, a, o, u

A distinctive feature of Minangkabau pronunciation is the realization of word-final -VC as /-iə/-ua/-uə/, with or without glottal stop; thus Malay/Indonesian *duduk* 'sit' is realized in Minangkabau as /duduəʔ/; *baik* 'good' as /baʔiəʔ/. Cf.

Malay *timor* 'east' – Minangkabau /timua/; Malay *laut* 'sea' – Minangkabau *lauik*; Malay *gunung* 'mountain' – Minangkabau *gunuang*. A final /r/ elided in this way may reappear as medial /r/ after affixation: e.g. *tidur* /tiduə/, 'sleep' – *ka.tidur.an* 'dormitory'.

MORPHOLOGY AND SYNTAX

Noun

Largely as in Malay/Indonesian. A plural form may be made by reduplication: *rumah-rumah* 'houses', *anak-anak* 'children'; or by coupling congruent nominals: *bujang-gadih* 'boy–girl' = 'young people'.

Derivative nominals are made by means of affixation: e.g. *-an* makes collectives, resultatives: *ganggam* 'fist' – *ganggaman* 'a handful'. The circumfix *ka...an* indicates locus of action: e.g. *katiduran* 'dormitory'; or makes abstract nouns: *elok* 'good', *ka.elok.an* 'goodness'. *Pa(m/n)-* indicates the agent: e.g. *buru* 'hunt', *pamburu* 'huntsman'; *duto* 'lie', *panduto* 'liar'.

ARTICLES
si is used for proper names, and may be extended to natural phenomena: e.g. *si puti malam* 'princess of the night' = 'the moon'.

The genitive relationship, or general qualitative relationship between two nominals is expressed by juxtaposition, the qualifier following: e.g. *rumah abak* 'father's house'; *jalan kampuang* 'the village street'; *bintang Timua* 'star of the east'; *pulau Sumatera* 'island of Sumatra'.

Adjective

Usually with *nan* = Malay/Indonesian *yang* (relative pronoun): e.g. *buku nan itam* 'black book'; *gadih nan rancak* 'pretty girl'.

Pronoun

Singular 1 *den* = Ind. *aku*; *ambo* = Ind. *saya*, + several literary grades; 2 *ang* (masc.), *kau* (fem.) are familiar; *kalian* is an acceptable familiar form for both genders; *awak* + *ang/kau/kalian* is polite. 3 *inyo* or *baliau*.

Plural: 1 *kami* (excl.), *kito* (incl.); 2 (*awak*) *kalian*; 3 as singular. The literary third person form is *mereko* (cf. Ind. *mereka*). The third person also has an enclitic form *-nyo*, with variants.

Awak 'body', may replace any personal pronoun.

DEMONSTRATIVE PRONOUN/ADJECTIVE
Two general forms, *a* and *anu*; three other pronouns are graded for relative distance from referent: *ko* 'this' – *itu* 'that' *nin* 'that (yonder)'.

INTERROGATIVE PRONOUN
sia 'who?'; *baa/ma* 'what?'.

nan: e.g. *rumah nan baru dibuek* 'the house which has just been built'.

Numerals

1–10: *ciek, duo, tigo, ampek, limo, anam, tujuah, salapan, sambilan, puluah*. 11 *sabaleh*; 12 *duobaleh*; 20 *duopuluah*; 100 *saratuih*; 200 *duoratuih*.

Verb

Simple, reduplicated, or composite bases; many of the latter involve echo words; e.g. *inga-binga* 'be noisy', or antonyms, e.g. *kalua-masuak* 'go out and in'. As in Malay/Indonesian, specific meanings are generated from bases by means of prefixes, suffixes, and circumfixes; the inventory in Minangkabau of these formants is larger than in Malay. Some are associated with transitive verbs only, others with statives. Some again are coded for subject focus, others for object focus.

Tense and aspect are indicated by specific markers, e.g. *lai* or *alah* for perfective, *indak* or *alun* for imperfective aspect; *kan* is a future marker; *panah* establishes past occurrence of action; *sadang* and *tatok* indicate that action is now proceeding. There are also potential, necessitative, and desiderative markers.

Word order

Word order depends on which element of the proposition is being stressed – subject, object, or predicate; any one of these can be sentence-initial, with a corresponding reordering of the remaining elements. Compare:

banyak urang mambali buah-buah di Padang
'many people buy fruit in Padang'

mambali buah-buah banyak urang di Padang
'buy fruit – many people – in P.'

di Padang banyak urang mambali buah-buah
'in P. – many people – buy fruit'

buah-buah **t**ambali **dek** banyak urang di Padang
'(it is) fruit (that) is bought by many people in P.'

tabali buah-buah **dek** banyak urang di Padang
'is bought – fruit – by many people in P.'

9 Jadi ingeklah ko, mintaklah, mangko kalian kadibari, carilah, mangko kalian kamandapek, guguahlah pintu, mangko pintu kadibukak untuak kalian. 10 Sabab satiok urang nan mamintak kamanarimo; urang nan mancari kamandapek, sarato urang nan mangguguah pintu, pintu kadibukakan untuak inyo. 11 Sia diantaro kalian nan manjadi bapak namuah mambarikan ula kapado anaknyo, jiko anaknyo mamintak ikan? 12 Ataupun mambarikan kalajangkiang jiko anaknyo mamintak talua? 13 Sajahek-jaheknyo kalian, tantu kalian tahu mambari barang-barang nan baiak kapado anak-anak kalian. Apo lai Bapak nan di sarugo, inyo ka mambarikan Rohnyo ka urang-urang nan mamintak kapadanyo!"

MINGRELIAN

INTRODUCTION

This language belongs to the Kartvelian (South Caucasian) group of languages. Together, Mingrelian and Laz form the Zan complex of Kartvelian dialects; both are closely related to Georgian. Mingrelian is spoken by about 360,000 in western Georgia, and in the Abkhaz Autonomous Soviet Socialist Republic. It is unwritten. *See also* **Laz**.

PHONOLOGY

As in Georgian, plus a glottal stop, /w/, and a schwa vowel which figures in the realization of consonantal clusters.

MORPHOLOGY AND SYNTAX

Noun

In general as in Georgian. There are, however, nine cases, adding an aditive, an ablative, and a destinative to the Georgian six. The ergative is marked by -*k*. Thus, e.g. *ķoči* 'man' (Georgian *ķaci*), with ergative *ķočǝk*, genitive *ķočis*.
   The plural marker is -*ep* (Georgian -*eb*): e.g. *ķočepi* 'men', erg. *ķočenk*.

Adjective

As in Georgian.

Pronoun

The personal series is: sing. 1 *ma*, 2 *si*, 3 (*e*)*tina/ina/mu*; pl. 1 *čki*, 2 *tkva*, 3 *tinepi/ inepi/munepi*.

Numerals

1–10: *arti, žiri, sumi, othi, huti, amšvi, škviti, ruo, čhoro, viti*.

Verb

For a general aperçu of the Kartvelian verb structure, *see* **Georgian**. A specific divergence in Mingrelian is the use of the ergative marker -*k* for the subject of both transitive and intransitive verbs in the aorist tenses of group II, for example. Thus, while the sentences

Bošik didas kemeču **uškuri** 'The boy gave an apple to his mother'

Ķočǝk dočaras kaɣardi 'The man wrote a letter'

are what one might expect in a South Caucasian language, the following sentence is not: *ķočǝk komortu* 'the man came'. Hewitt (1981: p.224) writes: 'the Mingrelian so-called ergative has become a redundant aorist marker, and the language no longer exhibits any true ergative construction'.

NEGATION
va(r) + verb: cf. *ma moko* 'I want'; *ma **varmoko*** 'I don't want'.

Word order

The order of components in a Mingrelian verb complex is: prefix (*a-*, *mo-*, *me-*, etc.) – augment (tense indicator) – personal prefix – modal characteristic – root – tense suffix – personal suffix.

MISKITO

INTRODUCTION

This is one of the three Meso-American languages grouped by Suárez (1983) in his Misumalpan category. It is spoken by 15,000–20,000 Indians on the Caribbean coast of Nicaragua, extending into Honduras. Miskito is unwritten.

PHONOLOGY

Consonants

stops: p, b, t, d, k, g, q
fricatives: s; r, l, h
nasals: m, n, ŋ
semi-vowels: w, j

Clustering, e.g. /dr, kl, pn, mk, tn/, occurs.

Vowels

a, aː, e, iː, ɪ, oː, ɔ, ɔː, u, uː
ai, au

/ɔ/ is notated in Berckenhagen (1894) as á. Long vowels are notated here with macrons, e.g. /iː/ = ī.

MORPHOLOGY AND SYNTAX

Noun

No gender; natural sex may be lexically marked: e.g. *līmi wainka* 'jaguar'; *līmi mairin* 'female jaguar'. There are definite – *ba* – and indefinite – *kumi* – articles. *Nani* is added to singular to make plural: *waikna* 'man', pl. *waikna nani*. An oblique case marker is -*ra*: e.g. *waiknara* 'to the man'.

POSSESSION
i and *m* are first/second personal markers; they may be infixed or affixed:

watla 'house': *waitla* 'my house', *wamtla* 'your house';
(*jang*) *lupi* 'my child': (*man*) *lupiam* 'your child';
twīsa 'tongue': *twīsi* 'my tongue', *twīsam* 'your tongue'.

third possession is marked by *-ka*, usually combined with *ai*: e.g. *ai aiska* 'his father'.

Adjective

As attribute, adjective follows noun: e.g. *waikna umpira ba* 'the poor man'.

Pronoun

INDEPENDENT PERSONAL

	Singular	Plural
1	jang	jang nani
2	man	man nani
3	witin	witin nani

There are specific possessive forms, e.g. *jawin* 'our'. An oblique case is formed by adding *-ra*, or by using infixed *ai* for first person, *mai* for second person, Ø for third person: e.g. *makabaia* 'to ask' – *maikabisma* 'you ask me'.

DEMONSTRATIVE PRONOUN/ADJECTIVE
naha 'this'; *baha* 'that'.

INTERROGATIVE PRONOUN
yā 'who?'; *dia* 'what?'.

RELATIVE PRONOUN
ya ya; *witin ba/na*.

Numerals

1–10: *kumi, wol, jumpa, wol-wol* (= 2×2); *matasip* 'handful' = 5; *matlalkabi* 'right hand on top of left hand' = 6; 7 *matlalkabi pura kumi*; 8 *matlalkabi pura wol*; 9 *matlalkabi pura jumpa*; *matawolsip* '2 hands full'; 20 *jawin aiska* 'our all' (i.e. fingers and toes); 40 *jawin aiska wol* 'twice our all'.

Verb

All Miskito verbs end in *-aia*, and there is only one conjugation (though certain phonetic changes occur). The root is the citation form minus *-aisa*; to this root, *-i* is added to form the first participle (unless root ends in *-i*). *-(a)n* is added to form second participle: e.g. *briaia* 'to have, hold' – *bri, brin*. The present tense is formed by adding first person *sni*, second *sma*, third *sa* to the first participle: e.g. *smalkaia* 'to teach' – *smalki sni, smalki sma, smalki sa*. *Sni, sma, sa* are the present-tense forms of the irregular verb *kaia* 'to be'. The plural forms are identical; the plural marker *nani* is optional: e.g. *yang (nani) sni* 'we are'. These forms – *sni, sma, sa* – are often replaced by *lika/mika/sika*, which appear to be interchangeable in the affirmative, and are so in the negative: cf. *jang lika/sika*

933

apia 'I am not/was not/have not been'.

Imperfect of *kaia*:	katna	katma	katta
Perfect:	kapri	kapram	kan
Future:	kamni	kama	kabia

Thus, taking the root of *smalkaia* 'to teach' – *smalk-*: present (as above);

imperfect: *smalkatni – smalkatma – smalkatta*
perfect: *smalkri – smalkram – smalkan*
future: *smalkamni – smalkma – smalkbia*

IMPERATIVE
In *-s* or *-ram*, e.g. *smalks, smalkram*

NEGATIVE
Root + *-ras*; the tense forms of *kaia* are used where necessary: e.g. *jang smalkras* 'I don't teach'; *jang smalkras katni* 'I wasn't teaching'; *jang smalkras kapri* 'I didn't teach'; *jang smalkras kamni* 'I shan't teach'. The future has an alternative form: affirmative + *apia*.

PROGRESSIVE FORM
Examples: *jang smalki* 'I am teaching'; *jang smalki katni* 'I was teaching'.

CONDITIONAL
Infinitive + imperfect: e.g. *jang smalkaia katni* 'I should/would teach'.

IMPERSONAL VERBS WITH DATIVE
Examples: with *daukaia* 'to make': *plun ai daukisa* 'I'm hungry' (*plun* 'food'; *ai* 'to me'); *japan ai daukisa* 'I'm sleepy'.

COMPOSITE VERBS
First participle + inflected form: e.g. *aisi kaikaia* 'to see, speaking' = 'to read'; *dābi kaikaia* 'to see, sucking' = 'to taste'.

PASSIVE
With second participle: e.g. *jang ai smalkan sa* 'I am being taught'; *jang ai smalkan katta* 'I was being taught'; *jang ai smalkan kabia* 'I shall be being taught'. Negative: e.g. *jang ai smalkras sa*. Many roots have paired forms for active and passive: e.g. *baikaia* 'to split', pass. *baiwaia*; *dringbaia* 'to break down', pass. *dringwaia*.

Prepositions

Some take personal markers infixed: e.g. *lāmāra* 'near': *laimāra* 'near me', *lammāra* 'near you'; *mata* 'for the sake of': *maita* 'for my sake', *mamta* 'for your sake'.

Word formation

-*ra* forms abstracts: e.g. *jamni* 'good' – *jamnira* 'goodness'.

Nouns from verbs: the formula is initial consonant + *a* + stem + *ra*, e.g. *smalkaia* 'to teach' – **sasmalkra** 'teacher'; *daukaia* 'to make' – **dadaukra** 'maker'.

Verbs with initial *ai* reduplicate: e.g. *aiklabaia* 'to fight' – *aiklaklabra* 'fighter'.

Adjectives: -*s* is privative, e.g. *nakra* 'eye' – *nakras* 'blind'; *bila* 'mouth' – *bilas* 'dumb'. -*kas* and -*kirra* are antonyms: e.g. *lalla* 'money' – *lallakas* 'poor' – *lallakirra* 'rich'. Example: *Jang sika lallakirra* 'It is I who am rich.'

Word order

SOV.

1 ¹ Blasi poli kat, baha Bila bara kan, baha Bila sin God wol kan, baha Bila sin God kan. ² Baha ba blasi polira God wol kan. ³ Diera nani sut witin mita daukan kan; witin apu kira diera kumi sin daukras kan, daukan bangwi ba tilara. ⁴ Witinra raya-kaia bara kan; baha rayakaia ba sin upla nani ingnika kan. ⁵ Baha ingnika ba sin timiara klauisa; timia ba sin sip baha alkras sa.

⁶ Waikna kumi balan, God wina blikan kan, ai nina Jon. ⁷ Witin lika witnis dukiara balan, ingni ba witniska aisaia, baku mika upla nani sut witin mita kasak lukaia kan. ⁸ Witin ba baha ingnika apia kan, sakuna balan, baha ingnika dukiara witnis aisaia.

MIXTEC

INTRODUCTION

Since the 1920s, the Mixtec dialect complex has been recognized as a branch of the Otomanguean phylum, which includes Zapotec, Popolacan, Otopamean, and other groupings. The Mixtec languages are spoken in Central Mexico by an estimated 250,000 people. The dialect described here is mainly that of Jicaltepec, following Bradley (1970). Some reference is also made to the dialect of San Miguel el Grande, as described by Dyk and Stoudt (1965).

PHONOLOGY

Consonants

> stops: p, b, t, d, k, g, q, ʔ; palatalized t', d'; and pre-nasalized mb, nd, nd', ŋg
> affricate: tʃ
> fricatives: s, ʃ, h
> nasals: m, n, ŋ, ɲ
> lateral and flap: l, r
> semi-vowels: j, w

/ß/ and /s'/ occur in Spanish loan-words.

In their description of the San Miguel el Grande dialect, Dyk and Stoudt (1965) use *h* to mark the hamza-like suspension following a checked vowel; thus, *uhu* = /uʔu/ 'to pain, grieve'. Also ¢ = /ts/ occurs in this dialect.

Vowels

> i, e, a, o, u

All occur nasalized: /ĩ, ẽ, ã, õ, ũ/; and checked: /i', e'/, etc. The checked vowels are characteristic of Mixtec, and very frequent. /ɪ/ is notated by Dyk and Stoudt, as *i*.

Tones

Three tones are distinguished: high, middle, and low. Dyk and Stoudt (1965) divide Mixtec words into three classes, according to their tonal valencies:

1. words which do not induce tonal change in other words;
2. words which always cause tonal change in following words: cf. *chāa vāha* 'good man' (*chaa* 'man'), but *suchí váha* 'good child', *uū chāa* 'two men', *cuūn cháa* 'four men';
3. words belonging to this class induce tonal change only if their own tones have not been changed: e.g. the third person feminine pronominal enclitic *-ña*: e.g. *quihīn.ña vína* 'she is going today', *quee.ñá vina* 'she will eat today'.

In the above, ' marks high tone and ‾ middle.

MORPHOLOGY AND SYNTAX

Bradley (1970) classifies parts of speech in Jicaltepec Mixtec as verbs, nouns, pronouns, numerals, adverbs, modifiers, markers, and interjections. A Mixtec word may be dependent or independent. Independent words are not monosyllabic, may stand in isolation, and may be complete sentences in themselves. Dependent monosyllables are obligatorily affixed to a preceding or following independent word.

Noun

Bradley lists five genders: masculine, feminine, sacred, animal, and inanimate or neutral. The taxonomy is alien to the Indo-European mind: e.g. *sáwí* 'rain' is masculine, *yóó* 'moon' is animal, *dósó yá'á* 'comet' is sacred, *yutū* 'tree' and *támá* 'famine' are inanimate.

Nouns are not marked for number; gender concord is overt in relationships between noun and verbal phrase, and in pronominal deixis. Nouns denoting parts of the body or members of the extended family are marked for inalienable ownership: e.g. *nű'ű kū* 'your tooth'.

Adjective

The attributive adjective follows its noun, preceding a demonstrative: e.g. *we'e kuta ka* 'that round house' (*we'e* house, *ka* is the neutral distal demonstrative).

Pronoun

Formal and familiar forms are distinguished:

	Singular			*Plural*	
	Formal	*Familiar*		*Formal*	*Familiar*
1	yú'ú	í	incl.	yoo	dí
			excl.	d'ú'ú	dí
2	yo'o	kū		d'o'o	do

The third person forms are derived from the demonstrative series, which has a three-way gradation for proximate, distal, and neutral, and which is marked for the five genders. Thus, *rá* and *ña* are respectively masculine and feminine proximate forms; similarly, *yá* is used for the sacred series, *ri* for the animal and *čí* for the inanimate/neutral.

All persons have enclitic forms. Thus the familiar first person *ruu* (in San Miguel el Grande) has the singular enclitic *-ri*, plural *ri.jinahan.ri*: e.g. *ni śasïn.de i.jínáhan.i* 'he separated them' (in this sentence, *śasïn* means 'to separate'; *de* is the third person masculine series pronominal enclitic, acting as subject; the *i.jínáhan.i* enclitic identifies the object as belonging to the neutral/ inanimate gender: 'he separated the children'). Substitution of *tï.jínáhan.tï in this sentence would identify the object as animals.*

Numerals

Mixtec has unit numerals and group numerals. The unit numbers 1–10 are: *ïï, úwí, úní, kúmí, ÿ'ÿ, íñú, účá, úná, ïï, účí*; the unit number for 20 is *ókó*. The group numbers include *šiko* 20; *s'edu* 100. Examples: *úwí kíwí* 'two days'; *kíwí úwí* 'the second day'; i.e. a numeral following a noun is an ordinal.

Verb

The Mixtec verb has three stems: imperfective, perfective, continuative. Verbs may be classified in terms of stems: in the first class, all three stems differ; in the fourth all are identical. In each of the other two stems, one stem differs from the others. With each stem a specific tone pattern is associated.

Aspect markers precede the stem, though the latter may, as explained above, itself determine aspect. These markers differ from one dialect to another. Examples from Jicaltepec are: *qá* (imperfective), *ní* (perfective); in San Miguel el Grande *na* is used for habitual action, *ni* for past perfective, *ná* for present progressive. Thus, with a two-stem verb: *ni juña.ná* 'I opened it'; *(na) juña.ná* 'I'm opening it'; *cuña.ná* 'I'll open it'.

Personal markers are affixed to the stem; the third person endings reflect the five-fold gender taxonomy. An example of an intransitive verb in Jicaltepec is: *qÿ'í* 'I am going' *qÿ'ú* 'you (familiar) are going'; *qÿ'á* 'he is going'. Cf. *ča'á.rá šÿ'ú* 'he is giving the money'; *kani'ï.rá duta* 'he carries water'.

The pluralizing prefix *ka.* is not used in the future tense: e.g. *ni yee.dé* 'he ate'; *ni kayee.dé* 'they ate'. The same pluralizer shows the number of the subject in stative verbs: e.g. *na'nu* '… is big'; *ka'nu* '… are big'.

NEGATION

The marker is *ñá*: e.g. *ñá ku'u.rá* 'he will not go'; *rái kuu.rá* 'he is a man'; *ñá kuu.rá rái* 'he is not a man'.

Prepositions

These are derived from nouns; cf. *xini* 'head' – *xini vehe* 'above the house'; *chii* 'stomach' – *chii ñuhun* 'below the ground'; *nuu* 'face' – *quihin.ná nuu yúcu* 'I'm going to the mountain'.

Word order

VSO is common.

MOLDAVIAN

INTRODUCTION

A member of the Romance branch of the Indo-European family of languages. Moldavian is Romanian written in Cyrillic. In other words, the language spoken in *Chişinău* is virtually identical to the language spoken in Bucharest, and owes its existence to the same original set of events – the Roman colonization of Dacia, and the subsequent spread of Low Latin to Wallachia, Muntenia, Bessarabia, and Moldavia.

Historically, 'Moldavia' was the name given to the most northerly province of the Romanian-speaking area, with its capital at Iasi. From 1919 to 1940 the region lying between the Prut and the Dniester formed part of the Kingdom of Romania, under the name of 'Bessarabia'. During the Second World War, this area was incorporated into the USSR as the Moldavian Soviet Socialist Republic (capital Chişinău). Here, 'Moldavian' is spoken by about 3 million people.

SCRIPT

Cyrillic since 1940. In a sense this is a return to origins, as Romanian was written in Cyrillic until the middle of the nineteenth century. Cyrillic ы is used to notate the specifically Romanian sound /â/î/ (/ɨ/); and the soft sign is used for final -*i*: e.g. *lucruri* = лукрурь. Romanian /ă/ is represented by э.

PHONOLOGY

See **Romanian**.

MORPHOLOGY AND SYNTAX

See **Romanian**.

Lexicon

A considerable number of recent Russian loan-words have found their way into Moldavian.

MON

INTRODUCTION

Mon belongs to the Mon-Khmer family of languages. It is also known as Talaing or Peguan. Old Mon (*mon pa-oeh*) is attested in an extensive corpus of inscriptions, which date from the sixth century AD to the sixteenth.

SCRIPT

The Mon version of the Brahmi script was taken over by the Burmese in the ninth century.

OLD MON

PHONOLOGY

Consonants

The consonantal system postulated for Old Mon includes the stops /p, b, t, d, k, g, ɖ, ɓ, ʔ/; four nasals, /m, n, ɲ, ŋ/; the affricates /tʃ, dʒ/; the fricatives /s, h/; and /r, l/. There is a series of glottalized consonants. The stops and affricates have pre-nasalized counterparts, which were lost in later stages of the language.

Vowels

The vocalic system was, basically /i, e, a, o, u/, with intermediate values and phonotactic restrictions.

MORPHOLOGY AND SYNTAX

As in Mon-Khmer generally, infixes and prefixes are the essential functional and syntactic formants. Examples:

-*m*/-V*m*/: nominal formant, e.g. *jnok* 'to be great' – *jumnok* 'who is/are great';
p-/*p*V-: causative formant, e.g. *das* 'to be' – *pdas* 'to create';
s(*i*)-: future formant, e.g. *das* 'to be' – *sdas* 'will be';
-*ir*-: forms deverbal nouns, e.g. *das* 'to be' – *dirdas* 'existence'.

941

Example: *Risi bisnū goḥ scuti nor dirdas* 'The rishi Vishnu will (*s-*) pass (*cuti*) from (*nor*) that existence.'

MODERN MON

INTRODUCTION

The modern Mon language is spoken by about half a million in Burma and Thailand. With Burmese, it shares the original Mon script (adapted in Burmese).

PHONOLOGY

Consonants

Mon retains the five consonantal series of the Sanskrit Devanagari system (*see* **Sanskrit**), though not all of the component sounds are pronounced as in Sanksrit. In particular, the third member of each series – the voiced member in Sanskrit – seems to be pronounced as the first (unvoiced non-aspirate), but in a deeper tone. Notation for the original retroflex series is present, though Mon has lost its retroflex phonemes.

Also present are: /j, w, r, l/ all with deep tone; /s, h/. Finally, the voiced labial /b/ plus its deep-tone counterpart, are added at the end of the consonantal series. Permissible finals are the nasals plus /p, t, k, j, w, h, a/.

Vowels

short: i, e, ε, ɪ, ə, a, ʌ, ɔ, u
long: i, e, a, ɔ, o, œ, u

/ε/ is notated as *ä*, /œ/ as *ö*. Long vowels are marked with macron.

MORPHOLOGY AND SYNTAX

As in Old Mon, prefixes and infixes are the key formants.

Noun

E.g. deverbal with *lV-* prefix, e.g. *nyat* 'to see' – *lenyat* 'view'; infix *-m-*, e.g. *klon* 'to work' – *kamlon* 'work'; *klot* 'to steal' – *kamlot* 'thief'.

NUMBER
Not necessarily marked, but, if required, various indicators are available, e.g. the verb *kemläng* 'to be many': *kon dung kemläng* 'people – country – many' = 'many citizens'.

Lexically indicated; there is no grammatical gender.

CASE
Postitional (SVO); modifier follows modified, possessor follows possessed: cf.

> *dait* 'water': *dait kamauh* 'cold water', *dait pateak* 'fresh water';
> *kwot* 'learning, craft': *kwot so* 'practice of medicine', *kwot reče* 'kingship',
> *kwot senangke* 'military knowledge';
> *mnih* 'man': *mnih kamlak* 'blind person', *mnih nge* 'farmer', *mnih penoit*
> 'trader'.

Pronoun

The invariable forms serve as subject, object, and possessive pronoun:

	Singular	*Plural*
1	oa	poe
2	be	mneh to'
3	nyeh/deh	nyeh to'/deh to'

To' is a pluralizing affix. There are honorific forms for second and third persons.

DEMONSTRATIVE PRONOUN
Examples: *ano'/ino'* 'this'; *akoh/ikoh* 'that'. These follow the noun.

Numerals

1–10: *moa, bā, pei, pon, msaun, taraō, thapoh, tečam, tečit, čoh*; 11 *čoh mao*;
20 *ba čoh*; 100 *klom*.

The numerals follow the noun: e.g. *pöt pei* 'the three Vedas'; *pasoit ekarāt
mesaun prakā* 'the five insignia of kingship' (*pasoit* 'insignia'; *ekarāt* 'monarch'
from Sanskrit *ekarāj*; *prakā* 'sort').

NUMERICAL CLASSIFIERS
Examples: *čekau* (persons), *tamä* (plants), *kanop* (books).

Verbs

Verbs in Mon are transitive or intransitive, and often occur in pairs, the
transitive/causative form being made from the intransitive by prefixation of e.g.
pa/ta/tha/te. Examples: *teim* 'to know' – *sateim* 'to inform'; *mok* 'to appear' –
tamok 'to show'.

Temporal, modal, and aspectual nuances are expressed by verbal prefixes and
affixes. Thus, prefixes *teh* (necessitative), *pa* (prohibitory), *nyong* (imperative),
sa (future tense and subjunctive).

Suffixes: e.g. *rao* (intrerrogative), *rong* (emphatic future), *lo* (perfective).

Preposition

Prepositions are plentiful: e.g. *akrā* 'between', *pano* 'in', *kau* 'with'.

MONGOLIAN, CLASSICAL

INTRODUCTION

The Mongolian literary language is something of an enigma in that no known form of spoken Mongolian can be conclusively shown to be its basis. When it first appears in the thirteenth century AD, the language is already equipped with a sophisticated writing system and a literary identity, pointing to antecedent development in circumstances that can only be guessed at. The pre-Genghiz Khan Kereits and the Khitans have been seen as possible sources; both of these peoples were in contact with Nestorian Christianity and Buddhism, and both were on a significantly higher cultural plane than the other Mongolian tribes.

The major work in literary Mongolian, the 'Secret History of the Mongols', was in fact written and transmitted, not in Mongolian script, but in Chinese characters. It dates from 1240, and marks the beginning of the Middle Mongolian or pre-classical period. The richest period in Mongolian literature followed upon the introduction of Buddhism in the sixteenth century. Thereafter the classical language was used for writing in both the Khalkha and the Buryat areas until the emergence of the modern literary languages in the twentieth century (*see* **Mongolian**, **Modern**; **Buryat**). According to Poppe (1964), the classical written language is still used by Khalkhas and Buryats for private purposes, e.g. correspondence.

SCRIPT

Derives ultimately from Aramaic via Sogdian and Uyghur; in use from the twelfth century onwards. As might be expected in the light of their Semitic origins, the letters have specific initial, medial, and final forms. The language written in the 'phags-pa character, based on Tibetan (thirteenth to fourteenth centuries), is not the same as Classical Mongolian proper.

PHONOLOGY

Classical Mongolian has characters denoting the following phonemes.

Consonants

stops: p, b, t, d, k, g
affricates: tʃ, dʒ
fricatives: γ, s, ʃ, χ, h
nasals: m, n, ŋ
lateral and flap: l, r
semi-vowels: j, w

Vowels

short: ɪ, ɛ, a, o, œ, y
long: i, e, a, ɔ, u, œ, y
diphthongs: ai, oi, ei, ui, yi

/œ/ is notated as *ö*, /y/ as *ü*.

VOWEL HARMONY
Front vowels are followed by front, back by back. /i/ is neutral.

MORPHOLOGY AND SYNTAX

Nominals

A frequent plural formation is in *-nar/-ner*: e.g. *blama* 'lama', pl. *blamanar*; *böge* 'shaman', pl. *bögener*. *-nad/ned* occurs in 'Secret History.' Other plural formations: *-n* drops before a plural in *-d*: e.g. *noyan* 'prince', pl. *noyad*; *ebügen* 'old man', pl. *ebüged*. Similarly, *-r* drops before *-n*: *nökör* 'friend', pl. *nököd*.

DECLENSION
Specimen declension of back vowel stem, *ulus* 'state':

genitive	ulus.un
dative	ulus.tur
locative	ulus.tu/a
accusative	ulus.i
ablative	ulus.ača
instrumental	ulus.iyar
comitative	ulus.luγa

Cases may be compounded: e.g, comitative + instrumental; *noyan.luγ.a.bar* 'together with the prince'.

Adjective

Any nominal can function as an adjective, and precede noun as attribute: e.g. *sayin nökör* 'good friend'; *sayin morin* 'good horse'. The attributive remains uninflected: e.g. *sayin morin.luγa* 'with the good horse'.

Pronoun

Sing. 1 *bi*, 2 *či*, 3 (not attested; *i?*); pl. 1 incl. *bida*, excl. *ba*, 2 *ta*, 3 (not attested: *a?*). These forms are declined in all cases; the base for the oblique cases in 1st singular is *min-/nam-*; for 1st person plural exclusive *man-*: cf. *mal.ača.manu* 'from our cattle'; *axa.luγa.tanu* 'with your elder brother'; *bayši.nar.ača.anu* 'from his/their teachers'.

DEMONSTRATIVE PRONOUN/ADJECTIVE
ene 'this', pl. *edeger*; *tere* 'that', pl. *tedeger*.

INTERROGATIVE PRONOUN
ken 'who?'; *yaγun* 'what?'.

RELATIVE CONSTRUCTION
Participial preceding headword.

Verb

Affixes are added agglutinatively to stem to form moods, tenses, verbal nouns, or participles; modal nuances are provided by converbs.

There are indicative, imperative, and optative (voluntative) moods.

The singular imperative = stem: *yabu* 'go!', pl. *yabuγtun*: e.g. *keleg.tün* 'please say!'. The third person imperative form is in *-tuγai*: e.g. *yabutuγai* 'he must go'.

Optative: *-suγai/sügei*: *yabusuγai* 'let me go', 'that I should go'.

INDICATIVE MOOD, TENSES
The present has two narrative forms:

(a) (link vowel) + *-mui/müi*, e.g. *yabu.muj* 'he goes';
(b) (link vowel) + *-nam/nem*, e.g. *yabunam*.

Past: has three forms:

(a) (link vowel) + *-ba(i)/be(i)*, e.g. *yabubai*;
(b) past definite: (link vowel) + *-luγa/lüge*, e.g. *yabu.luγa*;
(c) past anterior: (link vowel) + *-j/č-uqui/üküi*, e.g. *yabujuqui* 'he had gone (so it appeared)'.

VERBAL NOUNS

of agent: (V) + *γči/gči*, e.g. *yabuγči* (he) who goes';
of habitual action: (V) + *daγ/deg*, e.g. *yabu.daγ* '(he) who habitually goes';
of future action: *-qu/kü*, e.g. *yabu.qu* 'who will go, a future going ...';
imperfective: *-γa/ge*, usually with negative, e.g. *irege ügei* '... has not yet come';
perfective: *-γsan/gsen*, e.g. *yabuγsan* 'who went'.

CONVERBS
1. Verbal forms:

(a) conditional: (V) + *-basu/besü*, e.g. *yabu.basu* 'if (he...) goes';
(b) concessive: (V) + *-baču/bečü*, e.g. *yabu.baču* 'although (he) goes';
(c) concomitant: *-ju/jü*, e.g. *yabu.ju* '... going ...';
(d) modal: (V) + *-n*, e.g. *nisün irebe* 'he came flying';
(e) perfective: (V) + *γad/ged*, e.g. *yabuγad* 'after having gone'.

2. Petrified oblique cases of verbal nouns: e.g.

(a) terminative: *-tala/tele*, e.g. *yabu.tala* 'until (he...) goes';
(b) durative: (V) + *-γsagar/gseger*, e.g. *yabuγsagar* 'while (he...) was going';
(c) purposive: (V) + *-ra/re*, e.g. *yabu.ra* 'in order to go'.

Negatives: nominal, *ügei* or *busu*: e.g. *ende usun ügei* 'there is no water here'; *modon busu ...* 'not a tree but ...'; verbal, *ese*, *ülü*, *buu*: e.g. *manu bayši ese irebe* 'our teacher did not come'; *ülü medejü* 'not knowing'; *buu ire* 'don't come'.

Postpositions

These are nominal in origin, and govern either the base stem or an oblique case, usually genitive or ablative: e.g. *door.a* 'under', *dotor.a* 'in', *qoyin.a* 'behind': *aγula.yin qoyin.a* 'behind the mountain'.

Word formation

A great many derivatives, both denominal and deverbal, are made by suffixation; e.g.

  -liγ/-lig: indicates locus of object/action denoted by stem + notion of abundance: e.g. *čečeg* 'flower' – *čeče.lig* 'garden of flowers' (*-g-* drops); *bayan* 'rich' – *baya.liγ* 'wealth' (*-n-* drops).
  -tai/tei: owner, agent, e.g. *morin* 'horse' – *mori.tai* 'horseman' (*-n-* drops).
  -dal/del/tal/tel: form abstract nouns, e.g. *bayi* 'to be' – *bayidal* 'existence'; *sur* 'to learn' – *surtal* 'doctrine'.
  -lya/lge: process: *bari* 'to build' – *barilya* 'building'.

Appositional compounds: e.g. *γajar usun* 'earth-water' = 'territory'; *erdem soyul* 'science-civilization' = 'culture'.

MONGOLIAN
LANGUAGES OF CHINA

The collapse of the Yuan administration in the fourteenth century left a number of Mongol garrisons stranded in various parts of China. Thus originated several enclaves of Mongol speech in China which survive to the present day; they are:

> Dagur, spoken in Heilongjiang and the Inner Mongolian Autonomous Region; about 100,000 speakers.
> Santa (Dōngxiāng) spoken in Gansu; c. 280,000 speakers.
> Monguor, spoken in Qinghai by c. 160,000 people.
> Bao'an, also spoken in Qinghai, by c. 9,000 people.

Isolated as they are from the main area of Mongol speech and culture, these languages (a) share certain archaic features, and (b) show a tendency to adopt certain characteristics of their Sino-Tibetan linguistic environment.

Thus, in all four, the rules of vowel harmony, if not abolished altogether, are very much eroded. All four retain initial /x/ and /f/ where Literary Mongolian and Modern Mongolian have initial vowel: e.g.

Literary Mongolian

Dagur /xarbaŋ/	
Monguor /xarvan/	arban 'ten'
Santa /harwan/	
Bao'an /habraŋ/	
Dagur /xoːŋ/	on 'year'
Dagur /xulaːŋ/	
Monguor /fulaːn/	ulaγan 'red; Modern Mongolian *ulaan*
Monguor /fugʷor/	üker 'bull'

Final consonants tend to be reduced: in Dagur to -r/l, in Santa often to Ø. In Bao'an and Monguor, initial vowels have been replaced by *n*-: e.g.

		Khalkha
Monguor	nta 'to sleep'	untax
Bao'an	ndaŋ 'door'	üüden
	nde- 'eat'	idex

Finally, in all four the genitive and accusative case endings have fused: in Dagur, *-jī/-ī*, in Monguor *-ne*, in Santa *-ni/-ji*.

Some specific features in individual languages:

1. Monguor is unique among Mongolian languages in that the normal stress falls on the final syllable.
2. Like Kalmuk, Dagur adds the first and second personal pronouns to verb forms as personal markers: e.g. /xelsen.ta/ 'you said'.
3. In Monguor, verbs in the indicative present and past may be marked for person: /bi guledži/ 'I spoke', /či guledža/ 'you spoke'.
4. Monguor and Bao'an have developed an affixed indefinite article: e.g. Bao'an /kuŋ/ 'man' – /kuŋge/ 'a man'.
5. Santa has borrowed the Chinese copula *shì* following the subject, while retaining the Mongolian copula in final position: e.g. X **shi** Y **we** 'X is Y is'. This is perhaps the most surprising Chinese borrowing in Santa, more than a quarter of whose vocabulary, however, consists of Chinese loan-words.

All four languages are unwritten.

MONGOLIAN, MODERN

INTRODUCTION

Khalkha Mongolian is the official language of the Mongolian People's Republic, where it is spoken by about 2½ million people. Another 2 million speak it in the Inner Mongolian Autonomous Region of the CPR, with up to half a million in other areas of Northern China.

SCRIPT

For the Old Mongolian script, *see* **Mongolian, Classical**. In 1941 the Cyrillic alphabet was taken over en bloc for literary Khalkha, though not all of the Cyrillic letters are, in fact, required for the adequate representation of Mongolian phonemes. Two new letters had to be added: ө and ү. In comparison with the classical script, Cyrillic gives a closer, though still far from perfect, notation for Khalkha speech.

PHONOLOGY

Consonants

    stops: p, b, t, d, g
    affricates: ts, dz, tʃ, dʒ
    fricatives: v, s, z, ʃ, x
    nasals: m, n, ŋ
    lateral and flap: l, ł, r
    semi-vowels: j, w

An important distinction is made between vocalized consonants (the seven consonants /m, n, g, l, b, v, r/) and the non-vocalized (the remaining nine consonants). In what follows here, a *7* means one of the seven vocalized; a *9* means one of the others. The basic rule is that a *7* must be preceded or followed by a vowel; a *9* can follow a *7* without intervening vowel. Thus, if two consonants are in final position, the first must be a *7*, the second is *9*: e.g. *bold* 'steel'; *uls* 'country'.

In medial position, three consonants may be contiguous only if the middle one is a *9*: e.g. *boloxgüi* 'not allowed' = /bolxgwe/

Vowels

front: i, e
central: ə, u̇, ȯ
back: a, o, u

All occur both short and long, and all have several allophones. Thus the letter *i* for example, represents [i, ɪ, e]; *o* represents [ɔ, å, ɐ]. The symbol ʏ, represented here by *u̇*, is close to /ʉ/ when short, to /y/ when long; the symbol ө, represented here by *ȯ*, = /ə/ or /œ/: e.g, *ȯmȯn* 'south' /œmənə/, /œmᵊnə/.

Vowel length is phonemic: cf. *xol* 'far', *xool* 'food'. Long vowels are written doubled. Short vowels are given their full value only in first syllables; thereafter they tend to be reduced to /ə/. Final short vowels are notated in the script only after *g* and *n*. Thus *bagš* 'teacher' is actually /bagʃɪ/, which explains why the dative case is *bagšɪd*.

VOWEL HARMONY

The basic division is between front and back vowels; /i/ is neutral: e.g. *margaašaas* 'from tomorrow'; *ȯnȯȯdrȯȯs* 'from today'; *xoyordugaar* 'second'; *negdügeer* 'first'. Certain final particles, e.g. the negative *gùi* /gwe/, are not affected by vowel harmony.

Stress

On first syllable if the word has no long vowel; otherwise on first long vowel.

MORPHOLOGY AND SYNTAX

Mongolian has no grammatical gender and no articles.

Noun

Case inflection is by affix marked for vowel harmony. As illustration, declension of *mal* 'cattle, livestock':

nominative	mal	ablative	malaas
accusative	maliig	instrumental	malaar
genitive	maliin	comitative	maltai
dative	mald		

n-stems: in these, the so-called 'fleeting' *n* is dropped in the nominative, but surfaces in certain oblique cases: e.g. *mori* 'horse': dat. *morind*; abl. *morinoos*.

The comitative affix *-tai* is used to indicate possession: e.g. *bi xoyor mori.toi bain* 'I have two horses'.

NUMBER

Collective markers are affixed, e.g. *-nar*, *-uud*, *-čuud*: e.g. *nom* 'book', pl. *nomuud*; *zaluu* 'youth', pl. *zaluučuud*.

953

Double decension is frequent, with affixes strung together: e.g. *nòxòr* 'friend', gen. case *nòxriin* + dative ending *-d* → *nòxriind* 'at my friend's house'.

Adjective

As attribute, adjective precedes noun and is invariable: e.g. *ulaan nom* 'red book'; *ulaan nomuudtoi* 'having red books'.

COMPARATIVE

Made with the ablative case: e.g. *Ònòòdòr òčigdròòs dulaan* 'Today (it) is warmer than yesterday'.

Pronoun

The personal subject forms, with bases for oblique cases:

	Singular			Plural		
1	bi	obl. base except gen.	nad- min-	bid	obl. bases	bid-/man-
2	či		či-/ča-	ta		tan-

The third person forms are supplied by the demonstrative pronouns *ter* and *ene*, with plurals *ted*, *ed*; oblique bases: *tüü-*, *üün-*, *ted-*, *ed-*. The pronouns are declined in all cases. The plural form *ta* is used as the polite form of address for the singular.

INTERROGATIVE PRONOUN

xen 'who?'; *yu* 'what?'.

RELATIVE PRONOUN

None; for formation of relative sentences, *see* **Verb**.

Numerals

1–10; these are all *n*-stems except *xoyor* 2: *neg(en)*, *xoyor*, *gurav*, *dürüv*, *tav(an)* *zurgaan*, *doloon*, *naim(an)*, *ies(òn)*, *arav/arvan*; 11 *arvan neg*; 12 *arvan xoyor*; 20 *xori(n)*; 30 *guč(in)*; 40 *dòč(in)*; 100 *zuu(n)*.

Verb

The fundamental distinction is between perfective and imperfective aspects; each aspect has a tense system in which past is opposed to non-past. This yields four base forms, with each of which a specific affix is associated:

perfective past	*-v*	imperfective past	*-džee*
perfective non-past	*-laa*	imperfective non-past	*-na*

These forms are not marked for person and cannot be negated. For negation purposes, the verbal nouns are used plus the negative marker *-güi* /gwe/. Thus, the past system is negated by adding *gùi* to the verbal noun in *-san*: e.g. *ter irev* 'he came': *ter irsengùi* 'he didn't come'. The non-past system uses the verbal noun in *-x + gùi*: e.g. *bi meden* 'I know', *bi medexgùi* 'I don't know'. The verbal noun in *-dag* is used to denote customary or repeated action: e.g. *ter Ulaanbaatart suudag* 'he lives (is resident in) Ulaan Baatar Xot'.

IMPERATIVE
The bare stem serves as a peremptory imperative: e.g. *yav* 'go!'. The ending *-aarai* is used for a polite request: e.g. *saiŋ yawaarai* lit. 'go well!' = 'goodbye'.

CONVERBS
These forms, which are always used in conjuction with finite verbs, play a crucially important part in Mongolian syntax by linking one action to another in various aspectual, temporal, sequential, and modal ways: e.g.

> Converb in *-dž/č* (imperfective), used as holding device in sequence of verbs, closed by finite verb: *Bi doloon cagt bosodž ôglôônii xool idedž, nom unšiv* 'I got up at seven, ate breakfast and read a book' (lit. 'rising ... eating ... I read ...'); *Nar garč, dulaan bolon* 'When the sun rises, it gets/will get warm'; *nar garč, dulan bolov* 'When the sun rose, it got warm.'
> Converb in *-aad* (perfective) relates conclusion of one action to ensuing action(s): e.g. *Bid xuvcas ômsôôd, ôglôônii xool ideed, nomın sand orood, nom unšina* 'Having got dressed, eaten breakfast and gone to the library, we shall read books' (*xuvcas* 'clothes', *nomın san* 'library', *unšix* 'to read').
> *-saar* refers to passage of time since an action, or result of that action: e.g. *Deed surguuld orsoor xeden džil bolov?* 'Since going to the university, how many years is it?' (*deed* 'big', *surguul* 'school', *džil* 'year').

CONDITIONAL/CONCESSIVE
-bal, e.g. *cas orwol* 'if it snows'; *dulaan bolbol* 'if it turns warm'.

TERMINATIVE
-tal, e.g. *irtel* 'until ... come(s)'; *gartal* 'until ... go(es)'.

RELATIVE CLAUSES
Verbal nouns are treated as attributive adjectives, e.g. *unšix nom* 'a book which is to be read'; *nom unšidž baigaa xùùxed* 'the child who is reading the book'; *bidnii xiisen adžil* 'the work which we did'.

Postpositions

Postpositions follow nominative, genitive, ablative, or comitative cases: e.g.

> with nominative: *dotor* 'in', e.g. *tasalgaan dotor* 'in the room';
> with genitive: *tuxay* 'about', e.g. *šine baišingiin tuxay* 'about the new building';
> with ablative: *xoiš* 'after', e.g. *xuvisgalaas xoiš* 'after the revolution'.

Word order

SOV is basic.

31. Тэндэ Тӱни Эхэ ахá дӱнэт ирэт, газá бáйжи, Тӱни иргэхэ́ илэгэбэ.

32. Тэндэ улагхи Тӱни хажуда гхӱжи байсарá; зармінин Тӱндӱ: мэнэ Шини Эхэ ахадӱнэр, газá бáйжи. Шамáй бэдэрнэ, гэжи Тӱндӱ айлада.

33. Алатхада, Тэрэ зарлик болó: Мини Эхэ эгхэгэбэл, Мини дӱнэр хэт би?

34. Тпгэт Тӱни хажӱда гхӱкшиди ширтэн, пжи: мэнэ Мини Эхэ, Мини ахадӱнэр эдэ бáйна;

35. тэрэ юндаб гэхэдэ, Бурхани дӱрайги бӱтэкши, тэрэ Мини дӱ, ухин дӱ, Эхэм мӱн, гэжи зарлик болó.

(Mark 3: 31–5)

MORDVA
(MORDVINIAN)

INTRODUCTION

Mordva belongs to the Volgaic group of Finno-Ugric languages, and consists of two closely related languages, Erzyan and Mokshan. Erzyan is spoken in the eastern half of the Mordov Autonomous Soviet Socialist Republic, Mokshan in the western half, in each case with spill-over into Bashkir, Tatar, and Chuvash linguistic territory. Together, Erzyan and Mokshan are spoken by over 1 million people; the degree of mutual intelligibility is high, but not total. Each has a literary standard, used, since the 1930s, for a steady output in most fields of writing. Here, the description is mainly of Erzyan.

SCRIPT

Cyrillic.

PHONOLOGY

Consonants

The Erzyan inventory is as follows:

> stops: p, b, t, d, k, g; palatalized: t', d'
> affricates: ts, tʃ; palatalized ts'
> fricatives: (f), v, s, z, ʃ, ʒ, j, (x); palatalized s', z'
> nasals: m, n ɲ
> laterals: l, l'
> trill: r, r'

To this inventory, Mokshan adds five voiceless sonants: /l̥, l̥', r̥, r̥', j̥/.
  Both Erzyan and Mokshan allow some initial consonant clustering, a rare phenomenon in Uralic languages; e.g. Erzyan *kšni* 'iron'.
  Voiced consonants are not devoiced in final position: e.g. *kev* /kev/, 'stone'.

Vowels

> front: i, e
> mid: ɪ, ɛ, a
> back: o, u

In this article, *e* denotes soft, palatalized /e/; dotted *ę* denotes non-palatalized /ɛ/.

VOWEL HARMONY
Broadly, front followed by front, back by back. Palatalized consonants affect this sequence: e.g. *kudo.so* 'in a house', but *loman'sę* 'in a man'.

MORPHOLOGY AND SYNTAX

Noun

No gender. The noun is marked for number and case, and takes possessive affixes. Further, the noun is definite or indefinite, the definite marker being *-s'* in the singular: *kudo* 'a house', *kudos'* 'the (specific) house'. Each form, definite and indefinite, is declined in ten (definite) and eleven (indefinite) cases.

PLURAL
The indefinite plural marker is *-t/-t'* and appears only in the nominative; the other ten cases are not marked for number. Thus, genitive *kudon'* 'of (a) house(s)'; inessive *kudoso* 'in (a) house(s)'. The definite declension, however, has a full set of plural case forms; thus, *kudosont'* 'in the house'; *kudotnesę* 'in the houses'.

POSSESSIVE AFFIXES
These are added to the case endings. A distinction for singular/plural of possessed object is made in first and third persons singular nominative: e.g. *kudom* 'my house', plural *kudon* 'my houses'; declined in eight cases. Compare: *kudozo* 'his/her house', plural *kudonzo* 'his/her houses'; but *kudot* 'your house/ houses'; *kudonok* 'our house/houses'.

GENITIVE CONSTRUCTION
Examples: *cerïnent' knigazo* 'the boy's book'; where *cerïnent'* is definite declension of *cerïne* 'boy', *kniga.zo* 'his book'. Nouns denoting inalienable relatedness – e.g, of kinship, parts of the body – always take the possessive declension.

Adjective

As attribute, adjective precedes noun and is invariable. A comparative is made on the formula X.nom.–Y.abl.–adjective: 'X is ... than Y'.

Pronoun

PERSONAL INDEPENDENT

	Singular	Plural
1	mon	min'
2	ton	tïn'
3	son	sïn'

These are declined in eleven cases: e.g. *mon*, gen. *mon'*, dat. *monen'*, abl. *monden'*.

DEMONSTRATIVE PRONOUN/ADJECTIVE
te 'this', pl. *ne, netne*; *se* 'that', pl. *nonat*.

INTERROGATIVE PRONOUN
kie 'who?'; *meze* 'what?'.

RELATIVE PRONOUN
As interrogative.

Numerals

1–10: *veike, kavto, kolmo, nile, vete, koto, sisem, kavkso, veiksę, kemen'*. 11 *keveikee*; 12 *kemgavtovo*; 13 *kemgolmovo*; 20 *koms'*.

Verb

The basic division is into (a) indefinite (intransitive), and (b) definite(transitive, perfective) conjugations. In both, the verb form is marked for number, tense, and mood. In the indefinite conjugation, the verb ending indicates person of subject; in the definite conjugation, the verbal ending encodes the subject/object relationship.

There are seven moods: indicative, imperative, subjunctive, optative, hortative, conditional, subjunctive–conditional. Only the indicative has a full set of tenses; these are present–future, two past tenses, and a compound future, formed with the auxiliary *karmams* 'become, begin'.

The mood markers are:

indicative: Ø;
subjunctive: *-vl'/-vel'/-vol'*;
conditional: *der'a*;
optative: *-ksę*;
hortative: *-ze/-zo*;
imperative: 2nd sing. *-k/-t/-t'*; 2nd pl. *-de/-do*.

NEGATION
Either by means of invariable particle *a* preceding inflected affirmative form, or with inflected negating auxiliary *ęz-* preceding invariable form of sense-verb (cf. **Finnish** *en, et, ei*): e.g. *a mol'an* 'I shan't go' *a mol'at* 'you won't go'; *ęzin' mole* 'I didn't go', *ęzit' mole* 'you didn't go'. In Mokshan the invariable particle *af* negates the inflected present–future indicative. In other tenses, the verb form is invariable, *af* is conjugated: e.g. *af.olen' mole* 'I wouldn't have gone'.

SPECIMEN PARADIGM
kundams 'to catch', indefinite conjugation, indicative mood:

present–future: sing. 1 *kundan*, 2 *kundat*, 3 *kundɪ*; pl. 1 *kundatano*, 2 *kundatado*, 3 *kundɪt'*;

past I: e.g. *kundɪn'*, *kundɪt'*, *kundas'*;
past II: e.g. *kundɪlin'*, *kundɪlit'*, *kundɪl'*;
compound future: e.g. *karman kundamo*, *karmat kundamo*, *karmi kundamo*.

Definite conjugation, indicative mood; specimen forms: present–future: *kundasamak* 'you (will) catch me'; *kundatan* 'I shall catch you'; *kundasamiz'* 'you will catch us'. Similarly for both past tenses: e.g. *kundɪtin'* 'I caught you', and for other moods.

An active verb is made passive by *-v-* infix.

The infinitive ends in *-ms* or in *-mo/-me*; the endings are specific for certain usages. There are active and passive participles.

Stems are modulated by infixes to express causativity, reflexivity, reiteration, involuntary action, etc.: e.g. *-vt-* for causativity, *-zev-* for involuntary action.

Postpositions

These follow nouns in the nominative, genitive, or ablative case of all three types of declension (indefinite, definite, possessive). They take personal pronominal affixes: e.g. *marton* 'with me', *martonzo* 'with him'.

Word order

VS occurs with intransitive verb. SOV/SVO with transitive verbs.

1 Васня ульнéсь вáлъ, и вáлъ ульнéсь Пáзонь
2 кéце, вáлъ гáкъ ульнéсь Пáзъ. Сóнъ ульнéсь
3 васня Пáзонь кéце. Вя́се эсьпéльдензе лúсь,
4 и сонцшéмензе эзьлúсь мезея́къ, мéзе езьлúстъ.
4 Эстéнзе ульнéсь эря́мо, эря́мосъ гáкъ улнéсь
5 вáлдо ломáтьненень. Вáлдось гáкъ чóпудава
6 вáлдови; но чóпудась эзíзе сáйтъ сонзé. Улнéсь ломáнь, кучóзь Пáзонь пéлде. конáтань
7 лéмзе Iоáннъ. Те сáсь селменéемсъ, штóбы
8 вя́сетъ кéмевелтъ сонзé вя́лдестïа. Авóль
9 сóнць улнéсь вáлдось, но улнéсь кучóзь, штóбы ïôвтамксъ валдóде.

MUṆḌĀRĪ

INTRODUCTION

Muṇḍārī and Santali (*see* **Santali**) are usually grouped together under the name Kherwari, and are the two most important members of the Muṇḍa or Kol family in India. The name 'Muṇḍārī' is Hindi; the ethnonym is *horo-kaji*, the language of *horoko* 'the men'. The Muṇḍa languages certainly antedate the Indo-European invasion of India, possibly even the Dravidian presence. They are sited on the Chota Nagpur plateau in Bihar and Orissa; the total number of speakers may be around 5 million. The many dialects do not differ greatly. Since the 1950s there has been some writing in Muṇḍārī. The description given here is based on the grammar by J. Hoffmann (1903).

PHONOLOGY

Consonants

> stops: p, b, t, d, ṭ, ḍ, k, g
> affricates: ts/tʃ, dʒ
> fricatives: s, h
> nasals: m, n, ɲ, ŋ, ṇ
> lateral and flaps: l, r, ṛ
> semi-vowels: j, w

All the stops may be aspirated; /b/ and /d/ have nasalized forms. Retroflex phonemes are notated here with dots: e.g. ṛ.

Vowels

> long, short, neutral: a, e, i, o, u

All vowels are nasalized before /ḍ, ṛ/.

Peculiar to Muṇḍa are the 'checked' vowels, e.g. $á$ = /a.^{a}/ where the superscript a is a kind of ultra-short echo of the first a, which is itself choked off.

Stress

Stress is weak, normally on first syllable.

MORPHOLOGY AND SYNTAX

Noun

There is a basic dichotomy between animate and non-animate categories. Animate nouns have three numbers, non-animate have singular only. There are no articles.

A Muṇḍārī base can be treated either as a nominal with agglutinative suffixes, or as a verbal with markers for tense and person: e.g. *buru* 'mountain' (as nominal), 'to amass' (as verbal); *gapa* 'tomorrow'; as verbal, 'to procrastinate'.

The dual marker is *-king*, the plural *-ko*: e.g. *horo* 'man', *horoking* 'two men'.

CASE

Nominative, accusative, and dative are identical. Other cases are formed by postpositions. There are definite and indefinite locative cases: e.g. *sadom* 'horse'; *sadomre* 'on a specific horse'; *sadomtare* 'near a horse'.

Hoffmann explains the genitive formation in -(*ta*)*ren* as definite/indefinite locative marker + demonstrative -(*e*)*n*: e.g. *haturen horo* 'the "in-the-village man" ' = 'the man of the village'; *mundataren dasi* 'the "attendant-upon-the-chief" servant' = 'the chief's servant'.

Adjective

Invariable as attribute preceding noun: e.g. *bugin apai* 'good father'; *bugin sadom* 'good horse'

COMPARISON

A comparative is made with the definite ablative ending *-ete*: e.g. *sadomete hati marangal* 'than-the-horse the-elephant is-big'.

Pronoun

PERSONAL SUBJECT SUFFIXES/INFIXES

		Singular		*Dual*	*Plural*
1		ing	incl.	lang	bu
			excl.	ling	le
2		me		ben	pe
3		í		king	ko
	impersonal	á		á	á

These are suffixed to the copula following a sense-verb, or to the word immediately preceding predicate: e.g. *hijúlen.a.ko* 'they came' (*a* is copula); *hola.ko hijúlen.a* 'they came yesterday'. They are also infixed between tense marker and imperfective marker: e.g. *leltan.ing taeken.a* 'I was seeing it then' (*taeken* is imperfective marker; *-tan* is present marker). As direct object in definite present or imperfect they are infixed between the stem and the tense

962

sign: e.g. *lel.ko.tan.a.le* 'we are seeing them' (excl. pl.). In other tenses they are suffixed to the tense sign preceding the copula: *lel.keḋ.ko.a.le* 'we saw them'. Further, as indirect object preceded by *a*: e.g. *ne sadom.ko.ing om.ako.tan.a.ing* 'I give these horses to them' ('these horse-pl.-I give-to-them-present marker-copula-I').

The emphatic pronoun series: e.g. *aing* 'I', *am* 'thou', *aé* 'he' are used as the base for the possessives: e.g. *aiñá* 'my', *ama* 'your': *aiñá sadom = sadomtaing* 'my horse'.

DEMONSTRATIVE PRONOUNS
ne 'this', *en* 'that', *han* 'that yonder'; also a third person pronoun if the reference is to humans: e.g. *ní*, *niking*, *niko*.

INTERROGATIVE PRONOUN
okoe 'who?'; *oko* 'what?'.

RELATIVE PRONOUN
None; verbal form used attributively: e.g. *hola hijúlen horo* 'the man who came yesterday'.

Numerals

1–10: *miḋ, baria, apia, upunia, monṛea, turuia, ea, írilia, area, gelea*; 11 *gel miḋ*. 20 *hisi*; 30 *miḋ hisi gelea*; 40 *bar hisi*; 100 *monṛe hisi*.

Verb

The verb has voice, mood, and tense; this is the order of addition for the agglutinative particles: root – voice – mood – tense – copula (RVMTC + S = subject). The root remains unaltered in all forms. The active voice, the indicative mood, the imperative mood, the future, and the indeterminate tenses have null marker. The negative marker is *ka*.

Object infix: in definite present/imperfect, this appears before the tense marker: in all other tenses, after tense marker.

A minimal form is root + tense marker: e.g. *ol.ked* 'wrote, writing done in past'; *ol.ked horo* 'the man who wrote'. About a dozen tenses are made by adding markers to stem: e.g. simple past has *-ken-* for intransitive, *-ked-* for transitive: e.g. *sen.ken.aing* 'I went'; *lel.ked.aing* 'I saw it'.

All perfective tenses can be made imperfective by addition of *taeken*.

Personal constructions: the subject is a personal pronoun: impersonal constructions: the subject is the neuter pronoun *a*.

PASSIVE
This can be expressed in certain tenses by *ó* affixed to root, in others by replacing transitive marker by intransitive: e.g. *lel.led.aing* 'I had seen it'; *lel.len.aing* 'I had been seen'.

REFLEXIVE

-n affixed to root: link vowel shows vowel harmony (in consonantal stems): e.g. *dal* 'to strike' – *dalen* 'strike oneself'.

RECIPROCAL

-p following first vowel of transitive root, + resumption of that vowel: e.g. *om* 'to give' – *opom* 'to give each other'; *nel/lel* 'to see' – *nepel* 'to see each other'.

IMPERATIVE

Stem + Ø + second person pronoun: e.g. *sen.me* 'go!'; *sen.ben* 'you two go!'.

Precative, concessive, optative marker is *-k-*: e.g. *lel.ko.k.a.ing* 'let me see them!'. Further verbal examples: *om.a.ko.a.ing* 'I will give it to them' (the second *a* is copula); *lel.keḍ.ko.a.ing* 'I saw them'; *om.a.ked.ko.a.ing* 'I gave it to them'.

Postpositions

Simple or compound: e.g. *-re*: *hature* 'in the village', *sadomre* 'on the horse'; *-te* 'towards': *bir.te.ko niṛleṇa* 'they ran to the forest'. Verbal forms such as *chetan* 'to be above', *suba* 'to be below', coalesce with case endings: e.g. *mej subaṛe* 'under the table'; *daru sabate nirme* 'run under the tree'.

Word formation

For example by compounding: e.g. *uri-merom* 'ox-goat' = 'livestock'; *sadom-chatom* 'horse-umbrella' = 'affluence'; *sunum-bulung* 'oil-salt' = 'the necessities of life'. There are also bound forms: e.g. *-urum-* which is not used by itself: *lel.urum* 'to recognize by sight'; *aium.urum,* 'to recognize by sound'.

Word order

Basically SOV.

१ एनेटेःरे कजी तैकेनाय आड़ो कजी
ईश्वर लो तैकेनाय आड़ो कजी ईश्वर
२ तैकेनाय । इनी एनेटेःरे ईश्वर लो तैके-
३ नाय । सोबेना इनीआ होराते बैयना
आड़ो जेतन बैयाकन चीज इनीआ बेगर
४ का बैयना । इनीरे जीदो तैकेना आड़ो
एन जीदो होड़ोकोआ मर्सल तैकेना ।
५ आड़ो मर्सल नुबारे जुलतना आड़ो नुबा
एनाके काए चिनाकेदा ।

NA-DENÉ LANGUAGES

Geographically, this family of North American Indian languages occupies three very uneven zones. By far the largest stretches from Central Alaska to Hudson Bay, and from the Eskimo-speaking area in Mackenzie Territory down to the State of Washington. A second zone of Na-Dené speech centres on Arizona, New Mexico, and parts of Texas; the third and smallest stretches along the Pacific coast of Oregon and California.

The Na-Dené languages formerly spoken in this Pacific Coast zone are now all extinct; in the 1970s, Hupa had about 20 speakers. Around 22,000 speakers of some two dozen Na-Dené languages are to be found in the first zone, but, thanks to the presence of Navajo, it is in the comparatively small second zone that the largest number of Na-Dené speakers are located – about 120,000.

Linguistically, the 30 or 40 Na-Dené languages fall into two highly disparate groupings:

(a) Athabaskan, a well-defined grouping, which includes all of the main Na-Dené languages – Chipewyan, Sarcee, Carrier, and the Apachean sub-division comprising Kiowa-Apache, Navajo, Chiricahua, Mescalero, etc. Athabaskan accounts for at least 95 per cent of Na-Dené speakers.

(b) Non-Athabaskan: this grouping now consists virtually of one language, Tlingit, with about 2,000 speakers in south-eastern Alaska with spread into Canadian territory. A second member of this grouping, Eyak, is extinct. Haida, once treated as a Na-Dené language (e.g. by Edward Sapir in the 1929 edition of the *Encyclopaedia Britannica*), is now regarded as an isolate, with areal features aligning it with Athabaskan (Voegelin and Voegelin 1965).

The distinctive individuality of Na-Dené as a genetic unit is strikingly confirmed in Greenberg's (1985) classification, which retains this family intact, while consigning virtually all other American Indian languages to a vast conglomerate designated as 'Amerindian'.

See **Apache, Athabaskan, Chipewyan, Navajo, Tlingit**.

NAGA LANGUAGES

INTRODUCTION

The Naga languages belong to the Assam-Burmese branch of the Tibeto-Burman family. About 20 Naga languages, divided into five sub-groups, are spoken by three-quarters of a million people in the Indian state of Nāgāland (established 1961), which lies in the Naga Hills between Assam and Burma. All the Naga languages are tonal and agglutinative, but differ from each other to a very marked degree; intertribal communication is possible only in a corrupt form of Assamese.

The short description which follows is of two of the larger languages belonging to the Central group: *Ao Nāgā* and *Lhōtā Nāgā*; Ao is spoken by about 70,000 people, Lhota by about 40,000.

PHONOLOGY

Consonants

A generalized inventory for Ao and Lhota comprises the following phonemes:

> stops: p, b, t, d, k, g; k°
> affricates: ts, tʃ, dʒ
> fricatives: (f), v, s, z, (h)
> nasals: m, n, ŋ
> lateral and flap: l, r
> semi-vowels: j, w

To this basic inventory, Lhota adds an extensive series of aspirated stops, the fricatives /ʃ/, /ʒ/ and rolled /r/.

Vowels

The basic series in both languages is: i, ɪ, e, ɛ, a, o, ɔ, u, ə; to which Lhota adds three varieties of /a/: [aː, å, æ], /y/ and /œ/, and a nasalized series: /ã, õː, ɔ̃, ɛ̃/. /y/ and /œ/ are notated here as *ü*, *ö*; long vowels with macrons. Witter (1888) emphasizes the instability of the consonantal structure; alternation is frequent, e.g. /m–w, n–ŋ, m–p/. Thus the word for 'himself' appears as *ōmōmō* or as *ōpōpō*.

MORPHOLOGY AND SYNTAX

Noun

A morpheme which is probably a demonstrative pronoun is used in both languages as a postfixed article: Ao, *zi*; Lhota: *šī*, *čī*: e.g. Lhota *kāko šī ā pīā* 'give me the book'.

GENDER

Marked in Ao by specific particle: *ba* (masc.), *la* (fem.) (cf. Tibetan *po/mo*).

NUMBER

In Ao plurality inheres in the noun; the singular can be specified by such markers as *kati/ka*. Lhota has a pluralizer: *nčūā* for humans, *matcaŋa* for non-human referents. A plural demonstrative may also be used: e.g. *kyə̃ šīāŋ* 'these men' → 'the men'.

Traces of an old dual persist in both Ao and Lhota, and are present also in Angami; in Lhota, *ōnī* 'two': e.g. *Šīhā ātā ōnī šī šopheni īyā* 'He and (his) brother (two) have gone to the bazaar.' The Ao form is suffixed *-na ← ana*: e.g. *any.ita.na* 'the sun and the moon'.

CASE

In Lhota the subject of an active transitive verb is marked by *nā*: e.g. *koror.nā ōčāk cōālā* 'the horse (New Indo-Aryan loan-word) eats grass'. The genitive is positional. Other cases are marked by postfixed particles, e.g. in Ao *-n*VN for the dative; in Lhota, *nā* for ablative: *ā.kī.nā.rō.čo* 'I came from my house'; *-ī* for inessive, *-(l)o* for locative: *caŋthī ōtōŋ.o līā* 'the fruit is on the tree'.

Adjective

As attribute, adjective follows noun: e.g. Ao *nisung tazung* 'good man'; *nisung mazung* 'bad man'. The case marker may be transferred from the noun to the attributive adjective: e.g. Lhota *Ōtōŋ saphō.lo caŋthī mpāpā* 'There is fruit on the tall tree' (*saphō* 'tall'); *Ā korr etha.nā nūŋōr epāčo* 'My new pony kicked a boy' (*-nā* is the agentive marker).

Pronoun

The Ao personal pronouns are:

	Singular		Plural
1	ni	excl.	ozo(nok)
		incl.	asen(ok)
2	na		nenok
3	pa		parenok

The Lhota forms are: (all forms have several variants):

	Singular	Plural
1	ā, ai	e
2	nā	nī, nīno
3	hī, šī, čī	hīāŋ, sīāŋ

plus specific forms for various combinations: *enī* 'we (you and I)'; *šī ennī* 'we (he and I)'. As possessive forms these precede the noun: e.g. *ā kī* 'my house'; *nī kī* 'your house'.

DEMONSTRATIVE PRONOUN/ADJECTIVE
Ao has a two-degree series based on *a/i*. Lhota uses the forms shown above as third person pronouns: *hī, šī, čī* with plural forms.

INTERROGATIVE PRONOUN
Ao: *shir/shiba* 'who?'; *kechi* 'what?'. Lhota *ōčī/ōčō* 'who?'; *ntīō* (with variants) 'what?': e.g. *Ōčō rō.čo.lā* 'Who came?'

RELATIVE PRONOUN
Ao uses the interrogative pronoun; Lhota has a relative affix: *(wo)čü/či*, e.g. *nčö kyỡ e.rō.wōčü* 'the man (*kyỡ*) who came yesterday'.

Numerals

1–10:

Ao	ka	ana	asəm	pezə	pungu	trok	tenet	ti	təko	ter
Lhota	ekhā	ennī	eham	mezü	mūngo	tīrōk	ti.ing	tizā	tōkū	taro

12 in Lhota is *taro sü ennī*; 20 *mekwī*; 30 *thamdro*; 40 *züro*; 100 *ekha tāro*.

Verb

The stem is invariable. The Lhota tense system:

> Imperfective tenses: root + *ā* + *lā*, e.g. *nthāŋā ā.nā cō.ā.lā* 'I am eating now'. *Vān* 'is', may be added, e.g. *ā.nā cō.ā vān.ā.lā* 'I am going on eating'.
> Completed action: root + *ā./čo*, e.g. *ā.nā cō.ā = ā.nā cō.čo* 'I ate'.
> Future: root or root + *kā*, e.g. *ā.nā cō. (kā)* 'I shall eat'.
> Negation: *n/m* in high tone prefixed to verb, e.g. *ā.nā ń.cō* 'I am not eating'. The prohibitive particle is *ti*, e.g. *ti.cō.ā* 'do not eat'.
> Interrogative: the particle for yes/no questions is *ke* or *kung*, e.g. *Nno cō.ā.ke* 'Do you eat?'; *Nno cō.čo.ke* 'Did you eat?' (*nno = nā*)
> Causative: the particle is *tōk*, e.g. *ā.nā hī cō.tōk.ālā* 'I'm causing him to eat'.
> Potential: *kōk*, e.g. *ā.nā ń.cō.kōk* 'I can't eat'.
> Intentional: *kattō*, e.g. *Hī.nā ā theni cō.kattō yī.čo* 'He came to eat with me'.
> Inceptive: *sālā* added to a future form in *v/u*, e.g. *ā.nā cō.v.sālā* 'I'm about to eat'.

970

Directional prefixes: e.g. *čüŋ* 'upwards', *čō* 'downwards', *thrō* 'into', *čī* 'out of': *korr mānkwi čüŋ.wō.ā* 'mount the horse'; *čī yī.ā* 'go out'.

The verb is neutral as to voice; as in New Indo-Aryan, participial holding constructions are much used.

In Ao Naga, the verbal stem seems to be modulated by prefix and suffix to express tense: e.g. *ben*, a stem meaning 'to bring':

present	ben.er/ben.dage/ben.dar
perfect	a.ben.er
preterite	a.ben
future	ben.di/ben.tsə

Like Lhota, Ao has a very extensive inventory of auxiliary suffixes expressing potential, causative, durative, terminative, reiterative, etc. nuances: e.g. *ben.tet* 'able to bring', *bean.ma* 'to finish bringing', *ben.dak.tsə* 'cause to bring'.

Postposition

Both languages use postpositions: e.g. *ā sīlami roa* 'to come (*roa*) after (*sīlami*) me'; *hiṇa enī nūyī yīpālā* 'he sleeps between (*nūŋi*) the two of us'.

Word order

Basically SOV.

Thérriá ki Die u tuo, tsiu Die u Ihova zé 1
tuo, tsiu Die u Ihova tuo. Hawa thérriá ki 2
Ihova zé tuo. Pétékà puo ú chúlie ; tsiu ké- 3
chúkà dånu puo rei puo sciá chú mo. Puo dånu 4
kérheirà tuo ; tsiu kérheirà u thémiá kézie u
tuo. Tsiu kézie u kézei nu pézie shú ; tsiu 5
kézei u scú tsåliemoté. Thémiá puoá vårr, 6
Iohan za, Ihova kinu kétsé shú. Puo ú pétékà 7
pélélievi thiányú, puoá kézie u dzé zha pulievi
thiányú, puoá zha pu la vårr. Puoá kézie u mo, 8
sierei kézie zha pu shútuoú vårr.

NAHUATL

INTRODUCTION

Nahuatl is usually classified as belonging to the Uto-Aztecan branch of the Aztec-Tanoan family. Nahuatl-speaking groups appear to have reached the Valley of Mexico in the middle of the first millennium AD; the Aztec group is attested there from mid-thirteenth century onwards. The heyday of the Tenochtitlan Aztec Empire was from the fourteenth century to its destruction by Hernán Cortés in 1519–21.

As in the case of the Mayan languages, pre-Conquest literary works in Nahuatl took the form of the pictorial record, which was presumably used as an *aide-mémoire* to accompany the oral tradition. The use of the Roman script, introduced by the Spanish friars, played an invaluable role in preserving at least part of Aztec cultural tradition (much was, of course, also destroyed by the Spanish authorities). Here, the work of Bernardino de Sahagún (fl. c. 1530–90) is of cardinal importance. His great work – *Historia de las cosas de Nueva España* – provides an encyclopaedic survey of Aztec civilization, and contains many examples of Aztec historical, religious-ceremonial, and poetical writing. Other important works which have been preserved include the Annals of Cuauhtitlan, covering almost a thousand years of Nahuatl history (635–1519) and the Annals of Tlatelolco, part of which covers the period from 1250 to 1525.

Today, Nahuatl is spoken by about 1 million people in central Mexico. The description that follows is of Classical Nahuatl, the language of the Aztec Empire.

SCRIPT

The orthography is based on Spanish; e.g. /k/ is notated as *c* before *a*, *o* and as final; as *qu* before *i*, *e*. Syllable-final *-uc* = /k°/. /tʃ/ is notated as *ch*, /ʃ/ as *x*; /s/ is notated as *z* before *a*, *o*; as *c* before *i*, *e*.

PHONOLOGY

Consonants

stops: p, t, k (voiceless and non-aspirate); k° (unaspirated, labialized); ʔ
affricates: ts, tʃ, λ
fricatives: s, ʃ
nasals: m, n
lateral: l
semi-vowels: j, w

The glottal stop /ʔ/ is notated as *h*; /ƛ/ is notated as *tl*. Nahuatl has an extensive system of regressive assimilation.

Vowels

long and short: i, e, a, o

In some environments, /o, oː/ tend to /u, uː/.

MORPHOLOGY AND SYNTAX

Noun

Nouns are classified by their stem ending in the absolute state: *-tl, -tli, -li, -in, -Ø*; e.g. *oquichtli* 'man', *ocelotl* 'jaguar', *coatl* 'snake', *tlalli* 'ground' (this is an example of regressive assimilation: *tli → li* after *l*); *tochin* 'rabbit'. These endings are dropped when the noun changes status.

PLURALITY
Normally reserved for nouns denoting animates, and is indicated in one of the following ways:

(a) by reduplication: e.g. *coatl* 'snake', pl. *cocoah*; *coyotl* 'wild dog', *cocoyo*;
(b) by affix *-meh* or *-tin*: e.g. *oquichtli* 'man', pl. *oquichmeh/oquichtin*;
(c) by *-h*: *cihuatl* 'woman', pl. *cihuah* /siʔwaʔ/.

The noun has a vocative in *-é*: e.g. *Quetzalcoatlé* 'Oh Quetzalcoatl!' A locative ending is *-n*: e.g. *tla.cua.lo.ya.n* 'place where people eat' (*cua* 'to eat'; for form, see **Verb**, below).

Adjective

As attribute, the adjective often forms compound with its noun: e.g. *tlil-* 'black': *tlil.coatl* 'black snake'; *tlil.azcatl* 'black ant'.

Denominative verb stems in *-ti* provide a great many Nahuatl adjectives; e.g. *cihua.ti.c* 'he has become womanly' = 'he is effeminate' (*cihua.tl* 'woman'). Incapsulation of modifier (noun, etc.): e.g. *iztac* 'white' + *cuai* 'head': *t.iztac* 'thou art white'; *ti.cuai.ztac* 'thou art white-headed'; *chicahua* 'strong' + *yollo* 'heart': *ti.yollo.chicahua.c* 'thou art courageous'.

Pronoun

Personal independent forms + nominal (possessive), verbal subject/object prefixes:

	Independent	Nominal prefix	Verbal subject	Verbal object
Singular				
1	nehhua(tl)	no-	ni-	nech
2	tehhua(tl)	mo-	ti-	mitz
3	yehhua(tl)	i-	Ø	c/qui

973

Plural

1	tehhuan(tin)	to-	ti...h	tech
2	amehhuan(tin)	amo-	an...h	anmech
3	yehhuan(tin)	in-/i-	Ø...Ø	quim

Possessive prefixes: e.g. *no.yollo* 'my heart'; *to.cal* 'our house(s)'. Examples of verbal subject and object: *ti.nech.itta* 'thou seest me'; *ni.mitz.itta* 'I see thee'.

DEMONSTRATIVE PRONOUN
inin 'this', *inon* 'that'; with plural forms.

INTERROGATIVE PRONOUN
aquin(tin) 'who?'; *tlein* 'what?'.

RELATIVE PRONOUN
Example with identifying particle *in*: *in o.nech.ittac oquichtli* 'the man who saw me'; *in o.ni.qui.ttac oquichtli* 'the man whom I saw' (*o* is the past-tense marker); *No.tah.tzin in o.qui.ttac oquichtli* 'the one whom the man saw was my father' (*tzin* is honorific marker).

Numerals

The Nahuatl numerical system is vigesimal: $20 = 4 \times 5$, i.e. four sets of five items – the fingers and toes. The word denoting the fifth item in each set acts as the base for the following set; e.g. 1–5: *ce – ome – ei – nahui – macuilli*; a secondary form of *macuilli* acts as base for 6–10: *chicua.ce – chic.ome – chicu.ei – chiuc.nahui – mahtlactli*; 11–15: *mahtlactli once – mahtlactli omome ... caxtolli*; 16–20: *caxtolli.once – caxtolli omome ... cempohualli*. The count then proceeds *mod* 20 to 380; thereafter, *mod* 400 to 7,600, and *mod* 8,000 to 15,200. Intermediary numbers are stated in terms of these major sectors, with *ipan/m* as a linker; e.g. 2,000 is *nauhtzontli ipan centzontli* $= 4 \times 400 = 1,600 + 1 \times 400$.

The numerals can be treated as verbals, taking subject prefix and plural marker: e.g. **ti.chic.ome.n.tin** 'we are seven (5 + 2) in number'.

Verb

The Nahuatl verb consists formally of stem + affixes. The stem is marked for aspect (imperfective/perfective: in one class of verb, the two aspects are identical); and affixes indicate person, number, tense, mood, and voice.

ASPECT
Unless the two aspects are identical (e.g. *itta* 'to look at') the perfective is formed from the imperfective by dropping the final vowel and/or adding *h*: e.g. *ya* 'to go', perfective stem *yah*; *yoli – yol* 'to live'.

AFFIXES
Indicating person and number:

(a) Intransitive: the prefixes and suffixes are shown in the pronoun table above. Imperfective stems: *ni.notza* 'I call'; *ti.notza.h* 'we call'. Tense markers: present

Ø; habitual present *-ni*; imperfect *-ya*; future *-z*: e.g. *ni.notza.ya* 'I called'; *an.notza.ya.h* 'you (pl.) called'; *ni.notza.z* 'I shall call'. The future plural adds *-queh*: e.g. *t.ahuia.z.queh* 'we shall be content'. The indicative tenses may also be formed with the perfective stem.

OPTATIVE MOOD
Has present, past, and future forms, the present with Ø marker, the past with *-ni-*. The personal pronominal prefixes are as in the indicative mood, apart from the second person plural which has *xi-*: e.g. *Ma xi.qui.pia.ni.h* 'If only you (pl.) had guarded it' (root *pia* 'to guard').

ADMONITIVE MOOD
Like the optative, introduced by the particle *ma* 'let ...!' The mood marker is *-h-* or Ø, the plural takes *-tin* or *-tih*: e.g. *Ma ti.tla.cua.h.tin* 'Let us beware of eating' (root *cua* 'eat'; *tla* = third person object marker, indefinite).

(b) Transitive verbs: the object pronoun may be specific personal: these forms are set out in the pronoun table above. There are two non-specific object pronouns: *te* for an indefinite human referent, and *tla* for an indefinite non-human, animate or inanimate referent. Double- and triple-object sequences occur: e.g. *ni.**tla**.itta* 'I see something'; *ni.**quim**.itta* 'I see them'; *ni.mitz.**Ø**.maca* 'I give it to you'; *ni.mitz.**tla**.maca* 'I give something to you'. That is, a definite third person non-human referent is marked by Ø, an indefinite by *tla*.

PASSIVE
Passive is made in Nahuatl from active verb + object: this object becomes the subject of the passive form. The passive markers are *-lo, -o, -hua*, depending on final of active voice form: e.g. *Ø.tech.huica.h* 'they are accompanying us'; ***ti. Ø. huic. o*** 'we are being accompanied'.

NEGATION
ah/ahmo precedes personal subject marker, or focused modifier: e.g. *ah.ti.cuica.h* 'we are not singing'; *ah.huel an.cuica.h* 'not-well they sing' = 'you (pl.) sing badly'.

DIRECTIONAL MARKERS
hual indicates motion towards, *on* motion away from speaker or source; the aspect markers for the intentional form are also in directional contrast: *-t-* + *ihui/iuh* signals motion away from, *-/k/* + *o*, motion towards source: e.g. *Ni.cuica.t.iuh* 'I am going there in order to sing'; *Ni.cuica.c.o* 'I am coming here in order to sing'.

FREQUENTATIVE
A frequentative mode is made by reduplication: e.g. *cuih.cuica* 'to sing repeatedly'.

CAUSATIVE
Examples: verbs in *-i* change this to *-a*: *tomi* 'to be loose' – *tla.toma* 'to loosen something'.

Composite verbal themes are made by incapsulation of verbal stems (or other verbal form, e.g. a past tense) in primary stems. Similarly, a nominal can be incorporated in a transitive verb; the nominal then loses its object status, and becomes an associate theme in the new composite sense; e.g. the two components (a) 'it is X', and (b) 'we are doing Y', combine to form the composite verb 'we are doing Y as modified or pointed by X': e.g. *atl* '(it is) water'; *ti.qui.i.h* 'you are drinking it' (→ *ti.qu.i.h*) gives a composite form: *t.atl.i.h* 'you-are-drinking-water' (root *i* 'to drink'). Adjectivals and adverbials can also be incorporated in this manner.

Word order

Free.

OMOCHÎ: icuac ometzticatca ce yeyantli mo tlatlâtiliticatca, in yê omo tlamiti oqui ilhui ceme in i tlamachtilhuan : Tlâtoani é, xi tech machti ti tlatlatlâlizquê no yù quenami in Juan oquin machti in itlamachtilhuan.

2 In yêhuatzin oquin ilhui : icuac an tlatlâtiâ, zic itocan : To tâtzin é, máyectenehualo in motocatzin. Ma hualyâ in mo tlâtòcayotzin.

3 In totlaxcal mômoztla mômoztla totech monequi xi tech momaquili axcan.

4 Yhuan xi tech mo tlapôpolhuili into tlâtlacol quenami in Tehuantin ti quin tlapôpolhuiâ in tlatlacame tech tlâlla calhuiâ. Yhuan amo xi tech mo cahuili ti huetziz quê te nêyecoltilizpan.

(Classical)
(Luke 11: 1–4)

NAKH LANGUAGES

INTRODUCTION

The Nakh languages form the North-Central Caucasian group of the Ibero-Caucasian family, and comprise Chechen, Ingush, and Bats. The total number of speakers is about 800,000, of which Chechen accounts for about 75 per cent. Chechen and Ingush are very close to each other, indeed very largely mutually intelligible. Bats, spoken in northern Georgia by around 3,000 people, is divergent and unwritten.

PHONOLOGY

In sharp contrast to the minimal vocalic systems of the neighbouring Abkhaz-Adyge languages, the Nakh languages share a rich and highly differentiated vocalism. The basic vowel series, /i, e, a, o, u/, is extended by lengthening (/aː, eː/ etc.), by palatalization (/je, jeː/ etc.), by labialization (/wo, woː/ etc.), by nasalization (/ã, ĩ, jẽ, jẽː/ etc.), and by umlaut (/ɛ, ɛː, œ/ etc.).

In Chechen and Ingush this process of differentiation by secondary articulation gives rise to about 30 phonemes, 20 in Bats.

The Proto-Nakh language seems to have had only the basic series of vowels; that is to say, the differentiation process has taken place over the last thousand years (Desheriev 1979).

The consonantal inventory is virtually identical in all three; *see* **Chechen**.

MORPHOLOGY AND SYNTAX

Noun

The main characteristics of Nakh are:

1. The presence of noun classes, six in Chechen and Ingush, eight in Bats: class I comprises human males; class II females. All other nouns are distributed over the remaining four/six classes. The characteristic class marker is attached, not to the noun itself, but to the predicate and to certain qualifying material. Thus, verbs and modifiers are in concord with nouns by class, which in the noun is not overtly marked. All class markers are based on the phonemes /b, v, d, j/.

2. A well-developed conjugation system expressing class, tense, and mood. In Chechen/Ingush the verb is not conjugated for person, but personal endings have made their appearance in Bats, possibly under South Caucasian influence.

3. An elaborate case system – eight in Chechen/Ingush, 22 in Bats.

4. Three types of syntactic construction: nominative (with intransitive verbs), ergative (transitive verbs), dative (affective verbs).

See **Chechen** for a more detailed description of a Nakh language.

NAMA

INTRODUCTION

The most important of the Hottentot languages (Khoisan family), Nama is spoken by about 40,000 in south-west Africa, plus a further 50,000 Bergdama (who are non-Khoisan) in the same area. Nama is also spoken by a small group of Bushmen. Nama is the only Hottentot language with any form of writing (in Roman script).

PHONOLOGY

Consonants

```
p   m
t   n   tʃ   s   r
k   kʰ
h
```

CLICKS

These were defined by Beach (1938) in terms of 'influx' and 'efflux':

Four types of influx:

	Abrupt	*Affricate*
gingival	≠	/
post-alveolar	!	//

Five types of efflux:

		Glottal stop	*Glottal friction*
smooth velar	γ	ʔ	h
delayed velar	χ		

Plus nasalization, notated as *n*.

Combining these, we get the following grid of click sounds:

```
≠(γ)   ≠x   ≠ʔ   ≠h   ≠n
/(γ)   /x   /ʔ   /h   /n
!(γ)   !x   !ʔ   !h   !n
//(γ)  //x  //ʔ  //h  //n
```

Vowels

i, e, a, o, u

/a/ is reduced to [ə] before certain vowels

Tone

There are three tones, high, middle and low; high is indicated by an acute accent, low by a grave.

MORPHOLOGY AND SYNTAX

Noun

Three genders: masculine, feminine, and common. Three numbers.

	Singular	*Dual*	*Plural*
masculine	-p, -i	-khà	-ku
feminine	-s	-rà	-tì
common	-'ì	-rà	-ìǹ -ǹ

Examples: *íríp* 'male jackal'; *írís* 'female jackal'; *írí'ì* 'some jackal or other'. The female form may be suppletive: e.g. *tàtáp* 'father'; *màmás* 'mother'. Hagman (1977) points out an interesting transfer of gender marker to indicate departure from norm: *'oms* 'house'; *'omi* 'unusually large house'.

ASSOCIATIVE/GENITIVE RELATIONSHIP
The particle is *tì* following possessor, e.g. *'áop tì 'oms* 'the man's house'; *seetáfrikàp tí póótàp* 'the South African border'.

Adjective

Simple or derived. As attribute, adjective precedes noun, with *-xà* ending. Thus, from root *//aṁi* 'water', *//aṁxà !xáis* 'watery place'. The privative ending is *'o*: e.g. *//ám'o !xáis* 'waterless place'. Nama uses apposition also to express attribution: e.g. *∤ōāp ≠xaríp* 'the boy, the small one' = 'the small boy'.

Pronoun

As specimen, the masculine forms in three numbers of first, second, and third persons:

	1st person		*2nd person*	*3rd person*
	Exclusive	*Inclusive*		
singular	tiíta	—	saáts	//'ĩp
dual	siíkxṁ	saákxṁ	saákxò	//'ĩkxà
plural	siíke	saáke	saáko	//'ĩku

Similarly for feminine: e.g. *tiíta – saás – //'ĩs*; and common dual/plural: e.g. *siṁ*

– saárò – //'ūrà.

The common plural second person *saátù* yields the polite form of address.

POSSESSIVE PRONOUNS
tíí 'my', *sáá* 'your': e.g. *tíí 'oms* 'my house'.

DEMONSTRATIVE PRONOUN
nee 'this?'; *//nāā̂* 'that'.

INTERROGATIVE PRONOUN
tarî'ì 'who?'; *taré'ì* 'what?'.

Numerals

Decimal system: 1–10 are root words: */úí, /ám, !noná, hàká, kóro, !nání, huu, //xáísá, kxòese, tìsí*; 100 *káí tìsí* 'big ten'.
   'aa is used as an itemizer: e.g. *hàká tìsí !noná 'aa* '43 bits'.

Verb

Aspect and tense are distinguished by marker:

	Imperfective aspect	Perfective aspect	Tense
recent past	kòrò	kò hāā̀ 'ií	kò
distant past	kèrè	kè hāā̀ 'ií	kè
present	ra/ta	Ø hāā̀ Ø	Ø
future	nǐí ra	nǐí hāā̀	nǐí
indefinite	kàrà	kà hāā̀ Ø	kà

The personal pronouns can be used as verbal objects, but there is in addition a series of verbal suffixes marked for gender and person/number:

   1st person: masc. *-te, -kxm̀, -ke*; fem. *-te, -'m̀, -se*; common *-'m̀, -ta*;
   2nd person: masc. *-tsi...*
   3rd person: masc. *-pi...*

Cf. *//'ūku ke //'ūpà kè mũ̄ū = //'ūku ke kè mã̄ūpi* 'they saw him', where the first version uses the full pronominal form, the second the pronominal suffix.

PASSIVE
The marker is *-he*: cf.

   'áop ke tarásà pérépà kè màa
   'The man gave the woman bread'

   *tarás ke 'áop xaa pérépà kè màa**hè***
   'The woman was given bread by the man' (*xaa* is postposition 'by'; *màa* 'give').

There are also reflexive (*-sn*) and reciprocal (*-ku*) suffixes.

STATIVE VERB

Tense marker + predicate + copula (*'ií* or Ø): e.g. *'áop ke kè !a̋i'ií* 'the man was good'.

NEGATIVE

tama + *kè, kò, kà,* Ø + *ha̋a̋* + *'ií* (for past tenses): e.g. *na̋a̋s ke !a̋i tama ha̋a̋* 'that is not good'.

MODAL VERBS

(Aux.) e.g. *//xáa* 'be able'; *//'óá* 'be unable'; *≠áó* 'to want to'; *//'ūp ke nee /óa̋sà ra ≠áó* 'He wants this girl'.

Postpositions

Simple or compound: e.g. *'áí* 'on, at'; *!na̋a̋* 'in(to)'; */xáa* 'with'; *≠'oákunis /xáa* 'by plane'.

Word order

Structure of active verbal sentence: S + tense marker + (imperfective aspect marker) + active verb + (perfective aspect marker). The aspect markers are, of course, mutually exclusive.

Word order in general is flexible; items may be promoted or postponed for reasons of emphasis.

1 Koeroep nas ke koemssa ha ore koemss ke Tsoeikwap dewa hai, siihii koemss ke Tsoeikwaza.

2 Nees ke koeroep na Tsoeikwap dewa hai.

3 Howagoen ayip ka ke diihii, ooike ayip oossii goeigaree diitama, diihiikeenga.

4 Ayipnap ke oeiiba ha, oeiip ke kooin dii naapba.

5 Naapke kayp nara naa, oop ke kaypba nauoeg a bii tama ha.

6 Nabap ke kwii kooiba Tsoeikwapga ke tzii hii, tallip ons Johannip tamira kayhip.

7 Neep ke ha, naapgap nii hoeaaka, howan nii ayipga koemka.

8 Apip ke naatamaba, gaweep ke tziihii, naap gap nii mii ka.

NANAY

INTRODUCTION

This language, also known as Gold, belongs to the South-Eastern branch of the Tungus-Manchu family. There are at present some 7/10,000 speakers in the Khabarovsk and Primorski areas of the USSR, along with a small number in the CPR. The ethnonym *na nai*, meaning 'local man', is also that of the Ulcha people (see note on Ulcha, at end of this article).

SCRIPT

Since 1963, Nanay has been written in a far from phonetic adaptation of the Cyrillic script. It is, in fact, the only written member of the South-East Tungus group.

PHONOLOGY

Consonants

> stops: p, b, t, d, k, g
> affricates: tʃ, dʒ
> fricatives: f, v, s, x
> nasals: m, n, ɲ, ŋ
> lateral and flap: l, r
> semi-vowel: j

Vowels

The six notated vowels are *i*, *ı*, *ə*, *a*, *o*, *u*; these represent no fewer than 42 phonemes, each of the six letters serving as a nucleus or base for a series of allophones. Thus, *a* is realized as [a], [aː], and [ã], both independently and as a component in the diphthongs which proliferate in Nanay. The nasal allophone is word-final only. *U* and *a* are positionally realized as /θ/.

VOWEL HARMONY

This turns not so much on a simple back/front opposition as on relative height of vowel: the soft vowels /i, ε/ and one value of /u/ are higher than the hard vowels /ı, a/, and the [o] value of /u/. /i/ is neutral.

MORPHOLOGY

Noun

The plural marker is *-sal/sel*: e.g. *ogda* /ugda/, 'boat', pl. *ogdasal*; *dere* 'table', pl. *deresel*. Use of the plural marker is optional. There are specific plurals for kinship terms.

DECLENSION
ogda 'boat', singular:

nominative	ogda
accusative	ogda.va
instrumental	ogda.di
dative	ogda.do
locative	ogda.la
directive	ogda.či
ablative	ogda.dyadi

Plural: *ogda.sal* + same case endings as in singular, except for loc. *ogda.sal.dola*; with variants throughout.

There are two sets of possessive markers: the first by person (i.e. six forms), the second (reflexive) by number (i.e. two forms): e.g. first set: *mī ogda.i* 'my boat', *sī ogda.si* 'your boat'.

Adjective

As attribute, adjective precedes noun, and is invariable: e.g. *dāi khoton* /khoto/, 'big town'; *daī khotondu* 'in the big town'; *khoton.sal.pu dāi* 'our towns are big' (*-pu* is first person plural possessive marker).

Pronoun

INDEPENDENT PERSONAL
Sing. 1 *mī*, 2 *sī*, 3 *nyoani*; pl. 1 *bue*, 2 *sue*, 3 *nyoanči*. These are declined as nominals (first and second person forms on base with *-n*: e.g. *min-*, *sin-*).

DEMONSTRATIVE PRONOUN/ADJECTIVE
ei 'this, these'; *tei* 'that, those'.

INTERROGATIVE PRONOUN
ui 'who?'; *xai* 'what?'.

Numerals

1–10: *emun, dyuer, ilan, duin, toiŋa, nyuŋun, nadan, dyakpun, xuyun, dyoan.* 20 *xorin*; 30 *gučin*; 40 *dexi*; 100 *taŋo*.

Verb

Four types of base are distinguished by phonetic criteria. To these bases are added formants for voice, aspect, and mood, e.g. *-p-* for passive of a transitive verb: *Bue bit.pu kala.p.d'āra* 'Our life will be changed' (*-d'ara* is future marker).
There are indicative, imperative, and subjunctive moods.

Examples of tense formation in indicative mood (S = stem; + hard endings):

> present: sing. 1 *mī* S.*am.bi*, 2 *sī* S.*a.či*, 3 *nyoani* S.*ra*; pl. 1 *bue* S.*a.pu*,
> 2 *sue* S.*a.su*, 3 *nyoanči* S.*ra.l*;
> past: sing. 1 *mī* S.*ka.yi*, 2 *sī* S.*ka.si*, 3 *nyoani* S.*ka*; pl. 1 *bue* S.*ka.pu*,
> 2 *sue* S.*ka.su*, 3 *nyoanči* S.*ka.l*;
> future: sing. 1 *mī* S.*d'ām.bi*, 2 *sī* S.*d'ā.či*, 3 *nyoani* S.*d'āra*; pl. 1 *bue*
> S.*d'ā.pu*, 2 *sue* S.*d'ā.su*, 3 *nyoanči* S.*d'āra.l*.

The participle, both positive and negative, is a key component in Nanay morphology, discharging nominal, adjectival, and verbal functions. It is personal or impersonal, both of these forms being marked for tense (present–future and past). The personal participle, like the noun, is simple or equipped with the possessive marker (*-i, -si, -ni*, etc.). The simple form is usually attributive: e.g. *xola.i nai* 'the man who is reading', *xola.xan nai* 'the man who was reading' where *-i*[4] is a present marker, *-xan*[4] is a past. With possessive marker the participle is used predicatively: e.g. *nyoani xola.i.ni* 'he is reading'. The impersonal participle ending in *-v/-bo/-u* + tense marker is also used attributively: e.g. *xol.a.o.ri daŋsa* 'the/a "being-read" book; a book to be read'. The negative infix is *-(C)a/e*, where C is *r*, *d* or *t*: e.g. *d'obo.a.si* 'doesn't work' (verbal); 'not working' (attrib.); 'no work' (nominal). The indicative future can be negated by negative particle *em* + auxiliary *ta-* 'to do', + infinitive: e.g. *em d'obo.a tad'āči* 'you will/shall not work'.

Postpositions

Nanay uses postpositions.

Word order

SOV.

ULCHA AND OROK

Two minor languages belonging with Nanay to the Nanay sub-group of the South-Eastern Tungusic languages are Ulcha and Orok. The Ulcha, numbering about a thousand, none monoglot (all use Russian), live on the lower reaches of the Amur. Their language might be regarded as a dialect of Nanay. Orok is still spoken by a few families on the island of Sakhalin.

Both languages have vowel harmony by pitch factor, and both have typically Tungus declension and conjugation systems.

NEGATION

Orok uses the negative verb ę- + sense-verb in base form + affixes specific for each type of verb (four types are distinguished by ending): e.g. *bi ętčimbi ŋenę* 'I didn't go'. Ulcha uses specific negative affixes: -(*a*)*si*/(*ę*)*si*, e.g. *bi anāsimbi* 'I don't push', *si anāsisi* 'you don't push'; past: *bi ečie*(*l*) *anai* 'I didn't push', *si ečie*(*l*) *anasi* 'you didn't push'.

Дади экта эджсинни тактдагуй бэйда-ду ый халадди, тотора нуанво байтаку уфонди; тый джсарумъ нуанъ дидче горо бодди дольджсигумъ Соломонъ мыргэнъ хасэво, еду тае Соломонъ ди даиджсима.

Халь ирбапси ыре (амбанъ) найдди нигуми, пульсини му ана бо ди, дэрумсиво галиндыми, тотамда бавоси.

Тотора гисурини: мочогуйтамбе мэпъ джсогъ бару хавуйдди нигуха; дидюми. нуанво бари ктэунво, хапулухаво, эхири-хаво.

Тотора аными джсафый мынди ктой наданъ ырево, мэпди бади аяхтаво, игуми чалу тэнгагуй, тавуй найду осигуй хамеджсима бади орке джсулепчидди да. Туй осигуй ый джсаленгку халади да.

Nanay
(Matt. 6: 9–15)

NAVAJO

INTRODUCTION

Navajo, also spelled Navaho, belongs to the Apachean sub-group of the Athabaskan branch of the Na-Dené family. The Navajo call themselves *t'áá diné* 'the people', and the language is *diné bizaad* (*saad* 'words': *bi.zaad* 'his words'). Navajo is spoken by about 130,000 Indians in New Mexico, Arizona, Colorado, and South-East Utah. Almost alone among North American Indian languages it is on the increase, being widely used in the conduct of affairs in the Navajo Reservation, and in its local media, radio, journalism, and some literature.

SCRIPT

Roman alphabet plus ' for glottal stop in pre- or intervocalic position; consonants marked with ' are ejectives: *t'* = /t'/. Barred *l* is used for /ł/; the cedilla is used to mark nasalization. High tone is marked by an acute accent.

PHONOLOGY

Consonants

Authorities differ as to the exact composition of the Navajo consonantal inventory. The following phonemes are generally accepted:

> stops: p, t, k; th, kh; t', k', ʔ
> /p, t, k/ are non-aspirated, unvoiced and are notated as b, d, g; the aspirates /th, kh/ are notated as t, k; the glottal stop is the most frequent sound in Navajo.
> affricates: ts, ts', dz, tʃ, tʃ', dʒ
> fricatives: s, z, ʃ, ʒ, γ, ç, h, x, γ°, x°; j, w
> nasals: m, n
> laterals: l, ł, tł, tł', dl
> palatalization: the consonants k, g, t, x, h, are always palatalized before /e/ ké 'shoe' = /kh'é/ The same consonants are labialized before /o/: tó 'water' = /th°ó/.

Vowels

The basic series is:

> i, e, a, o

Young and Morgan (1976) give three vowel lengths: short, long, over-long (before /d, '/). Length is phonemic: e.g. *bita'* 'between them' – *bitaa'* 'his father'. All vowels occur nasalized. Long vowels are written as digraphs.

Tone

High or low, plus two glides, rising and falling. The high tone is marked by the acute accent, the low tone is unmarked. In digraph vowels, an acute on the first component indicates falling glide; acute on the second marks rising tone.

MORPHOLOGY AND SYNTAX

There is no grammatical gender: e.g. *bi* 'he, she, it'.

Noun

There is a fairly small inventory of basic monosyllables, e.g. *sǫ'* 'star', *kǫ́'* 'fire', *dził* 'mountain'. Nouns involving inalienable possession, e.g. the parts of the body, family relationships, are cited with the impersonal possessive prefix *'a/'á*: e.g. *'akee'* 'foot' (necessarily belonging to someone), *'ála* 'hand'. Certain verb forms may be used as derived nouns: *neest'ą́* 'it has matured' = 'fruit'; *ólta'* 'reading is completed' = 'school'.

COMPOUNDS
Example: noun + noun: *tózis* 'waterbottle' (*tó* + *zis*); postposition + verb: *bee'eldǫǫh* 'gun' (*bee* 'with it'; *'eldǫǫh* 'makes an explosion').

NUMBER
Navajo has singular, dual, and different categories of plural, including a distributive plural, conceived as a grouping of individual items rather than a mere plurality. These refinements emerge in the verb; the noun itself is rarely marked for plurality, e.g. *dził* 'mountain(s)'. Kinship nouns take a specific ending in *-ke*, e.g. in Mark, 3.34: *kǫ́ǫ́ shimá dóó shi.tsilíké* 'behold, my mother and my brethren'; *shiye'* 'my son' – *shiye'ké* 'my sons'.

POSSESSION
Phrases like 'the man's horse' are rendered as 'the man – his horse': *hastiin bi.łį́į́'*, where *bi-* is the third person possessive marker.

Adjective

Qualifying material is usually supplied by the third person forms of impersonal verbs – 'to be thick/sharp/green', etc. The relative formant *-ígíí* can be used: e.g. in Luke 5.36–9, 'new wine' is rendered as 'wine that is new': *wain ániid.íígíí*.

There are also a few adjectival suffixes: e.g. *-tsoh* 'big', *-chil(í)* 'small': *dinetsoh* 'big man'; *łį́į́chilí* 'small horse'.

Pronoun

The independent subject pronouns are:

	Singular	Dual	Distributive plural
1	shi	nihi	danihi
2	ni	nihi	danihi
3	bi	bi	daabi
3a	ho	ho	daaho

3a is the impersonal form. These forms are prefixed to nouns as possessives: normally low tone, but certain nouns require a preceding possessive prefix to be high tone, e.g.

low tone series: *shi.tsii'* '(it is) my head', *ni.tsii'*, etc.;
high tone series: *shí.la'* '(it is) my hand', *ní.la'*, etc.

shi.yáázh bi.chidí 'my son's car'.

The pronominal forms are also used predicatively: e.g. *'eii łį́į́' bí* 'That horse is his'; lengthened, + glottal closure, the same form indicates acquisition: e.g. *'eii łį́į́' bíí' silį́į́'* 'That horse became his'.

DEMONSTRATIVE PRONOUN/ADJECTIVE
díí 'this, these'; *'eii* 'that, those'; *'éí* 'that' (remote).

INTERROGATIVE PRONOUN
háa 'where?'; *háishą'* 'who?'; *ha'át'íishą'* 'what?'. Cf. Matthew, 12.48: *Háishą' shi.má nilį́, áádóó háishą' shi.tsilíké danilį́* 'Who is my mother and who are my brethren?' (*nilį́/danilį́* 'is/are').

Numerals

1–10: *łáá'ii, naaki, táá', dį́į́', 'ashdla', hastą́ą́, tsosts'id, tseebíí, náhást'éí, neezná.*
11–19: the format is, unit – *ts* – *'áadah*: e.g. 11 *ła'ts'áadah*, 12 *nakits'áadah*. 20 *naadiin*; 21 *naadį́į́ła'*; 22 *naadiinaaki*; 30 *tádiin*; 40 *dízdiin*; 100 *neeznádiin*.

Verb

For a general note on the structure of the Athabaskan verb, *see* **Athabaskan**.
Semantically and formally, Navajo verbs can be divided into two categories:

(a) Static verbs, including adjectivals; these have perfective or continuative form alone, and are thus conjugated.

(b) Dynamic or active verbs: these generally focus on certain physical properties of their objects, e.g. *shosh* 'to place slender, stiff objects side by side, e.g. planks across a stream', *mas* 'to roll a round object'. Here, dictionary definitions often appear to be no more than a catalogue of basic activities, but many of these roots yield impressive mytho-poeic metaphors in modern Navajo;

989

e.g. *'ááł* 'to handle a round, bulky object', is used of the sun-bearer, who 'carries the sun' across the sky.

Some active stems are coded for number; thus, the stem *teeł* 'to lie down' (with reference to a singular referent) – *tish* 'to lie down', (with reference to two persons) – *jah* (plural).

In both (a) and (b) the root is a monosyllable CV or CVC. The initial C is subject to consonantal sandhi at juncture with preceding prefixes and classifiers. The root itself is a variable which appears in several differentiations, each of which has specific aspectual and/or modal meaning. For active roots, these are future, imperfective, continuative, perfective, reiterative, optative, progressive, neutral, habitual. Not all of these are in use for every root. Those actually in use are listed, for any given root, in a Navajo–English dictionary. Thus, the entry for the root meaning 'to say (it)' appears in the Young–Morgan dictionary (1943: 165) as follows:

niił, niih (ni), niid, 'niih, ne'

these being the future, imperfective (continuative), perfective, reiterative, and optative bases. For each of these, the requisite personal prefixes are then listed. Six forms are normally sufficient to provide all twelve forms of the personal pronoun grid (*see* **Pronoun**, above): for *niił*: *dideesh, didíí, didoo, jididoo, didii, didooh*: the paradigm for the future base:

	Singular	Dual	Plural (three or more)
1	dideesh.niił	didii'.niił	dadidii'.niił
2	didíí.niił	didooh.niił	dadidooh.niił
3	didoo.niił	didoo.niił	dadidoo.niił
3a	jididoo.niił	jididoo.niił	dazhdidoo.niił

It will be seen that the six forms given in the dictionary cover the singular and the dual first and second persons. Thereafter, the same forms recur, with *da-* prefix in the plural, and syncope in 3a.

It should not be imagined that the pronominal prefixes given here are valid for other verbs: there are hundreds of variants: for example, the pronominal series for the future base of the root *t'ǫs – t'ǫs – t'ą́ą́z – t'ǫs – t'ǫǫs* 'to cut in spiral fashion', is: *náhidínées – náhidínííł – néidínóoł – náhizhdínóoł – náhidínííł – náhidínóoł*.

The tense system is based on the available stems, e.g. the present tense is formed from the imperfective or the continuative stem + a specific pronominal series: e.g. from *jił* 'to carry something along on one's back': sing. *yishjił – yiłjił – yoołjił*; dual: *yiiljił – ghołjił*. A past tense is formed from the perfective aspect, again with its specific pronominal series: e.g. from *ghal* 'to eat it': *yishghal – yinílghal – yoolghal*.

Certain periphrastic forms are available for future and past: e.g. *yishą́* 'I'm eating it' – *yishą́ą́ dooleeł* 'I'll be eating it' – *yishą́ą́ ńt'ę́ę́* 'I was eating it'.

NEGATION

By circumfix, *doo...da*: e.g. *dayoosdlą́ą́d* 'they believed'; *doo dayoosdlą́ą́d da* 'they did not believe'.

OBJECT PRONOUN

In the verbal complex, the object pronoun immediately precedes the pronominal prefix + base unit; the -*l*- classifier (see below) may intervene: e.g. *shi.didoo.niił* 'he will say it to me'; *bi.didíí.niił* 'you (sing.) will say it to him'.

CLASSIFIERS

These precede the stem: -*ł*- causative, -*l*- passive: cf. *hółbį́* 'you are building a hogan', *halbį́* 'a hogan is being built'; *ńdííłtłoh* 'you will make it wet', *ńdííłtłoh* 'you will get wet'
These examples are from Young and Morgan (1976).

PREFIXES

Navajo has a large inventory of verbal prefixes which confer specific modal and directional meanings on verb complexes: e.g.

> *'ahá*: conveys idea of bisection, e.g. *'ahádeeshgish* 'I'll cut it in two' (root *gish*);
> *ch'í*: making a linear exit, e.g. *ch'ídeesháál* 'I'll go out' (e.g. from a house) (root *gaal*);
> *hada*: downward motion, e.g. *hada.díí.tłish* 'you'll fall down' (root *tłish*).

Order of items in verbal complex: prefix – pronominal subject – object – classifier – stem.

RELATIVE CLAUSE

The relative formants *ígíí* and *ii* are widely used. *shił nizaad.ígíí* 'the one (place) that I think is far' (*shi.ł* 'according to me'; *nizaad* 'far').

Postpositions

Young and Morgan list about 50 of these; they are usually cited with the 3rd person pronoun *bi*-, e.g. *bi.k'ee* 'on account of him'; *bi.náká* 'through it'; *bi.ł* 'with him'; *bi.deijígo* 'above it': *góne'* in. *'atiin bi.deijígo tsin 'íí'á* 'Above the trail stands a tree.'
sodizin bá hooghan góne' ná'át'oh doo bee haz'ą́ą da 'smoking is not permitted inside the church' (where *sodizin bá hooghan* 'house of prayer', 'church'; *góne'* 'in'; *ná'át'oh* 'smoking'; *bee haz'ą́ą* 'permitted'; *doo...da* is negating circumfix.)

Word order

Free as regards S,V,O in nominal sentence; order of components in verbal complex is of course fixed.

Saad jílíinii

1 Hodeeyáadi Saad hojíló̧, 'éí Saad Diyin God bił hojíló̧, 'índa 'éí Saad Diyin God jílį́. 2 T'áá 'éí hodeeyáadi Diyin God bił hojíló̧; 3 t'áá'ałtsoní hanahjį' dahazlį́į́', 'índa dahólónígíí t'ááłá'í ndi t'áá hádingo t'áadoo ła' dahazlį́į' da. 4 'Iiná hwii' hóló̧, 'áko 'éí 'iiná nihokáá' dine'é bee bá 'adińdíín. 5 'Éí 'adińdíín chahałheełjį' 'adiníłdíín, 'áko chahałheeł doo bidééłnii da.

John 'adińdíín yaa ch'íhoní'ą́

6 Diné léi' John wolyéego, Diyin God bits'ą́ą́dóó yíl'a'. 7 T'áá hó hwee 'ééhózin doo biniyé jiníyá, 'adińdíín nilíinii baa ch'íhozhdoo'áałgo, diné t'áá'ałtso hanahjį' da'iidoodlą́ą́ł biniyé. 8 Hó 'éí doo 'adińdíín jílį́į da, ndi 'adińdíín t'óó baa ch'íhozhdoo'ááł biniyé jiníyá.

NAXI

INTRODUCTION

This Tibeto-Burman language is spoken by about 250,000 people in the Yangzi loop in Yunnan (CPR). Naxi is close to Yi, the genetic relationship being no doubt reinforced by many centuries of cultural and linguistic contiguity (*see* **Yi**).

SCRIPT

What makes Naxi unique among the Tibeto-Burman minority languages of south-west China is its possession of a remarkable literature and an even more remarkable script. The literature is religious and genealogical, with a fascinating creation myth. The script is pictographic, reminiscent at first glance of very early Egyptian, of Hittat Hieroglyphic, and of the Shang shell-and-bone inscriptions. Of particular interest is the rebus element in this script: primary graphs – pictograms – acquire secondary phonetic referents, and even come to be used as syntactic particles, e.g. tense markers. S.R. Ramsey (1987) quotes the example of *se*, whose primary referent is a kind of antelope and which is so depicted; in its secondary capacity, however, it is an aspect marker.

There is no one-to-one correspondence between discourse and script; often, several words in the story are left unnotated, and the written record is picked up again at a point where the officiating priest may require an aide-mémoire.

PHONOLOGY

Consonants

Naxi has 48 consonants. The core of the system is provided by the four-term series voiceless (stop/affricate) – aspirate – voiced – pre-nasalized voiced: e.g. /p, p', b, ᵐb; t, t', d, ⁿd; ts, ts', dz, ⁿdz/. This pattern occurs seven times: in the labial, dental, palatal, and velar stops, and in the dental, palatal, and retroflex affricates.

Vowels

Five basic + /ɪ, ə, y, ɑ/.

Tone

Naxi has four tones: three level – high, mid, and low – and one low rising.
The morphology is similar to that of the other Tibeto-Burman languages of
Yunnan.

NEGIDAL

INTRODUCTION

Negidal belongs to the Manchu-Tungus family, between the Northern and Southern branches of which it occupies an intermediate position, sharing certain characteristics with each. The language is unwritten, and is at present spoken by a small and diminishing group – between 200 and 300 people – in the Khabarovsk region of the USSR, and on the lower reaches of the Amur. Central to the vocabulary is the richly stocked semantic field connected with fish and fishing.

PHONOLOGY

Consonants

stops: p, b, t, d, k/q, g plus a palatalized d'
affricate: tʃ
fricatives: s, x, (χ, γ)
nasals: m, n, ɲ, ŋ
lateral: l
semi-vowels: j, w

Though /r/ figures in the inventory as usually presented, reflecting the extent of borrowing from Russian, the sound does not seem to occur in native Negidal words. /r/ in the closely cognate Evenki (*see* **Evenki**) is often reflected in Negidal by /j/ or zero; cf. Evenki *daran* = Negidal *dajan* 'alongside'; Evenki *kadār* = Negidal *kadā* 'rock'; Evenki *murir* = Negidal *mojil* 'horse'.

Vowels

front: i, iː, ɪ, ɪː, eː, a, aː
middle: œ, œː, ɛ, ɛː
back: ɔ, ɔː, o, oː, u, uː

In this article, /ɛ/ is notated by ẹ, /ɔ/ by ǫ, and /œ/ by ö.

VOWEL HARMONY

Negidal has two opposing harmonic groups, with a neutral third. One group contains /i, ɛ, œ/, long and short; the opposing group contains the rest of the vowels, apart from /u, uː/, which are neutral: cf. *d'ōdu* 'in(to) the house'; *ujkẹ* 'door'.

995

MORPHOLOGY AND SYNTAX

Noun

Plural markers are -*l*/-*sal*, with variants for vowel harmony: e.g. *d'ō* 'house', pl. *d'ōsal*; *amın* 'father', pl. *amtıl*; *ẹnin* 'mother', pl. *ẹntil*. There are nine cases; a distinction is made between definite and indefinite accusative: e.g. *d'ō* 'house': def. acc. *d'ōwa*; indef. acc. *d'ōja*.

POSSESSIVE ENDINGS
Examples: with *koto* 'knife': sing. 1 *kotow*, 2 *kotos*, 3 *kotonın*; pl. 1 *kotowun*, 2 *kotosun*, 3 *kototın*. Plural object possessed, e.g. *koto.l.bı*, *koto.l.sı*, *koto.l.nın*.

Pronoun

Sing. 1 *bi*, 2 *si*, 3 *noŋan*; pl. 1 *bu/butta*, 2 *su*, *noŋatıl*.

Numerals

1–10: *ömön*, *d'ūl*, *ılan*, *di(γ)in*, *ton'ŋa*, *n'uŋun*, *nadan*, *d'apkun*, *jẹγin*, *d'ān*; 100 *taŋgu*.

Verb

Has active, passive–reflexive, and reciprocal voices. The basic aspectual division into perfective/imperfective aspects is further sub-divided into such modalities as durative, inchoative, and reiterative.

Example of tense/mood system: stem *ana-* 'to be pushing/to push':

> aorist: sing. 1 *anam*, 2 *anas*, 3 *anajan*; pl. 1 *anajawun/anajan*, 2 *anajasun*, 3 *anaja*;
> past: the marker is -*ča-*, e.g. *ana.ča.w*, *ana.ča.s*, *ana.ča.n*;
> future: marker is -*d'a-*, e.g. *ana.d'a.m*, *ana.d'a.s*, *ana.d'a.n*;
> subjunctive: marker is -*mča-*, e.g. *ana.mča.w*, *ana.mča.s*;
> probable future: marker is *nā...dixẹ*, e.g. *anan.nā.m.dixẹ*, *ana.nā.s.čixẹ*, *ana.nā.n.dixẹ*.

NEGATION
Inflected auxiliary *ẹ-* 'not to be', + invariable form of verb in -*ja*, e.g. *ẹsim anaja* 'I don't/didn't push'; *ẹsẹsis anaja*, *ẹsin anaja*, etc. Future: *anad'an* 'he will push' – neg. *ẹtẹn anaja*; past: *ẹčeṇ anaja* 'he didn't push'.

Negidal has an extensive apparatus of participial forms, of crucial importance in the syntax.

Postpositions

Postpositions are used.

996

Word order

SOV.

NENETS

INTRODUCTION

Nenets belongs to the North Samoyedic group of Altaic languages. The 1970 census registered 24,000 speakers of the language, who now mainly inhabit the Nenets National Area in the Archangel administrative region. The Nenets speech area, however, extends as far to the east as the lower Yenisei. The Tundra dialect has been a written language since the 1930s, and now has a small literature, consisting chiefly of school books (there is a list in Hajdú 1963).

SCRIPT

Since 1937 Cyrillic + ' (nasal glottal stop) and " (oral glottal stop) for the two glottal stops; also ӈ = /ŋ/.

PHONOLOGY

Consonants

    stops: p, b, t, d, k, g, $\tilde{ʔ}$, ʔ
    affricates: ts, ts'
    fricatives: s, s', ß, j, h
    nasals: m, n ɲ, ŋ
    lateral and flap: l, l', r, r'

The palatalized stops: p', b', t', d' are used with front vowels.
    The nasal glottal stop /$\tilde{ʔ}$/ occurs only as word-final; the non-nasal glottal stop /ʔ/ can be either medial or final.

Vowels

    i, e, a, ɪ, ə, o, u

Vowel length is phonemic.
    Hajdú (1963) records 'phenomena reminiscent of vowel harmony'.

MORPHOLOGY

Noun

The noun is marked for three numbers, seven cases and for possession. The dual marker is *-xV*: e.g. *tɪ* 'reindeer': *texe*' 'two reindeer'; the plural marker is ": e.g. *tɪ*" 'reindeer' (pl.).

There are two declensions depending on word ending: (a) any consonant or vowel except the glottals; and (b) the glottals, with sub-groups for nasal and oral types.

pya 'tree', *pyaxa*' 'two trees', *pya*" 'trees':

> *Singular*
> genitive   pya'
> accusative   pyam'
> dative/aditive   pyan'
> locative/instrumental pyaxana
> ablative   pyaxad

The seventh case, *pyawna*, expresses motion along something.

In the plural, the oral glottal marker " moves in two cases from final position: loc./instr. *pyaxa"na*, and continuative *pya"amna*.

The possessive declension has only three cases: nominative, genitive, and accusative. This declension is used mainly with reference to inalienable relatedness or possession, e.g. parts of the body; the first person endings for singular object possessed are: sing. *-mi/-w*; dual *-mi*'; pl. *-wa*"; for dual or plural objects possessed: sing. *-ni*; dual *-ni*'; pl. *-na*".

Adjective

As attribute, adjective agrees in number with its noun; as predicate in person, number, and tense. The adjective has a specific form of negation, formed from the participle of the negative verb *nis'*.

Pronoun

Sing. 1 *man*', 2 *pɪdar*, 3 *pɪda*; with dual and plural forms, all declined. An accusative form in *si*" takes personal possessive endings: e.g. *si"mi tenevan* 'you know me'; *sidda" tenevadm*' 'I know you' (pl.).

t'uku 'this' – *t'ikɪ* 'that' – *takɪ* 'that (yonder)': i.e. three degrees of removal.

xib'a 'who?'; *ŋamge* 'what?'.

Numerals

1–7: *ŋob"*, *s'id'a*, *n'axar"*, *t'et*, *samlaŋg*, *mat"*, *s'i"iv*; 8 *s'idnd'et* = 2×4; 9 *xasuyu"*, from *xasawa yu"* 'Nenets ten'. If used independently, the numerals are declined as nouns. 10 *yu"*; 100 *yur"*.

Verb

The following moods are distinguished: indicative, imperative, subjunctive, presumptive, and an inferential necessitative. The indicative mood has null marker; the imperative, *-x*V; the subjunctive, *-i*; the presumptive, *-kɪ*. All markers have allophones depending on phonetic environment.

Three sets of personal endings are available for the conjugation of Nenets verbs. One of these sets – the objective conjugation – distinguishes a singular from a dual/plural object. This objective conjugation is used, however, only if and when the object is to be specifically emphasised. In the absence of such emphasis, a transitive verb may well take endings from the subjective set: cf. *manzaraθ* 'he works'; *mə"nada* 'he holds it' (something specific).

INDICATIVE

Three tenses: indefinite with Ø marker; past with *-s'* marker affixed to personal endings of indefinite tense; future with the marker *-ŋgo* etc. following the stem: as example, the singular present, past, and future of the verb *manzaras'* 'to work':

	Present	*Past*	*Future*
1	manzaradm'	manzaradamz'	manzaraŋgudm'
2	manzaran	manzaranas'	manzaraŋgun
3	manzaraØ	manzaras'	manzaraŋgu

Similarly for dual and plural. The first person dual is *manzarani'*, pl. *manzarawa"*.

There is no specific passive voice; the agent/patient relationship has to be deduced from context: cf. *pod'erpada tɪ* 'the reindeer which is harnessed'; *tɪm' pod'erpada xasawa* 'the man who is harnessing the reindeer'.

The four participles combine nominal with verbal properties, and have infixed or affixed markers defining action in process of completion (*-na/da*, see the sentence above), action already completed, action to be completed, and, lastly, action awaiting completion.

NEGATION

There are several negative formulae; *nis'* is in general use as an all-purpose negator. *Nis'* is inflected, while the sense-verb is in base form with non-nasal glottal stop: e.g. *Tɪm' nidm' mis"* 'I'm not giving back/didn't give back the reindeer.'

Postpositions

Postpositions serve to reinforce case endings. As a rule, they follow the genitive case; e.g. *id' ninya* 'on the water'; *id' nid* 'with water'.

Word order

SOV is typical. V is always final.

NEPALI

INTRODUCTION

In the *Linguistic Survey of India*, Grierson (1903–28) classified Nepali as belonging to Eastern Pahari (*see* **New Indo-Aryan**). The linguistic continuum in north-west India is one of great complexity; dialects overlap and merge into one another, with few hard and fast boundaries. Nepali itself seems to be a composite language consisting of (a) an Indo-Aryan substratum of Śauraseni type (*see* **Prakrit**), which was the language of the Khasa tribes in the Himalayan foothills some two thousand years ago, an ancestry which survives in the local name of the language – Khas Kurā (*kurā* 'speech'); (b) the related New Indo-Aryan language brought to Central Nepal by the Rajput invaders in the mid-eighteenth century, a development associated with the rise of the Gurkhas; (c) the new literary standard fostered by press and radio, which makes heavy demands on the Sanskrit reservoir; and finally, (d) one should mention the pervasive influence, especially in the more outlying colloquials, of the Tibeto-Burman languages – e.g. Newari – which have always surrounded the Pahari languages.

Nepali is now the official language of the Kingdom of Nepal where it is spoken by about 8 million people. It is also spoken by substantial minorities in Sikkim, Bhutan, parts of Assam, and in Darjeeling. The first tentative steps towards a literary language were taken in the eighteenth/nineteenth centuries along traditional Indian lines (a version of the *Rāmāyaṇa* by Bhānubhakta Ācāryā). The modern literary language is based on the Kathmandu norm.

SCRIPT

Devanagari.

PHONOLOGY

Consonants

> stops: p, b, t, d, ṭ, ḍ, k, g; all with aspirates: ph, th, etc.
> affricates: tʃ, dʒ with aspirates
> fricatives: v, s, ṣ, ʃ, j, h
> nasals: m, n, ṇ, ɲ, ŋ
> lateral and flap: l, r

Vowels

ə, i, e, a, o, u

All occur long and short, except /o:/ which is long only. All occur nasalized: nasalization is marked either by *candrabindu* or by *anusvār (see **Sanskrit**).* There are two diphthongs: /əy/, /əw/, also nasalized. Nasalization and stress are phonemic; length is not.

MORPHOLOGY AND SYNTAX

Noun

There are no articles. Gender plays little part in Nepali structure, though the markers of its historical presence could hardly be entirely absent from a New Indo-Aryan language. Very generally, in nouns denoting human beings, *-o, -ā* are masculine endings, *-ī* is feminine: e.g. *chorā* 'son', *chorī* 'daughter'. The basic opposition in Nepali is human/non-human, and this is reflected in the use of the acc./dat. marker *-lāī* (see below).

Plural: the all-purpose suffix is *-harū*, added to the singular form.

DECLENSION
Genitive: the affix is *-ko/kī* for masculine/feminine; *-kā* for plural: e.g. *chorāko kitab* 'the boy's book'; *Nepālkā šaharharū* 'the cities of Nepal'.

Acc./dat. *-lāī* marks the oblique case, with reference to human beings: e.g. *bābu choralāī lin.cha* 'the father takes the son'; *timīlāī* 'to you'; *bābu pustakØ lin.cha* 'the father takes the book'.

The instrumental/agentive marker is *-le*. The locative *-mā*: e.g. *Annapūrṇā paščim Nepālmā cha* 'Annapurna is in Western Nepal'; *may.le* 'by me'.

Adjective

As attribute, adjective precedes noun. Many are invariable; those in *-o* change this to *-ī* for feminine and *-ā* for plural. In the colloquial, the *-o* form suffices for both numbers: e.g. *rāmrā vidyārthī.harū* 'good students'; *rāmrī chorī* 'good girl'.

Pronoun

Socio-linguistically complex in that there are three possible forms for second and third persons, depending on social status of person spoken to or of:

first person: the sole form is *ma*, pl. *hāmī(harū)*;
second person: low grade *ta*; middle grade *timī*; high grade sing. *tapāĩ*, pl. *tapāĩharū*;
third person: low grade *u/yo*; middle grade *yinī/unī*, pl. *yinīharū/unīharū*; high grade *yahā̃/vahā̃*, pl. *yahãharū*. Example in high grade: *Tapāĩ.ko jāt ke ho* 'Sir, what is your caste?'

The gender distinction made in the verb, where the second and third persons have masculine and feminine forms, is not reflected in the pronominal system.

POSSESSIVE PRONOUN
The forms are *mero/-ī/-ā* 'my'; *hamro*, etc. 'our'; *tapāīko*, etc. 'your'.

DEMONSTRATIVE PRONOUN/ADJECTIVE
Sing. *yo*, pl. *yī* 'this, these'; *tyo*, *tī* 'that, those'.

INTERROGATIVE PRONOUN
ko 'who?'; *ke* 'what?'

RELATIVE PRONOUN
The *jo* (oblique *jas*)/*je* formula exists (*see* **Hindi**) but relative clauses are more idiomatically expressed by means of the participle in *-ne*, or the first perfect participle in *-eko*: e.g.

> Kāṭhmānḍəw **jāne** bas 'the bus which is going to Kathmandu'
>
> bholi **āune** vidyārthī 'the student who is coming tomorrow'
>
> hijo **āeko** mānche 'the man who came yesterday'

Numerals

1–10: standard New Indo-Aryan forms; beyond 10 the numerals are unpredictable as regards individual form, though the overall pattern agrees with that in other NIA languages, with decade + 9 linked to the following decade; e.g. 30 *tīs*; 38 *aṭhtīs*; 39 *unancālīs*; 40 *cālīs*, 100 *ek say*.

Verb

In certain features – personal and impersonal forms, finite and non-finite, simple tenses (stem + personal ending), compound tenses (participle + conjugated auxiliary) – the Nepali verb conforms to the standard New Indo-Aryan model. It has, however, three unique features: (a) specific negative forms for many tenses; (b) a future in *-lā*; (c) a semi-ergative construction with transitive verbs: the participial predicate agrees with the *subject*, which is, however, in the oblique (agentive) case.

The infinitive is in *-nu*: e.g. *garnu* 'to do', with secondary forms in *-na* (the verbal noun) and *-nā* (used with postpositions). From this, the primary base is found by dropping *-nu*. The following participles are formed on this base or on a secondary associated base:

1st perfect:	*-eko*
2nd perfect:	*-e*
imperfect:	*-da/do/dā/dəy*
conjunctive:	*-era, -ī, -īkana*
infinitival:	*-ne*

The two auxiliaries *cha* (locative, existential) and *ho* (copula) are fully conjugated. There are imperative, indicative, and optative moods.

INDICATIVE MOOD
Specimen tense formation of *garnu* 'to do', primary base *gar-*:

> simple indefinite: primary base + *cha*: e.g. *ma garchu* 'I do', *unī garcha* 'he does', *garche* 'she does'
> present continuous: imperfect participle + *cha*: e.g. *ma gardəy chu* 'I am doing'
> simple past: stem + endings: *-ē, -is, -yo*; pl. *-yə̄w, -yəw, -e*: e.g. **məyle garē** 'I did'
> two perfect tenses: 1st/2nd perfect participle + *cha*: subject in agentive: e.g. **məyle gareko chu/garechu** 'I have done'
> future: base + endings: *-ūla, -las, -la*; pl. *-əlwa, -əlwā, -lān*; e.g. *ma garūlā* 'I shall do'

IMPERATIVE MOOD
The honorific imperative is made by adding *-hos* or *-holā* to the infinitive: e.g. *garnu.hos* 'do!'; *Basnuhos/Basnuholā* 'Please take a seat' (*basnu* 'to sit'). This form is negated by prefixing *na-*: e.g. *na.garnu.hos* 'don't do!'.

OPTATIVE MOOD
The endings of the optative or injunctive mood are shown here, attached to *gar-*:

	Singular	Plural
1	garū̃	garə̄w̃
2	gares	gare
3	garos	garun

Example: *bholi pānī na.paros* 'Let it not rain tomorrow!' (*parnu* 'to fall').

PASSIVE
-i is added to the base: e.g. *garinu* 'to be done'; *sunincha* 'it is heard'; *dekhincha* 'it is seen'.

CAUSATIVE
-āu/-ā is added to base– e.g. *garāunu* 'to cause to do'.

NEGATIVE CONJUGATION
As mentioned above, all Nepali verbs have parallel negative conjugations. Thus the simple indefinite negative of *garnu* is:

	Singular	Plural
1	gardinā	gardəynə̄w̃
2	gardəynas	gardəynəw
3	gardəyna	gardəynan

The second and third person forms are masculine. The negative endings are added directly to consonantal stems such as *gar-*. Vocalic stems are nasalized before the endings are attached: e.g. from *jā-* 'to go': *ma jẵdina* 'I do not go'. The negative of *che* is *chəyna*; of *ho, hoina*.

Some grammars give as many as 24 tense/aspect paradigms in the indicative mood, about half of these being doublets; e.g. *gareko cha* 'he did/has done', with doublets *gare cha* and *gareko ho*.

Postpositions

Examples: *-mā* 'in', *-bāṭa* 'with, from', *-sita* 'at'. *Sita* is used to express the verb 'to have'; *sāga* is also used: e.g. *Ma.sāga pəysa chəyna* 'I have no money on me'; *gar.nā.ko lāgi* 'so as to do'

Word order

SOV.

NEW INDO-ARYAN
LANGUAGES (NIA)

For a background note on the genesis of the NIA languages in the tenth to twelfth centuries AD, *see* **Prakrit**, where the individual *prakrit* forms, from which the modern NIA languages arose, are listed, and where some detail is given of the phonological and morphological reductionist processes involved.

The term NIA applies to all of the Indo-European languages occupying the northern and central areas of the sub-continent, between the Iranian languages to the west, the Tibeto-Burman languages to the north and east, and the Dravidian languages in the south; it includes the two outliers, Sinhalese and Romany. Five of these languages are official languages of state – Hindi, Urdu, Bengali, Nepali, Sinhalese – and several more are regional languages of administration, e.g. Assamese, Gujarati, Marathi, Oriya, Panjabi, Sindhi.

The first genealogical classification of the NIA languages is that given by Sir George Grierson in the *Linguistic Survey of India* (1898–1928). Marginally amended on some points by the Bengali linguist S.K. Chatterji, this classification is still valid, and may be tabulated in its main outlines as follows:

1. North-Western group: Lahndā (Western Panjabi), Sindhi;
2. Southern group: Marathi;
3. Eastern group: Oriya, Bihari, Bengali, Assamese;
4. Mediate group: Eastern Hindi;
5. Central group: Western Hindi, Panjabi, Gujarati, Bhili, Khandeshi, Rajasthani;
6. Pahari group: Eastern Pahari (*see* **Nepali**), Central Pahari, Western Pahari;
7. Sinhalese;
8. Romany.

The total number of people speaking NIA languages approaches the thousand million mark.

All NIA languages share a basic vocabulary drawn from common Old and Middle Indo-Aryan stock, as modulated, pruned, and adapted in the apabhraṁśa period (*see* **Prakrit**). Words belonging to this fundamental stratum are designated by Indian philologists as *tadbhava* 'derived from that' (scil. Sanskrit). This core vocabulary is greatly extended by a stratum of direct borrowings from Sanskrit, usually retaining specifically Sanskrit (i.e. non-vernacular) phonological and morphological identity. These words are known as *tatsama* 'the same as that' (= Sanskrit). The tatsamas in the NIA languages provide a kind of linguistic cash-point facility, affording access to a virtually inexhaustible source of lexical enrichment. Words in NIA languages which are neither tadbhava nor tatsama are known as *deśya*, that is to say 'provincial'.

A second major source of lexical and cultural enrichment is provided by the Arabic and Persian element introduced by the influx of Islam in the Middle Ages. This is particularly marked in such languages as Urdu, but Arabic words are found in all NIA languages.

English, in its turn, has contributed a large number of everyday words and technical expressions, e.g. to Hindi and Bengali.

Separate articles on the following NIA languages will be found in this book: **Assamese**, **Bengali**, **Gujarati**, **Hindi (Urdu)**, **Lahndā**, **Marathi**, **Nepali**, **Oriya**, **Panjabi**, **Romany**, **Sindhi**, **Sinhalese**.

NICOBARESE

INTRODUCTION

Nicobarese is a Mon-Kher-type language tentatively classified as Austro-Asiatic, and is spoken at present by around 10,000 people in the Nicobar Islands.

PHONOLOGY

Consonants

The labial, dental, and velar stops: /p, b, t, d, k, g/, are present, with their associated nasals; the affricates tʃ, dʒ the semi-vowels /w, j/, the sibilants /s, ʃ/ and the sonants /l, r/. /h/ and /h°/ are also present.

Vowels

The vowel system is very rich: 18 values of basic series /a, e, i, o, u/ plus 4 diphthongs plus 14 nasal values.

MORPHOLOGY AND SYNTAX

Noun

Nouns are primary, derivative, or compound. Derivative nouns are made

(a) by prefix from verbs, e.g. *orī* 'to kill' – **horī** 'what is killed';
(b) by modification of prefix, e.g. *katôka* 'to dance' – **kentôka** 'dance';
(c) by infix, e.g. *-am-, -om-*: *kamatôka* 'dancer'; *kalô* 'to steal' – *kamalô* 'thief'.

Compounds: e.g. *fâp-mattai* 'coast' (*fâp* 'side'; *mattai* 'country').
There is no form of inflection; gender is lexical. Case relationships are indicated by syntactical means: the possessed precedes the possessor, the objective case is introduced by the particle *ten*, the agent by *tai*: e.g. *düe chīa chüa* 'my father's canoe' (*düe* 'canoe'; *chīa* 'father'; *chüa* 'I').

Adjective

Adjectives, often made by suffixation, precede or follow the noun.

Pronoun

Pronouns have three numbers: singular, dual, and plural (= three or more, *or* communal).

	Singular	Dual	3 +	Communal
1	chüa	heṅ	hē	yôl-chüa
2	meṅ	inâ	ifē	yôl-meṅ
3	an	onâ	ofē	yôl-an

As possessive pronouns these follow the noun: e.g. *düe chüa* 'my canoe'.

DEMONSTRATIVE PRONOUN/ADJECTIVE
Basic series in *nēe* 'this', *ane* 'that'. Nicobarese has an elaborate inventory of directional expressions related to the cardinal points of the compass (*see* **Verb**, below).

INTERROGATIVE PRONOUN
chi 'who?'; *chūa* 'what?'.

RELATIVE PRONOUN
ka 'who?': e.g. *paiyūh ka leät chūh* 'the man who went home' (*paiyūh* 'man'; *chūh* 'to go home'; *leät* = past tense marker).

Numerals

There are two systems depending in what is being counted: (a) money or coconuts; (b) anything else. The coconut series uses the word *tafūal* 'pair': 1–10: *hēang, hēang-tafūal, hēang-tafūal-hēang, aṅ-tafūal-hēang, lōe-tafūal, lōe-tafūal-hēang, fōan-tafūal, fōan-tafūal-hēang, tanai-tafūal*. After the *tafūal* stage, counting is by *inai* 'scores', finally by *momchīama*, 400.

NUMERICAL CLASSIFIERS
Examples: *yūang* for humans, *nōang* for animals, etc., *danoi* for vessels: e.g. *âṅ yūang Pigu* 'two Burmese'.

Verb

Nicobarese has primary stems like *dīan* 'run', *hēu* 'see'; derivative stems with prefixes, e.g. *ha/ka*: *hatēha* 'to sail' (← *hentēha* 'sail'); compound verbs e.g. *ong.yīang-chông* 'make a voyage'.

Causatives are made with *wī* 'to make': e.g. *wī-yōm* 'to cultivate' ('make garden'). *Ta-* is a frequent passive marker: e.g. *wī-hata* 'to make' – *ta-wīa* 'to be made'.

There is no inflection; auxiliary tense markers are used, e.g. *leät* for past, *yô/enyâh* for future.

The negative particle is *hat* which is combined with the personal pronoun: e.g. *chüa hat → chit*; *meṅ hat → met*; *chit dāk* 'I'm not coming'.

DIRECTIONAL VERBS/ADVERBS

These form an extensive and subtly differentiated network of expressions covering graduated motion, approach, withdrawal, ascent, descent, with reference to the four cardinal points and to a landing-place: e.g. in the series based on *ta-ngange* 'south': *keòid-ngare* 'to come a little nearer southwards'; *höl-ngare* 'to retreat southwards'.

Prepositions and postpositions

Both prepositions and postpositions are used: e.g. *oal* 'in': *oal mattai ane* 'in that village'.

Word order

SVO.

```
1   Mi·im ra-neh An ngam Ṙô; hol ngam Tēv
2   An in-rē, ngam Ṙô; Tēv An ngam Ṙô.  A-
3   nga-aṅ mi-im ra-neh, nö hol ngam Tēv.  Va-
    hī-lö Ò në ta-ṙòk-hö-re che-hen; öt hĕng
4   hang, töt va-hī-lö Ò, nö i në tö-vī-lö ngö.  In
    Ò ngam nô-mö; ngam nô-mö nö Ha-nāṅ-tö
5   ta-rik.  Yang ngam Ha-nāṅ-tö nö el sin-ngñ-
    lö; ngaich ngam sin-ngū-lö, nö öt kò tã e.
6   Hĕng ta-ka ök u-muh ta-rik ta-hīn-tö ngam
7   Tēv, ök tö-mi-në-nyu tö Yô-han.  A-nga-aṅ
    ya-mih nö eū-a; pòn hôk-tu nö a-meū-kö
    ngam Ha-nāṅ-tö,—hôiṅ ṙòk-hö-re, lök-ten in
8   ò, ṙā-tö el-lōn-re.  Ḳöön a-nga-aṅ an Ha-
    nān-tö; yih pö-ri a-nga-aṅ nö a-meū-kö ngam
```

NIGER-CONGO LANGUAGES

This, the largest of Greenberg's (1963) four major groupings of African languages, occupies virtually the whole of sub-Saharan Africa, excluding the Khoisan preserve in the Kalahari and Namibia. About 1,000 languages are classified as Niger-Congo; they are spoken by at least 100 million people, and are divided synchronically into six families:

1. Benue-Congo: c. 700 languages, of which 500 are Bantu. The remaining 200 non-Bantu languages are mainly located in Nigeria.
2. Adamawa-Eastern: c. 90 languages in and adjacent to the Central African Republic, e.g. Sango with 1½ million speakers.
3. Kwa: this demographically and culturally very important family centres on Nigeria and Ghana, and includes such major languages as Yoruba, Igbo, Akan, and Ewe.
4. Voltaic: also known as Gur; c. 70 languages, spoken in Mali, Ghana, and Bourkina Fasso.
5. West Atlantic: c. 40 languages, the most important being Fula(ni).
6. Mande: 20 languages, spoken in several West African countries, from Burkina Faso to Nigeria.

The noun-class system (*see* **Bantu Languages**), which is a cardinal, but not universal feature of the Bantu sub-group of Benue-Congo, is also found in West Atlantic, in Voltaic (where it is marked by suffix in contrast with the Bantu prefixal system), and its historical presence can be detected in Adamawa Eastern. Mande has no noun-class system. The number of noun classes varies very considerably from one language to another.

Tone is prevalent in Niger-Congo languages, but, again, not universal. A striking feature of the Kwa group is 'terraced' tone, which considerably extends the phonemic repertory. The Kwa languages are also notable for the presence of labio-velar double stops: /kp, gb/.

See **Bantu Languages, Swahili, Yoruba, Igbo, Akan, Ewe, Fulani, Bambara, Mande, Gurenne, Wolof, Kpelle, Margi**.

NILO-SAHARAN
LANGUAGES

This is one of Greenberg's four families of African languages. It comprises one major grouping – Chari-Nile, so called because its hundred or so members are sited in two belts of territory along the Upper Nile and along the River Chari, which flows into Lake Chad. This group is typologically sub-divided into Nilotic and Nilo-Hamitic.

The family also includes a collocation of some two dozen languages in Mali and Chad; some of these may be isolates.

In general, controversy surrounds the exact degree of relatedness between these groupings, and also the question of sub-classification within them. Only one language in the entire family can be studied diachronically – Nubian.

About 100 Nilo-Saharan languages are spoken by around 20 million people.

See **Masai, Dinka, Nubian.**

NIVKH

INTRODUCTION

Presumably an isolated Palaeo-Siberian language, Nivkh (also known as Gilyak) is of doubtful affinity. Some connection with American Indian languages and with the Tungus family has been pointed out. It is spoken by around 3,000 to 4,000 people on the lower Amur and on the island of Sakhalin.

SCRIPT

In the 1930s a Roman-based script was introduced, with a switch to Cyrillic in 1953: the following additional letters were used: *g*, *q*, *γ*, *оɉ*. At present, Nivkh does not appear to be written.

PHONOLOGY

Consonants

    stops: p, b, t, d, k, g, q, ɢ
    affricate: tʃ'
    fricatives: f, v, s, z, x, γ, χ, h, ʁ
    nasals: m, n, ɲ, ŋ
    lateral and trill: l, r, ř = ɾ
    semi-vowel: j

Palatalized t', d' occur, and aspirated p', t', k', q'; also t''.

CONSONANTAL ALTERNATION

This characteristic feature of Nivkh affects word-initial and suffix-initial consonants, the mutation being triggered by the final of the preceding word or syllable. Typical mutation series are: /p – v – b; t – r – d; t' – z – d'; k – γ – g/. There are about 20 such series; inspection of them shows, for example, that no Nivkh word has a citation form with voiced plosive initial: cf. *tɪf* 'house' (citation form): /t/ → /r/ after /k/, e.g. *ɪtɪk rɪf* 'father's house'; /t/ → /d/ after vowel, e.g. *oγlagu dɪf* 'children's home'.

Vowels

i, ɛ, a, ɪ, o, u

The long vowels /iː, aː, oː, uː/ also occur, mostly as a result of the elision of the velar and uvular spirants /ɣ/ and /ʁ/: e.g. [oːla] 'boy' < /oɣla/. In this article, /ɛ/ is notated as ẹ.

MORPHOLOGY AND SYNTAX

Noun

The noun is marked for number, case, and possession.
The plural marker is *-ku* + allophones *-xu*, *-gu*, etc. depending on the nature of the final consonant: e.g. ɪtɪk 'father', pl. ɪtɪk.xu; oɣla 'boy', pl. oɣla.gu. Reduplication is also used to form plurals.

CASE SYSTEM
Absolute/nominative + seven oblique, e.g. from ɪtɪk 'father': ɪtɪk.ax (dat./acc.), ɪtɪk.rox (dat./adit.), ɪtɪk.uin (loc,), ɪtɪk.ɣir (instr.).

POSSESSION
The markers are sing. 1 *n'i*, 2 *či*, 3 *p'i*; e.g. *n'rɪf* 'my house', *črɪf* 'your house'; *p'rɪf* 'his/her house; one's own house'. Third singular prefixes: *i-*, *e-*, *vi-*, etc. may also be used.

Adjective

Non-existent in Nivkh; all qualification is expressed verbally.

Pronouns

PERSONAL INDEPENDENT
Sing. 1 *n'i*, 2 *či*, 3 *yif*; dual 1 *mẹgi*; pl. 1 *n'ɪŋ* (excl.), *mer* (incl.), 2 *čɪŋ*, 3 *yivŋ*. There are several variants for these, especially for the third person plural. The pronouns are declined in all cases: e.g. in first person singular: *n'ax* 'to me/me' (acc.); *n'ux* 'from me'; *n'iɣir* 'by me', etc.

DEMONSTRATIVE PRONOUN/ADJECTIVE
tɪd' 'this' (prox.); *(a)hɪd'* (distal); *kud'* 'that' (absent, but formerly mentioned).

INTERROGATIVE/RELATIVE PRONOUNS
aŋ/aɣ 'who(m), whose', *sid'* 'what'; *řad'* 'who, which of several, whose': cf. *Tɪd' řad' rɪvŋa* 'Whose house is this?'; *Aŋ nɪd'nɪ.dox q'aud'*, *hɪd' yin'.dox q'aud'* 'He who does not work, does not eat' (for negative construction with *-dox q'aud'*, see below).

Numerals

Nivkh has specific sets of numerals for the enumeration of various categories of objects – boats, people, animals, fishing-nets, small round objects, long thin objects, etc. Panfilov (1962) lists 26 such sets. For example, 'three' with reference to people is *t'aqr*; to animals, *t'or*; to boats, *t'ęm*; to sweep-nets, *t'for*; etc. It is noteworthy that the palatalized *t'* remains stable as initial in all variants, and the same stability applies in other numbers. Thus, *n'* is the initial for the 26 variants of *n'im* 1, and *m* is the initial for all variants of *mim* 2.

Verb

The Nivkh verb has voice, aspect, mood, and tense in affirmative, negative, interrogative, and affective versions. Quantitative aspects of the action may also be expressed.

VOICE
Active, hortative, reflexive, reciprocal. There is no passive voice as such: thus, *xa n'ivx* 'the man who is shooting' *or* 'the man being shot at'.

The base or active voice comprises intransitive verbs, two sets of transitive verbs (the first set with the object in absolute case, the second with the object in dative/aditive case), and the reflexive verbs with a *p'*- prefix: e.g. *ıtık vid'* 'father goes'; *Muinı n'ivx p'alɣazid'* 'The sick man resigned himself to his fate.'

ASPECT
Perfective, reiterative, habitual, durative; e.g. the perfective aspect is marked by *-ɣɪt*, often plus reduplication of base: *Utkuoʁla mu xorixori.ɣɪt.t'* 'The boy stopped rowing the boat.' Reiterative, intensifying, and habitual aspectual forms also show reduplication, the latter plus *-xɪ*: e.g. *ıtık vivi.xɪ.d'* 'father likes to walk'. Aspect markers may be compounded.

Intensification of action or quality may also be expressed by phonetic change: initial surd → related voiced stop: e.g. *tuzla-* 'cold' – *duzla-* 'very cold'.

A general indicative mood marker is *-d'/t'* (cf. the demonstrative endings), to which the pluralizing affix *-ku/xu/gu* etc. may be added. Tense: past/present marker is null; future has *-nɪ*. The verb is marked for person only in the imperative mood which shows 1, 2, 3 sing., 1, 2, 3 plural, and 1 dual.

Other moods include an inferential or presumptive, made with the endings *-uvr/ɪvr* etc. + *iaɣalo*: e.g,. *Čai q'avd'avr iaɣalo?* 'The tea is (presumably) hot?'; also a conditional and a concessive.

Nivkh has a wide range of participial and gerundial forms which retain tense, aspect, and voice identity, are not declined, and make a plural form by reduplication. For example, a temporal clause formant in *-(f)kę*: *Či mat'kakę čıtık mud'* 'When you were small, your father died'; and a form in *-pa/-ba* meaning 'as soon as': *yif tıftox p'rıba* 'as soon as he comes home'.

NEGATION

E.g. by affix *-tox/-dox* + *q'aud'* as auxiliary: *yif p'rɪdox q'au.γit.lę* 'he didn't come', *lɪx kɪdox q'au.ŋan* 'when it doesn't rain'; and as attribute: *pil.dox q'au dɪf* 'a not-so-big house'. Used by itself *q'aud'* means 'is/are not': e.g. *Naf toluin čo q'aud'* 'Now there's no fish in the sea' (*čo* 'fish').

Postposition

Nivkh uses postpositions.

Word order

SOV is normal. There is no ergative construction in Nivkh.

NORSE, OLD

INTRODUCTION

This language belongs to the Scandinavian sub-division of the Germanic branch of the Indo-European languages. The umbrella term Old Norse covers Old Norwegian, Old Icelandic, Old Swedish, and Old Danish. From the third to the eighth century these were hardly differentiated from each other, and it was only in the Viking period from 700 to 1100 that dialectal differences began to appear. The oldest Old Norse is attested, from the third century onwards, in inscriptions in the runic *fuþark*, a script, probably of Black Sea Gothic origin, which seems to be based partly on Greek and partly on Latin characters. The great majority of runic inscriptions are to be found in Sweden (about 2,000). The oldest of the very few examples found in Iceland dates from no earlier than the twelfth century. A fifth-century inscription from Norway (Gordon 1927: 163) reads:

> ðagaR þaR runo faihiðo
> (I) Dag these runes fashioned (where R denotes a sound intermediate between r and z)

It was in the period from 1100 to 1500 that Old Icelandic finally emerged as incomparably the most important of the old Scandinavian dialects. The colonization of Iceland from Norway, which began in the mid-ninth century, was triggered by the Norwegian King Harold Fairhair's demand that all Norwegian 'small kings' (*smákonungar*) should submit to him as overlord, and pay tax on their land holdings. These were restrictions which Norwegian free-men could not readily accept, and the exodus to Iceland began. The Icelandic *Landnámabók* ('Book of Settlements') records the names and genealogies of some 400 Norwegian aristocrats who preferred to make a fresh start in the wilderness, rather than adapt to Harold's new order.

Ari Þorgilsson, known as *hinn fróði* 'the learned', asserts in his *Íslendingabók* (c. 1130) that Iceland (i.e. the coastal strip) was 'all settled in sixty winters'.

This socio-politically motivated emigration had a very important literary dimension – the large-scale transfer of Norwegian literacy and literary skills to Iceland, where the scene was thus set for the emergence, over the next three centuries, of one of the world's great literatures.

Old Norse poetry is known from two main collections:

(a) the Edda of Snorri Sturluson (1178–1241), a manual of poetics, written for professional *skalds* or court poets;
(b) the so-called *Poetic Edda* (the *Codex Regius* in Copenhagen), which

contains most of the great Eddic lays (early fourteenth century); these can be broadly divided into mythological (e.g. the 'Völuspá', a Nordic vision of the creation and the doom of the world; the 'Hávamál', a book of gnomic wisdom; the 'Grimnismál', Odin's paean to Valhalla; and the 'Þrymskviða', the story of how Thor retrieved his hammer from the realm of the giants) and heroic, lays in this category centring on the figure of Sigurður Fáfnisbani, the Germanic Siegfried. Most of this poetry, of course, antedates the collections which preserve it, by several centuries.

The language of Old Norse poetry is, in general, highly stylized, a key feature being the *kenning*, an often far-fetched circumlocution for an everyday object. Thus, a *branda elgr*, 'beaked elk', is a ship; *heiðis stallr*, 'hawk's perch', is the hand; *oddbreki*, 'sword(point)-wave' is blood.

PROSE

The great age of the Icelandic *saga* ('something said'; pl. *sögur*) is from the twelfth to the fifteenth century. Formally, the saga is presented as a historical narrative, into which the writer (usually anonymous) skilfully and artistically weaves much that is fictitious, very frequently in the form of conversation. W.A. Craigie divided the saga literature into the following three groups:

(a) historical sagas dealing with Iceland and Greenland in the tenth and eleventh centuries: e.g. *Hrafnkels Saga*, *Egils Saga*, *Laxdæla Saga*, and the crowning masterpiece, *Brennu-Njáls Saga*;
(b) historical sagas relating to Norway: here, Snorri Sturluson's *Heimskringla* stands unrivalled, both as a historical source-book and as a splendid piece of writing;
(c) mythical and romantic sagas: e.g. the *Völsunga Saga*, whose theme is the Nibelung story, best known in its Middle High German version.

SCRIPT

Old Icelandic used the Anglo-Saxon version of the Latin alphabet, with the additional letters ǫ and ø.

PHONOLOGY

Consonants

stops: p, b, t, d, k, g; palatalized: k', g'
fricatives: f, θ/ð, s, h, ḥ
nasals: m, n, ŋ
lateral and flap: l, r
semi-vowels: j, v

[x, γ], are positional allophones of /g/. *R* = 'Czech /ř/' occurred in inscriptions only. /l/ and /n/ are devoiced following a voiceless consonant: e.g. *vatns* 'of the lake' → [vatn̥s]. Double consonants are separated, not held: -*kk*- = [k.k]

Vowels

short: front: i, y, e, ø
   back: ɑ, u, o, ɔ
long: front: i, y, e, œ, æ, ɑ
   back: ɑ, u, o

The letter *e* represents both /e/ and /ɛ/; the corresponding long vowels are /eː/ and /æː/. Some authorities give /ɔː/.
   There were three diphthongs: /au, ei, ey/.

MORPHOLOGY AND SYNTAX

Old Norse had three genders, masculine, feminine, and neuter; two numbers, though a dual is preserved in the pronominal system; four cases: nominative, accusative, genitive, dative.

Definite article

Free or bound (suffixed): singular masc. *inn*, fem. *in*, neut. *it*; plural masc. *inir*, fem. *inar*, neut. *in*. For example:

		Free		*Suffixed*	
		Masculine	*Feminine*	*Masculine*	*Feminine*
Singular	nom.	inn	in	úlfr.inn 'the wolf'	grǫf.in 'the pit'
	acc.	inn	ina	úlf.inn	grǫf.ina
	gen.	ins	innar	úlfs.ins	grafar.innar
	dat.	inum	inni	úlfi.num	grǫf.inni
Plural	nom.	inir	inar	úlfar.nir	grafar.nar
	acc.	ina	inar	úlfa.na	grafar.nar
	gen.	inna	inna	úlfa.nna	grafa.nna
	dat.	inum	inum	úlfu.num	grǫfum.num

The suffixed article is generally used, unless an adjective precedes the noun: e.g. *inn hrausti víkingr* 'the brave Viking'; *ins hrausta víkings* 'of the brave Viking'.

Noun

Strong and weak declensions.

STRONG DECLENSION
a-/ja-/wa- stems are masculine or neuter; *o-/jo-/wo-* stems are feminine only; *i-* stems are masculine or feminine, *u-* stems are masculine only. Below are given paradigms of masculine and neuter *a-* stems: *harmr* (masc.) 'sorrow'; *barn* (neuter) 'child':

	Singular	Plural	Singular	Plural
nom.	harmr	harmar	barn	bǫrn
acc.	harm	harma	barn	bǫrn
gen.	harms	harma	barns	barna
dat.	harmi	hǫrmum	barni	bǫrnum

CONSONANT STEMS

Usually with *i*-mutation of root vowel in plural nominative and accusative: e.g. *maðr* 'man', pl. *menn*; *bók* 'book', pl. *bækr*; *bondi* 'yeoman', pl. *bændr*; *broðir* 'brother', pl. *bræðr*.

WEAK DECLENSION

an-/jan-, ōn-/jōn, īn- stems: e.g. *bogi* 'bow' (*an-* stem):

singular: nom. bogi, acc./gen./dat. boga
plural: nom. bogar, acc. boga, gen. boga, dat. bogum

Adjective

Strong or weak declensions; weak after definite article or demonstrative. Example of strong declension: *gamall* (masc.), *gǫmul* (fem.), *gamalt* (neuter) 'old':

	Singular				Plural				
masc.	gamall	gamlan	gamals	gǫmlum	gamlir	gamla	gamalla	gǫmlum	
fem.	gǫmul	gamla	gamallar	gamalli	gamlar	gamlar	gamalla	gǫmlum	
ntr.	gamalt	gamalt	gamals	gǫmlu	gǫmul	gǫmul	gamalla	gǫmlum	

The weak declension has normally four forms: singular: nom. and acc./gen./ dat.; plural nom./acc./gen. and dat.: e.g. masc. sing. *langi – langa*; pl. *lǫngu – lǫngum* 'long'. Examples: *sumir inna hraustu víkinga* 'some of the brave Vikings'; *inna gǫmlu kvenna* 'of the old women': *gamalla kvenna* 'of old women'.

COMPARATIVE

The comparative is in *-ari*: e.g. *ríkr* 'rich' – *ríkari*. The usual suppletive forms are present: *góðr* 'good' – *betri*, *lítill* 'small' – *minni*, *mikill* 'great' – *meiri/œðri*; *gamall* 'old' – *ellri*.

Pronoun

PERSONAL PRONOUNS

First and second person have dual forms:

singular	1 ek	dual	vit	plural	vér
	2 þú		þit, it		þér, ér

These are declined in four cases; e.g. for first person singular: *ek – mik – mín – mér*. First person dual: *vit – okkr – okkar – okkr*; first person plural: *vér – oss – vár – oss*. The third person pronoun is marked for gender: masc. *hann*, fem. *hon*,

neut. *þat*; with plural forms, *þeir*, *þær*, *þau*.
   Use of dual: e.g. in 'Þrymskviða':

> vit skulum aka tvau   í iǫtunheima
> we two will go   to Giant-land
> (*tvau* 'two' is neuter because the protagonists are of different gender –
> masculine and feminine)

POSSESSIVE ADJECTIVES
Marked for gender, number, and case. The first person forms are: singular masc.
minn, fem., *mín*, neut., *mitt*; plural *mínir – mínar – mín*. Similarly for *þinn*, etc.
(second singular) and the dual and plural first and second persons *okkarr*,
ykkarr, *varr*, *yðarr*. The third person forms, *hans – hennar – þeira*, are
indeclinable adjectives. Examples: *vinir mínir* 'my friends'; *vinir varir* 'our
friends'; *með vápnum yðrum* 'with your weapons'.

DEMONSTRATIVE PRONOUN/ADJECTIVE
Masc. *sá*, fem. *sú*, nt., *þat*; declined in four cases with singular oblique and all
plural forms on the third person pronominal model; e.g. for *sá*: acc. *þann*, gen.
þess, dat. *þeim*.

INTERROGATIVE PRONOUN
Masc./fem. *hverr*, 'who?', neuter, *hvat* 'what?' Both declined in four cases.

RELATIVE PRONOUN
(*sá*) *er*, (*sú*) *er*: i.e. marked for gender; *sem* also used. For example:

> svá er maðr   sá er manngi ann ('Hávamál')
> 'so is the man   whom nobody loves'
> (*manngi* 'no one'; *ann* is third person singular present of *unna* 'to love')
>
> veiztu, ef þu vin átt   þanns þú vel trúir ('Hávamál')
> 'know you, if you have a friend   whom you can indeed trust'
>
> þar er hon nú, Unnr, er ek sagða þér frá (*Brennu-Njáls Saga*, chapter 2)
> 'there now is Unn, whom I was telling you about'

Numerals

1–4: *einn*, *tveir*, *þrír*, *fjórir* are declinable: e.g. *þeir váru úti **þrjár** vikur* 'they
were three weeks at sea'.
   5–10: *fimm*, *sex*, *sjau*, *átta*, *níu*, *tíu*; 11 *ellifu*; 12 *tólf*; 13 *þrettán*; 20 *tuttugu*; 30
þrír tigir; 40 *fjórir tigir*; 50 *fimm tigir*; 100 *tíu tigir*; 110 *ellifu tigir*; 120 *hundrað*;
240 *tvau hundrað*; 960 *átta hundrað*.

Verb

Strong and weak; the Old Norse verb had two voices, active and middle, and
three moods, indicative, subjunctive and imperative; present and past
participles.

THE STRONG VERB

Seven conjugations are distinguished, depending on ablaut series. The principal parts, from which all other forms of the verb may be derived, are: infinitive – third person singular and plural of preterite – past participle.

Representative members of the 7 ablaut classes are:

1	stíga	– steig, stigu	– stiginn	'step, walk'
2	bjóða	– bauð, buðu	– boðinn	'offer'
3	bresta	– brast, brustu	– brostinn	'break'
4	bera	– bar, báru	– borinn	'carry'
5	gefa	– gaf, gáfu	– gefinn	'give'
6	fara	– fór, fóru	– farinn	'go, journey'
7	ganga	– gekk, gengu	– genginn	'go'
	fá	– fekk, fengu	– fenginn	'get'

The personal endings of the strong verb in the active voice may be illustrated with the Class 6 verb *fara* 'to go, journey':

	Indicative		Subjunctive	
	Singular	*Plural*	*Singular*	*Plural*
present:	1 fer	1 fǫrum	1 fara	1 farim
	2 ferr	2 farið	2 farir	2 farið
	3 ferr	3 fara	3 fari	3 fari
past:	1 fór	1 fórum	1 fœra	1 fœrim
	2 fórt	2 fóruð	2 fœrir	2 fœrið
	3 fór	3 fóru	3 fœri	3 fœri

Imperative: sing. 1 *far*; pl. 1 *fǫrum*, 2 *forið*
Present participle: *farandi*; past participle: *farinn*; supine: *farit*

WEAK VERB

Three conjugations are distinguished: (a) with *i*-mutation, either in present only or throughout; the past tense formant is -ð-; (b) no mutation; the past tense formant is -að-; (c) no mutation; -ð- formant. For example, *kalla* (class b): first personal forms:

present: sing. *kalla*, pl. *kǫllum*; subjunctive: *kalla – kallim*
past: sing. *kallaða*, pl. *kǫlluðum*; subjunctive: *kallaða – kallaðim*

MIDDLE VOICE

-*sk*(mk) < reflexive pron. *sik*, *sér*; this ending is added to the active forms; the resultant form is (a) passive, (b) middle (medio-passive), (c) a semantic extension or innovation.

(a) passive:

vápnum ok váðum skulu vinir gleðiask ('Hávamál')
'friends should enjoy themselves with weapons and garments'
auðigr þóttumk 'I thought myself rich' (Hávamál)

(b) middle:

þa reiddisk þorvaldr 'then Thorvald grew angry' (*Brennu-Njáls Saga*)

(c) shift in meaning:

em með þvi at dýrit brauzk um fast 'and because the animal struggled hard' (*Grettis Saga*)

The supine – the neuter past participle – is used with the auxiliary *hafa* 'to have' to form a perfect tense: e.g. *Norrænir víkingar hafa farit til margra landa* 'Norse vikings have fared to many lands.'

Negation

The negative adverbs are *eigi/ekki*: e.g. *eigil vil ek eyða fé þínu* 'I don't want to use up your money' (*Brennu-Njáls Saga*, 21). In verse, negative enclitics are used: *-a/-at/-gi*: e.g.

sáka ek brúðir   bíta breiðara ('Þrimskviða')
'I saw not brides   bite more widely'
(*sáka = sá.ek.a* 'I saw not'; *ek* then repeated)

Preposition

Some prepositions govern specific cases, e.g. *til* 'until', takes the genitive, as does *innan* 'before'. *Áf* 'from', takes the dative. Several take dative or accusative, depending on whether rest in a place (dative) or motion into or towards a place (accusative) is implied: e.g. *á haugi* 'on the hill'; *á þingi* 'at the althing' – *á þing* 'to the althing'.

See further examples in the passage from *Brennu-Njáls Saga* quoted below.

Word order

A short passage from *Brennu-Njáls Saga*, section 2, will serve as illustration:

Síðan ganga þeir til lǫgréttu. Mǫrðr gígja mælti lǫgskil ... ok gekk heim til búðar sinnar. Hǫskuldr stóð upp ok Hrútr ok gengu til búðar Marðar ok inn í búðina. Mǫrðr sat í innanverðri búðinni. Þeir kvǫddu hann.

They walked on to the court-house. Mord-Fiddle was expounding the law ... and (then) he went home to his booth. Hoskuldr stood up, and Hrutr (did), and they went to Mord's booth and went into the booth. Mord was seated inside the booth. They greeted him.

NORTH AMERICAN
INDIAN ISOLATES

Strung along the Pacific coast of British Columbia, on Vancouver Island, and extending through the state of Washington into Oregon, Idaho, and Montana are about 30 languages which do not seem to be related to other North American Indian stocks. They fall into three groups:

(a) Salishan: extends from Bella Coola on the coast of British Colombia to Kalispel and Cœur d'Alene in northern Montana and Idaho. There are two dozen Salishan languages, several extinct, the rest moribund.
(b) Wakashan: six languages centred round Vancouver Island. The name is also used to designate a cultural area, to which the Salishan Bella Coola language belongs.
(c) Haida: this isolate was formerly regarded as a member of the Na-Dené family, with one member of which – Tlingit – it shares several features.

A major component in the native cultures of the Salish – Wakash – Haida area is or was the potlatch – a ceremonial gathering at which important personages vied with each other in conspicuous largesse and frivolous waste. Like fishing and hunting, the potlatch generated its own specific vocabulary in several of these languages.

SALISHAN

INTRODUCTION

The group is illustrated here through Squamish /skwɔmɪʃ/, a Coast Salishan language, now extinct, which was spoken in Howe Sound, just to the north of Vancouver.

PHONOLOGY

Consonants

The stops /p, t, k, q/, the affricate /ts/, and the labialized velar/uvular /k°, q°/, have matching ejectives: /p', t'/, etc. (notated here with subscript dots). The fricatives include /s, ʃ, x, χ, h/. The lateral series has /l/, and two sounds which Kuipers (1967–9) notates as ʎ and ʎ̣ = /ɬ, ɬ/? The nasals are /m, n/; the semi-vowels /j, w/, and there is a glottal stop.

Vowels

i, ə, a, u

Each has timbre and register spread; e.g. /i/ includes [e], /u/ includes [o].

MORPHOLOGY AND SYNTAX

Squamish has an elaborate system of articles which distinguish temporal (present and non-present) and spatial (proximate and distal) degree, and affective grade (strong/weak); also gender.

	Present			Non-present	
	Strong		*Weak*	*Strong*	*Weak*
	Proximate	*Distal*		*Proximal*	*Distal*
masculine	ti	taj'	ta	k°əci	k°a
feminine	ci	'aλi	λa	k°əλi	k°λa

PERSONAL AFFIXES

			Possessive	*Subject*	*Object*
singular	1		'n	-(a)n	-c/mš
	2		'ə	-(a)x°	-umi
	3		-s	-as	Ø
plural	1		čat	-(a)t	-umuλ
	2		'ə...jap	-a(ja)p	-umi(j)ap
	3		-s wit	-as wit	-wit

Examples: *'n.snəx°iλ* 'my canoe'; *'ə.snəx°iλ.jap* 'your (pl.) canoe'.

VERBAL COMPLEX

Intransitive verb: the formula is: *č* + subject marker + nominal/verbal stem (+ tense marker): e.g. *č.n.swi'qa* 'I am a man'; *č.x°.swi'qa* 'thou art a man'; *č.ap.sw'qa* 'you are a man'.

Transitive verb: *č* + subject marker + stem + object marker (Ø if third person): e.g. *č.x°.çawat.c* 'you (sing.) help me'; *č.ap.çawat.umuλ* 'you (pl.) help us'

There are factual and relative (hypothetical) paradigms: e.g. *na.çawat.c* 'one who helps me'; *na.çawat.c.as* 'he is one who helps me'; *Ø.çawat.c.as* 'if he helps me'; *s.çawat.c.as* 'that he helps me'.

Predicative clitics include *wa* (durative aspect), *'aq/'iṭ* (future tense), *t* (past tense), *'u* (conditional), *λ* (relative).

Numerals

Squamish has specific series for objects, persons, and animals: cf. *čanat* 'three objects'; *ča.čn'at* 'three animals'; *čn.čanat* 'three persons'.

WAKASHAN

INTRODUCTION

This small group is illustrated here by Kwakiutl, formerly spoken in the northern part of Vancouver Island and in adjacent seaboard areas of British Columbia.

PHONOLOGY

Consonants

As described as Franz Boas (1911): the surd – sonant – ejective (fortis) – (spirant) series is present, as in Tlingit, Haida, and the Salishan languages. There is a three-fold palatal–velar series, notated by Boas as follows (Boas uses ! to mark the fortis/ejective):

velar: q, G, q!, x
palatal: k(w), g(w), k!(w), x̣(w)
pre-palatal: k′, g′, k′!, x′

Kwakiutl has similar dental/alveolar, affricate, labial, and lateral series, the latter notated as: L, Ḷ, L!, ł. There are two nasals, m and n, two semi-vowels j, w, and the glottal stop; no /r/.

Vowels

The frequently occurring indeterminate vowel /ə/ is notated as E. In addition, Kwakiutl has a front vowel which ranges from /i/ to /e/, and a back vowel ranging from /u/ to /o/. a/ā is also present.

MORPHOLOGY AND SYNTAX

Kwakiutl has a large number of affixes which form words from stems. In this process a key part is played by assimilation, both progressive and regressive, at junctures: e.g., in regressive assimiliation, a final surd is hardened to fortis status, or weakened to voiced: $p \rightarrow p$ or b:

qap 'to upset'
qapalōd 'to upset on rock'
qabes 'to upset on the beach'

'nEmōk 'one person'
'nEmōḳus 'one person on the ground'
'nEmōgwis 'one person on the beach'

Focal points in discourse are linked in sequence in accordance with the rules for assimilation, to form integrated complexes which are often hardly susceptible to analysis. Stems are neutral, and become formally verbs or nouns via suffixation; many of the suffixes are themselves neutral; others have specific nominal or verbal valency. The suffixal structure is very rich, and Kwakiutl has a most elaborate inventory of locative and temporal determinants. Boas (1911) speaks of 'an exuberant development of localization'.

Boas uses the simple (in Indo-European terms) sentence 'My friend is sick' to illustrate the Kwakiutl need for closer definition: is 'my friend' present or absent, visible or invisible? What does 'is' mean? Is he or she in an enclosed space, in a canoe, on the beach, up river? Does his or her illness come as a surprise to me, or can I say 'I told you so!' (*-Emsk"*)? The Kwakiutl sentence will take all these aspects of the situation into account.

Boas lists just under 200 Kwakiutl suffixes, classified as follows:

1.   final completive suffixes;
2.   (a) primary suffixes denoting space limitation (general and local);
      (b) temporal suffixes;
      (c) affective, i.e. those involving subjective judgement.

Some examples:

1.   Final completive suffixes: e.g. *-d* added to stem; denotes initiated and carried through, action, especially of transitive verbs, e.g. *lāxtō.d* 'to reach the top' (*xta* 'top').
2.   (a) Spatial suffixes, e.g.

     -xsa 'motion through something': *la* 'to go' – *la.xsa* 'to go through';
     -aGō 'extreme point' – *Ḻās.aGō.d* 'to put farthest out to sea' (*Ḻās* 'seaward';
        -d: see 1 above);
     -'usdēs 'up from the beach' + *qās* 'to walk': *qās'usdēs* 'to walk up from the beach';
     -s 'on the ground in front of house': *lEq"* 'fire': *lEq!us* 'fire on ground outside of house', *k!wa* 'to sit': *k!wās* 'to be seated on the ground'.

     Parts of body may be used as spatial modal parameters; e.g. *-ēg'* 'back' + *la* 'to go': *lēg'a* 'to follow'.

     (b) Temporal suffixes:

     -uł: denotes remote past, e.g. *la* 'to go' – *loł* 'he went long ago'; *ōmp* 'father' – *ōmpwuł* 'long deceased father'.
     -x"id: recent past marker; also inceptive, e.g. *lax"īd* 'he went';
     -L: future, e.g. *xwāk!unaL* 'a canoe that will be built'.

There are two continuative suffixes: one, *-l(a)*, for continued action; the other, *-āła*, denoting maintenance of a position.

Pronoun

The pronominal system is of great complexity. Basically, three persons are distinguished; inclusive and exclusive forms are available for first person. As suffixed to verbs, these pronominal suffixes are:

1		En(L)	-k'/-g'a
	incl.	Ens	
	excl.	Enu'ҳu	
2		Es	-ōx/-ō'
3		–	-ēq/-ē'

The base forms in the left-hand table above are extended by the demonstrative markers for the visible/invisible dichotomy, shown in the right-hand table.

In addition, relative distance can be expressed by forms indicating proximity (a) to speaker, (b) to addressee, (c) to referent (third person). This refinement is particularly characteristic of third person deixis.

The pronoun as subject is not specifically marked; the objective marker is -*q*, the instrumental -*s*. Again, use of the objective and instrumental markers is particularly characteristic of third person.

Action by first person on third is expressed in composite pronominal forms with -*a*- link: e.g. *EnL.a.q* 'I' acts on 'him'; *Ens.a.q* 'we (incl.)' acts on 'him'; *EnL.a.s* 'I' acts 'with, to him'. Examples: *wuL.Ens.a.q* = 'we (incl.) ask (*wuL*) him'; *law.ad.EnL.a.s.ik'* 'I have him to husband' (*law* 'husband'; *ad* = suffix indicating 'having'; (*i*)*k'* is the first person demonstrative pronoun in visible category). Similarly, *EnLōL* expresses first person acting on second person: e.g. *GaGak'!inLōL* 'I try to marry you (sing.)' (this example illustrates the tentative mode, made by reduplicating the nominal, in this case *Gek'!* 'wife' – *GaGak'!* 'try to make wife').

Distributive plurality is also expressed by reduplication, with a great many variant forms dictated by the phonetic data: e.g. *hānaḶEm* 'arrow', pl. *hāhānaḶEm*; *'nEmōkᵘ* 'friend', pl. *'nē'nEmōkᵘ*. The reduplicated stem of a nominal component is also used with certain verbs, e.g. -*g'* 'to eat', with *Gēwas* 'venison': *GEGēwas.g'* 'to eat venison'.

HAIDA

INTRODUCTION

Formerly regarded as a member of the Na-Dené family, this language is now treated as an isolate with areal features linking it to its neighbours. Most Haidas, c. 1,500, live in the Queen Charlotte Islands off the coast of British Columbia; a few hundreds live in Alaska. The language is still spoken, in Northern and Southern dialect forms, by between 100 and 200 older people. The Southern – Skidegate – dialect, the subject of this note, was described by J.R. Swanton in Boas (1911).

PHONOLOGY

Consonants

A typical areal feature is the series surd – sonant – fortis (ejective) – (spirant – nasal), which Haida shares with Tlingit, Kwakiutl, and the Salishan languages:

e.g. in Haida, the dental row: /t – d – t' – s – n/. The labial series has only /p, b, m/. Swanton distinguishes between the palatal series /k, g, k!, x', n/, and the velar series /q, G, q!, x/ (no nasal). (As in their articles on Tlingit and Kwakiutl, Swanton and Boas use *!* to mark the fortis/ejective). The lateral series is notated as *L, Ḷ, L!, ł, l*: pronounced as /tl, dl, t'l'/, etc. There is no /r/ sound; /n/ and the lateral series give Haida its typical phonological contour.

Vowels

As in Kwakiutl, there is a central vowel /a/; the front vowel ranges from /i/ to /e/, the back from /o/ to /u/; all three may be long or short. Swanton notates the indeterminate vowel as /ᴧ/. Doubled vowels with a slight break between them form a characteristic feature of Haida: /a'a, i'i/, etc.: e.g. *l'su'us* 'he said'.

Tone

Haida is tonal (high vs low).

MORPHOLOGY AND SYNTAX

Most stems are monosyllabic. A clear distinction is made between nominal and verbal stems, though a few are ambivalent: e.g. *wāłGal* 'potlatch', or, 'to hold a potlatch'; *na* 'house' or 'to live'. Examples of nominal stems: *su* 'lake', *qait* 'tree', *Gai* 'blood', *q!An* 'grass', *Lga* 'land', *Lu* 'canoe', *łga* 'rock', *Gāyao* 'the sea'. Verbal stems are active (transitive) or neutral: e.g. *wa* 'to do, make', *ta* 'to eat', *su* 'to say', *dao* 'to go to get something', *xao* 'to fish', *L* 'to touch'. Neutral stems: e.g, *k!ot!a* 'to die'; *łGoa* 'to fear'; *gao* 'to be absent'.

Nouns are classified by their specific characteristics – length, flatness, thinness, etc., though nominal-class difference is not reflected or recapitulated in the verb stem. This stem may, however, vary for number, e.g. *qa* 'to go' (singular referent), *(is)dal* 'to go' (plural referent); *tia* 'to kill' (singular referent), *L!da* 'to kill' (plural referent).

The nominal itself is not usually incorporated in a polysynthetic complex; a specific index or marker, correlated with the class of noun, is sufficient. Word complexes contain the following formants:

(a) mode of instrumentality, agency;
(b) nominal referent: subject of intransitive verb, object of transitive;
(c) predicate;
(d) contingent modalities.

Such a complex is followed by temporal, modal, and other suffixes. Swanton gives the following example: *dAŋgīdālL!xasGa* 'canoe being hauled seawards' (*dAŋ-* 'by pulling'; *-gī-* is the classifier for canoes or similar objects; *dāl* 'to move'; *L!xa* 'toward something'; *sGa* 'seawards'). *Da-* suggests motion outwards by being pushed, e.g. by the hands: *lA L! daḶsLgawas* 'they pushed him down' (*lA* 'him'; *L!* 'they'; *Ļ* = classifier for human shape; *sL* 'to put, place'; *s* is the participial ending). Similarly, *q!o-* indicates that something is being done by means of the teeth: e.g. *lA ga q!oĻdAsis* 'something (alive) held him tight in its mouth' (*lA* 'him'; *ga* 'something'; *-Ļ-* = classifier for animates; *dAs* 'to hold'; *-is* = participial ending).

Nominal classifiers of form include, e.g. *tšī*, indicating full containers like bags, pillows, bellies: e.g. *ga k!ēdji tšīq!ēda* 'some (*ga*) (people) with big (*q!ēda*) bellies (*k!ēdji*)'. Similarly, *ska-* for round objects, *sq!a-* for long objects, *q!ōl-* for flexible objects in skein formation: e.g. *k!AldA q!ōlgueła* 'clump of branches (*k!AldA*) fall down!' (*gue* 'fall'; *ła* is the imperative marker).

A third group in the complex contains verbal stems, free or bound. These may be in initial or final position, e.g. *gAn* suggesting collective action: *lA stA L! gAndaxitdjiłasi* 'they all started away from her' (*stA* 'from'; *da* 'to go'; *-xit is* inceptive; *djił* is emphatic).

Contingent modality markers include: *da* 'to cause'; *dal* indicates movement relative to concomitant action; *Gaya* 'to know how to do something'.

Locative suffixes: e.g. *-tš!a* for motion into something, *-gua* motion out of something, *-t!adj* motion across water, *-sgien* motion across a strip of land, etc.

Temporal markers: e.g. *-gAn* past definite (non-inferential), *-aGAn* past inferential, *-gin* habitual past, *-sga* future.

The general negative marker is *GAn*.

Pronouns

PERSONAL PRONOUNS
Subjective and objective:

	Singular		*Plural*	
	Subjective	*Objective*	*Subjective*	*Objective*
1	ł	dī	t!alAn	iL!
2	da	dAɲ	dalAɲ	dalAɲ
3	la/nAɲ	la/nAɲ	L!/ga	L!/ga

-lAn in the plural first and second person forms is also used to pluralize kinship terms, e.g. *yāGa.lAn* 'parents'.

The subjective forms are used with active verbs in general, often without an overt object, and specifically with transitive verbs. The objective forms provide the subjects of neutral verbs. Both subject and object forms precede the complex (some examples will be found in the illustrative sentences above).

POSSESSION
The marker is *-Ga*. Where the possessor is not the subject of the sentence, the possessed object is preceded by the objective personal pronoun: e.g. *dī.Gōn.Ga* 'my father'; *ľ.djā.Ga* 'his wife'. In the case of alienable possession, the pronoun and *-Ga* fuse and precede or follow noun: e.g. *Luā.i lāGa* 'his canoe' (in this construction, the noun takes *-i*).

Numerals

The old blanket-count of the Haida ran as follows:

1 sGoansiɲ;	2 stiɲ	3 łGunuł	5 Lēił
	4 stʌnsiɲ	6 LGʌnuł	10 Lāał
	8 stansʌɲxa		9 LaałiɲgisGoansiɲGo = 10 minus 1.
7 djīguaGā;			

11 *Lāał waigi sGoansiɲ* = 10 + 1; 12 = 10 + 2; 20 *lʌguał sGoansiɲ*; 30 *lʌguał sGoansiɲgo waigi Lāał*; 40 *lʌguał stiɲ*; 100 *lʌguał Lēił*

Word order

The verb is final.

NORTH AMERICAN
INDIAN LANGUAGES

The first known contact between Europeans and the native inhabitants of the New World took place soon after 1000, when Leif Eiríksson stepped ashore in 'Vinland' (probably Labrador, but almost anywhere between there and Maine is possible) and met *skrælingar* (meaning doubtful: 'screechers'?) whom he describes as *smáir menn* ('short fellows'). It is not clear whether the short fellows were Eskimos or Indians; not long afterwards, Leif's brother, Thorwald, was killed by a *skræling*'s arrow. Four centuries later, Jacques Cartier was negotiating with Iroquois speakers in Quebec; and by the 1620s settlers from England were in touch with Indians – again, it seems, Iroquois speakers – in New England.

From the outset of the Anglo-French influx, Indian words, mainly Iroquoian, e.g. the numerals, were recorded by explorers and missionaries, and even the genetic relationship between different forms of the Iroquois family was correctly identified (Father Paul le Jeune, 1635). But in general the attention paid to North Indian languages was fragmentary, and there is nothing to compare with the Motul Dictionary in the Mesoamerican field (*see* **Maya**). Systematic study of the North American languages was stepped up in the nineteenth century and culminated in the work of Franz Boas (1858–1942), whose cultural anthropology, a fertile mix of descriptive linguistics and ethnology, set the scene for the tremendous upswing in the scientific study of American Indian languages through the twentieth century.

About 300 North American Indian languages were in use when the European colonization of the area got under way, in the sixteenth/seventeenth century. Their subsequent history is one of erosion, decimation, and, in many cases, extinction. Today, between 50 and 100 languages are still spoken, for the most part by aged and dwindling populations, often to be reckoned in dozens, at best in hundreds.

Five languages – Choctaw, Muskogee, Dakota, Cherokee, and Pima-Papago – each have between 10,000 and 20,000 speakers, and two – Cree and Ojibwa – can muster 40,000 to 50,000. The odd man out in this saga of the vanishing Indian, however, is Navajo: not merely stable, but apparently actually increasing its already impressive total of over 100,000 speakers.

The first general classification of the North American Indian languages was that of Major J.W. Powell, the founding director of the Bureau of American Ethnology, who, in 1891, divided the languages into 58 stocks, on a somewhat rough-and-ready basis of lexical similarity. Subsequent classifications – Sapir (1921/9), Mary Haas (1958), Voegelin and Voegelin (1965/6) – are based on the very detailed and highly technical identification and analysis of phonological correspondences. By means of such techniques, definitive genetic relationships have been established for many North American languages, and ancestral models have been reconstructed – Proto-Algonquian, Proto-Athabaskan, Proto-Iroquoian, etc.

None of these reconstructions, however, has so far thrown any light on the question of an Indian Urheimat. Are the Indians native to the Americas, or did they come from somewhere else? A Bering Straits/Aleutian Islands passage from Asia is still postulated as a likely provenance, and it is true that, over the last two thousand years, the movement of Indian tribes seems to show a general drift from north to south.

It is noteworthy, however, that in the latest general classification of the world's languages, J. Greenberg relates only one of his North American Indian groups, Eskimo-Aleut, to his Euro-Asiatic phylum, which includes the Indo-European and the Altaic languages, Japanese, and Korean. The North American Indian languages proper are classified by Greenberg as (a) the Na-Dené family, a small group with a highly distinctive genetic profile; and (b) Amerindian, a vast conglomerate comprising all the remaining families.

For practical descriptive purposes it is convenient to use a revised version of Sapir's 1929 classification, as adopted by David Crystal (1988). The North American families are listed as follows:

1. Na-Dené;
2. Eskimo-Aleut;
3. Macro-Algonquian;
4. Macro-Siouan;
5. Penutian;
6. Aztec-Tanoan.

In addition, a virtually extinct group of isolates on the north-west Pacific Coast, and the Hokan cluster of languages in California, Arizona, and Mexico, should be mentioned.

See **Na-Dené**, etc. as listed above: **North American Indian Isolates**; **Athabaskan**; and the following individual languages: **Apache, Arapaho, Blackfoot, Cherokee, Chipewyan, Choctaw, Cree, Dakota, Hopi, Menomini, Nahuatl, Navajo, Tlingit, Zuni**.

NORWEGIAN

INTRODUCTION

Norwegian is a member of the Scandinavian branch of the Germanic family of the Indo-European languages. It is spoken by about 4 million people.

From the fourteenth to the early nineteenth century Norway was part of Denmark, and Danish was the written, and, at least as far as the educated and urbanized classes were concerned, the spoken language of the country. With the end of Danish hegemony in the nineteenth century, nationalistic demands began to make themselves heard for 'pure' or 'rural' Norwegian, harking back via the many dialects to the Old Norse of the Middle Ages, in preference to the alien, though genetically very closely connected, Danish. Groups of intellectuals explored the potentialities of various dialects in search of a basis for a *landsmål* or popular speech, to replace the Danish norm of the *riksmål* or state language. Here, a crucial part was played by Ivar Aasen, whose grammar, based on the very conservative West coastal dialects, appeared in 1864, to be followed by a dictionary in 1873. Of course, a Doric, however pure linguistically, was bound to have an uphill struggle against the social prestige and the economic use-value of the Dano-Norwegian *riksmål*, and it took the rest of the century for a somewhat artificial construct like *landsmål* to emerge as a serious contender. The Nynorsk, 'New Norwegian', that took shape from Aesen's pioneer work, received official sanction in 1884; and by 1892 individual schools were empowered to choose it as language of instruction, in preference to Standard Norwegian. In 1907, an orthographical reform changed the Dano-Norwegian intervocalic voiced plosives *b*, *d*, *g* to their unvoiced counterparts *p*, *t*, *k*, thus falling into line with actual Norwegian pronunciation. A further reform in 1917 brought more sectors of *riksmål* – or *bokmål* as it was by then known – into line with *landsmål* usage. In 1938–9 an attempt was made to create a new unified norm – *samnorsk*. This never got off the ground.

Today, both Standard Norwegian and Nynorsk are joint official languages of Norway. Theoretically, they have equal status, and are used at all levels and in all walks of life. In practice, however, Standard Norwegian remains very much in the ascendant. Only about 16 or 17 per cent of Norwegians – resident mainly in the coastal fringe and in the central mountains – actually speak Nynorsk as mother tongue, and this percentage is reflected in Nynorsk's share of the media. The urban population remains solidly committed to Standard Norwegian, the leading language of administration, business, and the media.

In all linguistic matters, the Norsk Språkråd acts in an advisory capacity for the Norwegian government.

Since formally *bokmål* differs little from Danish (*see* **Danish**), Nynorsk forms are mainly considered here.

SCRIPT

The Roman alphabet + *æ*, *ø*, *å*.

PHONOLOGY

Consonants

  stops: p, b, t, d, k, g
  fricatives: f, v, ç, s, ʃ, j, h
  nasals: m, n, ŋ
  lateral and flap: l, r

Retroflex /ʈ, ɖ, ɳ, ɭ/ occur in *bokmål* and in eastern dialects. Geminated consonants are long.

Vowels

Notated as *i, y, e, ø, æ, a, å, u, ʉ*; all occur long or short *i* represents /i/ and /ɪ/; *e* represents /e/ and /ɛ/; *ø* = /œ/; *å* = /ɔ/. Unstressed *e* tends to become /ə/. Diphthongs: /ei, œ, ai, aʉ, ɔy/. That is, Nynorsk retains Old Norse diphthongs.

Tones

Two tones or pitch contours are distinguished: one is a rising tone (single tone) used in all monosyllables; the other is a falling–rising tone (double tone) used in polysyllables.

Stress

Nearly always on first syllable.

MORPHOLOGY AND SYNTAX

Noun

Uniquely among the Scandinavian languages, Nynorsk retains a distinct feminine gender with a specific indefinite article: masc. *ein*, fem. *ei*, neut. *eit*. Masculine and feminine definite articles coalesce into *den*; neuter, *det*.

DECLENSION
Typical series for three genders: indefinite, definite with affixed article, plural indefinite, plural definite with affixed article:

1036

masc.	ein fiskar	fiskaren	fiskarar	fiskarane	'fisherman'
fem.	ei jente	jenta	jenter	jentene	'girl'
nt.	eit hus	huset	hus∅	husa	'house' (*huset* = /husɛ/)

Umlaut of the stem vowel takes place in certain types of masculine and feminine nouns: masc. *son* 'son' – *søner*; *bonde* 'farmer' – *bønder*; fem. *hand* 'hand' – *hender*; *bok* 'book' – *bøker*

The old *-i* declension of feminine nouns is retained in certain dialects: e.g. *ei sky* 'a cloud': *skyi – skyer – skyene*.

Adjective

Typically, the Nynorsk adjective is marked for masculine/feminine (common form), neuter and plural in strong form: e.g. *hard – hardt – harde* 'hard'; *ny – nytt – nye* 'new'; and by *-e* for all three genders and both numbers in the weak form: e.g. *den, det, dei, harde* ...

COMPARISON

The comparative is made with *-are*: e.g. *farleg* 'dangerous' – *farlegare*. As in other Germanic languages certain adjectives have suppletive comparative forms: e.g. *god – betre – best*; *liten* 'small' – *mindre*.

Pronouns

		Singular			*Plural*		
		Subject	Object	Possessive	Subject	Object	Possessive
1		eg	meg	min	vi/me	oss	vår
2		du	deg	din	de/De	**dykk/Dykk**	**Dykkar**
3	masc.	han	han/honom	hans			
	fem.	ho	henne	hennar	dei	dei	deira
	nt.	det	det	(dess)			

Min, din, vår are inflected for gender and number: e.g. *min*, fem. *mi*, neut. *mitt*, pl. *mine*.

There is a tendency in Nynorsk to insert possessive pronouns such as *hans* and *hennar* between the nouns in a genitive relationship: e.g. *far hans Per* 'Per's father'; *bror hennar Lise* 'Lise's brother'.

DEMONSTRATIVE PRONOUNS

denne – dette – desse 'this, these'
den – det – dei 'that, those'

The latter is used as definite article for an adjective + noun complex: *den gamle mannen* 'the old man'; *det nye huset* 'the new house' (i.e. duplication of marker).

INTERROGATIVE PRONOUNS
kven 'who?', *kva* 'what?'

RELATIVE PRONOUN

som, *då*. These are invariable; *som* can be omitted if it is not the subject of a relative clause.

Numerals

1–10: *ein/ei/eitt*; *to*, *tre*, *fire*, *fem*, *seks*, *sju*, *åtte*, *ni*, *ti*; 11 *elleve*; 12 *tolv*; 13 *tretten*; 20 *tjue*; 30 *tretti*; 40 *førti*; 100 *hundre*.

Verb

Strong/weak, transitive/intransitive. Extreme reductionism: all verbs have one form for all persons in the present, and, similarly, one past form.

Compound tenses are made with the auxiliaries *å vera* 'to be', *å ha* 'to have'. The present and past forms of these are: *vera*: *er*, *var*; *ha*: *ha*, *hadde*.

There are four formal classes of weak verb: e.g.

1. Single ending *-a(r)*: *å fiska* 'to fish': pres. *fiskar* /fiska/; past *fiska*; pp. *fiska*.
2. Four endings: *å kjenna* 'to know': pres. *kjenner*; past *kjende*; pp. *kjent*.
3. Four endings, sometimes with umlaut: *å spørja* 'to ask': *spør – spurde – spurt*.
4. Four endings: *å bu* 'to dwell': *bur – budde – butt*.

STRONG VERBS

Two- or three-stage ablaut is found in virtually all strong verbs in Nynorsk. The past has no dental ending; the present has no ending, apart from stems ending in a stressed vowel, which take *-r*: e.g. *få* 'get', pres. *får*. Main ablaut patterns (infinitive – past tense – past participle):

e – a – o: vera 'to be' – var – vore
e – a – e: lesa 'to read' – las – lese
i – ei – i: gli 'to glide' – glei – glide
e – a – u: brenna 'to burn' – brann – brunne
y – au – o: krypa – 'to creep' – kraup – krope

PAST PARTICIPLES

These behave as adjectives ending in *-en* (masc./fem.), *-e* (neuter), *-ne* (pl.): e.g. *komen – kome – komne* 'arrived'.

mannen er komen frå ... 'the man has come from ...'
barnet er kome 'the child has come'
dei er komne 'they have come'

FUTURE

Expressed by auxiliaries such as *skal* and *vil* + infinitive. These auxiliaries are often omitted with verbs of motion.

PASSIVE

The -*st* passive is characteristic of Dano-Norwegian rather than of Nynorsk. Usually, the auxiliaries *verta*, *bli*, or *vera* + past participle combine to give a passive sense: e.g. *huset vert bygt* 'the house is being built' (or, *huset blei bygt*).

Negation

The general particle of negation is *ikkje*.

Prepositions

For example, *bak*(*om*) 'behind', *gjennom* 'through', *kring* 'around', *med* 'with', *på* 'on', *åt* 'for'.

Word order

SVO.

---

1 I opphavet var Ordet, og Ordet var hjå Gud, og Ordet var Gud. ² Han var i opphavet hjå Gud. ³ Alt vart til ved han, og utan han vart ikkje noko til av alt det som er til. ⁴ I han var liv, og livet var ljoset åt menneska. ⁵ Og ljoset skin i mørkret; men mørkret tok ikkje imot det.

⁶ Det stod fram ein mann, send av Gud; Johannes var namnet hans. ⁷ Han kom for å vitna; han skulle vitna om ljoset, så alle skulle koma til tru ved han. ⁸ Det var ikkje han som var ljoset; men han skulle vitna om ljoset.

(Nynorsk)

NUBIAN

INTRODUCTION

At present, this Nilo-Saharan language is spoken by about a million people in Egypt and the Sudan. Between the eighth and the fourteenth centuries AD, Christian homiletic texts were translated from Greek into Old Nubian, and written in the Coptic script, with three additional letters (borrowed from Meroitic) to denote /ɲ, ŋ, w/. For the texts, see Griffith (1913).

OLD NUBIAN

PHONOLOGY

Consonants

    stops: t, d, p, b, k, g
    affricate: dʒ
    fricatives: s, ʃ, h
    nasals: m, n, ɲ, ŋ
    lateral and flap: l, r
    semi-vowels: j, w

f, *ph*, *x*, *ps*, *th* occur in Greek loan-words.

   There is extensive consonantal assimilation, especially of /l, r, n, p/; e.g. /p + s/ → /ss/, /l + d/ → /dd/, /r + d/ → /dd/, /l + k/ → /kk/.

Vowels

    i, e, a, o, u

Diphthongs: ai, au, oi

MORPHOLOGY AND SYNTAX

Noun

Most root nominals are monosyllabic; e.g. *i(t)* 'man', *uk* 'day', *ur* 'head', *ag* 'mouth', *ngod* 'lord', *sal* 'word'.

   Affixation produces derived nouns: e.g. abstracta in *-it*: *pig.it* 'light', *tusk.it* 'trinity'; in -*kape*: *pis.kape* 'joy', *on.kape* 'love'; in -*e*: *al.e* 'truth', *di.e* 'death'.

Compounds: e.g. *it.onkape* 'man–love' = 'philanthropy'; *mašal.n.oski* 'sun–rise' = 'the orient'.

Subject marker -*i* is added to consonantal final: e.g. *skit.i* 'the earth', *kosmos.i* 'the world', *harm.i* 'the heavens, sky'.

The definite article is -*l*: e.g. *ngod.i.l* 'the Lord'; *ag.i.l* 'the mouth'; *istauros.i.l* 'the cross'.

The locative postposition -*lo* often functions as a focusing particle for indefinite nouns: e.g. *Parthenos.i.l.lo tu.lo džunt.u.ng.arr.a* '(Behold) a virgin shall be with child' (Matthew, 1.23) (where *parthenos* is a Greek loan-word; *tu* is 'stomach'; and the root *džunt.ung-* 'to become pregnant'). Cf. *Kosmos.la.lo dul.l.ana* 'These are in the world' (John, 17.11) (root *du-* 'to be resident in').

NUMBER
The plural marker is -*gu*: e.g. *uru* 'king', *uru.gu* 'kings'. Similarly, *i.gu* 'men', *tauk.gu* 'times'.

CASE RELATIONS
The genitive marker is -*n(a)*: e.g. *ngod.in angelos* 'the angel of the Lord', *ted.in tidžkanel* 'the fulfilment of the Law', *sagar.in ngal* 'son of Sagar'.

OBLIQUE MARKER
-*ka*: e.g. *ngape.gu.ka* 'the sins' (acc.).

Adjective

The adjective is treated as a nominal or as a verbal participle, and, attributively, follows the noun to which it is connected by the relational marker -*u*: cf. *istauros.u ngok.ko* 'the glorious Cross' (*ngok* 'glory'), *murt.u ngulu* 'a white horse'.

Pronoun

As regards both subjective and objective forms, the Old Nubian paradigm agrees with the modern one (see below, p. 1045). Old Nubian has an exclusive first person plural in *er*.

POSSESSIVE
The forms are: sing. 1 *an*, 2 *en*, 3 *tan*; pl. 1 incl. *un*, excl. *en*, 2 (not attested), 3 *ten*: e.g. *ngod.u.an.ni* 'my Lord', *tan.na magidel* 'his suffering'.

DEMONSTRATIVE PRONOUN
in (proximate), *man* (distal) for both singular and plural: e.g. *in ted.gu* 'these laws', *man dippi* 'that town'.

INTERROGATIVE PRONOUN
is: e.g. *Is.lo is.s.na?* 'What was there?'

RELATIVE PRONOUN
The relational marker -*u* is used to form relative or appositional clauses: e.g.

tar.u ... 'he who...', *ter.u* ... 'they who ...', *ngod.u till* 'the Lord God', *parthenos.u ngiss.u Maria* 'the holy Virgin Mary', *ogidždž.u tillil unil* 'a man (*ogidž*) whom God (*tilli*) loves (*on-/un-*)'.

Numerals

1, 2, 3, 4, 7, are attested, and are as in modern Nubian (see below); 10 is *timinigu*.

Verb

Most verbal roots are monosyllabic: e.g. *el-* 'find', *ok-* 'call', *on-* 'love', *i-* 'say', *ar-* 'take', *ken-* 'bring', *kap-* 'eat', etc. Compound stems: e.g. *ko.džu* 'to take away' (*ko* 'have' + *džu* 'go away').

ASPECT
In the oldest form of the language, aspect is expressed thematically in two participles, an imperfective (characteristic *-i-*) and a perfective (characteristic *-o-*). Thus, *iar.i* 'knowing' – *iar.i.l* 'he who knows'; *ān.i* 'living' – *añ.i.l* 'the living one'; with variant *-u-*: e.g. *ngal.u* 'seeing'.

Perfective: e.g. *di.o.l* 'he who has died'; *do.o.l* 'he who has gone out'.

In literary Old Nubian, this aspectual distinction survives only in certain auxiliary verbs.

TENSE STRUCTURE
Old Nubian had present, aorist, preterite, and two future tenses, with traces of a perfect and a pluperfect. Present, aorist, and preterite are attested in two versions, indicative (independent) and subjunctive (dependent): e.g. present endings:

	Indicative		Subjunctive	
1	-r.e	—	-e.r.i	-r-u
2	-(i)-na	-r-o	(-i-n)	-r-u
3	-na	-r-ana	-i.n	-r-an

Examples: indicative *ki.r.e* 'I come', *pes.i.na* 'thou sayest', *dul.l.ana* (< *dul.r.ana*) 'they remain'; subjunctive *padž.e.r.i* 'while/as I direct'.

The aorist, with an *-a-* characteristic, is sparsely attested.

Preterite: endings:

	Singular	Plural
1	(i).s-e	s.o
2	(i).s.na	—
3	(i).s.na	s.ana

The preterite subjunctive has an *-i-* characteristic. Examples: indicative *džu.s.e* 'I went out', *den.dži.s.na* 'thou gavest me'; subjunctive *on.e.s.i.n* 'that thou didst love'.

The first future has an *-ar-/-an-* infix: e.g. *au.ar.r.e* 'I shall do'. The second future has a *-d-* infix: e.g. *kid.d.r.e* 'I shall come'.

NEGATION

Originally by means of negative prefix *m-*: e.g. *on* 'to love', *m.on* 'not to love'. In later Nubian, the negative auxiliary *m.en* 'not to be' is used: *ulg-* 'to hear' – *ulg.r.i.men* 'not to hear something'.

Postpositions

Zyhlarz (1928) divides these into several functional categories: directional/locative, circumstantial, emphasizing, etc. Some examples follow:

1. Directional/locative:

    -la 'in': e.g. *ngog.la* 'in the house', *kosmos watto.la* 'in the whole world';
    -lo/-ro 'in, at' (spatial/temporal): e.g. *tan wiñdž.i.ka mašal.(n).osk.i.lo nga.s.in kas.s.o.si.n* 'we have seen his star (*wiñdž*) in the east and have come ...' (Matthew, 2.2) (*tan* 'his'; *ka* oblique marker; *ngal-* 'see'; *kin* 'come'). (For use of *lo* as focusing particle, *see* **Noun**, above.)
    -gil.(le) 'to(wards)': e.g. *ai.gil* 'towards me'; *is.gil* 'whither?'

2. Circumstantial:

    -dal 'with': e.g. *tad.dal* 'with him';
    -džun 'because of': e.g. *ngape.k au.e.s.i.lo.džun* 'because I have sinned' (*ngape* 'sin'; *au* 'do, make');
    -ketal 'from': e.g. *kim.m.a sion.i.a.ketal aul.el* 'from Zion the saviour (*aul*) will come' (*kin* 'to come').

A remarkable feature of Nubian structure is the nominalization of auxiliary clauses of time, place, etc.: e.g.

   en añdž.na saite.n.gu.n.ngadždž.il.do ak.in
   lit. 'our Saviour's when-he-was-on-the-mount-of-olives'

The long compound being a noun: i.e. 'when our Saviour was on the Mount of Olives ...' (*añdži* 'saviour'; *saite* 'olive tree'; *gu* 'time'; *ngadždži* 'hill').

   an.na kosmos.i.lo džo.a.r.a men.e.r.i.kello
   lit. 'as my I-am-not-of-this-world' (John, 17.16)

i.e. 'even as I am not of the world' (*džo* 'to issue from'; *men* 'to be not'; *kello* 'even, as').

Word order

SOV is usual in transitive context: e.g. *till.il tan tot.ka itir.s.na* 'God sent his son' (*tot* 'son'). VS occurs (cf. *-ketal* example above).

MODERN NUBIAN

PHONOLOGY

Consonants

> stops: b, t, d, k, ğ
> affricates: tʃ, dʒ (ǰ)
> fricatives: f, s, ʃ, z, h
> nasals: m, n, ɲ, ŋ
> lateral and flap: l, r
> semi-vowels: w, j

ASSIMILATION
Example: /b/ + /k/ → /bb/, /n/ + /f/ → /ff/, /d/ + /g/ → /tt/, /n/ + /l/ → /nn/: *tan fāb* /taffaːb/, 'his father'.

Vowels

> short and long: i, e, a, o, u

/e/ = [e] and [ɛ]; /o/ = [ɔ].
Diphthongs: either long–short, e.g. /aːi, oːu/, etc., or short–long: /aiː, eiː/, etc.

MORPHOLOGY AND SYNTAX

Noun

Typical nominal stems are CVC, CVCCV: e.g. *kid* 'stone', *fāb* 'father', *mas* 'good', *šareb* 'the moon', *murti* 'horse', *dessi* 'green'. Some stems end in a long vowel: e.g. *tī* 'cow', *kō* 'lion', *sū* 'milk'.

There is no grammatical gender; *ondi* 'male', *karrē* 'female', may be used to distinguish natural gender: e.g. *murt ondi* 'a stallion', *murti karrē* 'mare'.

NUMBER
Nubian has a variety of plural markers, e.g. *-ī*, *-(i)rī*, *-gū*, *-nji*: *fāb* 'father' – pl. *fābī*; *nogirī* 'houses'; *tīgū* 'cows'; *kittū* 'stones'; *karrēnjī* 'women'.

GENITIVE
The linking particle is -(V)*n*, e.g. *fāb.in ur* 'the father's head'; *idēn.in burū* 'the woman's daughter'; *burū.n ukki* 'the girl's ear'. If the possessed object is not overtly expressed, *-ni/-nan* is used: e.g. *Tirana Gaisarkā Gaisar.ni.gā* 'Render unto Cæsar what is Cæsar's' (Mark, 12.17.) This sentence also illustrates the indirect object marker *-kā*, and the direct object marker *-gā*: cf. *bahar.kā īgatiron* 'he said to the sea' (Mark, 4.39). Other case relationships are expressed with the help of postpositions.

Adjective

As attribute, adjective follows noun: e.g. *burū ašri* 'beautiful girl', pl. *buruwi ašrigū*.

Pronoun

The basic personal forms, with objective forms, are:

	Singular	Plural
1	ai; aigā	ū; ugā
2	ir; ikkā	ur; ukkā
3	tar; takkā	ter; tekkā

A specific series is used with postpositions: *annā, innā, tannā; ūnnā, unnā, tennā*.

POSSESSIVE PRONOUNS

anni, inni, or *an.gā, in.gā, tan.gā*, with variants: e.g. *murt anni = murt an.gā* 'my horse'. With kinship terms, however, the possessive pronoun precedes the noun: e.g. *tan.gar* 'his son'; *uf.fāb* 'our father'.

DEMONSTRATIVE PRONOUN

in(ī) 'this'; *tar* 'that'; *man* 'that' (further away): e.g. *inī.n sibal.l.ai kis* 'because of this (with -*n* linker) I came' (*sibal.la* 'because of' (postposition)).

INTERROGATIVE PRONOUN

nai 'who?'.

RELATIVE PRONOUN

See **Verb**, below.

Numerals

1–10: *wēr, ūwo, tusko, kemso, dija, gorǰo, koloda, iduwo, oskōda, dime(r)*; 11 *dime wēra*; 12 *dimer ūwo*; 20 *aro*.
From 30 *talatīn* onwards, Arabic numerals are used. The Old Nubian forms seem to have been: 20 *ar.ūwo*; 30 *ar-tusko*; 100 *imil*.

Verb

The Nubian verb is marked for voice, tense, number, and person. Use of the personal pronouns is therefore optional. The present, the preterite, and the first future are the main flectional paradigms; other tenses and moods are indicated by the addition of affixes.

Typical stem forms are: *nadde* 'to fall', *dēn.e* 'to give', *ǰān.e* 'to buy'; *dīe* 'to die', *fīe* 'to be'. Stems in -(*k*)*kire* are causatives: e.g. *fāwire* 'to kill', *kullikire* 'to teach'.

Examples of tense formation: *fāie* 'to write': Lepsius' (1880) forms:

	Singular	*Plural*
Present indicative:		
1	fāi.r	fāi.ru
2	fāi.nam	fāi.rokom
3	fāi.n	fāi.nnan

Preterite (narrative tense):		
1	fāi.s	fāi.su
2	fāi.onam	fāi.sokom
3	fāi.on	fāi.san

First future *nīe* 'to drink':		
1	nī.dil	nī.dillu
2	nī.dinnam	nī.dillokom
3	nī.din	nī.dinnan

There are perfect and conditional forms; a second future is made by prefixing *fa-* to the present tense.

PASSIVE
This formed by inserting *-takk-* between the stem and the personal ending: e.g. *ai tokki.takk.ir* 'I am shaken' *urī fa.tōg.takk.irokom* 'you will be beaten'.

INTERROGATIVE CONJUGATION
The tense marker (*r-* present; *s-* preterite; *r-* future) + long vowel: e.g. *Ai tōg. sē* 'Did I strike?'

NEGATIVE CONJUGATION
The marker is *mun/min*, which takes personal endings, and is affixed to the stem: e.g. with present tense of *ukkire* 'to hear':

	Singular	*Plural*
1	ai ukku.m.mun	ukku.m.munu
2	ir ukki.m.minam	ukku.m.munokom
3	tar ukku.m.mun	ukku.m.minnan

The markers *dēn/dēnǰ* and *tir/tiǰǰ* are infixed in verbs which take an indirect or dative object, e.g. the Arabic loan-word *gafre* 'to forgive'. *Dēn* is used with the first person singular, *denǰ* with first person plural; *tir* with second and third singular, *tiǰǰ* with second and third plural. These markers are stems of the verbs *dēne* and *tire*, both of which mean 'to give': *ir gafra.dēn.inam* 'you (sing.) forgive me'; *gafri.takka.dēn.in* 'I am forgiven'; *ū īga.tis.su* 'we said to you/him'.

A participial form in *-i* (sing.), *-kāl-kū* (pl.) often serves as relative-clause formant: e.g. *serif wē irnyo-ī nōrin mulukkā* 'a nobleman who waited for the kingdom of God' (*irnye* 'to wait'; *nōr* 'God'; *muluk* 'kingdom' (Arabic); *serif* 'nobleman' is also an Arabic loan-word.

Postpositions

About equally divided between those following the genitive link -*n*, and those attached to the stem: e.g. with genitive case: *sibal.la* 'on account of', 'so that'; *kabire.n sibal.la* 'that ... may eat'; *lotōn* 'by', *Gatis.takk.on Iūhannā.lotōn* 'He was baptized by John.'

Word order

SOV is normal, but not obligatory.

Koyallo were dasum. Wide were artigo-Ba$\underline{2}$ don dasum. Wide were arti ter esum. In 2 were koyallo artigodon dasum. Haja male 3 tekked awtakkisum. Tenna masirgon haja wekkon awtakkikomnum awbulloton. Ted- 4 der ayar dasum. In ayarkon zolina nur ter esum. In nurkon dulumar adawen. Dulu- 5 magon tekki gebladti monsum.

Zol wer dasum. Artinaiton ishinbusum. 6 Tenn erigon Hanay esan. In tasum sheha- 7 danai, nurki shehedetirri an, tekked male amnew an. Ter nurna kid ter ekomnum. 8 Ama nurki shehedetirri an tasum.

Modern Nubian

OCCITAN

INTRODUCTION

The Occitan-speaking, or *langue d'oc*, areas of France lie to the south of a line drawn roughly from Lyon to Angoulême, and to the west of a second boundary running from Grenoble down to Nice. The many dialects, sub-dialects, and patois forming the continuum lie for the most part in peripheral bands of mutual intelligibility, and French is widely used as a supra-dialectal language of communication, and, of course, for all official purposes.

Six main dialectal divisions can be identified:

(a) Lemosin in the north-western corner of the continuum, around Limotges (Fr. Limoges) and Peirigús (Fr. Perigueux);
(b) Auvernhat (Fr. Auvergne): a north-central strip running from Clermont Ferrand down to Rodés (Fr. Rodez);
(c) Provençal Alpin: between the Middle Rhone and the Alps;
(d) Provençal: from Niça (Fr. Nice) to Nîmes and Avinhon (Fr. Avignon);
(e) Lengadocian: from Montalban southwards through Albi to Carcassona (Fr. Carcassonne) and Perpinyà (Fr. Perpignan);
(f) Gascon: occupies the south-west corner from Bordèu (Fr. Bordeaux) down to the Pyrenées. This is the most widely divergent of the six main dialects.

The daunting task of providing a literary norm with a standardized orthography, acceptable to the 2 or 3 million people who speak one or another form of Occitan (none are monoglot), has been undertaken by the Institut d'Estudis Occitans, based in Toulouse. Lengadocian has been chosen as the most appropriate base for this standard. Historically, however, by far the most important of the Occitan languages is Provençal, of which a short description now follows.

As Provence gradually succumbed to military, political, and religious pressure from northern France and Italy (Angevin dynasty from 1246 onwards), Classical Provençal fell from its mediaeval pre-eminence as the unified language of a rich culture, and degenerated into a cluster of more or less divergent dialects. Perhaps it would be more accurate to say that several dialects which had been submerged by the unified literary language, now reasserted themselves; and some of these, e.g. Gascon, were to be used for literary purposes over the next 500 years.

The dawn of a new era in the history and development of the Provençal language can be very precisely dated: on 21 May 1854, in the Castelet de Font-Ségugne, a small group of poets who were working in Avignon, launched the Félibrige – a society devoted to the promotion of Provençal language and culture. Among them was Frédéric Mistral, whose labours on the standardization of the language culminated in his great two-volume dictionary *Lou Tresor dóu Félibrige* (1876–86). The impetus provided by Mistral and his colleagues (Théodore Aubanel, Joseph Roumanille, etc.) met with wide popular support, and by the mid-twentieth century hundreds of novels, plays, poems, and farces had been written in Provençal. The language is now taught in schools in a unified form, though the orthography remains a disputed area.

SCRIPT

The Latin alphabet minus *k, w, x, y*. Grave and acute accents are used and the cedilla.

PHONOLOGY

Consonants

Consonantal inventory as in French, but *ch* = /ts/.

Vowels

    i, e, ɛ, a, ɔ, o, u, y

/u/ is notated as *ou*, /y/ as *u*.

    All vowels can be nasalized by following *-n*. The vowels thus nasalized retain their non-nasalized position: thus *en* is /ɛ̃/, not /ã/ as in French.

    /o/ is always stressed; pre- and post-tonic /o/ is [u]: *sortído* = [surtídu].

MORPHOLOGY AND SYNTAX

Noun

Nouns are masculine or feminine. *-e* is a typical masculine ending, *-o* a typical feminine. With very few exceptions, Provençal nouns have the same gender as their French counterparts. Singular and plural forms are identical.

DEFINITE ARTICLE
Masc. *lou*; fem. *la*; pl. (both genders) *li* (*lis* before vowel): e.g. *lou jouvènt* 'the young man'; *li jouvènt* 'the young people'.

INDEFINITE ARTICLE
un, uno, with a plural form *de/d'* corresponding to French *des*.

Adjective

As attribute, adjective may precede or follow noun; if it follows it is invariable. Preceding the noun, the adjective is marked for gender; fem. in *-o*. Cf. *bèu – bello* = Fr. *beau, belle*; *egau* 'equal', fem. *egalo*; *nou* 'new', fem. *novo*.

Plural adjectives in *-e* change this to *-i* before consonant-initial noun; to *-s* before a vowel: e.g. *de grandi bèsti* 'large animals'; *li bons ange* 'the good angels'; *la liuenchénco estello* 'the distant star'; pl. *li liuenchénquis estello*.

COMPARATIVE
This is made with *mai* or *plus* (pronounced /pys/).

Pronoun

There are no subject pronouns corresponding to French *je*, *tu*, etc. as the Provençal verb is conjugated without pronouns. The oblique series are:

direct object: *me*, *te*, *lou/la*; pl. *nous*, *vous*, *li/lèi* (precede verb except *lèi*);
indirect object: *iéu*, *tu*, *éu/elo*; pl. *nautre*, *vautre*, *éli* (all precede verb).

The indirect series may be used for emphasis: e.g. *iéu parle* = Fr. *moi, je parle* 'I'm speaking'.

POSSESSIVE ADJECTIVES
These are marked throughout for number and gender: 1 *moun/ma*, 2 *toun/ta*, 3 *soun/sa*, pl. 1 *noste/nosto*, 2 *voste/vosto*, 3 *soun/sa*; object both genders: sing. *mi*, *ti*, *si*; pl. *nòsti*, *vòsti*, *si*.

DEMONSTRATIVE PRONOUN
aqueste 'this', *aqueu* 'that'; both declined for gender and number.

INTERROGATIVE PRONOUN
quau 'who?', *(de)que* 'what?'

RELATIVE PRONOUN
que; *lou quau*, *la qualo*; pl. *liquau/qualo*: e.g. *Fai forço quau amo forço* 'Who loves much does much.'

Numerals

1–10: *un(o)*, *dous/dos*, *tres*, *quatre*, *cinq*, *sièis*, *sèt*, *vue*, *nòu*, *dès*; 11 *vounge*; 12 *douge*; 13 *trege*; 20 *vint*; 30 *trento*; 100 *cènt*.
   In Provençal, as in Portuguese, 'two' is marked for gender: e.g. *dous brau* 'two bulls'; *dos chato* 'two girls'.

Verb

The Provençal verb is conjugated without personal pronouns. The auxiliaries *èstre* = Fr. *être* 'be', and *avé* = Fr. *avoir* 'have', are used in the formation of compound tenses. Verbs are divided into three classes by ending: *-a*, *-i*, *-e*.
   The main parts of *èstre* are as follows (first person singular forms): present: *siéu*; imperfect: *ère*; past: *fuguère*; future: *sarai*; subjunctive present: *que fugue*; imperative: *fugues/siegues*
   Main parts of *avé* (first person singular): present: *ai*; imperfect: *aviéu*; past:

aguère; future: *aurai*; subjunctive present: *qu'ague*; imperative: *agues*.

TENSE

-*a* conjugation, *canta* 'to sing':

		Present		Past preterite
sing.	1	cante	1	cantère
	2	cantes	2	cantères
	3	canto	3	cantè
pl.	1	cantan	1	canterian
	2	cantas	2	canterias
	3	canton	3	cantèron

-*i* conjugation: the present inserts -*iss*- formant: *legisse*; past: *legiguère* (*legi* 'to read').

-*e* conjugation: present: *entènde*; past: *entendeguère* (*entèndre* 'to hear').

PARTICIPLES

Example: in -*a* conjugation: present: *cantant*; past: *canta(do)*. Agreement is not necessary: e.g. *la cansoun qu'ai cantado/canta* 'the song which I have sung'.

The passive voice is made with *èstre* + past participle: e.g. *soun estado amado* 'they (fem.) have been loved'. Choice of auxiliary verb with verb of motion appears to be optional: one can say *nòstis ami an parti*, or *soun parti* 'our friends have gone'.

The present participle is used to form the equivalent of a subordinate temporal clause: e.g.

L'ivèr **arribant**, es mestié d'acampa sis óulivo
'When winter comes, one must gather in one's olives.'

Negation

Pas follows the verb: e.g. *siéu pas riche* 'I'm not rich'. *Noun* belongs to the literary style: e.g.

Au travai qu'noun s'abrivo, es carogno touta vivo.
'He who does not throw himself into his work is dead while he's still on his feet.'

Prepositions

These are used, in general, as in French.

Word order

SVO/VSO.

Es vengu lou tèms di marcat li bèsti
'The time has come to take the animals to market.'

1. Au coumençamen èro lou Verbe e lou Verbe èro emé Diéu e èro Diéu lou Verbe.

2. Èro dins lou principe emé Diéu.

3. Tout ço qu'eisisto es esta fa pèr éu, e, de tout ço qu'es esta fa, rèn l'es esta sènso éu.

4. En éu èro la vido e la vido èro la lumiero dis ome :

5. E la lumiero dins la sournuro clarejo, em'acò la sournuro i'a rèn coumprés .

6. l'aguè 'n ome manda de Diéu, que ié disien Jan .

7. Aquéu venguè sus l'estiganço de rèndre temouniage à la lumiero, pèr que tóuti sus sa paraulo aguèsson fe.

(Provençal dialect)

OIRAT

This form of Western Mongolian is spoken by about 200,000 people in the Mongolian People's Republic and China. Some estimates put the number of Oirats as high as 250,000; uncertainty here being in part at least due to the fact that the Chinese authorities do not make any distinction between Buryats and Oirats but classify them together as 'Mongolian'.

The Kalmyk, who migrated to the west in the seventeenth century and settled on the lower Volga, formed part of the Oirat group, and the two languages are related. *See* **Kalmyk**.

The Oirats who live in the MPR use Khalkha as their written language, Oirat itself being unwritten.

OLD CHURCH
SLAVONIC

INTRODUCTION

This is the oldest attested form of Slavonic, in many ways close to Common Slavonic as reconstructed from the evidence provided by the daughter languages. It has to be distinguished from Church Slavonic, which is the liturgical language used in the Orthodox churches of the Slavonic-speaking countries. Old Church Slavonic is the language of a fairly extensive corpus of translated and original material dating from the ninth century AD (though the manuscripts which have come down to us are of slightly later date). Most of these texts are the work of the 'Slavic Apostles', the brothers Constantine and Methodius, who were active as missionaries and linguists in Moravia from 863 to 867. Their mission to Moravia was undertaken at the behest of the Byzantine Emperor Michael the Third, in answer to a request from the Moravian prince.

The language is not entirely homogeneous. Since Constantine and Methodius came from the Macedonian–Bulgarian dialect area around Thessalonika, it is not surprising to find South Slavonic features in their work. However, some of the material – manuscripts found in Kiev – shows West Slavonic characteristics, while the fragments known as the Freising texts (in Latin script) are usually claimed to be Old Slovene.

The main Old Church Slavonic texts extant are: two translations of the Gospels, the *Codex Zographensis* and the *Codex Marianus* (both in Glagolitic script); the *Psalterium Sinaiticum* (also in Glagolitic); the longest of the liturgical texts is the *Codex Suprasliensis* (in Cyrillic), an ecclesiastical calendar for the month of March, containing hagiographic material.

After the expulsion of the original Cyrillo-Methodian mission from Moravia (885), various centres using Old Church Slavonic as a literary and liturgical language were established, e.g. at Lake Ochrid and at Preslav, the Bulgarian capital. In the following centuries, a dialectal difference, already present, deepened and was polarized as Old Bulgarian and Old Macedonian.

SCRIPT

It is known that Constantine and Methodius took the necessary step of working out a suitable notation system, before setting out for Moravia. This was presumably the Glagolitic script in which the main codices were first written, though they were later transliterated into Cyrillic. The latter script seems to have been invented at the end of the ninth century or early in the tenth. Use of Glagolitic persisted in Serbia until the twelfth century, in Croatia till well into modern times. The two scripts have very largely the same inventory of letters, but four (*ja*, *je*, *ks*, *ps*) are missing in Glagolitic.

PHONOLOGY

Consonants

> stops: p, b, t, d, k, g
> affricates: ts, dz, tʃ
> fricatives: f, v, s, z, ʃ, ʒ, x
> nasals: m, n, ɲ
> lateral and flap: l, l', r, r'

/s/ and /z/ may have palatalized allophones.

Vowels

> oral: i, ɪ, ɛ, æ, y, a, ɔ, u, o
> nasal: ɛ̃, ɔ̃

/ɛ̃/ and /ɔ̃/ are notated here as *ę* and *ǫ*. *y* = Russ. ы.

The palatalized vowels /je, ję, ja, jǫ, ju/ are notated in Cyrillic, and, partly, in Glagolitic.

In the section on morphology which follows, Cyrillic hard sign ъ is transliterated as *ŭ*, the soft sign ь as '.

MORPHOLOGY AND SYNTAX

Noun

There are three genders, three numbers, and seven cases.

Specimen declensions: masc. *o*-stem, *gradu* 'city'; fem. *a*-stem, *žena* 'woman':

	Singular	*Dual*	*Plural*
nom.	grad**ŭ**	grad**a**	grad**i**
voc.	grad**e**	grad**a**	grad**i**
gen.	grad**a**	grad**u**	grad**ŭ**
dat.	grad**u**	grad**oma**	grad**omŭ**
acc.	grad**ŭ**	grad**a**	grad**y**
instr.	grad**om'**	grad**oma**	grad**y**
loc.	grad**æ**	grad**u**	grad**æxŭ**
nom.	žen**a**	žen**æ**	žen**y**
voc.	žen**o**	žen**æ**	žen**y**
gen.	žen**y**	žen**u**	žen**ŭ**
dat.	žen**æ**	žen**ama**	žen**amŭ**
acc.	žen**ǫ**	žen**æ**	žen**y**
instr.	žen**ojǫ**	žen**ama**	žen**ami**
loc.	žen**æ**	žen**u**	žen**axŭ**

The genitive–accusative is used for masculine nominals in *-u, -'*: e.g. *iskaaxǫ že isusa* 'they sought Jesus'; and as the direct object of a negated verb: e.g.

Ne minte æko pridŭ razornitŭ zakona li prorokŭ (Matthew, 5.17)

'Think not that I am come to destroy the law or the prophets'

Adjective

Hard and soft stems; definite and indefinite declensions; the definite = the indefinite declension + relevant third person pronominal forms. e.g. from *slæpu* 'blind':

	Indefinite	*Definite*
dative	slæpu;	slæpu.jemu
genitive	slæpa;	slæpa.jego

Pronoun

PERSONAL
Base forms:

	Singular	*Dual*	*Plural*
1	azŭ	væ	my
2	ty	va	vy

These are declined, *azŭ* on base *men-*; *væ* and *my* on base *na-*; e.g. from *azŭ*: gen. *mene*, dat. *m'n'æ*, instr. *mŭnojǫ*; from *my*: gen. *nasŭ*, dat. *namŭ*, instr. *nami*.

Oblique cases of the etymological third person (*j*)*i, je, ja* are used, but the nominative cases are supplied from the *tu, to, ta* or *on, ona, ono* series of demonstratives.

RELATIVE PRONOUN
This is provided by the *ji, je, ja* pronominal form plus the particle *-že*. Thus, gen. sing. masc. *jego.že*, fem. *jeję.že*; cf. (John, 11.3): *Sei jego.že l'ubiši bolitŭ* 'He whom thou lovest is sick'; *zvezda jǫže videšę na vŭstoce* 'the star which they saw in the east'.

Numerals

1 *jedinŭ/jedino/jedina*; 2 *dŭva/dŭvæ*; 3 *tr'je/tri*; 4 *četyre/četyri*; 5–10 *pęt', šest', sedm', osm', devęt', desęt'*; 11 *jedinŭ/o/a na desęt'*; 12 *dŭva/æ na desęt'*; 20 *dŭva desęti* (both components declined); 30 *trije desęte*; 40 *četyre desęte*; 100 *sŭto*.

Verb

Two major categories, with sub-divisions:

(a) present stem has *-e-* in third person singular;
(b) present stem has *-i-* in third person singular.

A third and much smaller category comprises the athematic verbs with null marker between stem and ending. Imperfective and perfective aspects. There are indicative and imperative moods; the tense structure has a present, two or three aorists, an imperfect. The imperfect is made almost solely from imperfective verbs, the aorists mostly from perfectives. There are present and past, active and passive participles.

Specimen paradigm: *nesti* 'to carry':

		Singular	Dual	Plural
present	1	nesǫ	nesevæ	nesemŭ
	2	neseši	neseta	nesete
	3	nesetŭ	nesete	nesǫtŭ
imperfect	1	nesæaxŭ	nesæxovæ	nesæaxomŭ
	2	nesæaše	nesæašeta	nesæašete
	3	nesæaše	nesæašeta	nesæaxǫ
1st aorist	1	nesoxŭ	nesoxovæ	nesoxomŭ
	2	nese	nesosta	nesoste
	3	nese	nesoste	nesošę
sigmatic aorist	1	næsŭ	næsovæ	næsomŭ
	2	nese	næsta	næste
	3	nese	næste	næsę

Imperative: sing. *nesi*; pl. *nesæte*.

Participles:

		Masculine	Feminine	Neuter
active:	present	nesy	nesǫšti	nesy
	past	nesŭ	nesŭši	nesŭ
passive:	present	nesomŭ	nesoma	nesomo
	past	nesenŭ	nesena	neseno

All participles are declined for gender, number, and case.

Future tense: as in Russian, future time may be expressed by the present tense of a perfective verb. *Načęti* 'to begin' is used to make imperfective future: e.g. *nač'nǫ pisati* 'I shall write'.

Prepositions

Prepositions govern the accusative, genitive, dative, instrumental, or locative. There is also one postposition: *radi* 'for the sake of', which takes the genitive: e.g. *Radujǫ sę vasŭ radi* 'I rejoice for your sake.'

Word order

Rather free.

Въ началѣ бѣ Слово, и Слово бѣ къ Бг҃у, и Бг҃ъ бѣ Слово.

в҃. Сей бѣ искони къ Бг҃у.

г҃. Вся тѣмъ быша, и без негѡ ничтоже бысть, еже бысть.

д҃. Въ томъ животъ бѣ, и животъ бѣ свѣтъ человѣ_кѡмъ.

е҃. И свѣтъ во тмѣ свѣ_тится, и тма егѡ не ѡбятъ.

ѕ҃. Бысть чл҃вѣкъ посланъ ѿ Бг҃а, има ему Iѡаннъ.

з҃. Сей прiйде во сви_дѣтельство, да свидѣтель_ствуетъ ѡ свѣтѣ, да вси вѣру имутъ ему.

ORIYA

INTRODUCTION

This Eastern New Indo-Aryan language is the official language of the state of Orissa, and is one of the fourteen officially recognized local languages of India. In Orissa it is spoken by between 20 and 25 million people, and there are sizable Oriya-speaking communities in Andhra Pradesh, Madhya Pradesh, and Bihar. The ethnonym is *ōḍrī*. Like Bengali and Assamese, Oriya derives via Apabhraṁsa from the Māgadhī Prakrit (*see* **Prakrit**). The earliest writings in what is identifiably Oriya date from the twelfth/thirteenth centuries. The classic work of Oriya literature is the fourteenth-century adaptation of the *Mahābhārata* by Sāralā Dās.

SCRIPT

A derivative of Brahmi; many ligatures. Sanskrit phonemes are notated in tatsamas and tadbhavas, though not realized in Oriya pronunciation.

PHONOLOGY

Consonants

The Sanskrit inventory is largely retained. The three Old Indo-Aryan sibilants are preserved in the script but reduced in pronunciation to the dental /s/, and the palatal affricates tend to be dentalized. /ṭ, ṭʰ/ are present, also /ḷ/.

Vowels

As in Bengali, the vowel inherent in the base consonant is /ɔ/. The six basic vowels are /i, e, a, ɔ, o, u/ with nasal correlatives, except /o/. The Oriya script distinguishes long and short values, but the distinction is not made in the spoken language and is non-phonemic. A kind of vowel harmony appears to operate in Oriya.

MORPHOLOGY AND SYNTAX

Noun

Natural gender is distinguished for animates, either lexically or by Sanskrit ending: e.g. *kānta* 'husband', *kāntā* 'wife'; cf. *puruṣa.loka* 'men', *strī.loka* 'women'. There are no articles.

NUMBER

Animates add *-māne* for the plural, e.g. *mantrīmāne* 'ministers', *śramikamāne* 'workers'. Non-animates add a variety of affixes, e.g. *-gurie*, *-gurika*, *-lucā*, *-taka*, e.g. *kitābagurie* 'books'. Plural is not marked if context suffices.

DECLENSION

Specimen declension of *purușa* 'man':

	Singular	*Plural*
nom.	purușa.	purușa.māne
acc./dat.	pursaku	purușa.mānanku
gen.	purușara	purușa.mānankara
instr./loc.	purușare	purușa.mānankare
abl.	purușaru	purușa.mānankaru

Examples: *Oriśāra itihāsa* 'the history of Orissa'; *ehi nagarare* 'in this town'.

Adjective

Hardly distinguished from the noun. Adjective precedes noun as attribute, and is not declined: e.g. *chota pilā* 'small boy'; *chota pilāku* 'to the small boy'.

COMPARISON

A comparative is made with *-țhāru*: e.g. *Ehi āmba sehi āmba.țhāru mițhā* 'This mango is sweeter than that mango.'

Pronoun

The basic series is: sing. 1 *mū*, 2 *tume*, 3 *se*; pl. 1 *āme*, 2 *tumemāne*, 3 *semāne*. First and second singular honorific forms are *āmhe* /aːmbhe/; *tumhe* /tumbhe/, to which *-māne* is added for the equivalent plural forms. A polite form of address is second person singular *āpaṇa*, pl. *āpaṇamāne*.

The pronouns have accusative/dative and genitive cases; e.g. the oblique base of *mū* is *mo-*: acc./dat. *mote/mate*, gen. *mo(ra)*: *mora pustaka* 'my book'; *āmha.mānaṅ.ka mitra* 'our friend'.

The third person forms are associated with the demonstrative pronoun/ adjective series: *ehi/ei/e* and *sehi/sei/se*. These are not declined when qualifying a noun: e.g. *sehi koțhāre* 'in that building', but *sethire* 'in this'; *ehigurika* 'these'.

INTERROGATIVE PRONOUN

kie (with variants) 'who?'; *ki* (with variants) 'what?'

RELATIVE PRONOUN

yāhā ... tāhā, ye/yie...se: e.g.

Yāhā yoga thāe, tāhā avaśya hue
'What is prepared by fate is bound to happen'

Kali ye āsithilā se mo bhai
'He who came yesterday is my brother'

The verb *thibā* 'to be' may also be used: e.g. *nikaṭare thibā lokamāne* 'people who were nearby', i.e. 'bystanders'.

Numerals

1–10: *eka, dui, tini, cārī, pañca, chaa, sāta, āṭha, naa, daśa*; 11 to 19 are unpredictable forms connected with the units: e.g. *egāra, bāra, tera*; 20 *korie*; 30 *triśa*; 40 *caḷiśa*; 100 *sata/sahe*.

Verb

The impersonal forms in *-ibā, -l*, and *-ā* are of great importance as they provide the bases for the tense system. The verbal noun in *-ibā* is the citation form, and has both participial and gerundial significance. It can be active or passive, and takes case endings: e.g. *karibā* 'doing': *karibāku, karibāre*, etc.: cf. *Se saudā kiṇibāku galā* 'He went to buy goods'; *Sethāku yibāku rāstā nāhī* '(There is) no way of getting there'; *Āmaku seṭhāre yibāku heba/hela* 'We have/had to go there.' In genitive case: *Māku kāndibāra dekhi ...* 'Seeing that the mother was weeping ...' See Karpushkin (1964: 101–7) for a detailed analysis of the absolute (impersonal) forms, with many excellent examples; cf. *Inrejī na jāniḷe cākiri ghaṭibā baṛa muṣkil thilā*: 'Without knowing English it was very difficult to count on getting a job'.

The imperfective gerund is in *-u/ū*, the perfective in *-i*: e.g. *eha śuni* 'having heard this'; *karū* 'doing'.

PERSONAL FORMS
Example: from *karibā* 'to do': indicative present, plain and honorific forms:

	Singular	Plural
1	mū kare	ame, āmhemāne karū
	āmhe karū	
2	tume kara	tum(h)emāne kara
	āpaṇa karanti	
3	se kare/karanti	āpaṇamāne karanti
		semāne karanti

Past tense: the personal endings are sing. 1 *-i/ū*, 2 *-u/a*, 3 *-ā/e*; pl. 1 *-ū*, 2 *-a/e*, 3 *-e*: e.g. *mū kali, tumhe kala*.

Future tense: e.g. *mū karibi, āmhe karibū, tume kariba, se karibe*. The pronoun *āpaṇa* takes plural form of verb in all tenses.

There are imperative and conditional moods. The imperative has present and future forms, the latter being identical to the indicative future forms.

Compound verbs may be (a) nominal + *karibā* 'to do', or *hebā* 'to be'; (b) participial form of sense-verb + auxiliary in finite form: *yibā* 'to go', *asibā* 'to come', *debā* 'to give', etc. These forms provide one way of expressing aspect in Oriya. Cf.

pakṣīṭi uṛi galā 'the bird flew away' (perfective)

pakṣīṭi uṛiyiba 'the bird will fly away'

pakṣīṭi uṛi yāuchi 'the bird is flying away' (imperfective)

NEGATION

nāhī follows verb: e.g. *Dāsī kichi kahipārilā nāhī* 'The serving girl could give no answer.' The imperative is negated with *nā*.

Postpositions

Some retain their original nominal, verbal, or adverbial significance. Others have become fossilized as syntactic markers without individual meaning. Most Oriya postpositions follow the genitive case: e.g. *ghara ṭhāru bāhāribā* 'to come out of the house' (*ṭhā-* 'place'); *pāhāṛa upare* 'on the mountain'.

Word order

SOV; impersonal constructions are very common.

---

୧ ଆଦ୍ୟରେ ବାକ୍ୟ ଥିଲା ବାକ୍ୟ ଈଶ୍ଵରଙ୍କର ସହିତ ଥିଲା ସେ ବାକ୍ୟ

୨ ସ୍ୱୟଂ ଈଶ୍ଵର । ସେ ଆଦ୍ୟରେ ଈଶ୍ଵରଙ୍କ ସହିତ ଥିଲା । ତାହାଙ୍କଠାରୁ

୩ ସମୁଦୟ ସୃଷ୍ଟ ହୋଇଲା ପୁଣି ତାହାଙ୍କୁ ଛଡ଼ା କୌଣସି ଏକ ସୃଷ୍ଟବସ୍ତୁ ସୃଷ୍ଟ

୪ ନୋହିଲା । ତାହାଙ୍କଠାରେ ଜୀବନଥିଲ ସେହି ଜୀବନ ମନୁଷ୍ୟର ଜ୍ୟୋତିଃ

୫ ସ୍ୱରୂପ । ଅନ୍ଧକାରରେ ସେହି ଜ୍ୟୋତିଃ ପ୍ରକାଶମାନ ହୋଇଲା ପୁଣି ଅନ୍ଧକାର ତାହାଙ୍କୁ ଗ୍ରହଣ ନ କଲା ।

୬ ଈଶ୍ଵରଠାରୁ ଯୋହନ ନାମରେ ଜଣେ ମନୁଷ୍ୟ ପେଶିତ ହୋଇଲା ।

୭ ତାଂହାର ଦ୍ୱେର ସମସ୍ତେ ଯେମନ୍ତ ବଶ୍ଵାସକରନ୍ତି ଏହି ହେତୁ ସେହି ଜ୍ୟୋତିଃ

୮ ବଷୟରେ ପ୍ରମାଣ ଦେବାକୁ ସେ ସାକ୍ଷିସ୍ୱରୂପ ହୋଇ ଆଇଲା । ସେ ଆପେ ସେହି ଜ୍ୟୋତିଃ ତାହା କୋହେ ପୁଣି ସେହି ଜ୍ୟୋତିଃର ବଷୟରେ ପ୍ରମାଣ

୯ ଦେବାକୁ ଆଇଲା ।।

OROK

See under **Nanay**.

OROMO

INTRODUCTION

Also known as Galla, this Cushitic language is spoken by around 8–10 million people over a huge area stretching from Somalia through north-eastern Ethiopia to Kenya. There are many dialects; the one described here, following Owens (1985), is the Harar dialect of Ethiopia.

SCRIPT

Both the Ethiopic syllabary and the Roman alphabet have been used to notate Oromo.

PHONOLOGY

Consonants

> stops: p, b, t, d, k, g, ʔ; glottalized p', t', k', d'
> affricates: tʃ, dʒ; glottalized tʃ'
> fricatives: f, s, z, ʃ, x, h
> nasals: m, n, ɲ
> lateral and flap: l, r
> semi-vowels: j, w

Glottalized sounds are notated here with dots.

Vowels

> long and short: i, e, a, o, u

Final vowels tend to /ʔ/.

Tones

There are two tones, high and low/normal. Tone is essentially unpredictable, but there are certain regularities; for example, verbs are low-toned: *sēn* 'enter', *ark* 'see', *dēm* 'go'. In nominals, a high tone is primarily associated with the penultimate, and hence by a rule of Oromo phonology, with the final syllable. In particular, nominals ending in a long front vowel tend to have high tone on the penultimate: e.g. *hárré* 'donkey; *ḳúmbí* 'tusk'. Citation forms vary predictably in specific contexts.

MORPHOLOGY AND SYNTAX

Noun

Nominals are marked for number, gender, and case.

GENDER

Nouns in Oromo are masculine or feminine. Certain endings appear to be gender-related, e.g. many feminine nouns end in a long front vowel. Specific affixes are available for some nouns denoting persons: cf. *obbol.esa* 'brother'; *obbol.ēttī* 'sister'.

NUMBER

Nouns are rarely marked for plurality. Nouns denoting human beings take *-ōta* or *-ani*; *ḳottū* 'farmer', pl. *ḳotōta*.

CASE

The absolute form is unmarked. Nouns ending in -V̄ take *-n* in nominative, *-nī* (masc.) and *-tī* (fem.) are added to other nouns (a short *-a* is discarded). A genitive form is made by tonal change. Owens (1985) gives the example: *jōllé'* 'children' – *xun xa jóllēɸ* 'this is the children's' (note loss of final glottal closure). This genitive form acts as base for other cases: e.g. gen. + *-(ti)ni* – instrumental, gen. + *(ti)fi* – dative.

POSSESSION

Alienable or inalienable constructions, the latter with reference to integral parts of whole, e.g. of body. The personal possessives are marked for gender: *x*-masc./*t*- fem. in first and second persons: 1 *xiyya/tiyya*, 2 *xe/te*, 3 masc. *isa*, *xasa*, fem. *isī*, *xasī*; pl. *xennya/tennya*, 2 *xēsani/tēsani*, 3 common *isāni/xasāni*: e.g. *farda.n jāla xiyya = jāla xiyya farda.n isa* 'my friend's horse'.

There is a locative form in *-tti*: e.g. *magalātti* 'at the market'.

Adjective

The Oromo adjective is marked for gender: masc. *-ā*, fem. *-ō*, *-tū*, e.g. masc. *hamā* 'bad', fem. *hamtū*; *furdā* 'fat', fem. *furdō*. A plural form may be made by reduplication, optionally accompanied by *-ō*: e.g. *dīmā* 'red', pl. *diddīmō*. As attribute, the adjective follows the noun and is in concord: cf. *ḳottū gārī* 'good farmer'; *ḳotōta gaggari* 'good farmers'.

Pronoun

Base and nominative forms:

		Singular		Plural	
		Base	Nominative	Base	Nominative
1		na	ani	nu	nu
2		si	ati	isini	isini
3	masc.	isa	innī	isāni	isāni
	fem.	isī	isī.n		

The nominative forms are used as object pronouns: e.g. *innī **na** arke* 'he saw me'.

DEMONSTRATIVE PRONOUNS
The nominative forms are *xuni/tuni* for proximate, 'this, these'; *suni* for remote, 'that, those'.

INTERROGATIVE PRONOUN
ēnyū 'who?'; *māl* 'what?'.

RELATIVE PRONOUN
The head-word is followed by the associative form of the demonstratives, *xani/ tani*: e.g. *intal.tī tan innī arke* 'the girl he saw'.

POSSESSIVE PRONOUN
The series is marked for gender throughout (*x*- masc., *t*- fem.).

Numerals

1–10: *tokko, lama, sedi', afuri, shani, jaha, torba, sadēti, sagali, xuḍani*; 11 *xuḍa tokko*; 12 *xuḍa lama*; 20 *did.dami*; 30 *sod.domi*; 40 *afur.tami*; 100 *ḍibba*.

Verb

The verb is marked for person, number (second and third persons), gender (third person), tense, and voice.
    Conjugation is simple or periphrastic. The tense markers are: past *-e*, imperfect *-a/-i*, dependent *-u*: e.g. the past tense of *bēx* 'to know':

		Singular	*Plural*
1		bēxe	bēxne
2		bēxte	bēxtani
3	masc.	bēxe	bēxani
	fem.	bēxte	

Imperfect: *bēxa, bēxta*; dependent: *bēxu, bēxtu*.

NEGATIVE
Made with prefix *hin → n* (after vowel). The first person plural form is used for all seven forms in past negative: *himbēxne* (*n → m* before *b*). The negative imperfect has the *hin-* prefix on positive dependent forms: e.g. *himbēxu, himbēxtu*, etc.

The passive infix is *-am-*: e.g. *nyāt* 'to eat' – *nyātame* 'it was eaten'.

CAUSATIVE
The marker is *-s-/-sīs-*: e.g. *ani magalā dēme* 'I went to market'; *isa.n magalā dēmsīse* 'I made him go to market'.

VERBAL NOUN
The verbal noun in *-ū, -ā* is used in the formation of compound and periphrastic tenses, with the auxiliaries *jir-* 'to exist', *ture* 'was': e.g. *innī dēmū jira* 'he is

going'; *innī dēmūti njiru* 'he is not going'; *dēmū hin.tur.re* 'he wasn't going'; *khudrā bit.ā jira* 'he is buying vegetables (*khudrā* is an Arabic loan-word).

Postpositions

Examples: *jala* 'under', *gubbā* 'above', *jiddū* 'between', *waji* 'along with': *jāla xiyya waji* 'along with my friend'.

Word order

SOV is basic.

፩፤ ዾልቀባኒ ፡ (ይ.ራ.ቲ ፡) ሰገለን ፡ ቱሬ ፡፡ ሰገሊ
ኒቢ ፡ ዋቃዮ ፡ ቢራ ፡ ቱሬ ፡፡ ዋቅኒቢ ፡ ሰገለ ፡ ቱሬ ፡፡

፪፤ ኩኒቢ ፡ ዾልቀባኒ ፡ (ይ.ራ.ቲ ፡) ዋቃዮ ፡ ቢራ ፡
ቱሬ ፡፡

፫፤ ሁንይ.ምቱ ፡ ኢ.ባቲ ፡ ተኤ ፡፡ ኢ.ባ ፡ መለ ፡
ሃኒታኔ ፡ ወይማ ፡ ከን ፡ ተኤ ፡ ሁንይ.ማኑ ፡፡

፬፤ ኢ.ባይን ፡ ፈይማኒ ፡ ቱርቲ ፡፡ ፈይማኒቢ ፡ ኢ.
ፈ ፡ ያርማ ፡ ቱርቲ ፡፡

፭፤ ኢ.ፈኒቢ ፡ ይ.ክፈን ፡ ኢ.ብሳ ፡፡ ይ.ክፈስ ፡ ኢ.ቢ
ን ፡ ሃንቢምኔ(ሃፈርጌኔ) ፡፡

፮፤ ነማኒ ፡ ቶኮ ፡ ዾራይ ፡ ሐዋቃዮ.ቲ ፡ ኤርገማ ፡፡
መቀኒስ ፡ ዮሐንቢ ፡፡

፯፤ ኩኒ ፡ ይ.ጋይፉ ፡ ይ.ፈ ፡ ኢ.ፈ ፡ ሃሙደፈ ፡፡ ሁ
ንይ.ምቱ ፡ ኢ.ባ ፡ አክ ፡ አመኑፉ ፡፡

፰፤ ኢ.ፈ ፡ ኢ.ፈኒ ፡ ማቲ ፡፡ ይ.ቢን ፡ ገሬ ፡ ኤርገማ ፡
ኢ.ፈ ፡ ሃሙይ ፡፡

OSSETE

INTRODUCTION

Ossete belongs to the North-Eastern Iranian branch of Indo-European, and is spoken at present by about half a million people in the central Caucasus (the North-Ossete Autonomous Soviet Socialist Republic and the South-Ossete Autonomous Region). Ossete is a residual language of the Scythian group of Iranian languages, brought into the Caucasus area by various Pontic tribes, including the Alans, some 2,000 years ago. There are two main dialects, Iron and Digor, the latter being the more archaic. The majority form, Iron, has provided the basis for the modern literary language, the impetus for which came very largely from Kosta Khetægkaty (1859–1906), who wrote most of his works in Russian but still ranks as the greatest Ossete poet (*Iron Fændyr*, 'The Ossete Lyre', 1899). One of the best versions of the Nart saga is preserved in Old Ossete.

SCRIPT

After various false starts using Cyrillic and Georgian letters, a definitive Cyrillic script was adopted in the mid-nineteenth century. Only one non-Cyrillic graph is used – *æ*.

PHONOLOGY

Consonants

The core of the stop system is provided by the series aspirate surd – voiced non-aspirate – ejective surd, with similar series in the affricates.

    stops: p, b, p', t, d, t', k, g, k'; q
    affricates: ts, dz, ts', tʃ, dʒ, tʃ'
    fricatives: f, v, s > ʃ, z > ʒ, x, γ
    nasals: m, n
    lateral and flap: l, r
    semi-vowels: j, w

The ejectives may be due to the influence of contiguous Caucasian languages.

Vowels

The stable vowels, /i, e, a, o, u/ are contrasted with the unstable sounds æ = /ɛ/ and /ɪ/ both of which tend to [ə].

Vocalic alternation is found, e.g. in the plural formation: *xox* 'mountain', pl. *xæxtæ*. Consonantal assimilation occurs word-internally and is notated: e.g. unvoiced to voiced, *tɪx* 'power' – *ædɪx* 'powerless'. *æ* is transcribed in this article as *ä*.

Stress

Weak; the semantic phrase is stressed rather than syllable.

MORPHOLOGY AND SYNTAX

There are no articles, but a disyllable, with stress on the second syllable in the citation form, can be made definite by transfer of stress to the first: e.g. *bälás* 'tree': *bãlas* 'the (specific) tree'.

Noun

No gender; case endings are added agglutinatively to the stem; nominative has null marker.

PLURAL
The marker is *-t(t)-*; stems ending in *-t* take *-(w)ɪ-* link: e.g. *dur* 'stone': *durtä* 'stones'; *cäst* 'eye': *cästɪtä* 'eyes'.

Specimen declension: *don* 'water, river'; pl. *dättä*:

genitive	donɪ	inessive	donɪ
dative	donän	adessive	donɪl
allative	donmä	essive	donaw
ablative	donäi	comitative	donimä

To the plural form *dättä*, the same endings are added (but allative is *dättäm*).

Adjective

As attribute, adjective precedes noun and is not declined: e.g. *bärzond urs xox* 'high white mountain', pl. *bärzond urs xäxtä*. An intensive form is made by reduplication: *urs-ursid* 'very white' (cf. Turkish *bembeyaz*).

COMPARATIVE
The form is made with *-där*: e.g. *saw* 'black', *sawdär*.

Pronoun

The full personal forms for first and second persons are: sing. 1 *äz*, 2 *dɪ*; pl. 1 *max*, 2 *smax*. These are fully declined as nominals, *äz* on the suppletive base *män-*. For the third person the demonstrative pronouns are used.

The enclitic series: these have no nominative forms as they are used only as possessive markers and in the objective case. The non-emphatic forms are: sing. *mä*, 2 *dä*, 3 *yä*; pl. 1 *nä*, 2 *wä*, 3 *sä*: e.g. *mä bäx* 'my horse', *dä činɪg* 'your book'; emphatic form: e.g. *acɪ bäx max u* 'this horse is ours'.

DEMONSTRATIVE PRONOUN/ADJECTIVE

a/ai, pl. *adon* 'this, these'; *wi*, pl. *udon* 'that, those'. These are declined in all cases. The attributive forms, *acɪ*, *ucɪ* are indeclinable.

INTERROGATIVE PRONOUN

či 'who?'; *cɪ* 'what?'.

RELATIVE PRONOUN

The interrogatives may be used with finite forms of verb, e.g. *Či cɪ agurɪ, wi ɪssarɪ* 'he who wants something will find it'. A participial construction is also possible.

Numerals

1–10: *yu, duwä, ärtä, cɪppar, fondz, äxsäz, awd, ast, farast, däs*; 11 *yuändäs*; 12 *duwadäs*; 20 *ɪssädz*. From 20 onwards two systems operate, decimal (literary) and vigesimal (everyday). Thus, 21 is either *ɪssädz yu* (demical) or *yu ämä ssädz* (vigesimal); 40 is *cɪppur* (decimal) or *duwissädzɪ* (vigesimal). 100 *sädä*.

Verb

As in Farsi, the two-base system – present and past – is fundamental. The past base is marked by the presence of *t/d* between the present base and the personal ending, and very frequently by umlaut + mutation of final consonant of present base: cf.

Present base	Past base	Present base	Past base
käs 'look'	kast	fid 'pay'	fɪst
kus 'work'	kwɪst	cär 'live'	card
zon 'know'	zɪnd	cäwu 'go'	cɪd

There are three moods: indicative, imperative, subjunctive. The indicative and the subjunctive have each three tenses: present, past, future.

TRANSITIVITY

The *a/ä* alternation distinguishes many pairs of intransitive/transitive verbs: cf. *mälɪn* 'to die', *marɪn*, 'to kill'; *täfsɪn* 'to get warm', *tavɪn* 'to heat up something'; *kälɪn* 'to run out', *kalɪn* 'to pour' (trans.).

ASPECT

Affects the formation of past and future tenses. Some formations are suppletive, e.g. *dädtɪn* 'to give' (imperf.), *radtɪn* 'to give' (perf.), but most are by prefixation. The main prefixes are: *a-, ba-, är-, ärba-, ra-, ni-, cä-, fä-, ɪs-*. Apart from marking aspect, these have a two-fold directional function, indicating (a) in what direction something is moving, and (b) how an observer is spatially located with reference to that movement (cf. **Georgian**): e.g. *a.cıd* 'he went out' (from interior space in which observer is situated), *ra.cıd* 'he went out' (into exterior space in which observer is situated). In the present tense the pre-verb becomes purely directional, descriptive of spatial locus, or modal (reiterative, semelfactive, etc.): e.g. *fäbaddzınän* 'I'll stay sitting' (*badın* 'to sit'). This sense is also achieved by reduplication: eg. *radzur.badzur-känın* 'have a long chat'.

Specimen conjugation of transitive verb: *dzurın* 'to say something': indicative:

> present: sing. 1 *dzurın*, 2 -*ıs*, 3 -*ı*; pl. 1 *dzuräm*, 2 -*ut*, 3 -*ınc*;
> past: sing. 1 *dzırd*(*t*)-*on*, 2 -*ai*, 3 -*a*; pl. 1 *dzird*(*t*)-*am*, 2 -*at*, 3 -*toi*;
> future: sing: 1 *dzurdz-ınän*, 2 -*ınä*, 3 -*än*; pl. 1 -*ıstäm*, 2 -*ıstut*, 3 -*ıstı*.

The past tense of intransitive verbs varies slightly.

There are similar sets of endings for the present and past subjunctive: e.g. *dzurin* 'that I should/might speak'; 1st p. pl. *dzurikkam*.

PARTICIPLES
Present in -*äg* (usually active); past in -*t*/-*d* (passive); future in -*inag* (active or passive): e.g. *fıssaeg* 'writing, writer'; *fıst* 'written'; *fıssinag* 'intending to write' or 'about to be written'.

PASSIVE VOICE
Participle + *cäwın* 'to go', as auxiliary, e.g. *ävdisın* 'to show' – *ävdıst cäwın* 'to be shown'.

NEGATION
nä is the all-purpose negative particle for the indicative mood: *wi män nä zonı* 'he doesn't know me'. Imperative negative with *ma*.

COPULA
Sing. 1 *dän*, 2 *dä*, 3 *u*/*w*; pl. 1 *stäm*, 2 *stut*, 3 *stı*: e.g. *max lägtä stäm* 'we are men'.

Postpositions

A number of nouns are used as postpositions, e.g. *sär* 'head': *stolı sär* 'on the table'. Nearly all postpositions follow the genitive case, and can be declined: e.g. *bälası bın* 'under the tree'; *bälası bınäi* 'from under the tree'.

Word order

SOV is normal.

1. Фуᴅᴅагæj ỹді Дурᴅ, æмæ Дурᴅ ỹді Хуцаỹмæ,
2. æмæ Дурᴅ ỹді Хуцаỹ. Ỹj ỹді Фуᴅᴅагæj Ху-
3. цаỹмæ. Jỹỹлдæр Ỹмæj сусту, æмæ æнæ Ỹj онун
4. ніцу рајдуᴅта, цу сусту ỹдонæj. Ỹмæ ỹді цард,
5. æмæ цард ỹді адæму рӯхс. Æмæ рӯхс ꚉалунᴅу
6. рӯхсꚉæну; æмæ іл ꚉалунг нæ æрбаꚉухсті. Ху-
7. цаỹæj æрвуст лæг ỹді, jæ ном Іоанне. Ỹj æрцу-
   ді æвдісæнᴅінаᴅу ꚉуххæj, цæмæj æвдісæнлæỹỹа
8. рӯхсу ꚉуххæj, цæмæj æпꚉбæꚉу баỹрна ỹмæj. Ỹj
   рӯхс нæ ỹді, фæлæ æрвуст ỹді, цæмæj æвдісæнлæỹỹа рӯхсу ꚉуххæj.

OTOMANGUEAN LANGUAGES

In terms of its territory, this group of Mesoamerican languages is very small, being restricted to the Oaxaca area of Mexico. Demographically, however, it outstrips far more extensive groupings such as Ge-Pano-Carib. Three of its languages – Otomi, Mixtec, and Zapotec – are each spoken by at least a quarter of a million people. Like the Na-Dené family (*see* **Na-Dené languages**) the Otomanguean languages have a very specific genetic profile, which seems to have little in common with the great majority of American Indian languages. The Otomanguean proto-language has been very exhaustively reconstructed (Rensch 1973: 76, 77). According to Rensch, this proto-language had no labials or voiced stops; /t, k, k°/ were present, along with /s, n, j, w, h/ and the glottal stop, with three vowels /e, a, u/. It had four tones.

All Otomanguean languages have tones, both level and glides. In many members of the family, nasalization plays a phonemic role.

See **Mixtec**, **Zapotec**.

PALAEO-SIBERIAN LANGUAGES

This heading designates (a) a group of five genetically related languages – the Chukotko-Kamchatkan family, comprising Chukchi, Koryak, Itelmen, Alyutor, and Kerek – and (b) three singletons which have no genetic connection and do not share typological features either with the Chukotko-Kamchatkan family, or with each other: these are Nivkh (or Gilyak), Ket, and Yukagir.

The Palaeo-Siberian languages do not even form a coherent geographical unit; the Chukotko-Kamchatkan languages are spoken in a strip of territory 1,000 miles long, stretching from the Bering Straits down to the tip of Kamchatka; Nivkh is spoken on Sakhalin Island and the adjacent coastal strip, Yukagir in two tiny enclaves far to the north, between the Yanskiy Zaliv and the Kolym area, and Ket a couple of thousand miles to the west, on the middle Yenisei. In other words, the grouping lumps together languages which do not fit in anywhere else.

The designation 'Palaeo-Siberian', however, is apt, as some of these languages, e.g. Yukagir and Ket, are clearly residual members of families which were formerly larger and far more widely distributed. Only Nivkh seems to be a true isolate. About 20,000 people speak Palaeo-Siberian languages.

See **Chukchi**, **Itelmen**, **Ket**, **Koryak**, **Nivkh**, **Yukagir**.

PALAUNG

INTRODUCTION

This Mon-Khmer language is spoken by about 150,000 people in the Shan State of Burma.

PHONOLOGY

Consonants

> stops: p, b, t, d, k, g; aspirates: p', t', k'
> affricates: tʃ/tʃ', dʒ
> fricatives: f, v; s, s', z, ʃ, x, h
> nasals: m, n, ɲ, ŋ
> lateral: l
> flap: r
> semi-vowels: j, w

As final, /r/ → [rr]; final /k, p, t/ → ∅.

Vowels

> long and short: a, ʌ, ɛ, e, ɪ, i, o, ɔ, u, œ, y, au, ai

h + C is characteristic: e.g. *hl, hm, hn, hr, hw*. /œ/ is notated here as *ö*; /y/ as *ü*.

MORPHOLOGY AND SYNTAX

Noun

Two numbers, singular and plural. The plural marker is *gē*, unless a numeral or other distinguishing item is present: e.g. *s'or* 'mountain', *s'or gē*.

Where necessary, gender may be indicated by such lexical items as *ī-mē* 'male', *ī-pạn* 'female': e.g. *vā ī-mē* 'younger brother', *vā ī-pạn* 'younger sister'.

The Palaung noun is not inflected in any way. Possession is denoted by apposition, possessed preceding possessor: e.g. *ō-yīn mā ɔ* 'my mother's garden' (*mā* 'mother'; *ɔ* 'I').

Adjective

As attribute, adjective follows noun: e.g. *jāng jār* 'high tower'; *gāng tā s'ạ-t'ē* 'the house of the rich old man' (*tā* 'old man').

Pronoun

Sing. 1 *ɔ*, 2 *mī*, 3 *ạn*; pl. 1 *yɛ̄*, 2 *pɛ̄*, 3 *gɛ̄*. Dual forms: *āī* is used for dual involving 1st person; *gār/pār* are used for various combinations of second and third persons. The numeral *ār* 'two' seems to underlie these forms.

The same forms are used for the possessive pronouns, with *hā* as linking element (*hā* is often omitted): *mā ɔ* 'my mother'; *mā ạn* 'his/her/its mother'.

Once pronominal deixis has been established, it can be resumed and copied by *dē* 'self': e.g. *ạn dāh ta p'ŏm dē* 'he said in his heart' (*dāh* 'say'; *ta* 'in').

The pronominal subject forms are also used as object: e.g. *kwɔn rạk ɔ* 'the child loves me'.

DEMONSTRATIVE PRONOUN
(*i*)*ŏ* 'this'; (*i*)*tāī* 'that'; (*i*)*dīn* 'that yonder'.

INTERROGATIVE PRONOUN
a-s'ē, 'who'; *s'ī* 'what?'.

Numerals

1–10: *ū/hlēh, ār, u-āī, p'ōn, p'ạn, tɔr, pūr, tā, t'īm, kŏr*. 11 *kŏr na ū*; 12 *kŏr na ār*; 20 *ār kŏr*; 100 *ū pạ-ri-āh*.

The numeral may precede or follow noun; there is a large number of numerical classifiers; e.g. *ngyāng* (with allophones) for long objects; *kɔn* for certain parts of the body; *pŏn* for skins, books, blankets, etc.

Verb

Neutral as to voice, mood, tense, person, and number. The stem is also the imperative: *lɔh* 'to go; go!' The stem without marker is also the present tense: *ɔ lɔh* 'I go'. The past marker is *hwɔ-i: ɔ hwɔ-i lɔh* 'I went'. Future: *c'ạng, dī*, etc.: e.g. *A-hnạp yɛ̄ dī lɔh hyạng mŭk* 'Tomorrow (*a-hnạp*) we shall go to herd (*hyạng*) cattle.'

MODAL AUXILIARIES
bɛ/pēn 'can'; *bạp/bŏn* 'must', *lō* 'want': e.g. *ɔ bɛ̄ ɔ rŏr = ɔ pēn ɔ rŏr* 'I can work'.

NEGATIVE
The general negative particle is *ka/kɔ*: *ɔ ka lɔh* 'I'm not going'; *māī* negates the imperative: e.g. *mī māī grāī ta ɔ* 'don't speak to me'.

Prepositions

Example: *ta* 'in, at, to' (as indirect object marker): (*Ạn*) *vēng rɔt ta vāng hɔ-k'ạm* 'He went back and arrived in/at the court of the king'; *hɔ-k'ạm dāh ta nāng* 'the king said to the lady'.

Word order

SVO.

PALI

INTRODUCTION

As the only Middle Indo-Aryan language to become the vehicle of a major religion and culture, whose influence and distribution are now global, Pali is by far the most important of the Prakrits (*see* **Prakrit**).

Gautama Buddha (sixth to fifth century BC) seems to have preached in an eastern form of Middle Indo-Aryan, perhaps Ardhamāgadhī, and it is likely that the original codification of his teachings and mission – at the First Council, held about a hundred years after his death – was in the same language. This original version is lost. The canon as it now stands was codified in the early centuries AD, and is in a western form of Middle Indo-Aryan, though it contains many eastern features.

The main body of the canon is known as the *Tipitaka* 'the Three Baskets' (the first Basket contains rules of conduct, the second sermons, the third philosophical theses). The Pali described here is that of the second pitaka. 'Dh.' following an example indicates that it is taken from the Dhammapada.

SCRIPT

Originally written in Brahmi, Pali came to be notated in the various national scripts of the southern Indian and south-east Asian countries where Buddhism took root: Sinhalese, Burmese, Thai, Cambodian, Cham, and Lao. It can also be written in the romanization used here.

PHONOLOGY

Consonants

Labial, dental, retroflex, palatal, and velar series as in Sanskrit (*see* **Sanskrit** for tabulation)

Vowels

  i, iː, eː, a, aː, o, u, uː

Principles of vowel gradation are as in Sanskrit. The syllabic liquids /r/ and /l/ are missing in Pali.

Though the phonological inventories of Sanskrit and Pali are very close to each other, the phonological complexity of the former is greatly reduced in Pali. Consonantal clusters tend to be reduced to a single or geminated member: e.g. Skt *kṣatriyaḥ* 'warrior' = Pali *khattiyo*; *putraḥ* 'son' = *putto*; *mārgaḥ* 'way' = *maggo*; *bahuvrīhi* 'having much rice' = *bahubbīhi*.

SANDHI

Essentially as in Sanskrit: cf. *kaṭṭha + udakam → kaṭṭhodakam*; *su + ākāre →
svākāre*; *kusalaṃ + ti → kusalanti*; *ha + eva → heva*.

MORPHOLOGY AND SYNTAX

Noun

Pali has three genders (masculine, feminine, neuter), two numbers (singular, plural), and eight cases. There follow specimen declensions of a masculine *a*-stem and a feminine *ī*-stem:

	Singular	Plural	Singular	Plural
nominative	purisa 'man'	purisā	nadī 'river'	nadiyo
accusative	purisaṃ	purise	nadiṃ	nadiyo
instrumental	purisena	purisehi	nadiyā	nadīhi
genitive	purisassa	purisānaṃ	nadiyā	nadīnaṃ
dative (usually equals genitive, but see note following paradigm)				
ablative	purisā	purisehi	nadiyā	nadīhi
locative	purise	purisesu	nadiyā	nadīsu
vocative	purisa	—	—	—

Masculine and neuter nouns in *-a* have a specific dative form in *-āya*, which implies purpose: *gāmaṃ piṇḍāya pāvisi* 'he entered the village (*gāma*) for alms (*piṇḍa*)'.

Examples of case usage:

nominative: *Gotama āgacchati* 'Gautama approaches';
accusative: *so dhammaṃ deseti* 'he teaches the dharma', *imaṃ lokaṃ āgantvā* 'coming into this world';
instrumental: *khattiyo jātiyā ahosi* 'he was a kṣatriya by birth';
genitive: *tathāgatassa parinibbānaṃ* 'the Tathāgata's attainment of Nirvana';
ablative: *pāpā cittaṃ nivāraye* 'let him restrain his mind from evil' (Dh. 116);
locative: *evaṃ gāme munī care* 'so let the wise man dwell in his village' (Dh. 49).

Adjective

As attribute, adjective usually precedes noun; if there is a string of adjectives the sequence may be split, one preceding, the rest following: e.g. *Evaṃ subhāvitaṃ cittaṃ rāgo na samativijjhati* 'Even so, passion does not invade a well-ordered mind.'

Pronoun

The personal pronouns are: sing. 1 *ahaṃ*, 2 *tvaṃ*, 3 masc. *so*, fem. *sā*; pl. 1 *mayaṃ*, 2 *tumhe*, 3 *te*/*tā*. These are declined in seven cases. The first person stem for oblique cases is *ma(d)-*, and second and third, *ta(d)-*.

DEMONSTRATIVE PRONOUN
Masc./fem. *ayaṃ*; neuter: *idaṃ*; pl. *ime- – imā – imāni*. These are declined.

INTERROGATIVE PRONOUN
ko – kā – kiṃ 'who? – what? – which?'; declined.

RELATIVE PRONOUN
The stem is *yad*: masc. *yo*, fem. *yā*, nt. *yaṃ*/*yad*; pl. *ye – yā – yāni*, resumed by personal pronoun: e.g.

> **Yo** ca ... sīlesu susamāhito ... **sa** ve kāsāvam arahati
> 'He who is ... grounded in all virtues, he is worthy of the yellow robe' (Dh. 10)
>
> **Yo** mukhasannato bhikkhu ... madhuraṃ **tassa** bhāsitam
> 'The monk who controls his tongue, his utterance is sweet' (Dh. 363)

Numerals

1–10: the base forms are *eka, dve/dvi, ti, catur, pañca, cha(ḷ), satta, aṭṭha, nava, dasa*; 11 *ekādasa*; 12 *dvādasa*: 13 *teḷasa*: 20 *vīsati*: 30 *tiṃsa*: 40 *cattārīsa*; 100 *sataṃ*.

Inflection of these varies: *eka* behaves largely like the relative pronoun; *ti* is marked for gender and behaves like an adjective; *dve* and all numerals from 5 to 18 inclusive are used as adjectives and have one set of inflections for all three genders. Of the decades, some are feminine singular (e.g. *vīsata*), others (e.g. *tiṃsa*) are neuter singular.

Verb

The verb has finite and non-finite forms, and is marked for aspect, voice, mood, tense, number, person; partially for gender (e.g. in participal forms).

Aspect can be expressed periphrastically by means of auxiliaries. Voice is as in Sanskrit: *parassapada* (Skt *parasmaipada*), active forms, are contrasted with *attanopada* (Skt *ātmanepada*) middle forms, the latter being much less frequent than they are in Sanskrit.

Ten conjugations are distinguished, including a denominative, an intensive, and a desiderative. Examples of third person singular formation from root follows:

I	the root is strengthened to guṇa grade: e.g. *bhū – bhavati* 'to be';
II	root + nasal + *-a-*: e.g. *bhuj – bhuñjati* 'to eat'; *muc – muñcati* 'to become free';
III	root + *-ya-*: e.g. *man – maññati* 'to think'; *jan – jayati* 'to be born';
IV	root + *-ṇo-*; only one stem in use: e.g. *su – suṇoti* 'to hear';
V	root + *-na-*: e.g. *ji – jinati* 'to win'; *ki – kiṇati* 'to buy';
VI	root + *-o-*: e.g. *kar – karoti* 'to do'; *sak(k) – sak(k)oti* 'to be able';
VII	root is strengthened to guṇa/vuddhi grade + *-e-*: e.g. *kam – kāmeti* 'to love';
VIII	denominative: as VII, e.g. *sukha – sukheti* 'to be happy'.

Intensive conjugation: reduplication of root; desiderative conjugation: partial reduplication + *-sa-*, e.g. *man-* 'to think' – *vimaṃsati* 'to desire to think out/through'.

TENSE SYSTEM
In the present tense, the personal endings are: sing. 1 *-mi*, 2 *-si*, 3 *-ti*; pl. 1 *-ma*, 2 *-tha*, 3 *-nti*: e.g.

> Idha socati, pecca socati, pāpakāri ubhayattha socati
> 'The evil-doer sorrows in this world and in the next, he sorrows in both'
> (Dh. 15)

Future tense: the same inflections are added to the strengthened root + *-iss/ess-*: e.g. *labhissāmi* 'I will get'; *bhavissanti* 'they will be'. Aorist tense: specific set of personal endings added to root, perhaps with augment: e.g. from *bhās* 'say, speak'; *abhāsi* 'he spoke'; or, *-s-* added to VII conjugation present stem in *-e*: *kath* 'to relate' – *kathesi*.

PARTICIPIAL FORMS
Past: *-(i)ta* added to root which may be modified, e.g. *gam* 'to go': *gata – tathā.gata* 'thus-gone' (epithet of the Buddha); *bandh* 'to bind' – *baddha* 'bound'; *chid* 'to cut' *chinna* 'cut'; *dā* 'give' – *dinna*. This is formally the passive past participle (in contrast to the active past participle in *-tavant*) but it often functions as active, especially in the case of intransitive verbs. There is also a future passive participle.

GERUND
Formed from stem + *-(i)tvā* with variants, and indeclinable: e.g. *upasaṃkamitvā* 'having approached'; *chinditvā* 'having cut'. The gerund is very extensively used as a holding device in a series of narrative clauses, the finite verb being reserved to close the principal clause: ... *upasaṃkamitvā ... pavisitvā ... abhivādetvā ... vatvā ... gata* 'having approached ... having entered ... having greeted ... having said ... he went'.

AUXILIARY VERBS
as and *bhū*: *as* is extremely irregular.

PASSIVE SENTENCES
With past participle, subject in instrumental: e.g. *evaṃ me sutaṃ* 'thus by-me was-heard'.

Word formation

Compound formation as in Sanskrit:

> *Tappurisa* (Skt *tatpuruṣa*): the components may stand in any case relation-
> ship to each other; AB, where A limits B, e.g. *rājaputto* 'king's son';
> *candaggāho* 'eclipse of the moon'; *kittisado* 'word of praise'.
> *Kammadhāraya*: AB in apposition, e.g. *dhammāudhamma* 'the Dharma
> and all that appertains to it'.
> *Bahubbīhi*: adjectival compound, often equivalent to relative clause, e.g.
> *bahubbīhi (deso)* '(a country) having much rice' = 'a prosperous
> country'; *chinnapapañca (Buddho)* 'Buddha, who has cut through
> obstacles'.

Word order

SOV is normal.

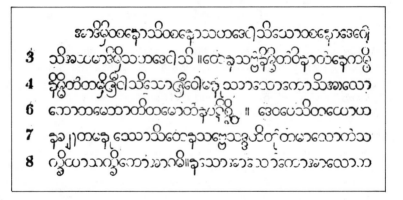

PAMIR LANGUAGES

INTRODUCTION

This group of Eastern Iranian languages comprises the following homogeneous dialect complexes: (1) Shughn-Roshan; (2) Yazgulyam; (3) Vakh; (4) Ishkashim; (5) Mundzi. All are unwritten.

Shughn-Roshan and Yazgulyam are spoken in the Pyandž River valley and in contiguous areas of the Gorno-Badakhshan Autonomous Region in Tadzhikistan. Shughn-Roshan dialects spread into Afghanistan, where Ishkashim is spoken by about 2,000 people. Most speakers of Vakh also live in Afghanistan. There are two outliers: Sarikoli, a member of the Shughn-Roshan sub-group, is spoken by a small number of people in Xīnjiāng in China; Mundži by a few hundred in Afghan Badakhshan. About 60,000 people speak Pamir languages, with Shughn-Roshan accounting for at least half of this total.

For a short account of the phonology and morphology of a Pamir language, *see* **Shughn-Roshan**.

Two other members of the group may be briefly mentioned.

YAZGULYAM

PHONOLOGY

The Shughn-Roshan phonological inventory is extended by a labialized series: /k°, g°, q°, x°, χ°, γ°/, + palatalized /k'/ and /gθ/.

Vowel alternation is frequent in plural formation: e.g. *kŭd* 'house', pl. *kadaθ*. There are several plural markers, e.g. *-aθ, -en, -ežg*.

MORPHOLOGY AND SYNTAX

Pronoun

Sing. 1 *az*, 2 *tow*, 3 *u/āy*, with oblique forms which are marked for gender in the third person: masc. *way/day*; fem. *im/dim*. The oblique form of the first person singular is *mŭn*. The plural forms, 1 *mox*, 2 *təmox*, 3 *(d)if*, are both nominative and oblique.

Verb

Two-base system + movable particles (*see* **Shughn-Roshan**). The particles are: sing. 1 *-əm*, 2 *-at*, 3 *-(ay)*; pl. 1 *-an*, 2 *-əf*, 3 *-an* for intransitive, *-əf* for transitive: e.g. *az.əm šod* 'I went'; *mox.an šod* 'we went'; *əm-zext* 'I took'; *-an zext* 'we took'.

In the transitive past tense, the subject is in oblique case, the object has an accusative marker *ž-/š-*: e.g. *mŭn ž-im wint* 'I saw her'.

ISHKASHIM

PHONOLOGY

The Shughn-Roshan phonological inventory is extended by a retroflex series: ṭ, ḍ, ṭṣ, ṣ, ẓ, ḷ.

MORPHOLOGY AND SYNTAX

The general plural marker is *-o*; kinship terms have a specific plural formant in *-(g)ən*: e.g. *štok* 'girl', pl. *štokən*. Use of the objective marker *-(y)i* is optional.

Pronoun

Sing. 1 nominative *az*, oblique *mak*; 2 *tə, fak*.

Verb

The personal endings are: sing. 1 *-əm*, 2 *-i*, 3 *-u*; pl. 1 *-on*, 2 *-əv*, 3 *-on*. The movable particles (*see* **Shughn-Roshan**) are identical.

TENSE SYSTEM

Two-base + perfect: e.g. present *γažəm* 'I speak'; past *γaždəm*; perfect *γaždŭkəm*. Compound tenses + *wəd*: e.g. pluperfect *γaždŭkəm wəd*, pl. *γaždŭkon wəd*.

Both prepositions and postpositions are used.

PANJABI

INTRODUCTION

Panjabi is the most important of the North-Western group of New Indo-Aryan languages. It is the official language of the Indian state of Panjab, and the major language in the Panjabi province of Pakistan. Estimates of the total number of Panjabi speakers vary from 40 to 70 million. It may be taken that the higher figure includes the estimated 20 million speakers of the closely related and contiguous language Lahnda (*see* **Lahnda**). No statistics appear to be available for the number of Panjabi speakers in Pakistan.

On the religious and cultural plane, the language has a very special significance for the Sikhs, whose holy book, the Adi Granth, is the oldest text in the Gurmukhi script (1604). The word *Gurmukhi* means 'from the mouth of the guru'. There is a considerable body of mediaeval literature, but, in general, Panjabi had to wait until the late nineteenth century before it stood much chance of competing with Urdu as a medium for literature. Today, the language is the natural medium in the state of Panjab for education, the media, and a large and flourishing literature.

The colloquial language falls into three fairly well-defined groupings:

(a) Central: the Mājhī (Amritsar/Lahore) dialect which provides the basis for the literary language;
(b) the Ḍōgrī group in northern Panjab;
(c) the more markedly divergent western dialects which gradually merge into Lahndā.

SCRIPT

The Gurmukhi script is derived from Brahmi, and is set out in the same arrangement as the Devanagari. The vowel inherent in the base form of the consonant is short *a*. Other vowel signs are added as in Devanagari.

Tone

Three tones are distinguished; the even tone is unmarked, the other two are indicated in the script as follows: the letter *h*, or a voiced aspirate, signals a low tone on the following vowel; the *h* is mute, the aspirate is devoiced, e.g. script form *ghoṛā* 'horse', realized as /kòṛaː/. The same signals following a vowel mark it as high, e.g. script form *cah* 'tea', realized as /cá/.

PHONOLOGY

Consonants

> stops: p, b, t, d, ṭ, ḍ, k, g; with aspirated surds ph, th, ṭh, kh
> affricates: tʃ, tʃh, dʒ
> fricatives: f/v, s, ʃ, z, x, h
> nasals: m, n, ṇ, ɲ, ŋ
> lateral and flap: l, ḷ, r, ṛ
> semi-vowels: j, w

The voiced aspirates *bh*, *dh*, etc. do not figure in the phonological inventory though they occur in the script, e.g. as tone markers (see above). /dʒ/ is represented here as *ǰ*.

Vowels

> short: ɪ, ə, u
> long: i, e, ɛ, a, ɔ, u

In this article, /ɪ/ is represented by *i*, /ə/ by *a*, and /ŭ/ by *w*. All vowels have nasalized allophones.

Stress

Stress is a function of the qualitative/quantitative distribution of vowels.

MORPHOLOGY AND SYNTAX

Noun

Two grammatical genders, masculine and feminine. Typical masculine endings are *-ā*, *-ã̄*: *kamrā* 'room'. Most nouns in *-ī* are feminine: e.g. *roṭī* 'bread'. The gender of inanimates is not always stable.

NUMBER
Masculine nouns ending in a consonant remain unchanged; those in *-ā* change this to *-e*: e.g. *ghoṛā – ghoṛe*. Typically, feminine nouns in *-ī* add *-ã̄*: e.g. *billī* 'cat' – *billīã̄*.

DECLENSION
Analytic. Postpositions are added to the oblique base of the noun, which is, e.g., *-e/-ē* for masculines in *-ā/-ã̄*. Feminine nouns and all masculines with consonantal final remain unchanged for oblique case.

Plural oblique forms: *-iã̄* for masculines in *-ā/-ã̄*; *-ã̄* for most other masculine and feminine nouns alike. Examples of these forms: *mwṇḍā* (masc.) 'boy': *mwṇḍe nū* 'to the boy, the boy (acc.)', *mwṇḍiã̄ nū* 'to the boys, the boys (acc.)'; *kwrsī* 'chair': *kwrsiã̄ ute* 'on the chairs'.

Genitive: the affix is *dā* following the oblique case; the affix *dā* is in concord for gender, number, and case with the possessed object: e.g. *mwṇḍe dā ghoṛā* 'the boy's horse'; ***mwṇḍe de ghoṛe*** 'the boy's horses'; *mwṇḍe diā̃ ghoṛiā̃ nū* 'to the boy's horses'.

Other case markers are: *nū*, dat./acc.; *ne*, agentive; *to*, ablative; *(u)te*, locative.

Adjective

Adjectives ending in *-ā* are declined like nouns in *-ā*: e.g. *navā* 'new': *nave ghar dā* 'of a new house'. Adjectives ending in a consonant, e.g. *lāl* 'red', are indeclinable.

COMPARISON
A comparative is made by adding *-erā* to the base: e.g. *vaḍḍā* 'big' – *vaḍḍerā*. If the adjective ends in *-ṛā*, the retroflex *ṛ* is transferred to the affix: *-eṛā*.

Pronoun

PERSONAL
The direct personal forms are:

	Singular	Plural
1	/mɛ̃/	asiŋ
2	tū; āp	twsiŋ

The oblique forms are *mɛ̃, tɛ̃, asā̃, twsā̃*.

The third person forms are supplied from the demonstrative series.

POSSESSIVE PRONOUNS
merā 'my', *terā* 'thy', *sāḍā* 'our', *twāḍā* 'your': declined as adjective.

DEMONSTRATIVE PRONOUN
There are several sets, with two degrees, proximate and less proximate: the opposition *e/o* is basic.

INTERROGATIVE PRONOUN
/kɔŋ/ 'who?'; *kī* 'what?'

RELATIVE PRONOUN
jo + correlative *wh*, etc. in principal clause: e.g. *Mɛ̃ jo/jeṛā nāval kharīdiā wh chetī gwmm ho giā* 'The novel which I bought soon went lost.'

Numerals

1–10: *ikk, do, tinn, cār, panĵ, che, satt, aṭṭh, nɔ̃, das*; from 11 to 99 the forms are unpredictable. As in several other New Indo-Aryan languages, decade + 9 is based on following decade: e.g. 30 is *tīh*, 38 is *aṭṭhī*, but 39 is *wntālī*, anticipating *cālī* '40'. Similarly, 49 is *wnanĵā*; 50 *panĵāh*; 100 /sɔ/.

Verb

The infinitive ending is *-ṇā/-nā*: e.g. *jǎṇā* 'to go', *laṛnā* 'to fight'.

SIMPLE (SYNTHETIC) FORMS
These are limited in Panjabi to the imperative: e.g. *kar/karo* 'go' (familiar); with more formal requests expressed by the endings *-ī/-īo*: e.g. *twsiŋ bēṭhīo* 'please sit'. The subjunctive: *mɛ̃ karǎ, tū karē*, etc.; and the simple future: *-gā, gi*, pl. *ge, gīǎ* added to the subjunctive: e.g. *mɛ̃ karǎ.gā*.

COMPOUND TENSES
These are made by combining the imperfective participle in *-dā*, and the perfective participle in *-iā* of the sense-verb, marked for gender and number, with the copula *hoṇā*: e.g.

> with the imperfective participle: present indicative: *mɛ̃ bēṭhdā/dī hǎ̃* 'I (masc./fem.) am sitting'; pl. *asiŋ bēṭhde/dīǎ̃ hǎ̃* 'we (masc./fem.) are sitting';
> with the perfective participle: perfect: *mɛ̃ bēṭhiā/ī hǎ̃* 'I (have) sat'.

In all tenses formed with the perfective participle, the logical subject of a transitive verb is in the oblique form followed by the postposition *ne*. The participle shows gender and number concord with the object, the verb is in third person: e.g. *Tobi ne kapṛe toe* 'The washerman washed the clothes.'
There are suppositive, subjunctive, and conditional moods, all made from the participles plus auxiliaries.

PASSIVE VOICE
A specific participle in *-īdā* can be used; or an analytical form, the perfective participle of a transitive verb + *jǎṇā* 'to go': e.g. *Pāṇī mwṇḍe to pītā jāndā hɛ* 'Water is drunk by the boy' (*pāṇī* is masc.). A two-fold gradation in ending turns intransitives into transitives, and thence into causatives: e.g. *dekhṇā* 'to see', *dikhāuṇā* 'to show', *dikhvāuṇa* 'to cause to be shown'.
Various verbs are used as auxiliaries to generate aspectual and modal nuances – inceptive, reiterative, intensive, terminative, etc.: e.g. *bannh rakhiṇā* 'to bind strongly'; *dass uṭṭhṇā* 'to start speaking'.

Postpositions

Dā, nū, and *ne* have already been mentioned. There are many more.

Word order

SOV is normal; indirect object precedes direct.

ਪਿਰਥਮੇ ਬਚਨ ਸਾ; ਅਰ ਬਚਨ ਪਰਮੇਸੁਰ ਦੇ ਸੰਗ ਸਾ; ਅਰ ਕਾਂਡ

ਬਚਨ ਪਰਮੇਸੁਰ ਸਾ। ਇਹੋ ਪਿਰਥਮੇ ਪਰਮੇਸੁਰ ਦੇ ਸੰਗ ਸਾ। ੨

ਸਭ ਕੁਛ ਉਸ ਤੇ ਰਚਿਆ ਗਿਆ; ਅਤੇ ਰਚਨਾ ਵਿੱਚੋਂ ਇੱਕ ੩

ਵਸਤੁ ਉਸ ਤੇ ਬਿਨਾ ਨਹੀਂ ਰਚੀ ਗਈ। ਉਸ ਵਿੱਚ ਜੀਉਣ ਸਾ; ੪

ਅਰ ਉਹ ਜੀਉਣ ਮਨੁੱਖਾਂ ਦਾ ਚਾਨਣ ਸਾ। ਅਤੇ ਉਹ ਚਾਨਣ ੫

ਅਨੇਰੇ ਵਿਖੇ ਚਮਕਿਆ; ਪਰ ਅਨੇਰੇ ਨੈ ਤਿਸ ਨੂੰ ਕਬੂਲ ਨਾ

ਕੀਤਾ।   ਪਰਮੇਸੁਰ ਦੀ ਵਲੋਂ ਜੂਹੰਨਾ ਨਾਮੇ ਇੱਕ ਮਨੁੱਖ ੬

ਭੇਜਿਆ ਹੋਇਆ ਸਾ। ਉਹ ਸਾਖੀ ਨੂੰ ਆਇਆ, ਜੋ ਚਾਨਣ ੭

ਉੱਪਰ ਸਾਖੀ ਦੇਵੇ; ਤਾਂ ਸਭ ਲੋਕ ਉਸ ਦੇ ਵਸੀਲੇ ਤੇ ਪਤੀਜਨ।

ਸੋ ਆਪੇ ਉਹ ਚਾਨਣ ਨਹੀਂ ਸਾ; ਪਰ ਉਸ ਚਾਨਣ ਦੀ ਉਗਾਹੀ ੮

ਦੇਣ ਆਇਆ ਸਾ।

PAPUAN LANGUAGES

INTRODUCTION

This term refers to the non-Polynesian and non-Melanesian languages spoken in Papua New Guinea and some neighbouring islands: i.e. the term is exclusive, and does not refer to a homogeneous 'family' or related group of languages. The term also covers the languages of the Bismarck Archipelago, New Britain, and some of the Solomon Islands, especially Bougainville. The total number of languages covered by the heading is probably close to a thousand, with a total number of speakers estimated at about 2½ million, of which more than 1½ million are in Papua New Guinea. The languages are not entirely hetero-geneous. From 60 to 100 small groupings can be identified, each grouping comprising anything from a couple to a few dozen languages showing certain common features, and each such language being spoken by a small or very small number of people. A few groupings, however, comprise some dozens of languages, each of which is spoken by 100,000 or more. It is a linguistic situation in which pidgins were bound to be generated as contact with the outside world increased, and two of these are widespread – Pidgin English and Police Motu.

SCRIPT

If notation is required, the English alphabet is used.

PHONOLOGY

Consonants

Special features are: pre-glottalized consonants i.e. the glottal stop + sonant); pre-nasalized consonants; labialized consonants; lateral ejectives. Leont'iev (1974) gives the following table of consonants in Fore:

p, t, k, q: these are aspirates: /ph/, etc.;
pː, tː, kː: long, held/tense consonants;
^{m}p, ^{n}t, ^{n}k, ^{n}k°: pre-nasalized consonants, the fourth also labialized;
s;
m, n;
qm, qn: pre-glottalized consonants;
qw, qj: pre-glottalized semi-vowels.

In contrast, the Asmat language of Flamingo Bay has only eleven consonants: /p, t, c, k, f, s, m, n, r, w, j/, where c is the alveopalatal voiceless plosive.

Some Papuan languages are tonal.

Vowels

Fore has six:

i, e, a, A, o, u

/A/ is open middle.

MORPHOLOGY AND SYNTAX

Noun

Declension is either absent or very rare. Many languages make plural forms which are usually collectives. Sometimes, number is expressed in an adjectival attribute, not in the nominal itself. Suppletive forms occur, e.g. in Banning. Elsewhere, specific suffixes for animates are found, with reduplicated forms for inanimates. In Ava, for example, we find *iyan* 'dog'; *iyatare* 'two dogs', *iyataro* 'three dogs', *iyamari* 'many dogs'.

Nouns are sub-divided by class. Here there is much variation. In Abelam, for example, all nouns denoting inanimates are masculine except four: the sun, river, sea, and sedge. In the same language, small animals, insects, and birds are included in the class of inanimates. Such taxonomies are evidently based upon criteria which escape non-Papuan perception.

Asmat has five classes: (1) erect objects (trees, people, etc.), (2) sedentary objects (houses, women); (3) recumbent objects (fallen trees, small animals, the sun or moon at rising); (4) floating objects; (5) flying objects (birds, etc.).

Banning has eight classes, including not only a partitive denoting pieces of a whole, but also a potential partitive – the class of wholes which could be separated into parts. Each class has a specific index marker.

Pronoun

Typically, there are three series: independent, bound, and ad-verbal. Kamoro has six series, Veri has twelve, including benefactive, comitative, and emphatic forms.

Among the categories distinguished in the pronominal series are: subjectivity/ objectivity, possession (general, with specific forms for kinship and other inalienable relationships), gender (in second and third person), inclusivity/ exclusivity, number (including duality, trinity), emphatic/non-emphatic. Veri, for example, has the following independent pronominal system:

	Singular	Dual/triple	Plural
1	ne	tenip 'we two without you'	ten 'we without you'
		tepir 'we two and you'	tëar 'I and you'
		tëarip 'I with you two'	
2	në	arip 'you two'	ar 'you'
3	pë	përip 'they two'	pët, pëar 'they'

DEMONSTRATIVE PRONOUN

Here Papuan has an elaborate spatial deictic system, referring not only to relative distance but also to relative plane – vertical, horizontal, etc. Some languages have multidimensional systems, e.g. Keva: *go* 'this here'; *mo* 'that over there'; *so* 'this up here'; *no* 'this down here'. The deictic system distinguishes movement relative to a surface, e.g. along it, along under it, along upon or over it; movement from a locus towards ego and vice versa, again with several ways of specifying particular permutations.

Numerals

Many Papuan languages have designations only for 1 and 2. Systems based on 4 (Keva), 5 (Elmek, Bongu), 6, and 10 also occur. Telefol counts from one hand via the neck and head to the other hand.

Verb

As a rule, person is marked, either by prefix or suffix; the object of a transitive verb is usually incorporated in the verb form, as the subject may also be: i.e. the verb may be polypersonal; the subject of a transitive verb may have a different marker from that of an intransitive verb. There is no passive voice in any Papuan language.

The tense marker is often of extreme complexity. The past is compartmentalized and ordered in ways strange to us: Tairora, for example, has two past tenses, the second of which is used with reference to events which took place more than a few weeks ago. Nasioi has nine past forms, including one referring to anything that has happened since the previous sunset.

A basic pattern has a narrative tense, which is differentiated into such forms as past imperfective, past perfective, future: e.g. in Ono: present *ari maile* 'I go'; *ari kole* 'I went' (remote past); *ari le* 'I went' (recent past); *ari kale* 'I shall go'.

MODALITY

Durative, semelfactive, completive, and repetitive modes of action are distinguished. In Asmat, for example, *-em/-om* indicates the act of standing up or lying down, i.e. changing class posture.

The subject/object grid may be illustrated from Marind, with the verb 'to carry':

Subject	Object	
sing.	sing.	e.vik.e.v
sing.	pl.	e.vik.**a**.v
pl.	sing.	**re**.vik.e.v
pl.	pl.	**re**.vik.**a**.v

Some languages can take dual or triple objects.

Telefol (spoken by some four thousand people in New Guinea) has several modal markers expressing such affective reactions as neutrality *vis-à-vis* a given action, familiarity therewith, impatience or surprise concerning it. These markers take various forms, depending on whether they are used indicatively, interrogatively, or in the imperative. Further sub-division is possible; e.g. there are specific forms for a general imperative (*a*), peremptory command (*eit, ehe'*) or request (*ehee'*).

Postpositions

Many Papaun languages have postpositions indicating spatial, temporal, modal relationships with the nouns they follow: e.g. in Gadsup, *-po* identifies the means or instrument of an action: *ikA-po yunka* 'boil by (means of) fire'. Similarly in Abelam *-t* is used: e.g. *tabA-t* 'by hand'; in Ono *-no*: e.g. *vesi.no* 'by means of a stone'; in Ava *-taten*: e.g. *sogi.taten* 'with a knife'.

Gadsup has a similative postposition *-ke*: e.g. *akinta ben ano.ke beni* 'the girl (*akinta*) is (*beni*) like (her) mother (*ano*)' (*ben* 'she', recapitulates the subject).

Word order

SOV is almost universal; e.g. in Telefol: *beeyo nimi nangkoola* 'he – me – me-he-beats' = 'he beats me'. SVO is found in a few, e.g. in Morari.

PASHTO

INTRODUCTION

Pashto belongs to the Eastern Iranian branch of the Indo-European family of languages. Since 1936 it has been the official language of Afghanistan (along with Dari/Farsi Kabuli) and is now spoken in Afghanistan and north-west Pakistan (Pashtunistan) by around 15 million people. The main dialect split is between Eastern (Mašriqi, Pešawari) Pashto and Western (Kandahari).

Writing in Pashto began in the sixteenth century. The seventeenth century produced the national poet of Afghanistan, Khushḥāl Khān Khaṭak; also many mystical *dīwāns* of Sufi inspiration. Typical of the rich Afghan folk literature is the *landey*, a short pithy verse form which has been compared to the Japanese haiku. The twentieth century has seen a rapid growth in political and social journalism and other contemporary genres, with concomitant innovation in language.

Pashto is rich in Arabo-Persian loan-words.

SCRIPT

The Arabic script, plus the Persian innovations, is further extended by specific letters for the following Pashto sounds: /ṭ, ḍ, ṇ, ts, dz, ʒ, ṛ, ʃ, e, əj/.

PHONOLOGY

Consonants

stops: p, b, t, d, ṭ, ḍ, k, g, q, ʕ, ʔ
affricates: ts, dz, tʃ, dʒ
fricatives: f, s, z, ʃ, ʒ, (ʂ, ʐ), x, γ, h
nasals: m, n, ṇ
lateral and flap: l, r, ṛ
semi-vowels: j, w

The retroflex fricatives /ʂ, ʐ/ are characteristic of Western Pashto. Retroflex sounds are represented here with dots.

Vowels

i, e, a, aː, ə, o, u

Vocalic length is not phonemic; /ə/ is always stressed.

Stress

Stress is on any syllable, movable and phonemic.

MORPHOLOGY AND SYNTAX

Noun

Pashto has two genders – masculine and feminine – and two numbers – singular and plural. Typical masculine endings are *-aj*, *-ə*, *-u*; nearly all nouns ending in a consonant are masculine. Feminine endings are *-a*, *-ā*, *-i*, *-o*, *-əj*. Examples: masc. *saṛaj* 'man', *plār* 'father'; fem. *koṭa* 'room', *ārzo* 'wish'.

NUMBER

Consonantal endings take the plural marker *-una* (*-ān* for animates); nouns in *-aj* change this to *-i*; feminine nouns in *-a* take *-e/-i*: e.g. *kor* 'house' – *koruna*; *saṛaj* 'man' – *saṛi*; *koṭa* 'room' – *koṭe*; *mdzəka* 'country' – *mdzəki*.

Phonetic assimilation of various kinds occurs at junctures; suppletive forms and the Arabic broken plural are also found.

CASE

There is a simple opposition between the direct (nominative) and oblique forms. In practice, the oblique form of masculine nouns in *-ə*, *-i*, *-u*, or with consonantal ending, is identical with the direct form; the singular oblique of all other masculine and all feminine nouns equals the plural direct; and all plural obliques are in *-o*: e.g. for the masculine noun *špun* 'shepherd': pl. direct = sing. oblique *špānə*, pl. oblique *špano*; and for *lmundz* 'prayer': pl. direct = sing. obl. *lmāndzə*; pl. obl. *lmandzo*. Each of these examples shows umlaut of the stem in the formation of the plural and the oblique case; this is very frequent in the Pashto nominal system.

POSSESSION

The marker is *də* preceding the possessor in the oblique case: e.g. *də koṭe war* 'the door (*war*) of the room'; *də halək plār* 'the father of the boy'.

Adjective

As attribute, adjective precedes the noun. Where phonetically possible, the adjective takes gender and number concord, with stem umlaut. At most, an adjective can have four forms (masc. sing./pl.; fem. sing./pl): e.g. *soṛ – saṛ – saṛa – saṛe* 'cold'; *loj kor* 'big house'; *loja koṭa* 'big room'; *loji koṭe* 'the big rooms'.

COMPARATIVE

Made with *tər*, which functions as a preposition governing the compared object, not as the normal Iranian adjectival affix: e.g. *Ahmad tər Madmud məšr dəj* 'A. is older than M.' (cf. Persian: *A. az M. mosenntar ast*).

Pronoun

The direct personal forms have oblique and enclitic forms:

		Singular			Plural	
		Direct	*Oblique*	*Enclitic*	*Direct/oblique*	*Enclitic*
1		zə	mā	-mi	muž	-mu
2		tə	tā	-di	tāsi	-mu
3	masc.	daj	də	-e/je	duj	-e/je
	fem.	dā	de			

In addition to their function as direct objective pronouns, the oblique forms appear in the ergative construction (see below); they also take postpositions. The enclitics are used as possessive markers, and as direct objects in the present and future tenses; they may also replace the oblique forms in the ergative construction: e.g. *hewād **mi*** 'my homeland'; *zə **di** winəm* 'I see you'; *də **duj** žəba* 'their language'.

DEMONSTRATIVE PRONOUN/ADJECTIVE
Three degrees of removal: *dā* 'this' – *daγa* 'that' – *haγa* 'that (yonder)'; these have oblique forms.

INTERROGATIVE PRONOUN
cok 'who?'; *ča* 'what?'.

RELATIVE PRONOUN
čə: e.g. *saṛaj **čə** num je Mahmud dəj* 'the man whose name is M.', i.e. with resumptive enclitic: ... *num je* 'his name'.

Numerals

1–10: *jau, dwa, dre, calor, pindzə, špaž, owə, atə, nəh, las*; 11 *jawolas*; 12 *dwolas*; 13 *djārlas*; 20 *šəl*; 30 *derš*; 40 *calwešt*; 100 *səl*.

Verb

All forms are derived from two bases, the present and the past. The past base of most verbs is identical to the infinitive base; the present base is not predictable, and suppletive forms are frequent. Compare:

Infinitive/past base	Present base
wistəl 'to take out'	bās-
tləl 'to go'	dz-
lidəl 'to see'	win-

TENSE STRUCTURE
The present tense is made from the present base, the past from the past base. The present indicative endings are, for *wājəl* 'to say':

	Singular	Plural
1	wājəm	wāju
2	wāje	wājəj
3	wāji	wāji

PAST TENSE

(a) Intransitive verbs: the personal endings (as in present tense, except for third person) are added to the infinitive, i.e. the past base: in the third person, gender is distinguished: e.g. *rasedəl* 'to arrive':

		Singular	Plural
1		rasedələm	rasedəlu
2		rasedəle	resedələj
3	masc.	rasedə	rasedəl
	fem.	rasedəla	rasedəle

(b) Transitive verbs: here the ergative construction is used; the agent is in the oblique case, the object in the nominative/direct; the verb agrees in gender and number with the object: e.g. *saṛi šədza lidəla* 'by-the-man the-woman seen' = 'the man saw the woman'.

The ergative construction is also used with certain intransitive verbs denoting human reactions and affective states: e.g. *mā žaṛəl* 'by-me wept' = 'I wept'.

ERGATIVE CONSTRUCTION WITH A PRONOMINAL OBJECT
Example: *zə je lidələm* 'I by-him my-(being)-seen' = 'he saw me'; future: particle *bə* + present, e.g. *zə bə tā winəm* 'I shall see you'.

ASPECT
The perfective aspect of a simple imperfective verb can be made by prefixing *wu-*: e.g. *wu-rasedəm* 'I arrived' – *zə šār ta wu.rasedəm* 'I reached the town'; but many verbs have suppletive perfective forms: e.g. imperfective *kawəl* 'to do, make' – perfective *kṛəl*; imperfective *kedəl* 'to become' – perfective *šwəl*.

PASSIVE VOICE
The auxiliary is *kedəl/šwəl*: e.g. *lidəl kedəl* 'to be seen'.

CAUSATIVE
The characteristic is *-wəl* affixed to the present stem: e.g. *lwastəl* 'to read' – *lwalawəl* 'to have someone read'.

There are also imperative and optative moods, and a conditional form.

PARTICIPLES

(a) Present: the infinitive ending *-əl* is replaced by the characteristic *-unk-* + singular/plural masculine/feminine endings: thus from *tləl* 'to go', *tl.unk.aj* 'going' (masc. sing.); *tl.unk.i* (plural referent of either gender).
(b) Past: *-aj* is affixed to the infinitive: e.g. *tləlaj* 'having gone'. This form is used to make a perfect tense with the auxiliary *jəm*; the participle is inflected for feminine singular and for common plural: e.g. *rasedəlaj jəm* 'I have

arrived'; *rasedəli di* 'they (masc./fem.) have arrived'.

NEGATION

The general negating particle is *na/nə*; the imperative is negated by *ma*.

Modal auxiliaries are used much as in Persian.

Prepositions and postpositions

Both are found in Pashto (e.g. *be* 'without', *tər* 'on', which are prepositions; *ta* 'to(wards)', postposition following the oblique case) but the usual form is the circumfix: e.g. *pə... ki* 'in', *pə šār ki* 'in the town'; *tər...lāndi* 'under', *tər mez lāndi* 'under the table'; *lə...na* 'from, out of', *lə šār na* 'out of the town'.

Word order

SOV.

> ١ آ په ابتدا کښ کلمه وه او هغه کلمه الله ځنه وه او هغه کلمه الله وه
>
> ٢ ر دغه په ابتدا کښ الله ځنه وه ب ټول څيزونه په دې سره وشول او بي
>
> ٣ له هغي هيڅ شي له هغو نه چه شوي دي و نه شه ج په هغي کښ ژوندون
>
> ٥ وه او هغه ژوندون نور د انسان وه د او نور په تياري کښ ځليده او تياري
>
> ٦ هغه و نه پيژاند د يو سړي له جانب د الله نه واستولي شه چه نوم ئي يوحنا
>
> ٧ وه ح هغه د شاهدئ دپارَ راغي تا چه په نور شاهدي ولي تا چه ټول دده
>
> ٨ په واسطي ايمان راوړي د دي هغه نور نه وه بلکه راغي چه په نور شاهدئ
>
> ولي

PEGUAN

See **Mon**.

PEHLEVI
(Middle Persian)

INTRODUCTION

This term covers the written and spoken language of Iran in the period between Old Persian/Avestan and the emergence of New Persian – i.e. from the fourth century BC to roughly the ninth century AD: a period covering the great cultural flowering of the Sasanid Dynasty (AD 224–651), the birth of Manichaeism, and the diffusion of both Manichaean and Zoroastrian religious literature. For example, the Dēnkart and the Bundahišn, encyclopaedic works embodying the beliefs and dogmas of Zoroastrianism, the traditional history of Iran, and Iranian mythology, astronomy, and eschatology, were composed in this period, though they are known to us only from much later copies. Inscriptions in Pehlevi date from the reign of Ardashir (224–41) onwards. Apart from one work in Pehlevi, the Manichaean texts are written in Aramaic.

The word *Pehlevi* is derived from *pahlav* < /parθava/, which originally denoted the Sasanid style of writing. Later, the word *Parthian* came to be used with reference to the North-West dialect of Middle Persian. Pehlevi is specifically the South-West form.

SCRIPT

Underlying the Pehlevi script is an Aramaic basis of 22 letters, denoting consonants and long vowels. In a gradual process of deformation, these 22 letters were reduced to 15, several of which were multivalued, requiring the introduction of specific diacritics. The resultant script had two main complications: (a) a large number of often arbitrary ligatures; and (b) the presence of Aramaic ideograms: e.g. the graph *mlk* (the Semitic root denoting 'king, kingship, to rule', etc. was used in Pehlevi, but read as /ʃaːh/, the Iranian word *shah* 'king, emperor'. Similarly, the Aramaic graph *lḥm* (the Semitic root denoting 'bread') was read as /naːn/ 'bread' in Iranian. These Aramaic ideograms were used to denote stems, to which inflections were added in phonetic Pehlevi script. (Cf. Japanese use of kanji + kana. For the extension of the Pehlevi script to Avestan, *see* **Avestan**.)

PHONOLOGY

Consonants

stops: p, b, t, d, k, g
affricates: tʃ, dʒ
fricatives: f, v, ß, θ, ð, s, z, ʃ, ʒ, x, γ, h
nasals: m, n
lateral and flap: l, r
semi-vowel: j

The stops /p, t, k/ in intervocalic position are typical of pre-Sasanid Pehlevi. In Sasanid Pehlevi they became the corresponding voiced fricatives /ß, ð, γ/: cf. Aršacid *pitar* > Sasanid *piðar* 'father'; Aršacid *kartan* > Sasanid *karðan* 'to do'.

Vowels

long and short: i, a, u

/eː/ and /oː/ represent Old Iranian diphthongs and have no short forms.

Stress

Regularly on final syllable.

MORPHOLOGY AND SYNTAX

Noun

The analytical structure of Modern Persian is already clearly emergent in later Pehlevi. In the oldest period of the language, two cases – direct and oblique – survived from the Old Persian inventory of eight; and these two were contrasted only in the singular of nouns and adjectives, and in the first person singular pronoun. Over the ensuing centuries the direct case ousted the oblique everywhere except in the first person singular pronoun, where, on the contrary, the oblique form – *man* – came to replace the direct form, *az*. The Modern Persian form is *man*.

The plural markers are *-ān* and *-īhā*. These are used for nouns and some pronouns; *-ān* is more frequent than *-īhā*: e.g. *pitarān* 'father'; *ātaxšān* 'fires'. Indefinite status of a noun could be indicated by the affix *-ē*: e.g. *pus.ē* 'a son' (cf. Modern Persian, *pisar.ī*).

Adjective

As attribute, adjective may precede the noun, e.g. *mastūk mart* 'drunk man', but usually follows, connected to noun by the *izafe -i-*: e.g. *pus-i-mas-i- Arðavān* 'Artavan's eldest son'; *kunišn-i-nēvak-i-tō* 'your good actions' (*nēvak* 'good').

COMPARATIVE

In -*tar*: e.g. *saxt.tar* 'harder'; but a few make a comparative by internal flection: *kam* 'few', comp. *kēm*; *vas* 'much', comp. *vēš*.

Pronoun

PERSONAL

	Singular		Plural	
	Full	Enclitic	Full	Enclitic
1	az (obl. *man*)	-m	amāh	-mān
2	tō	-t	smāh	-tān
3	avē	-š	avēšān	-šān

The enclitics are added to conjunctions and to the relative pronoun *i*, to denote possession, direct/indirect object: e.g. ***u-m** māt Spandarmāt,* ***u-m** pit Ōhrmazd* 'and my mother is S., my father is Ō'; ***u-š** guft Ōhrmazd* 'and O. said to him'; *Pāpak **kā-š** ān sax^wān ašnūt* 'when Papak heard these words'; *ān x^wamn **i-m** dīt* 'the dream which I saw'. They may also function as the subject of intransitive verbs, and of transitive verbs in non-past tenses.

DEMONSTRATIVE PRONOUN

ēn/ēt 'this'; *ān/ōj* 'that'. These take the izafe: e.g. *ēn-i, ēt-i; ēt-i-tō* 'this-of-you' = 'yours'; *Az ham **ēt-i-tō** humat ut hūxt ut huvaršt **i-t** mēnīt ut guft ut kart* 'I am your good thoughts, words and deeds, which you thought, said, and did.'

INTERROGATIVE PRONOUN

kē 'who?'; *čē* 'what?': e.g. *Tō kē hēh?* 'Who are you?'

RELATIVE PRONOUN

i (*see* above); *čē* was also used as relative: e.g. *Har čē tō framāyēh kunam* 'I shall do all that you tell me to do.' See also Passive, below.

Numerals

1–10: *ēvak, dō, sē, čahār, pandž, šaš, haft, hašt, nō, dah*; 11 *yāzdah*; 12 *duvāzdah*; 20 *vīst*; 30 *sīh*; 40 *čihil*; 100 *sat*.

Verb

Underlying the verbal structure is the two-base system – a present base generating the present–future tense, the imperative, and subjunctive moods; and a past base providing the past tense, the participial forms, and the infinitive. This past base represents the Old Persian past passive participle: e.g. *kart.an* – *kun*; *raft.an* – *raft*.

There are four moods: indicative, imperative, subjunctive, optative; and two voices.

INDICATIVE MOOD

The personal endings are sing. 1 -am/-ēm, 2 -ēh, 3 -ēt; pl. 1 -ēm, 2 -ēt, 3 -and/-ēnd. The auxiliary verb h- has the following present–future tense: sing. ham, hē(h), hast; pl. hēm, hēt, hand. Thus, present–future of kartan 'to do', present base kun-: e.g. kunam, kunē(h), kunēt; pl. kunēm, kunēt, kunēnd. The past tense of raftan 'to go', past base raft: e.g. raft ham, raft hē(h), raft Ø; i.e. the auxiliary is dropped in third person singular. A perfect tense is made with the auxiliary ēstātan: e.g. raft ēstēt 'he has gone'.

SUBJUNCTIVE

A present tense (present base + specific endings) and a past (past participle + subjunctive form of h- auxiliary) are partially attested.

IMPERATIVE

Second person singular = stem; second plural + -ēt /-e:ð/. The imperative takes enclitic pronominal object: e.g. bōž.əm, bōž.ēð.əm 'save me'.

PASSIVE

Formally, a passive present tense is made by infixing the formant -īh- between the present stem and the personal endings: e.g. kartan: kun.īh.ēt 'it is (being) done'. A past tense with the same formant + specific ending is attested only in third person singular. An analytical passive – the past base (= past passive participle) following the personally inflected relative/izafet particle i – is very common: e.g. i.m kart 'done by me' = 'which I did'; i.mān kart 'which we did'. Here, the pronominal enclitic is the logical subject. Cf. Dānist kū ān x^wamn i-m dīt, rāst būt 'We understood: that dream seen-by-me (i.e. which I saw) was true.'

CAUSATIVE

The formant is -ēn-: e.g. rasītan 'to arrive' – rasēnītan 'to deliver'.

PARTICIPLES

Present: present stem + -ēnd, e.g. kunēnd 'doing';

Past: (a) = past stem (see above); (b) past stem + -ak, e.g. nišastak 'having sat down'.

INFINITIVE

Past stem + -an: kartan 'to do'. A short form, without -an, is used with modal verbs (see below).

MODAL VERBS

Examples: šāyistan 'to be possible, able': e.g. šāyēt kart 'it can be done'; apāyistan 'to be necessary': e.g. apāyēt 'it is necessary'; apāyēt raft.

VERBAL PRE-FORMANTS

Examples: andar: andar šutan 'to go into'; apāč: apāč vaštan 'to turn round'; frāč: frāč raftan 'to move forwards'.

PREPOSITIVE VERBAL PARTICLES

Example: bē as perfective aspect marker: bē āmōxtan apāyēt 'one must (have) learn(ed)'. The particle ē underlies the future aspect in the present–future tense.

NEGATION

The general particle for all tenses and moods except the imperative is *nē*; *mā* negates the imperative.

Prepositions

Examples:

> *andar* 'in': e.g. *andar Pārs* 'in Fars'; *andar šap* 'by night';
> *hač* 'from': e.g. *hač nazdīk...hač dūr* 'from near...and far';
> *pat* 'in, at, about', e.g. *pat-aš guft ēstēt kū...* 'of him it was said that...'

There is one important postposition – *rāð*, used *inter alia* to mark direct object and to express the verb 'to have': e.g. *Pāpak rāð pus-ē hast* 'P. has a son'.

Word order

Normally SOV.

PENUTIAN LANGUAGES

In sharp contrast with such compact, genetically well-defined families as Na-Dené, Algonquian, and Athabaskan, Penutian is a loose and controversial grouping of highly disparate American Indian languages, scattered over a vast area which some authorities construe as extending from British Columbia to Chile. Geographically, this Macro-Penutian can be sub-divided as follows:

1. North-West Canadian group: Tshimshian, spoken in British Columbia by about a thousand people.

2. Western USA:

(a) Californian group: Yokutsan, Maiduan, Wintun, Miwok-Costanoan;
(b) Oregon group: Klamath-Modoc, Sahaptian (including Nez Perce), Coos, Takelma, Chinook.

Apart from Sahaptin which has a few hundred speakers, these languages are all extinct. It is from the words for the numeral 'two' in certain Californian languages that the name of the family is derived: *pen* (in Wintun and Maiduan) + *uti* (in Miwok-Costanoan) → *pen-uti-(an)*, selected by Dixon and Kroeber in 1913.

Edward Sapir's Penutian stock contained only these two groups, with an extension into Mexico to include the Mixe-Zoque languages. In 1965/6 Voegelin and Voegelin added Zuni to the family and the languages in 3.

3. The Mayan languages in Mexico and Guatamala. This addition gave Penutian what is by far its most important member, both from a demographic and a cultural point of view: the Mayan group has some 3–4 million speakers, and two of its members – Yucatec Maya and Quiché – have classical literary languages. The outstanding works are the 'Books of Chilam Balam' in Yucatec Maya, and the *Popol Vuh* in Quiché. Quiché also preserves the sole example of pre-Conquest drama, the *Rabinal Achi*. A third Mayan language, Cakchiquel, has preserved historical Annals of the Cakchiquel people.

4. The controversial South American Penutian stock includes several small groupings in Ecuador, Peru, and Bolivia, and one major language, Mapudungu, spoken by about a quarter of a million people in Chile and Argentine.

The Penutian languages are heterogeneous, ranging from inflectional/analytical languages like Coos and Mapudungu to polysynthetic languages like Chinook.

See **Mam, Mapudungu, Maya, Quiché, Zuni**.

PERSIAN

INTRODUCTION

Persian belongs to the South-West Iranian branch of the Indo-European family. The name 'Persia(n)' derives from Parsa, the province from which the Sasanid Dynasty originated. The language is also known as Farsi, which is an Arabicized form of Parsa (Arabic has no /p/ sound). Persian is spoken by about 30 million people in Iran, and, in slightly variant form, by 5 million in Afghanistan (known here as Dari), and by about 3 million in the Tadzhik Soviet Socialist Republic. There are a number of important dialects within Iran itself (e.g. Luri, Bakhtyari, Mazandarani).

The development and use of Middle Persian (*see* **Pehlevi**) was interrupted in 642 when the Arabs conquered Iran. When Persian reappears in the tenth century it is not based on any one identifiable Middle Persian dialect, it is rich in Arabic loan-words and it is written in the Arabic script. It should be pointed out, however, that Persian was Arabicized only as regards the appropriation of Arabic lexical items, including the broken plural and the derived stems (*see* **Arabic**). Thus, while the root *'ZL*, for example, is not conjugated in Persian, its passive participle appears in compound verbs plus auxiliary: e.g. *ma'zul shodan* 'to be dismissed', *ma'zul kardan* 'to dismiss'. There are thousands of such Arabo-Persian complexes in the language, but Persian structure itself was hardly modified to accommodate this new and inexhaustible influx.

A thirteenth-century writer like Sa'dī uses both languages, e.g. in the *Golistan*, but separately, a *hikāyat* (tale) in Persian being often followed by a *bayt* (couplet) in Arabic. Writing three centuries earlier, Ferdousi could consciously eschew Arabic words in his nationalistic epic, the *Shāhnāme*.

The great classical period of Persian literature runs from the tenth to the fourteenth centuries. Apart from Ferdousi, the national poet, the list of great names includes Rūdakī (ninth/tenth centuries), Nāṣere Khosrou (eleventh century), Neẓāmī and Omar Khayyām (eleventh/twelfth century) Aṭṭār, Jalāloddin Rūmī, Sa'dī (thirteenth century), Ḥāfeẓ (fourteenth century).

SCRIPT

Arabic with the addition of four letters for sounds which do not occur in standard Arabic: /tʃ, ʒ, g, p/. Retention of certain Arabic letters without their original phonemic values (e.g. Arabic /ḍ/ > Persian /z/) has led to considerable duplication in notation: there are four letters for /z/, three for /s/. The Arabic emphatics are found only in Arabic loan-words.

PHONOLOGY

Consonants

stops: p, b, t, d, k, g, ɢ, ʔ
affricates: tʃ, dʒ
fricatives: f, v, s, z, ʃ, ʒ, x, γ, h
nasals: m, n
lateral and flap: l, r
semi-vowel: j

The hamza onset /ʕ/ occurs medially in such verb forms as the second person plural imperative, e.g. *beguʕíd* 'say'.

Vowels

The long vowels *i, a, u* = /iː, ɔː, uː/ are notated in the Arabo-Persian script; the short vowels, not notated, are /æ, ɛ, ɔ/; there are two diphthongs /ɛi/ and /ɔu/.
   In this article /ɔː/ is notated as *ā*; *a* without a macron is /æ/.

Stress

Stress falls on final syllables, excluding enclitics, in nouns, pronouns, adjectives, verbal infinitives, and verbal forms without prefixes. Stress shifts to prefix *mi-* in imperfective tenses, and thence to preceding negative marker, if this is present: cf: *xarídam* 'I bought' – *mí.xaridam* 'I was buying' – *ná.mi.xaridam* 'I was not buying'.

MORPHOLOGY AND SYNTAX

Noun

Persian has no grammatical gender and no articles. The unmarked noun denotes a class of objects rather than a single element of that class: *man ketāb xōš dāram* 'I like books'. The noun is made specific by the addition of unstressed *-i*: *ketāb.i* 'a book'.
   For specific plurality there are two markers, *-ān* and *-hā*. In classical usage, a distinction was (and is) made between *-ān* for humans, and *-hā* for inanimates and animals. The modern tendency is for *-hā* to be used indiscriminately. Both *-ān* and *-hā* are stressed.
   The Arabic broken plural coexists in Persian with *-ān/-hā*. Thus, *ketāb* 'book' may be pluralized as *ketābhā*, or as *kutub* (Arabic broken plural). In a few cases, the Arabic plural alone is used: e.g. *xabar* 'news' – *axbār*; *hadd* 'frontier' – *hodūd*.
   The marker *-rā* serves to identify a noun as the object of a transitive verb: e.g. *bačče.rā díd* 'he saw the child'. *-rā* may follow *-i*: *pādešāh.i.rā šonidam, ke...* 'I heard of a king, who ...' (Saʕdī, *Golestan*, l.).

POSSESSION

The formula X's Y is expressed in Persian as Y-*e* X; the unstressed -*e* link is known as the *ezāfe*: e.g. *doxtar.e ān mard* 'that man's daughter'; *tamām.e tājer.hā.ye doulatmand.e šahr* 'all the rich merchants of the city' (where the attributive adjective, *doulatmand* 'rich', is also connected to its preceding noun by the ezāfe). In this example, if the word *tājer.hā* 'merchants' is to be the object, -*rā* must be affixed, not to *tājer.hā* but to *šahr*: i.e. the whole ezāfe phrase is felt to be a unit, which must, as a unit, be rounded off by the objective marker.

Adjective

As attribute, adjective follows noun, to which it is linked by the ezāfe, and is invariable: e.g. *manzal.e bozorg* 'the big house'; *melal.e mottahad* 'the United Nations'; *dāneš.ju.ye irānī* 'the Iranian student'; *kuh.hā.ye boland* 'high mountains'.

COMPARATIVE

In -*tar*: e.g. *Īn ketāb az ān ketāb bozorg.tar ast* 'This book is bigger than that book.'

Pronoun

Independent personal forms with enclitics:

	Singular		Plural	
	Independent	Enclitic	Independent	Enclitic
1	man	-am	mā	-emān
2	to	-at	šomā	-etān
3	u	-as	išān	-ešān

The objective pronouns are the same as the independent forms above, with the exception that *man* becomes *mā*: e.g. *mārā dīd* 'he saw me'. The enclitics may also be used as object pronouns: e.g. *be.u goftam = goftam.aš* 'I said to him'.

The enclitics are used as possessive markers: e.g. *ketāb.am* 'my book' (this may also be expressed as *ketāb.e man*, i.e. independent form with izāfe link). The plural pronoun *šomā* provides the polite form of address for second singular; similarly, *išān* is used as the polite form of reference to a singular third person (with plural concord).

DEMONSTRATIVE PRONOUN/ADJECTIVE

in 'this, these'; *ān* 'that, those'. They take the plural marker -*hā*: e.g. *ānhā kord.and* 'these (people) are Kurds'.

INTERROGATIVE PRONOUN

ki 'who?'; *če* 'what?': e.g. (*porsidand*) *ke haqiqat.e tasawwaf čist* (← *če ast*) '(asked) what is the true meaning of Sufism' (Golestan, 2.24). The particle *āyā* initiates a sentence requiring a yes/no answer.

RELATIVE PRONOUN

The linking particle *ke* follows the head-word: e.g. *mardi.ke diruz raft* 'the man who went off yesterday'; *manzel.i.ke ānjā manzel mi.konam* 'the house in which I live'.

Numerals

1–10: *yak, do, se, čahār, panǰ, šeš, haft, hašt, noh, dah*. 10–19: unit + *dah*, the units varying slightly: e.g. *yazdah, davāzdah, sizdah*; 20 *bīst*; 30 *sī*; 40 *čehel*; 100 *sad*.

Verb

The two basic oppositions are: (a) between present and past stems; (b) between perfective and imperfective aspects.

The infinitive ending is *-tan/-dan/-idan*: the *-an* is dropped to give the short infinitive, which is also the past stem, e.g. from *xaridan* 'to buy', *xarid* = past stem = third person singular past, 'he/she bought'.

Theoretically, the present stem is obtained by dropping the whole of the infinitive ending: in the case of *xaridan*, *-idan* is dropped, leaving *xar-*. There are, however, very many irregular formations: e.g. from *āmadan* 'come', *ā-*; from *raftan* 'go', *raw-*; from *kardan* 'do, make', *kon-*.

The personal enclitic markers used in conjugation are: sing. 1 *-am*, 2 *-i*, 3 *-ast/-ad*; pl: 1 *-im*, 2 *-id*, 3 *-and* (humans), *-ast/-ad*.

The auxiliary used in the formation of composite tenses is *budan* 'to be', whose present stem is *bāš-*. All Persian verbs are constructed and conjugated on this model; the only irregularity lies in the formation of the present stem.

ASPECT

Briefly, imperfective forms are marked by a prefix: *mi-*, *be-*; perfective forms have no prefix. Thus from *xaridan* 'buy':

> Imperfective aspect, present or past stem: *mí.xarim* 'we are buying'; *bé.xarim* 'that we may buy' (subjunctive); *mí.xarid.im* 'we were buying'.
> Perfective aspect, past stem: *xaríd.im* 'we bought'; *xaridé.im* 'we have bought'; *xāhim xaríd* 'we shall have bought/we shall buy'.

All of these forms are negated by prefixing *na-*, except in the case of the subjunctive, where the *be-* is dropped before *na-* is prefixed: thus *na.mi.xarim* 'we are not buying'; *na.∅.xarad* 'he is not to buy'.

A passive voice can be made with the auxiliary *šodan* 'to become': e.g. *koštan* 'to kill' – *košte šodan* 'to be killed', where *košte* is the past participle. The passive form cannot be used in Persian if the agent is specified.

IMPERATIVE

Prefix *be-* + present stem: *be.xar* 'buy!', pl. *be.xarid*. Necessitative and potential forms are made with the subjunctive; the former uses the third person singular of *bāyestan* 'to have to': *bāyad be.xarim* 'we have to buy'; *bāyad be.ravim* 'we must go'. The potential forms are made with *tavānestan* 'to be able': *mi.tavānam be.ravam* 'I can go'.

Several other Persian verbs are used as auxiliaries with Persian or Arabic nominals or verbals, especially *kardan* 'to do, make' (present stem, *kon-*); cf. with *šodan* 'to become': *vāred šod* 'he entered'; *xārej šodand* 'they went out', where *vāred* and *xārej* are Arabic active participles.

Prepositions

Some, e.g. *az* 'from', *tā* 'until, as far as', *bar* 'on', *ba* 'with', do not need the ezāfe: e.g. *az šahr* 'from the town'; *tā emruz* 'till today'. Others, such as *bedun* 'without', *pošt* 'behind', *ru-* 'on', require the ezāfe: e.g. *ru.ye miz* 'on the table', *bālā.ye kuh* 'up on the mountain'

Word order

SOV.

بود در ابتدا کلمه و انکلمه نزدخدا بود و ان کلمه خدا بود * وهمان درابتدا نزد خدابود* ومرچیز بوساطت او موجودشد وبغیر ازو هیچ چیزازچیز هاۓ که موجودشده است وجود نیافت * دراوحیات بودوان حیات روشناۓ انسان بود * وان روشناۓ درتاریکی میدرخشید وتاریکی درنمییافتش * شخصی بودکه ازجانب خدا فرستاده شده که اسمش یہی بود * واوبراۓ شهادت امدتاانکه شهادت بران نوردهدتا انکه همه بوساطت او ایمان اورند * واوخودروشناۓ نبود بلکه امده بود که براۓ روشناۓ شهادت بدهد *

PHOENICIAN

INTRODUCTION

A member of the Canaanite branch of the North-West Semito-Hamitic family, Phoenician was spoken in colonies scattered all over the Mediterranean area, from Lebanon and Syria in the east through Sicily, Sardinia, and Spain to North Africa in the west. The oldest records date from the second half of the second millennium BC. Key Phoenician settlements were Byblos and the Sidonian kingdom (*ṣidōnī*) with its capital Tyre, and Carthage. The most recent records are dated around the second century AD in the east, about 200 years later in the Carthaginian area.

SCRIPT

Phoenician was written in a linear script (right to left) which had many variants over 2,000 years. Basically, it is a version of the North Semitic script, developed in the early second millennium BC in Palestine, consisting of 22 consonantal signs. These signs represent consonantal phonemes, their geminates, and any contiguous vowel(s). Thus, △ in the Classical Phoenician script represents *da*, *di*, *du*, *dd*, *id*, *ud*, *ada*, *adda*, etc.

Some indication of Phoenician pronunciation (i.e. including vocalization) is retrievable from glosses in cuneiform Akkadian texts (for the early period), and from passages in Punic in Plautus' comedy *Poenulus* (for the Carthaginian period). There is also a corpus of Punic inscriptions in Greek and Latin characters.

PHONOLOGY

Consonants

stops: p, b, t, d, ŧ, k, g, ḳ, ʔ
fricatives: θ, ð, s, z, ś, ṣ, ʃ, γ, ḫ, ħ, h, ʕ
nasals: m, n
lateral and flap: l, r
semi-vowels: j, w

Vowels

> long and short: i, a, u
> plus mobile values y; o, o:

/y/ is notated as *ü*.

MORPHOLOGY AND SYNTAX

Noun

Phoenician had two genders – masculine and feminine – and three numbers, including a dual. The noun is in absolute or construct (conjugate) state.

CASE SYSTEM

The evidence suggests a direct case in *-u*, a genitive in *-i*, and an accusative in *-a*, as in Classical Arabic. In late Phoenician, these endings seem to have been discarded.

As elsewhere in Semitic, the feminine singular marker is *-t*. Designations for paired members of the body, and for certain natural phenomena are also feminine: e.g. *jd* 'hand', *šmš* 'sun'. There are some anomalies in comparison with general Semitic, e.g. *jm* 'day', is feminine, while the Hebrew form *jom* is masculine.

NUMBER

The dual ending is *-aj^{i/a}m*. The masculine plural ending is on the model *-Vm*: e.g. *khn* 'priest' – *khnim*; *mlk* 'emperor' – *mlkm*. The feminine plural is in *-ūt̠*: e.g. *alōnūt̠* 'goddesses'. *alonim valonuth* 'gods and goddesses' (Plautus) (v- is a connective particle)

CONSTRUCT

Example: *'š ṣdn* 'a man of Sidon' (Hebrew *'iš*). Lack of vocalization in Phoenician conceals the difference, if any, between absolute and construct states. Shifman (1963) points out that the epithet of the Carthaginian goddess Tinnit, *pn b'l*, was pronounced as /pane: ba:l/ 'adornment of Baal'; i.e. the plural *-im* changes to *-ē* in construct.

Pronoun

The independent personal forms are fully attested in the singular, partially (first common and third masculine) in the plural. The nominal and verbal enclitics are close to each other and to the equivalent Hebrew forms; e.g. the nominal series for the singular is: 1 *-i/-ī*, 2 masc. *-k*, fem. *-ki*, 3 masc. *-h/-w*. In the plural, the enclitic verbal series is attested only by third masculine *-hm/-m*. Plautus writes the first person independent form as *anech*.

DEMONSTRATIVE PRONOUN

Takes various forms based on *z* (masc.), *zt* (fem.). The common plural form seems to have been *'ilü*, rendered by Plautus as *ily*. The article in *-h* was a late development in Phoenician. In Punic, *-h* > *-'*.

INTERROGATIVE PRONOUN
mē/mī 'who?'; *mnm/mū* 'what?'.

RELATIVE PRONOUN
z; or, as in Hebrew, *'š/s*.

Numerals

The forms 1–10 are standard North Semitic: *'ḥd, šnm/'šnm, šlš, 'rb'/rb', ḥmš, šš, šb', šmn, tš', 'šr*.

Verb

The Phoenician verb expresses aspect rather than tense. Few forms are known for certain. The perfect aspect is marked by suffix, e.g. 1st p. sing. common *-tī*, 1st p. pl. *-nū*, 3rd p. common *-ū*.

The imperfective, marked by prefix and circumfix, is attested in the singular for the 1st, 2nd masc., and 3rd masc./fem., and in the plural for the 3rd p. masc.: cf. *t.rgz.n* 'thou (*t-*) troublest me (*-n*)' (Hebrew *rāgaz* 'to trouble').

Optative forms are frequent: e.g. *ḻ.brk* 'may he be blessed!'.

Passive: Plautus gives a form *dubirth* (root *DBR* 'to speak'), which shows a typical passive vocalic pattern (cf. Arabic *kutiba*).

Participial forms are also found in Plautus, e.g. *dobrīm* (masc. pl.), (*DBR*). Shifman (1963: 46) gives an inventory of probable *binyanim* in Phoenician.

The negating particle is *bl*.

Prepositions

Standard North Semitic.

PIDGINS AND CREOLES

Typically, a pidgin originates when and where speakers of mutually unintelligible languages encounter and seek to communicate with each other for mutually advantageous purposes – primarily the exchange of goods and services. Initially, gesture and mimicry play a crucial role in such encounters. Utterances accompanying mime will tend to fall into either of two categories: (a) an initially small class of phonemes, which increases as, by a process of trial and error, more and more phonemes appear to be associated with desired results; and (b) a much more extensive background of sounds, whose relationship with the transaction remains obscure. As they multiply, the phonemes in (a) provide a basic lexicon of roots for the emergent pidgin; that is, they become lexemes. If highly inflected languages are involved in the encounter, much of the accidence of either or both will be relegated to (b), though some of its features may persist as reflexes both in the pidgin and in a subsequent creole: cf. *zòt* in Haitian Creole, where *z-* reflects both *vous* and *les* in French: i.e. *vous autres* /vuːz.oːtr/ > *zòt* 'you'; *les autres* /leːz.oːtr/ > *zòt* 'they, them'.

Pidgins naturally proliferate along trade routes and lines of colonial diffusion. On both counts, a founding partner in nearly all successful pidgins is one of the five European languages primarily associated with imperialist expansion: English, Spanish, Portuguese, French, and Dutch. One of the earliest examples is Amerindian Pidgin English which was used in the mid-seventeenth century between settlers in the New England colonies and the local Iroquois and Algonquian Indians. Similar pidgins, involving French and local Indian languages took shape in eastern and central Canada. Through the nineteenth century, about a hundred thousand people in north-west Canada communicated with each other by means of the Chinook Jargon, an elaborate pidgin with English, French, Salishan, and Wakashan components (*see* **North American Indian Isolates**). In Central and South America, and in the Caribbean, many pidgins based on Spanish and Portuguese arose. In general, in all of these cases, the European lexical input was paramount, but there were exceptions; for example, one of the most extensively used and culturally important pidgins in Brazil was the so-called *lingoa gêral*, which was based on Tupí–Guaraní. Mention should also be made of Mobilian, a trade language formerly widespread in the south-eastern states of the USA, which was based on Choctaw (*see* **Choctaw**).

In West Africa, an extensive string of English-based pidgins runs from the Gambia to Cameroon. Major English-based pidgins are also found in Papua New Guinea – Tok Pisin, with 1 million speakers, and Hiri Motu (Police Motu) – and in Fiji and Vanuatu: Bislama (< *bêche-de-mer*).

Some pidgins have a very short life, vanishing along with the particular circumstances in which they were generated: e.g. Vietnam Pidgin, a mushroom growth of the Vietnam War, and Bamboo English, a similar spin-off from the Korean War. Others, however, take root, and, in the course of succeeding generations, achieve first-language status. They are then known as creoles. By far the most prolific region for successful creoles has been the Caribbean, where Haitian French Creole, for example, is spoken by about 4 million people; Caribbean English Creole has about 3 million speakers in Jamaica, Trinidad and Tobago, and the Spanish–Portuguese–Dutch-based Papamiento has about fifty thousand speakers in Curaçao and adjoining areas. The manifold but predominantly English-based Hawaiian Creole is spoken by half a million people.

As should be clear from what has been said above, creoles derive from many and totally disparate matrices. It is all the more remarkable, therefore, that they often appear to treat appropriated material, from whatever source, in uniform fashion, almost as though creolization were a homogeneous linguistic process with its own combinatorial laws. In very general terms, a pidgin or creole simplifies its matrix or matrices (cf. Trader Navaho or Mobilian). But simplification by itself if not enough to explain the symmetrical correspondences found in the phonological and morphological systems of completely unconnected creoles.

A mature creole may find itself sharing a habitat with the intrusive language on which the ancestral pidgin was based. Thus, the official language of Haiti is literary French, from which the creole may reappropriate lexemes already present in reflex or pidgin form in its lexicon. Bilingualism in Haiti is extensive.

There follows a brief description of Haitian Creole.

HAITIAN CREOLE

INTRODUCTION

Haitian Creole dates from the mid-seventeenth century. The main component is French, representing an original pidgin plus an eighteenth-century influx of francophone colonists from all parts of France. There now remains little trace of either Carib or African elements. Virtually all of the slaves imported to the island came from West Africa – Senegal, Dahomey, and the Congo – and spoke Wolof, Mandingo, or Ewe.

PHONOLOGY

Consonants

  stops: p, b, t, d, k, g
  affricates: tʃ, dʒ
  fricatives: f, v, s, z, ʃ, ʒ, h
  nasals: m, n, ɲ, ŋ
  lateral and flap: l, r
  semi-vowels: j, w

/p, b/ are positionally aspirate or non-aspirate. Realization of /t/ and /d/ varies from dental to interdental, depending on following vowel. /r/ is lax, tending to /w/ with a voiceless allophone /ʐ/, notated as *r̥*. [w̥] is a voiceless allophone of /w/. Initial /j/ tends to be affricated; /j/ is notated as *y*.

Vowels

  oral: i, e, ɛ, a, ɔ, o, u, y
  nasal: ĩ, ɛ̃, ɑ̃, õ, ũ

/ɛ/ and /a/ are very open sounds; /e/ is closed. Here, /ɛ/ is notated as *è*; /y/ and /u/ as *u*; /o/ and /ɔ/ as *o*.

Tone

Homonyms may be distinguished by tone; e.g. *māmā* 'mother' *or* 'big', the latter meaning being distinguished by falling tone on the second syllable.

MORPHOLOGY AND SYNTAX

Noun

Nouns are invariable for number: e.g. *divē* 'wine' (< *du vin*); *tut divē* 'all the wines'. A number distinction is made in the post-fixed definite article, which is *-la/-a*; *-la/-a* for singular, *-yo* for plural; *ñu* 'one', is used as an indefinite article. Examples: *bèt-la* 'the animal', *bèt-yo* 'the animals'; *fãm-la* 'the woman', *fãm-yo* 'the women'. The article may be extended to express greater precision: e.g. *bèt-la-a* 'this particular animal'; *fãm-la-yo* 'the (specific) women' (*yo* is a third person plural pronoun marker; its use as a plural nominal marker is paralleled in certain West African languages).

The genitive relationship is expressed by juxtaposition: e.g. *r̥ad fãm-la* 'the woman's clothes/dress'; *kay žaluzi vèt-la* 'the house with the green shutters'.

The prefix *ti* (< *petit*) makes diminutives: e.g. *ti-pul* 'chicken'.

The French definite article appears in petrified form in some Creole nouns: e.g. *lāmè* 'the sea'; *zorèy* 'the ears' (< *les oreilles*).

Adjective

Most attributive adjectives follow the noun; a few common adjectives precede; there appears to be a difference in emphasis: e.g. *ñu gro madām* 'a large lady'; *ñu madām gro* 'a *very* large lady'. Some French feminine forms have become fixed for both masculine and feminine: e.g. *Ala kut solda-a kut!* 'How short the soldier is!' (*kut < courte*).

The adjective is reduplicated for emphasis: e.g. *li blāš-blāš* 'she is very white', which may, however, also mean 'she is whitish'. The difference in meaning can be expressed tonally: for emphasis, both adjectives are in citation tone; for diminution, the first takes a falling tone.

COMPARATIVE
Made with *pasé*: e.g. *U grā pasé.l* 'You're older than he is.'

Pronoun

	Singular	Plural
1	mwē/mṛē/m'	nu/n'
2	u	u/nu/zot/n'
3	li-l'	yo/y'/zot

M', *n'*, *l'*, *y'* function as subject prefixes before initial vowel: e.g. *m'vini b-matē* 'I came this morning'; *n'ap vini* 'we arrive'; *Zot fini?* 'Have you finished?' *M, n, l* are attached to vowel finals as objective pronouns: e.g. *bā-m sa* 'give me that'; *m'we-u* 'I see you'; *pòté-l vini bā-mṛē* 'bring it to me'; *m'viṛé-yo* 'I've returned them'.

POSSESSIVE MARKERS
Sing. 1 *-m*, 2 *-u*, 3 *-li*; pl. 1 *-nu*, 2 *-nu*, 3 *-yo*: e.g. *papam* 'my father'; *māmāu* 'your mother'; *sènu* 'our/your sister'.

DEMONSTRATIVE ADJECTIVE
sa-a follows noun: e.g. *fi sa-a* 'this girl'. Similarly, *sila-a* 'that', pl. *sila-yo*. These forms also function as demonstrative pronouns: e.g. *bā-m sila-a* 'give me that'; *m'pito sila-yo* 'I prefer those'.

INTERROGATIVE PRONOUN
ki 'who?'; *kisa* 'what?': e.g. *Kisa u fè?* 'What have you done?'; *Ak (< avec) kisa u māžé?* 'With what do you eat?'

RELATIVE PRONOUN
ki (invariable) functions only as subject: e.g. *fām ki vini wè-u la* 'the woman who came to see you'; but *fām u té vin wè-a* 'the woman whom you came to see' (for *té*, see **Verb**, below).

Numerals

As in French, with creolized spelling: e.g. *dé = deux*, *twa trois*.

Verb

The stem is invariable; nuance of tense and mood is expressed via auxiliary particles. The stem itself serves also as an imperative: e.g. *vini we* 'come and see'.

The collocation of subject plus verb (plus object) can refer to past or present action, definite or indefinite: e.g. *li vin koté-m* 'he/she comes/came to me'; *li tužu vin koté-m* 'he/she always comes to me'; *m'pa ṛēmē-u* 'I don't love you'; *m'tužu ṛēmē-u* 'I have always loved you'; *m'māžé* 'I eat/ate/have eaten'. The particle *té* preceding the verb denotes past, possibly habitual, action: e.g. *yo té-bwè rōm* 'they drank/were always drinking rum'; *yo té-bwè rōm-la* 'they had drunk the rum'. The particle *a/va/ava* denotes future action: e.g. *surit a-māžé-l* 'the mice will eat it'.

A conditional is made with *t'ava/té-va/t'a*: e.g. *N'té-kwè u t'a-vini* 'We thought you would have come'. *apé/ap* denotes imperfective aspect or progressive tense: e.g. *m'apé-māžé* 'I'm still eating'. *Pu* is a necessitative marker: e.g. *T ān, li pu-rivé* 'Wait, he's bound to come.' For the recent past, *fèk/fèk-sòt* can be used: e.g. *M'fèk-sòt-kōnē-l* 'I've just this moment made his acquaintance.'

Inceptive: *prā < prendre*, e.g. *Piti-la fèk-prā-tuse* 'The child has just started to cough.' Another inceptive formula is *apr'al* + verb: e.g. *M'apr'al-ékri* 'I'm starting/going to write.'

Māké (< manquer) is used in the sense of 'almost', 'just fail to': e.g. *M'māké-trāglé afòs ri* 'I laughed so much I almost choked.' *Sa* denotes possibility, ability: e.g. *m'sa-kōtré-l* 'I can/may meet him', negative: *m'pa sa-kōtré-l*. *Kapab* is used in the same sense: e.g. *m'kapab/kabli lèt-sa-a* 'May I read this letter?' *Fòk < il faut que*: e.g. *fòk li rivé* 'He'll have to come/he must come'.

Most Creole verbs are both transitive and intransitive, active and passive: e.g. *m'péyé-u* 'I've paid you'; *žorāš-la péyé* 'the orange is paid for'; *ašté* 'to buy/be bought'.

Prepositions

The great majority are French-based: e.g. *pu (< pour)* 'for', *ak (< avec)* 'with', *parapot (< par rapport à)* 'because of', *pādā (< pendant)* 'during'; *ña (< dans* 'in, among': *pi bèl ña tut médām-yo* 'the prettiest of all the ladies' (notice in *médām-yo* the reflex of French plural *mesdames*).

Word order

SVO: indirect object precedes direct.

1 Matamana negana ai Hereva vada e nohova; una Hereva na Dirava ida e nohova; una Hereva na Dirava. 2 Ia na matamana negana ai Dirava ida e nohova. 3 Ḡau iboudiai iena amo e vara: e vara ḡaudia ta ia murinai se vara, lasi vaitani. 4 Mauri be ia lalonai: una mauri na taunimanima edia diari. 5 Diari be dibura lalonai e hedinarai; bona dibura ese se habodoa.

6 Tau ta e vara, Dirava ese e siaia, ladana be Ioane. 7 Ia na hereva momokani igwauraina bona diari ihahedinaraina totona ema, taunimanima iboudiai ia dainai bae kamonai helaoreana.

8 Ia na dia una diari; to diari iharorolaina totona ema.

Motu

Bipo tru Tok i stap. Tok i stap wantaim God. Na 1
Tok em yet i God. / Bipo tru em i stap wantaim 2
God. / Em i wokim olgeta samting. Na i no gat wan- 3
pela samting i kamap long narapela rot. Nogat. Olgeta samting i kamap, em yet i wokim na i kamap. /
Laip i stap long em, na dispela laip em i lait bilong 4
ol man. / Dispela lait i save givim lait long tudak. Na 5
tudak i no bin karamapim em.

Wanpela man i kamap, nem bilong en Jon. God i 6
bin salim em i kam. / Em i kam bilong autim tok. 7
Em i autim tok long dispela lait, bilong olgeta man i
ken harim tok bilong em, na ol i ken bilip. / Em yet 8
em i no dispela lait. Nogat. Em i kam bilong autim
tok tasol long dispela lait.

Tok Pisin

POLISH

INTRODUCTION

Polish is usually regarded as the sole survivor of the Lechitic sub-group of West Slavonic languages, though some authorities treat the dialect form known as Kashubian as a separate language (*see* **Kashubian**). The written record in Polish begins in the fourteenth century – apart from the famous sentence found in a thirteenth-century Latin document: 'daj ać ja pobruczę a ty poczywa' (in modernized spelling), presumably uttered by a considerate miller to his spouse: 'I'll grind for a bit, you take a break.' The first great Polish writer is Jan Kochanowski in the sixteenth century, the author of *Treny*, a beautiful threnodic sequence on the death of his little daughter. The Romantic period produced at least four outstanding figures, all of whom spent most of their productive years in emigration: Adam Mickiewicz, the national poet of Poland, whose *Pan Tadeusz* (1843) is a splendid apotheosis, both of Polish aspirations and of the Polish past; Juliusz Słowacki, Zygmunt Krasiński, and Cyaprian Norwid. In the early years of the twentieth century two novelists produced masterpieces: Stefan Żeromski's *Popioły* ('Ashes'), a saga of the Napoleonic era in Poland, rich in rapturous and lyrical descriptions of the Polish countryside, and Władysłow Reymont's *Chłopi* ('The Peasants'), an encyclopaedic survey of Polish peasant life in the nineteenth century. This novel received the Nobel Prize in 1924; a previous Nobel laureate was Henryk Sienkiewicz (for *Quo Vadis?*) in 1905. An impressive school of post-Second World War poets includes such individual voices as Tadeusz Różewicz and Zbigniew Herbert. In 1980 the Nobel Prize for Literature went again to a Polish writer – Czesław Miłosz.

Today, Polish is spoken by some 40 million people in the Republic of Poland, of which it is the official language. In addition there are about 6 million Poles in the USA, and several hundred thousand elsewhere.

SCRIPT

The Roman alphabet, plus marked letters for specific Polish sounds: ą, ć, ę, ł, ń, ó, ś, ź, ż.

PHONOLOGY

Consonants

stops: p, b, t, d, k, g
affricates: tɕ, dʑ, ts, dz, tʃ, dʒ
fricatives: f, v, ɕ, ʑ, s, z, ʃ, ʒ
nasals: m, n, ɲ
laterals and flap: l, ł (→ w), r
semi-vowels: j, w

/tɕ/ (notated as *ć*) and /dʑ/ (notated as *dź*) are pre-palatal, in opposition to alveolar /tʃ/ and /dʒ/.

Vowels

oral: i, ɛ, a, ɔ, u
nasal: ɛ̃, ɔ̃

Vowels are not reduced in unstressed position, in contrast to Russian, for example. Final voiced consonants are unvoiced, e.g. *mąż* 'husband' → [mɔ̃ʃ]. There is also an elaborate system of assimilation, both preparatory and regressive, at junctures: e.g. with prepositions: *w Polsce* 'in Poland' → [f]*Polsce*; *pod tytułem* 'under the title' → *po*[t].*tytułem*]; *odporność* 'resistance' → *o*[t]*porność*.

Stress

Invariably on penultimate syllable, except in foreign words like *fábryka*, *polítyka*; the conditional particle *-by* does not affect stress: e.g. *zróbił* 'he did'; *zróbiłby* 'he would do'.

MORPHOLOGY AND SYNTAX

Noun

Polish has three genders, two numbers, and seven cases, if we include the vocative. There are no articles. Certain noun endings are coded for gender, e.g. most nouns in *-a* are feminine, as are all nouns in *-ość*; nouns ending in hard consonants are masculine; all in *-e* and *-o* are neuter.

DECLENSION
There are four main types:

1. *a*-stems (mostly feminine): e.g. *kobieta* 'woman', *noga* 'leg, foot';
2. *o*-stems (masculine): e.g. *pan* 'gentleman, Mr > you' (polite 2nd person);
3. *o*-stems (neuter): e.g. *miasto* 'place, town';
4. *i*-stems (feminine): e.g. *noc* 'night'.

An animate/inanimate opposition appears in *masculine o-stems*, where the accusative case of a noun denoting an *animate being* takes the form of the genitive, an opposition reflected in adjectival and pronominal concord: e.g. (*Pamiętam*) *mojego starego ojca* '(I remember) my old father' (*mój* 'my (masc.)', *stary* 'old', *ojciec* 'father'). In the plural genitive, this animate/inanimate opposition is replaced by a more restrictive one, which sets up an opposition between men on the one hand, and everything else on the other: cf. the following three masculine nouns: *chłop* 'peasant', *rolnik* 'farmer', *pies* 'dog': for the first two, the plural accusative = plural genitive: *chłopów, rolników*; but, *pies* has plural genitive *psów*, acc. *psy* = nominative.

Specimen declensions: *noga* 'leg, foot'; *pan* 'gentleman'; *noc* 'night'

	Singular	Plural	Singular	Plural	Singular	Plural
nom.	noga	nogi	pan	panowie	noc	noce
gen.	nogi	nog	pana	panów	nocy	nocy
dat.	no**dz**e	nogom	panu	panom	nocy	nocom
acc.	nogę	nogi	pana	panów	noc	noce
instr.	nogą	nogami	panem	panami	nocą	nocami
loc.	no**dz**e	nogach	panu	panach	nocy	nocach

Note consonant alternation in the declension of *noga*: *g/dz*. This is frequent in Polish inflection; cf. *ręka* ('hand') pl. *ręce*; *brat* 'brother', pl. *bracia*.

Adjective

As attribute, adjective normally precedes noun, and is in concord for gender, number, case. For example, the hard stem *pełny* 'full': masculine and feminine singular, plural for male persons:

	Masculine	Feminine	Plural (men)
nom.	pełny	pełna	pełni
gen.	pełnego	pełnej	pełnych
dat.	pełnemu	pełnej	pełnym
acc.	pełnego/pełny	pełną	pełnych
instr.	pełnym	pełną	pełnymi
loc.	pełnym	pełnej	pełnych

Examples:

każdego polskiego miasta 'of each Polish town'

Mamy piękną pogodę 'We're having fine weather'

naszym kochanym córkom 'to our dear daughters'

COMPARATIVE

(*ej*)*szy* added to base form: e.g. *stary* 'old' – *starszy*; *trudny* 'difficult' – *trudniejszy*. The comparative is, of course, declined as a normal adjective. The comparative may also be formed with the adverb *bardziej* 'more': e.g. *bardziej głęboki* 'deeper'.

Pronoun

PERSONAL

The independent personal pronouns are:

		Singular		Plural
1		ja		my
2		ty		wy
3	masc.	on	male persons:	oni
	fem.	ona		
	nt.	ono	others:	one

These are fully declined; e.g. the other cases of first person singular are: gen. *mnie*; dat. *mnie, mi*; acc. *mnie, mię*; instr. *mną*; loc. *mnie*. The polite second person form of address is *Pan/Pani*: e.g. *Proszę Pana, gdzie Pan teraz pracuje?* 'Excuse me (for asking), where are you working at present?'

POSSESSIVE

The first and second person possessive adjectives – *mój, moja, moje*; *twój, twoja, twoje* – with plural forms – *nasz, nasza, nasze*; *wasz, wasza, wasze* – agree with their referents in gender, number, and case. The third person forms, *jego, jej, jego*; pl. *ich* (all three genders), are invariable. The polite second person forms, *pana, pani*, with pl. *państwa*, are also invariable.

DEMONSTRATIVE ADJECTIVE

ten, ta, to 'this'; two plural forms: *ci* for male persons, *te* for everything else. *Tamten, tamta, tamto* 'that'. All forms are fully declined.

INTERROGATIVE PRONOUN

kto 'who?'; *co* 'what?' Fully declined. *Czy* is an introductory interrogative marker, requiring a yes/no answer: e.g. *Czy samolot często się opóźnia?* 'Is the plane often late?'

RELATIVE PRONOUN

który, która, które 'who'; *kto, co* 'which': e.g.

> chłopiec, który przyszedł pierwszy 'the boy who came first'
>
> chłopcy, których uczyłem 'the boys (whom) I taught'
>
> ten, kto to zrobił 'the one who did it'

Numerals

The Polish numerical system is of considerable complication. 1 *jeden*: this is a regular adjective, fully declined; 2 *dwaj*, gen. *dwóch* for male persons only; fem. *dwie*, other masculine and neuter, *dwa*; 3 *trzej, trzech* (male persons only); otherwise, *trzy*; similarly for 4 *cztery*. From 5 onwards, numbers have two forms only; a nom./acc. uninflected form for all referents except male persons; and an inflected form in *-iu* which provides all cases for male human referents, and the oblique cases for other nouns. Thus: *pięć biletów, pięć kobiet* 'five tickets', 'five women'; but, *pięciu mężczyzn* 'five men'. From 5 upwards, the noun is in the genitive plural, the verb in the singular (third person neuter): e.g. *pięciu panów* 'five men', *pięc kobiet* 'five women', *Pięc psów mieszka w tym domu* 'Five dogs live in this house.'

Verb

The Polish verb has imperfective, perfective, iterative, and semelfactive aspects; a periphrastic passive voice; three moods – indicative, imperative, and conditional; present, past, and future tenses; non-finite forms.

ASPECT

Formation of perfective from imperfective aspect is, typically, by addition of prefix, which often changes not only the aspect but also the meaning of the verb: cf. from *pisać* 'to write': perfective *napisać* 'to have written'; with change in nuance: *dopisać* 'to add to something in writing'; *podpisać* 'to sign'; *zapisać* 'to make a note of'.

Some perfective forms are suppletive: e.g. *brać* 'take' – *wziąć*; *mówić* 'speak' – *powiedzieć*.

Secondary imperfective forms are generated from the perfective aspect by lengthening of the stem: e.g. *dopisać*: *dopisywać*; or by ablaut: *odnieść* 'take' – *odnosić*.

The *-ywa-* infix is also typical of the iterative aspect: e.g. *pisywać*:

W młodości pisywał wiele listów
'When he was young, he was in the habit of writing many letters.'

Semelfactive: a characteristic ending of the semelfactive infinitive is *-nąć*: e.g.

Nagły, daleki, jadowity głos drgnął w lasach (Żeromski, *Popioły*)
'A sudden sound, far-off and baneful, stirred in the forest.'

Compare:

Ogary poszły w las. Echo ich grania **słabło** coraz bardziej aż wreszcie **utonęło** w milczeniu leśnym.
'The hounds had moved off into the woods. The echo of their belling grew fainter and fainter until at last it was submerged in the silence of the forest.'

In this sentence (also from *Popioły*) *słabnąć* is an imperfective verb describing a process – 'to weaken' – which is brought to an end by the perfective verb *utonąć* 'to sink'.

TENSE STRUCTURE

Indicative: the past tense distinguishes gender in the singular, and, in the plural, the male human preserve, characteristic of the nominal declension. Specimen paradigm: *czytać* 'to read':

Present: sing. 1 *czytam*, 2 *czytasz*, 3 *czyta*; pl. 1 *czytamy*, 2 *czytacie*, 3 *czytają*.

Past: sing. 1 *czytał.em/am*, 2 *czytał.eś/aś*, 3 *czytał/czytała/czytało*; pl. 1 *czytaliśmy/czytałyśmy*, 2 *czytaliście/czytałyście*, 3 *czytali/czytały*.

Future: sing. 1, 2, 3: *będę/będziesz/będzie czytał/a/o*; pl. *będziemy/będziecie/ będą czytali* (male humans only), *czytały* (others). Thus: *będziemy czytali* 'we shall read/be reading' (men speaking); *będą czytały* 'they (not men) will be reading.'

The future forms given here are *imperfective* only. The perfective future is made by adding the present imperfective endings to the perfective stem:

Jutro **na**pisze do niej list
'He'll write (= have written) a letter to her tomorrow.'

Compare:

ØPisze ten list od dwóch godzin
'He's been writing that letter for two hours.'

CONDITIONAL

The endings sing. *bym*, *byś*, *by*; pl. *byśmy*, *byście*, *by* are added to the third person singular and plural past tense of the sense-verb: the male human restriction is observed. Thus: *pisali.by* 'they (men) would write'; *pisały byśmy* 'we (not men) would write'.

IMPERATIVE

Often formed from third person singular present tense (imperfective) by dropping last letter: e.g. *pisze* 'he writes': *pisz!* 'write!', pl. *pisz.cie!*; or by dropping last letter of third person plural (verbs in *-ać*): e.g. *czytają* → *czytaj!*

PARTICIPLES

Present in *-ąc*: e.g. *niosąc* 'carrying'; *widząc* 'seeing'. These are declined as adjectives: e.g. *kochająca córka* 'a loving daughter'. When used adverbially, the participle is indeclinable:

Wchodząc do kościoła Mariackiego, Zosia podziwiała słynny ołtarz
'Entering the Maria Church, Zosia admired the famous altar.'

The past participle (perfective verbs) has the ending *-wszy/-łszy*: e.g. *wróciwszy na swe miejsce* 'having returned to his place'; *wyszedłszy* 'having gone out'.

PASSIVE VOICE

Formed analytically with the auxiliary *być* 'to be' (imperfective) or *zostać* 'to remain' (perfective), plus passive past participle in *-ny/-na/-ne*, *-ty/-ta/-te*: e.g. *wszystko było zamknięte* 'everything was closed'; *...został zastrzelony* '... was shot dead'.

Negative

The general marker is *nie*; double and triple negatives are frequent.

Prepositions

Most Polish prepositions govern the genitive case, including the partitive genitive; the accusative, locative, and instrumental cases are also used. Some prepositions take more than one case, depending on sense: e.g.

Samolot poleci nad miasto 'The plane will fly away over the town' (acc.)

Lecimy nad miastem 'We are flying above the town' (instr.)

Word order

SVO is general.

1 Na początku było Słowo, a Słowo było u Boga, a Bogiem było Słowo.

2 To było na początku u Boga.

3 Wszystkie rzeczy przez nie się stały, a bez niego nic się nie stało, co się stało.

4 W niém był żywot, a żywot był światłością ludzi.

5 A światłość w ciemności świeci, ale ciemność jéj nie ogarnęła.

6 Był człowiek posłany od Boga, któremu imię było Jan.

7 Ten przyszedł na świadectwo, aby świadczył o światłości, aby przezeń wszyscy uwierzyli.

8 Nie był ci on światłością, ale, aby świadczył o światłości.

POLYNESIAN LANGUAGES

Geographically, the Polynesian languages fall into the following three clearly defined groups:

(a) Western Polynesian: Tongan, Niue, Samoan, East Uvean, East Futunan, the Ellice Islands language, and Tokelau.
(b) Eastern Polynesian: Maori, Rarotongan, Tahitian, Tuamotuan, Marquesan, Hawaiian, Mangarevan, Rapanui.
(c) The outliers. The following languages are spoken in the neighbourhood of the Solomon Islands: Sikaianan, Luangiuan, Rennellese; in the neighbourhood of the New Hebrides: Pileni, Mae, West Futunan, Aniwan, Mele-Fila, Tikopian; Nukuoro and Kapingamarangi are northern outliers; West Uvean is spoken in the Loyalty Islands. There are several smaller languages.

Genetically, however, neither the exact provenance of the Polynesian languages nor their internal relationships are so clear. Until the 1930s, Polynesian, Indonesian, and Melanesian-Micronesian were regarded as the three branches of the so-called 'Austronesian' family, a viewpoint which has not been entirely discarded. In 1934–8 Otto Dempwolff argued on phonological grounds that Polynesian, Melanesian, and Micronesian should be regarded as forming a single unit, to which the name 'Oceanic' was given. A third hypothesis (Kähler, 1962) identifies Polynesian as an outlying sub-division of the Indonesian branch.

As regards internal relationships within the group, various classifications have been proposed: e.g. that of Pawley (1936), who distinguishes (a) Tongic, consisting of Tongan and Niue; (b) Samoic, comprising Samoan, Ellice Islands, Tokelau, East Futunan, and the outliers: (c) East Polynesian. In this classification, the New Hebridean languages form a specific group among the outliers.

The linguistic question is throughout beset by the problem of when and from where the various island groups were first settled. Tonga seems to have been the scene of the earliest colonization (before 1000 BC), by settlers coming from Indonesia and New Guinea, followed by Samoa (more than 2,000 years ago) and Niue. From the central springboards of Tonga and Samoa, penetration of eastern Polynesia proceeded over the subsequent 1,000 years (Hawaii in the eighth century AD, New Zealand about 1200). Many island groups have probably been subjected to several successive waves of colonization.

SCRIPT

Only one form of indigenous writing is known to have been used in Polynesia – the Easter Island script (rongorongo), which has not yet been deciphered (*see* **Rapanui**). Roman-based alphabets have been introduced for several Polynesian languages, usually in association with a translation of the Bible, in whole or in part.

PHONOLOGY

Consonants

The Proto-Polynesian consonantal system has been reconstructed as:

p, f, w, m; t, n, s, l, r; k, ŋ; h, ʔ

In contemporary Polynesian, Proto-Pol. /p, t, k, m, n, ŋ/, are retained unchanged in virtually all cases; /f, s, r/l/ are retained in approximately half; /w, h, ʔ/, are retained in about 15 per cent of daughter languages. Where these are not retained, /w/ > /v/, /h/ > Ø, /ʔ/ > Ø. The former contrast between /r/ and /l/ has been lost, so that these letters represent notation for one and the same sound. Vocalic systems have been retained almost unchanged. Extreme reductionism is found in Hawaiian where Proto-Pol. /t/ > /k/, /ŋ/ > /n/, and /r, h, ʔ/ are all reduced to Ø. This gives a total of eight consonants. Tongan (*see* **Tongan**) has the richest consonantal inventory. Certain consonantal clusters are found in some of the outliers, e.g. /mb, nd/ in Mae and in Pileni. These may be the result of Melanesian influence.

The extreme poverty of the consonantal structure means that very few monosyllabic forms are possible (in the case of Hawaiian, only 45). However, it is precisely these monosyllabic forms that provide the nominal and verbal particles which abound in Polynesian languages, and which are crucially important for their syntax. The great majority of Polynesian roots are bivocalic, of (C)V(C)V type.

Vowels

i, e, a, o, u

MORPHOLOGY AND SYNTAX

In parallel with the high degree of phonological isomorphism, there is also considerable structural similarity between the various Polynesian languages. Some generally valid points are here set out, with examples where helpful.

1. Authorities on Polynesian languages do not always agree as to what exactly constitutes a Polynesian 'word', since boundaries between 'words' tend to be fluid. However, three classes of items which go towards generating 'words' can

be distinguished: (a) the (open) class of auto-semantic roots; (b) the affixes which can be prefixed or suffixed to items in (a); (c) particles. Classes (b) and (c) are closed. Example in Tongan: *ko e nofo'anga'a Tolu* 'Tolu's dwelling-place' (where *nofo* 'to sit' is a root; *'anga*, location marker, is an affix; *Tolu* is a proper name; *ko* is introductory particle; *e* is defining particle; *'a* is attributive particle).

2. Reduplication (partial or total) occurs widely and is a highly productive way of expressing reiteration, plurality, intensification or diminution, semantic extension, etc.: e.g. reiteration: Samoan, *eva* 'talk' – *evaeva* 'talk a lot, spend (the evening) talking; intensification: Tahitian *roa* 'long' – *roroa* 'very long' (partial redup.); plurality: Tongan *lahi* 'big' – *lalahi* (pl. form of adjectival base); semantic extension: Tahitian *arui* 'night' – *aruiarui* 'twilight', Tongan *moho* 'cooked' – *momoho* 'ripe'.

3. Internal inflection. Rare: occurs as plurality marker: e.g. Tongan *fefine* 'woman' – pl. *fafine*; *tangi* 'weep' – *tengihia* 'weep for, lament'.

4. Nominal and verbal particles gravitate to left-hand side of nucleus; adverbial particles gravitate to right.

5. Preposited particles: examples from a West Polynesian (Tongan), and East Polynesian (Marquesan), and from an outlier language (Nukuoro):

Nominal particles:

(a) prepositions

	Tongan	Marquesan	Nukuoro
focus marker	ko	ko	go
agentive marker	'e	e	e
alienable possession	'a	a	a
inalienable possession	'o	o	o
relative marker	'i	i	i

(b) determinatives

	Tongan	Marquesan	Nukuoro
definite article (sing.)	he/'e	te	de
personal article	a	a	a

Verbal particles:

aspect/mood/tense markers

	Tongan	Marquesan	Nukuoro
(a) inceptive	ka	'aa	ga
(b) perfective tense	kuo	ua/uu	gu
(a) past	na'a, na'e, ne	i	ne
(b) non-past	e/'e, te	e	e

6. Pronouns: singular, dual, plural forms, with exclusive/inclusive contrast in first person preposited:

			Tongan	*Samoan*
singular	1	excl.	u/ou/ku	ou/'ou
		incl.	te	ta
	2		ke	'ee
	3		ne	'ee
dual	1	excl.	ma	maa
		incl.	ta	taa
	2		mo	('ou)lua
	3		na	laa
plural	1	excl.	mau	maatou
		incl.	tau	—
	2		mou	('ou)tou
	3		nau	laatou

7. Plurality markers are sited between determinative and nucleus: e.g. Tahitian *e **mau** fare* 'houses'; *te **mau** fare* 'the houses'.

8. Demonstratives. Triple-term series by degree of distancing in space or in topicalization: e.g. Tahitian *teie – tena – tera*; Maori *teenei – teena – teera*; Tongan *ni – na – ia*.

9. The numerals are largely isomorphic over the whole field. 1–10 in Tongan: *taha, ua, tolu, fā, nima, ono, fitu, valu, hiva, hongofulu*; Samoan: *tasi, lua, tolu, fa, lima, ono, fitu, valu, iva, sefulu*.

10. Alienable/inalienable possession. Practically all Polynesian languages make a distinction between alienable and inalienable possession: a distinction which has to do not so much with the nature of the objects thus apportioned as with the relationship between them and the natural or contingent owner. Typically, the alienable series is marked by *-a-* , the inalienable series by *-o-*. The taxonomy into *-a-* and *-o-* categories may vary from one socio-linguistic milieu to another, but essentially the key point remains that the *-a-* series is subject-related, the *-o-* series object-related. With regard to the situation in Maori, Biggs (1969: 43) writes: 'Possession of anything towards which the possessor is dominant, active or superior, is expressed by *a*; possession of things in respect of which the possessor is subordinate, passive or inferior, is expressed by *o*.' And Buse (1960: 123) offers the following interesting information on the Rarotongan series:

> as a rule, a person stands in an A-relationship to his or her descendants, employees, spouse, lover (all acquired relationships), animals (not the horses), food, crops, instruments, tools, machinery, movable property (not means of transport). He stands in an O-relationship to his ancestors, employers (relationships which he is not responsible for, or in which he does not play the controlling part), parts of the body, clothing, buildings, conveyances, abstractions. (BSOAS 23; quoted in Krupa 1982: 115)

For examples of the *-a-* and *-o-* categories in practice, *see* **Tongan, Samoan, Tahitian, Maori**.

11. Negation. Negative markers are usually accompanied by positional and structural readjustment of the positive order. In some languages the negative markers are coded for tense (*see* **Tahitian**). There are specific markers for prohibition.

12. Sentence structure. Both nominative–accusative and ergative constructions are found; some Polynesian languages have both. As in certain American Indian languages, an ostensible 'object' may be absorbed as a constituent of the verbal complex: 'he shoots (a) bird(s)' → 'he is-a-bird-shooter'. That is, an intransitive sentence results. See Krupa (1982: 122–33) for a full discussion of this interesting point.

13. Word formation. (a) root + affix (prefix or suffix); (b) reduplication; (c) compounding. Examples from Tahitian:

(a) *Fa'a* + root, e.g. *aogā* 'useful' – *fa'aaogā* 'to utilize'; *fa'asamoa* 'in Samoan'.
   Root + *a*, e.g. *nofo* 'to sit' – *nofoa* 'chair'.
(b) *Fulu* 'feather': e.g. *fulufulu* 'hair'.
(c) *Tusi* 'to write' + *tala* 'story': *tusitala* 'story-teller, writer'.

Word order

VSO is usual. SVO is found in certain outliers.

PORTUGUESE

INTRODUCTION

Portuguese belongs to the Italic branch of the Indo-European family. It is the official language of Portugal, where it is spoken by about 9 million people, and of Brazil, where the number of speakers is estimated at about 125 million. In addition, it is the language of administration in Angola, Mozambique, Guinea-Bissau, Cape Verde, and San Tomé e Príncipe. Other islands of Portuguese speech are Goa, East Timor, and Macao.

Roman occupation of the western seaboard of the Iberian peninsula lasted from 200 BC to the fourth century AD. Subsequently, Visigoths and Moors came and went, but the Vulgar Latin spoken in Roman Gallaecia and Lusitania had become firmly established, and, by the time the Moors were expelled (the reconquest was complete by 1267) it was spreading to the rest of what is now Portugal. The phonological complexities of Modern Portuguese were already inherent in the Vulgar Latin of Gallaecia, which retained the vocalic structure of Latin while at the same time discarding some of the key consonants which supported it. The Portuguese literary language (from the thirteenth century onwards) is based on the south-central dialect of Lisbon/Coimbra. The literature is extensive and rich in all genres; in the modern period, particularly strong in lyric poetry, the essay and the novel.

In the fifteenth/sixteenth centuries Portuguese was the first Indo-European language to spread to sub-Saharan Africa, and the first to rejoin its congeners in India.

SCRIPT

The Latin alphabet minus k, w, y; diacritics are used: acute, grave, circumflex, cedilla, and tilde, the latter to indicate nasalization in the absence of a nasal consonant. The correspondence between symbol and sound is weak: five vowel symbols do duty for 17 sounds, while 18 consonants have some 30 values. For example, the letter s is realized, depending on phonetic environment, as /s/, /z/, /ʃ/ or /ʒ/: cf. *todas as mesmas senhoras* 'all the same ladies', realized as: /todɛz.aʒ.meʒməʃ.sɪɲorəʃ/

EUROPEAN PORTUGUESE

PHONOLOGY

Consonants

stops: p, b, t, d, k, g
fricatives: f, v, s, z, ʃ, ʒ
nasals: m, n, ɲ
laterals and flaps: l, ɫ, ʎ, r, ʀ
semi-vowels: j, w

The affricate /tʃ/ appears in northern Portuguese. /b, d, g/ have allophones [ß, ð, ɣ]

Vowels

i, e, ɛ, a, ɐ, ə, ɔ, o, u

Basic series, expanded by diphthongs. All vowels occur nasalized (by tilde, or by presence of a nasal consonant). Assimilation and sandhi, both consonantal and vocalic, play a key role in Portuguese pronunciation, in conjunction with tonic stress, which is accompanied by marked reduction of unstressed vowels. The stress pattern is phrasal rather than local: Cf. *Esta manhã vou escrever umas cartas* 'This morning I'm going to write letters', realized as: /ɛʃtə mãɲã voʃ.krəver.uməʃ.kartəʃ/; *que se divirta bem* 'have a good time', /kəsədəvirtəbẽi/ – stress marked by bold print.

MORPHOLOGY AND SYNTAX

Noun

Nouns are masculine or feminine, singular or plural. Some nominal endings are gender-related, e.g. *-a, -ção, -são* are feminine, *-o* is masculine. Gender is not predictable from consonantal endings: thus, *amor* is masculine, but *cor* is feminine.

ARTICLES
Definite: *o* (masc.), *a* (fem.), pl. *os, as*; indefinite: *um, uma*; *uns, umas*.

PLURAL
The marker is -(V)*s* with a wide range of phonological adjustment at junctures, e.g. *a liçao* 'the lesson', pl. *as lições*; *a viagem* 'the journey', pl. *as viagens*; *o hotel* 'the hotel', pl. *os hoteis*.

CASE
Relations are expressed analytically with the help of prepositions, many of which coalesce with the article: *em* 'in' + *o* → *no*, *de* + *a* → *da*, etc.

Adjective

A basic opposition is Ø for masculine, -*a* for feminine, but many adjectives have identical forms for both genders. The attributive adjective may either precede or follow the noun; there is a preferred order for many adjectives. ANA is frequent: e.g. *um velho costume militar* 'an old military custom'.

Pronoun

(a) Strong: subject forms and emphatics:

sing.	1 eu	2 tu	3 masc. ele, fem. ela
pl.	1 nos	2 (*vos*, archaic;	3 masc. eles, fem. elas
		see **Polite address**,	
		below)	

The emphatic forms used with prepositions are identical except for first person singular which has *mim*: e.g. *para mim* /mī/ 'for me', and the second person singular which has *ti*.

(b) Weak: direct and indirect object: the direct object forms are:

sing.	1 me	2 te	3 masc. o, fem. a
pl.	1 nos	2	3 masc. os, fem. as

In the indirect object series, *me*, *te*, and *nos* are unchanged; *o* and *a* have the same indirect form, *lhe* /ʎe/; *os* and *as* have the form *lhes*.

POLITE ADDRESS
There are two forms: (a) *você(s)*; (b) *o senhor*, *a senhora*. Both of these forms require third person concord (cf. Sp. *usted*).

POSSESSIVE ADJECTIVE
Forms show gender throughout: e.g. *meu/minha*, *teu/tua*.

PRONOMINAL ORDER
In positive sentences, weak oblique pronouns are usually hyphenated to right-hand side of verb, indirect preceding direct: e.g. *ele dá-no-los* 'he gives them to us'; *ele dá-mo* 'he gives it to me' (*me + o → mo*). In negative, relative, optative, clauses, etc. the weak object precedes the verb: e.g. *quando a vi...* 'when I saw her ...'; *se me permite...* 'if you will allow me'.

A striking feature of Portuguese structure is that the oblique pronoun can be infixed between verb stem and personal ending, in the future and conditional tenses: e.g. *dar.lhe.iamos* 'we would give you/him'.

DEMONSTRATIVE PRONOUN/ADJECTIVE
Three degrees of removal: *este* 'this' – *esse* 'that' – *aquele* 'that (yonder)'. These are declined.

INTERROGATIVE PRONOUN
quem 'who?', (*o*) *que* 'what?'

RELATIVE PRONOUN

qual is declined for gender and number: *o qual, a qual*; pl. *os quais, as quais*. *Que* is invariable, with either singular or plural antecedent.

Numerals

1–10: *um/uma, dois/duas, três, quatro, cinco, seis, sete, oito, nove, dez*; 11 *onze*; 12 *doze*; 13 *treze*; 14 *catorze*; 16 **dezasseis**; 20 *vinte*; 100 *cem*. The *dois/duas* distinction of gender reappears in the hundreds for 200 onwards: e.g. *duzentos/duzentas*.

Verb

Three conjugations, characterized by infinitive ending: *-ar, -er, -ir*. There are active and passive voices; indicative, imperative, and subjunctive moods. The indicative active has six simple tenses (stem + personal ending) and four compound (auxiliary *ter* 'to have' + past participle). Typical personal endings are (here, for present of *-ar* verb): sing. *-o, -as, -a*; pl. *-amos, (-ais), -am*. Similar endings are added to the remaining tenses, whose first person forms are (*comprar* 'to buy'): imperfect *comprava*; preterite *comprei*; future *comprarei*; conditional *compraria*; pluperfect *comprara*; past participle: *comprado*: e.g. *tenho comprado* 'I have bought', *tem comprado* 'he has bought'.

The inflected infinitive: i.e. the infinitive plus the endings: sing. 1 Ø, 2 *-es*, 3 Ø; pl. 1 *-mos*, 2 *-des*, 3 *-em*. This peculiarly Portuguese construction is used to avoid subordinate clauses of various kinds: e.g. *ao chegar eu* 'when I arrive(d), will arrive'; *depois de (eles) chegarem* 'after they have/had arrived, will arrive'; *Acho melhor não fazeres questão* 'I think it will be as well if you don't make an issue of this'; *ouvi-os dizerem que...* 'I heard it being said that ...'.

Passive voice: is made with *ser* 'to be' + past participle.

THE VERB 'TO BE'

ser/estar: *ser* denotes essential, permanent properties; *estar* denotes a temporary and contingent state of affairs: *Lisboa é em Portugal* 'Lisbon is in Portugal'; *estamos em Lisboa* 'we are in Lisbon'. *Estar* is also used with the present participle to express continuous action: e.g. *está olhando para...* 'he/she is looking at ...'.

Negation

Não precedes the verb negated, often reinforced by second negative following verb: *não tenho nada* 'I have nothing'.

Prepositions

The basic series – *a* 'to', *ante* 'before', *após* 'after', *em* 'in', *para* 'for', etc. – is greatly extended by the use of nominals/adverbials + *de*: e.g. *abaixo de* 'below';

através de 'through'; *em lugar de* 'instead of'; *por detrás de* 'behind'.

Word order

SVO is normal.

BRAZILIAN PORTUGUESE

INTRODUCTION

About 120 million people speak Brazilian Portuguese (*brasileiro*) in a variety of dialects. The Paulista dialect (of São Paulo and district) and the Carioca dialect of Rio de Janeiro vary, for example, in the pronunciation of the sibilants /s, z/; Paulista /s/ = Carioca /ʃ/, Paulista /z/ = Carioco /ʒ/: e.g. *as ruas* 'the streets' – Paulista /ɐz.ʀuəs/, Carioca /ɐʃ.ʀuəʃ/.

PHONOLOGY

Portuguese was transplanted to the New World in the early sixteenth century. By the late seventeenth century phonological divergencies between the two languages, European and Brazilian Portuguese, had developed. Some of the more important are (EP = European Portuguese; BP = Brazilian):

1. EP /ʀ/ becomes a fricative in BP: /h, x, ʁ/: e.g. *dormir* 'to sleep' in BP is /duhmih/.
2. /t, d/ in EP become the corresponding affricates in BP, if followed by /i/: e.g. *bom dia* /bõ.dʒiə/ 'good day'; *sétimo* = /sɛtʃimu/ 'seventh'; *depressa* /dʒiprɛsə/ 'hurry'.
3. Clusters tend to be simplified in BP: e.g. *facto* → /fatu/; *secção* → /sesẽũ/.

MORPHOLOGY AND SYNTAX

Largely as in EP, but *haver* 'to have' has been completely replaced by *ter*, even in the impersonal usage: *Ha água gelada* → *Tem água gelada* 'There is iced water.' The weak pronominal object, which tends to follow the verb in EP, precedes it in BP: e.g. *Eu a vejo quase todos os dias* 'I see her almost every day.'

SECOND PERSON FORM OF ADDRESS
você(s) or *o senhor/a senhora*.

LEXICON
BP vocabulary differs from EP in two respects. Firstly, for many everyday objects and verbs BP often uses an alternative Indo-European root: e.g. EP *o comboio* 'the train' is *o trem* in BP; EP *o tabaco* 'tobacco' is BP *o fumo*; EP *pôr* 'to put' is BP *botar*.

Secondly, however, BP has borrowed a large number of words from various

African and South American Indian languages, especially from Tupian, with which Brazilian has been in close contact for centuries. Some outstanding Brazilian writers have drawn heavily on this exotic reservoir, which is particularly rich in terms for native fauna and flora, and, as a result, passages in their writings may be incomprehensible to an EP speaker, and indeed not always immediately clear to a BP speaker. For example, in his collection of short stories *Sagarana* (where *rana* is a Tupí affix meaning 'similar to, quasi', and *saga* is the Norse word), not only does Guimarães Rosa exploit the vocabulary peculiar to the *sertanejo* (the inhabitant of the *sertão*, the outback) but Portuguese morphology and syntax are drastically modulated to harmonize with this exotic element.

1 No Principio era a Palavra, e a Palavra estava junto de Deos, e a Palavra era Deos.

2 Esta estava no principio junto de Deos.

3 Por esta forão feitas todas as cousas, e sem ella se não fez cousa nenhuma do que fui feito.

4 Nella estava a vida, e a vida era a luz dos homens.

5 E a luz resplandece nas trevas; e as trevas não a comprehendê-rão.

6 Houve um homem enviado de Deos, cujo nome *era* João.

7 Este veio por testemunho, para que testificasse da Luz, para que todos por elle cressem.

8 Elle não era a Luz: mas para que testificasse da Luz.

(European Portuguese)

PRAKRIT

INTRODUCTION

The word Prakrit derives from the Sanskrit word *prākṛta*, which has two meanings: (a) 'appertaining to original (unmodified) form', and, hence, (b) 'natural' or, by extension, 'vulgar'.)

As codified by Pāṇini, Sanskrit was to remain the literary medium of Hinduism for some 1,200 years: a canonical hypostatization in phonological and morphological terms of the Vedic-Brahmin world-view. Throughout this long period, various forms of the spoken language which had emerged along with Sanskrit itself from the original Indo-Aryan matrix, continued to diverge, both from Sanskrit and from each other. These Indo-Aryan dialects are called Prakrits. The earliest Prakrits date from around the fifth century BC, and retain a number of synthetic elements (*see* **Pali**). Thereafter, the reductionism already present, even in Pali, gradually spreads to all areas of the phonological and morphological structure, and by the close of the Prakrit era (eleventh/twelfth centuries AD) the individual forms have already assumed the lineaments of the modern New Indo-Aryan languages (*see* **New Indo-Aryan Languages**).

The main forms of Prakrit are:

1. Old Prakrit: the language of the Asokan inscriptions.
2. Pāli: the language of the Buddhist canon.
3. Mahārāṣṭrī: used for verse passages in the Sanskrit drama; the ancestor of modern Marathi.
4. Śauraseni: the closest of the Prakrits to Classical Sanskrit; Śauraseni prose passages appear in the classical drama.
5. Māgadhī: an Eastern Prakrit, typically used by lower classes in the drama.
6. Ardhamāgadhī: the language of the oldest Jain (Śvetāmbara) sutras.
7. Jain-Śauraseni: the language of the Digāmbara canon (the Digāmbaras are the 'space-clad', those Jainas who believe that the body is 'space-clad' and needs no clothes; the Śvetāmbaras, the 'white-clad', wear white clothes).
8. Jain-Mahārāṣṭrī: the language of the non-canonical books of the Śvetāmbara.
9. Apabhraṁśa: the latest stage of Prakrit, marked *inter alia* by an increase in the non-Sanskrit Indo-Aryan element.

The following should also be mentioned: (a) Buddhist Hybrid Sanskrit, a highly Sanskritized artificial type of Prakrit known to us from central Asian manuscripts dating from the third to the fifth centuries AD; (b) Paiśācī, a somewhat mysterious form, once regarded as the language of demons.

According to the well-known tale in the Kathasaritsāgara of Somadeva, the Bṛhatkathā of Guṇāḍhya – the original source of the Kathasaritsāgara – was written in *paiśācī bhāṣā*.

It will be seen from the above that written Prakrit played a considerable part in three important fields:

(a) Religion: while literary Sanskrit remained the preserve of Brahmin Hinduism, both of the heterodox traditions, Buddhism and Jainism, were promulgated in Prakrit, the former in Pali, the latter in Mahārāṣṭrī and other forms (Mahāvīra, the founder of Jainism, is said to have preached in Ardhamāgadhī).

(b) Politics and statecraft: the Edicts of Aśoka (third century BC), promulgated in his capital city of Pāṭaliputra, were translated into various Prakrits and displayed on pillars throughout his kingdom.

(c) Literature: the Prakrits play a very important socio-linguistic role in the Sanskrit drama (c. second century AD onwards). While gods, heroes, and kings express themselves in literary Sanskrit, less exalted personages use various Prakrits. Thus, women talk in Śauraseni, but sing in Mahārāṣṭrī. Commoners use these and various other forms. At the bottom of the social scale are the menial types who speak in Māgadhī. One might compare the use of Low German by servants in the Hamburg opera of the eighteenth century.

SCRIPT

The Kharoṣṭhī script is found in the north-western inscriptions. Everywhere else, Brahmi script is the rule.

PHONOLOGY

In general, the phonetic inventory is fairly homogeneous over the whole field of Prakrit, and does not vary greatly from that of Sanskrit. The main divergences are:

1. The old diphthongs /aːi, aːu/, are reduced to /e, o/; /ṛ, ṝ, ḷ/ disappear.
2. Consonantal clusters are reduced:

    initial: there is a tendency towards single consonant initial only;
    medial: $C_1C_2(C_3)$ tend to become $C_x$geminate: e.g. *supta* > *sutta*; *satya* > *sacca*.

3. Intervocalic aspirates > /h/: e.g. *rudhira* > *ruhira* 'red'.
4. The Sanskrit sibilants /ś, ṣ, s/ are reduced to dental /s/.
5. Treatment of intervocalic stops:

    (a) Pali: stops retained;
    (b) Śauraseni and Māgadhī: voiced stops only;
    (c) Mahārāṣṭrī: stops disappear.

Thus, Skt *hita* 'placed, laid' – Śau. *hida* – Mah. *hiɵa*; Skt *prabhṛti* 'offering' – Śau. *pahudi* – Mah. *pahui*.

Loss of final consonants naturally eliminates most of the Sanskrit sandhi system. Hiatus is permissible, but vocalic sandhi at junctures is normally observed.

Magadhi is remarkable for two anomalies: the sibilant series is represented by /ś/; and /r/ becomes /l/, e.g. *lāāṇo* 'kings' (Skt *rājānaḥ*).

MORPHOLOGY AND SYNTAX

The reductionism characteristic of the phonological system is found also in the morphology. Paradigms shrink as specific inflections are lost, leading to a proliferation of variant forms with identical meanings.

Noun

The dual disappears, as does the consonantal declension. *a*, *i*, *u* stems remain (both long and short).

Specimen declension (Mahārāṣṭrī) of an *a*-stem: *putta* = Skt *putra* 'son'.

	Singular	Plural
nominative	putto	puttā
accusative	puttaṁ	putte/puttā
instrumental	puttena	puttehiṁ
dative	puttāa	—
ablative	puttāo	—
genitive	puttassa	puttāṇa(ṁ)
locative	puttammi/putte	puttesu(ṁ)

In feminine declension, singular genitive, locative, and instrumental coalesce. Thus *devīe* = these three cases of *devī*.

Adjective

Declined like other nominals.

Pronoun

Typical are:

	Singular	Plural
1	ahaṁ	amhe
2	tumaṁ	tumhe

Gender is distinguished in the third person masc. *sa*, neut. *taṁ*, fem. *sā*; pl. masc., neut. *te*, fem. *tāo*.

Verb

The effects of reductionism and erosion are more marked in the verbal system than in the nominal. The main changes are:

1. Disappearance of the dual number.
2. Virtual disappearance of the middle voice (ātmanepada) except in Pali. A passive form is retained.
3. Synthetic tense system reduced to present indicative and future (future in *-issa*).
4. Imperative and optative forms retained (opt. in *-ejja*).
5. Non-finite forms: participle (past passive) increasingly used in formation of past tense.
6. The ten classes of verb distinguished by Indian grammarians are reduced to two (*a*- and *e*-classes); to one single class in Apabhraṁśa.

PROVENÇAL

See **Occitan**.

QUECHUA

INTRODUCTION

Quechua belongs to the Quechuamaran branch of the Andean Equatorial grouping. The original habitat of the Quechua people seems to have been in the Apurímac–Ayacucho area of what is now Peru. Here arose the Inca Empire, which was known up the the Spanish Conquest as *Tahuaninsuyu* 'the four regions' (*tahua* 'four', *suyu* 'region'). Quechua, the predominant language of the empire, was spoken in two versions: the ruling caste spoke Inca Simi, which was presumably a high-caste register of the Kråmå type (*see* **Javanese**), although some authorities believe it to have been a secret language; the ordinary people spoke Runa Simi, or 'popular language'. From the mid-sixteenth century onwards, the tribal name Kechwa/Quechua came to be used to designate Runa Simi.

For several reasons, with proselytizing high among them, the Spanish establishment encouraged the spread of Quechua. The language was taught at the University of Lima (founded in 1551), and in 1560 Domingo de Santo Tomás produced the first Quechua grammar. At the same time, however, the active promotion of Quechua over a huge area extending from Ecuador to Argentine, led inevitably to its dilution and degeneration. It is now spoken in various dialect forms throughout Peru and Bolivia and in much of Ecuador, by something like 8 million people. During the 1970s, Quechua enjoyed a brief period of semi-official status, from which it was demoted in 1979.

There are two main dialect forms: Cuzco Quechua, the Bolivian standard, and Ayacucho Quechua, the Peruvian standard. The main difference between them is a phonological one – the presence in Cuzco Quechua of a three-way opposition in the stops and affricates: surd – glottalized (ejective) surd – aspirate surd, e.g. /p – p' – ph/. There are also minor grammatical differences, e.g. the 1st person plural (inclusive) pronoun is *ñoqanchik* in Ayacucho, *ñoqanchis* in Cuzco. The two dialects are mutually comprehensible. The description which follows here is essentially of Ayacucho Quechua.

The most important literary work in Quechua is the drama *Ollanta*, which is in the Cuzco dialect, and is probably post-Conquest in date.

SCRIPT

Runa Simi was unwritten. The first official Quechua alphabet was drafted in 1939 and adopted in 1946. It contains 21 letters of the Roman alphabet.

PHONOLOGY

Consonants

    stops: p, t, q, k
    affricate: tʃ
    fricatives: s, γ, χ, h
    nasals: m, n, ɲ
    laterals and flaps: l, ʎ, r, rr
    semi-vowels: j, w

/b, d, g, f/ occur in Spanish loan-words. /k/ and /q/ tend to be realized as fricatives /χ/ and /γ/.

Vowels

The basic phonemic vowel series is /i, u, a/. /i/ → [e, ɛ], and /u/ > [o, ɔ], in contact with uvular /q/.

Stress

Stress, if unmarked, is invariably on the penultimate syllable. A final syllable may be stressed and is then so marked: *arí* 'yes'. As suffixes are added cumulatively to the base, stress moves progressively to the right: e.g. *wási* 'house', *wasikúna* 'houses', *wasikunápaq* 'for the houses'.

MORPHOLOGY AND SYNTAX

There is no grammatical gender. Natural gender can be denoted by coded words, e.g. *warmi* for female, *qari* for male. Thus *wawa* 'child' – *warmi wawa* 'little girl'.

ARTICLES

No definite article. The suffix *-qa* acts as a topic marker. The numeral *huk* 'one' may be used as an indefinite article. The plural marker is *-kuna* suffixed to noun and followed by the case ending.

Noun

All Quechua nouns are declined according to one and the same paradigm: e.g. *wasi* 'house':

	Singular	*Plural*
nom.	wasi	wasi**kuna**
gen.	wasi**pa**	wasi**kunapa**
dat.	wasi**paq**	wasi**kunapaq**
	wasi**man**	wasi**kunaman**
acc.	wasi**ta**	wasi**kunata**
abl.	wasi**manta**	wasi**kunamanta**
iness.	wasi**pi**	wasi**kunapi**

In addition to *-kuna*, there is a plural form in *-s*, borrowed from Spanish, and used after vowel finals: e.g. *wawas* 'children', *warmis* 'women'.

POSSESSION

The possessed object takes the relevant personal possessive marker: e.g. *wasipa punkun* 'the door of the house'; *Incap ususin* 'the Inca's daughter'; *warminpa sutin* '**his** wife's name' (*-n* is the third person possessive marker (see below)).

INESSIVE

Used for both place and time: e.g. *wasipi* 'in the house'; *ñaupa ñaupa pachapi* 'long, long ago' (*pacha* 'time'). *-pi* is also used adverbially: e.g. *baratullapi rantiy* 'to buy cheaply'.

Adjective

The adjective precedes the noun and is invariable: e.g. *hatun wasi* 'big house' – *hatun wasikunapi* 'in the big houses'; *Pay sumaq llaqtaykiman rin* 'He goes to your beautiful village' (*pay* 'he'; *sumaq* 'beautiful'; *llaqta* 'village'; *-yki* is poss. ending 2nd p.; *-man* is dat. ending; *riy* 'to go').

COMPARATIVE

-manta + *aswan* 'than': e.g. *Qaqamanta aswan kapkam kay tantaqa* 'This bread is harder than rock' (*qaqa* 'rock', *tanta* 'bread').

Pronoun

The independent personal pronouns are:

	Singular	Plural
1	ñoqa	incl. ñoqanchik, excl. ñoqayku
2	qam (Cuzco: qan)	qamkuna
3	pay	paykuna

These are declined as nouns: e.g. *ñoqanchikpaq* 'for us'.

POSSESSIVE MARKERS

Sing. 1 *-i/-y*, 2 *-iki/-yki*, 3 *-n*; pl. 1 *-nchik* (incl.), *-yku* (excl.), 2 *-ykichik*, 3 *-nku*: e.g. *wasin* 'his/her house'; *wasiikichik* 'your (pl.) house'. For agent–patient markers, *see* **Verb**, below.

DEMONSTRATIVE PRONOUN/ADJECTIVE

Three degrees of removal: *kay* 'this' – *chay* 'that' – *wak* 'that (yonder)'.

INTERROGATIVE PRONOUN

pitaq 'who?'; *imataq* 'what?': e.g. *Pitaq yachachisunkichik runasimita?* 'Who is teaching you (pl.) *runa simi*? the verbal ending *-sunkichik* encodes action by 3rd person on 1st. *-chu* is an enclitic interrogative particle: e.g. *Pirwanuchu kanki?* 'Are you (sing.) a Peruvian?'

RELATIVE PRONOUN

mayqin, *ima*, *pi(chus)* are used especially in Cuzco Quechua: e.g. *chay warmi*

1145

mayqin.manta.chus rimani 'that woman of whom I am speaking'.

Participial construction: e.g. *yaku haypaq runakuna* 'the people who have received water (*yaku*)'; *ñoqa.pa risqay llaqtam* 'the village I am going to' (*llaqtam* 'village'; *riy* 'to go'); *llamkasqay chakra* 'the field which I tilled' (*llamkay* 'to till, work').

Numerals

1–10: *huk, iskay, kimsa, tawa, pichqa, soqta, qanchis, pusaq, isqon, chunka*. 11 *chunka hukniyoq*; 12 *chunka iskayniyoq*; 13 *chunka kimsayoq*; 20 *iskay chunka*; 30 *kimsa chunka*; 100 *pachak*; 200 *iskay pachak*.

Verb

The Quechua verb is fully conjugated for three persons in both numbers, singular and plural; in the first person plural a distinction is made between inclusive and exclusive. There are no irregular verbs; all verbs are conjugated according to one and the same paradigm. The three basic tenses are present, past, and future.

The infinitive ends in *-y*: e.g. *riy* 'to go'; *karunchay* 'to go away'; *llamtay* 'to work'.

Present tense: e.g. of *karunchay*:

	Singular	*Plural*
1	karuncha.ni	incl. karuncha.nchik; excl. -.yku
2	karuncha.nki	karuncha.nkichik
3	karuncha.n	karuncha.nku

Past tense: the same endings are added to the stem plus the past marker *-rqa-*, e.g. *karuncha.**rqa**.ni, karuncha.**rqa**.nki*. These endings are close to those of the possessive pronouns (*see* **Pronoun**, above).

Future tense: there are specific endings for first and third persons; second person is as above.

	Singular	*Plural*
1	karuncha.saq	incl. karuncha.sunchik; excl. -saqku
2	karuncha.nki	karuncha.nkichik
3	karuncha.nqa	karuncha.nqaku

A progressive tense is made by infixing *-chka-*: e.g. *Imatataq ruwa.**chka**.nkichik?* 'What are you (pl.) doing?': *hamu.chka.ni* 'I'm coming'.

CONDITIONAL

The affix is *-man-*: e.g. *apa.nchik.man* 'we would take'.

PAST NECESSITATIVE

Stem + *na* + personal ending + *mi* + *kara*: e.g. *ri.na.y.mi kara* 'I had to go'.

GERUNDS

The affixes are *-spa-*, *-stin-*, and *-pti-*, e.g. from *takiy* 'to sing': *Takistin llamka.chka.nku* 'While singing, they go on working'; *Taki.pti.n kusiku.ni* 'I am happy when (*pti*) he (*-n*) sings'; *tapu.wa.spa* '(he) having asked/asked me'.

The *-wa-* in this last example is the 1st person object marker; some further examples of the agent–patient pronominal infix/affix system: *uyari.**wa**.rqa.**nki*** 'you (sing.) listened (*rqa* for past tense) to me'; *uyari.**wa**.rqa.**nkichik*** 'you (pl.) listened to me'; *tapu.**y.ki*** 'I ask you (sing.)'; *tapu.**y.kichik*** 'I ask you (pl.)'; *yanapa.**su**.**nki*** 'he will help you (sing.)'; *yanapa.**su**.**nkichik*** 'he will help you (pl.)'.

Ignoring plural endings, the basic formulae, then, are: *-yki* 'I – you'; *-wanki* 'you – me'; *-wan* 'he – me'; *-sunki* 'he – you': e.g. *qam.ta Inca muna.sunki* 'the Inca loves you' (Ollanta 154).

IMPERATIVE

-y (sing.), *-ychik* (pl.); negated by *ama...chu*, e.g. *ama lloqsi.ychik.chu* 'don't go out' (*lloqsiy* 'to go out').

Quechua has a very extensive inventory of bound affixes which may be used with either nominals or verbals, and which confer all sorts of nuances – delimiting, concessive, dubitative, reassuring, etc. – on the thematic core. For example, *-si* added to the subject, with *-sqa* added to the verb, generates an inferential form: e.g. *pay.**si** llamta.**sqa*** 'it is said that he worked; he seems to have worked'.

NEGATION

The circumfix *manam...chu* is used: e.g. *manam yachan.nki.chu* 'you (sing.) don't know'; *manam payta tari.nku.chu* 'they don't find him'; *pay.**pa** mana tayta.**n** kan.chu* 'he has no father' (lit. 'of him – not – his father – is not').

Postpositions

The case endings are supported by various postpositions. Many of these can also be added directly to the stem: e.g.

- *-nta* 'by means of', e.g. *chaka**nta** mayu.ta chimpa.ni* 'I cross the river by the bridge';
- *-rayku* 'for the benefit of', e.g. *Mama.**y**.rayku tukuy tuta llamka.ni* 'I work all night for the sake of my mother' (*tuta* 'night');
- *-mantapacha* 'since, from', e.g. *wasimantapacha* 'from the house', *qayna watamantapacha* 'since last year'.

Word order

SVO, SOV.

1 Qallariynimpim Simi karqa, Simitaqmi Dioswan karqa, Simitaqmi Dios karqa. 2 Paymi qallariy-
nimpi Dioswan karqa. 3 Tukuy imakunam paywan
rikurirqa, ima rikuriqpas mana paywanqa manam
rikurirqachu. 4 Kawsaymi paypi karqa, kawsay-
taqmi karqa runakunapa kanchaynin. 5 Kanchaymi
akchirin tutayaypi, tutayayñataqmi mana hapirqa-
chu.

6 Diosmanta kachamusqa runam karqa, Juan
sutiyuq. 7 Paymi hamurqa testificakuypaq, kanchaymanta testificanampaq, chay hinapi paywan llapa-
llan iñinankupaq. 8 Payqa manam kanchaychu karqa, aswan kanchaymanta testificaqpaqmi.

(Ayacucho dialect)

QUICHÉ

INTRODUCTION

Quiché is one of the Mayan languages (Penutian family) close to Cakchiquel. This article gives a short description of Classical Quiché, the language of the *Popol Vuh* book, which was written down, using Spanish letters, by a native speaker of Quiché in the mid-sixteenth century. The original is lost, but several copies have survived. This invaluable document gives Quiché-Mayan accounts of the creation of the world, the heroic age, and the origins and history of the Quiché people.

Modern Quiché is spoken by over half a million people in Guatemala and Mexico.

SCRIPT

Popol Vuh is written in the Roman alphabet minus *d*, *f*, *s*. The orthography reflects Spanish practice, e.g. /k/ is written as *qu-* before *e*/*i*, as *c* before a hard vowel. ε and *g* denote the clicks (*see* **Phonology**, below).

PHONOLOGY

Consonants

    stops: p, b, t, k, g
    affricates: ts, tʃ, ts', tʃ'
    fricatives: (ß), s, ʃ, χ
    nasals: m, n, ŋ
    lateral and flap: l, r
    semi-vowels: j, w

Vowels

The vowels are notated as *i*, *e*, *a*, *o*, *u*.

MORPHOLOGY AND SYNTAX

There is no declension. A subject–object relationship is marked in the verb. Other cases are expressed by means of prepositions.

Nouns

Some Quiché nouns: *a* 'water'; *coh* /koχ/, 'puma'; *ixok* /iʃok/, 'woman'; *ic* 'moon'; *ɛaɛ* 'fire'; *huyub* 'mountain'. Compounds: e.g. with *ha* 'house': *balami ha* 'jaguar house'; *tihobal ha* 'house of ordeals'.

POSSESSION

'The X of Y' is rendered as 'his X – Y': e.g. *v gux cah* /u guʃ kaχ/ 'the heart of heaven' (for *v*~ /u/ see Possessive pronoun); *r amac Quiche vinac* 'the race of Q. people' (for *r* see Possessive pronoun); *v vinaquil huyub* 'the inhabitants of the mountains'.

The suffix -V*l* forms collectives: *huyubal* 'mountain ranges', *chumilal* 'the starry heavens'.

PLURAL

Typical ending is -V*b*, e.g. *achihab* 'men'; *Quiche.eb* 'Quiché people'; *capohib* 'maidens'.

Adjective

As attribute, adjective follows noun. Some adjectives have reduplicated plural forms: e.g. *poto* 'short', pl. *potopoto*.

Pronoun

The personal pronouns with their possessive forms are:

	Singular			*Plural*		
	Subject	*Possessive*		*Subject*	*Possessive*	
1	in	nu	v	oh	ca	c-, qu-
2	at	a	av	ix	iv	i-
3		u, v	r		qui	c-, qu-

The first set of possessives is used with consonantal initials; the second with vocalic: e.g. *nu vach* 'my face'; *v bi* 'his name'; *ca bi* 'our names'; *a chuch a cahau* 'your mother and your father'; *r echa* 'his food'; *iv echa* 'your food'.

DEMONSTRATIVE PRONOUN/ADJECTIVE

(*a*)*re*.

INTERROGATIVE PRONOUN

a(*pa*) *chinac*.

RELATIVE PRONOUN

ri(*j*) invariable: e.g. *Mavi utz ri c-u-bano* 'What he does is not good' (*mavi* 'is not'; for *c-u-bano*, see **Verb**); *Che ri tiquil pa be* 'The tree which is planted by the road' (*che* 'tree').

Numerals

The system is vigesimal. Key multiples, e.g. 20, 40, 60, 80, 100, are equated with specific measure-words, and act as group markers: e.g.

20 = hu.vinac 'one person'
40 = ca.vinac 'two persons'
60 = ox.gal 'three cocoa-measures'
80 = hu.much 'one heap'
100 = o.gal 'five cocoa-measures'

The units 1–10 are: *hun, cab, ox(ib), cah(ib), oo(b), vacac/quib, vucub, vahxac/ quib, beleh(eb), lahuh.*
The bracket governed by a particular marker begins at the previous marker: e.g.

40 = ca.vinac 'two persons'
41 = hun-r-oxgal '1 towards 60'
42 = cab-r-oxgal '2 towards 60'
50 = lahuh-r-oxgal '10 towards 60'
60 = oxgal

Verb

The Quiché verb is primary, e.g. *ban* 'to do, make', *ah* 'to wish', *ti* 'to eat', *ya* 'to give', or derivative, e.g. *camizah* 'to kill' (*-izah* is causative ending), *quiar* 'to increase in number' (*qui* 'many'); or composite: e.g. *ulu-cul* 'to come and sit down' (*ul* 'come', *cul* 'sit down'), *vinac-bitoh* 'to create men', *zac.bizan* 'to move animatedly' (*bizah* 'to move something'; *zac* 'white, bright'; hence intensification).

Verbs are transitive, intransitive, passive, absolute.

Pronominal subject series:

	Singular		Plural	
	Intransitive	*Transitive*	*Intransitive*	*Transitive*
1	in	nu	oh	ca
2	at	a	ix	i
3	Ø	u	e	qui

That is, the transitive subject markers are the possessive series.

TENSE FORMATION

(a) Transitive:

present indicative: the marker is *ca-*, e.g. *ca-nu-loεoh* 'I love'; *c-a-loεoh* 'thou lovest'; *ca-u-loεoh* 'he loves';

preterite: the marker is *x-*, e.g. *x-nu-loεoh, x-a-loεoh*;

future: marker is *xchi-*, e.g. *xchi-nu-loεoh, xchi-a-loεoh*;

iterative/durative: *chi/ch*; pronominal markers are above, except for 1st person singular, which is *in*.

imperative: *ch(i)*; pronominal markers as in iterative, e.g. *chi-c-oquibeh* 'let us attack!' *M-oh-i-zach-o* 'Do not forget us!'

(b) Intransitive:

the present marker is *ca/c/qu*, e.g.

	Singular	Plural
1	qu-i(n)-be 'I go'	c-oh-be
2	c-at-be	qu-ix-be
3	ca-Ø-be	qu-e-be

preterite: x marker, e.g.

	Singular	Plural
1	x-in-ul 'I came'	x-oh-ul
2	x-at-ul	x-ih-ul
3	x-Ø-ul	x-e-ul

future: e.g. xqu-in-ul, xc-at-ul, xch-Ø-ul.

PASSIVE

The *Popol Vuh* language has three forms of passive: a root passive, e.g. *x-e-muc* 'they were buried'; a rare form in *-tah*, e.g. *x-oh-chaca-tah-ic* 'we have been overcome'; and a form-V*x*, e.g. *x-tzon-ox* 'he was asked', *qu-ix-tzon-ox* 'you are asked'.

NON-FINITE FORMS

-ic is characteristic ending, e.g. of infinitive *ban* 'to do': *ban-ic* 'the act of doing', *xa-hou-ic* 'the dancing'. It may be passive, e.g. *ta-ic* 'the being heard'.

There are five participles: active, e.g. in *i/y* with variants: *camizai* 'killing'; and passive in *-(ta)lic/m*: *tzibam* 'written/painted'.

EMPHATIC FORMS

Composed from root + root vowel + root initial + *oh/ah*: e.g. *matz* 'to hide' – *matz.a-m-oh* '(... were) well hidden'; *von* 'to shine' – *e von-o-v-oh* 'they were shining brightly'. This form may take an intransitive preterite ending: e.g. *chac* 'to work' – *chac-a-ch-ax-inac* '(... were) very busy'.

The verbal noun is in -V*l*: e.g. *yac* 'to arise' – *yacal* 'existence'; *tzib* 'to paint' – *tzibal* 'picture'.

NEGATIVE

The particle is *ma/mavi*: e.g. *Ma c-u-bijh* 'She does not say so'.

Prepositions

Chi is an all-purpose preposition rendering 'in, at, from, between', etc.: e.g. *chila chi cah* 'there, from out of the sky'.

> 1 Pa ri ticbal-ré arè Tzij, ri Tzij g'o rug' Dios, ri Tzij arè Dios.
>
> 2 Aré wá pa ri ticbal-ré rug' Dios.
>
> 3 Ronojel ri jastak rumal aré xbantajic; we-ta-mat g'o aré majun ri banom xbantajic.
>
> 4 Rug' aré g'o-wi g'asle-mal, ri g'aslemal arè ri sakil quech winak.
>
> 5 Ri sakil cajuluwic pa ri k'ekum; ri k'ekum man xquichomaj taj.
>
> 6 Xg'ojicjun achi takom-lok rumal Dios, Xuan u bí.
>
> 7 Wà xpetic yal sakiri bal, rech cusakirisaj ri sakil, rech conojel quiqui-cojo rumal aré.

RAPANUI
(Easter Island)

INTRODUCTION

This language, the most easterly member of the Polynesian family, was spoken on Easter Island until the middle of the nineteenth century, when it was replaced by an imported hybrid language, a mixture of Tahitian and Spanish. Spanish is now the official language of the island.

Little is known about the original inhabitants of Easter Island. Their traditions tell of two races – the Long Ears, who came from South America, and the Short Ears, who were Polynesians. Alone among Polynesian languages, Rapanui had developed a form of writing. This script – known as rongorongo – has so far resisted all attempts at decipherment. It is largely pictographic, but some of the graphs appear to function as ideograms.

PHONOLOGY

Consonants

stops: p, t, k, ʔ
fricatives: v, h
nasals: m, n, ŋ
liquid: r

The glottal stop is phonemic: cf. *pua* 'flower'; *pu'a* 'cover up'. /r/ represents both [r] and [l].

Vowels

i, e, a, o u

There are several diphthongs.

MORPHOLOGY AND SYNTAX

Noun

As in other Polynesian languages, the class of nouns in Rapanui is determined by compatibility with the nominal particles. These are:

(a) Determinatives: (*ko*) *te*, the definite article: e.g. *te vaananga rapanui* 'the Rapanui language'. In other contexts, *vaananga* can be a verb meaning 'to speak'. Here, the presence of the nominal particle *te* fixes it as a noun. Verbs may also be nominalized by the affixes *hanga*, e.g. *te vaananga-hanga* 'speaking, speech'; *ngaa*, the plural definite article; *he*, the indefinite article; *a* the personal article.

(b) Prepositive nominal particles denoting case relationships: *ko*: as in Maori, Tongan, Raratongan, etc., this is the focus marker; *o, a te/tou* is the genitive relationship marker, where *o* signals inalienable, *a* alienable possession. The Rapanui distinction between what is and is not alienable is unstable (*see* **Polynesian Languages**). To judge from the examples in Englert's handbook of the language (1938), one's spouse may be alienable while one's clothes are not: cf. *te kahu o Mateo* 'Mateo's clothes'; *te vii'e a Mateo* 'Mateo's wife'. But Englert also gives the sentence: *te vii'e o tou tangata era* 'this man's wife'.

A dative is expressed by *ki*, and there are two benefactive particles, coded for possession: *mo/ma*.

Gender may be expressed lexically: e.g. *poki tama.aroa* 'son'; *poki tama.hahine* 'daughter'.

Adjective

Roots used as attributive adjectives follow the noun: e.g. *te tangata rivariva* 'the good man'.

Pronoun

The personal forms include a dual:

	Singular		*Dual*	*Plural*
1	(ko) au	incl.	taua	tatou
		excl.	maua	matou
2	koe		korua	korua
3	ia		ra'ua	ra'ua

POSSESSIVE PRONOUNS
to- and *o-* series, with vowel coded for alienable/inalienable possession: e.g. *ki tooku hare* 'to my house'. Similarly, in the benefactive series: *mooku/maaku* 'for me'; *moou/maau* 'for you'; *moona/maana* 'for him'.

DEMONSTRATIVE PRONOUNS
te me'e nei 'this'; *te me'e ena* 'that'; *te me'e ra* 'that' (distal); demonstrative adjective: e.g. *te...nei*: *te hare nei* 'this house'.

INTERROGATIVE PRONOUNS
ai 'who?'; *aha* 'what?'.

RELATIVE PRONOUN
The common Polynesian relative pronoun *i* is found; Englert gives an example with the *o-* series possessive: *te tangata oona te ha'u nei* 'the man whose hat this is'.

Verb

As in Polynesian generally, tense and aspect are marked by particles; the root itself is invariable.

TENSE

There is a broad division into past (marked by *i*) and non-past (*e*). The tense markers are prepositive: e.g. *ai i-tu'u-mai-nei?* 'who came here?' (*i-* is the past-tense marker); *e-turu au ki tai* 'I go down to the sea' (*tai* 'sea'; *turu* 'descend').

ASPECT

> perfective: *ku, ku...ana*, where *ana* seems to carry the result of perfective action in the past into the present: e.g. ***ku-rehu-ana** au taaku hoe* 'I have forgotten my knife';
> progressive: *e...ana*;
> inceptive: *ka*;
> conditional: *ana*, e.g. *ana uua mai* 'if it rains' (lit. 'if rain arrives').

IMPERATIVE

The marker is *ka, 'aa*, e.g. *ka.tata i te kahu!* 'wash the clothes!'

NEGATION

ina precedes proper nouns, and is used to denote absence, lack of: e.g. *ina o matou vai* 'we have no water'. *ina...eko* marks the prohibitive mood or the negative future: e.g. *in'au eko turu ki tai* 'I shan't go down to the sea'.

CAUSATIVE

haka- (cf. e.g. Maori *whaka-*, Samoan *fa'a*, Tongan *faka*): e.g. *mate* 'to die' – *hakamate* 'to kill'.

1157

ROMANIAN

INTRODUCTION

Romanian belongs to the Italic branch of the Indo-European family. It is spoken by around 20 million people in Romania, while 2½ million speak the morphologically identical, phonologically slightly divergent form known as Moldavian in the Moldavian Soviet Socialist Republic. Other forms of Romanian, spoken by small numbers of people, are: Aromanian in Greece, Albania, and Yugoslavia; Megleno-Romanian in the Greek–Yugoslav border areas, and Istro-Romanian in Istria.

The language described here is, genetically, Daco-Romanian: i.e. it derives from the Low Latin superimposed on a Dacian substratum in the Roman colony of Dacia between the second century BC and the third century AD. It is not clear how this original nucleus disintegrated into divergent and, geographically, widely separated forms. As regards Daco-Romanian itself, the main dialectal division is between Muntenian in the south, and Moldavian in the north and north-east. The modern literary language is based on Muntenian usage.

There is a rich body of oral traditional literature in Romanian, culminating in one of the world's great poems, the *Miorița* ballad. From the sixteenth century onwards, historians and theologians began to use Romanian in place of the Old Church Slavonic hitherto used for administrative and religious purposes in the Moldavian and Wallachian principalities. Modern writing in Romanian can be dated from the Romantic period in the early nineteenth century. The period from the late nineteenth century to the Second World War produced an extensive literature of very high quality, particularly strong in poetry and the novel.

SCRIPT

The Cyrillic script continued to be used until well into the nineteenth century, and is indeed still used for Moldavian in the Soviet Socialist Republic. In Romania, the language is written in the Roman alphabet, extended by the following letters for specifically Romanian sounds: ă, â, î, ş, ţ. â and î are both pronounced as /ɪ/ (*see* **Phonology**): â was the form in use until 1953, when it was everywhere replaced by î. In 1965, â was restored in all words belonging to the semantic–etymological field based on the word *român* 'Romanian': thus, *România, românește*.

PHONOLOGY

Consonants

stops: p, b, t, d, k, g
affricates: ts, tʃ, dʒ
fricatives: f, v, s, z, ʃ, ʒ, h
nasals: m, n
lateral and flap: l, r
semi-vowels: j, w

/ʃ/ is notated as ș, /ts/ as ț, /ʒ/ as j, /dʒ/ as ge/gi.

Exceptionally for a Romance language, Romanian tolerates initial clusters such as *mr-* (*mreajă* 'net trap'), *hl-* (*hleios* 'marshy'), *ml-* (*mlaștină* 'marsh').

Vowels

i, e = [e] or [ɛ], ı, ă = [ə], a, o = [o] or [ɔ], u

/ı/, notated as *î, â*, is central, closed, unrounded, and tense, produced in the velar region; represented in Moldavian ы. Final *-i* often indicates palatalization of final consonant: e.g. *munți* /munts'/ 'mountains'. There are several diphthongs.

MORPHOLOGY AND SYNTAX

Noun

Nouns in Romanian are masculine, feminine, or ambivalent; the latter behave as masculines in the singular, as feminines in the plural. Most words in this category, conveniently classed as neuter, denote inanimate objects. Consonantal endings are masculine or neuter; typical feminine endings are *-a, -e*, but some nouns in *-e* are masculine, e.g. *pește* 'fish', *cîine* 'dog'.

NUMBER
In general, masculine nouns take *-i*, feminine *-e/-i*, neuter, *-uri*. The masculine and feminine endings frequently induce phonetic change in the noun, e.g. regressive assimilation, accommodation of final consonant: e.g. *strada* 'street', pl. *străzi* 'student', pl. *studenți*; *masa* 'table', pl. *mese*; *carte* 'book', pl. *cărți*.

ARTICLES
(a) Indefinite: *un* (masc.), *o* (fem.), inflected for case and number:

masculine

un student bun 'a good student'
unui student bun 'of/to a good student'
unor studenți buni 'of/to good students'

feminine

> o maşină bună 'a good car'
> **unei** maşine bune 'of/to a good car'
> **unor** maşine bune 'of/to good cars'

Similarly, *un*, *unui*, *unor* for neuter nouns.

(b) Definite: uniquely for a Romance language, the definite article is affixed to the noun: masc. *-ul/-l*; fem. *-a*; neuter *-ul/-l*. The masculine form *-le* also occurs. Where an adjective is present, the suffixed article is often attached to the adjective: cf. *bunul student = studentul bun* 'the good student'. Plural *bunii studenţi*; oblique case sing. *bunului student* 'of/to the good student'; pl. *bunilor studenţi*. Similarly in the feminine: *bunei maşine* 'of the good car', pl. *bunelor maşine*; and neuter: *bunului hotel* 'of/to the good hotel', pl. *bunelor hoteluri*.

(c) The possessive article: masc./nt.: *al*, pl. *ai*; fem. *a*, pl. *ale*. These are used:

(i) in concord with the independent possessive adjectives:

> masc.: cîinele este **al meu** 'the dog is mine'
> fem.: cartea este **a mea** 'the book is mine'
> pl.: cărţile sînt **ale mele** 'the books are mine'

(ii) as resumptive linking agent in genitive construction, e.g. where an adjective intervenes:

> politica României 'Romania's policy'
>
> but:
>
> politica externă **a** României 'Romania's foreign policy'
> o clasă socială 'a social class'
>
> but:
>
> un studiu amănunţit **al** unei întregi clase sociale
> 'a detailed study of an entire social class'
>
> existenţa lumii materiale şi **a** sufletului
> 'the existence of the material world and of the soul'

It follows from the above that there are two sets of endings for Romanian nouns and adjectives, depending on whether they are definite or indefinite. The difference between the two sets is not great.

Adjective

As explained above, the adjective may follow the noun, but often precedes and then takes the article. The adjective is always in concord with the noun, and may have as many as four forms, due to inflection. Cf. *crud* 'raw, cruel': fem. sing. *crudă*; masc. pl. *cruzi*; fem. pl. *crude*.

Pronoun

The personal pronouns have each one subjective and four objective forms. Thus, for the first person singular:

sbj.: eu
direct obj. stressed: (*pe*) *mine*; unstressed: *mă*
indirect obj. stressed: *mie*; unstressed: *îmi*

Similarly for second and third persons. The third person masculine forms are: *el* – (*pe*) *el* – *îl* – *lui* – *îi/i*.

In the second person, *dumneata* is preferred for singular, *dumneavoastra* for singular/plural in polite address. The latter always takes the second person *plural* form of the verb.

The preposition *pe* precedes the stressed objective form, which is then accompanied by the unstressed form preceding the verb: e.g.

L-am văzut **pe** Ion lînga pod 'I saw John near the bridge'
Pe mine mă cunoaşte multă lume 'Many people know me'
Cine **te**-a învaţat **pe tine** să/că...? 'Who taught you to ...?'

In general, *pe* is used, like *a* in Spanish with nouns denoting animate beings, but cf.:

însuşirile **pe care** trebuie să **le** posede un scriitor
'the qualities which a writer must possess'

DEMONSTRATIVE PRONOUN/ADJECTIVE
acest(a) 'this'; *acel(a)* 'that'; the forms with -*a* follow the noun, which is then definite: e.g. *acel student = studentul acela* 'that student'. All forms are fully declined for gender, number, and case.

INTERROGATIVE PRONOUN
cine 'who?'; *ce* 'what?'

RELATIVE PRONOUN
care 'who, which'; fully declined.

al doilea din cei opt copii **ai** unei familii **al cărei** destin si **ale cărei** migraţii sînt ...
'the second of the eight sons of a family, whose fate and whose peregrinations are ...'

In *al cărei*, *al* refers to *destin* (masc.), *cărei* to *familia* (fem. in oblique); in *ale cărei*, *ale* refers to *migraţii* (fem.), *cărei*, again, to *familia* (in oblique). Dative forms are recapitulated by the unstressed indirect pronoun: *omul căruia i-am vorbit* 'the man to whom I spoke (to him)'.

Numerals

1–10: *un* 'one' is used as indefinite article (see above); as a numeral, it has the feminine form *una*. *doi* 'two' (masc.) has a feminine form *două*: e.g. *doi prieteni* 'two friends'; *două sticle* 'two bottles'.

The remaining numbers are invariable: 3–10: *trei, patru, cinci, şase, şapte, opt, nouă, zece*; 11 *unsprezece*, 12 *doi/două.spre.zece*; 20 *douăzeci*; 30 *treizeci*; 40 *patruzeci*; 100 *o sută*; 200 *două sute*.

Verb

It is customary to distinguish four conjugations, representing the Latin conjugations in *-ā, -ē, -e, -ī*: e.g. *a cîntá* 'to sing'; *a vedeá* 'to see'; *a fáce* 'to make, do'; *a auzí* 'to hear'.

There are indicative, imperative, subjunctive, and conditional moods. The indicative mood has simple (present, imperfect, preterite) and compound (perfect, two periphrastic future) tenses. The auxiliaries are *a avea* 'to have' and *a fi* 'to be'; *voi* 'to want' appears in the compound future.

The present tense of *avea* is: sing. *am – ai – are/a*; pl. *avem – aveţi – au*. Specimen paradigm of *a cînta* 'to sing' indicative present in full, thereafter first person singular.

> Present: sing. 1 *cînt*, 2 *cînţi*, 3 *cîntă*; pl. 1 *cîntăm*, 2 *cîntaţi*, 3 *cîntă*
> Imperfect: *cîntam*
> Preterite: *cîntai*
> Perfect: *am cîntat*
> Future: *voi cînta*; *am să cînt*. The form *am să cînt* consists of auxiliary + *să* + subjunctive: the subjunctive is identical to the present except in the third person singular where *cînte* replaces *cîntă*.
> Conditional: auxiliary (*aş – ai – ar*, etc.) + infinitive: *aş cînta* 'I'd sing'.

The stems of many first conjugation verbs are expanded in the present tense by the element *-ez-*: thus, *a lucra* 'to work', has: *lucrez, lucrezi, lucrează*; Similarly, fourth conjugation stems are expanded by *-esc*: e.g. *a lipsi* 'to be missing': *lipsesc, lipseşti, lipseşte*.

Passive: with auxiliary *a fi*: e.g. *casa a fost vîndută* 'the house was sold'; *casa ar fi fost vîndută* 'the house would have been sold'.

Imperative: the polite form = second person plural indicative present: *întrebaţi-l şi pe el* 'ask him too'.

The uninflected past participle is used, following the preposition *de*, in a gerundive or passive infinitive sense:

> Erau aici multe de văzut
> 'There were many things to be seen here'
>
> De auzit am auzit dar n'am înteles
> 'I heard what there was to be heard but I didn't understand'
>
> un studiu temeinic **al** căilor de urmat în vederea ...
> 'a thorough study of the ways to follow with a view to ...'

Negation

The negative marker throughout the verbal system is *nu*.

Prepositions

Primary prepositions – *sub* 'under', *în*, 'in', *după* 'after', *peste* 'on', etc. – govern the direct case, undefined (i.e. without the article) unless the noun is itself qualified by an adjective or numeral: e.g. *după război* 'after the war'; *după primul război mondial* 'after the First World War'; *în traducere* 'in translation'; *într' o traducere reușită* 'in a successful translation'.

Secondary prepositions beginning with primary prepositions like *de-*, *în-* etc. take the oblique case: e.g. *de.asupra clădirii* 'above the building'; *reacția îm.potriva convenţiilor* 'the reaction against the conventions'.

Word order

SVO; OSV is possible.

În început erà Cuvântul, și Cuvântul erà la Dumnezeu, și Dumnezeu erà Cuvântul. 2 Acesta erà în început la Dumnezeu. 3 Printr'însul tot fu făcut, și fără dânsul nu fu făcù nici măcar ceva ce este făcut. 4 Vieața erà intr'însul, și vieața erà lumina oamenilor. 5 Și lumina în întunerec se arată, și întunerecul nu o prinse. 6 Fost-a un om trimis, dela Dumnezeu, al cărui nume *erà* Ioan; 7 Acesta venì spre mărturie, ca să mărturisească pentru lumină, ca toți să crează printr'însul. 8 Nu erà acela lumina, ci *venì* ca să mărturisească pentru lumină.

ROMANY

INTRODUCTION

Until well into the eighteenth century the gypsies were something of an enigma, both as regards their origins and their language. The very fact that they were popularly supposed to have come from Egypt (the word *gypsy* is a corruption of *Egyptian*) was enough to invest the language with mystery. It is now clear that the gypsies (the ethonym is *roma*) emigrated from India in a succession of waves towards the end of the first millennium AD. One of these waves proceeded via Iran into Anatolia, South Russia, and the Balkans, to reach Western Europe by the fifteenth century, Britain by the sixteenth. A following wave seems to have taken a more southerly route via Iran, Syria, and the Mediterranean into North Africa and the Iberian Peninsula. By the twentieth century, groups of gypsies leading a more-or-less nomadic form of life were present in all European countries and in many other parts of the world, and the Romany language, originally a specific form of New Indo-Aryan, had been substantially differentiated into two or three dozen dialects – a process in which contact with the languages of the host peoples played a crucial role.

Three main factors have gone towards shaping the Romany language as it appeared in its nineteenth-century heyday:

1. progressive simplification of the Middle Indian phonological system;
2. erosion of synthetic forms and their replacement by analytical means;
3. assimilation of lexical items and phonological and morphological features belonging to the languages of the host countries.

The first two points are also characteristic of the new Indo-Aryan languages in the sub-continent. So is the third, up to a point, but to nothing like the same extent as in the case of Romany.

Vencel' and Čerenkov (1976) divide European Romany into eight main groupings:

1. ruska roma, lotfitka roma; in north Russia, Latvia, Estonia, central Poland;
2. sinti: Germany, France, Poland, Czecho-Slovakia, Austria, north Italy;
3. servika roma, ungrike roma: Slovakia and Hungary;
4. erlides, ursari, drindari: Bulgaria, Macedonia, Serbia, Romania, Crimea;
5. lingurari, zletari, kekavyari (grouped together as čačě rom): the Vlach areas of Romania and Moldavia;
   kelderari: originating in the Hungaro-Romanian border country, now scattered world-wide from USSR to Argentine;

lovari: belt extending from USSR across Europe to England, with spread to USA;
gurbeti: Bosnia and Herzegovina;
6. servi, plaščunuya: Ukraine;
7. fintike roma: Finland;
8. volšenenge kale: Wales.

Until the early twentieth century, gipsies were normally bilingual in Romany and the language of the host country. The latter has now succeeded in reducing Romany everywhere to the level of a domestic patois.

SCRIPT

Both Roman and Cyrillic have been used for the few publications, mainly of a religious nature, which have appeared in Romany. Gypsy folklore, tales and poems, have been collected and published in Eastern Europe and in Britain (by the Gypsy Lore Society).

PHONOLOGY

Consonants

stops: p, b, p', t, d, t', k, g, k'
affricates: ts, dz, tʃ, dʒ
fricatives: f, v, s, z, ʃ, ʒ, x, γ, h
nasals: m, n, ɳ, ŋ
laterals and flaps: l, ł, r, ɹ, ɽ
semi-vowels: j, w

/p', d', k'/ are aspirates. Most consonants including the aspirates, have corresponding palatalized values, /p', b', p''/, etc.

Vowels

front: i, e/ɛ
central: ɪ, ə, ɔ, a
back: o, u
diphthongs: ai, ei, oi, ui

Nasalized /ā, ū/ occur, e.g. in Romanian Romany. All vowels tend to /ə/ in unstressed position.

Stress

Varies from one dialect to another under influence of stress patterns in host language. Thus, it is transferred towards initial in Hungarian Romany, towards a long vowel in Latvian Romany. In pure Romany (New Indo-Aryan) words, the main stress is on the final syllable. In the oblique cases, this stress moves to the penultimate: e.g. in Russian Romany: *romá* 'gypsies', *roméstɪr* (ablative).

Treatment of Middle Indian sounds:

1. Aspirated voiced stops are devoiced: Skt *bhumi* > /p'uv/ 'earth'; *bhrāta* > /p'ral/ 'brother'.
2. Intervocalic /-t/ > /l,r/: Skt *bhrāta* > /p'ral/ 'brother'; *gata* > /gelo/ 'gone'; *gītā* > /gili/ 'song'.
3. Retroflex series disappears: Skt *vāṭa* > /bar/ 'enclosure'; *varṣa* > /bɛrʃ/ 'year'.
4. /s, s/ /s, ʃ/: Skt *kāṣṭha* > /kaʃt/ 'wood'.
5. /tr-/ is retained: Skt *triṇī* > /trin/ 'three'.

VOCALIC CHANGE
Some examples:

Sanskrit		Romany
agni	>	/yag/ 'fire'
caura	>	/cor/ 'thief'
mṛta	>	/mulo/ 'dead'
daśa	>	/deʃ/ 'ten'
śṛṇoti	>	/ʃunel/ 'hears'
hṛdayam	>	/yilo/ 'heart'

MORPHOLOGY AND SYNTAX

Article

The definite articles *o* (masc.) and *e* (fem.), singular and plural, are borrowed from Greek: the oblique form is *e* (with variants). Thus, *o rom* 'the gypsy', *e romeske* 'to the gypsy'.

Noun

The basic dichotomy is animate/inanimate; animates are masculine or feminine. There are two numbers. Formally, the animate/inanimate opposition, and the masculine/feminine opposition are differentiated only in the oblique base (i.e. inanimates have base form = accusative = nominative).

Plural: *-a, -e*: e.g. *rom* 'gypsy', pl. *roma*; *chavo* 'boy', pl. *chave*.

There are six cases; five of these have endings added agglutinatively to the base oblique form = accusative.

	Singular	Oblique	Plural	Oblique
masculine	rom	rom**es**	rom**a**	rom**en**
feminine	romn′i	romn′**a**	romn′**a**	romn′**en**

Thus, in Russian Romany:

	Singular	Plural
nominative	rom	roma
accusative	rom**es**	rom**en**
dative	rom**eske**	rom**enge**
locative	rom**este**	rom**ende**
ablative	rom**estɪr**	rom**endɪr**
com./intrumental	rom**essa**	rom**enca**

Genitive case: formed with -*ker*- + final vowel marked for gender:

romés.**ker.o** chavo 'the gypsy's son'
romes.**ker.i** chai 'the gypsy's daughter'
romes.**ker.e** chave 'the gypsy's children'
romen.**ger.o** chavo 'the gypsies' son'
romen.**ger.e** chave 'the gypsies' sons'

Adjective

Attributively, adjective precedes noun and agrees with it in gender and number. Case is restricted to two: nominative or oblique (group 6 (*see* **Introduction**) may decline adjective in all six cases): e.g. *baro rom* 'big gypsy', fem. *bari romn'i*; pl. *bare roma*; obl. *bare(s) romende*.

COMPARATIVE
A comparative is made in -(V)*d*V*r*, e.g. *baridir* 'bigger'.

Pronoun

Gender is distinguished in third person singular: sing. 1 *me*, 2 *tu*, 3 masc. *ov*, fem. *oi*; pl. 1 *ame*, 2 *tume*, 3 *on*. These are declined in six cases: base for first singular is *man*; for third masc. *łes*, fem. *ła*; pl. *łen*.

POSSESSIVE
    sing. 1 miró, mirí, miré (→ mo, mi, me)
        2 tiró, tirí, tiré (→ to, ti, te)
        3 masc. łéskiro, etc., fem. łesk'eri, etc.
    pl. 1 amaró, etc.; 2 tumaró, etc.: 3 łéngioro ...

DEMONSTRATIVE
adava 'this', *odova* 'that'. These vary widely in dialects. The Welsh forms are *kadava, kodova*.

INTERROGATIVE
ko(n) 'who?'; *so* 'what?'

RELATIVE
For Russian Romany Vencel' (1964) gives *savi*, pl. *save*.

Numerals

1–10: *ek'*, *dui*, *trin*, *štār*, *paṁž*, *šov*, *efta*, *oxto*, *en'a*, *deš*; 11 *deš.u.yek*; 12 *deš.u.dui*; 20 *biš*; 30 *tranda*; 40 *štar.var.deš*; 50 *paṁž'.var.deš*; 100 *šeł*.

Verb

Marked for person and number; gender is marked in participial form only. There are two moods, indicative and imperative; in some dialects a conditional–optative mood may be expressed analytically.

Four tenses are usually distinguished: present – future – past imperfective – past perfective. In certain dialects, the present has a future sense.

A reflexive form can be made from all transitive verbs.

Aspect is not a feature of the Romany verb, but certain prefixes associated with aspect in other languages have been borrowed, e.g. *za-* from Russian, *pše-* from Polish, and *fer-* from German. There are three conjugations.

Specimen paradigm: first conjugation verb, *čin-* 'write'; Russian Romany forms:

present: *čin.ava*, *-esa*, *-eła*; pl. *-asa*, *-ena*, *-ena*
past perf.: *čin-d'om*, *-d'an*, *-d'a*; pl. *-d'am*, *-dle*, *-dle*
past imperf.: *čin-avas*, *-esas*, *-ełas*; pl. *-asas*, *-enas*, *-enas*
future: in Russian Romany formed from present tense of *le-* 'to take' + *tə* + truncated present: sing. *łava tə činav*, *łesa tə čines*, *łeła tə činel*; pl. *łasa tə činas*, *łena tə činen*, *łena tə činen*.
imperative: second singular = root; second plural adds *-n*.

Present tense of auxiliary *ov-* 'to be': sing. *som*, *san*, *si*; pl. *sam*, *san*, *si*.

NEGATION
In general, indicative tenses are negated by *na* preceding verb; imperative by *ma*. In German Romany, a negative marker *či* or *gar* follows verb (influence of *nicht*?): Rmy *činava či/gar* = Gm. *ich schreibe nicht*.

PARTICIPLE
This is formed from third person plural base of past perfective: marked for gender and number: e.g. *bikindło*, *-i*, *-e* 'sold' (masc., fem., pl. common); *kerdo*, *-i*, *-e* 'done'; *dzindło*, *-i*, *-e* 'known'. The participle can be active or passive, and is neutral as to tense.

Prepositions

The nominal declension set out above refers mainly to nouns denoting animate beings. Other nouns are rarely declined in this way, and here prepositions are brought in to express syntactic relationships. In some dialects, a distinction is made between a dynamic situation (motion towards or into something) and a static (rest in a place). Thus, in servika/ungrike roma, *andro veš* 'into the forest'; *andro vešeste* 'in the forest'.

Word order

SVO is normal.

---

31. Atunči avile leski dey tay vi leske phral. Ašile avri tay tradine ekh vorba te avel avri lende. 32. Vi but žene bešenas kote tay phende, "Ašun, tyiri dey tay tyire phral si avri. Mangen tu te Žas lende." 33. Tay dya anglal o Isus, "Kon si muŕi dey tay muŕe phral?" 34. Tay dikhlya pe kodolende kay bešenas truyal leste tay phendya, "Katka bešen muŕi dey tay muŕe phral. Kongodi kerel e voya le Devleski, vo si muro phral tay muŕi phey tay vi muŕi dey."

Kelderari
(Mark 3: 31–5)

RUSSIAN

INTRODUCTION

This East Slavonic language is the official language of the Soviet Union, where it is spoken by about 160 million people as mother tongue, and, as second language, by the national minorities totalling around 60–70 million.

The dialectal split of East Slavonic into Russian, Ukrainian, and Belorussian dates from the end of the first millennium AD. The earliest writing in the Kievan and Mongol periods (eleventh to fourteenth centuries) was in Old Church Slavonic, i.e. a literary medium based on South Slavonic: an influence which was fortuitously promoted by an influx of South Slavonic clerics after the fall of Constantinople in 1453. Thus fortified, the written language, which had pre-viously permitted some intermingling with East Slavonic forms, remained aloof from the more and more divergent East Slavonic spoken language until the eighteenth century, when, as part of the modernization programme of Peter the Great, agreement on a standardized written and spoken norm was recognized as a most urgent necessity. What emerged was to some extent a compromise between written South Slavonic and spoken East Slavonic – a compromise which can still be traced in the modern Russian language, e.g. in the presence of doublets representing East and South Slavonic versions of Proto-Slavonic roots, e.g. ESlav. *golová* 'head', SSlav. *glavá* 'chapter'.

A main dialectal division in the Russian speech area is that between northern and southern pronunciation, and features of both have found their way into the standardized language. Thus, what is known as *akan'e*, the reduction of unstressed /o/ to [ə, a], is originally a southern trait, but is now a phonological component of standard Russian, one which is not, however, reflected in the orthography. *See* **Phonology**, below. On the other hand, the northern pronunci-ation of /g/ as [g] is now standard, versus the southern pronunciation [ɣ].

Modern Russian literature begins with the scholar, poet, and linguist Lomo-nosov in the eighteenth century; his Russian Grammar was published in 1755. A first high point was reached in the early nineteenth century with two outstanding poets: Alexander Pushkin and Mikhail Lermontov. Over the ensuing half-century, Turgenev, Gogol', Dostoievski, Tolstoy, and Goncharov wrote some of the world's best novels, and Anton Chekhov some of its best plays. A third efflorescence came in the very early years after the Revolution, with the experimental poetry of Blok, Mayakovsky, Khlebnikov, Mandel'stam, and others. From the 1930s until the advent of *perestroika*, writing in Russia has suffered from dual political pressure: on the one hand, internal in the shape of government decrees delimiting the writer's field (e.g. the Zhdanovščina), and, secondly, external, in that apparently non-conformist works have tended to be hailed for political reasons as masterpieces. From hundreds of names, those of Pasternak, Paustovsky, and Bulgakov rate special mention.

SCRIPT

Cyrillic. The 'civil alphabet' (*grazhdánskaja ázbuka*) was introduced in the place of the Church Slavonic script as part of Peter the Great's language reform in the middle of the eighteenth century. In 1917/18 certain redundant letters were discarded, and this is the form now in use.

PHONOLOGY

Consonants

    stops: p, b, t, d, k, g
    affricates: ts, tʃ
    fricatives: f, v, s, z, ʃ, ʒ, x
    nasals: m, n
    lateral and flap: l, r
    semi-vowel: j

With certain exceptions (noted below) all Russian consonants occur in pairs: one non-palatalized, one palatalized: thus, for example, the stops can be set out in two rows as /p, b, t, d, k, g/ and /p′, b′, t′, d′, k′, g′/ (though velar palatalization is rare). The exceptions are provided by the affricate /ts/ which is hard only, while /tʃ/ is always soft. The fricatives /ʃ, ʒ/ are always hard, the other fricatives are ambivalent, as are /m, n, l, r/. Finally, the Cyrillic letter щ, pronounced as /ʃ:/ has no hard counterpart. In the Cyrillic script, the soft sign ь is used to signal that an ambivalent consonant is palatalized: e.g. *den′* 'day'.

    It should be noted that *g* in masculine and neuter adjectival and pronominal genitive forms is pronounced as /v/: e.g. *jego* /yǝvo/, 'his'.

Vowels

Symmetrically divided into hard and soft series; specifically notated in the script.

    hard: i, ɛ, a, o, u
    soft: i, e, ja, jo, ju

As will be seen, the difference between /a/ja, o/jo, u/ju/ is one of palatalization only. In the other two cases, there is an additional difference in quality: /i/i, ɛ/e/.

    An extremely important feature of Russian phonology is the extensive reductionism which affects all unstressed vowels except /u/. Unstressed /o/, in particular, tends to become [a]; this phenomenon is known as *akan′e*. Where two or more unstressed vowels (not /u/) precede the tonic stress, the reductionist or neutralization process is graduated through more than one stage of the secondary vowel inventory. Again, this is particularly evident in the case of /o/; cf. *xorošo* /xərʌʃɔ/, 'well, good'; *golova* /gəlʌva/ 'head'. In this article, consonants preceding a soft vowel are understood to be soft (apart from exceptions noted above): e.g. *délo* /d'eła/, plural *delá* /d'əla/ 'affair(s)'; ы is notated as y.

Stress

Free, occurring on any syllable of a word. Stress is mobile within the inflectional system: cf. *oknó* 'window', pl. *ókna*; *délo* 'affair', pl. *delá*; *pisát'* 'to write': *ya pišú* 'I write', *my píšem* 'we write'.

MORPHOLOGY AND SYNTAX

Noun

Russian has no definite article. There are three genders, two numbers and six cases. Some endings are coded for gender: *-a* (fem.), *-o* (nt.), consonant (masc.).

Examples of declension: *a*-stem, *stena* 'wall'; masc. *o*-stem, *stol* 'table'; *i*-stem, *dver'* 'door'.

	Singular	Plural	Singular	Plural	Singular	Plural
nom.	stena	steny	stol	stoly	dver'	dveri
acc.	stenu	steny	stol	stoly	dver'	dveri
gen.	steny	sten	stola	stolov	dveri	dverjei
dat.	stene	stenam	stolu	stolam	dveri	dverjam
instr.	stenoi	stenami	stolom	stolami	dver'ju	dverjami
prep.	stene	stenax	stole	stolax	dveri	dverjax

Animate/non-animate opposition: for masculine singular nouns referring to living creatures, and for all plural animate nouns, the accusative = genitive. Compare

My posetili zavod 'We visited the factory' (acc. = nom.)

My vstretili molod**ogo** inžener**a** 'We met the young engineer' (acc. = gen.)

The genitive case is always used with the negated verb 'to be in a place' → 'to exist': e.g. *Otveta net/ne bylo* 'There is/was no reply.' This turn of phrase is also used to express the notion of 'having/not having': e.g. *U menja mašina* 'I have a car': *U menja mašiny net* 'I haven't got a car.' The object – especially if abstract – is usually in the genitive after negated verbs: e.g. *Oni ne obratili nikako**go** vnimanija na jego slova* 'They paid no attention at all to his words.'

Adjective

Adjectives have long attributive forms, preceding the noun, and short predicative forms; the long forms may also be used predicatively, very frequently in the instrumental case after the verb 'to be': e.g. *Mongol'skie voiny byli lovkimi i bespoščadnymi* 'The Mongol warriors were cunning and ruthless.'

Specimen declension of attributive adjective: masculine hard, *stary* 'old':

	Masculine	*Neuter*	*Feminine*	*Plural*
nominative	staryj	staroe	staraja	starye
accusative	stary/-ogo	staroe	staruju	starye
genitive	starogo	starogo	staroi	staryx
dative	staromu	staromu	staroi	starym
instrumental	starym	starym	staroi	starymi
prepositional	starom	starom	staroi	staryx

COMPARATIVE

The formant is *-ee/-ei/-e*: e.g. *sil'nyj* 'strong' – *sil'nee*. Before the comparative ending *-e*, consonant alternation takes place: e.g. *dorogoi* 'dear' – *dorože*; *krepkij* 'strong' – *krepče*; *suxoj* 'dry' – *suše*. A periphrastic form with *bolee* 'more than', can also be used: e.g. *Eta kniga interesnee, čem ta = Eta kniga bolee interesna, čem ta* 'This book is more interesting than that one.'

Pronoun

PERSONAL PRONOUNS

sing. 1 *ja*, 2 *ty*, 3 *on/ona/ono*; pl. 1 *my*, 2 *vy*, 3 *oni*

These are declined in six cases; e.g. for first person singular *ja*:

gen. *menya*; dat. *mnye*; acc. *menya*; instr. *mnoi*; prep. (*obo*) *mnye*

Throughout this pronominal declension, the accusative is identical with the genitive. The possessive adjectives are: *moi, tvoi, naš, vaš*, for first and second persons singular and plural. These are declined in six cases. The possessive pronoun of the third person is *jego* (masc., nt.), *jejo* (fem.), *jix* (pl.); these forms are indeclinable: *ja videl jego/jejo/jix brata* 'I saw his/her/their brother'.

DEMONSTRATIVE PRONOUN

etot/eta/eto, pl. *eti* 'this/these'; *tot/ta/to*, pl. *te* 'that/those'. Again, these are fully declined in six cases. However, only the neuter form *eto* can function by itself as a subject (i.e. without a noun): cf.

Eti knigi – učebniki 'These books are textbooks'

Eto – učebniki 'These (which we have here) are textbooks'

INTERROGATIVE PRONOUN

kto 'who?'; *što* 'what?' Both are fully declined.

RELATIVE PRONOUN

Masc. *kotoryj*, fem. *ktoraja*, nt. *ktoroe*: always agrees with referent in number and gender; case agreement depends on function of relative pronoun in sentence.

Ja xoču uspet′ na poezd, kotoryj otxodit v 10 časov
'I want to catch the train which leaves at 10'

Daite mnje knigi, kotorye ležat na stole
'Give me the books which are lying on the table'

Zavtra ko nam pridët tovarišč, kotor**ogo** my davno ne videli
'Tomorrow a friend of ours is coming to see us, whom we haven't
seen for a long time'

Ya uže pročital knigu, kotor**uju** on mnje dal
'I have already read the book which he gave me'

Numerals

1 *odin, odna, odno*; pl. *odni* can be used to mean 'some'. 2 *dva* (masc. and nt.),
dve (fem.). 3–10: *tri, četyre, p′at′, šest′, sem′, vosem′, dev′at′, des′at′*; 11
odinnadcat′; 12 *dvenadcat′*; 20 *dvadcat′*; 30 *tridcat′*; 40 *sorok*; 100 *sto*. The
numerals from *p′at′* to *dvadcat′* are declined like *dver′*.

Nouns following 2, 3, 4, or any numeral whose last digit is 2, 3 or 4, take the
genitive singular: *četyre doma* 'four houses'. Numerals upwards of 4, i.e. from 5
inclusive take the genitive plural: e.g. *šest′ knig* 'six books', *trëx sestër* 'three
sisters (acc.)'.

Verb

The Russian verb has two aspects (perfective, imperfective), two moods
(indicative, imperative), two tense forms (past and non-past), and two conjugations. Imperfective verbs have, in addition, a compound future tense.

ASPECT
In general, the imperfective form denotes incomplete action, action in progress
(present, past, or future) without specific cut-off point. The perfective aspect
denotes completed action, past or future: e.g.

My stojali (imperfective) pod derevom, poka ne končilsja dožd′
'We stood under the tree (process) until the rain stopped (cut-off point)'

Formation of perfective aspect:

(a) By prefixation: as in Polish, the prefix has a dual role: over and above
perfective aspect, it may also modify the root meaning, usually within the same
semantic field. Prefixes also serve to form inceptive and semelfactive verbs.

(i) simple perfectivity is illustrated by such pairs as *čitat′* 'to be reading' –
*pro**čitat′** 'to read through and finish'.

Včera učennik **sideli** **čital** ves′ den′
'Yesterday, the pupil sat and read all day'

Učennik **pročital** knigu i pošol gul′at′
'The pupil finished the book and went for a walk'

(ii) change of meaning: e.g. *pit'* 'to drink' – *vypit'* 'to drink up' – *zapit'* 'to take to drink'.

dat' (perfective) 'to give'   **vy**dat' propusk 'to issue a pass'
                                    zadat' vopros 'to put a question'
                                    otdat' knigu 'to return a book'
                                    podat' primer 'to set an example'

(iii) inception of action: e.g. *plakat'* 'to weep ' – **za**plakat' 'to start crying'; *dut'* 'to blow' – **po**dut' 'to start blowing'.

Ženščina **za**plakala 'The woman began to cry'

Podul silnyj veter 'A strong wind got up'

(b) Aspect is also generated by modulation of the verbal ending: e.g. imperfective forms are made from perfective by infixing -(*i*)/(*y*)*va*-: e.g. *vstat'* (perf.) 'to rise' – *vstavat'* (imperf.)

Segodnja ja **vstal** očen' rano 'Today I got up very early'

Letom ja často **vstaval** s vosxodom solnca
'In summer I often got up at sunrise'

(c) By alternation of *a*/*i*: e.g.

Imperfective	*Perfective*
rešat' 'to solve'	rešit'
končat' 'to finish'	končit'
pokupat' 'to buy'	kupit'

(d) By -*nu*- infix: e.g. *nagibat'* 'to bend' – *nagnut'*.

(e) Some perfective forms are suppletive: e.g. *brat'* 'to take' – perf. *vz'at'*.

PASSIVE VOICE
This is analytical: *byt'* 'to be', + passive participle in -*n*: e.g. *On byl soslan v Sibir'* 'He was banished to Siberia.'

TENSE STRUCTURE
Compared with that of Serbo-Croat, for example, the Russian tense system is simple, and depends for its amplification on the aspectual system. The two simple tenses may be described as past and non-past, the latter subsuming present and future. Only imperfective verbs can have a present tense in the exact meaning of the word; the formal equivalent made from a perfective verb has a future perfect meaning: cf. *on čitaet* 'he is reading'; *on pročitaet etu knigu* 'he will (have) read this book through'.

The past form is made by dropping the -*t'*/-*ti* of the infinitive, and adding the following endings: -*l* (masc.), -*la* (fem.), -*lo* (nt.), -*li* (pl. common): e.g. *on čital* 'he was reading'; *ona čitala* 'she was reading'; *oni čitali* 'they were reading'. And in the perfective *on pročital etu knigu* 'he read the book'; *ona pročitala*, etc.

Paradigms in illustration of these two tenses: conjugation I: *rabotat'* 'to work'

		Non-past
singular	1	ja rabotaju
	2	ty rabotaeš
	3	on etc. rabotaet
plural	1	my rabotaem
	2	vy rabotaete
		oni rabotajut

	Past
singular	ja, ty, on rabotal
	ja, ty, ona rabotala
	ono rabotalo
plural	my, vy, oni rabotali

Only regular forms have been shown here. There are many irregularities, involving consonantal alternation. Verbs in *-č'* make their past tense, for example, as follows: *moč'* 'to be able': past: masc. *mog*, fem. *mogla*, nt. *moglo*; pl. *mogli*.

DETERMINATE AND INDETERMINATE VERBS

Russian has 14 verbs of motion, each of which has two specific imperfective forms: one denotes vectorial motion (i.e. non-random), usually undertaken on purpose; the other, the indeterminate paired member, simply expresses the category of motion in a given modality ('walk', 'run', 'swim', 'fly', etc.) without a specification as to vector or intention: e.g. *xodit'* 'to go on foot' (indeterminate imperfective); *idti/itti* 'to go on foot' (determinate imperfective: directed motion) with perfective *prijti*, made from determinate imperfective: cf. *ja xožu medlenno* 'I am a slow walker'; *Ja prišol k vam pogovorit' o važnom dele* 'I've come to you to discuss something very important.'

Similar sets of paired verbs are:

Indeterminate	Determinate
jezdit' 'to go, not on foot'	jexat'
letat' 'to fly'	letet'
plavat' 'to swim'	plyt'

NON-FINITE FORMS

Russian has present and past participial forms, both active and passive: the present active participle has the formant *-ušč/-jušč, -ašč/-jašč*: *čita.jušč.ij* 'reading' → 'who is reading'; *govor.jašč.ij* 'speaking' → 'who is speaking'. The past active participle: the formant is *-vš/-š*: e.g. *čita.vš.ij* 'having read, who had read'.

These participles are declined as adjectives: e.g.

dl'a lic **govorjaščix** na russkom jazyke 'for people who speak Russian'

My besedovali s pisatelem, **napisavšim** povest' o ...

'We were talking with a writer, who has written a story about ...'

Passive participles: the formants are, for the present *-Vm*; for the past *-nn/-t*; e.g. *čita.em.yj* 'being read'; *pro.čita.nn.yj* 'having been read, which was read'. The formation of the passive participle of verbs ending in -*it'* involves extensive consonantal alternation: cf. *vozvratit'* 'to give back' – *voxvraščjonnyj*; *kupit'* 'to buy' – *kupl'ennyj*. Compare:

Čitatel' vozvratil knigu 'The reader returned the book'

čitatel' vozvrativšij knigu 'the reader who returned the book'

kniga vozvraščjonnaya čitatelem
'the book which has been returned by the reader'

IMPERFECTIVE AND PERFECTIVE VERBAL ADVERBS
Examples: *čitaja* 'while reading'; perfective: *pro.čitav* 'having read':

On sidel v sadu, čita**ja** knigu
'He was sitting in the garden, reading a book'

Zakončiv rabotu, on otdyxaet/otdyxal/budet otdyxat'
'Having finished work, he rests/rested/will rest'

Prepositions

The Russian prepositions are specifically associated with certain cases, e.g. *k* 'towards' with the dative, *ot* 'from', *bez* 'without', *dl'a* 'for' with the genitive, etc. Some prepositions take more than one case, and verbs may be followed by a variety of prepositions depending on nuance: *Mat' dumala o syne* 'The mother was thinking about her son'; *dumat'* **nad** *kakim-nibud' voprosom* 'to think a question over'.

Word order

Free; SVO, SOV are common; O(S)V occurs, e.g.

den'gi	rabočim	platili	neregul'arno
'money	to-the-workers	they-paid	not-regularly'

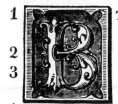

1 ъ началѣ было Слово, и Слово было у Бога, и Богъ было Слово.
2 Оно было въ началѣ у Бога. Все
3 Имъ получило бытіе, и безъ Него не получило бытія ничто,
4 что ни получило бытіе. Въ Немъ была
5 жизнь, и жизнь была свѣтъ человѣковъ. И свѣтъ во тьмѣ свѣтитъ; но тьма не объ-
6 яла его. Былъ человѣкъ, посланный отъ
7 Бога, именемъ Іоаннъ. Сей пришелъ для свидѣтельства, чтобы засвидѣтельствовать о свѣтѣ, дабы всѣ увѣровали чрезъ
8 него. Не *самъ* онъ былъ свѣтъ, но *былъ посланъ*, чтобы засвидѣтельствовать о свѣтѣ.

SAMARITAN

INTRODUCTION

A member of the Afro-Asiatic family, Samaritan was a written and spoken form of Western Aramaic. Three stages may be distinguished in the development of the language:

1. Fourth century BC to eighth century AD: in this oldest period, Samaritan was both a spoken and a written language. Samaritan translation of the *Targum*.
2. Ninth to twelfth century: mediaeval period; spoken Samaritan ousted by Arabic, though the language continued to be written.
3. Thirteenth century onwards: Samaritan no longer spoken; growth of a hybrid literary language, influenced by both Hebrew and Arabic.

The ethnonym is *šāmērim*; that is to say, 'those who take heed, are observant' (root ŠMR /ša:mar/, 'to watch').

When the Assyrians subjugated Judah in 721 BC, many Samaritans were not deported along with other Jews to Babylon, and it is to these people that the modern Samaritans trace their origins. After the Babylonian exile, when Cyrus gave permission for the Second Temple to be built, the Jews rejected Samaritan offers of help. Consequently, the Samaritans built their own temple in the town of Nābulus, a little to the north of Jerusalem; and Nābulus has remained their spiritual seat ever since. At present, a few hundred Samaritans live in Nābulus, and in Holon (near Tel-Aviv). Even as a cult language, Samaritan is moribund; the spoken medium is provided by Arabic in Nābulus and Ivrit in Holon.

SCRIPT

Consonantal, very close to its Phoenician original.

PHONOLOGY

Consonants

    stops: b, t, d, ŧ, k, g, q, ?
    fricatives: f, s, z, ᵴ, ʃ, ʕ
    lateral and flap: l, ł, r
    nasals: m, n
    semi-vowels: j, w

In contrast to Hebrew, the stops /b, d, t, k, g/ have no fricative values. /t, s̱, ɬ/ are emphatics (notated below as ṭ, ṣ, ḷ). /h/ and /ħ/ are missing: /h/ > /ʔ/, /ħ/ > /ʔ/ or /ʕ/.

Vowels

short: a, ɑ, e, ə, i, o, u

/ə/ and /o/ are short only; the others have long and overlong values. The overlong vowels represent the loss of intervocalic laryngeal ḥ, historically present, with consequent fusion. They occur only in open syllables: e.g. 'bhtn /aːbaːtan/, 'our fathers'. Shwa is not present in Samaritan.

MORPHOLOGY AND SYNTAX

Noun

Nouns in Samaritan are masculine or feminine; with two numbers, singular and plural; and three states, absolute, construct, and emphatic or definite.

Absolute state: the masc. sing. marker is null, the plural is -Vn/m; fem. sing. -h, pl. -n/wt.
Construct: here, the masculine singular = masculine absolute, with plural in -y /iː/; fem. sing. -t /at/, pl. -'t.
Emphatic: masc. sing. -h, pl. -yh/-'y/-ayya, 'ay/; fem. sing. -th; pl. -th/-'th.

Examples: masc. sing. yom 'day' – construct yom – emphatic yūma; pl. yūmᵉn – construct yūmi – emphatic yūmayya.

Adjective

Adjectives are marked for gender, number, and state.

Pronoun

The consonantal written forms are realized as:

		Singular		Plural	
		Independent	Enclitics	Independent	Enclitics
1		āna	-i, -ni	anan	-an, -nan, -nu
2	masc.	atta	-ak, -nak	atton	-kon, -innūkon
	fem.	atti	-ak, -nak	attᵉn	-kᵉn
3	masc.	ū	-e, -ne	innon	-on, -non
	fem.	ī	-a, -na	innᵉn	-ᵉn, -nᵉn

Each of the two series of enclitics is associated with a specific aspect: the first set with the imperfective and the imperative; the second with the perfective and the infinitive.

The first set also supplies the possessive affixes: cf. *malk.i* 'my emperor';

malk.an 'our emperor'; *mālēk.innan* 'our emperors'; and the conjunctive forms for use with prepositions: e.g. *l.i* 'to me'; *l.ak* 'to you'.

DEMONSTRATIVE PRONOUNS
dan/ād^en, with variants, 'this'; *'ā'u/'ā'i* 'that'.

INTERROGATIVE–RELATIVE
man 'who(?)' *man da-* 'he who...' (where *d-* is the relative particle): cf. *Fērāq.an ad.l^et l.an fāroq illa atta* 'Save us, "for that" we have no other saviour except thee.'

Numerals

The bases are standard Semitic. The numerals 1–10 are nouns, and may have four forms: absolute and construct, masculine and feminine. The form used for the enumeration of masculine objects has the feminine ending *-h* = /aː/; the form used with feminine objects is not marked for gender: e.g. for 3: with masc. referent, absolute *tālātā*, construct *talātat*; fem. referent, absolute *tālat*, construct *talāti*.

Verb

Triliterals are both strong and weak, the latter having a laryngeal, *w* or *j* in initial, medial, or final root position (*w* does not occur as final). A verb is also weak if second and third radicals are identical. The verbal structure is aspectual: perfective/imperfective. The perfective aspect is suffixal, the imperfective is basically prefixal, with circumfix in second person feminine singular and in plural second and third persons, both genders. Both aspects are marked for person and number; additionally for gender in second and third persons.

PERFECTIVE
(Past) tense has the following ending (phonetic realizations):

		Singular	Plural
1		-^et/-ti	-nu/-na
2	masc.	-ta	-tun
	fem.	-t	-t^en
3	masc.	-Ø	-u
	fem.	-a(t)	-i

IMPERFECTIVE
(Also expresses the jussive):

		Singular	Plural
1		a-	ni-
2	masc.	ti-	ti-...-on/-u
	fem.	ti-...-i	ti-...-an
3	masc.	yi-	yi- ...-on/-u
	fem.	ti-	yi-...-an

IMPERATIVE

The endings are masc. sing. -Ø, pl. -u; fem. sing. -i, pl. -an. In the *pe'al* (see Derived stems, below) the characteristic vowel following C_1 is normally *ē*, e.g. from *'BD*, *'ēbad* 'do!'

DERIVED STEMS

(Compare Hebrew forms):

		Reflexive–passive
base theme	pe'al	etpe'el
intensive	pa'el	etpa'al
causative	af'el	ettaf'al

NEGATIVE

The negating particle is *l'*, realized as /laː/

PARTICIPLES

Both active and passive are formed from *pe'al*, *pa'el*, and *af'el*: e.g. active: from *pe'al*, root *DBQ:* /daːboq/, 'saving', *YTB:* /yeːtob/, 'sitting', from *pa'el*, root *QBL:* /amqabb^{e}l/, 'receiving'. Passive: from root: *KTB* /akt^{e}b/, 'written', *GLY:* /galiː/ 'opened'.

INFINITIVE

The infinitive proper has the prefix *m*V-/-V*m*: e.g. *pe'al*, from root *LBŠ*: *malbaš* 'act of dressing oneself'.

Used as abstract noun, the infinitive takes the feminine ending:

> *pe'al*: *maštūqa* 'being silent, silence';
> *pe'al*: *sūbārot* 'forgiveness';
> *af'el*: *mīṭēba* 'beneficence'.

Prepositions

Stops in the consonantal script, e.g. *b-* 'in, *on*', are, where necessary, realized as the correlative fricatives: cf. *b.ṭwr syny* /af.ᴛor siːni/, 'on Mount Sinai'; *b.gw 'r'h* /af.gu aːra/, 'on earth'.

Word order

VSO in verbal sentences; in nominal sentences SVO or VSO.

SAMOAN

INTRODUCTION

Samoan belongs to the Malayo-Polynesian branch of the Austronesian family and is spoken by about 200,000 people in Samoa, New Zealand, and other parts of the Pacific area. Since 1962 Samoan has been the official language (along with English) of Western Samoa, and is used for education and journalism; there are several newspapers and periodicals. Literacy in Samoan dates from the 1830s, when work began on the translation of the Bible. The rich corpus of Samoan folk literature was preserved and transmitted orally.

SCRIPT

As English. The letter g = /ŋ/.

PHONOLOGY

Consonants

Three stops, /p, t, k/; three nasals, /m, n, ŋ/; fricatives, /v, f, s/; the lateral /l/ alternates with /r/. /h/ is found mainly in foreign words. The glottal stop /ʔ/ is also present, but is not stronger than a hamza pause.

Vowels

    short: ɪ, ɛ, ə, ɔ, u
    long: i, e, a, ɔ:, u

Represented by i, e, a, o, u. There are four diphthongs beginning with /a/ + glide to /e, i, u, o/; also /ei, ou/.

Stress

Usually on penultimate; on any final diphthong.

MORPHOLOGY AND SYNTAX

For note on general structure of Polynesian, *see* **Polynesian Languages**.

Noun

A few nouns have specific plural forms – e.g. *tamaloa* 'young man', pl. *tamalaloa* – but, in general, number is marked by specific articles. Thus, *le/lee* marks a noun as definite and singular, *se* as indefinite and singular. The corresponding plural markers are Ø and *ni*: e.g. *'o le fale* 'the house', *'o se fale* 'a house'; *'o fale* 'the houses', *'o ni fale* 'some houses'. In these examples *'o* is a focusing particle which introduces the (nominal) subject of discourse. It figures normally in initial position; i.e. in VSO order (typical of Polynesian) it is dropped.

POSSESSION

Possessed object precedes possessor: e.g. *'o le ulu o le tama* 'the boy's head'. Here, *o* is the possessive marker indicating inalienable possession, or possession which is independent of the possessor's wish or intention. In contrast, the *a* marker is used with contingent or vuluntary possession: e.g. *'o le solofanua a le tama* 'the boy's horse'. *See* **Polynesian Languages** for a general note on the *a/o* possessives.

Adjective

As attributive, the adjective follows the noun, and agrees with it in number. Many adjectives have specific plural forms, either by partial reduplication or by elision of one syllable: e.g. *lapo'ā* 'big', pl. *lapopo'a*; *manaia* 'beautiful', pl. *mananaia*; *puta* 'thick, fat', pl. *puputa*; *pa'epa'e* 'white', pl. *pa'pa'e*.

COMPARISON

A comparative can be made with the formula *'ua sili ona* ...: e.g. *'ua sili ona maualuga lenei mauga i lenei* 'This mountain is higher than that' (*maualuga* 'high'; *lenei* 'this/that'; *mauga* 'mountain').

Pronoun

The personal forms are:

	Singular	Dual		Plural	
		Inclusive	Exclusive	Inclusive	Exclusive
1	a'u/o'u/'ita	ta'ua/ta	ma'ua/ma	tatou	matou
2	'oe/e	oulua/lua		outou/tou	
3	ia/na	laua/la		latou	

These are both subject and object forms. Choice of long or short form may be positional: e.g. short form of first and second person pronouns is preferred immediately preceding a verb: e.g. *sa e nofo i se nofoa* 'you (sing.) sat in a chair'.

POSSESSIVE PRONOUNS

Formally associated with the pronominal series set out above. They take initial *l* for a singular possessed object, and drop this *l* for the plural; they are also marked in accordance with the *a/o* series. Thus: *lo'u* 'my (*o*-series object)', *la'u* 'my (*a*-series object)'; *'la'u ta'avale* 'my car', *'o a'u ta'avale* 'my cars'.

DEMONSTRATIVE PRONOUN/ADJECTIVE
lenei 'this', pl. *nei* 'these'. There are three forms for 'that': *lea – lenā – lelā*, with plural forms *ia – nā – lā*.

INTERROGATIVE PRONOUN
ai 'who?'; *'o le.a* 'what?', pl. *'o a*.

RELATIVE PRONOUN
'o le, pl. *o'e*; preceded by preposition: (*i*) *ai*, following the verb: e.g. *'o le teine sa o'u va'ai i ai* 'the girl whom I saw (her)'.

Numerals

1–10: *tasi, lua, tolu, fa, lima, ono, fitu, valu, iva, sefulu*; 11 *sefulu ma le tasi*; 12 *sefulu ma le lua*; 20 *lua sefulu*; 30 *tolugafulu*; 100 *selau*.

The numeral may precede or follow the noun it quantifies. If it follows, *e* is used as linking particle: e.g. *'o maile e tolu* 'three dogs'.

Verb

Three classes may be distinguished: (a) transitive verbs, (b) stative verbs, and (c) adjectival or qualitative verbs. Transitive verbs take a direct object, with or without the preposition *i*. Many verbs have a plural form, made by reduplication of the first or second syllable or of the whole word: e.g. *lafo* 'to throw', pl. *lalafo*; *alofa* 'to love', pl. *alolofa*; *tu* 'to stand', pl. *tutu*. Some plural forms are suppletive, e.g. *alu* 'to go,' pl. *o*.

A reciprocal form is made with the help of the prefix *fe* + suffix (*a*)*i*: e.g. *fealofa.n.i* 'to love one another'; *sa femisa'i i māua* 'we two were quarrelling'.

The suffixes *-ina*, *-a*, with allomorphs, added to the stem, produce a form traditionally described as 'passive voice': e.g. *amata* 'to begin' – *amataina* 'to be begun'; *alofa* 'to love' – *alofagia* 'to be loved'; *inu* 'to drink' – *inumia* 'to be drunk'. Since these suffixes are used, however, in contexts where a passive sense is impossible, they are now regarded rather as aspectual markers of completed action, and are so listed, e.g. in Arakin's grammar of Samoan (1973).

In itself, the verbal stem is neutral as to tense. Tense, or better, aspect, can be expressed by modulation of the stem by the prepositive verbal particles. The most important of these are:

e: imperfective, denoting present or future habitual action;
te: imperfective, denoting present or future indefinite action;
o lo'o: imperfective, denoting continuous action;
o le ā: imperfective, denoting future action;
'ua: perfective, denoting completed action in past, whose effect persists into present; also used with impersonal verbs;
sa/na: perfective, denoting completed action in the past

Examples: *'ua alu le va'a i Apia* 'the boat has gone to Apia' (*le va'a* 'the boat'); *o lo'o moe le tama* 'the boy is sleeping' (*moe* 'to sleep'); *o le ā'o'u alu i le tifaga* 'I shall go to the cinema'.

The prepositive particle *se'i* denotes the optative: *ina* + stem + *ia*, the imperative.

CAUSATIVE

The prefix is *fa'a*, e.g. *pa'ū* 'to fall' : *fa'apa'ū* 'to drop'; *aogā* 'useful' – *fa'aaogā* 'to make use of'.

NEGATIVE

The general marker is *lē*, preceding verb, e.g. *'ua lē sau 'o ia* 'he hasn't come' (*sau* 'to come').

DIRECTIONAL MARKERS

Example: *atu* denoting movement away from focus; *mai* towards focus. *A'e* can be used for upward, and *ifo* for downward motion in the same way.

Prepositions

Examples: *i* 'in, on', etc.: e.g. *i Apia* 'in Apia, to Apia'; *'o le tusi i le laulau* 'The book is on the table.' *I* also means 'about': e.g. *'o le tala i Samoa i Sisifo* 'the story about Western Samoa'. *E* marks the agent, animate or inanimate: e.g. *e le tamaaloa* 'by the man'; *e le afā* 'by the storm'.

Composite prepositions include *e aunoa ma* 'without', *seis o'o i* 'until'.

Word formation

Derivatives are made by affix or by compounding:

(a) Prefix + stem: e.g. the many *fa'a* words (see Causative, above).
(b) Stem + suffix: e.g. verb + suffix, *galue* 'to work' – *galuega* 'work'; noun + adjective, *matagofie* (*mata* 'eye' + *gofie* 'light') 'light on the eye' = 'pretty'.
(c) Compounding: noun + noun, e.g. *fuamoa* 'fruit–hen' = 'hen's egg', *potu.moe* 'room–sleep' = 'bedroom'; verb + noun: *tusi.tala* 'write–story' = 'writer'.

Word order

VSO is normal.

Sa i le amataga le Lo- 1
kou, sa i le Atua le
Lokou, o le Atua foi le
Lokou. Oia foi sa i le 2
Atua i le amataga. Na 3
ia faia mea uma lava; e
leai foi se mea e tasi sa
fai e lei faia e ia. O ia 4
te ia le ola; o le ola foi
lea, o le malamalamao ta-
gata. Ua pupula mai foi 5
le malamlama i le pouli-
uli, a e lei tali atu i ai, e
le pouliuli.

   Ua feauina mai, mai 6
le Atua, le tasi tagata, o
Ioane lona igoa. Ua sau 7
ia o le molimau, na te
faailoa mai i le malama-
lama, ina ia faalogo *i ai*
o tagata uma lava, ia te
ia. E le o le malama- 8
lama ia, a ua sau ia e faailoa mai i lea lava mala-
malama.

SANSKRIT

INTRODUCTION

Sanskrit belongs to the Indo-Aryan branch of Indo-European. The name is an anglicization of *saṃskṛta* 'polished, purified' (in contrast to *prākṛta* 'natural, unadorned', and hence by extension, 'vulgar, vernacular'; *see* **Prakrit**).

Indo-Aryan speakers seem to have entered India from the north-west during the second millennium BC. The Aryan kindreds are spoken of as 'immigrants' in the *Rig-Veda*, which was composed c. 1200 BC, and in this sense Ananda Coomaraswamy compared the *Rig-Veda* to the Old Norse *Landnámabók*. Vedic, the oldest stratum of Indo-Aryan, differs in several respects, mainly morphological, from the Classical Sanskrit described in this article. A note on these differences is appended.

The term Classical Sanskrit, the literary medium of the Hindu establishment and the Brahmin upper classes, covers the language and its literature from the fourth century BC (when the language was precisely and comprehensively codified by the unique linguistic genius of Pāṇini) to the twelfth/thirteenth centuries AD. Throughout this long period, spoken forms of Middle Indo-Aryan – already evident in the Aśokan inscriptions of the third century BC, and the Pali texts – went on diverging from *saṃskṛta*, which continued, however, to be written by scholars as a living language, and to function as a lexical reservoir for the emergent NIA languages. (*See* **New Indo-Aryan Languages**.) Sanskrit is still used to some extent as a suitable medium for scholarly writing, and, amazingly, a few thousand people in India still claim it as 'mother tongue'.

Periodization of Sanskrit literature:

1. 1200–200 BC. Composition of the Vedic corpus comprising (a) the liturgical canon: *Ṛgveda* (*Rig-Veda*), *Yajurveda*, *Sāmaveda*, *Atharvaveda*; (b) the exegetical texts: *brāhmaṇas*, *āraṇyakas*, *upaniṣads*, all dating from the second half of the first millennium BC.

   Both (a) and (b) are held to be *śruti*, i.e. 'heard' in the beginning by divinely inspired *ṛṣis* (in contrast to other authoritative but not divinely inspired texts which are *smṛti* 'remembered').

2. The two great epics, the *Mahābhārata* and the *Rāmāyaṇa*, composed and added to, from some years BC to about the eighth century AD.

3. The drama: AD 400–1000; the great figure here is Kālidāsā (fifth century AD) author of such plays as *Śakuntalā* and *Vikramorvaśīya*.

4. The *purāṇas*, composed from BC to about the fifteenth century AD; repositories of Hindu lore concerning the 'five essential themes' – the

creation of the universe, its destruction and regeneration, the genealogies of the gods, the solar and lunar kings, the progenitors of the human race.

5. The *tantras*: similar in substance to the *purāṇas*, but concerned mainly with *śakti*, the female principle inherent in the god Śiva.

SCRIPT

Devanagari, developed from *brāhmī*.

PHONOLOGY

Classification of the sounds of the language in terms of positional series is very important in Sanskrit philology, and is retained here: each series has five terms: voiceless non-aspirate, voiceless aspirate, voiced non-aspirate, voiced aspirate, homorganic nasal: the consonants, as set out in the Devanagari script, are accompanied by the short vowel -*a* = /ə/:

Consonants

velar:	ka	kha	ga	kha	ṅa
palatal:	ca	cha	ja	jha	ña
retroflex:	ṭa	ṭha	ḍa	ḍha	ṇa
dental:	ta	tha	da	dha	na
labial:	pa	pha	ba	bha	ma

In addition, Sanskrit has the sibilants *ś* (palatal), *ṣ* (retroflex), and *s* (dental); the voiced pharyngeal *h*, the dental liquid *l*, alveolar or retroflex *r*, and the semivowels *y* = /j/ and *v*. Voiceless *ḥ* in final position is known as *visarga*.

FINAL CONSONANTS

A Sanskrit word cannot have more than one final consonant, which must be one of the following: /k, ṭ, t, p, ṅ, n, m, r, ḥ/ (visarga is marked in the script as two dots :).

Any other etymologically legitimate final must therefore be converted to one of the permissible finals:

palatals and *h* → *k*, *ṭ*: e.g. *vāc* 'speech' → *vāk*; *samrāj* 'supreme ruler' → *samrāṭ*;
retroflex → *ṭ*: e.g. *prāvṛṣ* 'rainy season → *prāvṛṭ*;
dentals → *t*: e.g. *suhṛd* 'friend' → *suhṛt*;
labials → *p*: e.g. *kakubh* 'summit' → *kakup*;
s, r → *ḥ*: e.g. *kavis* 'poet' → *kaviḥ*.

SANDHI

May be external, i.e. between words in a sentence, or internal, between stem and affix. In both cases, the purpose is to avoid hiatus and to promote the smooth and homorganic assimilation of sounds. The system in Sanskrit is very elaborate; a few examples must suffice:

dental + palatal; vowel + vowel: e.g. *yat ca ucyate* → *yaccocyate* 'as it is said'; *tat jāyate* → *tajjāyate* 'that is born'; *tān jayati* → *tāñjayati* 'he conquers them'
dental + dental nasal: e.g. *jagat nāthaḥ* → *jagannāthaḥ* 'lord of the world'
retroflex + *h*: e.g. *dviṭ hasati* → *dviddhasati* 'the enemy laughs'

Vowels

i, iː, e, a, aː, o, u, uː
ai, au
syllabic ṛ /r̥/ and ḷ /l̥/ (r̥̄ is rare)

A vowel is nasalized by *anusvāra*, represented by superscript dot in Devanagari, and transliterated as *ṃ*; e.g. *taṃ* = /tə̃/.

MORPHOLOGY AND SYNTAX

Sanskrit has three genders, three numbers (including a dual), and eight cases.

Noun

Stems may be uniform or flexible.

1. uniform stems: e.g.

> *a*-stems: masc. *grāma* 'village', *deśa* 'country'; nt. *vanam* 'forest';
> *i/ī-*, *u/ū*-stems: fem. *nadī* 'river', *mati* 'thought, mind', *vadhū* 'woman, bride', *dhenu* 'cow'; masc. *muni* 'sage', *guru* 'teacher';
> ṛ-stems: masc. *pitṛ* 'father', and fem. *mātṛ* 'mother';
> consonant stems: dental: *suhṛd* (masc.) 'friend'; palatal: *vāc* (fem.) 'speech'; retroflex: *dviṣ* (masc.) 'enemy'.

Specimen paradigms: masc. *a*-stem: *grāma* 'village'; fem. *i*-stem: *nadī* 'river'; consonantal stem: *vāc* (fem.) 'speech':

	Singular	Dual	Plural
nominative/vocative	grāmah	grāmau	grāmāḥ
accusative	grāmam	grāmau	grāmān
instrumental	grāmena	grāmābhyām	grāmaiḥ
dative	grāmāya	grāmābhyām	grāmebhyaḥ
ablative	grāmāt	grāmābhyām	grāmebhyaḥ
genitive	grāmasya	grāmāyoḥ	grāmānām
locative	grāme	grāmāyoḥ	grāmeṣu
vocative	grāma	grāmau	grāmah

	Singular	Dual	Plural
nominative/vocative	nadī	nadyau	nadyaḥ
accusative	nadīm	nadyau	nadīḥ
instrumental	nadyā	nadībhyām	nadībhiḥ
dative	nadyai	nadībhyām	nadībhyaḥ
ablative	nadyāḥ	nadībhyām	nadībhyaḥ
genitive	nadyāḥ	nadyoḥ	nadīnām
locative	nadyām	nadyoḥ	nadīṣu

	Singular	Dual	Plural
nominative/vocative	vāk	vācau	vācaḥ
accusative	vācam	vācau	vācaḥ
instrumental	vācā	vāgbhyām	vāgbhiḥ
dative	vāce	vāgbhyām	vāgbhyaḥ
ablative	vācaḥ	vāgbhyām	vāgbhyaḥ
genitive	vācaḥ	vācoḥ	vācām
locative	vāci	vācoḥ	vākṣu

2. Flexible stems: for example, the reduplicated perfect active participle in -*vas* has three stems, e.g. *cakṛvas* '(he) having done': middle stem, *cakṛvat*; strong stem, *cakṛvāṁs*; weak stem, *cakruṣ*. The strong stem appears in the singular nominative, vocative, accusative, the dual nominative, vocative, accusative, and the plural nominative, vocative. Elsewhere, the middle or weak stem appears, the middle, for example, being used with the dual and plural instrumental and dative: *cakṛvadbhyām/-bhiḥ*.

There are, of course, many variants, and the declension system is further complicated by internal sandhi.

Examples of case usage:

Nominative: *sa pandito.bravīt* 'that pandit said'; *kalo gacchati* 'time passes'; *vyāghro māṇuṣam khadati* 'the tiger eats man'.

Accusative: *Dharmaṁ śrotum ihāgataḥ* '(I) have come hither to hear the law'; *brāhmaṇam.āyāntam.avalokya* 'seeing the Brahmin coming'; *paṭavam dadāti* 'it gives skill'.

Instrumental: *vyāghreṇa vyāpāditaḥ khāditaśca* '(was) seen by the tiger and eaten'; *kena.cit sṛgalena avalokitaḥ* 'was seen by a certain jackal'; *daivena deyam* '(to be) given by Fate'; *Balo mukhaṁ hastābhyām gūhati* 'The boy hides his face with his hands'; *prakṛtyā* 'by nature'.

Dative: *ācāryaḥ śiṣyebhyaḥ pustakāni yacchati* 'the teacher gives books to the students'; *yuddhāya gacchati* 'he goes to war'; *Kūpaṁ putrebhyaḥ khanati* 'He digs a well for his sons.'

Genitive: + noun replaces verb 'to have' in Sanskrit, e.g. *arīṇāṁ rathā bhavanti* 'the enemies have chariots'. Genitive absolute: used in contemptuous or slighting sense: e.g. *pasyato mūrkhasya* 'while a fool was looking on'.

Locative: *grīṣme* 'in summer'; *rājakuleṣu* 'in royal families'. Locative absolute: *tasmin nirgate* 'when he had gone out'; *astam gate savitari* 'when the sun had set'.

Ablative: *munir.vanāt gacchati* 'the sage goes from the forest'; *ahāryatvāt* 'because of (its) being unlikely to be stolen'.

Vocative: *Mitra – kuśalaṃ te* 'Friend – hail to thee!'; *Bho bho, paṇḍitāḥ śruyatām* 'Ho, pandits give ear!'

Adjective

Declined in concord with nominal and on same lines. Many adjectives are formed with the suffixes *-mat*, *-vat* (masc. forms) meaning 'possessed of', 'possessing': e.g. *jñāna.vat* 'possessing knowledge'; *rūpa.vant* 'having form' → 'shapely, handsome'.

Adjective + noun can often be rendered in Sanskrit by a compound: e.g. *su.janaḥ* 'a good man'; *dur.janaḥ* 'a bad man'.

Pronoun

PERSONAL

The base forms of the personal pronouns are:

sing.: 1 *aham*, 2 *tvam*, 3 *saḥ/sa/tat* (i.e. the third person distinguishes gender)
dual: 1 *āvām*, 2 *yuvām*, 3 *tau/te/te*
pl.: 1 *vayam*, 2 *yuyām*, 3 *te/tāḥ/tāni*

These are declined in seven cases. The oblique forms of first singular are based on *ma-*: *mām, mayā, mama*, etc. Similarly, for *vayam*: *asmān, asmābhiḥ*, etc.

DEMONSTRATIVE PRONOUN

ayam 'this', *asau* 'that': fully declined.

INTERROGATIVE PRONOUN

kaḥ (masc.), *kā* (fem.), *kim* (neuter) 'who?'

RELATIVE PRONOUN

yaḥ/yā/yat may be used, but Sanskrit often prefers to make a relative clause into an adjectival compound. Both forms are shown in this sentence from the *Hitopadeśa*:

asti kaścid evaṃbhūto vidvān **yo** mama putrāṇāṃ nityam.unmār-gagāminām- anadhigata.śāstrāṇām.idānīṃ nītiśāstropadeśena punar.-janma karāyituṃ samarthaḥ

Here, **yo** refers to *vidvān* 'learned man': 'is there any such learned man, **who** ... can (*samarthaḥ*) bring about (*karāyitum*) the rebirth (*punar.janma*) of my sons (*mama putrāṇām*) **who**-are-continually (*nityam*)-going-in-evil-ways (*un.marga.gāminām*) and-who-have-not-as-yet-studied-the-śāstras. (*nītiśāstra-upadeśa* 'instruction in social and political ethics': *-ena* is the instrumental case ending: 'by instruction in ...'; sandhi: -*a* + *u*- → -*o*-)

The interrogative *kah* forms may also be used: e.g. *parivartini saṃsāre mṛtaḥ ko vā na jāyate* 'who (when) dead (*mṛtaḥ*) in the round (*parivartin*) of existence (*saṃsāra*) is not born again ...'

Numerals

1–10: *eka, dvi, tri, catur, pañca, ṣaṣ, sapta, aṣṭa, nava, daśa*; 11 *ekādaśa*; 12 *dvādaśa*; 20 *viṃśati*; 30 *triṃśat*; 40 *catvāriṃśat*; 100 *śatam*.
  Eka is declined as a pronoun, *dvi* as an adjectival dual; 3 onwards as nominals.

Verb

VOICE
An active voice is opposed to a medio-passive. The active voice is known as the *parasmaipada* ('word for another'); the middle voice is the *ātmanepada* ('word for oneself'); the passive is identical to the ātmanepada, except in the present and imperfect tenses. There are indicative, imperative, and optative moods.

TENSE
The indicative mood has five main tenses, which can be formally divided into two groups: group 1 contains the present and the imperfect, in which the personal endings are added to the *base*, often with a linking agent; in group 2 the personal endings are added to the *root* (or root + sibilant); this group comprises the perfect, and aorist, and the future.
  The base to which the personal endings are added in group 1 is formed in ten different ways; in other words, there are, in this respect, ten classes of verb. The formation of these classes involves the important phenomenon of vowel gradation: briefly, normal grade vowels *a/ā, i/ī, u/ū, ṛ, ḷ,* are said to have a strengthened grade (known as *guṇa*) and a doubly strengthened grade (known as *vṛddhi*). The guṇa grade of *u/ū*, for example, is *o*, the vṛddhi is *au*; similarly, *i/ī* – *e* – *ai*; *ṛ* – *ar* – *ār*. For example, in class I: *budh* 'know' – *bodh, bodhati*: guṇa grade in present tense; in class III *bhṛ* 'carry': pres. (*bi*)*bharti* (guṇa), perf. *babhāra* (vṛddhi)
  In illustration of the personal endings, here are the parasmaipada and ātmanepada forms of the present tense of the first conjugation, class I verb *bhū* 'to be':

Parasmaipada			*Ātmanepada*		
Singular	*Dual*	*Plural*	*Singular*	*Dual*	*Plural*
1 bhavāmi	bhavāvaḥ	bhavāmaḥ	bhave	bhavāvahe	bhavāmahe
2 bhavasi	bhavathaḥ	bhavatha	bhavase	bhavethe	bhavadhve
3 bhavati	bhavataḥ	bhavanti	bhavate	bhavete	bhavante

Imperfect: with stressed augment: for example the singular parasmaipada forms are: 1 *ábhavam*, 2 *ábhavaḥ*, 3 *ábhavat*; plural: *abhavāma, abhavata, abhavan*.

Optative: characteristic *-e-*: sing. 1 *bhaveyam*, 2 *bhaveḥ*, 3 *bhavet*; pl. *bhavema, bhaveta, bhaveyuḥ.*

Aorist: sigmatic or non-sigmatic, both with augment: there are seven forms: e.g. from *diś-* 'to point'; *a.dik.ṣ.at* = third person sigmatic aorist

Perfect: by reduplication: e.g. *kṛ* 'to do', perfect, *cakāra*. Verbs which cannot be reduplicated make a periphrastic perfect, consisting of feminine noun in the accusative case + perfect of *kṛ* or of *as (babhūva)*: *bibharāṃ babhūva* 'he has been a-carrying'.

Future: *-sya-/-iṣya* added to stem: e.g. *da.syā.mi* 'I shall give'.

Ātmanepada forms may be construed as active or passive, depending on the context; often, parasmaipada and ātmanepada forms can be neatly opposed: e.g. in *Bhagavadgītā*, II. 19: *nā'yaṃ hanti na hanyate* 'that one neither slays nor is slain'.

Compounds

A characteristic feature of Sanskrit is the formation of compound words, sometimes of enormous length and intricacy, especially in the work of such late authors as Bāṇa (seventh century AD) and Subandhu (eighth century) where the facility is carried to excessive lengths. There are many types of compound; three are fundamental:

1. The *dvandva*: two members of equal status, or equally in focus, normally with dual ending: e.g. *mṛgakākau* 'a deer and a crow'.
2. The *tatpuruṣa*: the first member qualifies the second; often adjective + noun (then known as *karmadhāraya*): e.g. *nīla* 'blue' + *utpala* 'lotus' → *nīlotpalam* 'a blue lotus'; *dus* 'bad', + noun: *durjanaḥ* 'a wicked man'.
3. The *bahuvrīhi*: adjectival compound replacing relative clause. Theoretically, there is no limit to the number of component elements. A final noun loses its nominal character and takes adjectival status. Examples: *prāptajalo grāmaḥ*: this can be analysed as *sa grāmaḥ yaṃ jalaṃ prāptam*, i.e. 'the village which has been reached by water supplies'; *bahuvīraḥ deśaḥ* 'a country with many heroes'; *śāntomanāḥ muniḥ* 'the saga whose mind is at rest' (see also the example given in Relative pronoun, above).

Postpositions

Postpositions are virtually absent, as the elaborate case system meets most requirements. The following may be mentioned:

anu 'after', *prati* 'towards'; these follow the accusative case;
antar 'within' (with locative);
puras 'before' (with genitive);
ā 'from, up to': precedes ablative, and can also mean 'until'; cf. the following compound (from *Kathāsaritsāgara*, Chapter xvii: 'Story of Ahalyā'): *ā vanāntara.saṃcāri.rāghava.ālokana.āditi* 'until you come (*āditi*) to a

sighting (*ālokana*) of Rāghava (descendant of Rāghu, i.e. Rāma) wandering (*saṃcāri.n*) within the wood (*van.āntara*) = 'until you see Rāghava wandering in the woods'. A compound which illustrates the use of *ā* and the manner in which a prepositional relationship, which is felt to be a detached unit in English, is integrated with the rest of the concept in Sanskrit.

PREPOSITIONAL ADVERBS

These forms, which developed from the case system, are widely used in Sanskrit to express an extensive range of temporal and spatial relationships: e.g.

with accusative: *ubhayataḥ* 'on both sides of';
with instrumental: *samam* 'together with';
with ablative: *param* 'beyond, after';
with genitive: *agre* 'before, in the presence of'.

Word order

The concept is hardly applicable to Sanskrit, partly because of the preference for compounds.

श्रादौ वाद श्रासीत्, स च वाद ईश्वराभिमुख श्रासीत्, स **१**

च वाद ईश्वर श्रासीत् । स श्रादावौश्वराभिमुख श्रासीत् । तेन **२**

सर्व्वमुद्भूत, यद्यदुद्भूतं तन्मध्ये च तं विना न किमण्युद्भूतं । तस्मिन् **३**

जीवनमासीत्, तज्जीवनञ्च मनुष्याणां ज्योतिरासीत् । तज्ज्योति- **४**

ष्वन्धकारे राजतेऽन्धकारस्तु तन्न जग्राह । **५**

अथेश्वरसकाशात् प्रहितो नर एकः समुद्भभूव, तस्य नाम योहन **६**

इति । स साच्छ्यार्थमाजगाम, ज्योतिरधि तेन तथा साच्छ्यं दात- **७**

व्यमासीत्, यथा सर्व्वे तेन विश्वासिनो भवेयुः । स ज्योति नासीत्, **८**

श्रपि तु ज्योतिषि साच्छ्यदाने नियुक्तः ।

VEDIC

PHONOLOGY

Largely as in Sanskrit, plus two retroflex: /ḷ/ and /ḷh/.

SANDHI
Hiatus is acceptable in Vedic to a degree not tolerated in Classical Sanskrit.

MORPHOLOGY AND SYNTAX

There is some fluctuation in the case endings, e.g. -ena and -ā both occur as instrumental endings with a-stems, and there is similar alternation in locative endings. The dual nom./acc. is -au, as in Classical Sanskrit, or -ā. The paradigm for rathī 'charioteer' is given here:

	Singular	Dual	Plural
nom.	rathīs		
acc.	rathiam	rathiā	rathias
dat.	rathie	—	—
gen.	rathias	rathios	rathīnām
abl.	rathias	—	—
instr.	rathiā	rathībhyām	—
loc.	—	rathios	rathīṣu

Verb

In addition to the optative, Vedic has a subjunctive: e.g. from bhū: bhavāni, bhavāsi, bhavāti = first, second, third person singular parasmaipada.

Subjunctive, optative, and imperative moods are present, not only in the present system but in the aorist and perfect systems also.

Frequent use is made of the dative infinitive: e.g. pā.tav.e 'to drink', vas.tav.e 'to shine'.

Pitch accent is marked in the four Vedas, the main – rising – tone by its absence, the preceding low by ‿ under the syllable, the following falling tone by a vertical ' above the syllable: e.g. agnim īḷe purohítaṃ 'I laud/magnify Agni the appointed priest'.

SPECIMEN TEXT

The first stanzas of *Rig-Veda*, book X, hymn 129 (the so-called Creation Hymn):

नासंदासीन्नो सदासीत् तदानीं   नासीद्रजो नो व्योमा परो यत् ।

किमावरीवः कुह कस्य शर्मन्नम्भः किमासीद्गहनं गभीरम्   १

न मृत्युरासीवृमृतं न तर्हि   न राज्या अह्न आसीत् प्रकेतः ।

आनीदवातं स्वधया तदेकं   तस्मांद्धान्यन्न परः किं चनास   २

तम आसीत् तमसा गूल्हमग्रे   ऽप्रकेतं सलिलं सर्वमा इदम् ।

तुच्छ्येनाभ्वपिहितं यदासीत्   तपसस्तन्महिनाजायतैकम्   ३

TRANSCRIPTION

1. nāsad āsīn nosad āsīt tadānīm; nāsīd rajo no viomā paro yat.
   kim āvarīvaḥ? kuha? kasya sarmann?; ambhaḥ kim āsīd gahanam gabhīram?
2. na mr̥tyur āsīd, amr̥tam na tarhi; na rātriā ahna āsīt praketaḥ.
   ānīd avātam svadhayā tad ekam.; tasmād dhānyan na paraḥ kim canāsa.
3. tama āsīt tamasā gūḷham agre; apraketam salilam ā idam.
   tuchyenābhu apihitam yad āsīt; tapasas tan mahinājāyataikam.

TRANSLATION

1. Then, there was not the existent, nor the non-existent; space was not, nor the heavens beyond. What was latent? Where? By whom sheltered? Was water there, unfathomable, deep?
2. There was not death, nor was there non-death. The signal of day was not there, nor of night. That One breathed, breathless, by its own nature. Other than that, there was nothing beyond.
3. Darkness there was in the beginning, hidden in darkness; all was flux without sign. Covered by the void as it was, that One came into being through the great power of heat.

SANTALI

INTRODUCTION

Santali is the easternmost and most important of the Munda languages, spoken by about 5 million people in Orissa and Bihar, with smaller communities in Bangladesh. It was formerly grouped with Muṇḍārī and certain other small Munda languages as Northern Munda or Kherwari. Santali is rarely written, but when it is it can appear in Roman or Bengali script.

PHONOLOGY

Consonants

The labial series /p, ph, b, bh, m/ is paralleled by similar series of dentals, retroflex, palatals, and velars, plus related sonants. In addition, Santali has four glottalized stops, here marked p̱, ṯ, c̱, ḵ to distinguish them from the retroflex (with subscript dot).

Vowels

long or short: a, e, ɛ, ə, a, ɔ, o, u

All may be nasalized, and nasalization is phonemic. The short vowels /e, a, o/ have resultant (reduced) values in syllables contiguous with /i/ or /u/. There are no tones.

MORPHOLOGY AND SYNTAX

Words are not overtly marked for any specific function such as noun or verb, and most stems are multifunctional. Any Santali stem is, potentially, a verb. The class of particles and auxiliaries is exempt. Gender is not distinguished, though natural gender may be lexically marked: e.g. *herel* 'male', *maejiu* 'female'. The basic dichotomy is between animate and inanimate nouns, the former including astronomical bodies.

NUMBER
Singular, dual, and plural. The dual marker is *-kin*, the pl. *-ko*: e.g. *sadom* 'horse' – *sadomkin* 'two horses'; *oṛaḵ* 'house' – *oṛaḵko* 'houses'.

Syntactical relations are expressed by postpositions. The accusative form is the same as the nominative; *-ren* is affixed for the genitive: e.g. *Isorren hopon* 'the son of God'. A looser genitive relationship is expressed by -(re)ak: e.g. *bir.reak dare* 'a forest tree' (*bir* 'forest'; *dare* 'tree'). Other markers: -*then* (instrumental), -*khon* (ablative), -*re* (locative).

The unit numeral *mit* is used as an indefinite article: e.g. *mit hor* 'a man'. The demonstrative pronoun or demonstrative suffix may be used as definite article.

Adjective

Attributively, the adjective precedes the noun: e.g *(mit) boge hor* 'a good man'. Any Santali word ending in a vowel may add -*n* and function as a qualifier: *kaḍawa.n hor* 'a man who has buffaloes'.

COMPARATIVE
Made with the particle *khon*: e.g. *am khon maraṅ* 'bigger than you (sing.)'.

Pronoun

There are full (independent) and suffixed forms; also infixed forms used in transitive verbs, which differ from the suffixed forms only in the singular. The singular set is as follows:

	Full	*Suffixed*	*Infixed*
1	iṅ	-iṅ/-ṅ	-iṅ/-ṅ
2	am	-em/-m	-me
3	ac/uni/ona	-e/i	-e

The dual full forms are: 1 *alaṅ*, 2 *aben*, 3 *akin*; plural 1 incl. *abo(n)*, excl. *ale*, 2 *ape*, 3 *ako*. The suffixed and infixed forms are the same minus the *a-* prefix: e.g. -*laṅ*, -*ben*.

Analogous forms are used as possessive markers: e.g. *apuṅ* 'my father': *apu.ṅ orak.re* 'in my father's house'. Possession may also be expressed by putting the full-form pronoun before the noun: e.g. *am hopon* 'your (sing.) son'.

DEMONSTRATIVE PRONOUN
Here there is a very large inventory turning on the animate/inanimate dichotomy, with several degrees of distancing. Basically, an *n-* series for referents close at hand, a V*n-* series for those further away, an *h-* series for remote referents. There is a specific series for peripheral reference: 'on that side', and for visual or audible referents, e.g. *atekin* 'those two we/you can hear over there'.

INTERROGATIVE PRONOUN
Animate/inanimate distinction: *okoe* (animate) 'who?'.

RELATIVE PRONOUN
The interrogative form may be used: e.g. *mit(ten) hor, okoe* ... 'a man who ...'; or the relative clause may be transferred to attributive position before the noun: e.g. *senen hor* 'the person who went'. Santali prefers the latter construction.

Numerals

1–10: *miṯ, bar, pe, pon, mõṟẽ, turui, eae, irạl, are, gel*; 11 *gel miṯ*; 20 *miṯ isi/bar gel*; 40 *bar isi/pon gel*; 100 *miṯ sae/mõre isi*: i.e. either decimal or vigesimal.

Verb

The Santali verb is agglutinative. Affixes are added to the stem in the following order (for transitive verb, animate): tense or mood marker – object infix – possessive infix – finite marker, *a* – subject pronoun. The stem itself, while never inflected, is modulated to express reciprocity, reiteration, inception, etc. The subject pronominal marker can be attached to the word immediately preceding the verb: e.g. *apuṅ ṭheniṅ calaḵa* 'I shall go to my father'. If the full personal pronoun is used, it must still be recapitulated: e.g. *iṅiṅ calaḵa* 'I shall go' (or, *calaḵaṅ*).

There are three sets of suffixes for use with (a) transitive verb + direct object, (b) indirect object, and (c) intentional action. Again, these may be added to the word preceding the verb. In Santali, however, the verb itself can be a sentence, which then takes the pronominal affixes. For example, the verbal form *dal.ed.iṅ.ae* 'he beats me' consists of: *dal* = stem of verb 'to strike, beat'; *-ed-* is the present-tense marker *-eṯ-* (*ṯ* → *d* before vowel); *-iṅ* is the objective personal infix, first person singular; *-e* is third person marker.

Other tense markers are *-kan-* for the definite present, *-keṯ-* for simple past active. *Tahēkan* makes present tenses imperfect: e.g. *menkedae* 'he said' (*ṯ →d* before vowel).

CHANGES IN BASE

> reciprocal: *-p-* is added after first vowel of stem, + link vowel, e.g. *ṅel* 'to see' – *ṅepel* 'to see each other';
> reiteration: reduplication;
> causative: *-oco-*, e.g. *kiriṅ oco.ked.e.a.ṅ* 'I made him buy it' (*-ked-* is past marker; *-e-* is 3rd p. obj.; *-a-* is finite marker, *(i)ṅ* is 1st p. marker).

INDIRECT OBJECT

In present–future tense: *-a-* + pronominal infix if animate; *-aḵ-* if inanimate: e.g. *bengeṯaḵtakoae* 'he will have a look at what they have' (*-tako-* is 3rd p. poss.). In simple past: *-aṯ-*, e.g. *lai.aṯ.ko.a* 'he told them', *lai.ad.iṅ.a.e* 'he told me'.

INTENTIONAL FORM

This is used where the action of the verb is focused with reference to its effective completion. The marker in the intentional future is *-ka-* + pronominal infix for animate object or *-ḵ-* for inanimate object: e.g. *giḍi.ka.ḵ.a.e.* 'he will throw it away'.

IMPERATIVE

The infix forms of second person singular/dual/plural are added to the present–future tense form: e.g. *ạgu.ko.ben* 'you two bring them!'.

A prohibitive is made with the future definite + the negative *alo*.

Santali has a series of verbal suffixes which do not form part of the tense/mood system, e.g. *-re* 'during, while, when': *oṛakreko duṛup akan tahēkanre* 'while they were sitting in the house' (the subj. marker *-ko* 'they' is attached to *oṛak.re* 'in the house').

NEGATION
The general marker is *ba*: e.g. **Bako ataṅledea** 'They did not receive him.'

Postpositions

Some of these have already been seen in examples given above, e.g. *re* 'in': *bir.re* 'in the forest'. Cf. *mod.re* 'among': *abo modre miṭ hoṛ* 'a man among us' (*abon*).

১ :এদরে রড়ে তাহেঁকান৷, আর রড় ঈশ্বর তুলূইঃএ তা-হেঁকান৷, আর ওন৷ রড়দো ঈশ্বর। উনি :এদরে
২ ঈশ্বর তুলূইঃএ তাহেঁকান৷৷ উনি সানাম দ্বিরবে
৩ বেনাউকেদ৷, আর সানাꞏ বেনাউএন দ্বিরব তালারে উনি বেগর মিঠটাং দ্বিরবহঁ বাং বেনাউ-
৪ লেন৷। উনিরে জিওি তাহেঁকান৷, আর ওন৷ জিওি
৫ হড়কোরেআঃ মার্সাল। ওন৷ মার্সাল এꞏ, তালারে জোলোঃআ, মেনখান এꞏ ওন৷ বাং গডাউলাঃআ।
৬ ঈশ্বর কোলিঃ মিঃ গটেঃ হড়ে তাহেঁকান৷, উনিরে-
৭ আঃ এꞏতুম যোহন। উনি গাও৷ এমঃ লাগিৎ, বাংমা উনি লাসাণকেঁতে জতকো পাতিআউঃম৷, ওন৷ লাগিৎ
৮ নআ মার্সালরেআঃ গাও৷ এমঃএ হেঃএন৷। উনি আইঃতে ওন৷ মার্সালদো বায় তাহেঁকান৷, মেনখান ওন৷ মার্সালরেআঃ গাও৷ এমঃএ হেঃলেন৷।

SCOTTISH GAELIC

INTRODUCTION

Scottish Gaelic belongs with Irish and Manx to the Goidelic division of the Celtic branch of Indo-European; i.e. to Q-Celtic. Goidelic Celtic seems to have been brought to Scotland by the Scoti, an Irish tribe who settled in Central Scotland around the middle of the first millennium AD. Here, they formed an enclave between Brythonic Celtic speakers to the south, and the Picts to the north. Little is known about the Pictish language; it may well have been non-Indo-European.

The earliest writing in the Celtic part of Scotland is, naturally, in the Irish brought by the Scoti. Specifically Scottish Gaelic appears in the bardic poetry of the fifteenth/sixteenth centuries, preserved in part in such collections as the *Book of the Dean of Lismore*, and the *Red Book of Clanranald*. Both in tone and substance – panegyric, genealogy, lampoon, dirge, call to arms – this material is very reminiscent of early Arabic poetry. Some of the poems deal with the legendary hero Ossian. From the seventeenth century onwards Gaelic poetry falls into two main divisions: (a) folk-song accompanying such traditional occupations as waulking, reaping, herding, gathering sea-dulse, with love lyrics and laments; and (b) occasional poetry and political diatribe, the most notable exponents being Iain Lom of Keppoch (seventeenth century) and, in the eighteenth century, Rob Donn MacAoidh, Duncan Bàn Macintyre, and Alexander MacDonald. The twentieth century has seen something of a renaissance in Gaelic poetry (Sorley Maclean).

Gaelic is spoken today in western Scotland and the islands by just under 100,000 people; a few may be monoglot. It is used in television and radio services. Acquisition of Gaelic as a second language is actively, indeed enthusiastically promoted in Scotland and in Scottish communities (often third-generation émigré) in many parts of the world, especially in the United States and Canada.

SCRIPT

Roman alphabet, with acute and grave accents. Scottish Gaelic preserves traditional orthography (in contrast to Manx).

PHONOLOGY

Consonants

stops: p, b, t, d, k, g
affricate: tʃ, dʒ
fricatives: f, v, s, ʃ, χ, γ, h
nasals: m, n, ɲ, ŋ
laterals and flaps: l, ɫ, ʎ, r, r'
semi-vowel: j

Under certain conditions (*see* **Mutation**, below) the stops /p, b, k, g/ are pronounced as their homorganic spirants /f, v, χ, γ/ and are then notated in script as *ph, bh, ch, gh*; /t, d/ are pronounced Ø, but notated in script as *th, dh*.

Vowels

short: i, ɪ, ɛ, e, a, ʌ, ɔ, o, u
long: i, e, ɛ, a, ə, å, œ, u

These are basic values. Nasalization affects the vowels, and there is an extensive series of diphthongs and triphthongs, also nasalized, involving very subtle distinctions. Many digraphs and trigraphs are realized as single vowel sounds, e.g. *iù, ùi*, and *iùi* = /uː/; *eoi* = /ɔ/, *ea* = /ɛː/, etc. In general, correspondence between sound and symbol is weak; cf. Fhionnlaidh (a mountain in Ross-shire) which is pronounced /yūːɫa/: *fh* = /Ø/, *ionn* /jūː/, *dh* = /Ø/.

Stress

Stress is on the first syllable, unless specifically marked.

Mutation

As mentioned above, initial stops are, in certain environments, mutated into their homorganic spirants. The mutation takes place in the following conditions.

(a) in feminine nouns after the definite article *a', an*:

beinn /beːn/ 'mountain'	a' **bh**einn /ə veːn'/
caileag /kalak/ 'girl'	a' **ch**aileig /ə χalək/
faoileag /fœulak/ 'seagull'	an **fh**aoileag /ən œulak/
banarach /banərəχ/ 'milkmaid'	a' **bh**anarach /ə vanərəχ/

(b) in the formation of the past tense:

buail 'strike'	**bh**uail mi /vuːil mi/ 'I struck'
gearr 'cut'	**gh**earr /Øyar/
seas 'stand'	**sh**eas /heːs/

(c) relative future: *bi* 'to be': e.g. *a* **bh**itheas /ə viəs/, 'what will be'.

(d) after possessive pronoun:

    biadh /biə/ 'food'   mo **bh**iadh /mo viə/ 'my food'
    mac /maχk/ 'son'   a **mh**ac /a vaχk/ 'his son'

Here, it is worth pointing out that, on occasion, mutation plays a phonemic part as well as a purely euphonic one: *a* is the third person possessive pronominal adjective for both masculine and singular, but when *a* means 'her', the following noun does not mutate: *a mac* /a maχk/, 'her son' (contrast /a vaχk/ 'his son').

(e) in adjective after feminine noun:

    beag 'small, little'   Màiri **bh**eag 'little Mary'
    caoraich /kœur.iχ/ 'sheep, pl.'   caoraich **bh**àna 'white sheep'

(f) after certain adverbs:

    mor 'big'   glé **mh**or 'very big'
    salach 'dirty'   glé **sh**alach /haləχ/ 'very dirty'

(g) in masculine noun initial after simple preposition + article:

    cu 'dog'   leis a' **ch**u /leʃ.ə.xuː/ 'along with the dog'
    balach 'boy'   ris a' **bh**alach /riʃ.ə.vałəχ/ 'to the boy'

(h) in genitive of masculine nouns: e.g. *cnoc* 'hill': *mullach a' chnuic* /mulləx.ə.χnuiχk/, 'the top of the hill'.

(i) after *aon* 'one': *aon chu* 'one dog' (here, /d, t, s/ are not affected).

It will be seen that aspiration is a very important and far-reaching phenomenon in Gaelic structure. Almost as important is internal flection, which occurs (a) in feminine nouns after simple prepositions: e.g. from *brog* /bråk/, 'shoe', *air a' bhroig* /vråik/, 'on the shoe'; (b) in the genitive of both masculine and feminine nouns: e.g. *carn* 'a cairn': gen. *cuirn*; *each* 'horse': gen. *eich*; *grian* 'sun': gen. *greine*, etc. Aspiration and internal flection are only two features of a rather complicated phonological structure, which is not clarified by the orthography.

MORPHOLOGY AND SYNTAX

Noun

Gaelic has two genders: masculine and feminine. There are two numbers. The definite article: *an, am, a', 'n*, for masculine nouns, depending on case; for feminine nouns, *an, 'a, na*, again depending on case and following initial. Before masculine nouns beginning with a vowel it is *an t*': *an t'athair* 'the father'. The genitive plural form is *nan/nam*: e.g. *nan abhainn* 'of the rivers'.

PLURAL

Most Gaelic nouns add -*an*: e.g. *clach* 'stone' – *clachan*; *brog* 'shoe' – *brogan*. Internal flection is also frequent: e.g. -*i*- inserted after back vowel: *am bard* 'the poet': *na baird* /bairtʃ/. Further examples of ablaut: *fear* 'man' – *fir*; *duine* 'man' – *daoine* /dœunə/. Suppletive forms: *bean* 'wife' – *mnathan* /mna.ən/.

DECLENSION

In terms of Indo-European noun classes (or their reflexes) five declension models can be distinguished in Gaelic: the paradigm of the first declension (masculine -*o* stems) is given here:

	Singular	Plural
nominative	am bard 'the poet'	na baird
genitive	a' bhaird	nam bard
dative	a' bhard	na baird
accusative	am bard	na baird

2nd decl. fem. -*ā* stems: e.g. *làmh* 'hand', gen. sing. *làimhe*; pl. *lamhan*;
3rd decl. fem. -*i* stems: e.g. *suil* 'eye', gen. sing. *sula*; pl. *suilean*;
4th decl. -*u* stems: e.g. *guth* 'voice', gen. sing. *gutha*; pl. *guthan*;
5th decl. consonantal stems: e.g. *cathair* 'chair', gen. sing. *cathrach*, pl. *cathraichean*.

Adjective

As attribute, adjective usually follows the noun, with concord and specific rules for mutation. The following example shows a feminine noun with a mutating adjective, without the added complication of the article (*craobh* /krœuv/ 'tree'):

sing. *craobh mhor* 'big tree'; gen. *craoibhe moire*; dat. *craoibh mhoir*;

pl. *craobhan mora*, gen. *chraobh mora*, dat. *craobhan mora*.

COMPARATIVE

Can be made by using the relative form *na is* → *na's* 'which is' + the genitive singular form of the adjective; e.g. *Tha an cnoc seo n'as airde na an cnoc eile* 'This hill is higher than the other hill.' There are several suppletive forms: e.g. *math* 'good' – *feàrr*; *olc* 'bad' – *miosa*.

Pronoun

PERSONAL

The independent personal forms are:

		Singular	Plural
1		mi	sinn
2		tu	sibh
3	masc.	e	iad
	fem.	i	

These make emphatic forms with a sibilant affix: sing. *mise, tusa, esan* (masc.), *ese/ise* (fem.); pl. *sinne, sibhse, iadsan*.

POSSESSIVE ADJECTIVES

The base forms are: sing. 1 *mo*, 2 *do*, 3 *a*; pl. 1 *ar*, 2 *ur/bhur*, 3 *an/am*. *Mo*, *do* and *a* (masc.) are followed by mutation: the emphatic -*sa* is added to the noun: e.g. *do chu.sa* 'your dog', or to the attributive adjective: e.g. *mo chu dubh.sa* '*my black dog*'.

DEMONSTRATIVE ADJECTIVE

seo 'this'; *sin* 'that'; *siud* 'that yonder'. These follow the noun: e.g. *an cnoc seo* 'this hill'.

INTERROGATIVE PRONOUN

có 'who?'; *cia* 'what?'

RELATIVE PRONOUN

Positive and negative forms:

> Positive: *a, an, am* + dependent form of verb: *Seo am fear **a bha** anns a' mhonadh* 'This is the man who was on the moor.'
>
> Negative: *nach* + dependent form of verb: *Seo an gille **nach robh** anns an sgoil an de* 'This is the boy who was not at school yesterday.' Cf. *Seo an cnoc airan robh an fiadh* 'This is the hill the deer were on.'

Relative future form: *a bhitheas, na bhitheas* /vi.əs/, 'who, which, what will be'.

Numerals

The forms 1–10 preceding a noun are: *aon, dà, trì, ceithir, cóig, sia, seachd, ochd, naoi, deich* /tʃeːχ/: e.g. 'one man' *aon fhear*; 'two men' *dà fhear*; all the other numerals to 10 take the plural: e.g. *trì fir*.

'11 men' *aon fhear deug*; '12 men' *dà fhear dheug*; '13 men' *trì fir dheug*; '20 men' *fichead fear*; '21 men' *aon fhear ar fhichead*; '40 men' *da fhichead fear*; '100 men' *ciad fear*.

There is also an interesting series of numerical nouns (going up to 10): e.g. *aonar* 'one person'; *dithis* '2 persons'; *cóignear* '5 persons'; *deichnear* '10 persons'.

Verb

The Gaelic verb has independent and dependent (relative) forms. The independent form has two voices, three moods (indicative, imperative, subjunctive) and two basic tenses, past and future. A present and an imperfect tense are made analytically. The dependent forms are used in negative, interrogative, and conditional sentences. All tense forms are derived from the root which is identical with the imperative second person singular. All verbs are regular, apart from ten. Use of the personal pronouns is necessary, as verbal forms are marked for person only in the imperative and in the subjunctive first person singular and plural.

Before the modal and tense structure can be profitably set out, it is necessary to list the verbal particles which play a crucial role in that structure:

1. *do*: all Gaelic verbs, except the ten irregular verbs, make their past tense by softening the initial, and prefixing *do*; *do* → *dh'* if the initial is a vowel or *f*-: e.g. *seas* 'stand': past: *do sheas*; *ol* 'drink': past: *do dh'ol* /ɣåɫ/; *fag* 'leave': *dh'fhag* /ɣaːk/. *Do* may be omitted, but the initial mutation is obligatory.

2. *an*: interrogative particle, *am* before labials: e.g. *an do ghabh thu* 'did you take ...?'; *An robh Calum ag obair* 'Was Calum working?' (where *robh* is the dependent form of the past tense – *bha* is the positive – of the verb 'to be').

3. *cha*: negates all forms of the verb except the imperative; takes euphonic *n* before vowels: e.g. *Cha robh mi anns a' mhonadh* 'I was not on the moor'; *Chan e Calum ag obair* 'Calum is not working.'

4. *nach*: interrogative negative particle: e.g. *Nach (do) dh'ol thu do uisge-beatha* 'Didn't you drink your whisky?'

5. *ma*: conditional particle, followed by soft mutation: e.g. *ma bhuail mi ...* 'if I struck'. *na'n* is also used in this sense: e.g. *na'n robh mi ...* 'if I was/were'.

6. *mur*: conditional negative: e.g. *mur do bhuail mi* 'if I did not strike'.

7. *ged*: concessive: e.g. *ged a tha mi ...* 'although I am ...'. *Ged + nach*: negative concessive: e.g. *ged nach do bhuail e* 'although he did not strike'.

8. *gu'n*: relative conjunction: e.g. *Thubhairt cuideigin gu'n robh Calum ag iasgach* 'Someone said that Calum was fishing.'

9. *Nach do*: negative relative: e.g. *an duine nach do thuit* 'the man who did not fall'.

10. *na*: imperative negative particle: e.g. *Na treig a' Ghaidhlig* 'Don't forsake the Gaelic.'

TENSE AND MODAL STRUCTURE
Indicative mood:

> Past tense: mutation of initial, as explained above.
> Future: root + *-idh*/*-aidh*, depending on stem vowel: e.g.
>
> *cuir* 'put': future, *cuiridh mi* /kuːir.i.mi/
> *tog* 'raise': future, *togaidh mi* /toːki.mi/
>
> Analytic present: present tense of copula + verbal noun: e.g. *tha mi a' dol do'n bhaile* 'I'm going to town' (*dol* = verbal noun of *rach* 'to go'); *tha sinn a' dol do'n bhuth* 'we're going to the shop'.
> Analytic imperfect: e.g. *bha mi a' dol ...* 'I was going ...'
>
> Subjunctive: marked for first person singular and plural, e.g. from *buail* 'to strike': *bhualinn* /vuilinʲ/, 'I would strike'; pl. *bhuaileamaid* /vuiləmɪtʃ/.

Imperative: is marked for first and second person; no mutation; ***buail!*** 'strike!'

Passive voice: specific endings, without distinction of person, for past, future, imperative and subjunctive: e.g. ***bhuaileadh*** /vuːiləɣ/, 'was struck'; ***buailear*** 'will be struck'.

There are various periphrastic passive forms.

IRREGULAR VERBS
Most of the ten have suppletive stems: e.g.

> *abair* /apɪr/, 'to say'; past stem: *thubhairt* /huːərˈtʃ/; fut. stem: *their* /heːr/
> *dean* /dʒi.ən/, 'to make, do': past stem: *rinn* /rinˈ/; fut. *ni*;
> *cluinn* /kluinˈ/ 'to hear'; past: *chuala* /xuələ/
> *rach* 'to go': past: *chaidh* /xai/

PREPOSITIONAL PRONOUNS
Several basic prepositions, e.g. *aig* 'at', *air* 'on', *ann* 'in', *do* 'to', *gu* = 'till', *le(is)* 'with', *roimh* 'before', etc. combine with the personal pronouns: e.g. *aig*:

> sing. 1 *agam*, 2 *agad*, 3 *aige/aice*; pl. 1 *againn*, 2 *agaibh*, 3 *aca*

These are then used with verbs in many idiomatic senses: e.g.

> *the agam* 'I have': *tha cu dubh agam* 'I have a black dog'
> *tha eagal orm* 'fear is on me' = 'I am afraid' (*air + mi → orm*)
> *tha gradh agam ortsa* 'there is love at me on you' = 'I love you' (*air = tu → ortsa*)

Word order

VSO is typical.

AN toiseach bha am Focal, agus bha am Focal maille ri Dia, agus b'e am Focal Dia.

2 Bha e so air tùs maille ri Dia.

3 Rinneadh na h-uile nithean leis ; agus as eugmhais cha d'rinneadh aon ni a rinneadh.

4 Ann-san bha beatha, agus b'i a' bheatha solus dhaoine.

5 Agus tha 'n solus a' soillseachadh anns an dorchadas, agus cha do ghabh an dorchadas e.

6 Chuireadh duine o Dhia, d'am b'ainm Eoin.

7 Thàinig esan mar fhianuis, chum fianuis a thoirt mu'n t-solus, chum gu'n creideadh na h-uile dhaoine trìd-san.

8 Cha b'esan an solus sin, ach *chuireadh e* chum gu'n tugadh e fianuis mu'n t-solus.

SEMITIC LANGUAGES

INTRODUCTION

This group of related languages, formerly known as the Semito-Hamitic family, is now classified as part of the Afro-Asiatic family, whose other members, apart from Semitic, are:

(a) Egyptian; attested from the third millennium BC (Old Egyptian) to its latest stage, Coptic, still in use, up to a point, in the Coptic Church (*see* **Egyptian, Coptic**);
(b) Berbero-Lybian (*see* **Berber**);
(c) the Cushitic/Omotic languages in north-east Africa, whose best-known members are: Afar (Danākil), Oromo (Galla), Somali, Walamo (*see* **Oromo, Somali**);
(d) the Chadic languages: over a hundred languages in north-west Africa, including Hausa, Angas, Margi, Somrai (*see* **Hausa, Margi**).

Culturally, by far the most important of the Afro-Asiatic member groups is the Semitic, conventionally divided into:

1. North-East Semitic: Akkadian, Babylonian, Assyrian. Records begin c. 2350 BC and continue to c. 500 BC.
2. North-West Semitic: Ugaritic, Hebrew, Phoenician, Aramaic, Syriac, Samaritan, Mandaean; records from mid-second millennium BC. Represented today by Ivrit, Modern Assyrian (Syriac), Maltese.
3. South Semitic: Arabic, South Arabic (Sabaean-Himyaritic), Ethiopic and the modern Semitic languages of Ethiopia.

Semitic phonology, morphology, and lexicon provided the mould for the formulation, and, in part, the promulgation of the world's two great monotheisms, Judaeo-Christianity and Islam: twin Semitic mappings of the human condition and its metaphysical superstructure, which have achieved global significance, and which have influenced other languages and cultures to a degree hardly matched, if at all, by any other language system. Judaism and Islam agree, moreover, in conferring an extra-linguistic dimension upon their holy books by designating these as *ipsissima verba*, 'the Word of God'. In the Qur'ān it is explicitly reiterated that the Mosaic Law and the Christian Gospel are chronologically earlier but still valid revelations from the one God, which are now subsumed and sealed by the Qur'ānic text; and it is in this sense that the Jews and the Christians are accepted in the Qur'ān as *ahl al-kitāb*, 'the people of the Book'; *al-kitāb*, 'the Book', being the divine exemplar of Islamic theology, the uncreated Word of God (see Qur'ān XXVI, IV, V, XVII).

Semitic promulgation of Semitic monotheism was, however, reserved for Arabic alone. The scriptures of Judaism and Christianity were obliged to seek their wider audiences via translation into non-Semitic media – Greek (the Septuagint and the New Testament), Latin and, in due course, the European successor languages. For the Arabs, on the contrary, the Qur'ān inspired, informed and sustained the great wave of territorial, religious and cultural conquest, and the creation of a multilingual Islamic community. As L. Montgomery Watt puts it:

> In the century after Muḥammad's death many thousands accepted Islam in this way (*scil.* by becoming 'protected persons') and Muḥammad's little state became a vast empire. This could not have come about but for the Qur'ānic conception of the holy war, which in turn is linked with the distinctive conception of the Islamic community and polity. Thus the later Islamic state, even at the economic level, is in certain respects an embodiment of the Qur'ānic vision. 1968: 109)

Client and conquered communities alike acquired the Arabic script, along with at least a ritual participation in, at best a mastery of the Arabic language. Some of the linguistic results are to be seen in the wealth of Arabic words assimilated into a string of non-Semitic languages, ranging from Spanish and Portuguese to Swahili and Javanese, many of which still use the Arabic script. And, at the eastern extremity of the domain of Arabic expansion, it is intriguing to find, in the Buginese and Macassarese translations of the New Testament, the gospels each introduced by an Islamic exordium: in Arabic 'In the name of Allah, the Compassionate, the Merciful, and to Him we pray, to God most high.'

Today, the total number of people speaking Semitic languages is approaching 200 million, with Arabic in its various forms accounting for more than 160 million.

SCRIPTS

The earliest script used for a Semitic language – Akkadian – was the cuneiform borrowed from Sumerian. A consonantal cuneiform alphabet was used for Ugaritic in the second millennium BC. The consonantal Phoenician alphabet, dating from the late second millennium BC was also used for Hebrew, Moabite, and Samaritan. There was also a consonantal Aramaic script, from which was derived the square Hebrew character and the Classical Arabic script. Finally, the South Arabic scripts, from which is derived the Ethiopic syllabary used for Ethiopic, Amharic, Tigre, and Tigrinya.

VOWEL NOTATION

In part, present in Akkadian cuneiform (a, i, u, e). Specific notation of vowels in North-West and South Semitic appears much later: Masoretic in Hebrew, Estrangelo and Nestorian in Syriac, the Arabic short-vowel signs, were all introduced in the late first millennium AD. The Ethiopic syllabary, which notates seven vocalic values by modulation of consonantal base forms, dates from the fourth century AD.

Throughout the first millennium BC the consonants *y* and *w* were used in North-West Semitic to notate /iː/ and /uː/, while *h* was used to notate final *e*, *i*, *o*.

PHONOLOGY

Consonants

As reconstructed, the Proto-Semitic consonantal inventory is as follows:

stops: p, b, t, d, ŧ, đ, k, g, q, ʔ
affricate: ts
fricatives: θ, ð, s, ʃ, ç, ʂ, z, γ, χ, ħ, ʕ, h
nasals: m, n
lateral and flap: l, r

Nearly all of the Proto-Semitic consonants are retained virtually intact in all daughter languages where these sounds are present. One important exception is that Proto-Semitic /p/ became /f/ in South Semitic: cf. North Semitic *pqd* 'to seek' > Arabic *fqd*.

ASSIMILATION
Occurs in all Semitic languages. Two examples are: the sun letters in Arabic (*see* **Arabic**) and the stop → fricative process in Hebrew (*see* **Hebrew**).

Vowels

Proto-Semitic had three basic vowels:

long and short: i, a, u

Stress

The exact position and the nature of stress in Proto-Semitic are unknown.

MORPHOLOGY AND SYNTAX

The key genetic characteristic in the Semitic languages is the presence of the consonantal root: usually of three consonants, though bi- and quadriliterals are common: e.g. from Arabic: *HRB*, *QNʕ*, *SLM*, *SQṬ*.

There are phonotactic constraints on the identity of the three radicals: e.g. identical consonants cannot figure in first and second position, nor can consonants which, though not identical, belong to the same phonetic series.

It seems likely that both bi- and triradicals were present in Proto-Semitic, since biradical nominals – *yad* 'hand', *dam* 'blood', etc. – are found in the oldest Semitic strata.

Each root represents an undifferentiated semantic nucleus. Specific, i.e.

meaningful, differentiations within that semantic field are generated by set vocalic patterns, servile consonants, prefixes, suffixes. e.g. in Arabic: root *KTB*: *KaTaBa* 'he wrote'; *KaTaBtumā* 'you two wrote'; *yaKTuB* 'let him write'; *KiTāB* 'book'; *KuTuB* 'books'; *maKTaB* 'bureau', 'office'; *KāTiB* 'clerk'; *maKTūB* 'written'; *istaKTaBa* 'he wished to write'.

All Semitic languages have noun, pronoun, verb, adverb, adjective, preposition, conjunction.

Noun

Two genders, masculine and feminine, are found throughout the family. A typical feminine marker is -(a)t – -ā in Hebrew and Syriac. All members have examples of masculine nouns with feminine endings, and feminine nouns which have no feminine ending: e.g. Arabic: *khalifat^u* 'caliph'; *nafs* (fem.) 'soul'.

NUMBER

The dual is present, along with singular and plural. The dual is rare in Ethiopic. A characteristic trait is the formation of secondary plural from primary plural form: cf. Arabic: *balad* 'country, place'; pl. *bilād*; secondary pl. *buldān*. Plural forms may be external (sound) or broken (internally inflected). In North-West Semitic *-im* (masc.), *-ot* (fem.) are typical plural endings (Hebrew). The broken or internal plural is regularly found in South Semitic only; for examples *see* **Arabic**.

DEFINITENESS/INDEFINITENESS

In Hebrew and Arabic, definiteness is expressed by the definite article; in Syriac by the emphatic state in *-ā*. A suffixed article developed in Amharic. Both mimation and nunation are present in Akkadian, but are not associated with definiteness or indefiniteness. Neither is present in Hebrew, Syriac, Aramaic, Ethiopic. In Arabic, nunation marks indefiniteness.

DECLENSION

Three basic cases, nominative, genitive, accusative, marked in Akkadian and in Arabic in singular paradigm by *-u*, *-i*, *-a*. For diptotes this is reduced to *-u*, *-a*. North-West Semitic has lost inflection by ending.

POSSESSION

The typical pattern is the construct: possessed + article + possessor: e.g. in Arabic, *ibnu'l.malik^i* 'the king's son'. In North-West Semitic and in the Ethiopic successor languages' expression of possession by means of genitive particle replaces the construct: Syriac: *də*; Hebrew–Ivrit: *šel*; Amharic *ya...* (preceding possessor).

Adjective

Adjective follows noun and agrees with it in Akkadian, Hebrew, Syriac, and Arabic. Feminine form in *-t*. Usage fluctuates in Ethiopic.

Pronoun

The pronominal system is virtually isomorphic for the entire field. The only markedly divergent forms occur in Akkadian in the oblique cases. There are independent forms and suffixed forms, these serving as possessive markers and as pronominal objects. As example of isomorphism, cf. first person singular: Akkadian *anāku*; Ugaritic *ȧnk*; Hebrew *'ānōkī*; Syriac *'enā*; Arabic *'anā*; Ethiopic *'ana*.

DEMONSTRATIVE PRONOUN
Two-term series, distinguishing 'near' from 'far'.

INTERROGATIVE PRONOUN
Isomorphic for whole family: typical forms: *man* 'who?'; *min/ma* 'what?'.

Numerals

Decimal system. A curious and possibly unique feature is the reversal of gender which takes place when the numbers 3 onwards (i.e. excluding 1 and 2) are used with nouns: the feminine form of the numeral is used with masculine nouns, the masculine form with feminine nouns. For examples *see* **Akkadian**, **Hebrew**, **Arabic**. The system is eroded in Ethiopic.

Verb

From the bare root (bi-, tri-, or quadriliteral) further stems (versions) are generated by such devices as gemination of second radical, vowel lengthening, introduction of servile consonants, or combinations of these. These versions express modifications of the root sense: intensification, causativity, reciprocity, reiteration, etc. Not all possible versions are represented in all the Semitic languages, and the tendency over their recorded history is to reduce the inventory. Stem II (gemination of second radical), for example, is found in all members; stem III, however, seems to be in South Semitic only (lengthened first vowel). For derived stem paradigms, *see* **Akkadian**, **Hebrew**, **Arabic**, **Syriac**, **Ethiopic**.

A possible connection between the second vowel (in triliteral) and the dichotomy: action/state (contingent or permanent) is clearest in South Semitic; cf. Arabic: *kataba* 'he wrote' (action); *salima* 'he was well' (contingent state); *ḥasuna* 'he was good-looking' (permanent state).

The vocalic theme: $u - i - a$ denotes passivity: e.g. from root *QTL* 'to kill', *qutila* 'he was killed'.

CONJUGATION
The Semitic verb is aspectual rather than tense-related. The imperfective aspect is implicit in conjugation by personal prefix + suffix (coded for number); conjugation by personal suffix alone (again showing number) expresses the perfective aspect. Examples from Arabic: *yaktubāni* 'they two (masc. dual) are writing' (imperfective); *katabat* 'she wrote' (perfective). For aspects/tenses

peculiar to Akkadian, *see* **Akkadian**.

It is not entirely clear to what extent modal versions of the verbal system were present in Proto-Semitic. *See* **Akkadian, Ugaritic**.

In North-West and South Semitic, vocalic patterns generating the subjunctive and the jussive, the waw-consecutive in Hebrew, etc. are applied to the imperfective form. Thus, in Arabic, change of -*u* to -*a* + apocope of final -*ni*/-*na* gives subjunctive, apocope of final vowel gives jussive: e.g. *yaktubu* 'he writes'; *yaktuba* 'he may write'; *yaktubØ* 'let him write'. In Ethiopic the subjunctive is an imperfective form only. In Akkadian, however, modal patterns were applied to the perfective aspect also.

All Semitic languages have an imperative mood with prefix–suffix formation: e.g. Arabic: *uktub*, pl. *uktubū* 'write!'.

There is no consistency in the formation of the infinitive. All members of the group have active and passive participial forms.

Weak verbs are also found throughout the group. These involve *w, j* in any radical position, and verbs with the glottal stop. Verbs may be doubly weak, e.g. hollow verbs with initial hamza. In doubled verbs, the second and third radicals are identical: e.g. *SRR* 'to please', *MRR* 'to pass'.

By negative particle: *lo, lā, lan, ul(a)*, etc. In Ethiopic, by prefix *i*-. There are specific forms for the negative of the copula: e.g. Hebrew *ayin*, Arabic *laisa*.

Prepositions

The *b*- series, meaning 'in/by', etc., *l*- series, meaning 'to', *k*- series, meaning 'like', etc., and *mn*- series, meaning 'from', are all isomorphic throughout the family. In Ethiopic daughter languages, a tendency has developed to introduce postpositions, sometimes with preposition as well; e.g. Amharic ... *lay* 'on'; *ba...wəsṭ* 'in'.

Word order

Nominal sentences SVO; verbal sentences VSO. SOV is found in Akkadian; SVO appears in Assyro-Babylonian.

SENECA

INTRODUCTION

This Northern Iroquois language is today spoken by about 200 people, mainly in New York State. The Seneca were one of the Five Nations of the Iroquois League, a political and military alliance of some importance in the colonial wars of the seventeenth century and in the American War of Independence. (The other four were the Cayuga, the Onondaga, the Oneida, and the Mohawk; later joined by the Tuscarora.)

SCRIPT

Bible translation in Roman script was in progress from the early nineteenth century on.

PHONOLOGY

Consonants

No labial stops; /t/d/ and /k/g/ are present; as finals, /k/ and /t/ → [ʔ]. Also present are: /ts/tʃ, w/m, s/ʃ, j, n, h, ʔ/.

Vowels

long and short: a, æ, e, i, u + 2 nasals ẽ, ũ

There are nine oral and five nasal diphthongs. All vocalic realizations are dependent on phonetic environment: /ẽ/ varies from [œ̃] to [ɛ̃], /ũ/ from [ɔ̃] to [ɑ̃].

MORPHOLOGY AND SYNTAX

Noun

In the singular there are three genders: masculine, non-masculine, and common. The last two coalesce in the dual and plural. Women are included in common gender. Formally, nouns are divided into five classes by prefix, each class containing specific markers for the three singular and two dual/plural genders. Thus, for example, in class I, masculine singular is marked by *ha-*, e.g. *ha.tecēs* 'medicine man'; non-masculine singular is marked by *(w)a-*, e.g. *wa.kayūh* 'something old' (root *-kayūh* 'old'); common gender is marked by *yū*, e.g. *yū'tanyuhkwa* 'fishing rod'.

An example of a class V noun in masculine plural is *hēnūkwehshū'* 'Indians, men'; non-masc. pl. *wēnūkwehshū'* 'women' (where *-shū'* is a plural marker (redundant, as *hēnū-* itself marks the word as plural).

POSSESSIVE
Prefixes correspond to the five noun classes, with class distinction in the third person: e.g. for class I:

		Singular
1		aka-, e.g. akā.ūta 'my ear'
2		sa-
3	masc.	hu- (also for non-masc.)
	common	ku-

Plus dual and plural markers. There are similar sets for classes II–V.

Adjective

Adjectives are usually provided by attributive suffix, e.g. *'a* 'little'; *-es* 'big'; e.g. *yeksa* 'girl' – *yeksa'a'* 'little girl'; *-(u)nūta* 'mountain' – *unūtes* 'high mountain' (with elision of *-ta-*).

Pronouns

Basic forms, personal: 1 *(ne')i*, 2 *(ne')is*, 3 *(ne')we*. (*See* Verbal subject prefixes, below).

DEMONSTRATIVE ADJECTIVES
hikē/ne'/nēkē: e.g. *hikē hūkweh* 'that man'; *nēkē kanūhsut* 'this house'; *hikē hēnūkwehshū'* 'those men'.

INTERROGATIVE PRONOUN
sū 'who?', pl. *sūshū'*; *na'ut* 'what?'.

Numerals

The base forms 1–10 are: *skat, tekni, sēh, kei, wis, yei, catak, tekyū', tyuhū', washē*. 11 *skaskai*; 12 *tekniskai*; 20 *tewashē* (i.e. dual form of *washē*). These are used for counting objects; there are specific sets for enumerating male persons, female persons, and animals; e.g. *skat kait* 'one tree'; *shaya'tat haksa'a* 'one boy'; *syeya'tat yeksa* 'one girl'.

Verb

Like the noun, the verb is formally divided into five classes. There are two versions: subjective, with agent focused; and objective, with target focused. The objective version is often related to past tense. There is also a compound version, focusing both agent and target. All three versions have forms for present, past, and future tenses:

present: simple verbal form, often with -' final;
future: ē-/ēci- + present form, e.g. *ēkahtēti* 'I will go';
past: objective form of present, e.g. *akahtēti* 'I went'.

NEGATIVE

The marker is *te'/ta'* (with variants) + -*h* suffix: e.g. **te'katistaeh** 'I do not speak'; **te'ēkahtētih** 'I'm not going'. The past negative varies for subjective/objective versions; the subjective version has the present negative with change of ending to -*ūū'*: e.g. **ta'kahtētyūū'** 'I didn't go'.

SUBJECT PREFIXES

The grid sets out five classes of 15 personal forms. By way of illustration, here are the first and second person singular rows for the five classes:

	I	II	III	IV	V
1	ka-	k(e)-	ke-	ki-	ku-
2	sa-	s(e)-	se-	si-	su-

The equivalent rows for the objective series are:

1	aka-	ake-	ake-	aki-	aku-
2	sa-	sa-	sa-	sē-	su-

e.g. *aka.thūte'* 'I hear (something)'; *sa.thūte'* 'you hear (something)'.

COMPOUND FORMS

Example: action of 1st sing. on 2nd: *kūya*; 1st sing. on 3rd masc.: *heya*; 2nd sing. on 1st: *ska*; 3rd sing. on 1st: *haka*. Examples: **kūyathūte'** 'I listen to you'; **heyathūte'** 'I listen to him'; **sknūūkhwa'** 'you love me'.

The subjective/objective prefixes coalesce with other formants, especially tense markers and negative. Reflexive and reciprocal moods are made by infixing -*t*-, -*tat*-.

Word order

VSO or SVO.

NEH ne chi o heh sho No wăă noh ne shon da'wah-saa wăh; neh kuh ne dc ya'di noh' Na wĕn ni yòh No wăă noh; neh gwah huh No wăă noh neh ne'huh Na wĕn ni yòh.

2 Neh' ne sha'yah daat' sho ne chi wa'ceh shon da'-wah sa wăh de ya'di noh Na wĕn ni yòh.

3 He yò'i wa gwe goh' ha o hwah' ho dyă nohk'dah oh; neh kuh na'găă noh' neh huh' dc o'ye ăh', dch tah'gwïs-dăh deh o'des yo niih', he ni yoo ne' gas yo nii.

4 Neh huh' kuh haa yah da deh i waat' nc' yoh heh; neh' kuh nc' yoh heh de o dih hat'hes dah' goh noo'-gweh.

5 Neh ne dc yòh hat heh oh son'da gooh dyòt gont' he yo dă'ăh goot, neh gwaa' ne de yò'dah son da i goh tăh ăh deh o ye noos'ooh ne de yòh'hat heh.

6 ¶ Da neh' ne toh hah oh Na wĕn ni yòh noo'gweh, neh' ne John ha'yaa soh.

7 Neh shah gaat' na i'wa gwa'ih sos no yos'oh, neh ă a'i wa gwa'ih sahs' ne Dc yòh hat heh; ne ga gwee goh' i găă no gweh a ye'i wa gwĕn ni yòs', on'da weeh dak' haa yah'da deh.

8 Tăh ăh naeh neh na'o hwah ne De yòh'hat heh; neh gwaa' sho ne to wah'hah oh ne'neh ă a'i wa gwa'-ih sahs' ne De yòh'hat heh.

SERBO-CROAT

INTRODUCTION

This South Slavonic language is the most important language of Yugoslavia. It is spoken by about 18 million people, and has been present in the Balkans since the sixth/seventh centuries. Since the Middle Ages the area has been divided on two planes – socio-linguistically between Orthodox (Serbia) and Catholic (Croatia), with a Moslem component in the south; and dialectally between Štokavian (east, centre, and south-west), Kajkavian (north) and Čakavian (west). These names are derived from the words for the interrogative pronoun 'what?', which are respectively *što*, *kaj*, and *ča*. In the early nineteenth century Vuk Stefanović Karadžić chose Štokavian as the basis for the reformed Serbian literary standard at the same time as Ljudevit Gaj was engaged on a similar project for Croat. In 1850 a Literary Accord was signed in Vienna, recognizing Štokavian as the basis for the new unified language, Serbo-Croat. Not that this accord put an end to dialectal variation; on the contrary, new Štokavian itself falls into three mutually intelligible dialect forms: Ekavian (in Serbia), Ijekavian (western Serbia and Croatia) and Ikavian (Dalmatia and parts of Bosnia). The latter is no longer used as a literary language, but the other two, centring respectively on Belgrade and Zagreb, are about equally distributed and used interchangeably. They differ lexically, on some morphological points (see below) and, most noticeably, in the pronunciation of the mid front vowel *e*: e.g. Belgrade *sneg* 'snow' = Zagreb *snijeg*; *reka* 'river' = *rijeka*; *lep* 'beautiful' = *lijep*.

Writing in both forms of Serbo-Croat dates from the eleventh/twelfth centuries. Pride of place must go to the Serbian folk epic – the *srpske narodne pjesme*. There are two main cycles, one centring on the disastrous Battle of Kosovo, the other on the heroic figure of Marko Kraljević. Recited by wandering minstrels to the accompaniment of the gusla, through the centuries of Ottoman domination, the *narodne pojesme* came to the attention of Western writers in the late eighteenth century and were enthusiastically received by protagonists of the Romantic movement, such as Herder and Goethe. Much of the corpus was recorded in 1933–4, an enterprise sponsored by Yale and Columbia and edited by Béla Bartók.

From the mid-nineteenth century onwards through the twentieth century a large, high-level output in all literary genres has been sustained in both languages. Among them, the names of the Nobel laureate Ivo Andrić in Serbian, and of Miroslav Krleža in Croat deserve to be singled out.

SCRIPT

In the Orthodox area, Cyrillic has been used since the twelfth century. The use of the Roman alphabet in the Catholic area (Croatia) dates from the fourteenth century. The 1818 dictionary of Vuk Stefanović Karadžić presented an adapted Cyrillic with additional letters, represented as digraphs in the revised Croat orthography: ħ /ć/; џ /dʒ/; ђ /đ/; љ /lj/; њ /nj/. The orthography for both forms was further standardized in the Pravopis of 1960.

PHONOLOGY

Consonants

stops: p, b, t, d, k, g
affricates: ts, tʃ, ć, dʒ, đ
fricatives: f, v, s, z, ʃ, ʒ, x
nasals: m, n, ɲ
laterals and flap: l, l' (ʎ), r
semi-vowel: j

/tʃ/dʒ/ are palato-alveolar, /ć/đ/ are palatal.

Vowels

i, e, a, o, u + syllable r

The pure vowels are long or short.

TONE

The combination of vowel length + rising/falling intonation yields four tones: long rising: ′; long falling: ^; short rising: `; short falling: `. The tones are not marked in written Serbo-Croat. Tone may shift and change within a word; e.g. *lèkar* 'doctor', acc. *lekára*. Tone is phonemic: cf. *grâd* 'city' – *grȁd* 'hail'. Consonant alternation and vowel gradation: e.g. *pisati* 'to write' – *pišem* 'I write'; *plakati* 'to weep' – *plačem* 'I weep'; *smrt* 'death' – *umreti* 'to die' – *umoreti* 'to kill'.

Stress

Stress is intimately bound up with tone; thus, monosyllables have only falling tone (short or long); in polysyllables, a falling tone can only be on the first syllable, a rising tone cannot be on the final.

MORPHOLOGY AND SYNTAX

Noun

Serbo-Croat has three genders, two numbers, seven cases, including a vocative. Four main types of declension are distinguished: *a*-stems, *i*-stems, masculine, and neuter *o*-stems. For example, the paradigms for *kuća* 'house' (*a*-stem), *selo* 'village' (neuter *o*-stem):

	Singular	Plural	Singular	Plural
nom.	kuća	kuće	selo	sela
voc.	kućo	kuće	selo	sela
gen.	kuće	kućā	sela	selā
acc.	kuću	kuće	selo	sela
dat.	kući	kućama	selu	selima
loc.	kući	kućama	selu	selima
instr.	kućom	kućama	selom	selima

Formally, the most interesting point in the declension system is the plural genitive in -*ā*. Dative and locative have virtually fused. In masculine singular nouns, the animate/inanimate distinction is preserved: e.g. *retko vidam tvog brata* 'I seldom see your brother' (acc. and gen. forms are identical). The locative case is also known as the prepositional (always used with a preposition).

Adjective

The indefinite adjective has survived in Serbo-Croat: e.g. *star čovek* '(an) old man', *stari čovek* 'the old man'; but is used mainly predicatively: e.g. *Dan je lep* 'It's a nice day.'

The attributive adjective precedes the noun and is fully declined in concord: e.g. *ovaj mladi čovek* 'this young man'; *ta mlada devojka* 'this young girl'; *naše leposelo* 'our beautiful village'.

The animate distinction is preserved for masculine singular: e.g. *ovog mladog čoveka* (acc. and gen. forms are identical) '(of) that young man'.

COMPARATIVE
-(*j*)*ji*/*a*/*e*, with palatalization in monosyllables as phonologically necessary: cf. *slab* 'weak' – *slabiji*; *jak* 'strong' – *jači*; *brz* 'fast' – *brži*; *sladak* 'sweet' – *slađi*.

Pronoun

sing. 1 *ja*, 2 *ti*, 3 *on*/*ona*/*ono*; pl. 1 *mi*, 2 *vi*, 3 *oni*/*one*/*ona*

These are declined in seven cases (with obvious omissions, e.g. no vocative in first person). The oblique cases of first singular are: *mene* (acc./gen.) *meni*, *meni*, *mnom*. Those of the third person singular and plural have *nj*- initial; e.g. for *on*: acc./gen. *njega*, dat. *njemu*, loc. *njemu*, instr. *njime*.

THE POSSESSIVE PRONOUNS
moj/*moja*/*moje*, *tvoj*/*tvoja*/*tvoje*, *naš*, *vaš*: 3rd sing. masc. *njegov*, fem. *njen*, pl. *njihov*, are fully declined in seven cases.

ENCLITIC PRONOUNS
These have genitive/accusative and dative forms. They can never take first place in a sentence, and the dative form always precedes the genitive/accusative: cf.

On će mi ga dati = daće mi ga 'he will give it to me'

On je rekao da će mi ga dati 'He said that he would give it to me'

Da li mu je rekao da nas je njegov drug video
'Did he tell him that his friend saw us?'

For the enclitic forms of the verb shown here (*ću* and *je*), *see* **Verb**, below.

DEMONSTRATIVE PRONOUN
ovaj, ova, ovo 'this (near me)'; pl. *ovi*; *taj, ta, to* 'this (near you)'; *onaj, ona, ono* 'that'; pl. *oni*. All are fully declined.

INTERROGATIVE PRONOUN
ko 'who?'; *šta/što* 'what?' – declined, without vocative.

RELATIVE PRONOUN
koji, koja, koje: e.g. *čovek koji je bio sa mnom* 'the man who was with me'. *Što* may also be used: e.g. *Što snaga ne može, pamet učini* 'What force cannot do, brains can.'

Numerals

jedan/jedna/jedno and *dva/dve/dva* (1 and 2); nouns following *dva/dve/dva* take -*a* for masculine (an old dual ending) and -*e* for feminine nouns: e.g. *dva dana* 'two days'; *dve godine* 'two years'.

The same endings follow *tri* 3 and *četiri* 4.

5–10: *pet, šest, sedam, osam, devet, deset*; 11 *jedanaest*; 12 *dvanaest*; 20 *dvadeset*; 30 *trideset*, 40 *četrdeset*; 100 *sto*.

From 5 on, the cardinals are followed by nouns in the plural genitive: e.g. *petnaest danā* 'fifteen days'.

Verb

The Serbo-Croat verb is notable for the presence of tense forms which cut across the essentially aspectual structure, e.g. an imperfect (formed from imperfective verbs) and an aorist (from perfectives), with both of these forms tending to lose ground to a composite perfect tense formed from verbs of either aspect. Remarkably, Serbo-Croat perfective verbs also form what is morphologically a present tense: cf. *dajemo* 'we are giving' (imperfective), *dok ne damo* 'until we give' (from perfective verb *dati*).

Verbs are divided into six classes by the joint criteria of infinitival ending and present tense. Thus, the very numerous class of -*iti* verbs has a present tense in -*im*: e.g. *govoriti* 'speak' – *govorim*; *držati* 'hold' – *držim*. Verbs in -*ati*: present in -*am*: e.g. *gledati* 'look at' – *gledam*; in -*ovati*, with present in -*ujem*: e.g. *putovati* 'travel' – *putujem*.

ASPECT
The root may be perfective or imperfective: e.g. *kup-* 'buy' is perfective, *pis-* 'write' is imperfective. Perfectives are made from imperfectives (a) by prefix,

syed、

e.g. *pisati – napisati* 'write'; *piti* 'drink' *– popiti* 'drink up'; (b) by change in stem: e.g. *skakati* (imperfective) – *skočiti* (perfective) 'to jump'. As in other Slavonic languages, prefixation often generates not only perfectivity but also a semantic change in the word.

Secondary imperfective verbs can be formed from perfectives by expansion of the stem: e.g.

| perfective | snábdeti 'to supply' | imperfective | snabdévati |
| | zaúzeti 'occupy' | | zaúzimati |

TENSE FORMATION

Present: e.g, of *ráditi* 'to work' (all Serbo-Croat verbs take -*m* in the first person singular present tense):

sing. 1 radim, 2 radiš, 3 radi; pl. 1 radimo, 2 radite, 3 rade

Imperfect: e.g. of *kupovati* 'to buy':

sing. 1 kupovah, 2 kupovaše, 3 kupovaše; pl. 1 kupovasmo, 2 kupovaste, 3 kupovahu

Aorist: naučiti (perf.) 'to learn':

sing. 1 naučih, 2 nauči, 3 nauči; pl. 1 naučismo, 2 naučiste, 3 naučise

Perfect: e.g. of *čekati* (imperf.) 'to wait':
The active participle of *čekati* is: sing. čekao (masc.), čekala (fem.), čekalo (neuter); pl. čekali, čekale, čekala. These forms are conjugated with the present tense of *biti*:

sing. 1 sam, 2 si, 3 je; pl. 1 smo, 2 ste, 3 su.

Thus: *čekao sam* 'I (masc.) have waited, have been waiting'; *čekale su* 'they (fem.) have waited, have been waiting'.

These enclitic forms may precede the subject; e.g. *svi su pokušaji propali, da* 'all efforts (*pokušaj* 'effort') to... failed' (*propasti* 'to fail'); *Taj je komad oštra satira gradskog života* 'The play is a biting satire on city life.'

Future: the short forms (enclitic) of the verb *hteti* 'to want' are used with the infinitive of the sense-verb:

sing. 1 ću, 2 ćeš, 3 cé; pl. 1 ćemo, 2 ćete, 3 će.

The auxiliary may precede or follow the infinitive: e.g. *ja ću imati = imaću posetiću vas kad dođem u Beograd* 'I'll visit you when I come to Belgrade'; *neću vas posetiti kad...* 'I shan't visit you...'.

Active participle: as illustrated in the perfect tense above, the participle is made by dropping -*ti* of the infinitive and adding -*o/-la/-lo*; -*li/-le/-la*. The passive participle in -*n/-na/-no*, -*jen/-jena/-jeno* is declined as an adjective: e.g. *kupovan, kupovana, kupovano* 'bought'.

The use of the infinitive after modal verbs, frequent in English and many other languages – 'I want/have/ought **to go**' – is avoided in Serbo-Croat, which, like Bulgarian, prefers a construction with *da* and a finite verb: *moram da idem* 'I have to go'; *neću da pitam* 'I don't want to ask'.

Negative particle: *ne*.

Prepositions

Govern genitive, accusative, dative, locative/prepositional, or instrumental cases. Some prepositions, e.g. *u*, *za*, take either the accusative, the genitive, or the instrumental: cf.

za with instrumental: *sedeti za stolom* 'to be seated at table'

za with accusative: *sesti za stol* 'to sit down/seat oneself at table'

za with genitive: *za turskog vremena* 'during the Turkish era'

Of particular interest is the series of paired prepositions, not found elsewhere in the Slavonic group of languages: *nad/iznad* 'on, above', *pod/ispod* 'under', *pred/ispred* 'in front of', *za/iza* 'behind', *medu/izmedu* 'among, between'. The simple forms take the accusative or instrumental depending on whether motion towards something is involved, or rest in a place: e.g.

ići pred pozorište 'to go to the front of the theatre' (acc.)

čekati pred pozorištem 'to wait in front of the theatre' (instr.)

The *iz-/is-* forms take the genitive, and may suggest comparison; cf.

nad gradom 'above the town' (instr.)

iznad prosečnog 'above average' (gen. case, with naunce of comparison; *prosečon* 'average')

Word order

Rather free; SVO/VSO are both frequent. The question of word order is complicated by the pronominal and verbal enclitics, which often require SOV.

У почетку бјеше ријеч, и ријеч бјеше у Бога, и Бог бјеше ријеч.

2. Она бјеше у почетку у Бога.

3. Све је кроз њу постало, и без ње ништа није постало што је постало.

4. У њој бјеше живот, и живот бјеше видјело људима.

5. И видјело се свијетли у тами, и тама га не обузе.

6. Посла Бог човјека по имену Јована.

7. Овај дође за свједочанство да свједочи за видјело да сви вјерују крозањ.

8. Он не бјеше видјело, него да свједочи за видјело.

SHILLUK

INTRODUCTION

This Western Nilotic language, spoken by about 110,000 people in southern Sudan, belongs to the Chari-Nile family (*see* **Nilo-Saharan Languages**).

PHONOLOGY

Consonants

    stops: p, b, t, d, k, g
    affricates: tʃ, dʒ
    frictives: f, s, ʃ, z, γ
    nasals: n, n, ɲ, ŋ
    lateral and flap: l, r
    semi-vowels: j, w

In addition, there is an interdental series, marked here as /t̠, d̠, n̠/, which has to be distinguished from the alveolar-dental series /t, d, n/.

The stops and the affricates have labialized and palatalized series: /k°, k′/, etc. Consonantal assimilation takes place at junctures, e.g. /k/ → [g] before a voiced consonant or a vowel.

Vowels

    i, ɪ, e, ɛ, ə, a, ʌ, ɔ, o, u

In this article, /ɛ/ by ẹ, and /ɔ/ by ọ.

Shilluk has three tones, high, middle and low, plus two glides, a rising and a falling. In this article, the glides are not marked.

MORPHOLOGY AND SYNTAX

Noun

There is no grammatical gender. Lexical items are used to distinguish natural gender: e.g. *ɲù ò̠twò̠n* 'lion', *ɲù mà̠t̠* 'lioness'.

Plural is marked by change of vowel quantity and/or quality, or of tone; also by elision or change of final vowel: e.g. *gwòk* 'dog', plural *gwók*; *tò̠ŋò̠* 'egg', plural *tò̠ŋ*.

POSSESSION

Possessor follows possessed: e.g. *woṭ* 'house', *jāgò* 'chief': *woṭ jāgò* 'the chief's house'. The endings *-jọ*, *-dọ*, *-gọ* change to *-ɲ*, *-n*, *-ŋ* in the construct relationship: e.g. *jāgò* 'chief': *jāŋ fōṭe wón* 'the chief of our country'. In the plural construct, *e* is added to the first component: e.g. *jākè fōṭe woṇ* 'the chiefs of our country'; cf. with *gwòk* 'dog', plural *gẁòk*: *gẁòkè jal ẹni* 'this man's dogs'.

Adjective

As attribute, the adjective follows the noun, whose final may be changed: *yaṭ* 'tree' – *yaṇ ṭēṇ* 'small tree'. The adjective may change for plural concord: cf. *yeṇ ṭōŋọ* 'small trees'.

The relative particle *má-* may be used to form attributive adjective: e.g. *woṭ má.dúọŋ* 'a big house'; *woṭ má.dòŋọ* 'big houses'.

Pronoun

	Singular			Plural		
	Absolute	Subject Prefix	Object and Possessive	Absolute	Subject Prefix	Object and Possessive
1	yán	yá̌	-à	wón	wá/wó	wón
2	yín	yí̌	-ì	wún	wú	wún
3	ẹn	(y)ẹ́/á	-è	gẹ́n	gẹ́	gẹ́n

Examples: *yá̌.kẹ̀dò* 'I go, am going'; *gwòg.à* 'my dog'.

VERB WITH OBJECT

    á čwòlà 'he called me'
    á cẁọlì 'he called thee'
    á cẁọlè 'he called him'
    á cẁọlì wón 'he called us'
    á cẁọlì wún 'he called you (pl.)'
    á cẁọlì gẹ́n 'he called them'

DEMONSTRATIVE PRONOUN AND ADJECTIVE

There are three degrees of relative distance: *àn* 'this', *ẹ́ni* 'that', *àčà* 'that yonder': these have plural forms. Tonal and consonantal change takes place at juncture; cf. *gwòk* 'dog' – *gwóŋ ẹ́ní* 'that dog'; *lyẹ́č* 'elephant' – *lyẹn án* 'this elephant'.

INTERROGATIVE PRONOUN
àmeṇ 'who?'; *ā́ŋọ* 'what?'.

RELATIVE PRONOUN
As well as *má* (*see* **Adjective**, above) *á* is also used, if the verb is in the past tense: e.g. *jal à bì auwa* 'the man who came yesterday'.

Numerals

1–10: *ákyḛl, áryàu, ádɔ̀k, ánwḛn, ábič, ábikyḛl, ábiyàu, ábidɔ̀k, ábinwḛn, pyằrɔ̀*;
11 *pyằrò wí ákyḛl*; 20 *pyằr áryàu*; 30 *pyằr ádɔ̀k*; 100 *pyằr pyằr*.

Verb

Conjugation is by pronominal marker + inflection + stem change: e.g. the
intransitive verb *kḛṭ* 'to go':

> Indicative present: *yá kḛḓò* 'I am going';
> past: *yá kḛṭ* 'I went';
> future: *yá ú kḛḓò* 'I'll go'.
> Imperative: *kḛ́ṭ* 'go!'; plural *kḛ́ḓùn*.

Inflectional endings vary if the verb has an object or target: e.g. *yá kḛ́ṭà gat*
'I went to the river'.

With reference to past action, Shilluk prefers to use a passive construction,
characterized by a falling glide on the stem vowel: e.g. *á čam* 'it was eaten';
where *čam* has the falling glide tone.

The possessive enclitic may be used to specify a pronominal subject: *á kwọpà*
'spoken by me' = 'I said'; *á kwọpì* 'spoken by you' = 'you said'.

If a nominal is the subject, the particle *yɪ* 'by' is used: e.g. *á čam yɪ jál ḛ́ní*
'eaten by this man' = 'this man ate'; *yá čwọ̀là jàl àn* 'I called this man'; *yá čwol yɪ*
jàl àn 'I was called by this man'.

NEGATION
The negating particles are *fà, bà*: e.g. *yá fā kḛ́ṭ* 'I didn't go'.

Prepositions

Prepositions in Shilluk are nouns which stand in a genitival relationship with the
noun governed: e.g. *báŋ* 'back' *báŋ rɪt* 'behind the king'; *dyḛr* 'middle' – *dyḛr*
wọ̀t 'in the house'.

Word order

SVO is the normal active construction; VSO is very frequent in passive forms of
the past tense.

1 Shon (keñ° shāk fiñ ki shwājō) Dok ayiñ°
ma nūt, de yiñ° yī God, de beid° God. 2 Bena
mugani kirīgen ayiñ° yī God shon. 3 Jum bein°
agwukī yī gon; eri tawg° kwuñ awāñ gin mā ūyūt
kirī gin a rūmī shwājō. 4 Neinō ayiñ° ya rigon;
de neinō ba shārō jī. 5 De shārō immeiñ° (itarō)
yī mūd°; de nūti nagī yī mūd°. 6 Jal (megō) abī
e shākā wūrī yī God, ñiñe ba Jon. 7 Abein° ena
ñanani kire be ñōtō mug adadīer, e shākā ñōtō
tielī shār, ū ter° shākā yeiyō kī shārō kī yigon.
8 E ba shākā yiñ shārō, de abein° be ñōtō mug
adadīer kī kaj shārō (fa rī shār).

SHUGHN-ROSHAN

INTRODUCTION

This, the most important sub-group within the Pamir language complex (*see* **Pamir Languages**), comprises the following languages or dialect complexes: Shughn, Roshan, Bartang, Oroshor, and Sarikoli. There is in general a high degree of mutual intelligibility, though Sarikoli is divergent: it is an isolate, spoken by a small number of people in the Xinjiang-Uygur Autonomous Region of China. All the others are spoken in the Gorno-Badakhshan Autonomous Region of Tadzhikistan. All are unwritten. The total number of speakers of Shughn-Roshan languages is about 60,000, with Shughn accounting for well over half of this total, Roshan for about 15 per cent of the remainder.

PHONOLOGY

Consonants

stops: p, b, t, d, k, g, q
affricates: ts, dz, tʃ, dʒ
fricatives: f, v, θ, ð, s, z, ʃ, ʒ, x, γ, χ, ʁ
nasals: m, n
lateral and flap: l, r
semi-vowels: j, w

Vowels

The Shughn inventory comprises the following:

long: i, e, ɛ, u, o, a
short: i, a, u

Shughn distinguishes an allophone of /u/, notated in textbooks as *ů*, which has been levelled to /u/ in Bartang and Oroshor. Sarikoli has lost the long/short opposition.

MORPHOLOGY AND SYNTAX

Noun

All Shughn-Roshan languages have number, and most have gender (masculine/feminine). Sarikoli has lost grammatical gender, but, alone in the sub-group, has retained an oblique case in the noun. The plural marker in Shughn-Roshan is *-ēn*. Sarikoli makes a distinction between nominative and oblique plural: *-xeul* (nom.) and *-ef* (oblique). Gender is not specifically marked in the noun, but is identifiable from concord expressed, e.g., in past tense of intransitives, in demonstrative pronouns, and in adjectives. Gender is partially coded for number; overt feminine gender, for example, implies singularity.

CASE

By preposition and postposition; Sarikoli has an oblique case. Possession is usually expressed by apposition: e.g. *mu pid čod* 'my father's house'.

Adjective

Not marked for number, but may show gender.

Pronoun

The Shughn personal pronouns in base form are: sing. 1 *wuz*, 2 *tu*; pl. 1 *māš*, 2 *tama*. The oblique case of *wuz* is *mu-*. The oblique cases of *tu*, *māš*, and *tama* are identical to the nominative. The third person forms are supplied from the demonstrative series.

DEMONSTRATIVE PRONOUNS

Three degrees of relative distance are distinguished in Shughn: sing. *yu/yā* (showing gender) is proximate; *yid*, middle term; *yam*, distal. These have oblique and plural forms.

INTERROGATIVE PRONOUN

čāy 'who?'; *čīz* 'what?': e.g. *Yid čīz* 'What's that?'

Numerals

1–10 in Shughn: *yīw, ðu, aray, cavōr, pīndz, xoγ, wūvd, waxt, nōw, ðīs*.

Verb

All Shughn-Roshan languages have the typically Iranian twin-base (present/past) system, plus a derivatory perfect base. The general model is: present base is the stem; past base is the stem + *-t/-d*; perfect is stem + *-č/dž*. There are many irregularities.

The past and perfect base of intransitive verbs show concord in gender and number with the subject.

Personal endings: sing. 1 *-um*, 2 *-ī*, 3 *-t/-d*; pl. 1 *-ām*, 2 *-ēt*, 3 *-ēn*. These are added to the present stem to form the present tense. A closely similar set of movable particles is added, not to the base but to the personal pronoun, to form the past and perfect tenses. Thus, *vār.um, vār.ī* 'I, you bring', but, *wuz.**um** tūyd* 'I went'; *wuz.**um** tūydž* 'I have gone'.

In Roshan and in some other Shughn-Roshan languages the pronominal subject of a transitive past tense is in the oblique case, and often the object as well: e.g. *munum mum/dum gudž zōxt/zoxč* 'I took/have taken this kid' (where *mun-* is the oblique case of *wuz* 'I', and *mum/dum* are oblique cases of the demonstrative pronouns *yu/yid*).

The general negative marker is *na*.

Prepositions

Examples: *as/az* 'from': *az mu zōxt* 'took from me', *az mu zurdi* 'stronger than me'; *pis/pas* 'as far as': *Satan čod pas čod* 'They went from house to house' (Roshan).

LOCATIVE POSTPOSITIONS
Examples: *-andi, -andīr, -and, -ard*: *čīd/čod.andīr* 'in(side) the house'; *tōbistůn.andi* 'during the summer'. These forms can also indicate possession: *mund* 'to me', 'I have'.

Word order

SOV.

SINDHI

INTRODUCTION

Sindhi belongs to the North-Western group of the New Indo-Aryan languages (NIA), and is spoken by between 6 and 10 million people in Pakistan and Baluchistan. After partition, over 1 million Sindhi speakers moved to India and settled in large cities such as Delhi, Bombay, and Poona. There are several dialects. The literary language is based on the central Vicoli dialect, which does not differ greatly from the Northern or Siraiki dialect. Though basically a New Indo-Aryan language, Sindhi shows very marked Islamic influence, with both Arabic and Iranian traits.

Writing in Sindhi began in the seventeenth century and even the earliest work shows the cross-culture eclecticism which is so striking in Sindhi literature of the eighteenth and nineteenth centuries. A classical high point is reached in the great *risālō* of Shāh 'Abdu'l-latīf Bhitā'ī. (1689–1752).

SCRIPT

In 1852, the Arabic script used to write Sindhi was augmented by signs for the following specific Sindhi phonemes:

the retroflex series: ʈ, ʈh, ɖ, ɖh, ɽ, ɳ
the aspirates: ph, bh, th, dh, ch, gh;
the nasals: ɲ, ŋ
the implosives: ɓ, ɗ, ʄ, dʒ(subscript dot indicates retroflex; /dʒ/ is implosive /dʒ/); Zograph (1982) notates these as *b̄*/b', *ḏ*/ḍ', *ȳ*/ĵ', *ḡ*/g'.

As in Urdu and Iranian generally, there is some redundancy in the script. Thus, /s/ has three graphs, /z/ has five.

PHONOLOGY

Consonants

stops: p, b, t, d, ʈ, ɖ, k, g, q; with corresponding aspirates /ph, bh/, etc., except /q/
implosive or recursive stops: ɓ, ɗ, ʄ
affricates: tʃ, dʒ; with aspirates: /tʃ', dʒ'/ and implosive /dʒ/
fricatives: f, v, s, z, ʃ, x, ɣ, h
nasals: m, n, ɳ, with corresponding aspirates: mh, nh, ɳh; ɲ, ŋ
laterals and flap/trill: l, lh, r, ɽ, ɽh
semi-vowel: j

In this entry retroflex sounds are indicated by a dot, implosives by subscript macrons.

Vowels

i, e, a, o, u

Short or long, apart from /o/ which is always long. The short vowels /i, a, u/ are realized as [ɪ, ə, ʊ]. /ɔ/ is represented by the diphthong [au]. All vowels occur nasalized.

A striking feature of Sindhi is the presence of short final vowels, which tend to be weakly articulated, but which have a phonemic function.

MORPHOLOGY AND SYNTAX

Noun

GRAMMATICAL GENDER

Masculine and feminine nouns share all five vocalic endings, but -*o* and -*u* are typically masculine, -*ī* and -*e* are typically feminine: e.g. *naru* 'man'; *nare* 'woman'.

NUMBER

Typically, masc. -*o* → -*ā*: e.g. *ghoṛo* 'horse' – *ghoṛā*; feminine in -(*i*)*iū*/-*ū̃*: e.g. *nare* 'woman' – *nareũ*.

DECLENSION

Direct and oblique forms are distinguished. The direct form is also the form used for the direct object; the oblique form provides the indirect object: e.g. from nouns in -*o*, oblique case -*e*, from fem. in -*ī*, oblique -*ia*. *See* **Postposition**, below.

Sindhi has an instrumental in -*ā̃* (with variants): e.g. *kamā̃* 'by work', *hathā̃* 'by hand'. Masculine singular nouns in -*u* have a locative case in -*e*: e.g. *hathe* 'in the hand'.

Adjective

As attribute, adjective precedes noun. Many adjectives are indeclinable, but those with vocalic endings are usually inflected for gender, case, and number. Partial inflection (e.g. gender and case, not number) is also found.

COMPARISON

A comparative is made with the oblique case + *khā̃*/*khõ*/*khũ*: e.g. *Hī chokaro hūa chokarē khā̃ caṇo āhē* 'This boy is better than that boy.' Sindhi also uses the Iranian comparative in -*tar*, and the Arabic elative of '*aF'aL* type.

Pronoun

PERSONAL

With gender distinction in third person singular: sing. 1 *mā̃*, 2 *tū̃*, 3 masc. *hū*/*hīu*; fem. *hūa*/*hīa*; pl. 1 *asī̃*, 2 *tavhī̃*, 3 *hū*. These have oblique forms, e.g. *mū̃*, *to*, *huna, hina*; and enclitics, sing. *-me, -i/-e, -se*; pl. *-ŭ/sŭ, -va, -ne*. The enclitics can be used as possessives, and with postpositions: e.g. *ḍaḍume* 'my grandfather'; *khē.me* 'to me'; *sãse* 'with him'.

DEMONSTRATIVE PRONOUN
hī 'this'; *hū* 'that'.

INTERROGATIVE PRONOUN
kēru 'who?', oblique, *kāhē*; *keharo* 'what?'

RELATIVE PRONOUN
Masc. *jo*, fem. *jā*, with oblique and plural forms, has a correlative in *so*: e.g. *Jo ḍauṛando so thakibo* 'Who runs quickly soon gets tired.'

Numerals

1–10: *hiku, ḅa, ṭī, cār, panja, cha, sata, aṭha, nav, ḍiaha*. 11–99: unpredictable; as is usual in NIA languages, decade + 9 is linked to the following decade: 20 *vēha*; 28 *aṭhāvēha*; 29 *uṇṭēha*; 30 *ṭēha*; 100 *sau*.

Verb

Infinitive is in *-aṇu* (intrans.): e.g. *halaṇu* 'to go'; *-iṇu* (trans.): e.g. *khāiṇu* 'to eat'.

Participles: imperfective in *-ando/-īndo*: e.g. *halando* 'going'. Perfective is in *-yo*: e.g. *paṛhio* 'having read'; this participle is active if the verb is transitive, passive if intransitive. A passive imperfective participle is made with *-ibo*: e.g. *paṛhibo* 'being read'.

Gerundial forms: e.g. in *-ē/-ī, khāē* 'eating'; in *-iṇo/-aṇo, vaṭhiṇo* 'requiring to be taken'.

Personal forms: Sindhi has imperative, indicative, subjunctive, and conditional moods. Tense forms are simple or compound.

Simple: e.g. the subjunctive, which consists of stem + personal ending: sing. 1 *halā*, 2 *halẽ*, 3 *halē*; pl. *halũ, halo, halane*: these forms are preceded by the personal pronouns.

Compound tenses: the format is personal pronoun + participle (imperf./perf.) + personal endings, *or*, + auxiliary: *huaṇu/tho/āh*: e.g. *mã halando hose* 'I was going'; *asī halandiũ huyŭsī* 'we were going' (first person plural, feminine).

About a dozen compound tenses are made in this way to express various shades of complete/incomplete, habitual, frequentative, action. There are two compound present tenses, which are virtually doublets: cf. *mã khāiã piã tho* 'I eat and drink' (regularly or all the time); i.e. the subjunctive of the sense-verb plus the auxiliary *tho*, marked for gender and number. The second compound present is made with the imperfective participle and the auxiliary *āh-*: *Kamlā ine madrāsīa khē piyār kandī āhē* 'Kamla is in love with this Madrasi.'

There are three futures: e.g. first future made from the imperfective participle with personal endings: *mã halanduse* 'I shall go.'

The perfective participle plus the first future of the verb *huaṇu* 'to be' is used with transitive verbs; the participle is marked for gender and number, the auxiliary for gender, number and person: e.g. *mã halyo hūnduse* 'I (masc. sing.) shall go'.

The negative participle is *na*.

Passive voice: the active base takes *-j̆/-ij̆* infix: e.g. *māriṇu* 'to beat', *mārj̆aṇu* 'to be beaten'.

Postpositions

One of the most important is *jo/jī*, plural forms *jā/j̆ū*, which provides the genitival link between a noun in the oblique case and a following noun: e.g. *chokarē jo nālo* 'the boy's name'; *hāriune jī zamīn* 'the peasants' earth'.

Khē marks direct and indirect object: e.g. *māṇhūa khē ḍisaṇu* 'to see the man'; *mū khē ḍiaṇu* 'to give to me'; *huna khē kamu karaṇo āhē* 'to him, work is to be done' = 'he has to work'.

Khã 'from', *sã* 'with', etc.

Word order

SOV.

مُنڊِ مِركَلِمُ هو ۽ كَلِمُ خُداءَ ساڻُ هو ۽ كَلِمُ پاڻ خُداءَ هو (٢) سو
أهو مُنڊِيءَ مِر خُداءَ ساڻُ هو (٣) ۽ سِيَيئِي شيُون تنهِ كان پَيدا ٿِي ۽
پَيدائِش مِرتنهِ ڏاران كا هِڪَڙي شيءِ بِ نَ پَيدا ٿِي (۴) تنهِ مِر جِيَاپو هو
سو جِيَاپو ماڻُهُنِ جو سوجهرو هو (۵) ۽ أهو سوجهرو أوندَهِ مِر پِئي چِمكِيو
پر أوندَهِ تنهِ كِي نَ ميِيو ؛

(٦) تَ هِڪَڙو جَڻو خُداءَ موكلِيو تنهِ جو نالو يوحَنُ هو (٧) أهو شاهِدُ
ٿِي سوجهرِي جي ساك پيرِٽ آيو سو انِهي لاءِ تَ سِيَيئِي تنهِ كري وِساهُ
آڻِينِ (٨) تَ أهو پاڻ سوجهرو نَ هو پر تنهِ سوجهرِي جي ساك پيرِٽ آيو ؛

SINHALESE (Sinhala)

INTRODUCTION

This Indo-Aryan outlier has developed over the last 2,000 years in isolation from its New Indo-Aryan congeners, and, not suprisingly, exhibits a number of unusual, not to say unique, features, due in part to Dravidian influence. The earliest records of literary Sinhalese date from the thirteenth/fourteenth centuries AD. This literary language has continued to be used into the twentieth century, and differs markedly from the colloquial Sinhalese which is described in this article. Much of classical Sinhalese literature is derivative, an ornate recycling of Indian motifs, e.g. the *sandeśa* ('message-poem') model and jātaka themes.

Sinhalese is now the official language of Sri Lanka, where it is spoken by about 12 million people. Its only close relative is the Mahl dialect spoken in the Maldive Islands.

SCRIPT

The Sinhalese script, introduced in the tenth/eleventh centuries derives from Grantha, a South Indian version of the Brahmi script, and is both influenced by and close to Dravidian scripts such as Telugu and Kannada.

PHONOLOGY

Consonants

stops: p, b, t, d, ţ, ḍ, k, g
affricates: tʃ, dʒ
fricatives: v/w, s, ş, ʃ, h
nasals: m, n, ṇ, ɲ, ŋ
laterals and flap: l, ḷ, r
semi-vowels: j, w (allophone of v)

The aspirates, stops, and affricates, /ph, bh/, etc. are retained in the script for the due notation of Sanskrit loan-words. Similarly, /ş/ and /ɲ/ occur only in Sanskrit loan-words. In the spoken language, /l/ and /ḷ/ have coalesced.

An interesting feature of Sinhalese phonology is provided by the semi-nasals, which occur in association with voiced consonants: e.g. *amba* 'mangoes'. In the verbal system, a semi-nasal occurring in citation form may acquire full nasal status in the past tense: cf. *baňdinavā* 'to tie' – past, *bändā*.

Vowels

i, e, ε, a/ʌ/ə/, o, u

These six short vowels have correlatives. /a/ as initial and in closed syllables is [a]; elsewhere it is [ʌ], [ə]; e.g. *kapanavā* [kapənəvaː] 'to cut'.

The realization of Sinhalese words in connected speech is marked by elision, crasis, and assimilation, aimed at avoiding hiatus and promoting euphony.

MORPHOLOGY AND SYNTAX

Noun

GENDER
The basic contrast is between animate and inanimates; animates are further subdivided into masculine and feminine. Characteristic masculine endings are: *-ā*, *-vā/-yā* added to the root. There is no specific feminine ending, but *-ī* is common, and there are several feminine affixes: e.g. *-dena*, *-ikāva*, *-dēviya*. Neuter, i.e. inanimate, nouns usually end in *-ya*, *-va*, *-a*.

NUMBER
Many masculine and some feminine nouns in *-ā* change this ending to *-ō* in the plural: e.g. *piyā* 'father', pl. *piyō*. Again, final *-ā* may change to *-u*, with gemination of final consonant: e.g. *putā* 'son', pl. *puttu*.

Neuter nouns often add *-val*: e.g. *pāra* 'way', pl. *pāraval*. Apocope is also frequent: e.g. *pota* 'book', pl. *pot*.

An indefinite form, corresponding in sense to the indefinite article in English, is made by suffixing *-(e/a)k*: e.g. *minihā* 'man' – *minihek* 'a man'; *puṭuva* 'chair' – *puṭuvak* 'a chair'.

DECLENSION
Various cases are listed in grammars; the basic cases, used also in the spoken language, are as follows: *minihā* 'man': acc. *minihā(vā)*; dat. *minihāṭa*; gen. *minihāgē*; abl. *minihāgen*; instr. *minihāvisin*. The plural of *minihā* is *minissu*, acc. *minissun*, to which form the genitive, dative, etc. affixes are attached.

Neuter: e.g. *puṭuva* 'chair': dat. *puṭuvaṭa*; gen. and loc. *puṭuvē*; abl. *puṭuven*. The plural of *puṭuva* is *puṭu* (nom. and acc.); the dative is *puṭuvalaṭa*, gen. and loc. *puṭuvala*, abl. *puṭuvalin*.

Adjective

The adjective precedes the noun and is indeclinable: e.g. *loku minihā* 'big man'.

Pronoun

INDEPENDENT PERSONAL FORMS
First person: *mama* or *man*; pl. *api*. These are declined: e.g. *maṭa* 'to me'. second person: for polite address, pronouns are avoided, and titles or kinship

terms (i.e. third person forms) are preferred; e.g. *mahattayā* 'Sir', is a suitable form of address for all males; the feminine counterpart is *nōnā* (*mahattayā*). third person: *eyā* is acceptable for 'he'; equivalent plural form *ē gollo*: e.g. *ē gollaṇṭa* 'to them'.

DEMONSTRATIVE PRONOUN
oya 'this'; *ara* 'that'; *ē* is a general demonstrative.

INTERROGATIVE PRONOUN
kavda 'who?'; *mokāda* 'who?'; *monavā* 'what?'. *-da* is an interrogative particle affixed to verb or to any other focused element in the sentence: e.g. *Eyā enne heṭa.**da**?* 'Is it tomorrow that he is coming?' (*enne* is relative present participle of *enavā* 'he is coming').

RELATIVE PRONOUN
See **Verb**, below.

Numerals

1–10: *eka, deka, tuna, hatara, paha, haya, hata, aṭa, namaya, dahaya*; 11 *ekolaha*; 12 *dolaha*; 13 *dahatuna*; 14 *dahahatara*; 20 *vissa*; 30 *tiha*, 40 *hataliha*; 100 *siyaya*.

Verb

The citation form is in *-navā*: e.g. *karanavā* 'to do, make'. In colloquial Sinhalese, this form serves as a present–future form for all three persons, singular and plural: e.g. *mama/eyā karanavā* 'I/he shall/will do'. Similarly, colloquial Sinhalese has a general preterite form in *-ā* for all persons and both numbers. Two conjugations are distinguished, according to the way in which this past tense is formed:

1. Verbs with present form in *-a.navā* change this to *-uvā* with stem ablaut: e.g. *ō → ē, o → e, ū → ī, a → ä*: e.g. *labanavā – läbuvā* 'received'; *hōdanavā – hēduvā* 'washed'.
2. Verbs with present form in *-i.navā* change this to *-iyā*, again with stem ablaut: e.g. *arinavā – äriyā* 'sent'. There are several irregular formations, e.g. *denavā* 'gives' – *dunnā*; *yanavā* 'goes' – *giyā*; *bonavā* 'drinks' – *bivvā* or *bunnā*.

An indefinite future with a potential nuance is made with the endings *-yi/-vi*: e.g. *Eyā mē väḍa kara.yi* 'He will/may do this job.'

PARTICIPLES

present: the *-vā* ending of the present is dropped: e.g. *kanavā → kana* 'eating';
past: made in various ways, e.g. from past tense with shortening of final vowel: e.g. *bässā* 'sat down' – *bässa* 'having sat down'; *giyā* 'went' – *giya* 'having gone'.

The participles are neutral as to voice: cf. *minihā kana bat* 'the rice the man is eating'; *bat kana minihā* 'the man who is eating rice'.

GERUND
The perfective gerund has the ending -(*al*)*ā*: e.g. *balanavā* 'looks at' – gerund, *balā/balalā*. The subject of the sentence is in the dative: e.g. *eyāṭa vāḍa hamāra karalā* 'when he has finished the work' (*väda* 'work'; *hamāra karanavā* 'to finish').

IMPERATIVE
Several endings, e.g. *-nna*, e.g. *karanna* 'do'. The imperative is negated by means of the particle *epā* following the infinitive in the dative case: e.g. *Mē karanṭa epā!* 'Don't do this!'

CAUSATIVE
The characteristic is *-va-*, with agent in dative: e.g.

>Lamayā vāḍakārayāṭa kiyāla aṁba kaḍavanavā
>'The boy is getting the servant to pick mangoes' (*lamayā* 'boy', *kaḍavanavā* 'picks', *aṁba* 'mango', *kiyāla* 'having said')

CONDITIONAL
The *-ā* of the past tense → *ot*(*in*): *keruvot* 'if … were to do', 'if … do/does'.

MODAL VERBS
Example: *puluvan* 'can', with dative subject: *maṭa mēka karanna puluvan* 'I can do this'; but the desiderative modal verb with *kämati* has the subject in the nominative.

COMPOUND VERBS
Sinhalese has a large inventory of compound verbs (noun + verb, verb + verb) giving reciprocal, benefactive, durative, etc., nuances to the sense: e.g. *sellam.karanavā* 'to play'; *gahā.gannavā* 'to fight' (reciprocal of *gahanavā* 'to strike').

NEGATIVE
The general marker is *nä*: e.g. *Gaha loku nä* 'The tree is not big.' *Nemeyi* is used to negate the gerundial forms: e.g. *balalā nemeyi* 'not having looked at it'.

In written Sinhalese, the following personal markers are added to stems to form a present tense: sing. 1 *-mi*, 2 *-hi*, 3 *-yi*; pl. 1 *-mu*, 2 *-hu*, 3 *-ti*: e.g. *mama kara.mi* 'I do'. The same affixes, with some variations, are added to the colloquial preterite to form a perfective tense: e.g. *karanavā* 'to do', coll. pret. *kaḷā*, lit. pret. *kaḷe mi/hi*.

Postpositions

These can take case endings: cf. *gaṅgin megoḍa* 'this side of the river'; *gaṅgin egoḍa.ṭa* 'to the other side of the river'.

Word order

SOV.

1. පටන්ගැන්මෙහිදී වාක්‍යයානෝ සිටිසේ
ක; වාක්‍යයානෝ දෙවියන්වහන්සේ සමග සිටිසේක;
2. ඒ වාක්‍යයානෝ දෙවියන්වහන්සේව සිටිසේක. එම
තැනන්වහන්සේ පටන්ගැන්මෙහි දෙවියන්වහන්සේ
3. සමග සිටියාස්ක. ඒ තැනන්වහන්සේ කරණකොට
ගෙණ සියල්ල මවනලද්දේය. මවනලද කිසිවක් උන්ව
4. හන්සේ නැතුව නොමවනලද්දේය. උන්වහන්සේ
තුළ ජීවනය සිබුනේය; ඒ ජීවනය මනුෂ්‍යයන්ගේ
5. ආලෝකය වූයේය. ආලෝකය අඳුරෙහි බබලන්නේ
ය. අඳුර ඒක පිළිගත්නේ නැත.
6. දෙවියන්වහන්සේ විසින් එවනලද යොහන් නම්
7. මනුෂ්‍යයෙක් සිටියේය. ඔහු තමන් කරණකොටගෙ
ණ සියල්ලන් විසින් අදහන පිණිස, ඒ ආලෝකයට සා
8. ක්‍ෂිදෙන්ට සාක්‍ෂිකාරයෙක්ව ආයේය. ඔහු ඒ ආලෝ
කය නුවුණේය; සුමුත් ඒ ආලෝකයට සාක්‍ෂිදෙන පිණි

SINO-TIBETAN LANGUAGES

Some authorities extend this grouping to include the Tai languages and the Miao-Yao languages. Usually, however, it is restricted to two very extensive language families, one of which – Sinitic – has, in fact, the largest number of speakers of any language on earth: more than 1,200 million people speak a Sinitic language in one form or another.

The second component family is Tibeto-Burman, whose 300 languages are spoken by about 40 million people. Its main divisions are:

1. Tibeto-Himalayan, or Bodic; the Himalayan languages are divided into:

    (a) pronominalized: i.e. verbs take affixes, which are coded for, or recapitulate subject/object;
    (b) non-pronominalized.

2. Assam-Burmese; includes Bodo-Garo, Naga, Kuki-Chin, Kachinic, Loloish, Rung, Abor-Miri-Dafla.

All Sinitic languages, and most Tibeto-Burman languages have phonemic tonal systems. Both families are, synchronically at least, monosyllabic. Sinitic is isolating, Tibeto-Burman is agglutinative.

See **Chinese, Archaic, Classical, Modern Standard**; **Yue, Min, Gan, Wu, Hakka, Zhuang**; **Tibetan, Burmese, Naga, Karen, Garo, Naxi, Yi**; **Tai Languages, Miao-Yao Languages**.

SLAVONIC LANGUAGES

INTRODUCTION

Within the Indo-European family, the Slavonic languages form a compact and, morphologically homogeneous group with a large common stock of basic vocabulary. Phonologically, the individual languages show more variation; the nasal vowels of Common Slavonic have been retained only in Polish, and tone is found only in Serbo-Croat and Slovene. The degree of homogeneity suggests that dialectal variation from a common Slavonic stock is fairly recent. This common parent language seems to have persisted into the early years of the first millennium AD; by about 600 the individual Slavonic languages were beginning to take shape. When the Old Church Slavonic literary language appears in the ninth century some of its characteristic features are identifiably South Slavonic. In the main, however, this literary language is still close to Common Slavonic. The original diffusion of Common Slavonic into Eastern, Western, and Southern dialects remains the basis for contemporary classification of the Slavonic languages: Eastern Slavonic comprises Russian, Ukrainian, and Belorussian; Western Slavonic, Polish, Czech, Slovak, Lusatian (also known as Sorbian or Wendish, with two literary and spoken norms, Upper and Lower); South Slavonic comprises Serbo-Croat, Slovene, Bulgarian, and Macedonian. Extinct Slavonic languages include Polabian (Lechic group of West Slavonic).

SCRIPT

Old Church Slavonic was written in two scripts, Glagolitic and Cyrillic, both expressly designed for its adequate notation. Glagolitic is no longer used. Slavonic languages are now written either in Cyrillic or Roman, depending on religious and cultural affinity. Russian, Ukrainian, Belorussian, Serbian, Bulgarian, and Macedonian, traditionally associated with the Eastern Orthodox Church, use Cyrillic; the others, under Catholic influence, use Roman.

PHONOLOGY

Three inter-connected phenomena are fundamental in the process whereby Common Slavonic became differentiated from the Indo-European matrix. These are: (a) the loss of final IE consonants; (b) the monophthongization of IE diphthongs, and the reduction of phonemic length in vowels to a neutral grade; (c) successive stages of palatalization.

(a) loss of final consonant: cf. Greek *hupnos* – Slav. *sunŭ*; Latin *axis* – Slav. *osĭ*; Latin *taurus* – Slav. *turŭ*.

(b) monophthongization: cf. Lithuanian *eīti* – Slav. *iti* 'to go'; Latin *cruor*, Greek *kreas* – Slav. *kruvĭ* 'blood, flesh'.

(c) By the first palatalization (which antedated the process detailed in (b)), the Indo-European phonemes /k, g, x/, if followed by IE front vowels, were mutated to /tʃ, dʒ, ʃ/. The second palatalization followed the monophthongization process; and monophthong reflexes thus produced caused preceding /k, g, x/ to become /ts, ʒ, s/ʃ/. Cf. as an example of the first palatalization IE *g°ĭuos*, Lith. *gývas* – Slav. *živŭ* 'alive'; of the second, Lith. *kaina* – Slav. *tsena* 'price'. A third palatalization produced the same mutations of /k, g, x/ *following* front vowels: e.g. Germanic *kuningaz* – Slav. *kŭnēžĭ*, Russian *kn'az'* 'prince'.

Vocalic system of Common Slavonic:

  i, ɪ, e, a, o, u; nasalized: ę, ǫ;

The jers: ъ = /ŭ/, ь = /ĭ/.

  Common Slavonic had the sequence C_1Vl/rC_2, where V is /e/ or /o/. The sequence is conveniently exemplified by *tort*, whose reflexes in the successor languages are then *torot* (the 'full vowel' – *polnoglasie* – form found in Russian), *trot/trat*. /e/ and /l/ can be inserted in the formula to produce analogous forms: *tolt* – *tolot* – *tlot/tlat*, etc.: e.g.

  Common Slav. *gordŭ* 'town'. The reflexes are:

  East Slav.: Russian: *gorod*, Ukrainian: *horod*
  West Slav. (a) Polish: *gród*; Lusatian: *hród/grod;* (b) Czech/Slovak: *hrad*
  South Slav.: Old Ch. Slav.: *gradŭ*; Serbo-Croat: *grâd*; Slovene: *grâd*; Bulgarian: *grad*

  Common Slav. *bergŭ* 'bank, steep slope'

  East Slav.: Russian: *bereg*; Ukrainian: *bereh*
  West Slav. (a) Polish: *brzeg* /bʒɛk/; Lusatian: *brjoh/brjog*; Polabian: *brig*; (b) Czech: *břeh*; Slovak: *breh*
  South Slav.: Old Ch. Slav.: *brěgŭ*; Serbo-Croat: *brêg/brîg/brijeg*; Slovene: *brêg*; Bulgarian: *brěg*.

  The *jers*, ъ and ь; these are the Common Slavonic reflexes of IE /*u, *i/: e.g. IE *supn-*, Skt *sup-*, Gk. *hupnos*, Slav. *sъnъ* /sŭnŭ/ 'sleep'. Reflexes in modern Slavonic languages:

  Common Slav. *sŭnŭ: Russian: son*; Polish and Crezh: *sen*; Lusatian: *són/ soń*; Serbo-Croat: *sȁn*; Slovene: *sán/sèn*; Bulgarian: *sŭn*.
  Cf. Common Slav. *dĭnĭ* 'day': Russian: *d'en'*; Polish: *dzień*; Lusatian: *dźeń/ źeń*; Czech: *den*; Serbo-Croat: *dân*; Slovene: *dân/dên*; Bulgarian: *den*.

  Reflexes of the nasalized vowels: e.g. from Common Slav. *rǫka* 'hand, arm': Old Ch. Slav.: *rǫka*; Russian: *rukà*; Polish: *ręka*; Czech: *ruka*; Lusatian: *ruka*;

Serbo-Croat: *ruka*; Slovene: *róka*; Bulgarian: *rŭkà*.

Stress was mobile in Common Slavonic, falling on any syllable. The situation in the modern languages is as follows:

(a) Russian, Ukrainian, Belorussian: stress is mobile;
(b) Slovene, Bulgarian: stress mobile, with certain restrictions;
(c) Serbo-Croat: mobile; in Common Slavonic cognates, the Serbo-Croat stress frequently falls on the syllable *preceding* the stress in the (a) and (b) languages: cf. Russian: *govorít'* 'to speak'; Slovene: *govoríti*; Serbo-Croat: *govóriti*; Russian: *ženà* 'woman'; Bulgarian: *ženà*, Serbo-Croat: *žéna*.
(d) Polish, Czech, Slovak, Lusatian: stress fixed; in Polish on the penultimate, in the others on the initial syllable.

In the closely associated Baltic languages, stress is free in Lithuanian but nearly always word-initial in Latvian.

MORPHOLOGY AND SYNTAX

Nominal system

Typically, the Slavonic languages have seven cases, including a vocative. A striking innovation in the declension system, *vis-à-vis* Indo-European practice in general, is the opposition 'masculine animate versus other' set up in the singular paradigm originally, but extended to the plural in Russian: cf. *ja vižu dom* 'I see a/the house' (*dom* 'house': acc. case = nom.); *ja vižu brata* 'I see the brother' (*brat* 'brother': gen. *brata*). That is to say, if the referent is a masculine animate, the objective case is assessed as a genitive, and so expressed.

The same assessment of the objective case as a genitive may take place if the verb is negated: e.g. *ja vižu dom* 'I see the house': *ja ne vižu doma* 'I don't see the house', though here there are specific restrictions.

The two Slavonic languages which have acquired a postpositional definite article – Bulgarian and Macedonian – have also discarded the case system.

A dual number is conserved in Slovene and in Lusatian.

Adjective

Originally Slavonic had weak indefinite and strong definite forms, the latter being made by the affixation of pronominal gender markers to the weak form: e.g. from *dobŭr* 'good': masc. *dobry.ji*, fem. *dobra.ja*, neuter *dobro.je* (*see* **Old Church Slavonic**).

Verb

As exemplified in Old Church Slavonic, the verbal system of Indo-European is reduced to one voice (active), two moods (indicative and imperative), and three formally distinguished tenses: aorist, present, past. The aorist was to vanish in Eastern and Western Slavonic, though it is preserved in South.

The comparative poverty of this inventory is successfully offset by the elaborate aspectual system, which is one of relatively recent date. The basic dichotomy in the aspectual system is that between perfective (completed) and imperfective action; beyond this, the system is capable of endless refinements and very subtle nuances.

The perfective future is expressed by the present-tense form of perfective verbs; an imperfective future is made with the help of an auxiliary verb.

An inferential mode has been developed in Bulgarian and Macedonian.

See articles on individual languages.

SLOVAK

INTRODUCTION

This West Slavonic language is joint official language (with Czech) of the Republic of Czechoslovakia. It is spoken by about 5 million in Slovakia and adjacent areas. In addition, there are sizeable Slovak communities in the USA and in Canada. Slovak is very close to Czech, the two languages being mutually intelligible.

A literary norm for Slovak was successfully codified in the mid-nineteenth century by L'udovit Štúr, who based his dictionary (1846) on the central dialect. Hardly had this advance been achieved, however, when the 1867 *Ausgleich* gave the Hungarians a free hand to pursue their policy of magyarization throughout their domains. Slovak cultural interests were severely restricted, and in 1875 the Matica Slovenská, a cultural institution roughly equivalent to a Slovak Academy, was forced to close – not to reopen till independence came in 1918. In the early part of this period, the journal *Slovenské Pohl'ady*, edited by S.H. Vajanský, played an important part in keeping Slovak cultural aspirations alive. Panoramic surveys and steadfast reaffirmations of Slovak beliefs and customs were provided by the poet Pavol Országh (Hviezdoslav) and the novelist Martin Kukučin, whose masterpiece *Dom v stráni* appeared in 1903. It was left to the poet Ivan Krasko to open European horizons to Slovak writers; and between the wars Slovak writing in general reflected the European cultural scene. Latterly, dissident writers like Ladislav Mňačko have attracted much attention.

SCRIPT

The Roman alphabet + diacritics: acute accent on long vowels; *č, ň, š, ž; l', t', d'; ô* = /wɔ/.

PHONOLOGY

Consonants

>   stops: p, b, t, d, k, g; /t/ and /d/ occur palatalized: t', d'
>   affricates: ts, dz, tʃ, dʒ
>   fricatives: f, v, s, z, ʃ, ʒ, x, ɦ
>   nasals: m, n, ɲ
>   laterals and flap: l, ʎ, r
>   semi-vowels: j, w

Final *v* = [u̯] or [w].

Vowels

i, iː, ɛ, ɛː, a, aː, e, eː, ɔ, ɔː, u, uː

/i, iː/ are notated as *i, í, y, ý*. Syllabic /l̩/ and /r̩/ are notated as *ĺ, ŕ*. Vowel length is phonemic.

THE RHYTHMIC RULE
In Slovak, two long syllables cannot be contiguous; e.g. *ženám* 'to the women' is permissible, but in *piesňam* 'to the songs' the *-ám* ending must be shortened to *-am*, as the diphthong *-ie-* of the first syllable is long. There are, however, several important exceptions to this rule.

Stress

As in Czech, stress is invariably on the first syllable.

MORPHOLOGY AND SYNTAX

Noun

Slovak has three genders, two numbers. In its basic patterns – nominal and adjectival declension, the pronominal system, the aspectual structure of the verb – the language is close to Czech. Both languages observe the animate/inanimate opposition, though Slovak goes further and agrees with Polish in treating male humans as a special category in the plural. In declension, Slovak has lost the vocative case which is retained in Czech. The Czech phenomenon known as *přehláska* – the fronting of /a, aː/, /ɔ, ɔː/ to /e, ie/ and of /u, uː/ to /i, iː/ – is unknown in Slovak: cf. Czech *duše* 'soul', acc. *duši*; Slovak *duša, dušu*. In the neuter soft declension, e.g. of *srdce* 'heart', where Czech has the forms pl. dat. *srdcím*, instr. *srdci*, loc. *srdcích*, Slovak has *srdciam, srdcami, srdciách*.

Specimen declension of masculine hard stem (animate) with adjective:

	Singular	Plural
nom.	dobrý chlap 'good chap'	dobri chlapi
gen.	dobrého chlapa	dobrých chlapov/xlapou̯/
acc.	dobrého chlapa	dobrých chlapov
dat.	dobrému chlapovi	dobrým chlapom
instr.	dobrým chlapom	dobrými chlapmi
loc.	dobrom chlapovi	dobrých chlapoch

Pronoun

The human male category is again singled out for special marking: 3rd p. pl. *oni* with reference to men, *ony* for other categories.

The first person singular pronoun *ja* has the following oblique forms: acc./gen. *mňa, ma*; dat. *mne, mi*; prep. (*o*) *mne*; instr. *mnou*.

POSSESSIVE ADJECTIVES

Example: *môj, môjho, môjmu*, where *-o-* is the labialized /ʷo/.

Numerals

Basically as in Czech, but Slovak has a specific set from 5 upwards, for use with animates: these forms have genitive/accusative cases: e.g. 2–5: *dvaja, traja, štyria, piati*, with gen./acc. forms *dvoch, troch, štyroch, piatich*: e.g. *Boli sme piati* 'There were five of us.'

Verb

All infinitives in Slovak end in *-t'*. Five classes of verb are distinguished:

1. *a*-conjugation: e.g. *volat'* 'to call' – present tense 1st p. *volám*, 3rd pl. *volajú*;
2. *i*-conjugation: e.g. *robit'* 'to work' – *robím* – *robia*;
3. *e*-conjugation: e.g. *niest* 'to carry' – *nesiem* – *nesú*;
4. *ne*-conjugation: e.g. *kradnút'* 'to steal' – *kradnem* – *kradnú*;
5. *uje*-conjugation: e.g. *pracovat'* 'to work' – *pracujem* – *pracujú*.

The only simple tense in Slovak is the present, the personal endings are:

sing. 1 *-m*, 2 *-š*, 3 Ø; pl. 1 *-me*, 2 *-te*, 3 *-ú/-jú/-ia*

In contrast to Czech, Slovak has only one ending for the 1st person singular: *-m*.

Specimen paradigm: *robit'* 'to work':

Indicative present:

	Singular	Plural
1	robím	robíme
2	robíš	robíte
3	robí	robía

The past tense is made by conjugating the auxiliary verb *byt'* 'to be' with the inflected past participle:

	Singular	Plural
1	robil, -a, -o som	robili sme
2	robil, -a, -o si	robili ste
3	robil, -a, -o Ø	robili Ø

Future: the future tense of *byt'* + infinitive of imperfective verb: e.g. *budem, budeš, bude robit'*. The perfective future is made by adding the present-tense endings (as above) to the perfective stem: e.g. *urobím, urobíš, urobí*.

Perfective aspect: formed from imperfective either by prefix, as in *robit'* – *urobit'*; by the ending *-nút'*, e.g. *siahat'* 'to touch, disturb' – *siahnút'*; by vowel change: e.g. *chytat'* 'to take' – *chytit'*; or by suppletion: e.g. *brat'* 'to take' – *vziat'*, *klást'* 'to put' – *položit'*.

Non-finite forms: from *robiť*: active participle *robiaci*; gerund *robiac*; passive participle *robený*.

Preposition

Most Slovak prepositions take the genitive case, e.g. *do* 'to, for', *bez* 'without', *namiesto* 'instead of', *spod* 'from under', etc.: e.g. *ísť do práce* 'to go to work'; *lístky do divadla* 'tickets for the theatre'. *Cez* 'through', and *pre* 'because of', take the accusative: e.g. *dívať sa cez oblok* 'to look out of the window'; *priniesol som to pre teba* 'I've brought this for you'.

Some occur in pairs, e.g. *medzi* with accusative or instrumental, *spomedzi* with the genitive: e.g. *dedina medzi horami* 'a village among the mountains'; *vyjsť spomedzi stromov* 'to come out from among the trees'; *ľudia spod Tatier* 'folk from the Tatra foothills'. Optionally, prepositions may be tripled: e.g. *s.po.pred, s.po.pod.*

Na 'on', *po* 'up to, after, along', etc., *o* 'about', *v/vo* 'in', take the accusative or the locative: e.g. *prišiel v poslednú chvíľu* 'he came at the last moment'; *v minulom roku* 'last year'. *Za* 'at the time of', 'during', 'at', etc. takes three cases: genitive, accusative, instrumental: e.g. *hovoriť za niekoho* 'to speak about, talk of someone'; *sadnúť si za stôl* 'to sit down at table'; *sedieť za stolom* 'to sit/be seated at table'.

Word order

SVO is basic, with considerable freedom, depending on emphasis, style, and nuance.

Na počiatku bolo Slovo, a to Slovo bolo u Boha, a to Slovo bol Bôh. ² To *Slovo* bolo na počiatku u Boha. ³ Všetko je skrzeu učinené, a bez neho nenie nič učinené, čo je učinené. ⁴ V ňom bol život, a ten život bol svetlom ľudí, ⁵ a to svetlo svieti vo tme, a tma ho nezadržala. ⁶ Bol *istý* od Boha poslaný človek, ktorému *bolo* meno Ján. ⁷ Ten prišiel na svedoctvo, aby svedčil o tom svetle, aby všetci uverili skrze neho. ⁸ Nebol on tým svetlom, ale *nato prišiel*, aby svedčil o tom svetle.

SLOVENE

INTRODUCTION

Slovene belongs to the South Slavonic group of the Slavonic branch of Indo-European. It is one of the three official languages of Yugoslavia, and is spoken by between 2½ and 3 million people. The earliest specimens of written Slovene date from the eleventh century. In fact the so-called *Brižinski spomeniki*, the 'Freising Monuments', provide the oldest known text in a Slavonic language in Latin script. Slovene literature proper begins in the sixteenth century, when Primož Trubar translated the Bible into Slovene. The greatest Slovene poet is generally taken to be Franc Prešeren (1800–49). The most distinguished modern writers are the novelist and playwright Ivan Cankar and the poet Oton Zupančič.

SCRIPT

Roman alphabet with diacritics: *č, š, ž*.

PHONOLOGY

Consonants

    stops: p, b, t, d, k, g
    affricates: ts, tʃ
    fricatives: f, v, s, z, ʃ, ʒ, h (x)
    nasals: m, n, ɲ
    laterals and flap: l, ʎ, r
    semi-vowels: j, w

A key point in Slovene phonology is the labialization of /v/ and /l/ in post-vocalic or syllable-final position to /w/: e.g. *bil* = [biw] or [biṷ]; *polno* [powno], [poṷno]. The voiced stops are devoiced in final position: *ubog* = [ubok].

Vowels

Notated as *i, e, a, o, u*, where *e* = /e/ and /ɛ/, *o* = /o/ and /ɔ/. Stress-bearing vowels may be long or short, unstressed vowels are always short. The neutral vowel /ə/ is notated as *e*: e.g. *poguben* 'ruinous', /pogubən/.

Tone

Dialectically, rising and falling tones affect long vowels. The modern tendency in the standard literary language is to neutralize this distinction.

Stress

Stress occurs on any syllable of a word. In general, it tallies with stress in Serbo-Croat, but there are many discrepancies: cf; SC *dèset* = Sl. *desèt* 'ten'; SC *júnak* = Sl. *junàk* 'hero'; SC *mèso* = Sl. *mesò* 'meat'.

MORPHOLOGY AND SYNTAX

Slovene has three genders: masculine, feminine, and neuter; and three numbers, the dual being retained in the noun, pronoun, adjective, and verb.

Noun

-u/-u stems have disappeared in Slovene; *-i* and *-a* stems are mainly feminine; *-o* stems are masculine; neuter stems are in *-o* or *-e*. Each gender has a specific plural characteristic: masc. *-i*, fem. *-e*, nt. *-a*. For example:

masculine: sing. *klobuk* 'hat'; dual *klobuka*; pl. *klobuki*;
feminine: sing. *žena* 'woman'; dual *ženi*; pl. *žene*;
neuter: sing. *mesto* 'place'; dual *mesti*; pl. *mesta*.

Example of masculine noun in six cases, three numbers:

	Singular	*Dual*	*Plural*
nom.	klobuk	klobuk.**a**	klobuk.**i**
gen.	klobuk**a**	klobuk.**ov**	klobuk.**ov**
dat.	klobuk**u**	klobuk.**oma**	klobuk.**om**
acc.	klobuk∅	klobuk.**a**	klobuk.**e**
loc.	klobuk**u**	klobuk.**ih**	klobuk.**ih**
instr.	klobuk**om**	klobuk.**oma**	klobuk.**i**

The direct object of nouns denoting animate beings takes the genitive form: e.g. *vidim mladega gospoda* 'I see the young man' (for the declension of the adjective see below). The accusative of feminine nouns in *-a* is in *-o*: e.g. *hiša* 'house': *Moj brat kupi to hišo* 'My brother is buying that house'; and the feminine plural genitive is the stem minus *-a*: e.g. *teh hiš∅* 'of these houses'.

Some irregularities occur in all three genders; e.g. fem. *hči* 'daughter', pl. *hčere*; neuter, *uho* 'ear', pl. *ušesa*.

Adjective

The adjective is in concord for gender, number, and case throughout as attribute, and has determinate form (cf. **Baltic Languages**): e.g. *lep vrt* 'nice garden'; *lepi vrt* '**the** nice garden'. Examples: *priden deček* 'diligent boy': gen./ acc. *pridnega dečka*; *s pridnim dečkom* 'with, by a diligent boy'.

DUAL

Example in feminine: *lepi ženi* 'two beautiful women'; *z lepima ženama* 'with the two beautiful women'.

DERIVED ADJECTIVES

Examples: *bratov klobuk* 'the brother's hat'; *sestrin klobuk* 'the sister's hat'; *bratovo obuvalo* 'the brother's footwear'.

COMPARATIVE

The formant is -(*ej*)*š*-: e.g. *lep* 'beautiful' – *lepši*; *hud* 'bad' – *hujši*; *sladek* 'sweet' – *slajši*. Slovene has a few suppletive formations for common adjectives: e.g. *dober* 'good' – *bolje/boljši*; *majhen* 'small' – *manjši*.

Pronoun

The independent personal forms are:

	Singular	Dual	Plural
1	jaz	midva	mi
2	ti	vidva	vi

The third person forms are marked for gender:

	Masculine	Feminine	Neuter
singular	on	ona	ono
dual	onadva	onedve	onedve
plural	oni	one	ona

All these forms are declined in six cases.

The possessive pronominal adjectives are: 1st p. sing. *moj*, pl. *naš*; 2nd p. sing. *tvoj*, pl. *vaš*; 3rd p. sing. masc. *njegov*; fem. *njen*; pl. common: *njihov*. For example: *mati in njen sin* 'the mother and her son'; *oče in njegov sin* 'the father and his son'.

The pronominal object is placed between the auxiliary and main verb in compound tenses: e.g. *jaz sem ga videl* 'I have seen him/I saw him'; *mi smo ga videli* 'we have seen him'.

DEMONSTRATIVE PRONOUN/ADJECTIVE

Marked for gender: *ta* – *ta* – *to*, i.e. the masculine and feminine forms are identical: e.g. *ta deček je majhen* 'this boy is small'; *ta deklica je majhna* 'this girl is small'. The plural forms are *tisti* – *tista* – *tisto*. All forms are declined.

INTERROGATIVE PRONOUN

kdo 'who?'; *kaj* 'what?'.

RELATIVE PRONOUN

kateri – *katera* – *katero*; with dual and plural forms, declined in all cases: e.g. *slon, od katerega dobivamo slonovo kost* 'the elephant from which we get ivory'.

Ki may also be used: e.g. *deček, ki dela* 'the boy who is working'; *deček, **ki mu** dam knjigo* 'the boy to whom I give a book'. *Kdor* is used to mean 'the one who ...': e.g. *kdor kupuje in prodaja ...* 'he who buys and sells ...'

Numerals

1 and 2 show gender: 1 *ed/en* (masc.), *ena* (fem.), *eno* (nt.); 2 *dva* (masc.), *dve* (fem./nt.). 3–10: *tri, štiri, pet, šest, sedem, osem, devet, deset*; 11 *enajst*; 12 *dvanajst*; 13 *trinajst*; 20 *dvajset*; 30 *trideset*; 40 *štirideset*; 100 *sto*.

Verb

The infinitive ends in *-ti* (with few exceptions). Grammars of Slovene divide verbs into six categories according to the characteristic linking the stem to the *-ti* ending:

			1st person singular present
1	-ni-:	dvigniti	dvignem 'I raise, lift (perf.)'
2	-e-:	želeti	želim 'I wish'
3	-i-:	govoriti	govorim 'I speak'
4	-a-:	delati	delam 'I do'
5	-ova/-eva:	kupovati	kupujem 'I buy'
6	-∅-:	nesti	nesem 'I carry, take (perf.)'

Consonant alternation occurs as in other Slavonic languages:

pisati 'to write': *pišem* 'I write'
hoteti 'to want': *hočem* 'I want'
lagati 'to tell a lie': *lažem* 'I lie'

For conjugation purposes, the six categories reduce to three types with characteristic vowels: *-a-, -e-, -i-*.

Specimen paradigm of regular *-a-* type: *delati* 'to do':

Present indicative:

	Singular	*Dual*	*Plural*
1	jaz delam	midva delava	mi delamo
2	ti delaš	vidva delata	vi delate
3	on dela	onadva delata	oni delajo

Past, future, and conditional are all formed by means of the participial form: sing. *delal*, dual *delala*, pl. *delali*, conjugated by the auxiliary verb *biti* 'to be': thus:

jaz sem delal 'I did', *midva sva delala* 'we two did';
jaz bom delal 'I shall do', *mi bomo delali* 'we (pl.) shall do';
on bi delal 'he would have done', *onadva bi delala* 'they two would have
  done'.

Irregular verbs may have suppletive forms, phonological irregularities, and synthetic tense-forms, e.g. *iti* 'to go':

> present tense: sing. *grem, greš, gre*; pl. *gremo, greste, gredo*;
> past: jaz sem šel, ti si šel
> future: jaz pojdem, ti pojdeš

ASPECT

As in other Slavonic languages, imperfective (including duratives) and perfective (including inceptives). Some examples of perfective/imperfective formations:

Perfective	Imperfective	Perfective	Imperfective
pasti 'fall'	padati	spoznati 'get to know'	poznati 'know'
skočiti 'jump'	skakati	kupiti 'buy'	kupovati 'buy often'
ukrasti 'steal'	krasti		

PASSIVE

Infrequent in Slovene, the active voice being preferred. The past participle in *-t*, *-en*, *-n*, is used; phonetic accommodation at junctures: e.g. *kupiti* 'buy' – *kupljen*; *nositi* 'carry, bear' – *nosen*.

NEGATION

The general marker is *ne*: e.g. *ne delam* 'I don't do'. *Ne sem* → *nisem* 'I'm not', *ne imam* → *nimam* 'I don't have'.

After a negated transitive verb, the genitive case replaces the accusative: e.g. *jaz nimam knjige/klobuka* 'I haven't got a book/hat'; cf. *Mojega očeta ni doma* 'My father is not at home' (*oče* 'father', gen. *očeta*).

Infinitive: use of the infinitive is avoided, especially where subject switch is involved: cf. *Prijatelj me prosi, (da) naj grem domov* 'My friend is asking me to go home' (*naj* is an optative particle).

Prepositions

Prepositions may govern genitive, dative, accusative, locative, or instrumental case. Several take two cases, depending on whether rest in a place or motion towards a place is involved. Thus, *jaz grem v šolo* 'I go to school' (acc.); *učenec je v šoli* 'the pupil is in school' (loc.); *v teh hišah* 'in these houses' (loc.).

Word order

SVO in principal clause, with inversions in subordinate clauses.

V začetku je bila beseda, in beseda je bila pri Bogu, in Bog je bila beseda.

2. Ta je bila v začetku pri Bogu.

3. Vse je po njej postalo, in brez nje ni nič postalo, kar je postalo.

4. V njej je bilo življenje, in življenje je bilo luč ljudém,

5. In luč v temi sveti, in tema je ni zapopadla.

6. Bil je človek poslan od Boga, kteremu je bilo ime Janez.

7. Ta pride na pričevanje, da priča za luč. da bi vsi verovali po njem.

8. On ni bil luč, nego da priča za luč.

SOMALI

INTRODUCTION

The Somali language (*afka Soomaaliga*) belongs to the Cushitic branch of the Afro-Asiatic family. Since 1973 it has been the official language of the Republic of Somalia, where it is the mother tongue of about 2½ million people; a further 1½ million speak the language in Kenya and Ethiopia. Until the twentieth century the rich corpus of Somali traditional poetry was preserved and transmitted almost exclusively by word of mouth. The declamation of poetry seems to be peculiarly well suited to the emotional needs of a nomadic society composed of contentious clans; and just as in early Arabic verse, the panegyric, the dirge and the lampoon figure prominently in Somali verse. Given the mass appeal and the tenacity of the oral tradition, it is not surprising that radio has proved a major factor in the contemporary development of Somali culture.

SCRIPT

Closely associated with the oral tradition and a distrust of innovation went a reluctance to commit Somali utterance to any form of imported script. Attempts made in the early twentieth century to introduce an adapted form of the Arabic script were not very successful. As in the case of Oromo, the Amharic syllabary was also tried; and two indigenous alphabetic scripts were invented in the 1920s and 1930s. In 1972 a standardized national orthography, based on the Roman alphabet, was introduced by the Somali Language Committee, and a year later Somali became the vehicle for education in Somalia. The immediate result was a spectacular increase in literacy. Since then, there has been a rapid upsurge in the output of Somali periodicals and books in all genres.

The standardized script has all the Roman letters except *p*, *v*, *z*. The letter *c* is used to denote the pharyngeal fricative 'ain (as in Arabic); ' denotes hamza. The following digraphs are used: *dh* = /d'/, *kh* = /χ/, *sh* = /ʃ/.

PHONOLOGY

Consonants

> stops: b, t, d, k, g, q, ʔ; /d'/ is a post-alveolar ejective
> affricate: dʒ
> fricatives: w, f, s, ʃ, j, χ, ʕ, h, ħ
> nasals: m, n
> lateral and flap: l, r

[p] and [ß] occur as allophones of /b/; [ɣ] of /g/; [tʃ] of /dʒ/.

Vowels

In broad transcription:

long and short: i, e, ɛ, a, ɔ, o, u

Length is phonemic. In close transcription, /ө/ and /ʉ/ are distinguished.

Tone

The question of tone in Somali is controversial; intonation is associated with tonic stress, and is phonemic: *árday* 'student' – *ardáy* 'students'.

MORPHOLOGY AND SYNTAX

Noun

Somali has two grammatical genders, masculine and feminine. The enclitic definite article is marked for gender: initial *k-* (masc.), *t-* (fem.), plus vowel series *-a/-ii/-u*. The initials assimilate with certain stem finals, thus producing masc. *g-/Ø-/h-* and fem. *d-/ḍ-/s-*: e.g. *nin.ka* 'the man'; *naag.ta* 'the woman'; *buug.ga* 'the book'; *aabba.ha* 'the father'; *gabadh.dha* 'the girl'. The *-a* forms are neutral, i.e. without special deixis. There is a tendency for the *-u* forms to be used as subject markers, provided the subject is not qualified: cf. *macallin.ka* 'the teacher' (citation form); *macallin.ku wuxuu oronayaa* 'the teacher is speaking' (*oro* 'to say'; for *wuxuu* see **Verb**, below). The *-ii* forms play a specific part in the formation of relative clauses: *see* Relative pronoun, below.

Focus markers are syntactically obligatory in indicative sentences. Thus, in answer to the question *Yaa yimid?* 'Who has come?' two answers are possible: *Axmed baa yimid*, or *Axmed waa yimid*. In the former, Axmed is in focus as the person who came; in the latter, the verbal fact of 'coming' is stressed. Cf.

> Axmed **baa** Jaamacadda buugag geeyay
> '**Axmed** took books to the University.'

> Axmed Jaamacadda buugag **waa** geeyay
> 'Axmed **took books** to the University.'

The two sentences differ only in the selection of focused component.

PLURAL FORMATION
There are several types:

(a) by partial or selective reduplication; this is the commonest form of plural formation for masculine monosyllables: e.g. *nin* 'man', pl. *niman*; *dab* 'fire', pl. *dabab*;
(b) by affixing *-(y)o*: e.g. *gabadh* 'girl', *gabdho*;
(c) masculines in *-e/-i* take *-yaal*: e.g. *shaqaale* 'worker', pl. *shaqaalayaal*;

(d) Arabic loan-words may take the Arabic broken plural, or the Somali -*o*: e.g. *miskin* 'poor man', pl. Ar. *masaakiin*, or Som. *miskiinno*.

It is interesting that many nouns taking the *k*- determinative series in the singular, have the *t*- series in the plural, i.e. show inverse polarity in gender (cf. use of numerals in Semitic generally). Thus: *buug.ga* 'the book', pl. *buugag.ta* 'the books'; *macallin.ka* 'the teacher', pl. *macallimiin.ta* 'the teachers'; *qaran.ka* 'the nation', *Qarammada Midoobey* 'The United Nations'.

POSSESSION
The noun denoting the possessor may precede or follow possessed object: e.g. *guri.ga naag.ta* 'the house of the woman'; *buugga Maryam = Maryam buuggeeda* 'Mary's book' (where -*geeda* (← -*keeda*) is the feminine possessive definite ending); *nolo.sha dad.ka Soomaalidu* 'the life of the Somali people' (*nolol* 'life').

Adjective

As attribute, adjective follows noun: e.g. *buugga cusub* 'the new book'; *meel fog* 'a far-off place'. The use of attributive adjectives is not typical of Somali, which prefers to rearrange the sentence in terms of stative verbs: e.g. *weyn.aa* 'was big'. An attributive adjective qualifying a plural referent is itself in plural form: e.g. *wiil weyn* 'a large youth', pl. *wiilaal waaweyn*; *buug cusub* 'a new book', pl. *buugag cususub*: *cashar fudud* 'an easy lesson', pl. *casharro fudfudud*.

COMPARATIVE
ka + positive: e.g. *ka weyn* 'bigger'; *ka yar* 'smaller'.

Pronoun

The personal pronouns with their enclitic, object and possessive forms are as follows:

			Subject		Object		Possessive
			Full (emphatic)	Enclitic	Simple	Prepositional	
Sing.	1		anigu/a	aan	i	ii	kayga
	2		adigu/a	aad	ku	kuu	kaaga
	3	masc.	isagu/a	uu	Ø	u	kiisa
		fem.	iyadu/a	ay			keeda
Pl.	1	incl.	innagu/a	aynu	(i)na	(i)noo	keenna
		excl.	annagu/a	aanu			kayaga
	2		idinku/a	aad	idin	idiin	kiinna
	3		iyagu/a	ay	Ø	u	kooda

For feminine possessed objects the possessive series has the *t*- prefix: e.g. *tayga*, *taaga*. For plural objects the possessive forms have infixed -*w*-: e.g. *kuwayga*, *kuwaaga*.

Use of objective forms: e.g. *u keen macallinka buugga* 'take the book to the teacher'; *buugaggii baa Axmed **kuu** keenay* 'Axmed took the books to you';

*buugaggii **baan kuu** keenay* 'I took the books to you'.

DEMONSTRATIVE PRONOUN/ADJECTIVE

The basic forms are: proximate *kan/tan* 'this', pl. *kuwan*; distal *kaas/taas* 'that', pl. *kuwaas*. There is assimilation at junctures: e.g. *buuggaas* 'that book'; *naag.taas* 'that woman'.

INTERROGATIVE PRONOUN

Formed from definite article + invariable interrogative marker *ma*: e.g. **Maxaad** *dhigaysaa?* 'What are you writing?'; **Muxuu** *dhigayaa?* 'What is he writing?'; **Kumaad** *araktay?* 'Whom did you see?'

RELATIVE CONSTRUCTIONS

There is no relative pronoun as such. The focusing particle, obligatory in principal clauses, is absent in the relative. *-kii/-tii* is affixed to the head-word in a relative clause involving action in the past, *-ka/-ta* similarly used for action in the present. El-Solami-Mewis (1987) gives the following examples:

> Nin**ka** gurigan dhisaya **waa** weyn yahay
> 'The man who is building this house is big'

> Nin**kii** gurigan dhisey **wuu** weyn yahay
> 'The man who built this house is big' (*guri* 'house'; *dhiso* 'to build'; *weyn* 'big').

Numerals

1–10: *kow, laba, saddex, afar, shan, lix, toddoba, siddeed, sagaal, toban*; 11 *kow iyo toban*; 12 *laba iyo toban*; 20 *labaatan*; 30 *soddon*; 40 *afartan*; 50 *konton*; 100 *boqol*.

The numeral precedes the substantive, which is in the singular if masculine; if feminine, the ending *-ood* (not a normal plural marker) is added; cf. *saddex cashar* = 'three lessons', *afartan qof* 'forty people'; but *saddex walaalood* = 'three sisters'.

Verb

The verb has affirmative and negative conjugations; three moods (indicative, imperative, subjunctive); and two basic tenses (present, past) with a compound future. The tenses are further sub-divided into simple and progressive forms. The verbal stem is identical to the imperative singular: e.g. *qaad* 'take'; *akhri* 'read'; the plural is in *-a*: e.g. *qaada* 'take!' (pl.) *akhriya* 'read!'.

Verbal endings encode gender (third person singular) number, tense, mood, and modality.

There are four conjugational types:

1. consonantal: e.g. *keen* 'to bring', verbal noun, *keenid*;
2. in *-i/-ii/-ee*: e.g. *iibi* 'to buy', verbal noun, *iibin*;
3. derivative medio-reflexive: e.g. *joogsan* 'to stop', verbal noun, *joogsasho*;
4. stative–attributive: e.g. *weynaan* 'to be big', verbal noun, *weynaansho*.

TENSES

General present, e.g. of *keen*:

		Singular	Plural
1		keenaa	keennaa
2		keentaa	keentaan
3	masc.	keenaa	keenaan
	fem.	keentaa	

Present continuous: sing. *keenayaa, keenaysaa, keenayaa/keenaysaa*; pl. *keenaynaa, keenaysaan, keenayaan*. Simple past: sing. *keeney, keentey, keeney/keentey*; pl. *keenney, keenteen, keeneen*.

In affirmative sentences the subject – verb – object complex is always accompanied by an inflected particle, e.g. *waxaa: anigu **waxaan** dhigayaa warqad* 'I am writing a letter'; *adigu **waxaad** dhigaysaa warqad* 'you are writing a letter'; *isagu **wuxuu** dhigayaa warqad* 'he is writing a letter'.

Future: this tense is formed from three elements: the infinitive of the sense-verb, the inflected particle *waa*, and the inflected present of *doonid* 'to want': e.g. *waan keen doonaa* 'I shall bring'; *waad keen doontaa* 'you will bring'; ***wuu** keen doonaa* 'he will bring'.

The characteristic of the subjunctive is *-o*: eg. *waan keeno, waad keento, **wuu** keeno*.

A compound form, consisting of the particle *leh* plus inflected forms of the verb *ahay* 'to be', is used along with *waxaa* to express the verb 'to have': e.g. *anigu waxaan leeyahay guri* 'I have a house'; *adigu waxaad leedahay guri* 'you have a house'; *isagu **wuxuu** leeyahay guri* 'he has a house'.

An impersonal passive is formed with the impersonal pronoun *la*: e.g. *guri.ga* *waa **la** dhisi* 'one builds the house' = 'the house is being built.'

USE OF SUBJUNCTIVE IN SUBORDINATE CLAUSES

Example: *Dawladda waxay ka codsatay guddiga inuu qoro buugagii dugsiyada hoose* 'The government requested the committee to write books for the elementary schools' (*dawlad.da* 'government'; *guddi.ga* 'committee'; *qor* 'write'; *dugsi.**ga** hoose* 'elementary school').

NEGATION

The general negating particle is *ma*; the imperative is negated by *ha*: e.g. *ha keenin* 'do not bring'. In the indicative tenses, *-o/-to* replace *-aa/-taa*, i.e. take subjunctive characteristics: e.g. *ma aan keeno* 'I do not bring'; *Muqdisho ma aan tago* 'I am not going to Mogadiscio'. The past form, *ma keenin* is invariable for all persons: e.g. *ma aan keenin* 'I did not bring'.

Prepositions

The prepositions combine with pronominal forms and with each other. Thus, *lagu* may be either the impersonal passive particle *la* plus the second person pronominal marker *-ku*, or, *la* + the preposition *ku* 'in, by means of': cf. *Maryam baa shaah **noo** keentay* 'Mary brought tea for us' (where *noo* is first person plural object marker *na* + directional marker *u*); *lacag.tii buu naga qaaday* 'he took the money from us' (where *naga = na* (as in previous example) + preposition *ka* 'from').

The prepositions *gud* 'on', *hoos* 'under', *ag* 'beside', etc. are treated as nominals and take the possessive markers: e.g. *gud.kiisa* 'on' (with masc.), *hoos.tooda* 'under' (with pl.), *hoos.teeda* 'under' (with fem.), *ag.tiisa* 'near him', *ag.teeda* 'near her'; *dariishad.da ag.teeda* 'beside the window'; *sariir.ta gud.keeda* 'on the bed'.

Word order

SVO is basic, but not obligatory; order is free, the inflected particles serving to articulate the logical structure of a sentence.

1 Horti waḥa jirey Hadal, Hadalkana waḥu lajirey Ilahey, Hadalkana waḥu aha Ilahey. 2 Kan waḥu lajirey Ilahey horti. 3 Kuli waḥa lugusubiyey kan. Waḥ walba olasubiyeyna masubsamen asaga laan tisa. 4 Guda hisana waḥa kujirtey nolol, noloshana wahay eheyd nurki dadka. 5 Nurkana waḥu kaiftima mugdiga daḥdisa mugdiga mauawodin. 6 Waḥa sobaḥey nin ousodirey Ilahey, magaisana wa Yohana. 7 Kan waḥu uimadey marag inu umaragkaọ nurka kuli hahelane iney kuaminan daradisa. 8 Asaga maeheyn nurka, ilowse waḥu uimadey inu kamaragkaọ nurka.

SPANISH

INTRODUCTION

Spanish belongs to the Italic branch of the Indo-European family of languages. It is the official language of the Kingdom of Spain, where it is spoken by about 50 million, and of a long chain of Latin American countries, running from Mexico to Argentina, giving a total of a little under 300 million speakers. This figure includes the Spanish-speaking population of Puerto Rico, certain areas in the USA, and a few enclaves in North Africa.

The Roman presence in the Iberian Peninsula – then inhabited largely by Celtic tribes – dates from the late third century BC. Through the first century BC to the seventh century AD, Hispania formed part, first of the Roman Empire and, after the third century AD, of the Visigothic Kingdom. Some traces of this Germanic influence remain in the Latinate vocabulary bequeathed by the Romans. A far larger alien component is provided by the Arabic brought in by the Moorish invaders from the seventh century onwards. There are still some 4,000 Arabic words in modern Spanish. By the eleventh century the main dialectal watershed between Castilian in the north and Andalusian in the south had taken shape, and the language of the twelfth-century epic *El Cantar de mio Cid* is already clearly Castilian. Through the succeeding three centuries Castilian consolidated and extended its status as the 'Spanish' language; a pre-eminence due in part to the fact that the Reconquista – the gradual expulsion of the Moors from Andalusia, leading finally to the unification of the country in the fifteenth century – was launched from, and successfully prosecuted by Castile.

The main dialectal division in the modern language is still that between north (Castilian) and south (Andalusian); other dialects, such as Aragonese, are moribund. Catalan is a language in its own right, and Galician is a Portuguese outlier. A key phonetic difference between Castilian and Andalusian is the phenomenon known as *seseo*: in Andalusia, *c* before *e/i*, and *z*, are pronounced as /s/ instead of the Castilian interdental fricative /θ/. *Seseo* is also characteristic of much of the Spanish spoken in Latin America, a plausible hypothesis here being that the language brought by the conquistadores to the New World in the sixteenth century and onwards was in fact *s*-Spanish; i.e. the /θ/ pronunciation was not lost in Latin American Spanish, it was never there.

A second key characteristic of Latin American Spanish is the pronunciation of *ll* – Castilian /ʎ/ as /j/ or /ʒ/. Practice here varies from one country to another; e.g.

calle 'street' is pronounced as /kaʎe/ in Peru, as in Castilian, becomes /kaje/ in Venezuela, and /kaʒe/ in Argentine and Uruguay.

The earliest recognizable Spanish is found in some tenth-century glosses to Latin texts. The subsequent history of Spanish literature can be periodized as follows:

1. Twelfth to fifteenth centuries: epic and romance; *El Cantar de mio Cid*, the story of Spain's national hero, Rodrigo Díaz, known as el Cid (from Arabic *sayyid* 'lord, master'). Also in this period fall the important encyclopedic works produced in the reign of Alfonso the Wise (thirteenth century) such as the enormous *General Estoria*, the *Siete Partidas* and the *Estoria de España*.
2. The *siglo de oro*, the Golden Age (sixteenth to early seventeenth centuries): ushered in (1499) by the humorous and realistic masterpiece *La Celestina*. This period includes three of Spain's greatest writers: Garcilaso de la Vega, Miguel de Cervantes, and Lope de Vega; the original picaresque novel, *Lazarillo de Tormes*; the early and fascinating accounts of life in the New World, e.g. the *Historia verdadera de la conquista de la Nueva España*, by Bernal Diaz del Castillo; and the works of the great Spanish mystics, Fray Luís de León, Santa Teresa de Avila, and San Juan de la Cruz.
3. The seventeenth century: Gongora and the movement for re-Latinization: *conceptismo* and *culteranismo*; one great writer – Calderón de la Barca.
4. The late nineteenth century; the revival of the novel: Benito Pérez Galdós.
5. Early twentieth century the 'generation of 1898': Azorín, Angel Ganivet, Pio Baroja, and Miguel de Unamuno: politico-social, religious, and cultural reassessment of the modern world in general and of Spain in particular.
6. The period of the Civil War: Federico Garcia Lorca, Camilo Jose Cela.

The late nineteenth and the twentieth centuries have seen a remarkable proliferation of distinguished writers in Latin America. Oustanding among so many are: Argentine: Jorge Luis Borges; Chile: Pablo Neruda; Mexico: Octavio Paz; Colombia: Gabriel Garcia Marquez; Nicaragua: Ruben Dario; Peru: Cesar Vallejo, Mario Vargas LLosa.

SCRIPT

Latin alphabet plus tilde (to mark palatal /ɲ/) and acute accent. Certain letters, e.g. *b*, *c*, *g*, have positional variant sounds; e.g. *c* = /k/ before a back consonant, /θ/ before a front; *b* = /b/ as initial, /ß/ between vowels; *g* = /x/ before *e*, *i*, otherwise = /g/. There are four digraphs: *ch* = /tʃ/, *ll* = /ʎ/, *qu* = /k/, *rr* = /r/.

Spanish introduces questions and exclamations with inverted markers: *¿a que hora termina Vd. el trabajo?* 'When do you finish work?'; *¡Que lástima!* 'What a pity!'

PHONOLOGY

Consonants

stops: p, b, t, d, k, g
affricate: tʃ
fricatives: f, θ, s, x
nasals: m, n, ɲ
laterals and flaps: l, ʎ, ɾ, rr
semi-vowels: j, w

/d/ has allophone [ð]. /s/ has [z] allophone, e.g. in *mismo* 'same', /mizmo/. /n/ has homorganic allophones before certain consonants: e.g. *enviar* 'send' = [ɛmbjar]; *incapaz* 'unable' = [iŋkapaθ]. *h* is silent: e.g. *hombre* 'man' = [ɔmbre]. /l/ and /r/ alternate in uneducated speech in Latin American: e.g. *calma*/*carma*.

Vowels

i, e, a, o, u
Diphthongs: ai, au, ei, eu, oi

Stress

Normally tends to the penultimate syllable, except in consonantal endings where final stress is frequent: e.g. *el algodón* 'cotton'; *el almacén* 'store'; but *el azúcar* 'sugar', *el árbol* 'the tree'. Final stressed vowels, e.g. in preterite, are marked by acute: *compré* 'I bought'. Antepenultimate stress also occurs: *lámpara* 'lamp', *póliza* 'policy, certificate'.

MORPHOLOGY AND SYNTAX

Two genders, masculine and feminine; two numbers.

Articles

	Masculine	Feminine	Plural
definite:	el	la	los/las
indefinite:	un	una	unos/unas 'some'

For example, *Los unos dicen que sí y los otros que no* 'Some say yes, the others no.'

In contra-distinction to usage in French and Italian, the Spanish definite article can be used pronominally: e.g. *mi libro y el de Pedro* 'my book and Pedro's'.

The plural marker is -(e)s.

Adjective

As attribute usually follows, but some common adjectives precede noun and may be truncated: *buen(o)* 'good', *mal(o)* 'bad': e.g. *Hace buen/mal tiempo hoy* 'It's good/bad weather today.'

Position of adjective may affect meaning, cf. *un hombre grande* 'a big man', *un gran hombre* 'a great man'.

COMPARATIVE

This is made with *más + que*: e.g. *Este libro es más barato que ése* 'This book is cheaper than that one.' Spanish has retained the Latinate suppletives: *bueno* 'good' – *mejor*; *malo* 'bad' – *peor*; *grande* 'big' – *major*; *pequeño* 'small' – *minor*; though *más pequeno* and *más grande* are used with reference to size.

Pronoun

PERSONAL

All the basic personal pronouns except first and second singular are marked for gender:

		Singular	Plural
1		yo	nosotros/nosotras
2		tu	vosotros/vosotras
3	masc.	él	ellos/ellas
	fem.	ella	

A polite second person form of address is provided by *Usted*, abbreviated in writing to *Vd.*, with plural *Ustedes* (*Vds.*), with third person verbal concord.

There are three sets of object pronouns in Spanish. The direct object set is:

	Singular	Plural
1	me	nos
2	te	os
3	le/la/lo	los/las

These precede the verb, unless this is in imperative or infinitive form: *le/les esperamos a Vd./Vds.* 'we are expecting you (masc. sing./fem. pl.)'. The *a* in this example is the so-called 'personal *a*', which must precede an object noun denoting a person; cf. *Tendré oportunidad de conocerle a Vd. personalmente* 'I shall have a chance to get to know you personally.'

The indirect object pronouns are the same as the direct, with the exception that the gender-marked forms for the third person are reduced to *le/les*: *le parece bien a ella* 'it seems OK to her'; *¿En qué puedo servirles?* 'What I can do for you (pl.)?' *Le/les → se* before an object pronoun with an *l-* initial: e.g. *se lo digo a Vd.* 'I say it to you' = 'I tell you'.

PREPOSITIONAL FORMS

These are identical to the subject forms, except in the first and second person singular which have *mí* and *ti*: *para mí* 'for me'; *un regalo para ti/para Vd.* 'a present for you'.

PREPOSITIONAL ADJECTIVES
The singular forms, *mi*, *tu*, *su*, have two-way marking for number: e.g. *mi libro* 'my book'; *mis libros* 'my books'. The first and second person plural forms are marked in addition for gender of possessed object: e.g. *nuestros libros* 'our books'; *nuestra casa* 'our house'.

DEMONSTRATIVE ADJECTIVE AND PRONOUN
Three-degree gradation:

> este, esta, estos, estas 'this, these' (associated with 1st p.)
> ese, esa, esos, esas 'that, those' (associated with 2nd p.)
> aquel, aquella, -os, -as 'that, those yonder' (associated with 3rd p.)

The pronominal forms are identical, but take an acute accent: e.g. *esa tienda y ésta* 'that shop and this one'.

INTERROGATIVE PRONOUN
quién 'who?', *qué* 'what?'

RELATIVE PRONOUN
que is both subject and object and is invariable: e.g. *los puntos que se han tratado hoy* 'the points which have been dealt with today'. For greater precision, *el cual/la cual*, *los/las cuales* may be used.

Numerals

1–10: *uno* (→ *un/una* before nouns), *dos*, *tres*, *cuatro*, *cinco*, *seis*, *siete*, *ocho*, *nueve*, *diez*; 11 *once*; 12 *doce*; 13 *trece*; 14 *catorce*; 15 *quince*; 16–19: *diez y seis*, etc.; 20 *veinte*; 30 *treinta*; 40 *cuarenta*; 100 *ciento* (→ *cien* before a noun).

Verb

Three conjugations are distinguished, in *-ar* (the great majority), *-er*, *-ir*. The verb has three moods: indicative, imperative, subjunctive.

Specimen regular paradigm: *tomar* 'to take':

		Present indicative	Present subjunctive	Preterite	Imperfect	Future
sing.	1	tomo	tome	tomé	tomaba	tomaré
	2	tomas	tomes	tomaste	tomabas	tomarás
	3	toma	tome	tomó	tomaba	tomará
pl.	1	tomamos	tomemos	tomamos	tomábamos	tomarémos
	3	toman	tomen	tomaron	tomaban	tomarán

Note: the second person plural is not shown in these paradigms, as it is of very limited use.

The conditional adds the endings: *-ía, -ías, -ía; -íamos, -ían* to the infinitive. The imperfect subjunctive has alternative endings: either *tomara, tomaras, tomara*; *tomáramos, tomaran*, or *tom-ase, -ases, -ase, -ásemos, -asen*.

The *-er* and *-ir* conjugations have virtually the same endings, with a few exceptions, e.g. in the imperfect, where *comer* 'to eat' has *comía, comías, comía*; *comíamos, comían*. The *-er* verbs can distinguish between the first plural forms in the present and the preterite: e.g. *comemos* 'we eat', *comimos* 'we ate'. Tenses based on the infinitive differ, as might be expected, in vowel pattern. Both tenses of the subjunctive are much used in Spanish.

Departures from the regular pattern are found, e.g. in root-changing verbs: *mover* 'move' – present *muevo, sentir* 'feel, hear' – *siento, dormir* 'sleep' – *duermo*, but many apparent irregularities are due to orthographical requirements: e.g. the alternation of $z/c = /\theta/$, g/gu, $c/qu = /k/$.

There are, however, many genuinely irregular verbs: e.g.

	Present	Past participle
decir 'say'	digo	dicho
hacer 'do'	hago	hecho
ir 'go'	voy	ido
saber 'know'	se	sabido
conocer 'know'	conozco	conocido

Continuous tenses are made with the auxiliaries *estar* 'to be', *ir* 'to go' plus present participle: e.g. *estoy hablando/estamos hablando* 'I/we am/are speaking'; *está escribiendo la carta* 'he is writing the letter'.

The distinction between the two verbs *ser* and *estar*, both meaning 'to be', is very important; broadly, *ser* is the copula, used of any permanent identity; *estar* denotes a contingent state of affairs: cf. *El señor López es español* 'Mr L. is Spanish'; *El Señor López está malo* 'Mr L. is ill'.

The perfect tense is made by conjugating the auxiliary verb *haber* 'to have' with the past participle of the sense-verb: e.g. *he hablado* 'I have spoken'; *han hablado* 'they have spoken'.

In contra-distinction to French and Italian, verbs expressing motion are conjugated in Spanish with the auxiliary *haber*: e.g. *he venido* 'I have come'; *he ido* 'I have gone'.

Negation

The negating particle is *no* preceding the verb, with resumption of negation in pronominal or other associated material: e.g. *no viene nadie* 'no one is coming'; *no tengo nada* 'I have nothing'; *no hace nunca frio* 'it's never cold'.

Prepositions

Worthy of particular mention is the combination of the preposition *con* 'with', with the pronominal forms *mí, ti*, and *si: conmigo* 'with me'; *contigo* 'with you'; *consigo* 'with oneself'.

Word order

Both SVO and VSO are regular.

---

1 En el principio era la Palabra; y la Palabra estaba con Dios: y la Palabra era Dios.

2 Esta en el principio estaba con Dios.

3 Todas las cosas fueron hechas por ella; y sin ella, nada se hizo en lo que ha sido hecho.

4 En ella estaba *la* vida; y la vida era la Luz de los hombres.

5 Y la Luz resplandece en las tinieblas; mas las tinieblas no la comprendieron.

6 Hubo *un* hombre enviado de Dios, llamado Juan.

7 Este vino como testigo, para dar testimonio acerca de la Luz, á fin de que todos creyesen por él.

8 No era él la Luz, sino *enviado* para dar testimonio de la Luz.

SQUAMISH

See North American Indian Isolates.

SUMERIAN

INTRODUCTION

One of the oldest known languages on earth, Sumerian was spoken and written in southern Mesopotamia from the beginning of the third millennium BC to the middle of the first millennium. It is not known when the Sumerians first settled in the area; the written record begins about 3000 BC. As far as is known, Sumerian is an isolate, with no congeners. Attempts have been made to link it with Ural-Altaic, with Georgian, and with Sino-Tibetan. From the middle of the third millennium onwards, the name Sumer referred specifically to the southern part of the Sumero-Akkadian Empire, in opposition to the northern part, which was called Akkad. Through the third and second millennia Sumerian seems to have been the official language of government, while at the same time, Akkadian was supplanting it as the everyday language of the people. As the language of religion and ceremonial, Sumerian lingered on into the first millennium. The main literary texts date from the second millennium. The most complete version of the great Sumerian Gilgamesh epic is in Akkadian.

Eme.sal

A slightly variant form of Sumerian, found in texts addressed to goddesses or uttered by goddesses or their female attendants, is known as *eme.sal*, 'women's speech'. It is possible that ordinary Sumerian – *eme.KU* – pronunciation was taboo for women; and it is precisely on the phonological plane that *eme.sal* differs to any extent from *eme.KU*; morphology and lexicon are largely identical. What is surprising is that Akkadian borrowings from Sumerian are often in *eme.sal* form.

SCRIPT

Sumerian was never written in hieroglyphs. The earliest examples of the script show not so much a writing system as a series of shorthand mnemonics for objects and the semantic fields associated with them, in some ways a practical script for the inventories typical of the oldest Sumerian. Gradually, the rebus-type signs became conventionalized into wedge-shaped – cuneiform – signs; and these came to represent not so much the object as its name: the ideogram became the logogram. A key step was taken when it was discovered that such signs could represent not only words but also the relationships between words, i.e. syntactic and morphological formants.

Sumerian had a large stock of mostly monosyllabic homonyms, almost on a Chinese scale. In transliteration, the practice is to give these reference index numbers, e.g. du_2 'to make', du_3 'to open', du_4 'to be beautiful'.

From about 2500 onwards, a Sumerian text consists of ideograms and logograms plus phonetic signs for syntactic and morphological relationships. The non-phonetic signs had more than one reading, and, conversely, a Sumerian word could be represented by more than one sign; so, a system was developed whereby the final consonant of a homograph was reduplicated to fix the requisite reading: e.g. both *gin* 'to go' and *gub* 'to stand' are written

so, *gin* was specifically written as *gin.na* 'going', *gub* as *gub.ba* 'standing'. Cf. the use of kanji + hiragana in Japanese.

Determinatives

These are generic set markers preceding or following nominals; e.g. *dingir* precedes the names of gods, *lu* is the set marker for people, *mul* for stars. Cf. Egyptian, and the radical system in Chinese.

PHONOLOGY

Consonants

The late Sumerian inventory has been reconstructed as:

stops: p, b, t, d, k, g
fricatives: s, z, ʃ, ẖ (χ, γ)
laterals and flap: ɫ, l, r
nasals: m, n, ŋ

The voiced stops are represented in Akkadian as *unvoiced*.

Vowels

Attested vowels are:

i, e, a, u

It is very likely that the spoken language had further vowel sounds.

Tone

Given the proliferation of monosyllabic homonyms, it seems probable that Sumerian had a system of phonemic tones.

SUMERIAN

MORPHOLOGY AND SYNTAX

Noun

Gender is not distinguished: e.g. *dingir* 'god, goddess'. Sometimes, words are followed by *nitah* to indicate masculine, by *mi* for feminine: e.g. *mašda.nitah* 'male gazelle', *mašda.mi* 'female gazelle'.

NUMBER
Several methods were used to indicate collectives; e.g. reduplication: *kur.kur* 'mountains/countries' *E.ne* is a collective marker for human beings and divinities: *dingir.e.ne* 'gods/goddesses'.

An attributive adjective may be used to indicate augmentation on various planes: e.g. *ning.gal.gal* 'large things'; *a.gal.gal* 'severe flood'.

DECLENSION
Several markers indicate various syntactic relationships; e.g. the subject as agent is marked by *e*: *lugal.e* 'the king ...(did...)'.

The genitive relationship usually takes the form of a compound: e.g. *e.ka* 'door-of-the-temple' = 'the temple door'; *e.dingir.ra* 'the temple of the god' (*e₂* 'house, temple'). The genitive is also marked by *a(k)/(a)k:* e.g. *lugal.kalam.ak.e* '(by) the emperor (*lugal*) of the homeland (*kalam*)' (intercalary *k* separates case endings); and a dative by *ra*: e.g. *lugal.kalam.ak.ra* 'to the emperor of the homeland'.

There are also comitative (*da*), ablative (*ta*), allative (*še*), locative (*a*) markers.

Pronoun

The independent personal forms are (exact forms are questionable):

	Singular	Emesal	Plural
1	nga.e	me	menden
2	za.e.	ze	menzen
3	a.ne/e.ne	–	a.ne.ne/e.ne.ne

The predicative pronominal endings are : sing. 1 *men*, 2 *men*, 3 *am/me*; pl. 1 and 2 as independent, 3 *meš*.

POSSESSIVE ENDINGS
Sing. 1 *ngu*, 2 *zu*, 3 *a.ni*; pl, 1 *nge* 2 *zu.ne*, 3 *ne.ne*(?). Examples: *uru.nge.a* 'in our city'; *ki.zu.ne.ne.ta* 'from your place'; *nga.e ˡᵘkin.gi.a.men* 'I am a messenger' (*kin.gi.a* 'messenger'; *lu* = determ.).

DEMONSTRATIVE PRONOUN/ADJECTIVE
e.ne/bi: e.g. *lu.bi* 'this/that man'.

INTERROGATIVE PRONOUN
a.ba 'who?'; *a.na* 'what?'.

1274

RELATIVE PRONOUN

-a is the relative characteristic; *see* **Verb**, below

Numerals

1: Sumerian used several words for 'one': e.g. *deš, aš, ge.* 2–10: *min, peš (eš,* etc.), *lim(mu), i, i.aš, i.min, i.us, i.us, l.lim, hu*; i.e. the system is *mod* 5. From 20 on, the system is sexagesimal: 20 *niš*; 30 *ušu*; 40 *ni.min*; 100: not attested.

Verb

The segmentation of time in the Sumerian verb is not clear. There is a broad dichotomy into past and non-past, perfective and imperfective; the perfective has a null marker, the imperfective has *-e*. There is no tense system of any kind. Cf. *e.mu.na.du.Ø* '... built a temple (*e.*) to him (*na*)' (*du* 'to build'); *mu.du.e* '... builds a temple' (*mu*: see below).

The Sumerian verbal complex, other than imperative, has the following ordered sequence of items: 1 mood markers, including negative: *nu*; 2 spatial and directional markers, including indirect object and case characteristics marked for person: e.g. for first person singular ablative *-ta-*, allative *-ši-*, comitative *-da-*; for third person singular the same cases are *-nta-, -nši-, -nda-*; 3 subject/object marker (*see* also 5 below); 4 verbal base; 5 in active verbs only, subject–object marker, or marker coded for agent/patient. The imperfective aspect marker *-e*, if used, is sited between 4 and 5.

The present–future or imperfective paradigm: stem + *.e* + personal marker: sing. 1 *en*, 2 *en*, 3 *Ø*; pl. 1 *enden*, 2 *enzen*, 3 *(e)ne*; e.g. *i.zu.e.en.de.en* → *i.zu.un.de.en* 'we shall learn' (*zu* 'to know, learn').

Verbal infixes in slot 2: these may be dative, locative, or directional: e.g. the dative markers for the singular are: 1 *-a-*, 2 *-ra-*, 3 *-na-*; the plural markers are hardly attested: *mu.na.du* 'he built it for him' (*-na-*).

A locative infix is *ni/ne*: e.g. *mu.na.ni.du* 'he has built for him there'.

The *mu* in these examples is a verbal prefix which acts as a topicalizer. This prefix takes many forms, of which two are basic: *mu* and *e-/-i*. There are several theories as to their exact significance; most agree that they have a directional element built into them, on the lines of German *hin/her*. Jestin (1951) adds a temporal distinction: *mu* refers to what is more remote in time, *e/i* to what is proximate: e.g. *e.mu.na.du* 'he built (then) a temple to him'; *nam.lugal e.na.si* 'he has given him the kingship'.

Neither voice nor mood is a relevant category in Sumerian, though certain particles are associated with e.g. the optative: first person *ga/γe*, second/third *he/hu/ha*: e.g. *γe/ga.na.tum* 'let me bring to him'; *he.gub* 'let him stand'.

In sharp contrast with the Indo-European division of transitive verbs into active and passive voices, Sumerian appears to have a neutral voice, in which the agent is so marked – *lugal.e* 'by the king' – and the logical object is in the nominative/absolute case while the verb, however, agrees with the *agent*.

D'akonov (1965) gives the example: *lu.e gidru i.n.gar* where *lu* 'man' has the agentive marker *e*: 'by the man', and *gidru* 'stick' is in the nominative; the verb, however, contains the class marker for persons *-n-* and is therefore in concord with *lu*: '(by) the man – placed – the stick'.

RELATIVE CLAUSES

The verb in a relative clause is always marked by *-a*, and the clause may be introduced by a head-word in apposition to the referent, *lu* for human beings, *nig* for things: e.g. *lugal dug.ga.na nu.gi.gi.da* 'the king whose word is not gainsaid' (*gi.gi* 'to gainsay'); cf. *N. e mu.du* 'N. built a temple', *N. e mu.du.a* 'N., who built a temple'; *lu.igi mu.bar.ra.zu* 'the man whom you are looking at' (where *zu* is the 2nd p. possessive marker; *bar* 'to look upon'; *a* is the relative marker).

Use of head-word *lu*: *Ur.^DNammu **lu** e.^DNannar in.du.a* 'Ur.Nannu, **he who** built (lit. building) the temple of Nannar'.

Postpositions

Some are circumfixes: e.g. *ki.e.ta* 'from out of the temple'; *egir.e.še* 'behind the temple'.

SUNDANESE

INTRODUCTION

Sundanese belongs to the Malayo-Polynesian branch of the Austronesian family, and is spoken by between 15 and 20 million people in west Java. The modern literary standard is based on the Bandung dialect.

The earliest folk literature in Sundanese dates from the fourteenth century. Since the middle of the nineteenth century the language has been the vehicle for a flourishing modern literature in all genres. It is also used in primary education and in the local media.

SCRIPT

Until the seventeenth century Sundanese was written in the Javanese script, known in this context as *cacarakan*. Conversion to Islam in the twelfth/ thirteenth century brought the use of the Arabic script. Since mid-nineteenth century romanization.

PHONOLOGY

Consonants

    stops: p, b, t, d, k, g
    affricates: tʃ, dʒ
    fricatives: s, h
    nasals: m, n, ɲ, ŋ
    lateral and flap: l, r
    semi-vowels: w, j

Final *k* as /k/, not /ʔ/ as in Indonesian. Similarly, final *d*, *g* = /d/, /g/. The affricates are notated as *tj* and *dj*.

Vowels

    i, ɛ, a, ə, œ/ʌ, o, u

/ɛ/ is notated as *e*, /ə/ as *ĕ*.

Stress

Stress is normally on the penultimate syllable, unless this has *ĕ*, when stress moves to final.

MORPHOLOGY AND SYNTAX

The more or less elaborate coding of respect levels, characteristic of Javanese, Madurese, etc., is also found in Sundanese, where four levels are distinguished: high *basa lĕmĕs*; neutral *basa sĕdĕng*; everyday *basa kasar*; low *basa tjohag*. Equivalents are not evenly distributed in the four levels. Thus, the verb 'to sleep' is expressible in all four: b. lĕmĕs *kulem*; b. sĕdĕng *sarè*; b. kasar *saré*; b. tjohag *molor*. However, *artos*, the b. lĕmĕs word for 'money' has a b. kasar equivalent, *duit*, but no equivalents in b. sĕdĕng or b. tjohag. Similarly, 'house' is *rorompok* in b. lĕmĕs, *bumi* in b. sĕdĕng, and *imah* in b. kasar, but has no b. tjohag equivalent. *See* **Pronoun**, below.

Many roots are formally neutral and can be syntactically exploited as nominals or verbals, e.g. *djalan* 'way' (nominal), 'to go' (verbal). This ambivalence extends to loan-words: e.g. *sakola* 'school; to go to school'.

Noun

Root, e.g. *imah* 'house', *djalma* 'man'; derivative: e.g. with prefixes *pa-*, *pi-*, *ka-*, circumfix *pa...an*, etc. All prefixes have variants, depending on initial of stem; e.g. *pa-* appears as *pa-*, *pam-*, *pang*, *pan-*, *panj-*. Thus are formed nouns of agency: e.g. *dagang* 'to trade' – *padagang* 'trader'. Also nouns denoting verbal action: e.g. *bantu* 'to help' – *pangbantu* 'help(ing)'.

The circumfix *pa...an* forms nouns denoting locus of action, or activity engaged in: *mandi* 'to bathe' – *pamandian* 'bath-house'; *madat* 'opium' – *pamadatan* 'opium-smoker'.

Partial reduplication and compounding are prolific sources of nouns: e.g. *sato* 'animal' – *sasatoan* 'cattle'; *ngomong* 'speak' – *mĕsin-ngomong* 'gramophone'.

The plural number can be indicated by complete reduplication, e.g. *djalma* 'man '– *djalmadjalma* 'people'; by partial reduplication + *-an*, e.g. *kembang* 'flower' – *kĕkĕmbangan* 'flowers'; or by infixed *-ar/al-*, e.g. *budak* 'child' – *barudak* 'children'.

Adjective

See **Verb**, below.

Pronoun

All four speech levels have complete sets of personal pronouns in three persons and two numbers. The b. kasar set for normal everyday usage is:

	1	2	3
singular	kuring, sim kuring	maneh, silaing	manehna
plural	kuring kabeh	maraneh, maneh kabeh	maranehna

In second and third persons, note the use of pluralizing infix *-ar-* mentioned above. Sundanese does not possess the personal pronominal enclitics for first and second persons found in Javanese and Bahasa Indonesia. The third person does, however, have *-na*: e.g. *imahna* 'his house'.

DEMONSTRATIVE PRONOUN
ieu 'this' – *eta* 'that' – *itu* 'that yonder'; *ieu* and *eta* may precede the noun, *itu* always follows.

INTERROGATIVE/RELATIVE PRONOUN
saha 'who?'; *naon* 'what?'.

Numerals

1–10: *hidji, dua, tilu, opat, lima, gĕnĕp, tudjuh, dalapan, salapan, sapuluh*; 20 *dua puluh*; 100 *ratus*.

Verb

As stative verbs, adjectives are included under this heading. All predicative forms can be marked for plurality by means of the *-ar/al-* infix: e.g. *geulis* 'be beautiful', pl. *galeulis*; *alus* 'be good', pl. *aralus*.

The verb is neutral as to aspect, mood, or tense, and is not marked for person except for third, which may take *-eun*. Various particles are used to articulate the course of action as narrated in the flow of speech: thus, *geus* and *parantos* suggest that ongoing action has reached a result, i.e. is 'perfective', while *(a)tjan* suggests that this point has not yet been reached. In other words, *geus* or *parantos* will normally refer to the past; but the aspectual distinction can apply to any time frame. The future can be more pointedly specified by the use of *bakal* or *baris*. The auxiliary *pating* indicates co-operative action; concomitant action is suggesting by *keur* or *nudja*: e.g. imperfective: **keur** *matja naon?* 'What are you reading?'; perfective: **geus** *dahar?* 'Have you eaten already?'; future: *Sabulan deui kuring **bakal** papanggih djeung manehna* 'I shall meet him in a month'.

VERB FORMATION
By prefix, suffix, infix, or circumfix:

By prefix: (the index indicates the number of possible variants)

   nga[4]- forms transitives, e.g. *nga.duruk* 'to burn something'; *nga.djawab* 'to answer';

   pi-/mi- make transitives from verbal roots, nouns or adjectives; e.g. *garwa* 'wife' – *migarwa* 'to take a wife';

   ba-/si- make reflexive verbs from intransitive roots, e.g. *ba.robah* '(be) change(d)';

   di- is a passive formant, e.g. *di.batja* 'to be read' – *eta buku dibatja ku kuring* 'this book is read by me' (*ku* is prepositional subject marker).

By suffix: e.g. *-an/-keun/-eun*. The latter denotes chance passivity, e.g. *hudjan.eun* 'to be caught and soaked in a downpour'. *-an* and *-keun* are transitive markers: e.g. *meupeuskeun gĕlas* 'to smash the glass'.

By circumfix: e.g. *nga*[4]-...*an*/*keun*; *pang...keun*: e.g. from *diuk* 'sit' – *nga.diuk.an* 'to occupy'; *lagu* 'song' – *nga.lagu.keun* 'to sing a song'.

NEGATIVE

The general negating particle is *teu*, preceding the verb.

MODAL AUXILIARY VERBS

Example: *hajang* 'to want to', *embung* 'not to want to'; *bisa* 'to be able to': e.g. *kuring teu bisa ... njuratan* 'I can't write'.

Prepositions

Examples: *di* 'in', e.g. *di pasar* 'in the bazaar'; *ti* 'from'; *ku* marks the subject or the instrumental, e.g. ... *dibatja ku kuring* 'read by me' = 'I read'; *ku kapaludara* 'by plane'; *ka* marks object, e.g. *kuring ngabantu ka indung* 'I help mother'.

Word order

Free: SVO, VSO, OVS. Qualifier follows qualified.

دِنَ اَوِتْنَ كِّسْ اَيَا فَقَنْدِكَ تَيِهْ اَرِي فَقَنْدِكَ تَيْبِيا اَيَنَا دِ اَللَّه

2. سَرْتَ فَقَنْدِكَ تَيْبِيا بَا اَللّه * اَرِي اَيْتَ تَيْبِيا دِنَ اَوِتْنَ

3. كِّسْ اَيَا دِ اَللّه * سَنِسْكَرَ بَا كُوْ اَيْتَ دِجَدِكَنْنَنَا اَرِي

سَكَبَنَا كُوْ اَيْتَ مَهْ هَنْتَ اَيَا فِسَنْ اَنْوْ دِجَدِكَنْ دِنَ

4. سَكَبِيهْنَ نُوْ كِّسْ دِجَدِكَنْ * دِنَ جَرِوْ اَيْتَ فَقْئِينَا هُرُوْف

5. تَيِهْ اَرِي اَيْتَ هِرُوْف تَيْبِيا بَا جَهَيَا مَنْوْس * دَمِي جَهَيَا

تَيْبِيا غَبِّيَرْ دِ نُوْ فُوَايِكْ اَرِي كُوْ فُوَايِكْ تَيْبِيا هَنْتَ دِتَرِمَا *

6. اَيَا هِجِ جَلِمَ نُوْ دِفِورَغْ كُوْ اَللّه جَنَفَنْنَنَا يَوْهَنَيِسْ *

7. فَقْسُوْمُفَقُنَ فِمَرْتِيلَكَنَنْ // بَدَيْ مَرْتِيلَكَنْ فَرُكَرَ جَهَيَا تَيْبِيا

SVAN

INTRODUCTION

Svan belongs to the Kartvelian (South Caucasian) group of languages. There are about 20,000 speakers in the Svanetia area of Georgia, which lies to the south of Mt Elbruz. The language is unwritten.

PHONOLOGY

Svan is phonetically conservative, retaining certain Old Georgian features, and dialectally fragmented. From other Kartvelian languages it is particularly distinguished by its vowel system: the basic five vowels have long and short values, and, in addition, the three umlaut values, /ɛ, œ, y/, both long and short, are present. This umlaut is induced by a following front vowel, /i/ or /e/, either actually or historically present. Svan also has /ə/.

MORPHOLOGY AND SYNTAX

Noun

Svan has six cases; endings vary considerably from one dialect to another. Thus the ergative marker is *-em* in one dialect, *-d* in two others, while a fourth uses both of these and adds a reduplicated version of its own – *ēmnēn*.

The plural affix is *-är/-ār*, *-äl/-āl*, etc.: e.g. *mār.e* 'man'; pl. *mar.äl* 'people'.

Adjective

The attributive adjective precedes its noun and may agree with it: e.g. *hoca māre* 'good man', erg. *hocām mārēm*.

Pronoun

	Singular	Plural
1	mi	nä(j)
2	si	sgä(j)

Third person forms are coded for relative distance from speaker.

DEMONSTRATIVE PRONOUN
al 'this'; *ez* 'that'.

jär 'who?'; *mäj* 'what?'. These, plus the particle *-väj*, are also used as relative pronouns: e.g. *jerväj*.

Numerals

1–10: *ĕshu, jori, semi, võsthv, vohvišd, usgva, išgvid, ara, č'hara, ješd*; thereafter, dialects vary between decimal and vigesimal systems.

Verb

For a detailed analysis of Kartvelian verbal structure, *see* **Georgian**. In Svan, the pre-verbs are, e.g., *an-* (motion towards speaker), *ad-* (motion away from speaker); some pre-verbs combine with postpositions, e.g. *ži-* (motion from below upwards). The pre-verbs also express aspect.

The prefixed/circumfixed subject and object markers show person and number; the first person plural makes the inclusive/exclusive distinction.

MOODS
Indicative, subjunctive, imperative.

TENSES
Basically, present, past, and future are distinguished. Formally, tenses and moods are classified in three series (*see* **Georgian**). Series I includes a present and a future perfective. From each of these bases, various imperfective and subjunctive tenses/aspects are formed. The second series centres on the past perfective, and makes a distinction between transitive and intransitive verbs. Series III includes the 'inverted' construction with transitive verbs (subject in dative case).

Ergativity in Svan is associated with the perfective aspect.

SWAHILI

INTRODUCTION

Swahili belongs to the North-East Coastal Bantu group of the Benue-Congo family. The name is derived from the Arabic *sawāḥil*, the broken plural of *sāḥil* 'coast'. Estimates of the numbers speaking Swahili vary from 50 to 70 million and upwards; the great majority of these are bilingual, with Swahili used as a second language alongside other Bantu mother tongues (Chinyanja, Shona, Luba, etc.) and as a lingua franca for speakers of non-Bantu languages. Swahili is the national language of Tanzania and of Kenya, and is a main language in parts of Zaire and the Congo. There are many dialect forms spread over an enormous area stretching from the Somali border to Mozambique, and from the Comoro Islands to the Congo. The first steps towards the creation of a standardized Swahili were taken in 1930, when the Inter-Territorial Language Committee was formed. African participation in this body began in 1946, with representatives from Kenya, Tanganyika, Uganda, and Zanzibar. The work of standardizing the language is now in the hands of the Institute of Swahili Research in Dar es Salaam.

Swahili has had a Moslem background since the period of the Zenj Empire (tenth to fifteenth centuries). The growth of Swahili as an international trade language dates from about the thirteenth century. Contact with Arabic and other languages is richly reflected in the lexicon. The classical verse literature, dating from the mid-seventeenth century and reaching a high point in the eighteenth/nineteenth centuries, was centred on the coastal strip of Kenya. During the twentieth century the centre of gravity in Swahili creative writing has moved to Tanzania, as English has gained the upper hand in Kenya.

SCRIPT

Until the late nineteenth century (and occasionally thereafter) Swahili was written in the Arabic script. The romanization now in use has all the letters of the English alphabet except *c*, *q*, and *x*.

PHONOLOGY

Consonants

stops: p, b, t, d, k, g
affricates: tʃ, dʒ → [dʲ]
fricatives: f, v, s, z, ʃ, h
nasals: m, n, ɲ, ŋ
lateral and flap: l, r
semi-vowels: j, w

/θ, ð, x, ɣ/ occur in words of Arabic origin.

Some grammars make a distinction between aspirate and non-aspirate /p, t, k/, and quote such pairs as /paa/ 'roof', /pʰaa/ 'gazelle'.

Vowels

a, ε, i, ɔ, u

All are short.

Stress is invariably on the penultimate. Exceptionally for a Bantu language, Swahili has no tones. A degree of vowel harmony characterizes suffixation: cf. *timia* 'to be complete', *kimbia* 'to run'; *tokea* 'to appear', *pokea* 'to receive'.

MORPHOLOGY AND SYNTAX

Noun classes

(*See* **Bantu Languages**.) Swahili has fewer classes than some of its congeners, owing to the fusion in Swahili of certain classes having phonetically similar prefixes. Traditionally, fourteen classes were distinguished, by allocating two classes, singular and plural, to each semantic field. This system can be simplified by putting both singular and plural in one class: e.g. the m-/wa- class,

Class 1 – people: *mtu* 'person', pl. *watu*; *mtoto* 'child', pl. *watoto*.
Class 2: singular marker *m-*, pl. *mi*; heterogeneous, includes plants, trees, various natural phenomena, e.g. *mti* 'tree', pl. *miti*; *mlima* 'mountain', pl. *milima*.
Class 3: heterogeneous, singular marker *ki-*, pl. *vi-*, e.g. *kitu* 'thing', pl. *vitu*; *kisu* 'knife', pl. *visu*.
Class 4: heterogeneous, singular marker Ø, *ji-*, pl. *ma-*, e.g. *jicho* 'eye', pl. *macho*; Ø*duka* 'shop', pl. *maduka*. Most nouns in this class have no concord in the singular.
Class 5: heterogeneous, known as the *n-* class, this is the largest noun class in Swahili, as it contains all loan-words. Singular and plural are identical: e.g. *nyumba* 'house(s)'; *nyoka* 'snake(s)'; *dakika* 'minute' (Arabic).
Class 6: heterogeneous, but many abstract nouns in *u-* sing., with no plural,

e.g. *usafi* 'cleanliness'; *uzuri* 'beauty'; *Udachi* 'Germany'.

Class 7: the locative class contains only one noun: *mahali* 'place', with a rather complicated system of concord involving the locus markers *p-, k-, m-*. See Location, below.

The class system outlined above, while characteristic of the Swahili noun, is cut across by a simple animate/non-animate opposition, in the sense that nouns denoting animates, especially rational animates, take class 1 concord in adjective and verb, whatever their own formal grammatical class. Thus, *ndugu* 'younger brother' is a class 5 noun, but 'a good brother' is *ndugu mzuri*, i.e. the attributive adjective *-zuri* 'good' takes class 1 concord, *m-*. *Samaki* 'fish' (Arabic) is also class 5; but 'small fishes' is *samaki wadogo*.

POSSESSION

The stem *-a* is marked for concord with the class to which the possessed object belongs. The order then is possessed object – class marker + *a* – possessor: e.g. *kitabu cha mtoto* 'the child's book'; *watu wa Tanzania* 'the people of Tanzania'; *nyumba ya mtu* 'the man's house'. An attributive adjective comes between the possessed object and the particle: e.g. *nyumba ndogo ya mtu* 'the man's small house'.

LOCATION

The markers *p-, k-, m-* take class concord: *p-* gives a definite fix, *k-* an indefinite, *m-* refers specifically to location within something. Thus, 'there' can be translated in more than one way, e.g. *upo pale* 'it is there' (definite fix, e.g. *mezani* 'on the table'); *wako kule* 'they are thereabouts'; *imo nyumbani* 'it is in the house' (different class concords are used in these examples).

The postposition expressing the locative case is *-ni*.

Adjective

The attributive adjective follows the noun qualified and has class concord: e.g. *mtu mwema* 'good man' (cl. 1); *kisu kikali* 'a sharp knife' (cl. 3); *watoto Wazungu wengi* 'many European children'. Comparatively few adjectives are of Bantu origin; many are borrowed from Arabic, and these are all indeclinable: e.g. *chumba ßsafi* 'clean room'.

Compound adjectives are formed with the *-a* linking particle marked for concord: e.g. *chakula cha kizungu* 'European food'.

COMPARATIVE

Periphrastic with *kupita/kuliko*: e.g. *Mlima wa Kilimanjaro ni mrefu kuliko mlima wa Kenya* 'Mount Kilimanjaro is higher than Mount Kenya' (*-refu* 'tall').

Pronoun

The subject prefixes for the *m-/wa-* class are: sing. 1 *ni-*, 2 *u-*, 3 *a-*; pl. 1 *tu-*, 2 *m-*, 3 *wa-*. The object infixes for the same class are: sing. 1 *ni-*, 2 *ku-*, 3 *m-*; pl. 1 *tu-*, 2 *wa-*, 3 *wa-*. For all other classes, the object infix equals the subject prefix; e.g.

for the *ki-/vi-* class, 'it' is *ki-/-ki-*; 'they' is *vi-*; 'them' is *-vi-*. In such sentences as 'he gave it to me', 'it' need not be expressed: e.g.

a.li.ni.pa *a-* = subject prefix, *m-* class, 3rd p. 'he';
            li = past-tense marker (*see* **Verb**, below);
            ni = indirect object, *m-* class, 1st p. 'to me';
            pa = root verb, 'to give'.

Cf. *ni.li.ki.nunua* 'I bought it', where the presence of *ki* indicates that I bought something specific belonging to the *ki-* class. Cf. *ni.li.m.wona* 'I saw him'; *a.li.ni.wona* 'he saw me' (*-ona* 'to see'; *w* is a euphonic glide).

THE INDEPENDENT EMPHATIC PRONOUNS
mimi – wewe – yeye; pl. *sisi – ninyi – wao*; these can never replace the subject prefixes, but have to be used e.g. in the habitual aspect which does not take subject prefixes.

POSSESSIVE PRONOMINAL MARKERS
Sing. 1 *-angu*, 2 *-ako*, 3 *-ake*; pl. 1 *-etu*, 2 *-enu*, 3 *-ao*. These are modulated by the appropriate class markers: eg. *vitabu vile vyangu* 'these books are mine'; *nyumba yetu* 'our house'; *Ørafiki wema wangu* 'my good friends'.

DEMONSTRATIVE PRONOUN
The proximate series is based on the particle *ha-* + class marker; the distal series by combining the class markers with *-le*. Assimilation and some anomalies occur in both series: e.g. *kijiji hiki* 'this village', *vijiji hivi* 'these villages'; *chumba kile* 'that room', *vyumba vile* 'those rooms'.

INTERROGATIVE PRONOUN
nani 'who?'; *nini* 'what?'.

RELATIVE PRONOUN
See **Verb**, Relative clause, below.

Numerals

The numerals are adjectives, and the units 1, 2, 3, 4, 5, 8 take class concord; 6, 7, 9, being Arabic, do not. 1 *-moja*; 2 *-wili*; 3 *-tatu*; 4 *-nne*; 5 *-tano*; 8 *-nane*. 6 *sita*; 7 *saba*; 9 *tisa*; 10 *kumi*. 11 *kumi na -moja*; 12 *kumi na -wili*; 20 *ishirini*; 30 *thelathini*, etc. (*see* **Arabic**); 100 *mia* (Arabic). Examples: *visu vitatu* 'three knives'; *visu Øsabu* 'seven knives'; *watoto wanne* 'four children'; *watoto kumi na mmoja* 'eleven children'.

Verb

The infinitive form for Bantu stems is *ku* – stem – *a*: e.g. *ku.fany.a* 'to do'. For Arabic stems: *ku* – stem – *e/i/u*: e.g. *ku.fikr.i* 'to think'.

INDICATIVE FORMS
The general formula is subject marker – tense sign – stem. The present

characteristic is -na-; the past, -li-; the future, -ta-: e.g. *ni.na.soma* 'I am reading'; *ni.li.soma* 'I read (past)'; *nitasoma* 'I shall read'. Other characteristics are: perfect -me-; subjunctive Ø; conditional -ki-. Examples: *i.me.fika* 'it has arrived'; *tu.Ø.ngoje* 'let us wait'; *ni.ki.kaa* 'if I wait'.

PASSIVE

The passive of transitive verbs is made by inserting -w- between stem and final: e.g. *ku.soma* 'to read' – *ku.som.w.a* 'to be read'; *ku.jua* 'to know' – *ku.ju.liwa* 'to be known'. The second example shows the expanded passive marker -uliwa- (four variants) added to stems ending in -ua/-oa.

CAUSATIVE

-sha is added to stem: e.g. *kutelemka* 'to go down' – *kutelemsha* 'to lower'.

HABITUAL MOOD

The characteristic is -hu-; subject markers are not used. Thus, e.g. **husoma** means '... is/are habitually reading'; and person must be specified by other means, e.g. the use of the emphatic personal pronouns.

THE PREPOSITIONAL FORM

Example: *a.na.wa.som.ea* 'he/she is reading to them': here, the ending -ea marks the prepositional form which is used when the verb is benefactive, i.e. the action is performed to or on behalf of someone else. Formally, i/e is inserted before the final vowel. As in the passive, -l- may figure as a euphonic glide component: e.g. -pata 'to get' – *patia* 'to get for someone'; -chukua 'to carry' – -chukulia 'to carry to/for someone'

NEGATION

For most tenses, negative subject markers are used which are prefixed directly to the stem in the present tense, i.e. dropping -na-: class 1, sing. 1 si-, 2 hu-, 3 ha-; pl. 1 hatu-, 2 ham-, 3 hawa-; the stem final changes to -i: e.g. **hasomi** 'he doesn't read'; **hatujui** 'we don't know'.

The -li- past is negated by -ku- with negative prefix: e.g. **ha.ku.soma** 'he did not read'. Future: *si.ta.kwenda* 'I shall not go'; *ha.ta.soma* 'he will not read'.

RELATIVE INFIX

An alternative form of the demonstrative pronoun in -o provides the base -yo for the relative infix, which is marked for concord (*yo* → *ye* in class 1): e.g. *ni.li.ye.soma* 'I, who read (past)'; *mtoto. a.li.ye.soma kitabu* 'the child who was reading a book'.

A second way of making a relative clause is to use the base *amba-* + relative marker, as above: e.g. *mtu ambaye a.na.soma* 'the person who is reading'; *watu ambao wa.na.soma* 'the people who are reading'. Thus, *ni.na.ye.soma* = *mimi ambaye ni.na.soma* 'I who am reading' (*amba-* cannot be sentence-initial).

IMPERATIVE

The stem alone provides an abrupt command. A polite request is made with the formula *u* – stem – *e*: e.g. *ufany.e* 'would you be so kind as to ...' (sing.); pl. *m.fany.e*.

Prepositions

Several nouns take the possessive *ya*: e.g. *juu ya* 'on', *ndani ya* 'inside'. Others take *na*: e.g. *mbali na* 'far from'; *karibu na* 'close to': e.g. *ni.na.kaa karibu na mji* 'I live close to the town'.

Word order

SVO is basic. In the verbal complex, the object infix precedes the stem, and may anticipate an overtly expressed object, thus conferring definite status on the latter: e.g. *ni.li.ki.nunua kitabu* 'I bought **it** the book' (i.e. a specific book).

---

1   Hapo mwanzo kulikuwako Neno, naye Neno aliku-
2 wako kwa Mungu, naye Neno alikuwa Mungu. Huyo
3 mwanzo alikuwako kwa Mungu. Vyote vilifanyika
     kwa huyo; wala pasipo yeye hakikufanyika cho chote
4 kilichofanyika. Ndani yake ndimo ulimokuwa uzima,
5 nao ule uzima ulikuwa nuru ya watu. Nayo nuru
     yang'aa gizani, wala giza halikuiweza.
6   Palitokea mtu, ametumwa kutoka kwa Mungu,
7 jina lake Yohana. Huyo alikuja kwa ushuhuda, ili
     aishuhudie ile nuru, na wote wapate kuamini kwa
8 yeye. Huyo hakuwa ile nuru, bali alikuja ili aishu-
     hudie ile nuru.

SWEDISH

INTRODUCTION

Swedish belongs to the East Scandinavian branch of Common Scandinavian (part of the Germanic branch of Indo-European). The Old Swedish period runs from the thirteenth to the early sixteenth century.

The emergence of the modern Swedish language and literature can be dated with some precision: in the 1520s King Gustav Vasa dissolved the union with Denmark, and, more importantly, Catholicism was replaced by the Lutheran Church. The first translation of the Bible into Swedish appeared in 1547. From the late-nineteenth-century realists and Strindberg onwards, Swedish literature has produced a large crop of distinguished writers, working mainly in the field of experimental poetry and in the critical analysis of society and the arts.

The literary language is based on the central (Stockholm) dialect. Some of the outlying dialects are highly divergent, e.g. that of Dalecarlia.

SCRIPT

The Roman alphabet + *å, ä, ö*.

PHONOLOGY

Consonants

> stops: p, b, t, d, ṭ, ḍ, k, g
> fricatives: f, v, ç, s, ṣ, ʃ, h
> nasals: m, n, ṇ, ŋ
> laterals and flap: l, ḷ, r
> semi-vowel: j

/p, t, k/ are aspirated; the retroflex series /ṭ, ḍ, ṇ, ṣ, ḷ/ plus the retroflex clusters such as /tṣ, ḍṣ, ṇṣ/, are generally signalled in the script by r + C: e.g. *mord* 'murder', /muːḍ/ (in close transcription [muːḍ]; *korn* 'grain', /kuːṇ/ ([kuːṇ]). Word-final /r/ has the same effect on a following initial /s/: e.g. *för sent* 'too late', /fəṣeːnt/. There is a tendency for /ʃ/ to become /ṣ/: e.g. *skinn* 'skin', /ʃin/ > [ṣin].

Vowels

Some 20 vowel sounds, differing in quantity and quality, are represented by nine letters: *i, e, a, o, u, y, å, ä, ö*; basically, they can be classified as:

(a) front unrounded: short ɪ, e, ɛ
   long i, e, ɛ
(b) central: short ʏ, a, œ/ɵ, ʉ, ə
   long ʏ, a, ø, ʉ
(c) back rounded: short u, ɔ
   long u, o

In close transcription, the following central rounded phonemes are distinguished:

/œ/, e.g. *først* /fœʂt/, 'first';
/ɵ/, e.g. *just* /jɵst/, 'just, exactly';
/ø/, e.g. *överens* /øːvərɛns/, 'agreed';
/ʉ/, e.g. *ju* /jʉ/, 'indeed'.

In the central rounded area, close transcription of Swedish will distiguish between /ɵ/ as in *upp* 'up' and /ə/ as in *törst* 'thirst' (with retroflex /ʂ/).

Tone

Two tones are distinguished: the single or falling tone, which affects mono-syllables (ignoring affixed endings, e.g. the definite article) and the double tone, the second component of which has a slightly higher onset pitch than the first. Both components have a downward glide. This second tone affects most polysyllables. Tone may be phonemic; the example usually quoted is *anden*; pronounced with single tone, this means 'the duck'; with double tone, 'the spirit'.

In speech, elision of final consonants is typical: e.g. *var vänlig och kom* 'do (be friendly and) come!', is realized as [va.vɛnli.o kom].

Stress

Normally, the main stress is on the first syllable, with secondary stress on the first syllable of a second component in a compound. Final unstressed vowels tend to be reduced to /ə/.

MORPHOLOGY AND SYNTAX

Noun

There are two genders: common and neuter. The indefinite article precedes: *en* for common, *ett* for neuter: e.g. *en blomma* 'a flower', *en bil* 'a car'; *ett barn* 'a child', *ett äpple* 'an apple'.

The definite article is suffixed: -(*e*)*n* for common nouns, -(*e*)*t* for neuter: e.g. *blomman* 'the flower', *bilen* 'the car'; *barnet* 'the child', *äpplet* 'the apple'.

Plural markers are: *-ar*, *-or*, *-er*, *-n*, *-Ø*: this gives five declensions: *häst* 'horse'

– hästar; flicka 'girl' *– flickor; tand* 'tooth' *– tänder; äpple* 'apple' *– äpplen; barn* 'child' *– barn∅.*

Umlaut may affect the stem as in *tand/tänder*; cf. *son – söner, bror – bröder.* To these plural markers, the plural definite article is affixed: *-na* for common, *-en* for neuter nouns: e.g. *flickor.na* 'the girls'; *barnen* 'the children'.

The demonstrative pronoun *den/det/de* is also used as a definite article, especially where an adjective intervenes: thus, *en stor bil* 'a big car', becomes in the definite form *den stora bilen* 'the big car', similarly, *den unga flickan* 'the young girl'; pl. *de stora bilarna* 'the big cars'; and in neuter: *det långa brevet* 'the long letter', *det vita huset* 'the white house'. That is, definiteness is doubly marked.

In modern Swedish the plural definite marker *de*, tends to be replaced by *dom*.

CASE SYSTEM
Of the old case system only the possessive *-s* remains. This can be added to the affixed article: e.g. from *flicka* 'girl': *en flickas* 'a girl's'; *flickans, flickors, flickornas.*

Adjective

Adjective precedes noun as attributive and is marked for neuter and for plural: e.g. *grön* 'green': *ett grönt hus, de gröna husen.*

COMPARATIVE
The comparative is in *-are* (indeclinable), often with umlaut in the stem: e.g. *stor* 'big' *– större; låg* 'low' *– lägre.*

Pronoun

PERSONAL
The third-person singular forms distinguish masculine/feminine. The subject forms with their objective correlatives are:

		Singular		*Plural*	
		Subject	*Object*	*Subject*	*Object*
1		jag	mig	vi	oss
2		du; ni	dig; er	Ni	Er
3	masc.	han	honom		
	fem.	hon	henne	de	dem
	nt.	det	det		

The *ni/er* forms tend to be avoided as somewhat old-fashioned, with a corresponding increase in the use of *du*. Periphrastic forms of address for second person are much in use.

DEMONSTRATIVE PRONOUN/ADJECTIVE
den/det/de have already been mentioned. Another form is *denna/detta/dessa.*

INTERROGATIVE PRONOUN
vem 'who?', *vad* 'what?'

RELATIVE PRONOUN
som; invariable: e.g. *mannen, som jag talade med* 'the man I was talking to'; *tabletter, som man löser upp i vatten* 'tablets which one dissolves in water'.

Numerals

1–10: *en/ett, två, tre, fyra, fem, sex, sju, åtta, nio, tio*; 11 *elva*; 12 *tolv*; 13 *tretton*; 14 *fjorton*; 15 *femton*; 20 *tjugo*; 30 *trettio*; 40 *fyrtio*; 100 *hundra*.

Verb

Transitive/intransitive, with active and passive voices. There are two moods: indicative and imperative. The indicative has two simple tenses, a present and past. The supine is used with the auxiliary *att ha* to form a perfect tense. The past participle is used only as an adjective: e.g. *en av Sveriges mest* ***lästa*** *författare* 'one of Sweden's most (widely) read authors'.

INDICATIVE MOOD
The present tense is made by adding *-r* to the infinitive for all persons: e.g. *att gå* 'to go', *jag går* 'I go'; *skriva* 'write', *jag skriver* (/a/ > /e/).

PAST TENSE
Here, there are three weak conjugations and one strong:

Weak

(a) past tense ending *-ade*, supine in *-at*: e.g. *jag kallade, jag har kallat*.
(b) past tense ending *-de*, supine in *-t*: e.g. *jag glömde, jag har glömt*.
(c) past tense ending *-dde*, supine in *-tt*: e.g. *jag trodde, jag har trott*.

The roots in these examples are, *kalla* 'to call', *glömma* 'forget', *tro* 'believe'.

Strong verbs: these show one- or two-stage ablaut: e.g.

	Present	*Past*	*Perfect*
skriva 'write'	skriver	skrev	har skrivet
ligga 'lie'	ligger	låg	har legat

Formerly, singular and plural forms of the past tense of strong verbs were distinguished, and these plural forms may still be found in the literary language: e.g. *skrevo* 'we/you/they wrote'; *lågo* 'we (etc.) lay'.

In the perfect tense, the auxiliary *har/hade* is often dropped: cf. *I södra Småland... stod en römålad kvarn med de största vingar, som någon* ***sett*** *i hela bygden* 'In southern Småland ... stood a red-painted mill, with the biggest sails anyone (had) ever seen in all the countryside' (V. von Heidenstam: *Fem Berättelser*).

MODAL AUXILIARIES

Examples: *må/måtte, kan/kunde, skall/skulle, vill/ville*, etc.

jag måste skriva hem i dag 'I must write home today.'
jag ville skriva hem i dag 'I wanted to write home today.'
jag kan inte skriva hem i dag 'I can't write home today.'

PASSIVE VOICE

Either the *-s* form or the form with *att bli* + supine: e.g. *brevet har skrivits* = *brevet har blivit skrivet* 'the letter has been written'. The *-s* form is much used in general statements, public announcements, notices and recipes: e.g. *affären stänges kl. 5* 'the shop closes at 5'.

Deponent verbs have the passive *-s* form with active meaning: *jag hoppas, att du...* 'I hope that you will ...'; *Minns du, var han bor?* 'Do you remember where he lives?'

Negation

Inte follows a finite verb, but is inserted between auxiliary and non-finite form, except in relative clauses, where it precedes auxiliary:

*han sade, att han **inte** kunde göra det* 'he said that he couldn't do that';
han har inte sett 'he hasn't seen';
jag kan inte skriva 'I can't write'.

Prepositions

As in English, a preposition can be placed at the end of a phrase: e.g. *Vilka program brukar de titta på* 'Which programme are they accustomed to look **at**?'

Word order

SVO is normal; VSO in principal clause if subordinate material or a relative clause begins the sentence: *Just när han ska stänga dörren, kommer någon springande* 'Just as he is about to close the door, someone comes running up'.

I begynnelsen var Ordet, och Ordet var hos Gud, och [1]*
Ordet var Gud. Han var i begynnelsen hos Gud. Allting [2]
har blivit till genom honom, och utan honom har ingen-
ting blivit till av allt det som finns till. I honom var liv, [4]*
och livet var människornas ljus. Och ljuset lyser i mörkret, [5]*
och mörkret har icke fått makt med det.
En man uppträdde, sänd av Gud; hans namn var Jo- [6]*
hannes. Han kom som ett vittne, för att vittna om ljuset, [7]*
för att alla skulle komma till tro genom honom. [8]

SYRIAC

INTRODUCTION

This North-Western Semitic language, centring on the north Mesopotamian city of Edessa, is one of the most important forms taken by written Aramaic. The oldest inscriptions in what is recognizably Syriac go back to the turn of the millennia; the oldest document is dated AD 243. From the second to the seventh centuries Syriac was the medium for a very rich and interesting Christian literature, representing both original writing and translation from Greek. The Peshitta Bible translation was carried out in the second century. Original writing through the third to fifth centuries includes the works of the Gnostic Bardaisan, the 'Odes of Solomon', the 'Acts of Thomas', and the polemical poems of Afrem directed against Julian the Apostate. The great schism between the Eastern and Western churches in the fifth century initiated a decline in Syriac writing, but there was a brief revival in the work of the thirteenth-century historian, Barhebraeus. In the fourteenth century Syriac was finally ousted by Arabic. As a liturgical language, Syriac is still in use in Iraq, Syria, and Lebanon.

SCRIPT

The basis is Aramaic. The oldest form is Estrangelo, which was used until the fifth century. The schism between the Eastern (Nestorian) and Western (Jacobite) churches led to a division: in the Persian Empire, the eastern Syrians used the Nestorian variant with pointing on the Hebrew model, while the Jacobite Church opted for the so-called *serṭo* linear script with reversed Greek letters as vowel markers.

PHONOLOGY

Consonants

> stops: p, b, p', d, t, t', k, g, q, ʔ
> fricatives: s, ṣ, z, ʃ, h, ḥ, ʕ, (+ ḫ in Western Syriac)
> nasals: m, n
> lateral and flap: l, r
> semi-vowels: j, w

As in Hebrew, the phonemes /b, g, d, k, p, t/ have spirant allophones marked as *b̲, g̲, d̲, k̲, p̲, t̲*, which are realized as [v, γ, ð, x, f, θ]. Thus the root *KTB* appears in the word for 'book' as /kᵊθaːˠaː/.

/ɬ/ is notated here as ṭ.

Vowels

long and short: i, e, a, o, u

Plus shwa written as ə. Short vowels in unstressed position tend to shwa: e.g. qᵊṭal 'he killed'.

Stress

Stress tends to fall on the second syllable.

MORPHOLOGY AND SYNTAX

Noun

Syriac has two genders, masculine and feminine. The typical masculine ending is Ø, the feminine is -aṯ/ā.

Nominals, including adjectives, appear in three states: absolute, construct, and emphatic: the following table shows the endings for masculine and feminine nouns, singular and plural, in three states:

		Absolute	Construct	Emphatic
masculine	sing.	Ø	Ø	-ā
	pl.	īn	-ai	-ē
feminine	sing.	aṯ ā	-aṯ	-tā
	pl.	ān	-āṯ	āṯā

Examples: masc. məleḵ 'emperor': emphatic sing. malkā; pl. malḵīn – malḵai – malḵē.

The tendency in Syriac was for the emphatic form to oust the other two, thus becoming identified with the nominal itself: e.g. malkā 'the emperor', malkē 'the emperors'; rīšā 'head'; yaumā 'day'; ʿammā 'nation', etc.

GENITIVE

The tendency to use the emphatic state of the noun in preference to the absolute or construct is very clear in the formulation of the genitive relationship: e.g. the construct form bar malkā 'the emperor's son', is possible, but the idiomatic Syriac way of expressing this is to use the emphatic state with the relative particle dᵊ: e.g. bᵊrā dᵊmalkā 'the emperor's son'; šᵊlāmā dᵊʿammā 'the peace of the nation'; bᵊyaumā dᵊrugz.eh 'in the day of his wrath'.

Adjective

As attribute, adjective follows noun and is in concord with it: e.g. bᵊṯūlā qaddīšā 'a blessed maiden'; talmīḏē zᵊʿōrē 'young pupils'.

Pronoun

The independent personal forms with their correlative enclitics are

		Singular			Plural		
		Independent	*Enclitic*	*Possessive*	*Independent*	*Enclitic*	*Possessive*
1		'enā	-nā	Ø	hənan	-nan	-an
2	masc.	'at	-at	-ak̲	'attōn	-tōn	-k̲ōn
	fem.	'at	-at	-ek̲	'attēn	-tēn	-k̲ēn
3	masc.	hū	-ū	-eh	hennōn	-'ennōn	-hōn
	fem.	hī	-ī	-āh	hennēn	-'ennēn	-hēn

The enclitics are used as personal markers in nominal sentences: e.g. *šappīrat* 'thou art beautiful'. Use of possessive markers: cf. *malkø* 'my emperor'; *malkāk̲* 'thy emperor'; *malk.ai.k* 'thy emperors'; *malkətāk̲* 'thy empress'; *malkātāk̲* 'thy empresses'.

A third set of enclitics, closely similar to the possessive markers, is used to provide objective pronouns in verbal sentences.

Use of the relative particle *dī* + the dative marker *l-* + personal endings, to form an independent personal possessive pronoun, is an innovation in Semitic morphology: e.g. *dīlī* 'mine'; *dīlak̲* 'yours'.

DEMONSTRATIVE PRONOUN/ADJECTIVE
hānā 'this' (masc.), fem. *hāde*, common pl. *hālēn*; *hau* 'that' (masc.), fem. *hāi*; pl. masc. *hanōn*, fem. *hanēn*.

INTERROGATIVE PRONOUN
man 'who?'; *mā(n)(ā)* 'what?'.

RELATIVE PRONOUN
dˀ: e.g.

> melt̲ā **dˀ** mallet̲
> 'the word that I spoke' (John, 12.48)
>
> ḥˀzain nāš **dˀ** mappeq sīd̲ē b.ašˀmā.k
> 'we saw one casting out devils in thy name' (Mark, 9.38)
>
> uaḥˀzā 'allāhā lˀnuhrā, **dˀ** šappīr
> 'and God saw the light that it was good' (Genesis, 1.4)

Numerals

1–10: these have masculine and feminine forms, and are nearly always used in the absolute state. The masculine forms are: *ḥad̲*, *tˀrēn*, *tˀlāt̲ā*, *'arbˀˁā*, *ḥamšā*, *'eštā*, *šabˁā*, *tˀmāniā*, *tešˁā*, *ˁesrā*; i.e. the masculine forms from 3 to 10 have feminine endings.

The teens take the form unit + 10: e.g. 12 *tˀreˁsar*; the decades end in *-īn*: e.g. 20 *ˁesrīn*; 30 *tˀlāt̲īn*; 100 (absolute state) *mā*, emphatic, *māt̲ā*.

Verb

(For the binyanim structure of the Aramaic verb, *see* **Hebrew**.) There are three basic active themes: the *PEAL*, the *PAEL*, and the *AFEL*; their reflexives (or passives) are: *ETPEEL*, *ETPAAL*, and *ETTAFAL*.

MOOD

The Syriac verb has two moods, indicative and imperative.

The indicative mood is basically aspectual, as in Arabic, with perfective and imperfective aspects. In the *PEAL* theme, there is an opposition in transitive verbs between -*a*- forms, which are perfective, and -*o/e*- forms, which are imperfective: eg. *qᵓṭal* 'he killed'; *neqṭol* 'he is killing, will kill'.

The imperative mood shares the -*o/e*- characteristic of the imperfective: e.g. *qᵓṭol* 'kill!'.

TENSE

In Syriac, a secondary analytical tense system has been developed; thus, a present tense is made from the active participle + enclitic: e.g. masc. *qāṭel.nā* 'he is a killer' = 'he is killing'; fem. *qāṭlā.nā* 'she is a killer' = 'she is killing'; *qāṭel* 'I am ...'; *qāṭlīn.nan* 'we are killing'; and a past imperfect: e.g. masc. *qāṭel.uā* 'he was killing', fem. *qāṭlā.uaṯ*. These have passive correlatives: *qᵓṭīl.ū* 'he is (a) killed (one)'; *qᵓṭīl.uā* 'he was killed'.

The primary themes of the strong verb are here illustrated in the third person singular masculine and feminine, main themes only; there are several more of rare occurrence.

> PEAL: perfective masc. *kᵓṯaḇ* 'he wrote', fem. *keṯbaṯ*; imperfective *nekṯoḇ* 'he writes', *tekṯoḇ*; imperative *kᵓḇoḏ* 'write?'.
> ETPEEL: perfective masc. *eṯqᵓṭel*, 'he was killed', fem. *eṯqaṭlaṯ*; imperfective *neṯqᵓṭel*, *teṯqᵓṭel*.
> PAEL (intensive theme): with gemination of second radical: perfective masc. *qaṭṭel*, fem. *qaṭṭᵓlaṯ*; imperfective *nᵓqaṭṭel*, *tᵓqaṭṭel*.
> ETPAAL: *eṯqaṭṭal*, etc.
> AFEL (causative): perfective masc. *'aqṭel* 'he caused to be killed'; fem. *'aqṭᵓlaṯ*; imperfective *naqṭel*, *taqṭel*.
> ETTAFAL: reflexive of AFEL, e.g. *ettaqṭal*.

The personal paradigm is purely suffixal in the perfective, prefix–suffixal in the imperfective, and is coded for gender in the second and third persons masculine and plural.

Prepositions

There is a rich inventory of prepositions, many of which are connected with verbal roots: e.g. *QDM* 'to precede' – *qᵓḏām* 'before'. The prepositions take the personal enclitic markers: e.g. *beh* 'in him', *bāh* 'in her'. Some add the formant -*āṯ*/-*ai* before the enclitic: e.g. *meṭṭul* 'because of' – *meṭṭulāṯ* 'because of her'.

Word order

Very free.

(Ancient)

(Modern)

TADZHIK

INTRODUCTION

Tadzhik is a South-West Iranian language. During the centuries of Turkic expansion in central Asia, the Eastern Iranian languages which had been established in Transoxania since the Achaemenian Dynasty, were gradually forced to retreat into the Pamir mountains (*see* **Pamir Languages**). A residue of West Iranian speakers remained in the Bokhara–Samarkand area, and these were the forebears of the Tadzhiks of today.

Tadzhik is extremely close to the Persian of Iran, and it is very difficult to separate the literary tradition of the one from that of the other; some great names are claimed by both, e.g. Rūdakī. The seminal figure in the history of modern Tadzhik literature (and indeed of Uzbek as well) is Sadriddin Aynī, whose prolific and valuable output of novels and verse culminated in his *Yoddoštho* ('Memoirs': = Persian, *yād.dāšt.hā*) (4 vols, 1949–54).

The language is spoken by about 3 million people in the Tadzhik Soviet Socialist Republic and in the adjacent Uzbek and Kirgiz SSRs.

SCRIPT

Arabic till 1930; since 1940 Cyrillic with supplementary letters.

PHONOLOGY

Consonants

stops: p, b, t, d, k, g, q
affricates: tʃ, dʒ
fricatives: f/v, s, z, ʃ, ʒ, x, γ, h
nasals: m, n
lateral and flap: l, r
semi-vowel: j

Vowels

A distinction is made between the three stable vowels, /eː, oː, uː/, and the three unstable vowels, /i, a, u/. /oː/ corresponds to Persian /aː/. The unstable vowels tend towards /ə/: e.g. *kitob* → /kᵊtop/.

Stress

Stress is usually on the final syllable of the root words, discounting ezafe and the indefinite marker. The verbal prefixes *me-* and *bi-* are stressed as in Persian.

MORPHOLOGY AND SYNTAX

Most basic points in Tadzhik morphology are identical with their Persian counterparts; a detailed description will be found in the article on Persian.

The suppositional mood in Tadzhik is worth special mention. This has entered Tadzhik under Uzbek influence; the marker is *-agi*: e.g. *kard.agi.stam* → *kard.ag.am* 'it seems that I did, probably I did'. The personal endings are: *-am*, *-i*, *-Ø*; pl. *-em*, *-ed*, *-and*: e.g. *kor me.kard.agi.st* 'he is very likely working'. The *-gi-* element reappears in past, present–future, and actual present participles: e.g. *xondagī* 'having read, having been read' (i.e. the form is neutral as to voice); *me.xondagī* 'reading, being read' (see Comrie 1981: 177).

---

1. ДАР ибтидо Калом буд, ва Калом бо Худо буд, ва Калом Худо буд.

2. Он дар ибтидо бо Худо буд.

3. Ҳама чиз ба воситаи Ӯ ба вучуд омад, ва ҳар он чи вучуд ёфт, бе Ӯ вучуд наёфт.

4. Дар Ӯ ҳаёт буд, ва ҳаёт нури одамиён буд.

5. Ва нур дар торикӣ медурахшид, ва торикӣ онро фаро нагирифт.

6. Шахсе аз ҷониби Худо фиристода шуда буд, ки Яҳьё ном дошт.

7. Вай барои шоҳидӣ омад, ки бар Нур шаҳодат диҳад, то ки ҳама ба воситаи вай имон оваранд.

TAGALOG

INTRODUCTION

A member of the Indonesian branch of Austronesian, and native to central and southern Luzon, Tagalog has spread far beyond its original confines, and is now the official language of the Philippines, taught in all schools and spoken, either as mother tongue or as second language by up to 40 or 50 million people (approaching 75 per cent of the total population).

A common stock of Malayo-Polynesian root words provides the central lexical core of Tagalog, but the language has been subjected to several cultural influences and these are reflected in the Sanskrit, Dravidian, Arabic, and Chinese loan-words it contains. Since the sixteenth century a large number of Spanish loan-words have been more or less completely assimilated, and there is a more recent and substantial Anglo-American component. Some native literature seems to have existed before the Spanish conquest, but this was destroyed without trace by the Catholic authorities. The first Tagalog book, a Spanish–Tagalog religious digloss, was published in 1593; a Tagalog Bible appeared in 1704. A notable contribution to the enrichment and propagation of Tagalog was made in the middle of the nineteenth century by Baltazar, known as Balagtas, who instituted the poetry contests known as *balagtasan* (the derived verb is *makipagbalagtasan*, 'to take part in a poetry contest'). The National Language Institute for the promotion of Tagalog was founded in 1936.

SCRIPT

From the late sixteenth century onwards, use of the Roman alphabet accompanied the spread of Catholicism. The letters *c, f, j, q, v, x, z* are not used. The digraph *ng* is used to denote /ŋ/.

PHONOLOGY

Consonants

> stops: p, b, t, d, k, g, ʔ
> fricatives: s, h
> nasals: m, n, ŋ
> lateral and flap: l, r
> semi-vowels: w, j

[d] and [r] are allophones of the same sound, and alternate with each other.

Vowels

i, e, a, o, u

Unstressed /i/ → [ɪ]; unstressed /o/ → [u]. There are half-a-dozen diphthongs closing on /y/w/.

Stress

There are five types of accentuation, known by Tagalog names; stress is phonemic:

1. mabilis: acute on last syllable, e.g. *anák* 'child', *bulaklák* 'flower';
2. malumay: stress on penultimate, not marked, e.g. *lalaki* 'man';
3. malumi: weak stress on penultimate + grave on last syllable, which has glottal stop, e.g. *batà* 'child';
4. maragsa: strong stress on final + glottal stop marked by circumflex, e.g. *masamâ* 'bad';
5. mariin: two stressed syllables, e.g. *pàgawáan* 'factory'.

MORPHOLOGY AND SYNTAX

Noun

No grammatical gender. Syntactic relationships between words are expressed by a series of articles/markers which identify the status of the noun (proper or common, focused or non-focused), its number (singular or plural), and governance (direct/indirect object, genitive or passive relationship). These articles are:

	Proper				*Common*			
	Subject	*Genitive*	*Indirect*	*Passive*	*Subject*	*Genitive*	*Indirect*	*Passive*
sing.	si	ni	kay	ni	ang	ng	sa	ng
pl.	sina	nina	kina	nina	+ mga			

ng is pronounced /naŋ/, *mga* as /maŋah/. Examples: *si Pedro ay lalaki* 'Pedro is a man'; ***ang mga** sapatos ay malilínis* 'the shoes are clean'; ***ang** bahay **ng** lalaki ay bago* 'the man's house is new' (*ay* is the copula).

Adjective

As attribute, adjective may precede or follow noun; the euphonic ligature /ŋ/ connects A with N, N with A: cf. *matandâ* 'old', *babae* 'woman': *matandang babae = babaing matandâ* 'old woman'; *ang baháy **na** malakí = ang malakíng baháy* 'the big house'. The plural of adjectives may be marked by partial reduplication: e.g. *matandâ* 'old', pl. *matatandâ*.

Pronoun

Pronouns have subject series, *ng* series (genitive, instrumental), and *sa* series used as indirect objects. The subject series is: sing. 1 *akó*, 2 *ikáw*, 3 *siyá*; pl. 1 incl. *táyo*, excl. *kamí*, 2 *kayó*, 3 *silá*; The possessive/oblique forms are pre- or postpositive; e.g. for singular 1, 2, 3, the prepositive forms are: *akin*, *iyo*, *kaniya*; postpositive: *ko*, *mo*, *niya*; thus, *ito ay aklat **ko** = ito ay aking aklat* 'this is my book'. Cf. *binasa **ko** ang aklat* 'read – by me – the book', i.e. 'I read the book'.

For *binasa*, see **Verb**, below.

DEMONSTRATIVE PRONOUN
Three degrees of removal, in the *ang* series: *ito* 'this', *iyan* 'that', *iyon* 'that' (further away); with *ng* and *sa* forms.

INTERROGATIVE PRONOUN
sino 'who?'; *ano* 'what?'.

RELATIVE PRONOUN
See **Verb**, below.

Numerals

1–10: *isá, dalawá, tatló, ápat, limá, ánim, pitó, waló, siyám, sampû*; 11 *labíng isá*; 12 *labíndalawá*; 13 *labíntatló*; 20 *dalawampû*; 30 *tatlumpû*; 100 *(i)sandaán*.

Verb

Formally, a Tagalog verb consists of a root (which may be reduplicated) and an affix or affixes (prefix, suffix, infix). Verbs are classified in terms of (a) aspect, and (b) their focus determinant affixes, such as *mag-*, *um-*, *i-*, etc. The affixes convey information on how the verb form is to be construed *vis-à-vis* the other items in the sentence; one might describe them as signposts marking the structure of the sentence with particular reference to the agent–patient–beneficiary relationship; depending on choice of affix, one of these three main participants in an action is said to be 'focused'. Furthermore, locational or instrumental factors in the action may be focused.

Aspect: four aspects are distinguished: neutral – perfective – imperfective – intentional (future); e.g. for base *tulog* 'sleep' the four forms are: *ma.tulog – na.tulog – na.tu.tulog – ma.tu.tulog*.

Combining the four aspects with the four focus patterns, we get a 16-term grid, which may be illustrated with the base *sulat* 'write':

	1	*2*	*3*	*4*
I	sumulat	sulatin	sulatan	isulat
II	sumulat	sinulat	sinulatan	isinulat
III	sumusulat	sinusulat	sinusulatan	isinusulat
IV	susulat	susulatin	susulatan	isusulat

Accompanying pronouns are selected, to show the appropriate deixis, from the *ang*, *ng*, *sa* series (*see* **Pronoun** above).

Tagalog has a preference for what in other languages would be called passive constructions, and for predicate-initial sentences. Thus the sentence 'the man is eating' can be rendered in the same order as *ang lalaki ay kumákain*, but more idiomatically as *kumákain ang lalaki*, where the copula *ay* is dropped. No distinctions for gender, person, or number are made (though certain prefixes can act as pluralizers). Some authorities describe the perfective/imperfective aspects as 'past' and 'present'.

The pilot role of the key affixes will become clearer from some comparative examples:

1. Agent is in focus: the affixes are e.g. *mag-*, *-um-*. *-um-* is an infix except in verbs with initial vowel. The structure is *-um-* verb + agent in *ang/si* form + adverb etc.: e.g. from root *dating* 'to come' (Indonesian, *datang*): *dumating si Pedro kahápon* 'Pedro came yesterday'; imperfective *dumarating*; perfective *dumating*; future *darating*. Cf. John XVI, 32:

> Marito, ang oras ay d**umara**ting, oo d**um**ating na
>
> 'Behold, the hour cometh (imperf.) yea, is now come (perf.)'

2. Patient is in focus: the affixes are: *-in*, *-an*, *i-*, *ma-*. The structure is *-in* verb + agent in *ni/ng* case + patient in *ang* case: **binasa ni Pedro ang aklat** 'Pedro read the book'. Main forms: infinitive *basain*; imperfect *binabasa*; perfect *binasa*; future *babasain*.

3. Location or direction of action is in focus: the affixes are *-in*, *(h)an*, *pag...an*. The structure is *-an/-in* verb + agent in *ni/ng* case + target in *ang*: e.g. **nilapitan ni Pedro ang bundok** 'Pedro drew near to the mountain.'

4. Beneficiary or instrument of action is in focus: the affixes are *i-*, *ipag-*, depending on whether active form of the verb has *-um-* or *mag-* (see 1 above). *I-* is correlated with *-um-*, *ipag-* with *mag-*. The structure is *i-/ipag-* verb + agent in *ni/ng* case + beneficiary in *si/ang* case + object in *ang* case: e.g. **ibinibili ko si Pedro ng aklat** 'I buy a book for Pedro.'

These examples may serve to illustrate the basic structure of the Tagalog verbal system. The following four Tagalog sentences can all be translated by the same English sentence; but the four different 'focusings' require four different verb forms in Tagalog, with related changes in the markers:

1. Bumibili *si Pedro* **ng** aklat sa lunsod para kay Fidel.
2. Binibili **ni** Pedro *ang aklat* sa lunsod para kay Fidel.
3. Binibilhan **ni** Pedro **ng** aklat *ang lunsod* para kay Fidel.
4. Ibinibili **ni** Pedro **ng** aklat **sa** lunsod *si Fidel*.

In each sentence the focused component is italicized. The general English translation is 'Pedro is buying a book in town for Fidel.'

There are, of course, many other affix patterns which generate other verbal senses: cf. *matúlog* 'to sleep'; *mátulog* 'to drop off unintentionally'; *makatulog* 'to be able to sleep'; perfective *nakatúlog*.

NEGATION

The general negating particle is *hindî*: e.g. *hindî magandá si Linda* or *si Linda ay hindî magandá* 'L. is not pretty'; *hindî siya magandá* 'she is not pretty'. The prohibiting particle is *huwág*: e.g. *huwág mong insulat* 'don't write' (*mong* 'by you').

RELATIVE CLAUSES

Introduced by the ligature *na/ng*: e.g. *si Pedro ang lalaking bumabasa/bumasa/babasa* 'P is the man who is reading/was reading/is going to read'.

Prepositions

sa is virtually an all-purpose preposition in Tagalog, either by itself or as extended by modifiers: e.g. *sa mesa* 'on the table', *sa lunsod* 'in town', *sa Maynilà* 'in, to, from Manilla'. *Sa gitna* 'between', *sa loob* 'inside', *sa labas* 'outside'.

Word order

There is a broad division into predicate-initial and non-predicate-initial sentences. Examples of both will be found in the foregoing.

1 Nang una'y siya'y Verbo na, at ang Verbo ay sumasa Dios, at ang Verbo ay Dios.

2 Ito sa pagpapasimulâ ay sumasa Dios.

3 Ang lahat nang manĝa bagay ay guina â niya; at alin man sa lahát nĝ manĝa guinauà ay hindi guinauà cung hindi siya'y cainalam.

4 Sa caniya naroroon ang buhay, at ang buhay ay siyang ilao nang manĝa táuo

5 At lumiliuanag ang ilao sa manĝa cadiliman; datapua't hindi napag-unauà ang ilao nang cadiliman.

6 Nagcaroon nang isáng táuo na sinugò nang Dios, at pinanĝanĝalanang Juan.

7 Ito'y naparitong sacsí upáng patotohanan ang ilao, at nang dahil sa caniya'y sumampalataya ang lahát.

8 Hindi siya ang ilao; cung di upang magpatotoo sa ilao.

TAHITIAN

INTRODUCTION

A member of the East Polynesian branch of Austronesian, Tahitian is spoken in the Society Islands and the Tuamotu Archipelago by about 60,000 people. It has also replaced the Rapanui language on Easter Island.

Tahitian has a rich oral traditional literature. A series of splendid hymns and chants recounting the myths of the creation, the strife and reconciliation between heaven and earth, the birth of Tane the man-god, the creation of man, and the deluge are preserved in T. Henry's *Ancient Tahiti* (1928).

SCRIPT

The Roman alphabet is used. The following letters, which figure in foreign loanwords, are all pronounced as /t/: *c*, *d*, *g*, *k*, *s*, *x*, *z*. *l* is pronounced as /r/, *j* as /i/, *b* as /p/.

PHONOLOGY

Consonants

There are eight consonants + glottal stop: /p, m; v, f; t, n, r; h; ʔ/.

Vowels

    i, e, a, o, u

Initial vowel may or may not have glottal onset, and the difference may be phonemic: cf. *'āu* 'to swim', *āu* 'good' (as isolates). One authority – M. Durand (1951) – detects four tones with phonemic significance in Tahitian. The Tahitian syllable can be V, VV, or CV.

Stress

On the first long vowel in the word, or on the first vowel of a diphthong; if neither a long vowel nor a diphthong is present, stress moves to penultimate syllable.

MORPHOLOGY AND SYNTAX

For a general note on the structure of Polynesian languages, *see* **Polynesian Languages**.

Noun

Gender is not marked and there is no change for plural number; plurality is indicated by the article (see below). The attributive adjective follows the noun. Some adjectives have reduplicated forms for dual and plural: e.g. *poto* 'short'; dual *popoto*; pl. *potopoto*.

The prepositive nominal particles include: (a) articles and plural markers; (b) demonstratives; (c) possessive markers; (d) syntactic markers, prepositions.

ARTICLES

> *te*: this is the definite article for singular nouns, e.g. *te fare* 'the house', *te ta'ata* 'the man';
>
> *te mau*: the plural definite article, e.g. *te mau fare* 'the houses';
>
> *te hō'e*: indefinite or restricted singular article, e.g. *te hō'e fare* 'a house';
>
> *te hō'e mau*: plural indefinite article, e.g. *te hō'e mau ta'ata* 'some men';
>
> *'o*: definite article for proper nouns, e.g. *'o Tahiti* 'Tahiti';
>
> *'e*: indefinite article, singular, *'e mau* plural indefinite: e.g. *'e fare* 'a house' – *'e mau fare* 'houses';
>
> *na*: dual article, e.g. *na mata* 'the eyes', *na rima* 'the hands';
>
> *nau*: proximate definite article, e.g. *nau fare* 'the houses here';
>
> *tau na*: distal and indefinite marker, e.g. *tau na feti'a* 'the stars';
>
> *'i*: marks direct object (not pronominal) after transitive verb. The form for proper nouns is *'ia*, e.g. *here 'ia Tahiti* 'to love Tahiti', *'ua tāpū vau 'i te vahie* 'I cut the wood' (*'ua* is past tense marker; *vau* 'I'; *tāpū* 'to cut'; *vahie* 'wood');
>
> *'ō, tō, nō/'ā, tā, nā*: these mark possession, the *o* series for inalienable, the *a* series for alienable possession (*see* **Polynesian Languages**);
>
> *'e*: animate agent marker; the inanimate equivalent is *'i*, e.g. *'e te ma'o* 'by the shark', *'i te tipi* 'with the knife';
>
> *'i* also figures as a prepositional particle linking action directionally or locationally to target, e.g. *hopu 'i te miti* 'to bathe in the sea', *haere 'i te tinema* 'to go to the cinema';
>
> *tei*: locative marker, e.g. *tei Pape'ete 'oia 'inanahi* 'he was in Papeete yesterday'.

Pronoun

DEMONSTRATIVE PRONOUN

Three degrees of deixis: *teie – tēna – tēra*: e.g. *teie fare* 'this house (near me)'; *tēna fare* 'that house (near you)'; *tēra fare* 'that house (near neither of us)'. These take a plural form in *mau*: e.g. *tēna mau ta'ata* 'those men'.

PERSONAL PRONOUN

	Singular	Dual		Plural
1	au, vau	tāua	incl.	tātou
		māua	excl.	mātou
2	'oe	'ōrua		'outou
3	'oia, 'ona	rāua		rātou

INTERROGATIVE PRONOUN

'o vai + noun/pronoun 'who?'; *'e aha* 'what?': e.g. *'o vai 'oia* 'Who is he?'

RELATIVE PRONOUN

Construction here depends on tense; *tei* and *ra* are past markers, *te* and *nei* indicate present or future action: cf. *te vahine 'e parau nei* 'the woman who is speaking'; *te vahine 'e parau ra* 'the woman who was speaking'; *'o vau te 'āu nei* 'it is I who am swimming'; *'o vau tei 'āu* 'it is I who swam'.

Numerals

1–10: *hō'e/tahi*; *piti, toru, maha, pae, ōno, hitu, va'u, iva, hō'e 'ahuru*; 11 *hō'e 'ahuru ma hō'e*; 12 ... *ma piti* ...; 20 *piti 'ahuru*; 30 *toru 'ahuru*; 100 *hō'e hanere*.

Verb

There are three basic groups: (a) transitives; (b) statives: these are incompatible with an object, and cannot take a passive form (they express location, motion, physical state, perception, natural manifestations); (c) qualitatives (adjectives): these can combine with nominal and verbal particles. Group (a) has active and passive forms, the latter marked by suffixes *-hia/-a*: e.g. *papai* 'to write' – *papaihia* 'to be written'; *'ua fa'atae hia mai te mau pua'atoro 'i Tahiti* 'cattle are imported into T.' (*fa'atae* 'to import': *see* Causatives, below; *mai* is a particle denoting movement towards speaker). Some verbs are root passives and do not require marking with *-hia*.

Causatives of (a) class verbs are formed by means of prefixes *fa'a, ha'a, ta*. The same prefixes may be used with nominals: cf. *tupu* 'to grow' – *fa'atupu* 'to rear'; *'ahu* 'clothes' – *fa'a'ahu* 'to clothe someone'. As transitives, these verbs are compatible with a direct object introduced by the particles (prepositive nominal) *'i* or *'ia*.

Distinctions of tense and/or aspect are generated with the help of pre- and postpositive particles. In the following, R = verbal root:

   imperfective aspect with reference to present: model is *te* + R + *nei* + subject, e.g. *te 'amu nei 'oe 'i te hō'e vi* 'you are eating a mango' (*'amu* 'to eat');

   imperfective aspect with reference to past: *te* + R + *ra* + subject, e.g. *te 'amu ra tāua 'i te mau vi* 'the two of us were eating mangoes';

   future reference: *'e* + R + subject, e.g. *'e haere au 'i te 'oire* 'I shall go to town';

perfective aspect: *'ua* + R + subject, e.g. *'ua pohe te tavana 'inanahi* 'the chief died yesterday';

perfective aspect, single completed action in past; *'i* + R + *na* + subject, e.g. *'i tupa'i na te ta'ata 'i te hō'e ma'o* 'the man killed a shark';

conditional: *ia* + R; intentional, e.g. *nō te* + R (+ *ra'a*).

NEGATIVE

There are five negative particles coded for tense; they precede the verb. *'aita* and *'aore* negate present or past tense; *'e'ita* and *'e'ore* negate the future. *'e'ere* is used for 'there/it is not'.

The directional markers *mai* (towards the speaker) and *ātu* (away from the speaker) are syntactically important. In addition, there are lengthy inventories of locational and benefactive markers.

Word order

VS (intransitive); VSO (transitive).

1 I vai na te Logo i te mata mua ra, i te Atua ra hoi te Logo, e o te Atua hoi te Logo.

2 I te Atua ra hoi oia i te mata mua ra.

3 Na'na i hamani te mau mea tea nei, aore roa e, e ere oia i te hoe mea i hamanihia.

4 Tei roto ia'na te ora, e taua ora ra to te taata ïa maramarama.

5 I anaana mai na te maramarama i te pouri, aita ra te pouri e farii adu.

6 I tonohia mai te hoe taata mai o mai i te Atua ra, o Ioane te ioa.

7 I haere mai taua taata ra ei ite, e faa ite i taua maramarama ra, ia faaroo te taata toa ia'na.

8 E ere ra oia iho i taua maramarama ra, i haere mai râ e faa ite i taua maramarama ra.

TAI LANGUAGES

Previously treated as forming part of the Sino-Tibetan family, the Tai languages are now regarded as typologically analogous but not necessarily genetically related to that family. The principal members of the Tai group are Thai and Lao (*see* **Thai**, **Lao**). Several Tai languages are spoken in southern China by about 20 million people. These are:

1. Juang (see separate article).
2. Buyi and Dai; spoken in Guizhou and Yunnan. The Buyi are linguistically close to Juang. There are about 1 million Dai in western Yunnan. Their language is close to Thai and is indeed written in a variant of that script.
3. Kam-Sui. Both Kam and Sui are phonologically notable: the former (spoken by c. 1½ million people in the Guizhou–Hunan border region) may hold the world record for tonal distinctions, as many as 15 in some dialects; and the latter has an exceptionally large consonantal inventory for a Tai language, including pre-nasalized and pre-glottalized stops and a nasal *h*. The Sui have a rudimentary form of script which includes Chinese characters in mirror-image i.e. reversed.
4. Mulam and Maonan; spoken in Guangxi.
5. Li. This is an umbrella term for the complex of Tai languages spoken in Hainan. Phonologically and particularly lexically they diverge from their congeners in mainland China and South-East Asia.

TALAING

See **Mon**.

TALYSH

INTRODUCTION

Talysh belongs to the North-Western group of Iranian languages. It is spoken by about 100,000 people in the south of the Azerbaydzhan Soviet Socialist Republic, and by about 60,000 in Gilyan province of sub-Caspian Iran. In the AzSSR all Talysh are bilingual in Azerbaydzhani and Talysh. Abortive attempts were made in the 1930s to provide the language with a script, but it is now unwritten.

PHONOLOGY

As Tadzhik + /k', g'/. The vocalic system shows an opposition between full (stable) and reduced (unstable) vowels, in place of the Classical Iranian opposition between long and short.

MORPHOLOGY AND SYNTAX

Noun

Nouns have direct (Ø marker) or oblique form: -(*n*)*i*. An optional plural marker is -*on*: e.g. *ka* 'house', pl. *kaon*. Possession is expressed usually by simple apposition: e.g. *dada ka* 'father's house'.

Adjective

The attributive adjective precedes the noun and takes the ending -*a*: e.g. *sǝa sef* 'red apple'; *xosa kina* 'nice girl'.

Pronoun

The personal pronouns have full direct and oblique forms plus enclitics:

	Singular			Plural		
	Direct	Oblique	Enclitic	Direct	Oblique	Enclitic
1	åz	mǝ (ni)	-ǝm	ama	amani	-ǝmon
2	tǝ	tǝ (ni)	-ǝ	šǝma	šǝmani	-on
3	aw	ay, avi	-ǝš	avon	avoni	-ǝšon

The oblique forms and the enclitics are used as subject forms in the ergative past-tense construction, which is a feature of Talysh.

Verb

The dual base system of past/present roots, characteristic of the Iranian languages, has been partially lost in Talysh. Thus, while root *kårde-* 'do' has two bases, past *kård-/kå-*, and present *ka-*, *månde* 'to stay', and *vote* 'to speak', for example, have only one: *månd-*, *vot-*.

The personal endings are: sing. *-m*, *-š*, *-Ø*; pl *-mon*, *-on*, *-n*.

Talysh conjugation shows a considerable number of simple and compound forms. In the past tense, intransitives show concord with the subject in the direct case. Transitives have their subject in the oblique case; the object is in the direct case and the predicate is the invariable past base, i.e. third person singular in *-e/-be*: e.g. *ay əm žen vində.š.e* 'he saw this woman' (*ay* is oblique case of *aw*); *Müallimi šagərt voyanda.š.e ba ka* 'The teacher sent the pupil home.'

NEGATION
The marker is *p(ə)-*: e.g. *av.əm gatá* 'I caught him' – *av.əm pə́gata* 'I didn't catch him'.

Syntactic relations are expressed with the help of a large number of prepositions and postpositions, often in combination.

TAMIL

INTRODUCTION

This South Dravidian language is spoken by about 50 million people in Tamilnadu, where it has had official language status since 1956. There are also up to 3 million speakers in Sri Lanka, and at least another million scattered through South-East Asia, Indonesia, Polynesia (Fiji), South Africa, and Guyana. Tamil has a long history, with an epigraphical record dating from more than 2,000 years ago. Ancient Tamil literature dates from about the same period, the main monuments being (a) the *Tolkāppiyam*, a grammar of the language and also a socio-linguistic document of great interest and importance; (b) the *Tirukkuṛal*, the 'Tamil Veda', a kind of handbook of secular wisdom by the fifth-century poet Tiruvaḷḷuvar; and (c) two vast collections of short poems, the *Pattupāṭṭu* ('Ten Songs') and the *Eṭṭuttokai* ('The Eight Anthologies'), which provide a psychologically detailed mapping of human life in terms of its key twin facets: love and war. Many of the war poems are quasi-historical and take up themes concerning wise governance, in the manner of the Sanskrit classics; the love poems are set in five existential 'landscapes', each with its specific tensions and solutions. With such a classical past, Tamil is not surprisingly one of the leading literary languages in the sub-continent today.

The word 'Tamil' covers a highly complex set of socio-linguistic levels and relationships. In the first place, there is a basic distinction between literary Tamil and spoken Tamil. The literary language can be further sub-divided into (a) Classical Tamil and (b) modern standard literary Tamil of press, radio, and literature. Spoken Tamil itself exists in half a dozen main dialects (the Sri Lankan form is the most archaic) with an East-Central form emerging as a spoken standard. Finally, on the socio-linguistic plane there is an opposition between a Brahmin high register with its own specific lexicon, and various lower-caste registers. There are signs that spoken Standard Tamil is becoming increasingly acceptable within the framework of the modern literary standard.

SCRIPT

The Tamil syllabary derives via Granth forms from the Brahmi script. The grid consists of 18 consonants × 12 vowels (including two diphthongs). Five Grantha letters are used for Sanskrit words, and there is a sign for the *visarga*. As in Devanagari, short *a* is inherent in the base form of the consonant.

PHONOLOGY

Consonants

The core of the Tamil consonantal inventory consists of the following eighteen phonemes:

stops: p, ṭ, t̪, k
affricate: tʃ
fricatives: j, v, z̦
nasals: m, n, ṇ, ɳ, ɲ, ŋ
lateral and flap: l, ḷ, r, ɽ

The phonemic distinction between dental /t/, alveolar /t̲/ and retroflex /ṭ/ is explicit in the script, with a different letter for each. Similarly, the five *n* sounds are each specifically graphed.

Positionally determined allophones, however, share one and the same graph with the core consonant on which they are based: cf.

Core phoneme	Allophone sharing graph
k	g, x
tʃ	dʒ, s, ç
ṭ	ḍ, ɽ
t	d, ð
t̲	ḏ, ɾ
p	b, ß

Thus, /tʃ, dʒ, s, ç/ are all notated as ச. The /tʃ/ value is found in medial position, in association with /ṭ/ or /t̲/; /dʒ/ is found medially following /ɲ/; /s/ is initial or intervocalic; /ç/ – which often approaches /ʃ/ – is found in loan-words.

Similarly, /t̲, ḏ, ɾ/ are all notated as ற. Colloquial pronunciation of /t̲/ as /t̲r/, that is, as a fusion of two allophones, has spread to the literary language: e.g. *kut̲t̲am* 'fault, blame' is pronounced as /kut̲t̲ram/ or /kuttram/.

In this article, the alveolar phonemes are marked by subscript macron; the retroflex phonemes by subscript dot: t̲/ṭ.

Vowels

Short and long values are distinguished in the script:

short: ɪ, ɛ, ʌ, ɔ, u
long: i, e, a, o, u

There are two diphthongs, both notated in the script: /ai/ and /au/.
Vowels are nasalized before a final nasal consonant, which is then not released: e.g. *pustakam* /puttaxã/ 'book'; *vantom* /vəŋdõ/, 'we came'.

Sandhi is of crucial importance in Tamil pronunciation, and may or may not be notated in the script. The insertion of a homogeneous linking element at junctures is particularly frequent.

Stress

Stress is weak and may fall on any syllable.

MORPHOLOGY AND SYNTAX

Noun

There is no definite article. The numeral *oru* '1', may be used as an indefinite article. Use of the accusative case of a neuter noun identifies it as definite.

GENDER
Tamil divides nominals into two classes: rational/human as opposed to non-human (neuter). Within the rational class, a distinction is made between masculine and feminine.

NUMBER
Singular and plural. A typical plural marker added to singular, is *-kaḷ*; the stem-final may be modified: e.g. *āḷ* 'person' – *āṭkaḷ* 'persons'; *nāy* 'dog' – *nāykaḷ*; *pasu* 'cow' – *pasukkaḷ*. Further plural markers occurring in the literary language are: *-r, -ār, -mār, -ir*. A typical plural marker in the spoken language is *-nga*: e.g. *āḷu* 'man', pl. *āḷunga*.

The formant *-tt(u)-* marks the oblique base of neuter nouns in *-am*: e.g. *paṭam* 'picture', oblique case *paṭatt-*, acc. *paṭattai*.

There are eight cases. All are predictable, given the singular oblique base and the plural nominative. As specimen declension, *pāl* 'milk':

nominative	pāl
accusative	pālei
instrumental	pālāl
comitative	pālōṟu
dative	pālukku
locative	pālil
genitive	pālin/pāl.uṭaya

Similarly, for *maram* 'tree': e.g. *maram, marattei, marattāl*. In the plural, the same endings are added to the plural marker *-kaḷ*, etc.

GENITIVE RELATION
Possessor precedes possessed: e.g. *Rāviṉ makaṉiṉ makaṉ* 'Rao's son's son'.

Adjective

A few forms deriving from Old Tamil neuter plural nominal forms are used attributively in Modern Tamil, preceding the noun and invariable: e.g, Old Tamil *periya* 'large objects' – Mod. Tamil 'large'; Old Tamil *nalla* 'good objects' – Mod. Tamil 'good': *periya paiyan* 'big boy'; *nalla sankati* /sangaðı/, 'good news'.

Pronoun

PERSONAL

		Singular	Plural
1		nāṉ	nām (incl.), nāṅkaḷ (excl.)
2		nī	nīr, nīṅkaḷ
3	masc.	avaṉ	} avarkaḷ
	fem.	avaḷ	
	neut.	atu	

Pronouns in Tamil are nominals and are so declined. Thus for first person singular *nāṉ*: e.g. acc. *eṉṉai*, dat. *eṉakku*, gen. *eṉ/eṉṉiṉ*.

DEMONSTRATIVE PRONOUN
Three degrees of relative distance: *inta* 'this' – *anta* 'that' – *unta* 'that (yonder)'. These are invariable: e.g. *inta maram* 'this tree'.

INTERROGATIVE PRONOUN
Unlike the demonstrative series, the interrogative series is marked for number, gender, and case. Thus, *evaṉ* 'who?' = 'what man?'; *evaḷ* 'who?' = 'what woman?'; *evar(kaḷ)* 'who?' = 'which people?'; *etu* 'what?'. Addition of final *-ā* turns an affirmative statement into a question: e.g. *maturaikku.p.pōvīrkal* 'you will go to Madura' – *maturaikku.p.pōvīrkaḷā?* 'Will you go to Madura?'

RELATIVE PRONOUN
None. For relative constructions, *see* **Verb**, Participles, below.

Numerals

oṉru, iraṇṭu, mūṉru, nāṉku/nālu, aintu, āru, ēḻu, eṭṭu, oṉpatu, pattu; 11–19: *patiṉ/paṉṉ* + units, e.g. 15 *patiṉaintu*. 20 *irupatu*; 30 *muppatu*; 40 *nārpatu*; 100 *nūru*; 200 *irunūru*.

Verb

There are personal and impersonal forms. Personal forms are conjugated in three moods (indicative, imperative, and optative); the indicative mood has present, past, and future tenses. The affirmative paradigm has a negative counterpart, which has the same three moods but no tenses. Both affirmative and negative paradigms have an extensive array of participial forms and verbal nouns.

The citation form of a Tamil verb is in dental consonant + *al*: e.g. *seytal* /seyðal/. Most roots are mono- or disyllabic. Inflected forms are made from two bases: (a) root = first base; (b) root + -(k)k formant.

> present: *ir/-ind/-itp* etc. added to second base;
> past: *-t/-tt/-nt* added to first base;
> future: *-p/-pp/-v* added to either base.

Specimen conjugation (affirmative) of *seytal* 'to do, make':

> present: *sey.k.iṟ.ēṉ, -āy, -āṉ/-āḷ/-atu; sey.k.iṟ.ōm, īṟkal, -āṟkaḷ, sey.ki.ṉṟaṉa*;
> past: *sey.t.ēṉ, -āy, -āṉ/-āḷ/-atu; sey.t.ōm, -īrkaḷ, -ārkaḷ, -(aṉ)a*;
> future: *sey.v.ēṉ, -āy, -āṉ/-āḷ/seyyum; sey.v.ōm, -īrkaḷ, -ārkaḷ, -(aṉ)a.*

Similarly, from root *iru-* 'to be': first person singular present, *iru.kk.iṟ.ēṉ*; past *iru.nt.ēṉ*; future *iru.pp.ēṉ*. These are, of course, written forms, pronounced e.g. /irɪɡireːn/ ... /seyxirəðɪ/.

Second person singular (impolite) = root: *sey!* 'do!'. Plural forms are used for polite request: *seyuṅkaḷ* 'please do'.

The markers are *-ka* or *-aṭṭum* on either base: e.g. *seyyaṭṭum* 'may he do'.

Participle in *-a* (present or past) *-um/-untu* (future): e.g. *seykira, seyta, seyyum*. The gerund has a dental marker (*t, tt, nt*) + back vowel; i.e. the form is that associated with past tense, but the tense of the gerund is that of the main finite verb.

A cardinal rule of Tamil syntax is that only one finite verb can figure in a sentence; any other verbs occurring in the sentence must be in gerundial form.

The participles can be both active and passive depending on context: e.g. *pāṭam paṭitta paiyaṉ* 'the boy who read the lesson'; *paiyaṉ paṭitta pāṭam* 'the lesson read by the boy'.

The infinitive is in *-a*. This is used, e.g., with the word *vēṇṭum* to express obligation: *poka.veṇṭum* 'must go'; *koṭukka.veṇṭumā?* 'must give?' (interrogative *-ā*).

There are synthetic and analytic forms. The (older) synthetic form adds personal endings directly to stem. Thus from *sey-*: *sey.y.ēṉ, -āy, -āṉ/-āḷ/-ātu; sey.y.ōm, -īr, -ār/-ā*. These forms are neutral as to tense.

The analytic forms: here, the positive singular neuter participle is combined with *illai* 'not', to form a negative series which is neutral as to person, number, and gender, but which has the tense markers: e.g. *nāṉ/nī, avaṉ* etc. *seykiratillai/ seytatillai* 'I/you don't do/didn't do'. There are other analytic negative forms.

As there is no relative pronoun, relative sentences are transferred to the left-hand of the head-word; the verb form is the past, present, or future third person neuter, minus *-tu*: e.g. *pāṭam sollukira paiyaṉ* 'the boy who is saying his lesson';

anta.p.paiyaṉ paṭitta pāṭam 'the lesson which that boy studied'; *nāṉ eẓutum kaṭitam* 'the letter which I shall write'.

Third-person pronouns may be added to participial forms as follows: *paṭitta.avaṉ* 'he who has read'; *paṭikkir.avaṉ* 'he who is reading'; *paṭikkir.avaḷ* 'she who is reading'; *paṭipp.avarkaḷ* 'they who will have read'.

Postpositions

Postpositions proliferate in many variant forms. They are used with both nominal and verbal stems; nouns are in nominative, accusative, genitive, dative, locative case: e.g.

nominative: *itu **mutal** atu **varai** patiyuṅkaḷ* 'read from here to there';
genitive: *kīẓ* 'under' – *atan.kīẓ* 'under it'; *māṭu* 'towards' – *eṉ vittu.matē.vāruṅkaḷ* 'come to my house';
accusative: *paṟṟi* 'about, concerning' – *atai.p.paṟṟi ninaivu* 'recollections of this';
dative: *appuṟam* 'after' – *sāpāttukkappuṟam* 'after eating'.

Tamil makes much use of onomatopoetic words and echo-words.

Word formation

(a) compounds: e.g. *paṇputtokai* compounds (=Skt *karmadhāray*), where one component defines the other: e.g. *kalluppu* 'rock salt' (*kal* 'stone'; *uppu* 'salt'); *marappeṭṭi* 'wooden box' (*maram* 'wood'; *peṭṭi* 'box'); *maruttuccalai* 'chemist's shop' (*maruntu* 'medicine'; *-calai* = suffix denoting place, institution).
(b) Many suffixes are used to make nouns from other nouns, and nouns from verbs.
(c) Lengthening of root vowel is also used: e.g. *pōr* 'war' (*poru-* 'to make war').

Word order

SOV is normal.

1 ஆதியிலே வார்த்தை இருந்தது, அந்த வார்த்தை தேவனிடத்திலிருந் தது, அந்த வார்த்தை தேவனாயிருந் 2 தது.—அவர் ஆதியிலே தேவனோடிருந் 3 தார்.—சகலமும் அவர் மூலமாய் உண் டாயிற்று; உண்டானதொன்றும் அவ ராலேயல்லாமல் உண்டாகவில்லை.— 4 அவருக்குள் ஜீவன் இருந்தது, அந்த ஜீவன் மனுஷருக்கு ஒளியாயிருந் 5 தது.—அந்த ஒளி இருளிலே பிரகாசிக் கிறது; இருளானது அதைப் பற்றிக் கொள்ளவில்லை.

6 தேவனால் அனுப்பப்பட்ட ஒரு மனுஷன் இருந்தான், அவன் பேர் 7 யோவான்.—அவன் தன்னால் எல்லா ரும் விசுவாசிக்கும்படி அந்த ஒளியை க்குறித்துச் சாட்சிகொடுக்க சாட்சி 8 யாக வந்தான்.— அவன் அந்த ஒளி யல்ல, அந்த ஒளியைக்குறித்துச் சாட் சிகொடுக்க வந்தவனாயிருந்தான்.

TANGUT

INTRODUCTION

The Buddhist state, established by the Tangut people (of Tibetan stock) in 1038, lasted for 200 years until 1227, when it fell to the Mongols. Its territory corresponded closely to that of the modern Autonomous Area of Ningxia Hui, which adjoins Inner Mongolia in the Gansu province of the People's Republic of China. To the Chinese, the Tanguts were known as the Xīxià (*Hsi Hsia*, 'the Western Hsia'). Inscriptions in the Tangut language had been known in the mid-nineteenth century, but it was only in the early years of the twentieth century that excavation in the dead city of Khara Khot yielded a valuable collection of manuscripts, including a Tangut–Chinese digloss – the so-called 'Pearl' text – which has proved of great assistance in the reconstruction of Tangut phonology.

SCRIPT

Tangut was written in a pseudo-Chinese script of great complexity, specifically invented for the language at the behest of the Tangut emperor, Li Yuan-hao. As in Chinese, ideograms are built up from

(a) basic strokes such as

丶 丿 ⁊ ∟ ∠ ∣

(b) basic units consisting of several strokes, e.g.

𝌧 ∠ 开 𥄂 ⼑ 丷 𠂢

Theoretically, the meaning of a Tangut character derives from the integrated meanings of its several component units. In practice, however, there is no one-to-one correspondence between component and concept, nor is there an agreed inventory of component units; estimates of their number vary from 317 (the Japanese scholar T. Nisida) to 650 (the Russian researcher Y.I. Kyčanov).

In his grammar of Tangut, M.V. Sofronov (1968) gives several examples of composite characters as semantic constructs: e.g. the character

pronounced /kê/ which means 'rule': here, the left-hand component, is the central element of the negative marker *mi*, while the right-hand one,

is part of a character meaning 'to cross over, to transgress'. The integrated meaning, then, is '(what is) not to (be) transgress(ed)'. Certain component units appear to function as determinants.

In an interesting departure from the Chinese norm, Tangut has components which are purely phonetic, for use in place-names, etc.

PHONOLOGY

Consonants

From internal Tangut sources and from Chinese and Tibetan transcription of Tangut characters, it has proved possible to reconstruct a theoretical inventory of Tangut phonemes. Sofronov lists 31 consonantal phonemes, including the stops /p, t, k, ?/, with aspirates /ph, th, kh/; the affricates /ts, tʃ, ndz/, with positional allophones; the fricatives /v, s, ś, ź, x/; the nasals /m, n, ŋ/ plus /mb, nd/; /l, r, j, w/. The sole consonantal final appears to be /-n/.

Sofronov distinguishes different degrees of palatalization, marked by -i̯- and -i̯-. Both degree and incidence of palatalization seem to have varied diachronically in Tangut. Here, it is marked by -i̯-.

Vowels

i, ɪ, e, a, o, u, ə; several diphthongs end in [ɯ].

Tone

In the early eleventh century Tangut had two tones, even and rising, in two registers, high and low, depending on whether the initial was voiced or unvoiced. By the end of the twelfth century, two further tones had been added, a 'departing' (Chinese fourth tone) and an 'entering'. Tone is not marked here.

MORPHOLOGY AND SYNTAX

Most morphemes are monosyllabic, represented by single characters:

e.g. 㑊化 = *mi̯e* 'house'.

A character may have more than one reading, and, vice versa; a morpheme may be notated by more than one character.

Compounds: e.g. *mə ldi̯ə* 'heaven–earth' = 'world'; *via ma* 'father–mother' = 'parents'; *rai zə* 'much–little' = 'quantity'.

Formant suffixes: e.g. *ldeɯ* makes nouns from transitive verbs: *ngwi* 'to get dressed' – *ngwi ldeɯ* 'clothes'. *Twu* designates the object of verbal action: e.g. *vi̯e* 'to love' – *vi̯e twu* 'favourite'.

Nominals

Number inheres in the nominal, as in Chinese. Where enumeration is essential, a pluralizing marker

pronounced /ni/ is available for use with nouns denoting persons, and with pronouns.

Numerical classifiers follow the noun: e.g.

pai for long objects, especially weapons, e.g. *so.a ldi̯e pai* '30 arrows' (*so* '3', *a* '10'; *ldi̯e* 'arrow');
ngu for weapons;
kho for anything connected with human speech;
ndzu for buildings: e.g. *mi̯e.a ndzu* 'one monastery'.

CASE SYSTEM
Positional plus certain auxiliary particles: e.g.

genitive: possessor precedes, e.g. *nɪn mi̯e* 'prince's house';

dative: the marker is 矛帝 = *in*, e.g. *tha.in ngwe lə* 'to think of Buddha';

the accusative is unmarked: *mi̯e lɪn* 'to see a dream' (*lin* 'to see');

other case suffixes are: instrumental *ngu*; ablative *mbu*; locative *ndo*: e.g. *nɪn mi̯e.ndo ndźi̯e* 'to live in a princely house'.

Adjective

The adjective is treated as a verbal, and may take tense and aspect markers.

COMPARATIVE
Made with *źi*: e.g. *nga* 'fine', comp. *źi nga*; or by reduplication: *nga nga*.

Pronoun

PERSONAL
The usual first personal forms are

nga 𘟣 or *a* 𗹦

There are other very rare forms. *Nga* is typically used as subject, *a* in oblique cases. Similarly,

ni 𘓐 is the subjective second person pronoun,

na 㑲 the oblique form.

Both forms, subjective and oblique, of the third person are read as *tha*, with a tonal difference:

㲼 *tha²* is subjective, 㲼 *tha¹* oblique.

DEMONSTRATIVE PRONOUN/ADJECTIVE
thi 'this?'.

INTERROGATIVE PRONOUN
swi 'who?'; *xwa* 'what?'.

Numerals

1–10: *ḷịə, nịə, so, ldịe, ngwə, tśhịeu, śịwa, ịa, ngịə, a*; these are all first tone, except *a* '10', which is second.

Verb

The verb in Tangut is transitive or intransitive; some verbs are directional, e.g. *la* 'to come', *śịə* 'to go away', *o* 'to go into', *lho* 'to come out of': e.g. *we lho* 'to come out of the town' (*we*).

TENSE MARKERS

> present: *ndɪn* (suffix);
> past: *vịə, rịə, tha*, which are prefixes; e.g. *tha ndo rịə śịe* 'they approached the Buddha';
> future: *in* (suffix).

ASPECT
Perfective *ki*; inceptive *na*; semelfactive *a*. The hortative marker is *phi*: e.g. *śịə phi* 'ordered ... to go'.

MOOD
Five prefixes are available to express an optative mood, and prefixes are also used for the permissive (*rịa*), the hypothetical (*ma*), and the concessive (*ldịə*). The necessitative mood marker is the suffix *ldeu*.

NEGATION
mi negates any tense; *min* negates the past. These precede the verb.

Postposition

Several are available to indicate locus in, on surface of, underneath, in front of, behind, among, etc.

TASMANIAN

INTRODUCTION

Between the mid-eighteenth and mid-nineteenth centuries, several travellers, clergymen, missionaries, and administrative officers, visiting or working in Tasmania, made small collections of native words, noted down in the course of their contacts with the inhabitants of the island. Naturally, there was much variation in spelling. The most extensive source is that provided by J. Milligan: *Vocabulary of the Aboriginal Tribes of Tasmania*, forming Vol. III of the *Papers and Proceedings of the Royal Society of Van Diemen's Land*, published in Hobart in 1859. This collection covers three of the five Tasmanian languages that were still in existence at the time. Milligan's lists were subsequently used by other writers (Carr 1887; Ling Roth 1890–9). On the basis provided by these sources – often questionable, as the authors were not primarily linguists – J. Schmidt distinguishes five Tasmanian languages, which he classifies in two groups:

1. (a) North-East, (b) East Central, (c) South-East. These languages seem to share a common vocabulary, and to use the nominal particle *na*. (b) and (c) appear to be closer to each other than they are to (a).
2. The West Coast language and the North Coast language. Instead of *na*, these languages both use a form *leā* as a nominal marker.

PHONOLOGY of Group 1 (b) and (c):

Consonants

> stops: p/b, t/d, k/g; palatalized: p', t', k'/g'
> fricatives: w, x
> nasals: m, m', n, n', ŋ
> lateral and flap: l, l', r, r'

All affricates and most fricatives appear to be absent. It seems likely that a glottal stop or hamza-like sound was present.

Vowels

Five open, five closed, plus nasalized vowels like /ᴧ/ in both 1 (b) and 1 (c).

Stress

Stress seems to have been mainly on the penultimate syllable.

MORPHOLOGY AND SYNTAX

Noun

No grammatical gender; there is no evidence for a plural form. The nominal affix may mark the closure of a syntactic unit.

To *lowa.na* 'woman', in the Eastern group, corresponds *nowa.leā* in the Western group. Similarly, *rī.na* 'hand' = *ri.leā*; *tara.na* 'kangaroo' = *tara.leā*.

GENITIVE CONSTRUCTION
Possessor precedes possessed in apposition; the noun denoting the possessor drops the nominal affix: e.g. *wurrawaØ lowa.na* 'the wife of one who has died'.

Particles marking a change of direction: *to/ta*, and an adverbial marker for manner have been identified: e.g. *lunamea ta* 'to my house'; *lene.re* 'backwards'.

Adjective

Adjective follows noun; some end in *-ne*, e.g. *pāwine* 'small'; others in *-ak*, e.g. *mawbak* 'black', *tunak* 'cold'.

Pronoun

		North-East	East Central
singular	1	mi(na)	mī(na)
	2	ni(na)	nī(na)
	3	nara	nara

The possessive pronoun follows the noun: e.g. *loa.mi* 'my woman' (EC). The position of object pronouns in indicative sentence is unknown; sources give only imperatives: e.g. *tiena.mia.pe* 'give me!'.

DEMONSTRATIVE PRONOUN
wa/we 'this'; *ni/ne* 'that'. *Wa* seems to occur as a copula: e.g. *Riena narra wa* 'This is my hand.'

INTERROGATIVE PRONOUN
Not attested in sources.

Numerals

1: a form /marᵣa(wa)/ is attested; similarly, a form /p'a(wa)/ for 2. There are doubtful forms for 3, 4, 5.

Verb

In SE the following endings of doubtful meaning occur:

/gara/, /gera/: e.g. *nunu.g(e)ra* 'wash', *tia.garra* 'keep', *nu.gara* 'drink';
/gana/, /gena/: e.g. *lon.gana* 'sleep', *poen.ghana* 'laugh', *win.ganah* 'touch';
te, *ne*, *be*

In CE the negative particle *noia* is attested: e.g. *noia meahteang meena neeto linah* 'I won't give you any water' (not – give – I – to-you – water).

Postpositions

Examples: *le*, *li* 'behind'; *ra* 'without'.

Some examples of Tasmanian words

father EC *nanga*	mother NE *poa*	
sun EC *pögölina*	moon EC *wīta*	star EC *romtöna*
bird EC *pö ön'ena*		tree *wī(na)*
mountain EC *poime(na)*	river NE *waltomona*	stone EC *nani*

TAT

INTRODUCTION

Tat belongs to the South-Western group of Iranian languages. The Tats, totalling around 30,000, appear to be the descendants of garrison troops posted to the western extremities of the Sassanid Empire and stranded there by the Arab onslaught in the seventh century (cf. the Mongolian enclaves in China). Today, the Tats fall into two main groups: the Moslem Tats in northern Azerbaydzhan and the Apšeron peninsula, and the Jewish Tats in Dagestan and some parts of Azerbaydzhan. The latter dialect has had a Cyrillic script since 1938, and there is some literature. The Moslem dialect is heavily influenced by Azerbaydzhani, to which it is losing ground.

PHONOLOGY

To a Tadzhik-type inventory, Tat adds a glottal stop. There are five simple vowels: /i, æ, a, u, y/, the latter a reflex of historical /i, u/.

MORPHOLOGY AND SYNTAX

Noun

The plural marker is -ha/-a for general purposes; animates may take the -un marker (Persian -ān). Nouns have direct and oblique forms, the latter in -ræ (Persian -rā) used for definite object: e.g. *kitabharæ vægi* 'take these (specific) books'.

One way of making the genitive relationship is on the Turkic model: e.g. *pijæ ræ xunæ.y.i* 'father (oblique) his-house' = 'father's house', cf. Turkish *babanın evesi*. The Iranian model, *xune.i piyær*, may be used.

Pronoun

The basic personal forms are:

	Singular	Plural
1	mæn	(i)mi(n)
2	tÿ	(i)šmu(n)
		(i)šun

With oblique forms: *mænæ, tÿræ*, etc. The third person singular is *i, ÿ*, or *u*, depending on dialect. The base forms can be used as possessives: e.g. *kitab šmun* 'your book' (Persian, *kitāb.e.šomā*).

Numerals

Common Iranian, with *æ*, *ÿ* for *o, u*: e.g. *nÿh* for *nuh* '9'.

Verb

Few simple verbs are in use. Most verbs are compounds, consisting of a sense-verb stem + the Azerbaydzhani participial ending *-miş* + Tat auxiliary: e.g. *sæxtæn* 'to do', *biræn* 'to give': e.g. *ud.miş sæxtæn* 'to swallow' (Azer. *udmag* = Turkish *yutmak*).

The tense system is standard Iranian: imperative, aorist, and future from present base, past (simple and habitual) from past base. The personal endings are: sing. 1 *-ÿm/-um*, 2 *-i*, 3 *-ÿ/-u*; pl. 1 *-im*, 2 *-ind*, 3 *-ÿnd/-und*. Examples: aorist *báfum* 'I weave'; future *mibafúm*; simple past *báftum*; past habitual *mibáftum*.

NEGATION

næ- is prefixed to verb form: e.g. *næ.mibaftum* 'I wasn't weaving'. A passive is made with the particular in *-æ* + *biræn* 'to give'; a causative with the same participle + *sæxtæn* 'to do, make'.

TATAR

INTRODUCTION

The term *Tatar* has had several different connotations:

(a) Loosely (English, Tartar) it has served as an umbrella term for all Moslems of Turkic race and speech inhabiting the large area extending from the Ukraine and the Crimea, through the lower Volga region, into central Asia.
(b) More precisely, it was used to designate the successor states of the Golden Horde, the Khanates of Astrakhan and Kazan on the lower Volga, their peoples, and their language.
(c) It now refers specifically to the inhabitants of the Tatar Autonomous Soviet Socialist Republic, including their kin who live in adjacent ASSRs (Bashkir, Chuvash, and Mordva), and to their language.
(d) The term *Tatar* is retained in official Soviet terminology for certain other Turkic groups within the USSR, e.g. the Crimean Tatars (deported in 1944 to Central Asia) and the Baraba Tatars in Siberia.

The Tatar ASSR was established in 1920. In Baskakov's (1966) classification, the language is assigned to the Kipchak-Bulgar group of Western Turkic. With over 6 million speakers it is the sixth largest language in the USSR.

Culturally and intellectually, the Volga Tatars have always been among the most advanced of the Turkic minorities, and the literacy index has been correspondingly high. The first Tatar printing press was established in 1800, the University of Kazan in 1804. As a medium for literature and publicity, Tatar reached its apogee in the first quarter of the twentieth century.

SCRIPT

Originally Arabic; after experiments with romanization, Cyrillic was adopted in 1939. There are six additional letters: ə, ү, θ, җ. ң, h

PHONOLOGY

Consonants

    stops: p, b, t, d, k, g, q, ʔ
    affricates: tʃ, dʒ
    fricatives: f, s, z, ʃ, ʒ, x, ɣ, h
    nasals: m, n, ŋ
    lateral and flap: l, r
    semi-vowels: w, j

Hamza is written as ə; /w/ as *y*, *ɣ*, or *b*. Several Russian phonemes occur in Russian loan-words.

Vowels

Proto-Turkic /e, o, œ/, generally preserved in Modern Turkic, are raised in Tatar to /i, u, y/; similarly, Proto-Turkic /i, u, ɪ, y/ are lowered in Tatar to /e, o, ə, œ/. In comparison with Kazakh, for example:

Tatar	Kazakh
tel	til 'language, tongue'
min	men 'I'
kön	kün 'day'
kul	kol 'hand'
kük	kök 'sky'

front long: ə, ɛ, y, i
front short: y, i
back long: o, a, u, ɪi
back short: u, ɪ

In this article /y/ is notated as *ü*, /œ/ as *ö*.

VOWEL HARMONY
Palatal with progressive neutralization of rounding: cf. *küz.e.bez* 'our eyes'.

MORPHOLOGY AND SYNTAX

Formally, the declension system, the possessive affixes, the treatment of the adjective, the pronominal system, and the numerals are all standard Turkic (*see* **Turkic Languages**). The plural marker -*lar*/-*lər* has a variant -*nar*/-*nər*.

Verb

Voice and mood formation are standard. Examples of tense formation, indicative mood, of *bar-* 'to go':

	1st singular	1st plural
present	bar.am	bar.abɪz
past definite	bar.d.ɪm	bar.d.ɪk
past progressive	bar.gan.mɪn	bar.gan.bɪz
past frequentative	bar.a idem	bar.a idek
future definite	bar.ačak.mɪn	bar.ačak.bɪz

There are also forms for presumptive future, inferential past, future in the past, and a remote past frequentative.

The conditional marker is -*sa*-: e.g. *bar.sam* 'if I go'; the optative marker is -*ɪi*: in first person *bar.ɪi.m* 'I'd (like to) go'; the negative marker is -*mV*-.

PARTICIPLES

present in -*učɪ*² or -*a* + *torgan*: e.g. *yaz.učɪ bala* = *yaz.a torgan bala* 'the boy who is writing';
past: -*gan*⁴, e.g. *yaz.ɪl.gan kəgaz* 'the paper that has been written on';
future: -*ačak*⁴, -*ase*, etc., e.g. *kil.əse keše* 'the man who is coming/will come'.

INFINITIVE

The ending is -(V)*rgə*²: e.g. *əšlə.rgə* 'to work'; *kür.ergə* 'to see'.

Postpositions

Postpositions follow base, in genitive, dative, or ablative case.

```
1    Зач. 1. Сюз äÿялтенок булган, Сюз Алла-
2 да булган, Сюз Алла булган. Ул äÿялтенок
3 Аллада булган. Бар нястя дя Анын арткылы
  булган, ней гня булса да, Аннан башка ич
4 нястя булынмаган  Анда терелек булган, ул
5 терелек кешелярга жакты булган. Жакты ка-
  рангыда жактырыб тора, карангы аны каблаб
6 бетермей. Алладан жибярелган бер кеше бул-
7 ган, аның исме Iоаннъ. Ул таныклык итярга-
  гя килган, аның арткылы барысы да ышан-
  сыннар диб, ул Жактыны таныкларга килган.
8 Ул ÿзе жакты булмаган, тик Жактыны таныкларга жибярелган.
  ларга жибярелган.
```

(Kazan dialect)

TELUGU

INTRODUCTION

This South-East Dravidian language is the language of the Andhra people. Since 1966 it has been the official language of the state of Andhra Pradesh, which was formed from the Telugu-speaking districts of the former Presidency of Madras along with the nine Telangana regions of the Nizam's Dominions. In terms of numbers, Telugu is certainly the largest Dravidian language, being now spoken by about 55 million people, 8–10 per cent of whom live in neighbouring territories, such as Karnataka and Tamilnadu. There are four main dialects, in all of which there is a marked distinction between colloquial forms and the literary language. The latter is itself divided between the older and heavily Sanskritized literary model, and the emergent Modern Standard Telugu.

Literature in the classical literary language goes back to the eleventh century AD; its first great monument is the *Mahābhārata* translation by Nannaya (thirteenth/fourteenth century). This early literature is in a language which is more than half Sanskrit. A major part in the revival of Telugu literature after several centuries of stagnation was played by K. Wirēśaliṅgam, the first Telugu writer to develop a modern prose style. While New Indo-Aryan words still abound in Telugu, the purely Sanskrit element is being reduced, and the modern literary standard tends to converge with educated use of the Central colloquial.

SCRIPT

The Telugu syllabary is derived from a variant of the Asokan Inscription character. The Devanagari order is maintained, and there are many composite ligatures. Strangely, there is no graph for the past-tense characteristic /æː/ (transcribed below, in the section on verbs, as *E*).

PHONOLOGY

Consonants

    stops, p, b, t, d, ṭ, ḍ, k, g
    affricates: ts, dz, tʃ, dʒ
    fricatives: v/w, s, ś, ʃ, h
    nasals: m, n, ṇ, ɲ, ŋ
    laterals and flap: l, ḷ, r

All of the stops have aspirated forms, found only in Sanskrit loan-words. The latter pair of affricates have aspirated forms. /ś/ occurs in Sanskrit loans, as do the latter two nasals.

The retroflex /ɽ/ found in Tamil, is missing. [ts] and [tʃ] are positional variants of one graph, pronounced [ts] before a front vowel, [tʃ] before a back. Similarly, the graph *v* represents /ß/ before a front vowel, /w/ before a back. In the spoken standard, *t*/*d* are realized as [θ/ð].

Vowels

> short: ɪ, e, a, o, u
> long: i, e, æ, a, o, u

VOWEL HARMONY

This category is not typical of Dravidian; in Telugu it reduces to a choice between /u/ and /i/ in certain affixes, e.g. the dative case ending *ku*/*ki*, *nu*/*ni*: cf. *bidda.ku* 'to the boy'; *tammuni.ki* 'to the younger brother'.

SANDHI

Notably by insertion of glide sounds (/j, v/) at short vocalic junctures, or by fusion/elision.

MORPHOLOGY AND SYNTAX

Noun

There is no definite article. The numeral *oka* '1' may be used as an indefinite article.

GENDER

In the singular, the opposition is between masculine and non-masculine, the latter category including all nouns denoting females; in the plural, the dichotomy changes to rational versus non-rational, with females promoted to rational status. Grammatical gender is not formally marked, but is made explicit e.g. by concord of noun with verb in third person which is gender-coded, or by the use of a similarly coded demonstrative pronoun.

A typical masculine ending is -*ḍu*, with a feminine correlative in -*rālu*: e.g. *snēhituḍu* '(male) friend' – *snēhiturālu*.

NUMBER

-*lu* is added to the singular: e.g. *bidda* 'boy' – *biddalu*. There are many variants, cf. *illu* 'house' – *īṇḍlu* 'houses'.

DECLENSION

There are four cases: a specimen declension follows, for *tammu*- 'younger brother':

	Singular	*Plural*
nominative	tammu.ḍu	tammu.lu
genitive	tammu.ni/ḍi	tammu.la
dative	tammu.niki	tammu.laku
accusative	tammu.ni	tammu.lanu

For most Telugu nouns, the oblique base = genitive base = nominative (minus *-ḍu*). Many nouns, however, have widely varying oblique bases; cf. *illu* 'house', obl. base, *īnṭi*; *yēru* 'river' – *yēṭi*; *pannu* 'tooth' – *paṇṭi*.

Adjective

The few genuine adjectives are indeclinable and precede the noun. They are Dravidian root words, e.g. *manci* 'good', *cheḍḍa* 'bad', *tella* 'white': *manci pustakam* 'good book'; *pedda ceṭṭu* 'big tree'.

Pronoun

The personal pronouns are:

	Singular		*Plural*	
	Direct	*Oblique base*	*Direct*	*Oblique base*
1	nēnu	nā	mēmu/manamu	mā/mana
2	nīvu	nī	mīru	mī

In the plural first person, *mēmu* is exclusive, *manamu* inclusive, with oblique forms as shown. The third person forms exhibit gender and are graduated for social status. They are, in addition, marked for relative proximity, the *i-* series referring to persons close at hand, the *a-* series to those further away. Thus:

	Familiar	*Respectful*	*Honorific*
masculine	vīḍu/vāḍu	itanu/atanu	vīru/vāru
feminine	idi/adi	īme/āme	vīru/vāru

Plural forms for both genders: *vīṇḍlu/vāṇḍlu*, *vīḷḷu/vāḷḷu*, *vīru/vāru*.

DEMONSTRATIVE PRONOUN/ADJECTIVE
The bases are in *i-* for proximate, *a-* for distal: *idi* 'this', *adi* 'that'.

INTERROGATIVE PRONOUN
The base is *ē-*: *ēvaḍu* 'who?' (masc.); *ēvi* 'what?'.

RELATIVE PRONOUN
None; for relative constructions *see* **Verb**, below.

Numerals

1–10: *okaṭi, reṇḍu, mūḍu, nālugu, aidu, āru, ēḍu, enimidi, tommidi, padi.* 11 *padakoṇḍu*; 12 *panneṇḍu*; 13 *padamūḍu*; 20 *iruvai*; 30 *muppai*; 40 *nalabhai*; 100 *nūru*, or *vanda*.

Verb

As in other Dravidian languages, there are positive and negative conjugations. Verbal bases are usually disyllabic, and the (C)VCCV formula (i.e. with gemination of the intervocalic consonant) is very common. There are indicative and imperative moods, and a basic series of present, past, and future tenses with analytical secondary forms. The tense system distinguishes number and person (with exceptions, e.g. in negative past). Gender is marked in the third person. The non-finite forms underlie the finite.

Thus, from the root *cheppu-* 'to speak', are derived the infinitive *cheppa*, the verbal noun *cheppa.ḍamu*, the verbal participles, present *cheppatu*, past *cheppi* (with elision of the *-a*) and the conditional verbal participle in *-te*. In connected speech or written narrative, all verbs are in such participial forms apart from the finite verb which winds up the sentence.

The participles provide formants for relative clauses, present e.g. *cheppa.tuna*, past, *cheppina*, indefinite *cheppē*: e.g. *chepputunna* '(he, etc.) who is speaking'; *cheppina* '(he, etc.) who was speaking'. Such forms are neutral as to voice: cf. *ataḍu campina puli* 'the tiger (*puli*) killed by him', *atanni campina puli* 'the tiger that killed him', where the same past participial form does duty for both active and passive sense: cf. *nēnu tāgina niḷḷu* 'the water I drank'; *mīr rāsin(a) uttaram* 'the letter I wrote'.

PERSONAL FORMS

The personal endings are: sing. 1 *-nu*, pl. *-mu*; 2 *-vu*, pl. *-ru*. In the third person singular masculine *-ḍu* is contrasted with *-di* (feminine and neuter); the plural form *-ru* covers masculine and feminine, i.e. the rational category reappears, contrasting with *-vi* for the irrational category. These endings are added to stem + present marker *-utu-* + *unnā* to form the present tense: e.g. *chepp.ut.unnā.nu/vu/ḍu*.

Past tense: here, the modern standard literary and colloquial characteristic is /æ:/, which has no specific graph in the script; here transcribed as *E*: e.g. *cheppE.nu/vu/ḍu*. The third person singular feminine varies: e.g. *chepp.in.di*. Analytical forms with the auxiliary *uṇḍu* denote continuous present/past tenses.

Future: unlike Tamil, Telugu does not have a specific future characteristic. The present form in *-ut* is used, without *-unnā*: e.g. *chepp.utā.nu/vu/ḍu* 'I etc. shall speak'.

NEGATIVE CONJUGATION

Present: the personal markers are affixed to the infinitive, e.g. *cheppa.nu/vu/ḍu* 'I, etc. do not speak'; or, analytically, e.g. *cheppa.ḍamu lēnu/lēvu/lēdu* 'I am not one who speaks'.

Past: infinitive + *lēdu* for all persons and both numbers: e.g. *nēnu cheppa.lēdu*, *nīvu cheppa.lēdu*; i.e. the personal pronouns must be used here, as the verb form is invariable.

PASSIVE

Grammars give a passive form made with the auxiliary *paḍu* 'to feel, suffer, fall', etc., but this does not seem to be much used. More idiomatic is the use of the past participle plus the auxiliary *un* 'to be'.

IMPERATIVE MOOD

The second person positive markers are, sing. *-u*, pl. *-aṇḍi*. The prohibitive is made by pre-fixing the negative marker *-k-* to these endings: e.g. *pāḍaṇḍi* '(please) sing'; *weḷḷakaṇḍi* '(please) don't go'.

CAUSATIVE

The marker is *-inc-*, e.g. *tāgu* 'to drink' – *tāgincu* 'to give to drink'. This marker is also used to make transitive verbs from nouns: e.g. *prēma* 'love' (Sanskrit) – *prēmincu* 'to love'.

Various affixes are to generate potential, necessitative, etc. modal forms: e.g. with *-galanu*: *cheppa.galanu* 'I am able to speak'.

Postpositions

Postpositions are very numerous in Telugu; all follow the oblique stem. They are either simple, e.g. *tō* 'with', *valla* 'by means of', or compound, e.g. *lōnunci* 'from, out of'; *taravāta* 'after', *venaka* 'behind': e.g. *Mā iṇṭi venaka tōṭa unnadi* 'Behind our house is a garden.'

Word order

SOV; indirect object precedes direct: e.g. *nēnu ataniki ā sommu istānu* 'I'll give him the money.'

1 ఆదియందు వాక్యముండెను వాక్యము దేవుని

2 యొద్దనుండెను వాక్యము దేవుడైయుండెను। ఆయన
ఆదియందు దేవునియొద్ద నుండెను సమస్తమును ఆ

3 వాక్యము మూలముగా కలిగెను। కలిగియున్న దేది
యు ఆయనవలననే తప్ప మరి యెవరివలన కలుగ

4 లేదు। ఆయనలో జీవముండెను ఆ జీవము మనుష్య

5 లకు వెలుగైయుండెను। వెలుగు చీకటిలో ప్రకాశిం
చుచున్నది గాని చీకటి దాని గ్రహింపలేదు.

6 దేవుని యొద్దనుండి పంపబడిన యొక మనుష్యుడు

7 వచ్చెను ఆతని పేరు యోహాను। ఆతని మూలముగా
అందరు విశ్వసించునటుల ఆతడా వెలుగునుగూర్చి

8 సాక్ష్యము చెప్పుటకు సాక్షిగా వచ్చెను. ఆతడా
వెలుగై యుండలేదు గాని యా వెలుగునుగూర్చి

THAI

INTRODUCTION

Thai is the official language of Thailand and is spoken by about 40 million people. It is the most important member of the Tai family which also includes Lao, Shan, and Yuan. From the twelfth to the twentieth centuries the country was known as Siam, the language as Siamese. In 1939 the country was officially designated *mɪang thai*, the Thai Kingdom.

There are four main dialects, differing mainly in tonal and phonological respects. The literary language is based on the central dialect, which includes the Bangkok standard. Thai contains many Sanskrit and Pali words, imported mainly in the Ayutthaya period (fourteenth to eighteenth centuries).

The oldest work in Thai literature is the Buddhist cosmography known as the *Traiphūm* (Sanskrit *tribhuvana*), which dates from the fourteenth century. Both the Thai version of the *Rāmāyaṇa*, the *Rāmakrien*, and the national epic, the *Khun Chāng Khun Phāēn*, are ancient in substance, but both are known only in nineteenth-century recensions. A very important sector of Thai literature consists of the historical chronicles known as the *Phongsāwadān* and the *Prachum Phongsāwadān*, edited and analysed by the great Thai polymath Prince Rajanubhab Damrong. Mention should also be made of the *nirāt* literature, devoted to man as migrant and wanderer, a favourite genre of Thai poets in the seventeenth to nineteenth centuries. During the twentieth century the social novel has come to the fore.

SCRIPT

The Thai script, dating from the late thirteenth century, seems to have been borrowed in part from the Khmer version of a South Indian script. It has no ligatures. The short vowel ɔ is inherent in the base form of the consonant. Degree of redundancy is high, with five graphs for /kh/, six for /th/, three for /s/, etymologically explicable but no longer phonetically necessary. Consonants are sub-divided into low, middle, and high class.

The division into classes is partially phonological, in that the unaspirated consonants are grouped as middle, the aspirated consonants as high or low class. Thus /k/ has a middle-class graph, /kh/ a high-class. The spirant surds appear in both high and low classes: of four letters denoting /s/ three, sited as in Devanagari between the semi-vowels and *h*, are high class; the fourth, placed in Thai in the palatal series, is low. The Thai letters corresponding in locus to the retroflex series in Devanagari, are very rarely used.

PHONOLOGY

Consonants

> stops: b, p, ph, d, t, th, c, (g), k, kh, (ʔ)
> affricates: tʃ
> fricatives: f, s, h
> nasals: m, n, ŋ
> lateral and flap: l, r
> semi-vowels: j, w

/c/ (or /tɕ/) is a voiceless, unaspirated fortis stop, sometimes described as close to /t'/ and often transcribed as its allophone /dʒ/: e.g. the future marker จะ = /dʒə/. /tʃ/ is the aspirated correlative.

Permissible consonantal finals are the nasals and /p, t, k, r, l/. As finals, /p, t, k/ are pronounced as unreleased [t]; /r/ and /l/ as [n].

Vowels

> front: i, e, ɛ
> back rounded: u, o, ɔ
> back unrounded: ɪ, ə, a

All vowels occur long or short; length is phonemic.

Thai has fourteen diphthongs and three triphthongs; distinctions here are very subtle.

Tone

There are five tones, three level and two oblique: middle – low – falling – high (acute) – rising. Some authorities sub-divide the high tone into (a) plain high, and (b) constricted high.

Tone in a Thai word is determined by certain factors, and is therefore predictable. The following factors are relevant: e.g. for a typical Thai morpheme C_1VC_2:

1. class of C_1 consonant: low, middle, or high;
2. presence or absence of tone marker: there are two tone markers, *mai-ek*, *mai-to*;
3. vowel length;
4. nature of C_2 consonant: nasal (/m, n, ŋ/) or /p/t/k/; /r/l/;

Thus, for a C_1VC_2 morpheme, where C_1 is a low-class consonant, the following possibilities arise:

1. no tone marker, C_2 is not /k, t, p/: tone is even (middle);
2. V is short, C_2 is /k/, /t/, or /p/; mai-to may be present: tone is acute (high);
3. C_1 is preceded by a high-class /h/, and mai-ek is present: tone is low;
4. C_1 is preceded by high-class /h/: tone is rising;

5. C_1 is preceded by high-class /h/, and mai-to is present: tone is falling;
6. V is long, with C_2 = /k/, /p/ or /t/: tone is falling.

Analogous rules apply for middle- and high-class initials, and for CV and $C_1C_2VC_3$ morphemes. In the latter case, if C_1 and C_2 cannot be pronounced together, i.e. there is a shwa between them, the word is treated as disyllabic and subject to tone rules for each component.

MORPHOLOGY AND SYNTAX

Noun

The FSI Thai Reference Grammar (1964) points out that this, the largest class of Thai words, is also the most open, as lexical innovations are usually generated in the form of nominals. Thai nouns are monosyllabic: e.g. *nam* 'water'; *vua* 'buffalo; *ma* 'horse'; or polysyllabic:

(a) by prefixation, e.g. *khua:m-* 'condition of being ...' used to make abstracta: e.g. *khua:mpak* 'love'; *khua:mru* 'knowledge'; *khua:mdi:* 'goodness';
(b) by compounding: e.g. *nam.ta* 'water-eye' = 'tears'; *khon.khrua* 'person-kitchen' = 'cook'; *cha:ŋ.ma:j* 'artisan-wood' = 'carpenter'.

There is no declension of any kind. Genitive relationships are expressed either by apposition, or by use of the particle *khɔ:ŋ*: e.g. *na:n khɔ:ŋ khaw* 'his work'; *khɔ:ŋ khraj* 'whose?'.

PLURAL
Distinguished, if at all, by numeral or a particle such as *la:j* 'many': e.g. *ci:n la:j khon* 'many Chinese'.

CLASSIFIERS
Example: *khon* (for people), *tua* (animals), *lem* (books), *ton* (plants). The order is: noun – classifier – numeral: e.g. *ma: sɔ:ŋ tua* 'two dogs'; *phu:jiŋ sa:m khon* 'three women'.

Adjective

As attribute, adjective follows noun: e.g. *ba:n jaj* 'big house'. The classifier may serve to identify a non-overtly expressed referent: e.g. *tua jaj* 'the big one' (scil. animal).

COMPARATIVE
Made with *kwa:*: e.g. *di: kwa:* 'better'.

Pronoun

The pronominal system is socio-linguistically complex. Some generally accept-able forms are shown here:

first person singular: *phom* (masc.), *dichan* (fem.) (these are formal); pl. *raw*;

second person singular: *khun/than* (these are formal); *thə:* informal;

third person: *khaw*.

For the plural second and third persons the singular forms may be used. Kinship terms and titles are often preferable.

DEMONSTRATIVE PRONOUN/ADJECTIVE
ni: 'this', pl. *law.ni:*; *nan* 'that', pl. *law.nan*. These follow the noun: e.g. *nai ro:ŋ.rɪan nan* 'in that school'; *caag rɪan ni:* 'from this house'.

INTERROGATIVE PRONOUN
khraj 'who?'; *'araj* 'what?'.

RELATIVE PRONOUN
thi may be used: e.g. *Pha:sa: thi khon thai phu:t khy: pha:sa: thai* 'The language which Thai people speak is the Thai language' (*khy:* is the copula).

Numerals

1–10: *nɪŋ, sɔ:ŋ, sa:m, si:, ha:, hog, jed, pɛ:d, kaw, sib*; 11 *sib.et*; 12 *sib sɔ:ŋ*; 20 *ji: sib*; 30 *sa:m sib*; 100 *rɔ:j*.

Verb

Thai verbs are monosyllabic, e.g. *tham* 'do', *paj* 'go', *ru:* 'know'; or polysyllabic, e.g. with prefix *pra-*, which acts as a transitivizing formant, *gan* 'to ward off' – *pra.gan* 'to insure', *lun* 'to wake up' – *pra.lun* 'to waken someone'; or compounds, e.g. verb + noun *tham.ŋan* 'to work', noun + verb *kham.tham* 'to question', *kham.tɔ:b* 'to answer'. In certain compounds the second component has lost its primary meaning, and, when a real object is overtly expressed, this umbral object is discarded: e.g. *kin.khaw* 'eat rice' – *khaw kin.khaw* 'he eats' (in general); but, *khaw kin ponlamaj* 'he eats fruit'.

RESULTATIVES
Example: *lɛ:hen* 'to see and recognize' (*lɛ:* 'to look at'; *hen* 'to see'); *nɔ:n.lap* 'to go to sleep' (*nɔ:n* 'to lie down'; *lap* 'to fall asleep'). The negative *maj* is inserted between the components of such a compound: e.g. *phom nɔ:n.maj.lap* 'I can't get off to sleep'.

ASPECT AND TENSE

the simple present is expressed by the verb alone: e.g. *khaw hen* 'he sees'; *Raw paj Hua.hɪn boj.boj* 'We often go to Hua Hin.'
past tense: the marker is *daj*, e.g. *khaw daj paj* 'he went';
future: the marker is *ca'*, e.g. *Wan ni: raw ca' pai du lakhɔ:n* 'Today we'll go to the theatre';
progressive: *kamlaŋ ... ju*, e.g. *chan kamlaŋ kin ju* 'I am eating';

perfective: *lɛ:w*; also a conjunction meaning 'and then', e.g. *Khaw kin.khaw lɛ:w pai tham.ŋan* 'Having eaten, he goes off to work.'

MODAL VERBS

Examples: *khuan* 'should, ought to'; *tɔŋ* 'must'; *ja:g* 'want to'; e.g. *Khaw khuan ca' paj thamŋan* 'He will have to go and work.'

NEGATION

The general negative marker is *mai*: e.g. *chan paj maj daj* 'I cannot go' (*daj* 'to be able'). The negative command is made with *ya:* 'do not'.

Prepositions

Examples: *naj* 'in' – *naj na:* 'in the field'; *thi* 'in, at' – *thi ba:n* 'at home'; *ta:m* 'along' – *ta:m khlɔ:ŋ nii* 'along this canal'.

Word order

SVO.

TIBETAN

INTRODUCTION

Tibetan belongs to the Bodish branch of the Sino-Tibetan family of languages. The ethnonym is *bod.pa* (whence Bodish) pronounced as /pœpa/. Tibetan is spoken by about 4 million people: 1½ million in Tibet, where it has joint official status with Chinese, 1 million in Nepal and India, the remainder in south-west China.

The literary language dates from the seventh century AD, when Buddhism began to penetrate into Tibet. The enormous task of translating the Sanskrit/Pali canon into Tibetan began in the eighth century and was not completed until the fourteenth. The Tibetan canon comprises two main divisions: the *Kanjur* (in Tibetan, *bKa'.'gyur* 'word-change', the Buddha's own words in translation) and the *Tanjur* (*bsTan.'gyur* 'treatise-change', i.e. the translation of the commentaries). The Tanjur alone is in 225 volumes. Part of the translators' task was to provide a lexicon of calques on Sanskrit technical terms, in consistent and one-to-one correspondence with their originals. A measure of the accuracy with which this was accomplished is given by the fact that it is often possible to reconstruct with some certainty Sanskrit originals, which have been lost, from their Tibetan calques.

The old literary language was used for a large output of philosophical, philological, and historical works till the nineteenth/twentieth century. Worthy of particular mention is the great mystic and poet Milarepa (Mi.la.ras.pa; eleventh century). Since the late nineteenth century a new literary language, approximating more to the spoken language, has emerged.

SCRIPT

In the seventh century King Srong.brTSan.sGam.po commissioned a group of scholars to study Indian writing systems with a view to finding a script for Tibetan. Brahmi was chosen as a suitable model. In the Tibetan version, the phonological series are ordered as in Devanagari, but the voiced aspirate member is missing, e.g. in the velar series, *ka – kha – ga – nga* (minus *gha*). As in Devanagari, the short vowel *a* is inherent in the base consonant. The other vowels are marked by superscript and subscript signs.

PHONOLOGY

Consonants

> stops: b, p, t, d, ṭ, ḍ, k, g; palatalized: k', g'
> affricates: ts, dz, tʃ, dʒ
> fricatives: s, z, ʃ, ʒ, h
> nasals: m, mh, n, ɲ, ɲh, ŋ, ŋh
> laterals and flaps: l, lh, r, rh
> semi-vowels: j, w

Vowels

Short /a/ inheres in the base consonant; the other four basic vowels are (in Tibetan order) /i, u, e, o/. Depending on phonetic environment these are realized as: [i, e, ė, ɛ, ɔ, o, u, y/ʉ, œ/ə, ȯ]. [ė] and [ȯ] are tense, closed.

In the remainder of this article, the standard transcription of Tibetan is used. For reasons of space, only selected words are shown in phonetic transcription. Tone is not marked.

Tibetan spellings which have already occurred above, require some explanation. The basic point is that prefixed letters may precede the word-initial consonant: these prefixed letters are themselves silent, but may affect the sound of the word-initial: e.g. in *bsTan.'gyur*, *T* is the initial of the first component, which is pronounced /tėn/. In the classical literary language, the verb *sTon* /tœœn/ has a past root which is spelled *bsTan*, the form found in this compound, which is pronounced as a whole /ten.kuu/.

This retention of the traditional and etymological orthography means that the correspondence between sound and symbol is very weak. For example, *kra*, *khra*, *gra*, *phra*, *bra*, *sGra*, *bsGra* are all ways of writing the phoneme /ʈa/.

In Tibetan dictionaries, words are entered under word-initial consonant, i.e. ignoring the prefixed letters. Taking C = consonant, V = vowel sequence *i, u, e, o*, P = prefixed letter, the dictionary entry sequence is CV, C*y*V, C*r*V, PCV, PC*y/r*V, PPCV. Final consonants are ordered in sequence.

Tone

There are four tonal phonemes: mid (neutral), high, low, falling. These are not marked in the script, but can be deduced from the initial consonant or consonant cluster + vowel. High and low tones inhere in consonants: in a four-term series (velar, palatal, dental, etc.) the first two have high, the second two low tone: e.g. *kā – khā – ga̱ – nga̱*; *cā – chā – ja̱ – nya̱*.

The inherent tone of an initial can be changed by a prefixed, superscript, or subscript consonant: e.g. *g* prefixed to a low-tone initial raises it to high; thus *ma* is a low-tone consonant, but *dMar* /maa/, 'red', is high tone.

Final consonants introduce a further complication by affecting the tone, quality and length of the base vowel; e.g. *na* is low tone, but addition of *-d*, e.g. in *nad* /nɛɛ̀/ produces falling tone.

Tibetan is very rich in two-, three- and four-term compounds. In these, assimilation and vowel attraction cross junctures in a kind of vowel harmony which is, however, not consistent: e.g. /re/ + /tuun/ gives /rintuun/, 'wish, desire'.

MORPHOLOGY AND SYNTAX

Noun

The lexical repertory of Tibetan consists of a large number of monosyllabic morphemes which are either independent or dependent (bound). Many independent morphemes serve as words in their own right, e.g. *ri* 'mountain', *mi* 'human being', *rta* 'horse', *'bri* /ʈi/ 'to write'. Bound morphemes comprise morphological and syntactic formants.

GENDER
There is no grammatical gender; certain particles may mark natural gender, e.g. *po/mo*: *grogs* /ʈhɔɔ/ 'friend' – *grogs.po* 'male friend', *grogs.mo* 'female friend'; *rgyal.po* /kɛɛ.po/ 'king'; *rgyal.mo* 'queen'.

ARTICLE
The demonstrative *'di/de* may be used as a definite article: the numeral *gCig* (with variants depending on final letter of noun) as indefinite: e.g. *mi 'di* 'the man'; *mi chen-po 'di* 'the big man'; *sTag.gCig* 'a tiger'.

NUMBER
The plural markers are *tsho* or *rNams*; the noun itself is invariable: e.g. *dMag.mi* /mɑ́ɑ.mi/ 'soldier' – *dMag.mi.tsho* 'soldiers'.

SYNTACTIC RELATIONS
Four linking particles are of crucial importance, and each of these appears in four different allophones, depending on the final letter of the previous word. They are the genitive/relating particle *gyi*; the agentive particle *gyis*; the gerundial particle *de*; the connecting particle *zhing*: e.g. *bod.kyi rang.bCan.gyi las.'gul* = /pœœ.ki rang.tseen.qi lenqyy/ 'Tibet's independence movement'.

Locational and other markers follow the genitive particle: e.g. *LHa.sa.i byang.phyogs.la* 'in the northern part of Lhasa'.

AGENTIVE
In Tibetan, the agentive case marks the subject of all tenses of an active verb, i.e. for a transitive verb with an object the marker (C)*s*: *bzo.pa mang.pos sha nyo.gi.yod/nyos.pa.red/nyo.gi.red* 'Many (*mang.po*) workers (*bzo.pa*) are buying (*nyo*) meat (*sha*)/bought meat/will buy meat.' (For structure of verb, see below.) Also *khyed.rang.gis las.ka byas.pa.red* 'by-you the work was done' = 'you did the work'; *sTag.gis gYag bSad.pa.red* 'The tiger (*sTag*) killed yaks.'

Adjective

As attribute, adjective follows noun, precedes plural marker, and is invariable.

COMPARATIVE

Can be made by isolating the first syllable: e.g. *yag.po* 'good'; *yag.* 'better'.

Pronoun

PERSONAL

		Singular		Plural	
		Standard	Honorific	Standard	Honorific
1		nga	—	nga.tsho	—
2		khyod	khyed.rang	khyod.tsho	khyed.rang.tsho
3	masc.	kho	khong	kho.rang.tsho	khong.rang.tsho
	fem.	mo	khong	mo.rang.tsho	khong.rang.tsho

Possessive forms: e.g. *nga.i*, *khyed.rang.gi*.

DEMONSTRATIVE PRONOUN/ADJECTIVE
'di 'this', *de* 'that': e.g. *mi 'di.tsho* 'these men'.

INTERROGATIVE PRONOUN
su 'who?'; *ga.re* 'what?': e.g. *'di su.i deb red?* 'Whose is this book?'

Numerals

1–10: *gCig, gNyis, gSum, bZHi, lNGa, drug, bDun, brGyad, dGu, bCu*. These are pronounced: /tsig, nyii, sum, si, nga, thuu, tyyn, kεε, qu, tsu/. 11 *bCu.gCig;* 12 *bCu.gNyis*; 21–99: unit + ten + specific formant for each decade: e.g. 45 *bZhi.bCu.zhe.lNGa*. 100 *brGya* /ka/.

Verb

Tibetan classifies verbs as follows:

(a) Active verbs, mainly transitive verbs with an object; the subject is in the instrumental case; e.g. *khyed.rang.gis las.ka byas.pa.red* 'you did the work'.
(b) Verbs of perception and of movement; the subject is in the nominative: e.g. *nga mthong.gi.'dug* 'I see'; *nga. Bod.la phyin.pa.yin* 'I went to Tibet'.

Copula and existential verb: the copula has *yin* for first person and *red* for second/third: e.g. *kho dmag.mi red* 'he is a soldier'; *nga bzo.pa yin* 'I am a worker'. The existential verb has *yod.* for first person, *'dug* or *yod* for second/third: e.g. *Bod.la zhing.pa mang.po yod.pa.red* 'There are many farmers in Tibet.'
  In Classical Tibetan, classes (a) and (b) have four temporal/modal stems characterized by vowel and/or consonantal change: e.g. for *gCod.pa* 'to cut':

Present stem	Past stem	Future stem	Imperative
gCod	bCad	gCad	CHod

In Modern Tibetan, the tendency is for the past and present stems to oust the other two.

TENSE STRUCTURE

The general formula is: stem + particle + auxiliary: e.g. *nga 'gro.gi.yod* 'I go'; *khyed.rang 'gro,gi.'dug* 'you go'; *nga.tshos gYag.mang.po nyo.gi.yod* 'we are buying many yaks' (*nyo* = 'to buy'); *ngas khang.pa.gCig nyo.gi.yin* 'I'll buy a house'; *khong.tsho lHa khang.la 'dug* 'they are in the temple'.

The formula -.*la* + existential verb is also used to express 'to have something': e.g. *Nga.la khang.pa zhig yod* 'I have a house'; *Phrug.gu/ṭhuqu/tsho.la smyug.gu/ñuqu/mang.po yod* 'The children have lots of pens.'

NEGATION OF TENSE

The negative particle *ma/mi* is introduced into the auxiliary slot: e.g. *nga 'gro.gi.yod* 'I go' – *nga 'gro,gi.med* 'I don't go' (*ma* + *yod* → *med*); *kho za.gi.'dug* 'he eats' – *kho za.gi.mi.'dug* 'he doesn't eat'; *'di gYag red* 'this is a yak' – *'di gYag* (*yin.pa*) *ma.red* 'this isn't a yak'.

The past tense of verbs of perception and involuntary action is made with the auxiliary *byung* /tshung/ or *song* (the former for first, the latter for second/third person), and is negated by placing negative particle *ma* between stem and auxiliary: e.g. *nga khyed.rang.gi grogs.po* /ṭhɔɔ/ *mthong.ma.byung* 'I haven't seen your friend'.

RELATIVE CLAUSES

Normally precede their antecedent to which they are linked by the genitive particle

(cf. Chinese 的 *de*):

e.g. *Khos bris.pai phyag.bris* /tshəəṭii/ *ga.par.'dug?* 'Where is the letter he wrote?'; *khyed.rang.gis nyos.pai shing.tog* 'the fruit you bought'; *nga.tshos lHa.sa.la bTang.bai yi.ge* 'the letter(s) we sent to Lhasa'. Note that the stem in itself is neither active nor passive, but combines both: e.g. *bTang.pai dNGul* 'the money which was sent (given)'; *dNGul bTang.pai mi* 'the man who sent the money'. Note also the formant *mkhan* 'the one who performs the verbal action': e.g. *'dir las.ka byed.mkhan.(tsho)* 'the person(s) who is/are working here'.

Honorifics

Like several other oriental languages, Tibetan is a two-tier language. Everyday words are paralleled by honorific forms for use in communication with or in reference to more or less exalted personages, and also in polite conversation with equals or strangers: e.g. *'gro.ba* 'to go' – hon. *phebs.pa*; *za.ba* 'to eat' – hon. *bZhes.pa*; *mig* 'eye' – hon. *sPyan* /tsɛɛn/.

An honorific term often serves as a kind of radical for a series of further terms in the same semantic field. For example, the honorific for the 'mind' (the everyday word is *sems*) is *thugs* /thuù/. On this word as basis, compounds are constructed as, for example: *thugs.smon* /thuqmyyn/, 'prayer'; *thugs.mos*

/thuqmœœ/, 'aspirations'; *thugs.bSam* /thuusəm/, 'thinking'.

Lexicon

As mentioned above, Tibetan Buddhist literature contains a large number of specialist religious and philosophical terms which are calques on Sanskrit terms. As an example, we may take the Tibetan term *shes.rab.kyi.pha.rol.tu.phyin.pa* which renders the Skt word *prajñāpāramitā* 'reaching the further shore of knowledge' = 'attainment of complete insight' (*shes.rab* '(great) knowledge'; *pha.rol* 'the other side'; *phyin.pa* 'attain'; *kyi* is the genitive particle; *tu* is a terminative particle).

Compounds

Very many Tibetan words are compounds of various kinds:

(a) synonymic (a.b, where a = b), e.g. *sgra* 'sound' + *skad* 'sound': *sgra.skad* 'sound', /ta.qɛɛ/;
(b) a.b, where a modifies b, e.g. *gNam.gru* /nəm.ʈu/, 'sky boat' = 'aircraft';
(c) a.b, where a is opposite or complement of b, e.g. *che.chung* 'big–small' = 'size'; *po.mo* 'male–female' = 'sex';
(d) a.b, where b modifies a, e.g. *blo.mTHun* 'mind – being in harmony' = 'comrade'.

Word order

SOV is basic, where S is often in the agentive case. There are several examples above.

༄༅།། །།ཡོ་ཏན་ནན་གྱིས་ཡི་གེར་བཀོད་པའི་འཕྲིན་བཟང་ཞེས་བྱ་བ་བཞུགས་སོ།།

[1]།དཀོན་མཆོག་གི་ཁྲོམ་མ་མེད་པའི་བཀའ་ལ་ཤུམ་ཤི་ཀའི་ངང་ན་མི་ནུ་གྲུབ་པ་དང་། ཡོ་ཏན་ནན་ཁྲུས་
གསོལ་མཁན་གྱིས་དེ་ལ་དཔང་བྱས་པ་དང་། དེའི་རྐྱེན་གྱིས་ཉེ་གནས་སྟ་མ་རྣམས་བོང་གི་དྲུང་དུ་འོངས་
པའི་ལོ་རྒྱུ་སྐྱེ་དང་ངོ་འོ། [2]།ཁྲོམ་མར་བཀའ་ཡོད་ལེགས་པ་དང་། བཀའ་དེ་ནི་དཀོན་མཆོག་གི་ཀླུན་
ཕྱུར་བཞུགས་པ་དང་། བཀའ་དེ་ནི་དཀོན་མཆོག་ལགས་པ་ཡིན། [3]།དེ་ནི་ཁྲོམ་མར་དཀོན་མཆོག་གི
སྐྱུན་རྟུར་བཞུགས་སོ། [4]།བཀའ་དེས་ནི་ཀྱི་ཡོད་པ་ཐམས་ཅད་མཛད་པ་ཡིན་ནོ། དེ་མེད་པར་ཅི་ཡང་མ
བྱུང་བ་ཡིན། [5]།དེའི་ནང་ན་གསོན་པ་ཉིད་འདུག་སྟེ། གསོན་པ་ཉིད་དེ་ནི་མི་རྣམས་ཀྱི་འོད་ཡོད་པ་ཡིན།།
[6]ཡང་འོད་དེ་ནི་མུན་པའི་ནང་དུ་སྣང་བར་མཛད་ཀྱང་། མུན་པས་དེ་འཛིན་པར་མ་ནུས་སོ། །
[7]མི་དཀོན་མཆོག་གིས་མངགས་པ་ཞིག་བྱུང་སྟེ། དེའི་མིང་ཡོ་ཏན་ནན་ཞེས་བཏགས་སོ། [8]།མི་དེ་དཔང
པོར་སླེབ་ནེ། འོད་ལ་དཔང་བྱེད་པའི་རྐྱེན་གྱིས་མི་ཐམས་ཅད་དད་པར་འགྱུར་བའི་ཕྱིར་དུ་བྱུང་ངོ། །

TIGRE

INTRODUCTION

A member of the Ethiopic branch of Semito-Hamitic, Tigre derives from a close congener of Ge'ez (*see* **Ethiopic**), and has preserved typically Ethiopic, i.e. Semitic, traits to a greater extent than Amharic, for example. The language is spoken by the Northern Tigre people in northern Eritrea; the Southern Tigre speak Tigrinya (q.v.). The number of speakers is put at half a million. There is some literature in Tigre, mainly poetry and folk tales, descriptions of the customs of the Mansaʻ tribe (who speak the main Tigre dialect) and translations of the scriptures. Raz (1983) provides interesting examples of material in Tigre broadcast by Ethiopian Radio.

SCRIPT

The Ethiopic syllabary.

PHONOLOGY

Consonants

stops: b, t, d, k, g; ejectives: t', q'; ʔ
affricates: tʃ', s': these are ejectives; dʒ
fricatives: f, s, z, ʃ, ʒ, ħ, ʕ, h
nasals: m, n
lateral and flap: l, r
semi-vowels: j, w

/x/ occurs in loan-words from Arabic.

It will be seen that the Tigre inventory is close to that of Ethiopic and Tigrinya, but lacks the labio-velar series present in each of these (though $q°$ occurs: e.g. *qor* 'depth', plural *aqwar*.

In this article, the ejective consonants are marked with subscript dot: ṭ etc.

Vowels

 i, e, a, aː, u, o, ə; with allophones.

Stress

Stress is phrasal. Primary stress is periodic with indeterminate incidence of intervening syllables.

MORPHOLOGY AND SYNTAX

Noun

The definite article is *la*, which is prefixed to the noun and is invariable: e.g. *lawalat* 'the girl'. If an attributive adjective is present, it takes the article: e.g. *lagəndāb 'ənās* 'the old (*gəndāb*) man'; it is also prefixed to a noun with the possessive pronominal suffix.

GENDER
Nouns are masculine or feminine; *-t* is a feminine marker in animate nouns: e.g. *wad* 'son'; *gabay* 'road' (fem.); *fəlit* 'heifer'; *walat* 'daughter'.

NUMBER
The plural is formed (a) by suffixation, (b) by internal flection (the broken plural): e.g.

(a) *-āt, -ot, -otāt*, etc.: *dār* 'house', pl. *dārāt*; *'āmat* 'year', pl. *'āmotāt*;
(b) e.g. *kətāb* 'book', pl. *akətbat*; *sayəf* 'sword', pl. *'asayəf*.

Where relevant, a noun may have a collective form as well as a plural: e.g. *gabilat* 'a tribe' – collective *gabil*; pl. *gabāyəl*. The collective takes singular masculine concord, as do the plurals of inanimate nouns. Plurals of animate nouns take full concord of gender and number.

GENITIVE RELATIONSHIP
The construct is found, but the usual formula is with the particle *nāy*: e.g. *nāy Sidamo ra'as dəgge* 'the principal town of Sidamo'.

Adjective

As attribute, the adjective usually precedes the noun, but may follow. Where concord is observed, the adjective takes the feminine form and the broken plural: e.g. *ḥačir* 'short'; fem. *ḥaččār*; pl. *ḥačāyər*.

Pronoun

Personal pronouns with pronominal suffixes (nominal and verbal):

		Singular			Plural	
		Personal	Nominal suffix	Verbal suffix	Personal	Nominal and verbal suffix
1		'ana	-ye	-ni	həna	-na
2	masc.	'ənta	-ka	-ka	'əntum	-kum
	fem.	'ənti	-ki	-ki	'əntən	-kən
3	masc.	hətu	-u	-o	hətom	-om
	fem.	həta	-a	-a	hətan	-an

The suffixes have variants depending on final letter of noun/verbal form: e.g. a final dental is palatalized before *-ye*: e.g. *'ad* 'village' – *'aǰǰe* 'my village'. The nominal suffixes combine with prepositions: e.g. *ḥaqo* 'after' – *ḥaqohu* 'after him'; *'ət* 'in, to' – *'əčče* 'to me'.

DEMONSTRATIVE PRONOUN
'əlli 'this', with feminine and plural forms; 'that' is *l* + V + *hay*, fem. *l* + V + *ha*; with plural forms in *lVhom/lVhan*.

INTERROGATIVE PRONOUN
man 'who?'; *mi* 'what?'.

RELATIVE PRONOUN
la- is prefixed to the verb: e.g. *'ət gəblat 'ətyopya latətrakkab* 'which is found in southern Ethiopia'; *dəgge … latətbahal* 'a village which is called …'.

Numerals

1–10: *woro(t)* 'one' (masc.), *ḥatte* 'one' (fem.); 2 *kəl'ot* (masc.), *kəl'e* (fem.); *salas, 'arba', ḥaməs, səs, sabu', samān, sə', 'asər*. 20 *'əsra*, 30 *salāsa*; 100 *mə'ət*. Teens: *'asər* (invariable) + *wa* + unit.

Verb

Stems are bi-, tri- or quadriliteral; they may be simple, or modified e.g. by gemination of the second radical, by lengthening the vowel following the first radical, or by combining these two modifications.

Derived stems are made with prefixed formants: e.g. *tə-* forms the passive of the simple stem: *mazzana* 'to weigh' – *təmazzana* 'to be weighed'; *'a-* is causative: *baharara* 'to be afraid' – *'abharara* 'to frighten'; *'atta-* is transitive–causative: *bela* 'to say' – *'attabala* 'to put about a report'.

There are indicative, jussive, and imperative moods, perfective and imperfective aspects, providing a present–future and past-tense system. The future trends to be expressed analytically by means of the jussive preceded by the particle *'əgəl*, and followed by *tu*: e.g. *'əgəl 'nigis tu* 'we shall go'.

PERSONAL ENDINGS

Example: from *mazzana* 'to weigh':

		Singular	Plural
Perfective			
1		mazzanko	mazzanna
2	masc.	mazzanka	mazzankum
	fem.	mazzanki	mazzankən
3	masc.	mazzana	mazzanaw
	fem.	mazzanat	mazzanaya
Imperfective			
1		'əmazzən	'ənmazzan
2	masc.	təmazzən	təmazno
	fem.	təmazni	təmazna
3	masc.	ləmazzən	ləmazno
	fem.	təmazzən	ləmazna

Stems with laryngeals and weak stems with semi-vowels are subject to modification. Many verbs are irregular.

COPULA

The copula is the same as the independent personal pronouns, except in the third person, where the prefixed *hə-* is dropped, leaving *tu/ta/tom/tan*.

The existential verb is *halla* (present tense), *ala* (past); negated by *'i-*: e.g. *'i ala* 'there was not'. The verb in general is negated by *'i*: e.g. *ḥaza* 'he wished' – *'iḥaza* 'he didn't wish'.

Prepositions

These take the pronominal suffixes (see above).

Word order

Basically SOV.

፶፡ ቃል፡ እብ፡ መአምበት፡ 0ለ፥ ወለቃል፡ ጎ፡ ረቢ፡ 0ለ፥ ወለ
ቃል፡ ረቢ፡ ቱ። ፮፡ እሊ፡ እብ፡ መአምበት፡ ጎ፡ ረቢ፡ 0ለ። ፫፡ ክሉ፡
እቡ፡ ገአ፡ ወለገአ፡ ለቱ፡ እምበል፡ እቡ፡ ሴማ፥ ለገአ፡ አላቡ። ፬፡ ሐ
ዮት፡ እቱ፡ 0ለት፡ ወሐዮት፡ በርሀት፡ አዳም፡ 0ለት። ፭፡ ወበርሀት፡
እት፡ ጽልመት፡ ተበርሀ፡ ወለጽልመት፡ አ_ረክበታ።

፮፡ የሐንስ፡ ለልተበሀል፡ እናስ፡ እብ፡ ረቢ፡ እንዶ፡ ትለአኩ፡ ቀን
ጸ። ፯፡ ክሉ-ም፡ እቡ፡ እት፡ እምነት፡ እግል፡ ልብጹሕ፡ ሀቱ፡ ክምሰል፡
ሰመዕ፡ እብ፡ ለበርሀት፡ እግል፡ ልስመዕ፡ መጽአ። ፰፡ ሀቱ-ዲ፡ እብ፡
ለበርሀት፡ እግል፡ ልስመዕ፡ ትለአኩ፡ ደኢ_ከን፡ ሂሱ፡ በርሀት፡ ኢ_0ለ።

TIGRINYA

INTRODUCTION

Tigrinya belongs to the Ethiopic branch of the Semito-Hamitic family, Afro-Asiatic phylum. Spoken in Tigre Province and in Eritrea by about 3 million people, it forms a dialect continuum deriving from Ethiopic (Ge'ez) or from a closely related congener. In the early nineteenth century some poetry was written in Tigrinya, and missionary activity, both Catholic and Protestant, led to prose writing as well. The Asmara Press was particularly active in this respect. A Tigrinya version of *The Pilgrim's Progress* appeared in 1934.

SCRIPT

The Ethiopic syllabary is used.

PHONOLOGY

Tigrinya has virtually the same phonological structure as Ethiopic.

ɛ, u, i, a, e, ə, o

Consonants

stops: b, t, d, t' (ejective) k, g, q, ʔ
affricates: (tʃ, dʒ, tʃ': rare in Tigrinya)
fricatives: s, z, ṣ, ʃ, ʒ, ʕ, h, ḥ
nasals: m, n
lateral and flap: l, r
semi-vowels: j, w
labio-velars: k°, g°, q°

Tigrinya /ḥ/ represents Ethiopic /ḫ/ and /h/; ṣ is emphatic ejective.

Vowels

In terms of the traditional Ethiopic vowel orders: 1st order *ä*; 2nd order *u*; 3rd order *i*; 4th order *a*; 5th order *e*, *ẹ* = /ɛ/, /e/; 6th order *ə*; 7th order *o*.

Positional allophones: of 1st order: *å* (in contact with /w/); of 6th order: *ŭ* (in contact with /w/).

/ə/ is unrounded and may be long or overlong.

MORPHOLOGY AND SYNTAX

Masculine and feminine genders are distinguished; a typical feminine ending is *-t*. Gender concord extends to demonstrative/article, adjective, and verb.

The demonstrative pronoun series, *ətu, əta, ətom, ətän,* serves as definite articles: e.g. *ətu färäs* 'the horse', *əta lam* 'the cow'.

NUMBER

By suffixation: *-(t)āt,* or by internal flection (broken plural): e.g. *säb* 'man' – *säbāt; färäs* 'horse' – *äfräs; näbri* 'leopard' – *änābər.*

GENITIVE RELATION

The construct formula may be used – e.g. *mängəstä sə mayat* 'the kingdom of heaven' – but is felt to be archaic. More usual is the use of the particle *nay* preceding the possessor: e.g. *nay ḥawway kälbi = kälbi nay ḥawway* 'my brother's dog' (the *-y* ending here is 1st p. poss.).

DIRECT OBJECT

Position is normally sufficient to identify the object, but it can be specifically marked by the particle *nə*: e.g. *nə.ḥawwa.y ṣ̌awwʿä* 'he called my brother'. *Nə* also marks the indirect object: e.g. *nə.särawitu* 'to the soldiers'.

Adjective

As attribute, the adjective usually precedes the noun: e.g. *əta səbbəq.ti gʿal* 'the beautiful girl', but *ḥade säb habtam* 'a rich man'.

Pronoun

The independent personal pronouns with their enclitic correlatives are:

		Singular		Plural	
		Independent	Enclitic	Independent	Enclitic
1		ane	-(V)y	nəhna	-na
2	masc.	nəssəxa	-xa	nəssatkum	-kum/-x
	fem.	nəssəxi	-xi	nəssatkən	-kən/-xən
3	masc.	nəssu	-u	nəssatom	-om
	fem.	nəssa	-a	nəssatän	-än (etc.)

nəss- in these forms derives from the Ethiopic *nefs* 'spirit' (cf. Arabic *nafs*). Examples: *kälbəxa* 'thy (masc.) dog'; *kälbəxi* 'thy (fem.) dog'; *gäzana* 'our house'.

Closely similar to the enclitic possessives are the objective personal markers; the indirect object is marked by *-l-* preceding the direct-object set: e.g. *mäskiromu.l.ka* 'they bore witness on thy behalf'.

DEMONSTRATIVE PRONOUN AND ADJECTIVE

The proximate series has a *z-* characteristic, the distal series a *t-* characteristic:

proximate: əzuy, əziʿa; plural: əziʿom, əziʿen/än
distal: ətuy, ətiʿa; plural: ətiʿom, ətiʿen/än

The -y, -ʿa, -ʿom, -ʿen/än endings of the distal series are dropped to form the demonstrative adjective which functions as definite article: əta lam 'the cow'.

INTERROGATIVE PRONOUN
män 'who?'; pl. mänmän.

RELATIVE PRONOUN
zə with perfect or imperfect: negative form zäy: e.g. zə.säbärä 'he who has broken'; zäy.säbärä 'he who has not broken'. The first and second singular verbal prefixes of the imperfective drop after zə: e.g. *zə.əsäbbər → zəsäbbər 'I who break'; zəsäbärä säb 'the man who has broken'.

Numerals

ḥadę (fem. ḥantit), kələttę, sälästęs 'arbaʿtę, ḥammuštę, šudduštę, šob'attę, šommäntę, töšʿattę, ʿassärtę; 11 'assärtę ḥadä, 12 ʿassärtę kələttä; 20 ʿasra, 21 ʿəsran ḥadän; 30 salasa, 40 'arbaʿa, 50 ḥamsa; 100 mi'ti.

Verb

Triliterals which have a geminate second radical are distinguished from those which do not; a third class has long ā after the first radical.
Derived forms, e.g. from säbärä; passive täsäbärä; causative asbärä.

THE PAST TENSE ENDINGS
Sing. 1 säbär.ku, 2 masc. -ka, fem. -ki, 3 masc. -ä, fem. -ät; pl. 1 säbär.na, 2 masc. -kum, fem. -kən, 3 masc. -u, fem. -a. This tense is negated by the circumfix ay ... n: e.g. säbärku 'I broke' – aysäbär.ku.n 'I did not break'.

Where there is a pronominal enclitic marker following a plural form, the nominal plural marker -at may be inserted: qäbäru.w.at.o 'they have buried him'; qäbäru.n.at.i 'they have buried me'; qäbäru.k.at.a 'they have buried thee'.

IMPERFECT(IVE)
This is a prefix formation, with change of ending in the plural second and third persons and in singular second person feminine: sing. 1 əsäbbər, 2 masc. təsäbbər, fem. təsäbri, 3 masc. yəsäbbər, fem. təsäbbər; pl. 1 nəsäbbər, 2 təsäbru/a; 3 yəsäbru/a. That is, the forms with gemination do not mark person in the ending.

Kə + imperfect + the copula provides a future tense: e.g. näb tämähari bet kə.käyyəd.əyye 'I shall go to school'.

COPULA
The copula has the following present forms: sing. 1 əyye, 2 masc. əka, fem. əki, 3 masc. əyyu, fem. əyya; pl. 1 ina, 2 masc. əkum, fem. əkən, 3 masc. əyyom, fem. əyyän. Examples: ətu mäṣḥäf ḥaddis əyyu 'this book is new'; negative ḥaddis aykonän; habtam aykon.ku.n 'I am not rich'.

Kə + imperfect provides a subjunctive form. There are also imperative and jussive forms.

PASSIVE PARTICIPLE
Masc. *səbur*, fem. *səbərti*; pl. common, *səburat*.

The infinitive is *məsbar* 'to break', or 'the act of breaking'; the negative is *zäy.məsbar*, or *ay.məsbar.ən*.

Prepositions

Examples: *bə* 'with', *nə* 'for'; prepositions of this type have specific bases for pronominal affix: *bə'a*, *nə'a. ab* 'at': e.g. *ab tämähari.bet allo* 'he is at school' (*allo* is the existential verb); *bəzäy* 'without'.

The preposition may precede the genitival link element: e.g. *kab nay astämharəka gäza* 'from the teacher's house'.

Word order

SOV is frequent: e.g. *'anbäsa səga yəbällə'* 'The lion eats meat.'

፩።	ብመጀመርያ፡ ቃል፡ ነበረ፡ ቃል፡ ድማ፡ አብ፡ እግዚአብሄር፡ ነበረ፡ እቲ፡ ቃል፡
፪።	ከአ፡ እግዚአብሄር፡ ነበረ። እዚ፡ ብመጀ
፫።	መርያ፡ አብ፡ እግዚአብሄር፡ ነበረ። ኩሉ፡ ብኡ፡ ኮነ፡ ብጀክአ፡ ዝኾነ፡ የልቦን፡ ካብ፡
፬።	ዝኾነ፡ ኩሉ። ህይወት፡ አብኡ፡ ነበረት፡
፭።	ህይወትውን፡ ብርሃን፡ ሰብ፡ ነበረት። ብር ሃን፡ ከአ፡ አብ፡ ጸልማት፡ የብርሁ፡ ጸል ማት፡ ድማ፡ አይተቐበሎን።
፮።	ሓደ፡ ሰብአይ፡ ተላዕለ፡ ካብ፡ እግዚአብ
፯።	ሄር፡ እተላእከ፡ ሽሙ፡ ዮሃንስ። ንሱ፡ ን ምስክር፡ መጸ፡ ምእንቲ፡ ብርሃን፡ ኪ.ምስ
፰።	ክር፡ ኩሉ፡ ብኡ፡ ኪአምን። ነሱ፡ ብር ሃን፡ አይነበረን፡ ምእንቲ፡ ብርሃን፡ ኪ.ምስ ክር፡ ተላእከ፡ እምበር።

TLINGIT

INTRODUCTION

This Na-Dené language is spoken in south-eastern Alaska and adjacent parts of Canada by about 2,000 people, an estimated 10 per cent of the total Tlingit population. Tlingit is of considerable interest as the sole living Na-Dené language lying outside the Athabaskan sub-division (*see* **Na-Dené**, **Athabaskan**). Haida, with which Tlingit shares certain areal features, is now treated as an isolate.

PHONOLOGY

Consonants

As in Haida, a typical positional series consists of surd – sonant – ejective: e.g. /t – d – t'/. The dental series extends this row with a spirant (/s/) and a nasal (/n/). This /n/ is in fact the only nasal in Tlingit, though /m/ may occur in onomatopoetic words. /l/ and /r/ are missing, as is the entire labial series apart from /w/. On the other hand, the language has four laterals, which Swanton (in Boas 1911) notates as *L* (surd), *Ļ* (sonant), *L!* (ejective), and *ł* (spirant); also three sets of sibilants, two of which are affricates. All positional series have the ejective member. Swanton lists a pre-palatal *k·!* but points out that this sound is hardly distinguishable from the palatal *k!*.

Swanton's notation is used here for the ejectives: *k!* etc.

Vowels

/i/e/ and /u/o/, long and short, appear to be allophones of the same sounds. /aː/a/ is present, plus an indeterminate vowel which Swanton notates as *A* and describes as = /ə/ + /a/ nuance.

Tone

Short vowels have high tone; long vowels have high or low.

MORPHOLOGY AND SYNTAX

The key role in Tlingit structure is played by affixation, mainly by prefix. The great majority of both nominal and verbal stems are monosyllabic; e.g. nominals: *a* 'lake', *iš* 'father', *as!* 'tree', *tan* 'sea-lion', *ta* 'stone', *tat* 'night', *dis* 'moon', *yāk°* 'canoe', *q!an* 'fire', *hit* 'house'; verbals: *na* 'do', *qox* 'go by canoe', *tī* 'be', *qa* 'say', *yex* 'make', *tsis* 'swim'.

In general, the distinction between nouns and verbs is real; i.e. nouns cannot be used as verbs, and vice versa. Swanton mentions a few exceptions, e.g. *sa* 'name/to name'.

Noun

Nouns are not marked for plurality, but there is a collective suffix *q!(i)*, which is also used to denote unusual size: e.g. *lingit* 'man/men' ('Tlingit'), *lingitq!* '(large) group of men'; *q!āt!* 'island', *q!āt!q!i* 'group of islands'.

In compound nouns, the qualifier precedes the qualified: e.g. *qa.djin* 'human (*qa*) hand'.

There is no form of inflection. The Athabaskan predilection for close definition of locus and posture is reflected in a large inventory of locational adverbs and postpositions.

POSSESSION

A nominal or a possessive pronoun precedes the possessed noun, to which a personal marker is suffixed, unless the referent is a part of the body or a kinship term. This marker is *-(y)i* after front vowels, *wu/wo* after back: e.g. *yao te.yi* 'herring rock', *xuts! nu.wu* 'grizzly-bear fort', *du.hit.i* 'his house' (*du* 'his'; *hit* 'house'); but *du.La ∅* 'his mother', *Ax.iš ∅* 'my father'.

Pronoun

PERSONAL PRONOUN

The subject, object, and possessive forms are:

		Subject	Object	Possessive
singular	1	x, xa	xAt	Ax
	2	i	i	i
	3	—	a, du, Aš	du
plural	1	tu	ha	ha
	2	yi	yi	yi
	3	—	a, hAsdu	hAsdu

Examples: *i.xa.si.tīn* 'I saw you (sing.)' (where *i* is 2nd p. obj.; *xa* is 1st p. sbj.; *si* is modal perfective marker, neutral as to tense); *xAt.yi.si.tīn* 'you (pl.) saw me'.

DEMONSTRATIVE PRONOUN

Four-degree gradation: *he – ya – yu – we*; the first three denote referents which are visible but vary in distance; *yu*, theoretically for distal but still visible referents, now approximates to an article. A referent denoted by *we* is both very remote and never visible.

INTERROGATIVE PRONOUN
adūsa 'who?'; *dāsa* 'what?'.

Numerals

1–10: *Lēq!, dēx, nats!k, daq!ūn, kēdjin, Lēdušu, daxadušu, nats!kudušu, gušūk, djinkāt.* 100 *kedjin qa.*

Verb

The verbal complex consists of an ordered sequence of prefixes, a stem, and suffixes (temporal and other).

There are three sets of modal prefixes; if a nominal prefix is used (e.g. *q!a* 'mouth') it occupies the first position in the complex. The pronominal subject marker is inserted between the first and second sets of modal prefixes; e.g.

> Lēł wu.xa.sA.gōk yāndat!Atš
> 'I cannot swim' (*Leł* 'not'; *wu* is a modal prefix; *xa* marks 1st p. sing.; *sA* is a neutral tense marker, *gōk* 'be able').

> a.ya.u.si.qa
> 'he said to her' (*a* is 3rd p. sing. sbj. marker; *ya* belongs to the first set of modal prefixes, and denotes continued action; *u*, a second-set prefix, fixes the action as past; *si* is perfective; *qa* 'to say').

> a.o.dzi.ku
> 'he came to know it' (*dzi* belongs to the third set of modal prefixes and denotes change of state; *ku* 'to know').

> Lēł ye a.wu.s.ku du.yīt sA.tī.yi
> 'he did not know it was his son' (*yīt* 'son'; *sA/s/si* is a third-set prefix denoting state or action, neutral as to tense; *tī* 'to be'; *yi* is a participial suffix; *yīt* 'son').

The first set of modal prefixes includes *ka*, the causative; *ya*, the progressive; and *gu/gA*, the future marker. The second set includes *du*, which gives a meaning approximating to the English perfect, and *na*, a marker for concomitant action. Three aspectual markers are in the third set: *wa* (perfective), *di* (inceptive), and *l/li* (iterative).

Suffixes: *nutš* denotes habitual action:

> A.šutš.nutš du.yet.k!^{u}
> 'She was in the habit of bathing her child' (*šutš* 'bath'; *yet* 'child'; *k!^{u}* is a diminutive).

k^u is a participial suffix which may be used to form nominals from verbals, e.g.

> yu.q!a.ya.tAn.k^u
> 'The one that could talk' (*yu* is a demonstrative; *q!a* 'mouth'; *ya* is the progressive prefix; *tAn* 'talk').

LOCATIONAL ADVERBS

Examples: *dāk,* 'outward bound (to sea)'; *dāq* 'shoreward'; *nēl* 'into the house'; *yu(x)* 'out of doors'.

Postpositions

Swanton points out that some of the postpositions, e.g. *t* 'to', *n* 'with', *x* 'from', *q!* 'at', are phonetically unstable, and tend to fuse with the preceding nominal, which thus appears to be inflected.

TOBA

See **Batak**.

TOCHARIAN

INTRODUCTION

In some ways the discovery of Tocharian in the early years of the twentieth century is comparable with Herschel's discovery of Uranus; in both cases an established and neatly bounded system was suddenly and surprisingly expanded. But there the similarity ceases. Upon investigation, Uranus was found to be a fairly normal major planet situated obligingly close to where Bode's Law might have predicted it to be. Tocharian, on the other hand, turned out to be an anomaly: the wrong planet, one might say, in the wrong orbit. There was every reason to expect that an Indo-European language spoken in the Turfan area in the middle of the first millennium AD, would show either Iranian or New Indo-Aryan features; at least it would be a satem language. The script was Brāhmī, the content Buddhist. But it soon became clear that Tocharian was, in fact, a centum language, with morphological features linking it to Celtic and Italic rather than to its Indo-European neighbours. At least one Indo-European root, reconstructed as *$k^w ljo$ and meaning 'young girl', is attested only in Irish and Tocharian.

The name Tocharian is itself questionable. We may never know who the speakers of this language were, or where they came from, but it seems clear that they cannot be identified with Strabo's 'Toxaroi', who were probably Iranians.

There is a clear division into two dialects: dialect A, Turfanian or Eastern, and dialect B, Kuchean or Western. The fact that most of the non-liturgical material discovered – correspondence, accounts, caravan passes, and so on – is in West Tocharian, suggests that this may have been the living language, while East Tocharian was an older stratum preserved for cultic purposes.

SCRIPT

The Brāhmī syllabary is used for both dialects. The syllabary preserves the velar, palatal, retroflex, dental, and labial five-term series of Devanagari, though Tocharian had lost the retroflex series altogether, and had reduced the others to two terms – surd stop and nasal, e.g. /k, ŋ/. There is an additional symbol for /ts/.

PHONOLOGY

Consonants

The most notable feature of the phonology of Tocharian is the reduction of Indo-European labial, dental, and velar series to single values: e.g. /p, ph, b, bh/ to /p/.

1367

stops: p, t, k; palatalized p', t', k'
affricates: ts, ts'
fricatives: s, ś, ṣ
nasals: m, n, ɲ, ŋ (m')
laterals and flap: l, ʎ, r
semi-vowels: j, w

Some of these phonemes, e.g. /p', k', ts', m'/ are specific to the B dialect. /t'/ is notated as *c*: e.g. *pācar* = /paːt'ər/ 'father'.

Vowels

There are two series, oral and nasal, the latter marked by anusvar. Each series contains /i, e, a, o, u/, short and long. A short unstable vowel is notated as *ä*.

Diphthongs: /ai, ey, au, aːu/. These are characteristic of West Tocharian (B dialect).

MORPHOLOGY AND SYNTAX

Noun

There are three genders, though the neuter appears only in the demonstrative pronoun. In the absence of overt marking, the gender of a noun may be identifiable only from adjectival or demonstrative pronominal concord. Some nouns take masculine concord in the singular, feminine in the plural: e.g. *säs oko* 'this fruit' (masculine concord); *toṣ okontu* 'these fruits' (feminine concord).

NUMBER

There are two dual endings, one for natural pairings, e.g. parts of the body, and another for chance pairing: cf. *aśäm* 'two eyes'; *peṃ* 'two feet'; *wī pwāri* 'two fires'. Plural endings agree in both dialects: e.g. -(*w*)*al-ā, -na, -ūna, -nta*.

CASE

There are three primary cases: nominative, oblique (these two often coincide), and genitive; these are inflectional cases. Secondary cases – e.g. the perlative – are formed by attaching postpositions to the oblique case form.

Example of B dialect declension of *nyem* 'name':

	Singular	Plural
nominative	nyem	nyemna
oblique	nyem	nyemna
perlative	nyemca	nyemnasa
genitive	nyemance	nyemnamc

A and B declensions of *pācer/pācar* 'father':

	Singular		Plural	
	A	B	A	B
nominative	pācar	pācer	pācri	pācera (pātärn')
oblique	pācar	pātär	pācräs	pācera (pātärn')
perlative	pācrā	pātärsa	—	pacerasa (patärn'ca)
genitive	pācri	pātri	pācräśśi	pāceraṃc (pātarn'c)

Suppletive forms occur, e.g. the oblique case of B *walo* 'king' is *lānt*.

Examples of cases: acc. (obl.) B *prāśśäṃ prek-* 'to ask a question'; genitive A *ptānyäkte nyom klyoṣluneyā* 'hearing the name of Buddha'.

Several examples in Krause-Thomas (1960) show how the perlative was gradually extended in meaning to include the simple locative and the instrumental: e.g. *oŋkälmā lyäm* 'seated himself on the elephant'; *śāmñe kantwasa wemtsi* 'to speak with human tongues'.

Other cases, at least partially attested in Tocharian, include a comitative in *-áśśäl*, an allative in *-ac*, and an ablative in *-äṣ*; this latter is used, for example, in comparison: *Vipul ṣuläṣ lyutār tpär* 'higher than the Vipul mountain'.

Adjective

The ending *-ṣṣe* (+ alternants, declined for gender and number) can be added to any noun in nominative or oblique case: e.g. *waṣamo* 'friend' → *wāṣmoṣṣe* 'friendly'. The ending *-cce* 'endowed with' is very common in B: e.g. *kokalecce* 'having a carriage'. The feminine is in *-a*, the pl. masc. in *-i*, the fem. in *-ana*: e.g. *orocce* 'big', fem. *orocca*, masc. pl. *oročči*, fem. pl. *oroccana*. B has another series of adjectival endings based on *l'*: e.g. *-lye, -lya, -lyi*.

Pronoun

		Singular		Suffixed	Plural
		Full form			
		B. *Masculine*	A. *Feminine*		
1		nyäś	nyuk	-ny	wes
	obl.	nyäś	nyuk	—	wes
	gen.	nyi	nānyi	—	wesi
2		twe		-č	yes
	obl.	ci			yes

DEMONSTRATIVE PRONOUN

Masc. *su*, fem. *sa*, nt. *tu* 'this'; *samp, somp, tamp* 'that'. For *su* (= Skt *saḥ*) an alternative form is *se* (= Skt *ayam*). *Samp* = Skt *asau*. These are used for third person pronoun, with oblique forms *ceu* and *comp/cwimp*, etc.

INTERROGATIVE PRONOUN

kuse 'who, what?'.

RELATIVE PRONOUN

In West Tocharian as interrogative, with an oblique form *kuce*. In East Tocharian, the particle *ne* is added: e.g. *kuc sumas ne* 'for which reason ...' West Tocharian has also a relative/interrogative pronoun *mäksu* (fem. *mäksāu*, nt. *mäktu*) with oblique and plural forms in the masculine and feminine.

Numerals

1–10: *se, wi, trai, śtwer, piś, ṣkas, ṣukt, okt, ñu, śak*. *ṣe* has feminine *sana*; *trai* has *tarya*; and *śtwer* has *śtwāra*. 11–13: *śak ṣe, śak wi, śak trai*; 20 *ikäm*, 30 *täryaka*, 40 *śtwārka*. 100 *kante* (*känt*).

Verb

Active and passive voices; in Tocharian, the medio-passive ending in *-r*, found in Latin and in Celtic is extended in the present to all persons and numbers. There are present, preterite, and future/subjunctive stems, the latter two being usually identical. A causative stem is made for all verbs. As specimen, the present active and deponent-passive forms of root *kälp-* 'to get, reach', B dialect:

		Active	*Causative*	*Deponent-passive*
singular	1	kälpāskau	kalpäskau	kälpāskemar
	2	kälpāst	kalpäst	kälpāstar
	3	kälpāṣṣäṃ	kalpäṣṣäṃ	kälpāstär
plural	1	kälpāskem	kalpäskem	kälpāskemtär
	2	kälpāścer	kalpäścer	kälpāstär
	3	kälpāskeṃ	kalpäskeṃ	kälpāskentär

The active participle is *kälpāṣṣenyca*; passive *kạlpāskemane*.
Preterite of root *prek-* 'to ask', B dialect:

		Active	*Deponent-passive*
singular	1	prekwa	parksamai
	2	prekasta	parksatai
	3	preksa	parksate
plural	1	prekam	parksamte
	2	—	parksat
	3	prekar	parksante

Preterite participle: *peparku*.

Prepositions

Both pre- and postpositions are used: e.g. *śle* 'with' and *snai* 'without' are prepositions in B dialect (the A forms are *śla* and *sne*). (*e*)*ṣe* is a B dialect postposition meaning 'together with'.

TONGAN

INTRODUCTION

Tongan belongs to the West Polynesian branch of Malay-Polynesian, and is spoken in the Kingdom of Tonga by about 100,000 people. It has a fairly extensive body of traditional literature.

SCRIPT

Roman alphabet, standardized orthography since 1943. The customary order of the letters is: *a, e, i, o, u, f, ng, h, k, l, m, n, p, s, t, v, ʻ.*

PHONOLOGY

With twelve consonants, Tongan is phonologically the most richly endowed of the Polynesian languages. There are four labials, four alveolars, and two velars, + /h/ and the glottal stop /ʔ/. The five vowels occur both long and short; the difference is phonemic.

Stress

Stress is flexible, moving to the final syllable of a defined or topicalized complex: cf. *fále* 'house', but *kuo nau fakataha ʼi he falé* 'they have assembled in the house' (where *kuo* is past-tense marker; *nau* is 3rd p. pron.; *fakataha* 'to assemble'; *ʼi* is prep. 'in, at'; *he* is def. article). Similarly: *fále* 'house'; *ʼi he fale akó* 'in the school building'; *ʼi he fale ako motuʼá* 'in the old school building'. That is, as qualifying material is added, the defining stress for the semantic group moves to the concluding syllable.

MORPHOLOGY AND SYNTAX

Noun

As is the case elsewhere in Polynesian languages, the boundaries between parts of speech are fluid. Most verbs can function as nouns, many verbs are adjectives as well. A stem introduced by a preposition is, typically, a noun; the same stem following a tense marker is a verb.

Definite: *'e* is usual, *he* after certain prepositions. Indefinite: *ha*. There is also an emotionally coloured form: *si'a*.

Proper names take the article *a/a'*. Churchward (1953) points out that proper names and place names may be used without the definite article, as can certain common nouns which Tongans construe as being equivalent to emblematic place names: e.g. *moana* 'deep sea', *tahi* 'sea', *taulanga* 'harbour'.

NUMBER
The dual marker is *ongo*; the plural marker for persons is *kau*, for things *ū*. Internal inflection also found: e.g. *feline* 'woman', pl. *fafine*; *motu'a* 'parent', pl. *matu'a*. Plural by partial reduplication is also common.

Adjective

As attribute, adjective usually follows noun, but may precede it in special cases: e.g. *ha me'a lahi* 'a big thing'; *ha me'a si'i* 'a small thing'. Some adjectives have specific plural forms: e.g. *lahi* 'big' – pl. *lalahi*; *si'i* ('small') – pl. *iiki*.

As is the norm in West Polynesian, Tongan has a dual set of personal pronouns: full forms (which can function both as subject and as object) and short forms. A specimen row is (first person inclusive and exclusive):

	Singular		Dual		Plural	
	Full	Short	Full	Short	Full	Short
incl.	kita	te	kitaua	ta	kitautolu	tau
excl.	au	ou/ku/u	kimaua	ma	kimautolu	mau

Examples of their use will be found in the section on transitive/intransitive verbs below.

Pronoun

POSSESSIVE PRONOUNS AND ADJECTIVES
Tongan has a very elaborate system of possessive forms (Churchward's grammar gives 146 forms). As formal illustration we may take *he'eku* 'my', where *he* represents the definite article, *'e* defines the type of possession, and *ku* is the personal marker. Thus, *he'eku tohi* 'the-my-knife' = 'my knife' (alienable possession); similarly, *ha'aku tohi* 'a-my-knife' = 'a knife of mine'; and similarly for all persons in three numbers.

The term 'type of possession' requires explanation. There are two series, marked respectively by *-a-* (which may become *-e-* in Tongan) and *-o-*. The *-a-* series denotes alienable possession on the nominal plane, and is subject-related on the verbal plane. The *-o-* series denotes inalienable possession and reflects action on the subject, i.e. is object-related. Thus, *'eku taki* 'my leading', *'ene taki* 'his leading'; *hoku taki* 'my being led', *hono taki* 'his being led'. Further informative examples, also from Churchward, are: *'eku kātoanga* 'the feast I give'; *hoku kātoanga* 'the feast given in my honour'; *'ene lao* 'the law he makes';

hono lao 'the law by which he is governed'.

As regards nouns, it is not always predictable which items a Tongan will regard as alienable/inalienable. Thus, *pa'anga* 'money' and *puaka* 'pig' are alienable, while *vaka* 'boat' and *kofu* 'clothes' are inalienable. (For more detail on the alienable/inalienable contrast, *see* **Polynesian Languages**.)

Furthermore, there are in Tongan (a) an emotive series of personal possessive markers in *si-*: e.g. *si'eku* 'my special, precious...)'; and (b) a postpositional series of possessive adjectives.

As noted above, the full pronominal forms can function both as subject and as object in a sentence. As subject they are preposed; as object postposed: e.g. *'oku ne taki au* 'he leads me' (*'oku* is present-tense marker; *ne* 'he, him'; *au* 'I, me').

DEMONSTRATIVE PRONOUNS
There is a threefold gradation by distance in space or relative topicalization: *ni – na – ia*; usually preceded by *e/he*. Thus, the series *ni, eni, heni, peheni* 'this (nearby, in focus)' is first person related.

INTERROGATIVE PRONOUNS
hai 'who?'; *hā*, 'what?'

Numerals

1–10: *taha, ua, tolu, fā, nima, ono, fitu, valu, hiva, hongofulu.* 20 *uofulu*; 30 *tolungofulu*; 100 *teau*.

When used as attributive adjectives, these are preceded by *'e/e*: e.g. *'oku 'i fē 'a e kato 'e onó?* 'Where are the six baskets?' (note shift of stress).

Verb

Verbal and nominal particles precede verb, i.e. are in left-hand slots; adverbial particles (directional, locational) modality markers follow verb. Verbal particles include the tense markers; these precede subject pronoun (if any):

> present: *'oku*
> past: *na'a, na'e → ne*
> perfect: *kuo*
> future: *te, 'e, ka*

Examples: *'oku ne lea* 'he is speaking'; *kuo ne lea* 'he has spoken'; *'oku lea 'a Sione* 'John is speaking'.

NOMINAL PARTICLES
Example: the *'a, 'o* possessive markers, *'e* agentive marker, *'a* subject marker, *'i* object marker, *ko* focusing particle.

Adverbial particles following verb: e.g. *mai* 'hither', *ma'u* 'still', *nai* 'maybe'.

Most verbs are either transitive or intransitive, but some fluctuate in usage. What is, from the Indo-European viewpoint, the *object* may be syntactically coupled with the verb in such a way that an intransitive sentence results. Churchward's example: 'I don't drink kava' becomes in Tongan 'I am not a kava-drinker' (*cf.* **Maya**).

Both transitive and intransitive verbs can be used impersonally; transitive impersonals may be equivalent to Indo-European passives:

> transitive personal: *'oku ne taki au* 'he leads me';
> impersonal: *na'a taki au* 'led me' = 'I was led';
> intransitive personal: *na'a ne lea* 'he spoke';
> impersonal: *na'e'uha* 'it rained'.

Subject and object pronouns: cardinal pronouns may precede verb as subject. All other types of subject are postpositional to the verb, e.g. *'e* + def. article + common noun, *'e* + demonstrative pronoun.

All pronominal objects are postpositional: e.g. *'a* + def. article + common noun, *'a* + demonstrative pronoun.

Some examples of transitivity, ergativity: *na'e tangi 'a e fefine* 'the woman wept'; *na'e tangi 'a e fefine ki he tangata* 'the woman wept for (lit. 'be-wept') the man'; *na'e tengihia 'a e tangata 'e he fefine* 'the man was 'be-wept' by the woman'. Example of agentive: *na'e tosi 'e he manu 'a e ika* 'the bird pecked the fish' (*manu* 'bird'; *ika* 'fish').

NEGATIVE
The usual marker is *'ikai (te)*: e.g. *na'e 'ikai te u 'alu* 'I didn't go'. The prohibitive particle is *'oua (te)*; e.g. *'oua te ke hū ki hono fale* 'Don't go into his house!'

Prepositions

An example of purely functional preposition is provided by *'a*. *'a* introduces the postposed subject of an intransitive verb, or the postposed object of a transitive verb: e.g. *na'e lea 'a Tolu* 'T. spoke'; *na'e tāmate'i 'a Tolu* 'killed Tolu' = 'Tolu was killed'.

Ko is also a functional preposition; it serves to focus a topic. Churchward's (1953) example: *Ko e 'aho ni, ko e 'aho mahu'inga ia ki Tonga ni* 'This day, (it) is an important day for (this) Tonga' (where *ko* is the focusing marker, resumed by *ia* 'it').

Examples of locative preposition: *'i, 'ia, 'iate* 'in, at'; *ki, kia, kiate* 'to, into'.

Word formation

(a) By suffix: e.g.

> *'anga* denoting location: *nofo* 'dwell' – *nofo'anga* 'dwelling';
> *-'ia* denotes possession: e.g. *koloa* 'goods' – *koloa'ia* 'affluent';
> *-'aki*: e.g. *'otua* 'god' – *'otua'aki* 'to worship'.

(b) By prefix: e.g. *faka-* as causative, 'appertaining to'; *totonu* 'straight' – *fakatotonu* 'to make straight'; *tu'i* 'king' – *fakatu'i* 'regal'. *Faka-* may be used with nominal phrase: e.g. *fonua lahi* 'large country' – *fakafonualahi* 'big power' (adjective). *Kaungā* = con-/... *ngāue* 'to work' – *kaungāngāue* 'to collaborate'.

Word order

VSO and VOS are used in transitive sequences. VO is possible (i.e. no S is expressed): e.g. *'oku taki au* 'leads me', i.e. 'I am led' (where *'oku* is present-tense marker; *taki* is the transitive verb to 'lead'; *au* is the first person pronoun).

NAE *i mua* i he kamataaga ae Folofola, bea nae i he Otua ae Folofola, bea koe Otua ae Folofola.

2 Ko ia ia nae *i mua* i he kamataaga moe Otua.

3 Nae gaohi eia ae mea kotoabe; bea nae ikai ha mea e gaohi kae iate ia be.

4 Nae iate ia ae moui; bea koe moui koe mama ia oe tagata.

5 Bea nae ulo ae mama i he bouli; ka nae ikai mau ia e he bouli.

6 ¶ Nae ai ha tagata nae fekau mei he Otua, ko Joue hono higoa.

7 Nae hau ia koe fakamooni, ke fakamooni ki he Mama, koeuhi ke tui iate ia ae kakai kotoabe.

8 Nae ikai koe Mama koia ia, ka koe fakamooni ki he Mama koia.

TRUKESE

INTRODUCTION

Trukese belongs to the Micronesian branch of Malayo-Polynesian. It is one of three closely related languages spoken in Trust State (Federated States of Micronesia) – the other two are Mortlockese and Puluwatese – and is spoken by about 25,000 people. The ethnonym is Chuuk: *chóón Chuuk* 'a Trukese person', *fóósun Chuuk* 'Trukese language'.

SCRIPT

The Roman alphabet was first supplied by missionaries in the late nineteenth century for purposes of Bible translation. The original orthography was revised and standardized in the 1970s.

PHONOLOGY

Consonants

    stops: p, t, k
    affricates: tʃ
    fricatives: f, s
    nasals: m, n, ŋ
    lateral and flap: l, r
    semi-vowels: w, j

/p, tʃ, m/, have labialized allophones: [p°, tʃ°, m°].

    Extensive assimilation takes place at junctures: e.g. final /-n/ → [t, ch, s, r], depending on following initial consonant: e.g. *ree.n* 'about' – *ree.t timma* 'about the boat'.

Vowels

Notated as *a, á, e, é, i, o, ó, u, ú*; and realized as:

    aː, a, ɛ, ʌ, i, o, ɔ, u

The last notated vowel, *ú*, is described as 'high, central, unrounded', i.e. close to /ɪ/ but further back.

MORPHOLOGY AND SYNTAX

Noun

Words have full and contracted forms: e.g. *sáát* 'sea', in construct *seti-*. Not only stems, but particles also mutate. Stems can be classified according to their specific modulation patterns in the process of affixation.

Four main combinatorial patterns are recognized. For example, the base *pé* 'to blow (of the wind)' lengthens its stem vowel when followed by the directional particles *tiw* 'westward', *wu* 'northward', *nong* 'southward': *péé.tiw* 'to blow westerly'.

The relational/genitive linker is *-n*: e.g. *iimw/imwa* 'house': *imwe.n assak* 'copra-drying shed'; *imwe.n semwmwen* 'hospital'; *néwú.n nááyif* 'his knife'.

The possessive suffixes are: sing. 1 *-y*, 2 *-b*, 3 *-n*; pl. 1 incl. *-c*, excl. *-m*, 2 *-mi*, 3 *-r*: e.g. *nii.n* 'his tooth'; *mékúre.y* 'my head'; *waa.r* 'their canoe'. Addition of the possessive suffixes may be accompanied by modification of the base. Thus, from *naaw* 'child': *neyi(y)* 'my child', *nowu.mw* 'thy child' (*mw* is an allophone of *b*), *néwú.n* 'his child'.

Adjective

As attribute, adjective precedes noun, to which it is linked by *-n*: e.g. *emen watte.n iik* 'a big fish'.

Pronoun

Independent:

	Singular	Plural
1	ngaang	incl. kiich; excl. áám
2	een	áámi
3	iiy	iir

Subject pronominal prefixes used with verbs:

	Singular	Plural
1	wú	incl. si; excl. ewu
2	ke	ewu
3	e	re

These forms are prefixed to the aspect markers: thus, from *wu* 'I': *wúpwe* 'I shall ...'; *wúsapw* 'I shall not ...'; *wúpwene* 'I intend to ...'; perfective: *wúwa* 'I have (completed action) ...'; *wúse* 'I have not (completed) ...'. Similarly with *re* 'they': e.g. *repwe* 'they will ...'; *resapw* 'they will not ...'

DEMONSTRATIVE PRONOUN/ADJECTIVE

There are five degrees of proximate/distal gradation in space and time, ranging from (1) near speaker, now, to (5) remote from both speaker and audience in space and time: e.g. *eey* 'this': (1) *eey*, (2) *ena*, (3) *een*, (4) *enaan*, (5) ewe, with plural forms. These forms may also be added to certain nominals, e.g. to *iimw* 'house': *imweyeey* 'this house near me at present'; *imwekkewe* 'that house, far away, which I once told you about' (or similar meaning). Demonstratives may precede or follow noun, differing slightly in form.

INTERROGATIVE PRONOUN
iyé 'who?'; *meet* 'what?'.

RELATIVE PRONOUN
menne/minne.

Numerals

The base forms for 1–10 are *eet, érúúw, één, fáán, niim, woon, fúús, waan, ttiw, engoon*. An associated series of prefixes is used in the enumeration of various classes of objects. The prefixes are *e-/i-/o-, rúwé-, wúnú-, fé-/fa-, nime-, wono-, fúú-/fii-, wanú-, ttiwe-*; thus: *féfóch* 'four long objects'; *faché* 'four flat objects'; *wonossak* 'six pieces of copra'; *wonowo* 'six bunches of bananas'.

Verb

Stative or active: the stative marker is *meyi*: e.g. *eey mwáán meyi wátte* 'this man is big'.

Active verbs may be subject or object focused. The coded endings for object focus may be illustrated with the verb stem *nnii-* 'to hit':

	Singular	Plural
1	nnii.yey	incl. nnii.kich; excl. nnii.keem
2	nniyu.k	nnii.kemi
3	nnii.y	nnii.r

Cf. *kúná.á.yey* 'sees me', *kúnó.ó.k* 'sees you'. Positive and negative particles indicate tense; e.g. *ke* (future positive), *saq* (future negative).

Causatives are made by prefixing harmonic vowel and affixing object particle: e.g. *par* 'red' – *a.par.a* 'to redden (something)'.

Directional markers follow the object-marking endings: e.g. *-nó* (indicating motion away from referent), *-tá* (motion upwards or towards the east).

NEGATIVE
sapw is the negative copula; *-se* is a general aspect negator. Modal markers precede subject, e.g. *itá*, expressing desire or intention: *Itá wúpwe áni ewe kkón ngé wúse toongeni* 'I wanted to eat that breadfruit but was not able to' (*áni...kkón* 'to eat breadfruit').

Word order

SVO is general.

1 1 Le popün mi wor Kapas en Kot, nge ewe Kapas a nonom ngeni Kot, a pwal eäni sok ün Kot ewe Kapas,

2 a nonom ngeni Kot le popün.

3 Metoch meinisin ra för ren, nge ese wor och metoch a för lükün.

4 Mine a för, a manaü ren, nge manaü saram en aramas kana.

5 Iwe, ewe saram a titin lon rochopwak, nge rochopwak esap amwöchü.

6 **A** wor eman aramas, a künö me ren Kot, itan Johanes.

7 Ätewe a feito, pwe epwe pwäri, mine a let; a wis en pwärata usün ewe saram, pwe ir meinisin repwe lükülük ren.

8 Ätewe sap ewe saram, nge a wis en pwärata usün ewe saram.

TUPÍ

INTRODUCTION

Tupí is a member of the Tupí-Guaraní group of the Andean-Equatorial family. This description of Old Tupí is based on Lemos Barbosa (1956), who gives an account of the language as recorded by Portuguese and other missionaries and travellers in the sixteenth and seventeenth centuries. More precisely, it is the language of the Tupinambá, a large and warlike group of tribes, extending from the Ceará area southwards along the seaboard and deep into the interior, who seem to have practised cannibalism, not only for religious and social, but for connoisseur reasons as well.

Tupí languages are spoken today by between 2 and 3 million people in eastern Brazil. The first half of the twentieth century saw a very sharp decline in their numbers.

Old Tupí was unwritten.

PHONOLOGY

Consonants

stops: p, t, k, ʔ
fricatives: ß, s, ʃ, γ, ɦ
nasals: m, n, ɲ, ŋ
flap: r
semi-vowels: notated here as î, û, ŷ: *see* **Vowels**, below.

The voiced stops occur in the clusters /mb, nd, ng/. In intervocalic position, *g* is realized as the voiced fricative allophone /γ/. Initial *g* is /ng/.

Vowels

open: e, a, o
closed: i, u, y

All occur nasalized.

/y/ is described as a laryngeal or pharyngeal /ɪ/, ending in a slight degree of friction as though /g/ were to follow. The lips are immobile, and the cheek muscles are retracted as though for a smile. One should then apparently try to pronounce /y/, though the realization must be unrounded /ɪ/. *See* **Guaraní**. The nasalized allophone [ỹ] is the characteristic sound of Tupí-Guaraní.

Consecutive vowels are separated by a hamza-like suspension: e.g. *mbae* = /mba.e/.

The semi-vowels *î*, *û* = /j/, /w/; the semi-vowel *ŷ* combines the /ɪ/ sound described above, with a preceding or following vowel.

MORPHOLOGY AND SYNTAX

Noun

Tupí has no grammatical gender, nor is number distinguished, though reduplication is occasionally used: e.g. *abá* 'man', *abá.abá* '(many) people'. In post-Conquest Tupí, increasing use was made of *etá* 'many'.

Nouns can have future- and past-related forms, by the addition of such verbal markers as *pûera* and *rama*: thus, from *ybá* 'fruit': *ybá.pûera* 'what was a fruit'; *ybá.rama* 'what will be a fruit'.

POSSESSIVE RELATIONSHIP
As in Guaraní, by inverse construct: e.g. *îagûara* 'jaguar' + *akanga* 'head': *îagûar.akanga* 'jaguar's head'; *gûyrá pepó* 'bird's wing'.

CLASS MARKERS
t- for human beings, *s-* for everything else: thus, from stem *eté* 'body': *teté* 'human body', *seté* 'body of an animal'; *t.ugûy* 'human blood'. The *t-* marker is movable (*cf.* **Guaraní**): e.g. *t.ayra* 'son' – *xe r.ayra* 'my son'.

Adjective

The adjective is invariable, and follows noun, which may then lose last syllable if word is paroxytone: e.g. *ybaka* 'sky' – *yba' piranga* 'red sky'; *s.oby* 'blue' (bird, etc.); *itá* 'stone' – *itá tinga* 'white stone'.

Pronoun

Tupí has several sets of pronouns, each set having specific functions:

Set (a): the personal subject/agent prefixes: sing. 1 *a-*, 2 *ere-*, 3 *o-*; pl. 1 *îa-* (incl.), *oro-* (excl.), 2 *pe-*, 3 *o-*. These are obligatory in the indicative, the optative, and the conditional, unless the verb has a first or second person pronominal object: e.g. with third person pronominal object, *î*: *a.î.pysyk* 'I hold, catch him/them'; *ere.î.pysyk* 'you hold, catch him/them'.

Set (b): the predicative personal markers: sing. 1 *xe*, 2 *nde*, 3 *i/o/s*; pl. 1 *îande* (incl.), *oré* (excl.), 2 *pe*, 3 *i/o/s*. These are used in stative verbs (Tupí has no copula): e.g. *xe marangatu* 'I am good', *nde marangatu* 'you are good'. They can be governed by postpositions, e.g. *xe suí* 'of me'; and are also possessive pronouns, e.g. *îande ygara* 'our canoe', *xe pó* 'my hand'.

Set (c): objective personal pronouns. If the subject is third person singular/plural the objective series is the same as (b) above. There are variant sets for first and second person subjects. The third person pronominal object form used before a vowel-initial stem is s-: e.g. *a.s.ausub* 'I love him/them'; *a.s.ausub abá* 'I love the Indian'.

If a noun, as direct object, is placed after the verb instead of between pronoun and verb, the lacuna must be filled by a third person anticipatory pronoun: e.g. *ere-paranā-epîak* = *ere-s-epîak paranā* 'you saw the sea'.

DEMONSTRATIVE PRONOUN
iko (close at hand, visible): *ā/ang*, *iā/iang* (remote, invisible).

INTERROGATIVE PRONOUN
abá 'who?'; *mbaé* 'what?'. The interrogative phrase marker is *-pe*: e.g. *Ere-îuká-pe?* 'Did you kill him?' *Aba* is also used as a relative pronoun.

Numerals

1–4 are attested: (*m*)*oîepé*, *mokõî*, *mosapyr/t*, *irundyk*.

Verb

The Tupí verb is not marked for person, number, or tense. Personal deixis depends on the use of the personal pronouns. Tense can be indicated by such adverbial particles as *pûera* for past, *rama* for future: thus, from root *bebé* 'fly', *a-bebé-pûera* 'I flew'; future *a-bebé-rama*.

NEGATION
nda/nd' + stem + *-i/-î*: e.g. *nd'a-î-kuab-i* 'I don't know (it)'. The negative affix *eyma* is used to negate past and future tenses: e.g. *a-bebé-pûer-eyma* 'I didn't fly'.

The conditional marker is *-mo-*: e.g. *a-î-pysyk-mo* 'if I were to take it/could take it'.

CLASS PREFIXES
In the absence of an explicit nominal/pronominal object, a transitive verb in Tupí must be marked with either *poro* or *mbae*. Thus, the verb *a-î-kuab* needs neither, as the *-i-* pronoun provides an explicit third person object. One cannot, however, say **a-kuab* 'I know'; but either *a-poro-kuab* 'I know someone/ people', or *a-mbae-kuab* 'I know something'; *a-poro-îuka* 'I kill people', *a-mbae-îuka*. The prefix *t-* is associated with *poro*, prefix *s-* with *mbae*; see **Noun**, above.

PARTICIPLES
Examples:

> active: in *-bae*, e.g. *o-îuká-bae* 'he who kills him';
> *bora* (active), *pora* (passive): these take the past and future markers, e.g. *roy-bor-ûera* 'he who was cold';

-pyra makes a passive participle, e.g. *s-ausub-pyra* 'he who is loved', *s-ausub-pyr-ama* 'he who will be loved';

-(s)aba indicates the locus, the means, or the nature of the action, e.g. *îuká-saba* 'the place of killing';

-sûara/-ndûara expresses an habitual state of affairs in a given location, e.g. *kori.ndûara* 'what is habitual today: contemporary', *paranã-me-ndûara* 'what is in the sea'.

RELATIVE CLAUSE FORMATION
Example:

nd'a-î-kuab-i abá o-manó-bae-pûera
'I don't know who died' (*nd'a-î-kuab-i* 'I don't know him'; *aba* 'who'; *o* = 3rd p. sbj. pronoun; *manó* 'to die'; *bae* = relative connective; *pûera* = past-tense marker).

Cf. *O.mano.bae.pûera ixe* 'It was I who died'; *O.mano.eym.bae.pûera ixe* 'It was I who did not die'; *Nda o.mano.bae.pûera ruã ixe* 'It was not I who died.'

Postpositions

Some examples:

suí 'from, out of', e.g. *a-sem taba suí* 'I went out of the village';
r-upi 'while', e.g. *xe nheenga r-upi* 'while I was talking';
supé 'for, to', e.g. *a-î-meeng nde r-uba supé* 'I gave it to your father';
pupé 'in', e.g. *oré taba pupé* 'in our village'.

They may take the class markers: e.g. *t-enondé* 'before someone'; *s-enondé* 'before something'.

Word order

Very free: SVO, SOV, OSV, VOS. In all cases, however, the verb contains a nominal or pronominal (anticipatory) referent. As shown above, the verbal complex may encapsulate the 'sentence' as SOV; or the object may follow the verb, with an anticipatory objective pronominal infix: S–(O)–V–O.

1. Ijipwimehe uiko Zeemg,Zeeng uiko Tupan
iruramo,Zeeng uiko Tupan. 2. Ae zote uiko
ijipwimehe Tupan upe. 3. Ae uzapo roko
parapi maewe;ae-im nuerekoi hemiapo-kwerawe.
4. Ae rehe uiko ekwehau,ekewehau uiko zane-
kwera ara. 5. Ara uhiapo pitunahi rehe,
pitunahi nukwaui ara. 6. Uhem piteii awa
Tupan temimonokari,hera Zuwo heramo. 7. Ae
uuri purumue-mae ramo,umue aram au ara rehe
aramwi,maearam mura-u parapi uweruzari hehe.
8. Ae nuikoi kwei ara zote. Ae uiko umue
aram kwei ara rehe aramwi.

TURKIC LANGUAGES

The Turkic branch of the Altaic family comprises about 30 languages spoken over a vast area extending from Istanbul and the Balkans to the frontier areas of the People's Republic of China, and to Yakutia in the far north-east of Siberia. The total number of speakers lies between 80 and 90 million, with Osmanli Turkish accounting for about half of this figure; in second place come Kazakh and Uzbek, each with around 12 million, followed by Tatar and Azerbaydzhani with 5 million, and Chuvash, Kirgiz, and Turkmen with about 1½ million each.

Apart from Chuvash, whose specific peculiarities point to its early separation from mainstream Turkic, and Yakut, which has been considerably affected by its Tungusic neighbours, the family, as a whole, is remarkably homogeneous, lexically, phonologically, and morphologically. Thus, some degree of mutual intelligibility is possible over the whole field, which can, indeed, be seen as a dialectal continuum, with few, if any, sharp boundaries between contiguous representatives.

It is this very homogeneity of the Turkic languages which complicates any attempt at internal classification. Several classifications are available, based on phonological, morphological, and historical criteria. The following classification is that given by the Soviet Turkologist, N.A. Baskakov (1966): the names of dead languages are in parentheses:

A. Western Hunnic
1. Bulgarian (Old Bulgarian), Chuvash.
2. Oguz

    (a) Oguz-Turkmen: (Oguz), Turkmen, Trukhmen;
    (b) Oguz-Bulgarian: (Uz, Pecheneg), Gagauz;
    (c) Oguz-Seljuk: (Seljuk, Old Turkish) Azerbaydzhani, Osmanli Turkish, some dialects of Crimean Tatar.

3. Kipchak

    (a) Kipchak-Oguz: (Kipchak, Polovets), Kumik, Karaim, Karachaev-Balkar;
    (b) Kipchak-Bulgarian: (Golden Horde Western language), Tatar, Bashkir;
    (c) Kipchak-Nogay: Nogay, Kazakh, Karakalpak.

4. Karluk

    (a) Karluk-Uygur: (Karakhanid and post-Karakhanid Turkish);
    (b) Karluk-Khoresmian: (Chagatay, Golden Horde Eastern language, Old Uzbek), Uzbek, Uygur.

B. Eastern Hunnic
1. Uygur group:

(a) Uygur-Tukuy (Old Uygur, Old Oguz, Old Kirgiz), Tuvin;
(b) Yakut;
(c) Khakass, Shor, Chulim Tatar, Altay (northern dialects);

2. Kirgiz-Kipchak group: Kirgiz, Altay.

Synoptic table of the Turkic consonantal inventory (based on Baskakov (1966)):

stops: p, b, t, d, k, g, q, G: + hamza /ʃ/ and palatalized t', d', k', g'
affricates: ts, dz, tʃ, dʒ; palatalized ts' dz' tʃ' dʒ'
fricatives: f, v, θ, ð, s, z, ʃ, ʒ, x, γ, h, ɦ; palatalized: s', z' x', ʃ' ʒ'
nasals: m, n, ɲ, ŋ
laterals and flaps: l, ł, r, ʀ
semi-vowel: j

About 60 per cent of these phonemes will be found in the inventory of the average Turkic language.

COMMON FEATURES

1. Agglutinative structure, root + affixes; the roots are remarkably stable over the whole field and over long periods of time.
2. Vowel harmony is characteristic of the whole group, and even tends to persist in the *spoken* form of languages, in which it has been discarded as a component in the literary standard, e.g. Uzbek. Basically, Turkic vowel harmony reduces to the rule that front vowels in a linguistic unit – e.g. stem plus endings – are followed by front vowels, back vowels by back. Specific treatment of the category of rounded versus unrounded vowels varies from one language to another within the family. In many members, roundedness tends to be neutralized through a vowel sequence initiated by a rounded vowel: e.g. in Turkish *öneri* 'suggestion'; *görüşme* 'interview'.

In Kirgiz, on the other hand, a four-fold pattern involving front rounded, front unrounded, back rounded, back unrounded vowels is strictly adhered to (*see* **Kirgiz**, for details).

A convenient shorthand for such patterns is the index notation, e.g. -*lVk*⁴ which indicates that the vowel (V) in the suffix -*lVk* has four variants: in Turkish, *lik/lık/luk/lük*.

Consonantal sandhi at junctures may increase the number of possible permutations to twelve: again, for examples *see* **Kirgiz**.
3. There are no articles.
4. There is a total absence of grammatical gender.
5. The adjective precedes the noun; there is no concord.
6. Typically, the postposition is preferred to the preposition.
7. Relative clauses are recast as participial constructions and placed to the left of the head-word, i.e. in adjectival position.

8. Typically, verb forms are negated by a negative marker infix, which almost never carries stress.
9. The verb is usually final.

The following specimen of agglutinative build-up shows Kazakh forms, but an equivalent expansion could be provided for any Turkic language:

džaz	'write' (base = second singular imperative)
džaz.u	'letter, writing'
džaz.u.šɪ	'writer'
džaz.u.šɪ.lar	'writers'
džaz.u.šɪ.lar.ɪm	'my writers'
džaz.u.šɪ.lar.ɪm.ɪz	'our writers'
džaz.u.šɪ.lar.ɪm.ɪz.da	'appertaining to our writers'
džaz.u.šɪ.lar.ɪm.ɪz.da.γɪ	'that (quality, thing) which our writers have'
džaz.u.šɪ.lar.ɪm.ɪz.da.γɪ.lar	'those (qualities, things) which our writers have'
džaž.u.šɪ.lar.ɪm.ɪz.da.γɪ.lar.dan	'from those qualities (etc.) which our writers have'

TYPICAL PARADIGMS
1. Nominal declension: formula + three specific realizations:

	Formula	Kirgiz	Bashkir	Turkish
nominative	-Ø	köz 'eye'	bala 'child'	ev 'house'
genitive	-(d/t/n)V n/n	köznün	balanɪn	evin
accusative	-(d/n) V	közdü	balanɪ	evi
dative	-(k/g/γ) V	közgö	balaγa	eve
ablative	-d/t/n V n	közdön	balanan	evden
locative	-d/t/C V	közdö	balala	evde

where V depends on vowel harmony

2. Personal pronouns with possessive pronominal endings, front-vowel forms:

	Singular	Plural
1	ben ...m	biz ...(i)miz
2	sen ...n/n	siz ...(i)niz
3	o ...(s)i	onlar ...i

3. Verbal system: formulae with Azerbaydzhani realization in first person singular:

Infinitive	m + V + k/g	almag
Imperative	Ø	al; alın
Present/aorist	V + r	al.ır.am
Future	acak/ecek	al.aca.γ.am
Past	d-t + V	al.dı.m
Inferential past	miş	al.mış.am
Conditional	sa/se	al.sa.m
Optative	(j) V	al.a.m

Necessitative	malı/meli	al.malı.j.am
Present participle	V n	al.an
Past participle	d V k/g	al.dɪɣ.ım
Gerund	ıp/ ip	al.ıb
Passive	ı/i l/n	al.ın.mag
Causative	d/t + ı/i + r(t)	al.dɪrt.mag

4. Personal endings: basic forms: I present, future, aorist; II past, conditional:

	I		*II*	
	Singular	*Plural*	*Singular*	*Plural*
1	-im	-iz	-m	-k
2	-sin	-siniz	-n	-niz
3	-(dir)	-(dir)ler	Ø	-ler

All endings are affected by the rules of vowel harmony.

TURKISH

INTRODUCTION

Anatolian Turkish, described here, is classified by Baskakov (1966) as a member of the Oguz group of the Turkic family (*see* **Turkic Languages**); apart from Turkish, this group contains Azerbaydzhani, Gagauz, and Turkmen (the so-called *s*-group). Turkish is spoken by about 50 million people in Turkey, by about 120,000 in Cyprus, where it is co-official language with Greek, and by an estimated million in large Turkish minority groups in Bulgaria, Greece, and Yugoslavia.

The earliest literary records in Turkish date from the thirteenth century and already show substantial Arabo-Persian influence, a component which was to increase so markedly through following centuries that literary Ottoman Turkish is largely an artificial construct, remote from spoken Turkish. This Classical Turkish literature culminates in two great poets – Bakî and Fuzulî (both in the sixteenth century). In the wake of the political and social reform movement known as the Tanzimat (mid-nineteenth century) Turkish writers were introduced to Western models, a widening of mental and technical horizons which bore fruit most notably in the work of Ekrem Recaizade, Namik Kemal, and Tevkif Fikret. The associated movement for the erosion of the Arabo-Persian element in favour of native Oguz words antedates the switch from Arabic to Roman script by some twenty years. Modern Standard Turkish is based on the Istanbul dialect.

SCRIPT

From the outset until the late 1920s, Turkish was written in the alien and quite unsuitable Arabic script. Since 1928/9 the Roman alphabet has been used, minus *q*, *w*, *x* but with the additional letters *ç*, *ğ*, *ş*, *ı*, *ö*, *ü*. *ç* denotes /tʃ/, *ş* /ʃ/, *c* /dʒ/; *ğ* lengthens a preceding vowel, with attendant reduction of following vowel: e.g. *ağır* = /aː(ı)r/ > /aːr/ 'heavy'. Undotted *ı* = /ɪ/, *ö* = /œ/, *ü* = /y/.

The circumflex is found mainly in the loan-words from Arabic and Persian; it serves (a) to indicate a long vowel, and (b) to mark a preceding *l*, *k*, *g* as slightly palatalized.

PHONOLOGY

Consonants

  stops: p, b, t, d, k, g; ? occurs in Arabic loan-words
  affricates: tʃ, dʒ
  fricatives: f, v, s, ʃ, z, h
  nasals: m, n
  lateral and flap: l, r
  semi-vowel: j

/k, g, l/, have palatalized values: /k', g', l'/.

CONSONANT ASSIMILATION
Example: final /p, tʃ, t/ are voiced at junctures preceding a vowel: e.g. *kitap* 'book', accusative *kitabı*; *ağaç* 'tree', genitive *ağacın*; *gitmek* 'to go', aorist stem *gider*. Final /k/g/ > [ğ] before a vowel: e.g. *ekmek* 'bread', accusative *ekmeği*.

Vowel

  front: i, ɛ, œ, y
  back: ı, a, o, u

All are normally short; long vowels appear (a) as lengthened by -ğ- (see above) and (b) as reflexes of original long vowels in Arabic or Persian loans.

VOWEL HARMONY
Basically, front vowels are followed by front, back by back. If the vowel initiating a harmonic sequence is unrounded, so are the following vowels; if the leading vowel is rounded, following vowels are rounded or unrounded. Some examples: *evde* 'in the house'; *ormanda* 'in the forest'. The suffix *lVk*, for example, appears in four forms: *-lik, -lık, -luk, -lük*; e.g. *işçilik* 'workmanship'; *pazarlık* 'bargaining'; *çoğunluk* 'majority'; *ölümsüzlük* 'immortality'. It is convenient to write such a suffix as *-lik*[4], indicating that four variants occur.

Stress

In citation form, stress is usually on the final syllable. In connected speech, and especially in the verb, the allocation of stress is complicated; the presence of the negative marker *-me/ma-* fixes stress on the preceding syllable.

MORPHOLOGY AND SYNTAX

Noun

Turkish has no grammatical gender, and there is no definite article. The numeral *bir* 'one', may be used as an indefinite article. A nominal in the accusative case is regarded as definite.

The plural marker *-lar/-ler*, depending on stem vowel: e.g. *elmalar* 'apples'; *dersler* 'lessons'.

DECLENSION
The paradigm is invariable for all Turkish nouns: it is exemplified here by a back-vowel stem, a front-vowel stem, and a vocalic ending:

	Back vowel	Front vowel	Vocalic ending
nominative	baş 'head'	ev 'house'	oda 'room'
genitive	başɪn	evin	odanɪn
dative	başa	eve	odaya
accusative	başɪ	evi	odayɪ
locative	başta	evde	odada
ablative	baştan	evden	odadan

Choice of *t/d* initial in the locative/ablative ending depends on word final; the voiced consonant, for example, follows a voiced final or a vowel. In vocalic stems *-y-* and *-n-* are inserted before the affix.

The same paradigm applies to the plural form: the endings follow the plural marker: e.g. *baş.lar.ɪn* 'of the heads'; *ev.ler.de* 'in the houses'.

POSSESSION
The formula is: possessor in genitive, followed by possessed object with possessive suffix: e.g. *bu adam.ɪn kalem.i* 'of this man his-pencil' = 'this man's pencil'; *köpeğin rengi* 'the colour of the dog' (*köpek* 'dog' $k \rightarrow g$)

Adjective

As attribute, adjective precedes noun and is invariable. The indefinite article is normally between the adjective and the noun: e.g. *kɪrmɪzɪ bir gül* 'a red rose'; *ünlü bir kahraman* 'a famous warrior/hero'.

COMPARATIVE
Made with *daha* 'more' + ablative case: e.g. *Bu kitap şu kitaptan daha iyi* 'This book is better than that one.'

Pronoun

The personal pronouns are:

	Singular	Plural
1	ben	biz
2	sen	siz
3	o	onlar

These are fully declined in all cases: e.g. for first person singular: gen. *benim*, dat. *bana*, acc. *beni*, loc. *bende*, abl. *benden*

POSSESSIVE MARKERS
These are affixed to the noun: sing. 1 -(i)m[4], 2 -(i)n[4], 3 -(s)i[4]; pl. 1 -(i)miz[4],

2 -(*i*)*niz*[4], 3 -*leri/ları*: e.g. *lokanta.nız* 'your restaurant'; *lokanta.nız.ın ismi* 'the name of your restaurant'; *Türkiye (bizim) vatan.ımız dir* 'Turkey is our motherland'; *Türkiye toprak.ları.nın büyük bir kısm.ı* 'a large part of Turkey's lands'.

DEMONSTRATIVE PRONOUN/ADJECTIVE
bu 'this'; *şu* 'that'; fully declined.

INTERROGATIVE PRONOUN
kim 'who?'; *ne* 'what?'; declined.

RELATIVE PRONOUN
None; *see* **Verb**, Relative clause, below.

Numerals

1–10: *bir, iki, üç, dört, beş, altı, yedi, sekiz, dokuz, on*; 11 *on.bir*; 12 *on.iki*; 20 *yirmi*; 30 *otuz*; 40 *kırk*; 50 *elli*; 100 *yüz*.

Verb

(See *also* **Turkic Languages**.) A typical Turkish verb form is constructed as follows: stem – aspect and/or tense marker – personal ending: e.g. *gel.i.yor.um* 'I am coming' (where *gel-* is the stem of *gelmek* 'to come': -*i*- is a connective vowel: -*yor*- is the characteristic of the present continuous tense; and -*um* is the first person singular personal marker); *gel.ebil.e.ceğ.im* 'I shall be able to come' (-*ebil-* is the potential aspect marker; *cek-* → *ceğ-* is the characteristic of the future tense).

There are three sets of personal endings, all close to the possessive series set out above. One set provides the endings for the existential verb: sing. 1 -*im*[4], 2 -*sin*[4], 3 -*dir*[4]; pl. 1 -*iz*[4], 2 -*siniz*[4], 3 -*dirler*[4.2]: e.g. *evde.siniz* 'you are in the house'. With certain exceptions these are also the affixes for the present continuous, the aorist, the future, and the inferential past; the third person marker is Ø: e.g. *gel.i.yor.um* 'I am coming'; *gel.i.yor∅* 'he is coming'.

A very similar set of endings used in the past definite and in the conditional mood has one anomalous form: -*k* in the first person, e.g. *geldik* 'we came'; *gelsek* 'if we were to come'.

The third set of endings is used with the subjunctive mood: sing. 1 *eyim*, 2 *esin*, 3 *e*; pl. 1 *elim*, 2 *esiniz*, 3 *eler*.

The main tense characteristics are: present -*yor*-; future -*cek*[2]-; definite past -*di*[4]-; inferential past -*miş*[4]-; aorist -*r*-; conditional -*se*[2]-. Some examples:

present: *ver.i.yor.sunuz* 'you are giving (pl.)'
future: *ver.e.cek.ler* 'they will give'
past definite: *ver.di.k* 'we gave'
inferential past: *ver.miş.siniz* '(it seems that) you gave'
aorist: *ver.i.r* 'he gives'

conditional: *ver.i.yor.sa.m* 'if I am giving'
subjunctive: *ver.el.im* 'that we may give'

NEGATIVE CONJUGATION

The negative marker *-me/ma-* precedes the tense characteristic; stress is transferred to the syllable immediately preceding this marker. There are specific rules for stress in the aorist negative. Examples:

present: *gör.mü.yor* 'he is not seeing'
future: *gel.mi.ye.cek* 'he will not come'
aorist: *gel.mez* 'he doesn't come'
past definite: *al.ma.dı.m* 'I didn't take'
inferential past: *bul.ma.mış.ım* '(it seems that) I didn't find'

NEGATIVE COPULA

Made with *değil*: e.g. *hasta değil.im/değil.sin* 'I am/you are not ill'. The existential verb is negated by *yok*: e.g. *yok(tur)* 'there is not':

Dedim: bayram mıdır? Söyledi: yok, yok.
'I said: is there a festival? He said: no, there is not.' (Emrah: nineteenth century)

This line of poetry also illustrates the interrogative conjugation; the marker is *mi*[4], which follows the focal point in the verbal complex. Again, the preceding syllable is stressed: e.g. *Ver.i.yor **mu**.sunuz?* 'Are you giving?'; *Bil.mez **mi**.siniz?* 'Don't you know?'; *Bana yardım eder.**mi**.siniz?* 'Will you help me?' (*yardım* 'help'; *bana* 'to me'; *etmek* 'to do').

PASSIVE VOICE

The marker is *-il*[4]*-/-in*[4]*-*: e.g. *görmek* 'to see' – *görülmek* 'to be seen'.

CAUSATIVE

-dir[4]*-*: e.g. *ölmek* 'to die' – *öldürmek* 'to kill'.

NECESSITATIVE

-meli[2]*-*: e.g. *gel.meli.y.im* 'I ought to come'.

RELATIVE CLAUSE

Various participial forms are used: e.g. with present participle in *-en*[2]*-*, *gel.en adam* 'the man who is coming'; *gel.e.cek (ol.an) adam* 'the man who will come'; *gel.miş (ol.an) adam* 'the man who is said to have come'.

The participial form made from the past definite tense is in *-dik*; this is very extensively used in all sorts of relative clauses. Some examples: *gel.**diğ**.i zaman* 'when he comes' (*-dik* → *diğ* before third person marker *-i*: *zaman* 'time' → 'when ...'); *ev.e dön.**düğ**.üm zaman* 'when I (*-üm*) reach(ed) home'; *üzerinde yaş.a.**dığ**.ımız topraklar* 'the land(s) on which we live(d)'; *harabeler gör-.**ül.dük**.ten sonra* 'after the ruins have been viewed ...'; *bizim öğrenci vizesi ver.**diğ**.imiz kimselerden istediğimiz şey* 'what we want from those people to whom we have given student visas'; *hiç bir parti çoğunluğu kaza-na.ma.**dığ**.ın.dan sonra* 'since no party won a majority'.

Postpositions

The last example above shows a postposition following the ablative case: *sonra* 'after'. Other postpositions are used with the nominative (e.g. *gibi* 'like', *için* 'for') and the dative (e.g. *göre* 'according to', *kadar* 'as far as', *karşı* 'against').

Word order

SOV is basic; the inverted sentence (*devrik cümle*) is possible, with certain reservations.

---

1 İpuaada Kelâm var idi, ve Kelâm Allahın nez-
2 dinde idi, ve Kelâm Allah idi. O, iptidada Alla-
3 hın nezdinde idi. Her şey onun vasıtasile ol-
du, ve olmuş olanlardan onsuz hiç birşey olmadı.
4 Hayat onda idi, ve hayat insanların nuru idi.
5 Nur karanlıkta parlıyor, ve karanlık onu yenmedi
6 Allah tarafından gönderilmiş bir adam çıktı, onun
7 ismi Yahya[1] idi. Bu adam şehadet için geldi,
ta ki o nur hakkında şehadet etsin de bütün in-
8 sanlar onun vasıtasile iman eylesinler. Kendisi o
nur değildi, ancak o nur hakkında şehadet etmek
için geldi.

TURKMEN

INTRODUCTION

Turkmen belongs, in Baskakov's (1966) classification, to the Oguz-Turkmen group of Turkic. It is spoken by between 2 and 3 million people in the Turkmen Soviet Socialist Republic and in the adjoining Uzbek, Tadzhik, and Kazakh SSRs; also in the Karakalpak ASSR. Turkmen is an umbrella term for a continuum of dialects which are very numerous and which differ rather widely among each other, both phonologically and morphologically. There are two main groupings – central/major dialects and outliers. The literary language represents a consensus between the major dialects.

SCRIPT

Arabic until the 1920s; Cyrillic since 1940, + several additional letters.

PHONOLOGY

Consonants

    stops: p, b, t, d, k, g, q, G
    affricates: tʃ, dʒ
    fricatives: f/v, s, z, ʃ, ʒ, (x, γ) h
    nasals: m, n, ŋ
    lateral and flap: l, r
    semi-vowels: j, w

Vowels

    front: i, iː, ɛ, (ɛː), əː, (ə), y, yː, œ, œː
    middle: ɪ, ɪː
    back: a, aː, o, oː, u, uː

Length is not marked in script. /y/ is notated as *ü*; /œ/ as *ö*.

VOWEL HARMONY
Palatal harmony is observed throughout; the case of labial harmony is less clear; it is not notated in the script, and seems to be neutralized in third and subsequent syllables (not in all dialects).

MORPHOLOGY AND SYNTAX

Noun

Standard Turkic forms in declension, possessive affixes, treatment of the adjective, the pronominal system and the numerals.

In the possessive affix system, one form $-sɪ^2/-ɪ^2$ does duty for both singular and plural; thus, while *kitabɪm* is specific (first person singular) *kitabɪ* has to be further clarified: e.g. *olun kitabɪ* 'his book'.

Verb

The infinitive marker is standard: *-mak/-mek*. The negative infinitive, however, is in *-mazlɪk*: e.g. *yaz.mazlɪk* 'not to write'.

VOICE AND MOOD
Inventory and format are standard.

TENSE SYSTEM

> indicative present: the marker is *-yar/yər-*: e.g. *oka.yar.ɪn* 'I read'; *išle.yər.in* 'I work', negative *oka.ma.yar.ɪn*;
> past: the marker is $-dɪ^4$;
> future indefinite: $-ar^2$-;
> future definite: $-džak^2$- with an unusual negative using the particle *dəl*: *men ayt.džak dəl* 'I shan't say'.

PARTICIPLES
Largely standard, e.g. *gid.edžek poezd* 'the train about to leave ...' (*poezd* is a Russian loan-word). The present participle has a $-yan^2$- marker: e.g. *gidiyən adam* 'the man who is going'. Confusingly for Osmanli Turkish speakers, the *past* participle is in *-an/-en*: e.g. *gelen adam* 'the man who came' (= 'the man who *is coming*' in Turkish).

TUVINIAN (Tuva)

INTRODUCTION

Tuvinian belongs to the Uygur-Oguz group of Northern Turkic languages. It is spoken by between 140,000 and 160,000 in the Tuva Autonomous Soviet Socialist Republic, which was established in 1961. From 1921 to 1944 the Tuvinians enjoyed a brief spell of independence in the Tannu-Tuva People's Republic, which was taken over as an autonomous province within the Russian Federal Republic in 1944. Some Tuvinians also live in the Mongolian People's Republic.

Tuvinian preserves certain archaic features which relate it to Old Turkic; and it also shows considerable Mongolian influence, e.g. many loan-words adopted in the long period of Tuvinian-Mongolian contiguity from the twelfth century onwards. The literary language dates only from the 1930s – first in romanization, then, from 1941, in Cyrillic plus θ, γ, ӊ. The language is used in the local media.

PHONOLOGY

Consonants

    stops: aspirated: p', t'; non-asp. p, b, t, d, k, g
    affricates: ts, tʃ, dʒ
    fricatives: f, v, s, z, ʃ, x, γ
    nasals: m, n, ŋ
    lateral and flap: l, r
    semi-vowel: j

Vowels

Tuvinian has what is for a Turkic language an unusually complex vocalic system with 24 values = 3×8 basic vowels:

    i, e, ɪ, a, o, œ, u, y

The three series are: (1) short vowels; (2) long – then written doubled; (3) pharyngealized, marked with Cyrillic hard sign: here '. The pharyngealized vowels occur only in mono- or first syllables: e.g. a't 'horse', o't 'grass'.

VOWEL HARMONY

The normal Turkic pattern (front with front, back with back, rounded with rounded) is observed with certain exceptions; e.g. the aditive affix *-že/-če* is invariable as regards the front vowel: *dagže* 'to the mountain'.

MORPHOLOGY AND SYNTAX

The nominal declension, the possessive markers, the pronominal system, and the numerals are all more or less standard Turkic.

The plural marker is *-lar*[8], with initials *l-/d-/t-* and *-e/a-* depending on vowel harmony. The declension includes, as mentioned above, an aditive case in *-že/-če* (invariable). The demonstrative pronouns are *bo* 'this', *dŏ* 'that'.

There are various ways of expressing a comparative/intensive form; e.g. from *kɪzɪl* 'red': *kɪzɪŋgɪr/kɪzɪlgɪr/kɪp-kɪzɪl*.

In the numerals, note *čērbi* '20'; *üžen* '30'; *dörten* '40'; *čüs* '100'.

Verb

With six aspects, five voices, and four moods, the Tuvinian verb is remarkably rich in forms. The voice formants are regular: e.g. causative *-dɪr*; reciprocal *-ɪš*; passive *-ɪl* (with vowel-harmony variants).

ASPECT

> perfective: *-ɪvɪt*, e.g. *körüvüt* 'to have seen';
> imperfective: *-p + tur-*, e.g. *bidžip tur men* 'I am writing';
> frequentative: *-gɪla*, e.g. *nomčugula-* 'to read a lot';
> terminative: *-basta*, e.g. *adžilda.vasta* 'to stop working'.

The definite past tense is standard: e.g. *aldɪm* 'I took', *aldɪn*, *aldɪ*. Four compound past tenses are made on a different model: stem + aspect/gerundial marker – first/second personal marker – (particle): e.g. in past indefinite, *ber.gen men* 'I gave', *ber.gen sen* 'you gave'. In these forms the third person marker is Ø: e.g. *ber.gen* 'he/she gave'. Similarly, the inferential past: *kɪl.ɪp.tɪr men* 'it seems that I did'; and the past assertive: *kördžük men čop* 'the fact is, I saw ...' (+ particle).

There is a future marker *-galak/-kelek*: e.g. *keskelek bis* 'we're expecting to mow'.

The conditional marker is *-zɪ-* + personal marker + *za*: e.g. *aitɪr.zɪ.m.za* 'if I ask'; *aitɪr.zɪ.ŋ.za* 'if you ask', *aitɪr.Ø.za* 'if he/she asks'.

Tuvininan also has subjunctive and imperative moods. Several of the participial and gerundial endings have been illustrated in the examples above.

NEGATIVE

The negative marker *ma* (with variants e.g. *pa/ba/ve/be*) is always stressed, a rare phenomenon in Turkic languages; cf. *albádɪm* 'I did not take'.

Postpositions

For example, *udžun* 'because of', *udur* 'against', *bile* 'with'.

Word order

SOV is frequent.

TWI

See **Akan**.

UBYKH

INTRODUCTION

Ubykh belongs to the North-West Caucasian or Abkhaz-Adyge sub-group of Caucasian languages. The Ubykh people migrated from the Caucasus to Turkey in the 1860s, when they numbered several thousand. The language is now extinct, the few Ubykh who survive speaking Kabard-Cherkes or Adyge. The transcription used here is based on that of Kumaxov (1967).

PHONOLOGY

Consonants

With its 80 phonemes, Ubykh had the most extensive consonantal inventory of all the Caucasian languages. A recurrent pattern in the stops and affricates is voiced non-aspirate – aspirate surd – ejective surd, with labialized or pharyngealized values: e.g.

labial, simple: b, p, p'; pharyngealized: ḅ, p̣, p̣'
dental affricate, simple: dz, ts, ts'; labialized: dz°, ts°, ts'°

The velar series lacks the voiced member, but has both labialized and palatalized values: /q, q'; q'', q''; q°, q'°/. The velar spirants /x, γ/ also have labialized and palatalized values.

In 1963 H. Vogt published a frequency count of Ubykh phonemes based on a connected text totalling 10,000 consonants. Just over 50 per cent of this total was provided by the eight consonants /n, q', j, w, γ, d, g', m/; 39 consonants appeared less than 50 times, 18 of these less than 10 times. *ṃ, p̣, p̣', q°* were not found in the sample.

Vowels

/ə/a/: these take on different colourings, depending on phonetic environment. Thus /a/ may be realized as [a, ε, o]; /ə/ as [w, y].

MORPHOLOGY AND SYNTAX

Noun

The noun is marked for definite/indefinite status, the former with *a-*: e.g. *ša* 'head'; *a.ša* 'the head'.

CASE

Nominative and ergative, the latter as subject of transitive verbs; the ergative marker is *-n*: e.g. *č'ə* 'horse'; erg. *č'ən*; plural marker *-na*.

Possessive markers are prefixed to nouns and provide one way of indicating plurality: e.g. *sa.č'ə* 'my horse'; *sö.č'ə* 'my horses'.

Adjective

The adjective is hardly differentiated from the noun. In compound with a noun, the adjective follows: e.g. *čəbž'əja* 'pepper' + *płə* 'red': *čəbž'əjapłə* 'red pepper'.

Pronoun

	Singular	Plural
1	səɣ°a	š'əɣ°ała
2	wəɣ°a	s°əɣ°ała

These are not declined.

Numerals

1–10: *za, t'q°a, śa, p'łə, š'xə, fə, błə, ɣ°a, bɣ'ə, ž°ə.*

Verb

For general structure, *see* **Abkhaz-Adyge Languages**, **Kabard-Cherkes**, **Abkhaz**. Some examples of Ubykh verbal structure follow:

> *s.k̯'a.n*: subject – root – tense marker, 'I go';
> *sə.w.pła.n*: subject – object – root – tense marker, 'I look at you';
> *sə.wə.na.ťə.n*: direct object – indirect object – subject – root – tense marker, 'they give me to you';
> *š'ə.k''a.jə.fa.na.mə.t*: subject – root – reflexive marker – potential marker – number marker – negative marker – tense marker, 'we shall not be able to go back';
> *azbəj.öt* 'I'll see him';
> *azbəja.nöt* 'I'll see them';
> *azbəj.ö.mə.t* 'I shan't see him';
> *azbəja.nö.mə.t* 'I shan't see them'.

UDEGE

INTRODUCTION

The Udege sub-division of South Eastern Tungusic comprises two languages: Udege itself, and Oroch. Udege is spoken by a few hundred people who live near the confluence of the Amur and the Ussuri rivers in the Khabarovsk region; Oroch by about 500 people in roughly the same area. Neither language is written.

PHONOLOGY

Consonants

The consonantal inventory of Oroch is identical to that of Nanay (*see* **Nanay**). To this inventory Udege adds an unstable pharyngeal /ʀ/, and a uvular pair (stop + fricative).

Vowels

In both languages, a simple series of basic vowels is greatly extended by intermediate values, including, in Udege, the so-called 'interrupted vowels', *a̒* = /a'a/; and aspirated vowels, /aʀa/ → /aː/. Both languages have elaborate systems of vowel harmony.

MORPHOLOGY AND SYNTAX

Noun

The nominal system is based on the human/non-human dichotomy. There are seven or eight cases: e.g. in Oroch, declension of *inaki* 'dog': sing. nom. *inaki*; acc. *inaki.ma*; instr. *inakin'.ži*; dat. *inakin.dụ*. The locative ending is *-dula*, the ablative *-žiži*. Plural markers exist but are hardly ever used. In Udege, kinship terms have specific plural markers.

In Udege, the possessive declension makes a distinction between alienable possession and inalienable relatedness. For the latter, the endings are added directly to the case ending; where alienable property is concerned, the suffix *-ŋi* (with variants) is infixed between case ending and personal marker. Sunik (in Jazyki Narodov SSSR VI, 1968) gives the example: *dili.ni* 'his (own) head'; *dili.ŋi.ni* 'his head' (e.g. of an animal, as trophy).

Pronoun

The first person plural distinguishes inclusive and exclusive forms. The base series in Udege is: sing. 1 *bi*, 2 *si*, 3 *nuani*; pl. 1 incl. *bu*, excl. *minti*, 2 *su*, 3 *nuati*.

Verb

In Oroch the aspectual system is highly developed, and includes semi-modal forms expressing intention, feasibility, etc. Tense is generated by combining participial forms with tense markers specific to type of base (seven types are distinguished): e.g. for a type I base, i.e. ending in a vowel, *-i* is the present marker, *-xa(n)/-xen/-xon* is a past marker, and *-ža(n)* a future.

In Udege, two types of base are distinguished – vowel or consonant final. Examples of tense formation in Udege for stem *ana-* 'to push', indicative mood, singular:

> present: 1 *ana.mi*, 2 *ana.ʀi*, 3 *ana*;
> past: 1 *ana.'a.i*, 2 *ana.'a.ʀi*, 3 *ana.'a*;
> future: 1 *ana.ža.mi*, 2 *ana.ža.ʀi*, 3 *ana.ža*.

For negation in both languages the negating verb *ę-*, /ɛ/, is used + stable form of the sense-verb, e.g. in Udege: *ėʀimi digana* 'I don't speak', *ęʀini digana* 'he doesn't speak'. In Oroch: *bi ęsimi ŋęnęję* 'I don't go'; *bi ęčimi ŋęnęję* 'I didn't go'; *bi ęžēmi ŋęnęję* 'I shan't go'.

Postpositions

Both languages use postpositions.

UDMURT

INTRODUCTION

Previously known as Votyak, Udmurt belongs to the Permian group of Finno-Ugric languages, and is spoken by over half a million people in the Udmurt Autonomous Soviet Socialist Republic. Created in 1934, this ASSR lies between the Komi-Permyak National Area to the north, and the Tatar and Bashkir ASSR to the south. Décsy (1965) describes the Udmurt as the only Finno-Ugric people still resident in their original homeland. The language shows the influence of many centuries of contact with Turkic languages (Volga-Bulgar, Chuvash, Bashkir, etc.).

Written Udmurt dates from the late nineteenth century. The first newspaper in the language appeared in 1913. The creation of the ASSR greatly stimulated Udmurt cultural expression, and the language is now used in higher education and in the media (three or four dozen newspapers and periodicals), with a considerable output of books in technology and the arts.

SCRIPT

Cyrillic plus *ö* (= /œ/) and the modified Cyrillic letters й, ӝ, ӟ, ӵ. ӝ and ӵ notate the hard affricates /dʒ/ and /tʃ/ whose correlative soft, i.e. palatalized, values are /dʒ'/ and /tʃ'/, notated as ӟ and ч. й is used in opposition to и to indicate that preceding *d, t, s, z, n, l* are hard: cf. син /s'in/, 'eye'; сйль /sil'/, 'meat'.

PHONOLOGY

Consonants

> stops: p, b, t, d, k, g; palatalized: t', d'
> affricates: tʃ, dʒ; palatalized tʃ', dʒ'
> fricatives: v, s, z, ʃ, ʒ, s', z', j
> nasals: m, n, ɲ
> laterals and flap: l, l', r

Vowels

> i, ɪ, e = [ɛ], a, œ, o, u.

/ɛ/ following a palatalized consonant is written as *e*; otherwise as э. In the section on morphology below, both are represented by *e*; i.e. *e* following a soft consonant is /yɛ/; following a hard consonant, *e* is /ɛ/.

In the case of /i/, as explained above, the graph *ӥ* is used to signal that the preceding consonant is not soft. In this article, such a consonant is transcribed with a subscript dot: *ḍ*.

Stress

Stress is mainly on the final syllable.

MORPHOLOGY AND SYNTAX

Noun

No articles, no grammatical gender. The noun is marked for number and case, and for individual or collective possession. The plural is *-os/-yos*: e.g. *gurt* 'village', pl. *gurtyos*; *gurez'* 'mountain', pl. *gurez'yos*.

The noun is declined in fifteen cases: six of these are spatial, and do not apply to nouns denoting humans: e.g. *lud* 'field':

	Singular	*Plural*
nominative	lud	luḍyos
accusative	ludez	luḍyostɪ
genitive	ludlen	luḍyoslen
disjunctive	ludles'	luḍyosles'
dative	ludlɪ	luḍyoslɪ
privative	ludtek	luḍyostek
instrumental	luden	luḍyosɪn

Examples of locative cases: *ludɪn* 'in the field'; *luḍyosɪ* 'to the fields'; *ludɪs'* 'from the field'.

POSSESSIVE ENDINGS
Individual (singular object): 1 *-e*, 2 *-ed*, 3 *-ez*; (plural object): 1 *-ɪ*, 2 *-ɪd*, 3 *-ɪz*. Collective possession (singular object): 1 *-mɪ*, 2 *-dɪ/-tɪ*, 3 *-zɪ/-sɪ*; (plural object): 1 *-mɪ*, 2 *-tɪ*, 3 *-sɪ*: e.g. *lud.mɪ* 'our field'; *luḍyos.mɪ.tek* 'without our fields'.

GENITIVE RELATIONSHIP
Possessor in genitive, possessed with possessive marker, e.g. *Ivan.len pi.ez* '(of) John his-son'. The endings tend to be dropped, so this could also be expressed as *Ivan pi*.

Adjective

As attribute, adjective precedes noun, and does not take case endings, unless the discriminatory/isolating infix *-ez-/-z-* is used: e.g. *iz korka* 'stone house'; *syör* *murt* 'strange man' = 'stranger'; *vɪl' korka.len* 'of a new house'; *vɪl'ez.len korkalen* 'of the (particular) new house'.

COMPARATIVE
-ges/-gem: e.g. *vɪl'* 'new' – *vɪl'gem* 'newer'.

Pronoun

PERSONAL INDEPENDENT
Sing. 1 *mon*, 2 *ton*, 3 *so*; pl. 1 *mi*, 2 *ţi*, 3 *soos*. These are declined in seven non-locative cases: e.g. *mitek* 'we, being absent'; *soosɪn* 'by them'.

DEMONSTRATIVE PRONOUN/ADJECTIVE
ta 'this/these', *so* 'that/those'.

INTERROGATIVE PRONOUN
kin 'who?'; *ma* 'what?'.

RELATIVE PRONOUN
As interrogative: e.g. *Kin ke ug uža, so ug sɪɪ* 'Who doesn't work doesn't eat' (for negative with *ug*, see **Verb**, below; *užanɪ* 'to work'; *sɪɪnɪ* 'to eat').

Relative clauses may also be made with the relative pronoun *kuḍiz* 'who, which', e.g. *ad'amios kuḍyosɪz kuz' ludɪn užalo* 'the men who worked in the long field'; or with participial construction, e.g. *zavodɪn užasez brate* 'my brother who works in the factory'; *zavodɪn užasezlɪ bratelɪ* 'to my brother who ...'.

Numerals

1–10: *oḍig, kɪk, kuin', n'ɪl', vit', kuat', siz'ɪm, t'amɪs, ukmɪs, das*. 11 *das oḍig*; 12 *das kɪk*; 20 *kɪz'*; 30 *kuamɪn*; 40 *n'ɪl'don*; 100 *s'u*. The cardinals may take the discriminatory *-ez-*.

Verb

The infinitive ends in *-(y)ɪnɪ* or *-(y)anɪ*, giving two conjugations: e.g. *puk.ɪnɪ* 'to sit'; *už.anɪ* 'to work'.

There are three moods: indicative, imperative, conditional. The indicative has present, future, and two past tenses, all with negative versions, as in Mari and the Balto-Finnic languages. As illustration, the present, past definite and future of *mɪnɪnɪ* 'to go':

present: sing. 1 *mɪnis'ko*, 2 *mɪnis'kod*, 3 *mɪne*; pl. 1 *mɪnis'kom(ɪ)*, 2 *mɪnis'kodɪ*, 3 *mɪno*;
negative: sing. 1 **ug** *mɪnis'kɪ*, 2 **ud** *mɪnis'kɪ*, 3 **ug** *mɪnɪ*; pl. 1 **um** *mɪnis'ke*, 2 **ud** *mɪnis'ke*, 3 **ug** *mɪno*;
past: sing. 1 *mɪnɪ*, 2 *mɪnɪd*, 3 *mɪniz*; pl. 1 *mɪnim(ɪ)*, 2 *mɪnidɪ*, 3 *mɪnizɪ*;

negative: sing. 1 *öy*, 2 *öd*, 3 *öz*; pl. 1 *öm*, 2 *öd*, 3 *öz* + *mɪnɪ* in singular, *mɪne* in plural;

future: sing. 1 *mɪno*, 2 *mɪnod*, 3 *mɪnoz*; pl. 1 *mɪnom(ɪ)*, 2 *mɪnodɪ*, 3 *mɪnozɪ*;

negative: sing. 1 *ug*, 2 *ud*, 3 *uz* + *mɪnɪ*; pl. 1 *um*, 2 *ud*, 3 *uz* + *mɪne*.

The inferential past has an *-em-* marker, e.g. *mɪnemed* 'it seems that you went'; with an invariable negative marker *övöl*, e.g. *övöl mɪnemed* 'so you didn't go'.

IMPERATIVE
Second person singular: *mɪn*; second person plural: *mɪne*. Negative: *en mɪn/mɪne*

CONDITIONAL
mon/ton/so mɪnɪsal; pl. *mɪnɪsalmɪ*, *-dɪ*, *-zɪ*: i.e. the singular form requires the personal pronouns; the plural forms are conjugated.

The reflexive marker *-(i)s'k-* also supplies the passive voice: e.g. *ḍis'anɪ* 'to clothe' – *ḍis'as'kɪnɪ* 'to clothe oneself/be clothed'.

CAUSATIVE
The marker is *-t*: e.g. *pukɪnɪ* 'to sit' – *puktɪnɪ* 'to seat someone'.

There are markers for semelfactive and reiterated action; the perfective/imperfective contrast is achieved by means of auxiliary verbs: e.g. *kutskɪnɪ* 'to set about', *bɪḍestɪnɪ* 'to complete'.

PARTICIPLES
Present in *-is'/-as'*: e.g. *užas' ad'ami* 'working man'; past in *-em/-am:* e.g. *užam ad'ami* 'a man who worked'. The participle in *-mɪn/-mon* is used as predicate only: e.g. *kniga lɪdžemɪn* 'the book has been read'; but its negative can also be used attributively: *lɪdžɪmte kniga* 'a book that has not been read'.

Postpositions

Postpositions express spatial, temporal, causal, etc. relationships: e.g. *žök vɪlɪn* 'on the table', *žök s'örin pukini* 'to sit at table'; *už s'arɪs'* 'about the work'.

Word order

SOV.

1 Вальлянӥсенӥк Кыл вылэм, Кыл Инмарын
2 вылэм. Со Кыл Инмар вылэм. Со вальлянӥсенӥк
3 Инмарын луэм. Коть ма но Со вамен луэм, ма
гынэ луиз-ке но, Со сяна номре но кылдымтэ.
4 Со бордын улэп-улон вылэм, со улэп-улон адями-
5 ослы люгыт луэм. Люгыт пеӥмытын люгдыса улэ,
6 пеӥмыт сое шобыртыса уг бытты. Инмарлэн лэзем
7 одӥг муртыз вылэм, солэн нимыз Іоаннъ. Со ды-
шетыны лыктэм; со вамен ваньзы но мед оскозы
8 шуса, со Люгытэз тодытыны лыктэм. Со ачыз люгыт луымтэ. только Люгытэз тодытыны лэзьысь-
кемын вылэм.

UGARITIC

INTRODUCTION

Ugaritic belongs to the North-Western branch of the Semitic family, and is the language of Ugarit, and of its surroundings, a trading centre on the Mediterranean coast of Syria. The site is now known as Ras eš-Šamra. There are two firm dates in Ugarit history: a big earthquake in 1365 BC, and the destruction of Ugarit, by invaders from the sea, in 1200 BC. Most of the extant material in Ugaritic dates from the period between these two events, but there are frequent references to earlier times and traditions; the area seems to have been settled by Semitic-speaking tribes about the middle of the third millennium BC. Ugaritic shares certain features with the Canaanite languages.

SCRIPT

Perhaps the most interesting thing about Ugaritic is its unique writing system, in which the Akkadian cuneiform is used to provide a left-to-right alphabetic script, reflecting the letters of the Old Phoenician linear alphabet. The script is consonantal, but has three signs for aleph, as vocalized by /a, i, u/. Thus, *ugrt* (the name of the city) is written:

꠷꠷꠷ ꠷ ꠷꠷꠷ ꠷

Words were divided from each other by a small vertical wedge.

PHONOLOGY

As in Arabic, but Ugaritic has /p/ and /g/.
   The vowel system shows the basic inventory of North-West Semitic:

   long and short: a, i, u

MORPHOLOGY AND SYNTAX

Nominals

Ugaritic had no articles. The class of nominals includes nouns, adjectives, pronouns, and the numerals. There are two genders – masculine and feminine – three numbers showing absolute and construct states, and three cases – nominative, genitive, and accusative. Most known roots are triliterals, plus a few bi- and quadriliterals. The feminine marker is -*t*. The dual is marked by -*m*, reconstructed as masculine -*ami*, oblique -*emi*; feminine -*tami*/-*temi* (*cf.* **Arabic**: -(*t*)*ani*/-(*t*)*ajni*). The masculine plural is also marked by -*m*, realized as -*uma*/-*ima*; feminine: -*atu*/-*ati*.

In construct, the -*m*- of the masculine sound plural is dropped (cf. elision of -*n* of Arabic sound plural in construct). The feminine marker -*t* is not elided, i.e., the feminine absolute and construct are identical.

CASES
As in Arabic, nominative in -*u*, genitive in -*i*, accusative in -*a*.

Pronoun

The attested forms, independent with adnominal affixes, and reconstructed realizations are (in the singular)

		Independent	*Affix*
1		an/ank	-j
2	masc.	at = /ʔattaː/	-k = /kaː/
	fem.	at = /ʔatti/	-k = /ki/
3	masc.	hw = /huwa/	-h = /huː/
	fem.	hj = /hija/	-h = /haː/

DUAL
No independent forms attested; the affixes are doubtful, but seem to be 1 -*nj*, 2 -*km* (cf. Arabic *kumā*), 3 -*hm* (Arabic *humā*).

PLURAL
All forms except the first person affix -*n*, /naː/, are doubtful. The common second person form seems to be *atm* (cf. Arabic *'antum*), the third person *hm* (Arabic *hum*). Postulated forms for the second and third person affixes are: 2 -*kn*, 3 -*hm*/-*hn* (cf. Arabic: -*kum*/-*kunna*; -*hum*/-*hunna*).

RELATIVE PRONOUN
In -*d*/-*dt*; cf. Arabic *du*, Hebrew *z*(*u*).

Numerals

Roots as in Arabic, e.g. 5 *ḤMŠ*, 10 ʿ*ŠR*. The vocalizations as reconstructed, are also close to Arabic: *ḤaMiŠa*, ʿ*aŠRu*.

Verb

There are three persons; singular, dual, and plural forms. Gender is distinguished in the second and third persons. Aspectually, Ugaritic is typically West Semitic, with standard suffixes providing the perfective (past), and prefixes the present–future imperfective: i.e. on the model of *QaTaLa* 'he killed', *yaQTuLu* 'he kills'.

There are indicative, jussive, and imperative moods. An intensive version is obtained by gemination of R_2, i.e. the second radical. Active and passive voices are present, but are difficult to distinguish from each other, because of the consonantal script.

NEGATIVE

The marker is *l* /la/, usually written together with the following word. The particle *al* with the jussive forms a prohibitive: e.g. *al trgm* 'do not speak'.

Prepositions

Mono-, di- or trisyllabic: e.g. *b* /ba/, 'in'; *l* /la/, 'to'; *mn* /min/, 'from'; *ʿd* /ʿad/, 'to'; *bʿd* /baʿda/, 'after'.

UKRAINIAN

INTRODUCTION

The name of this Eastern Slavonic language derives from *ukraina*, the 'border area', the domain of the Cossacks, which lay between the Slav principalities to the north and west, and the Turkish hordes to the south. Today, the language is spoken by about 50 million in the Ukrainian Soviet Socialist Republic, and by considerable numbers in contiguous areas of Poland, Czecho-Slovakia, and Romania, and in Canada, the USA, and Australia. The total number of speakers is probably around 60 million.

Three main dialect areas are distinguished: northern, south-western (including Galicia and Bukovina), and south-eastern. The modern literary language is based on the Middle Dniepr dialect, and Kiev usage. Like Russian and Belorussian, Ukrainian derives from the Slavonic languages spoken in the early Middle Ages in the area between the Black Sea and the Baltic – the Kievan state, or *Rus'*. Specifically Ukrainian features can be detected in documents dating from the twelfth century, and by the fourteenth century the sound shifts and morphological innovations typical of Ukrainian are established. The literary language was, of course, strongly influenced by Old Church Slavonic. Two literary registers can be detected, one largely shared with Russian, the other a specifically Ukrainian variant, with some intake from the spoken Ukrainian language: the so-called *prosta mova*. Translation into *prosta mova* includes the Peresopnitskoe Evangelie (mid-sixteenth century). Towards the end of the sixteenth century the first printed books in Ukrainian appeared. An ever-present source of lexical and morphological enrichment lay in the rich oral literature generated during the struggles for national liberation against the Poles and Turkic invaders.

The consolidation and development of literary Ukrainian in line with the spoken language gathered impetus through the eighteenth century, a process which culminated in the mid-nineteenth century in the impressive figure of Taras Shevchenko (1814–61), whose literary and philological work was of crucial importance for the western Ukraine (i.e. the Austro-Hungarian lands). For the last thirty years of the nineteenth century the use of Ukrainian as a written language was prohibited in the eastern – Russian – part of the Ukraine.

SCRIPT

Cyrillic, with the additional letters є, *i*, *ï*.

PHONOLOGY

Consonants

stops: p, b, t, d, k, g; **t′, d′**
affricates: ts, dz, tʃ, dʒ; **ts′, dz′**
fricatives: f, (v), s, z, ʃ, ʒ, x, h; **s′, z′**
nasals: m, n; **ɲ**
lateral and flap: l, r; **ʎ, r′**
semi-vowels: **j**, w

The nine consonants and the semi-vowel shown in bold type are invariably soft.
/p, b, k, g, tʃ, dʒ, f, v, ʃ, ʒ, m, x, h/ are soft if followed by /i/; i.e. their palatalization is conditional.

Vowels

hard: ɪ, ɛ, a, o, u; /o/ and /u/ are labialized;
soft: i/yi, yɛ, ya, yo, yu

Confusingly, the hard /ɛ/ is notated in the script as *e*; the soft /yɛ/ as ε. Similarly, hard /ɪ/ is и, soft /i, yi/ *i* or *ï*. The other three soft vowels are denoted as я, ьо, ю.

Some notable features of Ukrainian phonology:

1. The presence of long soft consonants: e.g. *žitt′a* 'life', [ʒɪt′t′a]; *znann′a* 'knowledge', [znan′n′a]. A hard consonsant may be assimilated to a soft to produce a long soft cluster: e.g. *holosn′išatɪ* 'to get louder' = [holos′n′iʃatɪ].
2. Common Slav. /*ĕ/ (giving /ĕ/ in Russian) has an /i/ reflex in Ukrainian: cf. Russ. *leto* 'summer' – Ukr. *lito*; Russ. *les* 'forest' – Ukr. *lis*; Russ. *xleb* 'bread' – Ukr. *xlib*.
3. Vowels in unstressed position are not reduced as in Russian; unstressed /e/, however, tends to [i]: e.g. *selo* 'village', [seilɔ].

Stress

Free, on any syllable. Stress does not always coincide with Russian: cf. Russ. *mályj* 'small' – Ukr. *malíi*.

MORPHOLOGY AND SYNTAX

Noun

As in Russian, there are three genders and two numbers; the noun has six cases plus a vocative.

Nouns are divided into hard and soft declensions. Nouns with a final consonant are mainly masculine; *-a/-ya* are typically feminine endings, though many in *-ya* are neuter; *-o* and *-e* are typically neuter. Four declensions are distinguished.

Specimen paradigms: *voda* 'water' (fem. *-a* decl.); *stil* 'table' (masc.)

	Singular	Plural	Singular	Plural
nominative	voda	vodı	stil	stolı
accusative	vodu	vodı	stil	stolı
genitive	vodı	vod	stola	stoliw
locative	vodi	vodax	stoli	stolax
dative	vodi	vodam	stolu	stolam
instrumental	vodoju	vodami	stolom	stolami

The accusative form depends on whether the referent is animate or inanimate; if animate, accusative = genitive as in Russian: e.g. *Ja ne znayu cıx studentiw* 'I don't know these students'; *Vin zustriw brata* 'He met (his) brother.' In the colloquial language, the use of the genitive form is extending to the inanimate sector.

The genitive is used after negative verbs: e.g. *Ja ne znaju c'oho učitel'a* 'I don't know this teacher'; *Tut nemaje paperu* 'There's no paper here.'

Adjective

As attribute, adjective precedes noun and agrees with it in gender, number, and case: e.g. the paradigm of *ridne selo* 'native village' (*selo* is neuter):

	Singular	Plural
nominative	ridne selo	ridni sela
accusative	ridne selo	ridni sela
genitive	ridnoho sela	ridnix sel
locative	ridnomu seli	ridnix selax
dative	ridnomu selu	ridnim selam
instrumental	ridnim selom	ridnimi selami

COMPARATIVE

The marker is *-(i)š*: e.g. *xolodnıi* 'cold' – *xolodnišıi*; *starıi* 'old' – *staršıi*. Example with consonant alternation: *vısokıi* 'high' – *viščıi*. Some are suppletive: *velıkıi* 'big' – *bil'šıi*; *dobrıi* 'good' – *kraššıi*.

Pronoun

PERSONAL

    sing. 1 *ja*, 2 *tı*, 3 masc. *vin*, fem. *vona*, nt. *vono*;
    pl. 1 *mı*, 2 *vı*, 3 common, *vonı*

These are declined in six cases: e.g. for first person singular: acc. *mene*, gen. *mene*, loc. (*na*) *meni*, dat. *meni*, instr. *mnoju*.

The oblique forms of the third person are based on *-(n)jo-*: *joho* 'him', *jii* 'her':

e.g. *ja joho ne znaju* 'I don't know him'. The form *joho* is also the possessive pronoun for third masculine/neuter; *jii*, feminine. These are indeclinable. The possessive pronominal adjectives for the other persons are marked for number and gender: e.g. *miji – moja – moje – moji*.

DEMONSTRATIVE PRONOUN/ADJECTIVE
cei/cja/ce; pl. *c'i* 'this, these'; *toi/ta/te*; pl. *t'i* 'that, those'. Declined in six cases.

INTERROGATIVE PRONOUN
xto 'who?'; *ščo* 'what?'. Declined in six cases.

RELATIVE PRONOUN
kotrii/kotorii; used as in Russian.

Numerals

1–10: the base forms, as used in counting, are *odin, dva, tri, čotiri, p'at', šist', sim, visim, dev'at', des'at'*. 11 *odinadc'at'*; 12 *dvanadc'at'*, 20 *dvadc'at'*; 30 *tridc'at'*; 40 *sorok*; 100 *sto*. All cardinal numbers are declined.

Verb

As in Russian, the distinction between perfective (completed) and imperfective (durative/on-going) action is fundamental: cf.

ja čitaw gazetu 'I was reading the paper'

ja **pro**čitaw gazetu 'I read the paper (and finished it)'

Formation of perfective:

(a) By prefix: e.g. *pisati* 'write' – **na**pisati; *rozumiti* 'understand' – zrozumiti; *gotuvati* 'prepare, cook' – **pri**gotuvati.
(b) By change in stem: e.g. *l'agati* 'lie down' – l'agti.
(c) By stress change: e.g. *zdibati* 'meet' – zdibati.
(d) By means of *-nut'* (giving semelfactive meaning): e.g. *stukati* 'knock' – stuknuti.
(e) Suppletion: e.g. *brati* 'take' – uz'ati; *govoriti* 'speak' – skazati.

Voice, mood, and tense are, in general, as in Russian.

There are two conjugations. Conjugation I has a third person singular (present tense) in *-(j)e*, and third plural in *-(j)ut'*; the corresponding forms in conjugation II are *-t'/-jit'* and *-(j)at'*. As example, the present tense of the first conjugation verb *čitati* 'to read':

	Singular	Plural
1	čitaju	čitajemo
2	čitaješ	čitajete
3	čitaje	čitajut'

Second conjugation: e.g. from *bačiti* 'to see': 1 *baču*, 2 *bačiš*, 3 *bačit'*.

The past tense is marked for gender and number only, excluding persons:

	Singular	Plural
masc.	čɪtaw	
fem.	čɪtala	čɪtalɪ
nt.	čɪtalo	

A Ukrainian innovation is the synthetic future made from imperfective verbs, in parallel with the analytical future with the auxiliary *butɪ*; this synthetic future is unique in the Slavonic group of languages. It is made by adding *-m-* plus the personal endings of the present tense to the infinitive of the sense-verb; e.g. *robɪtɪ* 'to do':

1 *robɪtɪ.mu*, 2 *-mes*, 3 *-me*; pl. 1 *robɪtɪ.memo*, 2 *-mete*, 3 *mut'*

VERBS OF MOTION

As in Russian, there is a basic opposition between (a) determinate (vectorial) motion and (b) indeterminate (random). Both sets are further sub-divided to denote motion on foot or by means of transport. The aspectual distinction cuts across these categories; thus, (b) verbs are imperfective only, the other sets have both aspects: e.g. (a) *pɪtɪ* (perf.) – (b) *xodɪtɪ* (imperf.) motion on foot:

Vonɪ pišlɪ do mista 'They walked to town'

Vin xodɪt' povil'no 'He's a slow walker'

(a) *po-yixatɪ* (perf.) – (b) *yizdɪtɪ* (imperf.) motion by means of transport:

Vonɪ po.jixalɪ do mista 'They drove to town'

Vin jizdɪt' povil'no 'He's a slow driver'

Prepositions

Largely as in Russian. *V* 'in, at' and *u* 'at', distinct in Russian, have coalesced in Ukrainian.

Word order

Basically SVO.

Упочи́ні було́ Сло́во, и Сло́во було́ в Бо́га, и Бог було́ Сло́во.

2. Воно́ було́ в почи́ні у Бо́га.

3. Все ним ста́лося; и без не́го не ста́лося ніщо́, що ста́лося.

4. У іо́му житте́ було́: и житте́ було́ сві́тлом лю́дям.

5. И сві́тло у те́мряві сві́тить, и те́мрява іого́ не обня́ла́.

6. Був чолові́к по́сланий від Бо́га, имя́ іому́ Іоа́н.

7. Сей прийшо́в на сві́дкува́ннє, щоб свідкува́ти про сві́тло, щоб усі́ ві́рували че́рез не́го.

8. Не був він сві́тло, а щоб свідкува́ти про сві́тло.

ULCHA

See under **Nanay**.

URALIC LANGUAGES

The languages belonging to this family lie mainly in a broad band extending across northern Europe and Siberia, from Finland to the Taymyr Peninsula. On both sides of the Urals, the Uralic speech areas centre round the great rivers – the Ob and the Yenisei to the east, the Pechora and the Volga to the west. Still further to the west, a cluster of Uralic languages is found on the north-east Baltic seaboard. Hungarian, isolated from its congeners in central Europe, is the sole outlier.

Though they are structurally heterogeneous, there is no doubt that the Uralic languages are genetically related, and much research has gone towards reconstruction of the parent language and identification of its habitat. The presence of common roots denoting deciduous trees and terms connected with apiculture, suggest an Urheimat to the west, rather than to the east of the Urals. The absence of a common root for 'beech', however, which does not grow east of the Baltic–Black Sea line, may be taken as indicative of a western limit. Other notable lacunae are terms for the sea, rocks, sand, the tundra, and so on. On the whole, the evidence points to an original Uralic habitat between the middle course of the Urals and the Volga.

The first division of the parent language, into Proto-Samoyedic and Proto-Finno-Ugric, has been tentatively dated to the middle of the third millennium BC. A thousand years later, a similar split yielded Proto-Hungarian and Ob-Ugric on the one hand, Permic-Volgaic on the other. The family as it appears at present is internally classified as follows:

1. Samoyedic: Northern: Nenets, Enets, Nganasan;
             Southern: Selkup, Kamassian.
2. Finno-Ugric:

   (a) Ugric: Hungarian;
   (b) Ob-Ugric: Khanty, Mansi;
   (c) Permic-Volgaic: Komi, Udmurt, Mordva, Mari;
   (d) Balto-Finnic: Finnish, Estonian, Karelian, Ingrian, Veps, Vot, Liv;
   (e) Lappish.

Several of these languages were known by other names in the past; e.g. Ostyak (Khanty), Vogul (Mansi), Zyryan (Komi), Votyak (Udmurt), Cheremis (Mari).

Kamassian is now extinct (one speaker was known in 1970), and some of the Balto-Finnic minor languages are moribund. At present, about 23 million

1420

people speak Uralic languages, with Hungarian and Finnish accounting for about 80 per cent of this total.

For the hypothetical connection between Uralic and Dravidian, *see* **Dravidian Languages**.

See **Hungarian, Finnish, Estonian, Karelian, Balto-Finnic Minor Languages, Khanty, Mansi, Komi, Udmurt, Mordva, Mari, Nenets, Lappish.**

URARTIAN

INTRODUCTION

Urartian is the language of a slave-owning people who lived in the Lake Van area between 1500 and 500 BC. The capital city was Tušpa; the religious centre was Musasir. Urartia was at the height of its military and political power in the first half of the first millennium BC, at one time even threatening the Assyrians. Urartia is the Assyrian designation; the ethnonym was *Biaini-*:

LUGAL ^{KUR}bi.i.a.i.n.a.e alusi ^{URU}tu.uš.pa.a.e
'Emperor of the country of the Biaini(li) the ruler of the city of Tušpa.'

It seems clear that Urartian is a non-Indo-European language, genetically close to Hurrian, the language of the Mitamni people. The two languages share many phonological, morphological, and lexical features; D'akonov (in *Jazyki Azii i Afriki* 1979) treats them as variant forms of one language.

SCRIPT

The oldest inscriptions in Urartian date from the ninth century BC, when the cuneiform script seems to have been borrowed from the Assyrians. The script is read from left to right, and has signs for vowels, ideograms, and determinants. Assyrian (Sumero-Akkadian) ideograms are indicated in transcription, normally and here, by capital letters: e.g. LUGAL (Sumerian) 'emperor, king'. Determinants are also notated by capitals raised above the script line: e.g. KUR _____ 'country of'. The polyvalency characteristic of Assyrian usage is much reduced.

PHONOLOGY

Consonants

D'akonov gives a basic inventory of consonants including:

p, p', b; t, t', d; k, k', g; v/w, s, ʃ, ṣ = [ts], γ, ḫ = [χ], z; m, n, l, r; j

Vowels

Four vowels are notated: *i, e, a, u; o* may well have been present, but is not reflected in the cuneiform character.

MORPHOLOGY AND SYNTAX

Noun

Urartian had a defining particle -*ne*, affixed to nouns in any case, which acted as an article: e.g. *Ḫaldi.ne uštabe...* 'the god Ḫaldi appeared/acted...'

Nouns and adjectives normally end in -*i*, though other vocalic endings are possible: e.g. *pili* 'canal'; *ḫuradi* 'warrior'; *euri* 'lord/master'; *qiura* 'earth'; *u^SAL lutu* 'woman'; *gunuše* 'battle'; *LUGALtuḫi* 'kingdom'.

There is no grammatical gender. The noun has two numbers and about a dozen cases. A frequent plural marker is -*li*: e.g. *ereli* 'emperor', pl. *erelili*.

A noun in base form with the defining particle -*ne* is the subject of an intransitive verb or the object of a transitive verb. The logical subject of a transitive verb is in the ergative case in -*še*: e.g.

> ^Iišpuiniše ^ID sardureḫiniše ini E-é zaduni
> 'Išpuini, son of Sarduri, built this house' (where the affix -*ḫini* = 'belonging to'; cf. ^SAL taririaḫini(*li*) 'belonging to Tariria'; *ini* 'this'; E 'house' (Sumerian); *zadu*- 'to build').

GENITIVE CASE
Sing. -*i*/-*e*; pl. *a.w*: e.g. ^URU tušpae URU 'ruler of the city of Tušpa'; pl. ^KUR ebaninaw DINGIR '(to) the god of the countries'.

DATIVE CASE
-*i*/-*ə*, pl. *a.wə*: this ending is added to the nominative base + -*n*: e.g. ^LU ḫuradi 'warrior'; definite ^LU ḫuradinə; dat. ^LU ḫuradin.a.wə.

ADITIVE
-*e.də*, pl. *a.də*: e.g. *uštadi* ^KUR urmeedə 'I came to the country of Urme'.

There are also locative, ablative, essive, etc. case endings.

Adjective

-*usi* is a formant: *LUGAL(nu)si* 'imperial'; *urišḫusi(ni)* 'armed'.

Pronoun

The first person singular is attested in the ergative form: e.g. *iеše* 'by me'; *iеše ini pili agubi* 'by me this canal was built' = 'I built this canal'; and in the oblique form: e.g. *me* '(to) me': ^D ḫaldiš.me aruni 'the god Ḫaldi gave me ...'. The third person is *mani/manini*. The second person is not attested.

Two possessive affixes are known: sing. 1 -*uki* 'my'; 3 -*masi* 'his': e.g. ^KUR ebaniuki 'my country'.

DEMONSTRATIVE PRONOUN/ADJECTIVE
ini precedes the noun: e.g. *ini pili* 'this canal'.

RELATIVE PRONOUN

ali, erg. *aluše*: e.g. *aluše ini* DUB.*te tule* 'by whom this inscription is destroyed' = 'whoever destroys this inscription'.

Numerals

Only two numerals are known: 1 *šusini*; 10,000 *atibi*.

Verb

-u is the characteristic ending of transitive verbs: e.g. *aru* 'give', *zadu* 'create', *šidištu* 'build'.

The verb *du* 'to do', acts as a transitive formant: e.g. *welidu* 'to gather'. *-a* is a typical intransitive ending: e.g. *nuna* 'to come'. Thus, the same root may form a transitive in *-u* and an intransitive in *-a*: cf. *šiu* 'to bring'; *šia* 'to go/come' (with reference to motion, not direction).

The following past tense forms are attested:

> intransitive: sing. 1 *-di*, 3 *-bi/-e*; pl. 3 *-li*;
> transitive: sing. 1 *-bi/-li*, 3 *-ni/-me/-ali*; pl. 1 *-še*, 3 *-ituni/-li/-me*.

Direct and indirect pronominal object affixes are added to these endings: e.g. *artume* 'they gave me'; *ḫarḫaršituli* 'they destroyed them'. Cf. *šidištubi* 'I built it', *šidištuli* 'I built them'; *šidištuni* 'he built it', *šidištuali* 'he built them'; *šidištuše* 'we built'; *arubi* 'I gave it', *aruni* 'he gave it', *aruali* 'he gave them', *arume* 'he gave to me'; *alušme* BUZURtuḫə *arune* 'he who gave me the kingdom' (*alu.š.me* 'by-whom to-me').

The Urartian verbal complex contains the following ordered items:

1. stem + extensions (*-ar/-an* etc.);
2. aspect marker (narrative Ø; imperfective *-ed-*; perfective *-št-*;
3. transitive/intransitive marker: trans. *-u-/-i-*; intrans. *-a-*;
4. modal indices;
5. subject/object markers (these are movable).

An independent negating particle is *ujə*.

Postposition

A few postpositions are known: e.g. *-ka(i)* 'before'; *-pi* 'under, on condition of ...'; *-ištine* 'for': *ᴰḫaldia ištine* 'for the god Ḫaldi'.

URDU

Urdu is the official language of Pakistan, where it is spoken by about 10 million people. In India, it is spoken by many millions of people, either as mother tongue or as second language, in the Panjab and in the states of Uttar Pradesh and Andhra Pradesh; about 50 million is a reasonable estimate. Phonologically and morphologically, Urdu and Hindi are virtually one and the same language. For a description of this language, *see* **Hindi**.

Historically, this common language derives from the Khaṛī Bōlī group of dialects centred on Uttar Pradesh and the Delhi area, which served as a lingua franca between the local population and the Moslem invaders from the west. Through the Middle Ages, this lingua franca – known as *zabān-e-urdū*, the 'language of the camp/army' – gradually consolidated its position as the main inter-regional language of north India: a tribute, in a way, to the stability created by the Mughal dynasty. From being no more than a colloquial, it was able to graduate to the status of a literary language, used, along with Persian, in the Moslem courts (sixteenth to eighteenth centuries). Given the cultural affiliations of these courts, it is not surprising to find that large numbers of Arabic and Persian words entered the lexicon. From the late eighteenth century onwards the Farsi–Hindustani of the Mughal courts and their entourages is known simply as Urdu.

In other words, Farsi–Urdu, especially of the southern Indian courts, where it was known as *rextā* 'mixed', was a somewhat artificial product, whose specialized vocabulary hardly reached the Khaṛī Bōlī-speaking masses. In the late eighteenth century Hindu writers and scholars, nourished on native Indian tradition, rather than on Arabo-Persian culture, began to use Khaṛī Bōlī ('Hindustani') as a medium for literary expression in terms of Sanskrit–Hindu culture. This development had two corollaries: the use of the Devanagari script instead of the Arabic, and recourse to Sanskrit for lexical enrichment. By the mid-nineteenth century Hariścandra could use 'Hindi' as an effective and well-equipped vehicle for creative writing in the modern sense: that is, not simply as a vessel for the decanting of received tradition. Urdu and Hindi are, thus, cultural polarizations emanating from a common linguistic core.

Classical Urdu literature of the seventeenth/eighteenth centuries is rich and extensive, and some of it is of superlative quality: e.g. the ghazals of Mīr Taqī Mīr (1722?–1810). Today, Urdu is the vehicle of one of the sub-continent's most prolific and important literatures.

SCRIPT

The Arabic–Persian script is used, with additional letters for the retroflex series.

UYGUR

INTRODUCTION

In Baskakov's (1966) classification, Uygur is allocated to the Karluk-Khorezm sub-group of Hunnic (*see* **Turkic Languages**). The majority of Uygur speakers live in the Xinjiang-Uygur Autonomous Region of the People's Republic of China, where they form about 70 per cent of the total population, numbering about 4 million. About 100,000 Uygurs live in the Kazakh and Uzbek Soviet Socialist Republics of the USSR.

The name 'Uygur' has several linguistic connotations:

1. Modern Uygur: defined as above, and described in this article.

2. Old Uygur was the language of a Turkic people who were politically and culturally pre-eminent in central Asia from the tenth to the fourteenth centuries AD. They were connected with, but not certainly the forebears of the modern Uygurs. Old Uygur was the language of administration and literature, particularly during the Karakhanid period in the eleventh century and in the heyday of the Mongol Empire.

3. Yellow Uygur: this is an umbrella term for four linguistic groups in Gansu province of the CPR, only one of which speaks a Turkic language; the other three speak, respectively, Mongolian, Chinese, and Tibetan.

SCRIPT

The Old Uygur script (in use from the seventh century onwards) was based on a Sogdian model, and was in its turn borrowed by the Manchus and the Mongols. In the twelfth/thirteenth century the Arabic script was introduced into Transoxania by the Karakhanid Dynasty, while the older vertical script continued to be used by the eastern Uygurs.

In the CPR, Modern Uygur is written in the Arabic script with supplementary and amended letters for specific Uygur sounds. For example, /ə/ is represented by hamza on a bearer plus -*h*; /o/œ/ is represented by *waw*, /u/y/ by *waw* + hamza. In 1959, a romanized script was proposed for Uygur. Cyrillic is used by Uygurs in the USSR.

PHONOLOGY

Consonants

stops: p, b, t, d, k, g, q
affricates: tʃ, dʒ
fricatives: (f), s, z, ʃ, ʒ, x, ɢ, h
nasals: m, n, ŋ
lateral and flap: l, r
semi-vowels: j, w

Vowels

front: i, e, ə, œ, y
back: ɪ, a, o, u

Here /œ/ is notated as *ö*, /y/ as *ü*.

VOWEL HARMONY

In Uygur, as in Uzbek, vowel harmony is in a state of atrophy. The difference is that, whereas in Uzbek a declensional model based on back vowels has become the norm, the opposite has happened in Uygur, where the genitive, accusative, and ablative endings, for example, are, irrespective of stem, *-ning*, *-ni*, *-din*. A second, and very remarkable feature in Uygur vowel harmony is provided by regressive vocalic assimilation: a back stem-vowel may be fronted when a front-vowel affix is added: e.g. *mal* 'cattle'; but 'his cattle' is *mel.i*; *bala.lar* 'children' – *bal.i.lir.i* 'his children'. This phenomenon even affects root forms; cf. *beliq* 'fish' (common Turkic, *balɪq*). The form *beliq* also violates the common Turkic partition between the uvular phonemes /q/ɢ/ + back vowel, on the one hand, and the velar phonemes /k/g/ + front vowel on the other.

MORPHOLOGY AND SYNTAX

Plural formation, declension, personal affixes, possessive affixes, treatment of adjective, the pronominal system and the numerals are all standard Turkic (*see* **Turkic Languages**), at least in form, though the shift in vowel harmony produces some strange forms, and specific variants occur: e.g. the second person pronoun *sizler* has been reduced through *siler* to *silə*. The plural marker *-lar/-ler* also tends to *-lər*. Final *b* tends to become /v/ before a vowel: e.g. *kitab* 'book' + *-im* → *kitivim*.

The front vowel endings established in the declensional system have already been mentioned: cf. declension of *ana* 'mother': gen. *ananing*; loc. *anida*; dat. *aniɢa*; abl. *anidin*; acc. *anini*.

Verb

Some examples of tense formation, indicative mood:

preterite: *yaz.di.m* 'I wrote';

perfect: *yaz.ɢan.mən* or, more usually, *mən yaz.ɢan*: i.e. agglutinative personal marker is discarded in favour of neutral form + personal pronoun;

past narrative/inferential: *yez.ip.ti.mən* 'it seems I was writing' (note change of root vowel);

punctual past: *yezip yatar.edim* 'I was writing at the moment when...' (the -*ip* participle is followed by the aux. verb *yat-* 'to lie': realized as /yezivatattim/);

past frequentative: *yez.i.diɢan edim* 'I wrote (continuously/continually)';

present: the -*p* participle is used with auxiliaries *yat-* and *tur-*: e.g. *yezip yetip tuturmən* 'I am now writing': realized as /yezivatimən/.

Postpositions

Postpositions govern nominative, dative, ablative, or accusative.

UZBEK

INTRODUCTION

Baskakov (1966) allocates Uzbek to the Karluk-Khoresmian sub-group of the Karluk group of Western Hunnic (*see* **Turkic Languages**). Old Uzbek or Chagatay (also known simply as Turki) was one of the literary languages used at the Tīmūrid court in Herat in the fifteenth/sixteenth century by such distinguished writers as Alīshīr Navā'ī (1441–1501), the 'father of Uzbek culture'; and, later, by the Emperor Babur, whose delightful autobiography, the *Bāburnāma*, is a classic of world literature. Among outstanding writers and scholars native to the region, though they wrote in Arabic or Persian, is the polymath al-Bīrūni.

With around 12–13 million speakers, Uzbek is the third most widely spoken language of the USSR (after Russian and Ukrainian). Most Uzbeks live in the Uzbek Soviet Socialist Republic, with some spread into the adjacent Tadzhik, Kirgiz, and Kazakh SSRs. The language is used at all levels of education, and in the local media, with numerous newspapers and periodicals. More books appear in Uzbek than in any other language of the Moslem republics.

SCRIPT

The Arabic script was finally abandoned in 1927. After an experimental period of romanization, Cyrillic with additional letters was adopted in 1940.

PHONOLOGY

Consonants

stops: p, b, t, d, k, g, q
affricates: ts, tʃ, dʒ
fricatives: f, v, s, z, ʃ, ʒ, x, γ, h, j
nasals: m, n, ŋ
lateral and flap: l, r

Vowels

The six letters: *i, e, a, o, ŭ, u* represent the following sounds:

i, ɪ, ɛ, æ, a, aː, ə, ɔ, u, uː

In contact with a palatalized consonant, /u/ → [y]: e.g. *juda* 'very' = /dʒyda/. The sounds /ya, yo, ye, yu/, are denoted by the equivalent Cyrillic letters. Cyrillic hard sign is used to represent 'ain in Arabic words: the hard sign also lengthens the vowel: e.g. /fɛːl/ = Arabic *fa'ala*. /u/ is lengthened by the addition of Cyrillic в: e.g. *suv* /'water'/ = /suː/.

VOWEL HARMONY

Uzbek has lost the standard Turkic opposition between front/back, rounded/unrounded vowels, which determines the vocalic articulation of words throughout the family. Thus, where Turkish, for example, has *onlardan/sizlerden* Uzbek has back vowels in both: *ulardan/sizlardan*. The practical result is that, whereas elsewhere in the Turkic family there is at least a dual set of endings displaying concord with front or back stem vowels (and often more than two – e.g. in Altay, which has sixteen possible notations of the plural affix), Uzbek has only one set. Thus the infinitive ending, for example, is always *-moq*: e.g. *yozmoq* 'to write', *bermoq* 'to give'. Similarly, the negative infix remains *-ma-* for any root: e.g. *kelmadi* 'he didn't come' (contrast Turkish: *gelmedi*). On the other hand, the notation selected for the past tense, for example, favours a front-vowel spelling: *-dim, -ding, -di*; pl. *-dik, -dingiz, -dilar*, though there is a tendency to realize the *-i-* as *-ɪ-* after back vowel stems: e.g. *išladim* → [iʃladɪm].

MORPHOLOGY AND SYNTAX

In declension, the predicative personal affixes, the possessive markers, the treatment of the adjective, the pronominal system and the numerals, Uzbek has standard Turkic forms.

Noun

The accusative ending is *-ni*: e.g. *kitoblarni* 'books'. A stem-final /g/ɣ/ tends to become [k/q] before the dative ending, which then assimilates: e.g. *boy* 'garden' (Iranian loan-word) – *boqqa* 'to the garden'. Arabic words may take the Uzbek plural marker *-lar* or retain a broken plural: e.g. *taraf* 'side', pl. *taraflar* or *atrof*.

Examples of cases:

> genitive: *Toškent – Uzbekistonning eng katta šahari* 'Tashkent is Uzbekistan's biggest town', *Uzbek adabiyotning otasɪ* 'the father of Uzbek culture';
> accusative: *biz Tamarani kutubxonda kurdik* 'we saw Tamara in the library';
> dative: ... *menga xat yozdi* '... wrote me a letter';
> ablative: ... *keča Samarqanddan keldi* '... came yesterday from Samarkand'

Verb

Like the Uzbek noun, the Uzbek verb has a single set of endings, though here, as pointed out above, this single set often reflects a reductionist orthography rather than actual realization.

Tense structure is standard, as is the formation of the basic tenses: present–future in *-a-*, past in *-di*, future in *-adžak*, conditional in *-sa*. Uzbek, however, has several ways of making a present continuous tense: thus, from *yozmoq* 'to write':

yoz.a.yotir.man		(literary style)
yoz.a.yap.man	'I am in the process of writing'	(spoken language)
yoz.ib.turib.man		(continuity emphasized)
yoz.moqda.man		(not necessarily punctual)

The formation of the passive, reflexive, and causative forms is standard. The perfect marker is *-gan-*: e.g. *yoz.gan.man* 'I have written'.

PARTICIPLES

present: *-yot.gan/di.gan*;
past: *-gan*;
future: *-ar/-a.džak*.

These are used in the formation of relative clauses: e.g. *kel.a.yot.gan kiši* 'the man who is coming (now)'; *bu kitob.ni uqi.yot.gan bola* 'the boy who is reading this book'.

The participles are neutral as to voice: e.g. *kitob.ni ol.gan kiši* 'the man who took the book'; *ol.gan pul* 'the money that was taken'; *men borgan yer* 'the place I went to'.

RELATIVE CLAUSE
Example:

Rašida.ning kelgan.i.ni bil.a.man
'I know that Rašida has arrived' (*Rašida.ning* 'of R.'; *kel.gan.i* 'his coming'; *-ni* acc. ending after *bilaman* 'I know').

PASSIVE CONSTRUCTION
Example:

Eski uzbek tili.dan hozirgi zamon tili.ga kučir.il.di
'was translated from old Uzbek into the present-day language'.

Postpositions

Postpositions may follow nominative, genitive, dative, or ablative, and may take cases and possessive markers: e.g. *yoni* 'beside': *mening yonimda* 'beside me'; *sening yoningda* 'beside you'; *sizning yoningizda* 'beside you (pl.)'.

Word order

SOV.

۱ اوّل ده سوز بار ايردی وسوز خداده ايردی وسوز خدا ايردی⊙

۲،۳ اول سوز اوّل ده خداده ايردی⊙ بارچه نرسه آنينك برلان بولدی

۴ وهيچ بولغان نرسه آنسيز بولمادی⊙ آنينك ايچيده تيريكليك ايردی

۵ هم تيريكليك انسان لارنينك نوری ايردی⊙ ونور قارانغوليق ده

۶ ياقتيرادور ليكن قارانغوليق نورنی قبول قيلمادی⊙ خدا يباركان يحيی

۷ آتليغ بر كيشی بار ايردی⊙ بول شهادت اوچون كيلدی نور
خصوصيده شهادت بركای بارچه لار آنينك واسطه سی برلان ايمان

۸ كيلتورکای لار⊙ اول اوزی نور ايماس ايردی ليكن اول نور
خصوصيده شهادت برماککا (کيليب) ايردی⊙

VEDIC

See under **Sanskrit**.

VEPS

See under **Balto-Finnic Minor Languages**.

VIETNAMESE

INTRODUCTION

The genetic status of Vietnamese has been the subject of some controversy. For long, it was regarded as a member of the Sino-Tibetan family, and, certainly, there is a very substantial Chinese element in the language, which is hardly surprising, given the decisive influence of Chinese language and culture on Vietnam over some 2,000 years. Research in the nineteenth and twentieth centuries, however, has gone to suggest that this Chinese element is superimposed on a non-Sino-Tibetan substratum. What is controversial is the exact nature of the substratum. According to H. Maspéro (1912, 1916) Modern Vietnamese represents the fusion of a Mon-Khmer language with a Tai language; and, in view of the tonal structure of Vietnamese, the tonal Tai language was taken to be the decisive formant. Accordingly, Vietnamese was classified as a Tai language. In the 1950s, however, A.G. Haudricourt showed that Vietnamese did not acquire its tonal system till comparatively late in its history (probably during the first millennium AD) and that it was basically a Mon-Khmer language, belonging to the Austro-Asiatic phylum. This is now the accepted classification. About 65 million people speak the language in Vietnam, and at least another million speakers are scattered abroad, with large colonies in the USA, in Hong-Kong, Paris, and several Pacific islands.

Typical of Vietnamese classical literature is the *truyện thơ* or verse-novel, the most celebrated example of which is the *Truyện Kiêu* by Vietnam's greatest writer, Nguyên Du (1765–1820). Formally, the truyện thơ is composed in alternating six- and eight-syllable strophes, with a musical counterpoint between the two level tones and the four moving tones. The Tang seven-syllable line was also very popular in Vietnamese poetry.

DIALECTS

The main dialectal divisions have always tended to centre round the major cities – Hué, Hã-nôi, and Saigon (now Hô-Chí-Minh City). The modern literary standard combines the consonantal inventory of the central dialect with the tonal system of the northern.

SCRIPT

Diachronically, four main stages can be distinguished in the development of written Vietnamese:

1. Sino-Vietnamese: from BC to the tenth century AD. This period is characterized by the use of the Chinese script, and by Chinese pronunciation of Vietnamese words.

2. The medieval period, fourteenth to seventeenth centuries. In this period the writing system known as chữ nôm was developed by Buddhist scholar–priests. Chinese script continued to be used for Vietnamese pronunciation; and composite graphs were used, in which one component signals the pronunciation, while the other component indicates the meaning: e.g.

至典 = *đến* 'to come',

where

典

in Chinese, *diăn*, suggests the pronunciation, and

至

in Chinese, *zhì* 'to reach, arrive at', indicates the meaning. Again, a Chinese character denoting a semantic equivalent in Vietnamese, may be given a supporting Chinese graph to reinforce the equation; e.g. the non-Chinese graph

𡗶 = *trời* 'sky'

in which two Chinese characters

天 *tiān* 'sky', and 上 *shàng* 'above, up',

have been superimposed.

3. The Roman script was introduced by Catholic missionaries in the seventeenth century. It is extended by the use of diacritics to mark certain vowels and five of the six tones, and by the use of the letters *ơ*, *ư*, and *đ* = /d/; unbarred *d* = /z/.

4. In the twentieth century, more especially in its second half, this 'national script', quốc ngữ, has helped to extend literacy to all classes of Vietnamese society.

PHONOLOGY

Consonants

stops: p, b, t, d, k; aspirated stops: t', k'
affricate: tʃ
fricatives: f, v, s, z, ʃ, ʒ, x, ɣ
nasals: m, n, ɲ, ŋ
lateral: l

[g] is an allophone of /ɣ/. /p, t, k/ are non-aspirates and are unreleased as finals.

Vowels

i, ɪ, e, ɛ, ʊ, u, o, ɔ, aː, a, ʌ, ə

Correspondence between sound and symbol is weak; /z/, for example, is variously notated as *d*, *gi*, and *r*. The two most difficult vowel sounds are *ư* which is approximately /ʊ/ and *ơ* which is a wide, unrounded /ə/.

There are over 20 diphthongs and a dozen triphthongs, mostly containing /ʌ/.

Tones

There are six tones in the standard (northern) dialect:

1. mid-level: not marked in script, e.g. *tôi* 'I';
2. low falling: marked by grave accent, e.g. *rồi* (perfective marker);
3. high rising: marked by acute accent, e.g. *cá* 'fish'; *khách* 'guest';
4. low, rising after initial dip: marked by ˀ: e.g. *của* (genitive particle);
5. high broken: marked by tilde, e.g. *sẽ* (future particle);
6. low broken: marked by subscript dot, e.g. *lại* 'to come'; *lực* 'strength'.

Tones 5 and 6 are glottalized.

Tone is further modulated by intonation patterns of an affective nature.

MORPHOLOGY AND SYNTAX

As in Chinese, there is no inflection of any kind; meaning in a sentence depends on the due ordering of its components. The Chinese distinction between 'full words' (*shící*) and 'empty words' (*xūcí*) can be usefully applied to Vietnamese: 'full words' include nouns, pronouns, verbs, and quantifiers; 'empty words' are particles, connectives, and interjections.

Noun

Nouns differ grammatically from other words in Vietnamese in that they take classifiers: most importantly, *cái* for inanimate objects, *con* for animates. Other classifiers include: *chiếc* (for vehicles, boats, etc.) *quyển* (books) *người* (people), *vị* (important people), etc. Use of the classifier is obligatory if a numeral is present (apart from *một* '1'). The order is numeral – classifier – nominal: e.g. *hai con cá* 'two fishes'; *năm mươi sáu quyển sách* '56 books'.

NUMBER

The plural marker is *những*, which precedes the head-word: e.g. *những tiệm tạp-hóa* 'bazaars'. The pronominal plural marker is *chúng*: e.g. *chúng tôi* 'we'.

POSSESSION

The marker is *của*: e.g. *máy ảnh của tôi* 'my camera'; *Ai là bạn của chúng tôi?* 'Who are our friends?' Simple apposition is valid where possession is self-evident or inalienable: e.g. *cho nhà tôi và các cháu* 'for (*cho*) my wife and children'.

A focusing or topicalizing marker is *thì*.

Adjective

The predicative adjective is a stative verb. Attributively, the adjective follows the noun: e.g. *một lá cờ đỏ* 'a red flag' (*đỏ* 'red'; *cờ* 'flag': *lá* is a classifier); *các nước cộng-sản* 'Communist countries' (*các* is a pluralizing marker).

COMPARATIVE
Made with *hơn*: e.g. *lớn hơn* 'bigger'; *nhỏ hơn* 'smaller'.

Pronoun

Tôi is the usual first person singular form: pl. *chúng-tôi* 'we'. For the second person there is a fairly wide choice of socio-linguistic options, many forms being kinship terms. Generally, *ông* is used to males, *bà* to older women, *cô* to younger women. More familiar modes of address are: *anh* (elder brother), *chị* (elder sister).

Standard third person forms are: *ông ấy* 'he', *cô ấy/bā ấy* 'she': e.g. *Ông ấy nói tiếng gì?* 'What language does he speak?' (*nói* 'to speak').

DEMONSTRATIVE PRONOUNS
này 'this, these'; *ấy* 'that, those': e.g. *hôm này* 'today'; *ba cái bàn này* 'these three tables'.

INTERROGATIVE PRONOUNS
ai 'who?'; (*cái*) *gì* 'what?'. Several interrogative particles serve to round off sentences, e.g. *phải không* is equivalent to French *n'est-ce pas?*: e.g. *Ông muốn mua sách phải không?* 'You want to buy books, don't you?' (*mua* 'buy'; *sách* 'book').

RELATIVE PRONOUN
mà may be used where the referent is specifically identified: e.g. *cái nhà trắng ấy mà ông đứ ng đay thấy...* 'that white (*trắng*) house (*nhà*) which you can see (*thấy*) from this position...'. Where the referent is indefinite, no relative particle is necessary: e.g. *tôi gặp một người bạn ∅ đi...* 'I met (*gặp*) a friend (*bạn*) who was going...'; *tôi có em gái ∅ đang dạy ở...* 'I have a sister who is teaching in...'.

Numerals

1–10: *một, hai, ba, bốn, năm, sáu, bảy, tám, chín, mười*. 11 *mười một*; 20 *hai mươi*; 100 *một trăm*.

Verb

A characteristic of all predicatives in Vietnamese is that they can be negated. The general negating particle is *không*, which precedes the verb: e.g. *tôi không có tiến* 'I have no money'. *đâu* is a final negative particle.

Verbs are divided into active (functional) verbs, stative verbs, and co-verbs. Stative verbs include adjectives. The copula is *là*, which is negated by *không phải là* 'it is not true that...': e.g. *tôi là Mỹ, chứ không phải là người Anh* 'I am American, not British' (*Mỹ* 'American', cf. Chinese *měi*).

The existential verb *ở* is used to mean 'to be located in': e.g. *Ông Nam ở bên Pháp* 'Mr Nam is/lives in France'.

Verbs are not marked in any way for person, number, tense, or aspect. Various particles are used to give a temporal fix: e.g.

> *đã*: past-tense marker, preceding sense-verb, e.g. *chính-phủ Anh đã thay-đổi chính-sách* 'the English government has changed its policy (and will...)' (*chính-phủ* 'government'; *thay-đổi* 'to change');
> *chưa* 'not yet', e.g. *ông ấy chưa đến* 'he has not come yet';
> *sẽ*: future marker, e.g. *ông ấy sẽ đi Mỹ* 'he will be going to America';
> *sắp*: imminent future, e.g. *Chúng tôi sắp đi Hanoi* 'We are just about to go to Hanoi';
> *rồi*: perfective marker; this particle follows the sense-verb, e.g. *ông ấy đến rồi* 'he has already come' (Chinese: *le*);
> *đang*: progressive marker, e.g. *Cô ấy đang học tiếng Việt* 'She is at present studying Vietnamese'.

PASSIVE

Expressed by *bị* or by *được*; *bị* (cf. Chinese *bèi*) retains the true passive sense, suggesting that the patient is being subjected to something he or she cannot help or does not particularly enjoy: e.g. *Ông ấy bị vợ bỏ* 'His wife walked out on him.' Contrast: *Ông ấy được thăng chức* 'He was promoted.'

MODAL VERBS

Example: *phải nên* 'should, must'; *đừng (nên)* 'should/must not'; *được* 'to be able to/be allowed to' (depending on word order): cf. *bịnh-nhan được ăn* 'the patient was allowed to eat'; *bịnh-nhan ăn được* 'the patient was able to eat'.

Word order

SVO is basic; OSV is common.

¹Ban đầu trước hết có Ngôi Lời, và Ngôi Lời 1
ở cùng Đức Chúa Trời, mà Ngôi Lời là Đức
Chúa Trời. ²Ban đầu trước hết ngôi ấy ở cùng 2
Đức Chúa Trời. ³Mọi vật bởi ngôi ấy mà sanh 3
ra, và chẳng có sự gì đã làm nên, mà chẳng
phải bởi ngôi ấy. ⁴Sự sống ở trong ngôi ấy, 4
mà sự sống ấy là sự sáng soi thiên-hạ. ⁵Và sự 5
sáng ấy đã soi trong sự tối tăm, mà sự tối tăm
chẳng nhìn lấy sự sáng.

⁶Đức Chúa Trời đã sai một người tên là Jean. 6
⁷Ông ấy đến mà làm người làm chứng, để làm 7
chứng về sự sáng, hầu cho mọi người được tin
bởi ông ấy. ⁸Ông ấy chẳng phải là sự sáng ấy, 8
song ông ấy đến để được làm chứng về sự sáng.

VOT

See under **Balto-Finnic Minor Languages**.

WAKASHAN

See under **North American Indian Isolates**.

WELSH

INTRODUCTION

The Celtic people who colonized the British Isles in the second half of the first millennium BC were speakers of P-Celtic (*see* **Celtic Languages**). By the time the Romans arrived in Britain, this P-Celtic or Brythonic was the language of 'Britannia' = Brythonia, spoken from the Channel to the Clyde–Forth valley. The Anglo-Saxon invasions followed the Roman occupation, and by the seventh century AD the Celtic-speaking area was halved, with Anglo-Saxon established in a broadening swathe from the Tyne to the Channel coast as far west as Dorset, and Brythonic confined to a shrinking foothold in the western marches. Inherent in this process of break-up and tribal dispersion was the emergence of dialects – the earliest forms of Welsh and Cornish–Breton.

The Brythonic language spoken in what is now the Principality of Wales is usually periodized as follows:

Sixth to eighth centuries: primitive Welsh
Eighth to twelfth centuries: Old Welsh
Twelfth to fifteenth centuries: Middle Welsh
Fifteenth century to present day: Modern Welsh

The oldest text in what is recognizably the Welsh dialect of Brythonic is the *Gododdin*, a heoric lament for the Celtic warriors of the Kingdom of Edinburgh, who fell trying to take Catterick in Yorkshire from the Saxons. The poem has been attributed to Aneirin, one of the two celebrated Welsh bards of the sixth/seventh century. The other is Taliesin, whose figure was to blend in later Welsh literature with that of the mysterious and shadowy seer Merlin (< *Myrddin*).

From the eleventh century onwards Welsh poetry entered upon one of its greatest periods, that of bardic or courtly poetry. The bards – the *gogynefeirdd* – were attached to princely courts where they were organized in hierarchies, ranging from master singers to apprentices or disciples. Subject matter was prescribed and correlated with different grades within the hierarchy: thus, the production of eulogies was obligatory for a master bard, for whom, however, love was an unworthy and therefore taboo subject. A very high degree of technical skill in the handling of complicated prosodies was demanded, and, to ensure that such skills were duly cultivated and transmitted to posterity, a kind of competition – the eisteddfod – was introduced. The supreme master of the bardic style – Dafydd ap Gwilym (fourteenth century) – appeared, in fact, when the cult was well past its heyday; his influence both on the style and content of later Welsh poetry, and on the Welsh language itself, was enormous.

Two fourteenth-century manuscripts, *The White Book of Rhydderch* and *The Red Book of Hergest*, contain the text of the prose masterpiece of early Welsh literature – the *Mabinogion*, a collection of tales reflecting an interweaving of Celtic and Norman-French motifs and beliefs.

In 1547 the first Welsh printed book appeared. The importance of William Morgan's translation of the Bible (1588, revised 1620) for subsequent Welsh prose writing can hardly be overestimated.

Nineteenth-century Welsh literature was closely associated with religious revivals and movements. An outstanding figure is Daniel Owen, the Welsh Dickens.

The twentieth century has seen a remarkable revival in the use of Welsh for prose, poetry, and journalism; since the 1960s the language has enjoyed joint official status in the principality.

DIALECTS

There is a broad division into north and south dialects, which affects for example the pronunciation of certain vowels; the letter *u* is pronounced as /iː/ in South Wales, as /ɪ/, tending to /ʉ/, in North Wales.

SCRIPT

The Roman alphabet minus *k*, *q*, *v*, *x*, *z*. There are eight digraphs for specifically Welsh sounds: *dd* = /ð/, *ff* = /f/, *ng* = /ŋ/, *ll* = /ɬ/, *ph* = /f/, *rh* = /r̥/, *si* = /ʃ/, *th* = /θ/.

PHONOLOGY

Consonants

    stops: p, b, t, d, k, g
    fricatives: f, v, θ, ð, s, ʃ, x, h
    nasals: m, n, ŋ
    laterals and flaps: l, ɬ, r, r̥
    semi-vowels: j, w

/ɬ/ and /r̥/ are voiceless; the corresponding voiced sounds are /l/ and /r/. The affricate /dʒ/ occurs in loan-words.

Vowels

    short: ɪ, i, ɛ, a, ɔ, u
    long: i, e, a, o, u
    ə

In Welsh orthography, *w/ŵ* denotes /u, uː/: e.g. *cwm* 'valley' = /kum/; *y* denotes /ə/, /ɪ/, or /i/.

Diphthongs are rising (consonantal *j/w* + vowel) or falling (vowel + consonantal *j/w*): e.g. /ia, wo/ are rising; /ai, ey, aw/ are falling.

Stress

Stress is usually on the penultimate in polysyllables, but final stress is common.

Mutation

As in all Celtic languages, consonantal mutation plays a key role in Welsh phonology and morphology. The consonants which undergo mutation are the six stops: *p, b, t, d, c* = /k/, and *g*; also *m, ll,* and *rh*. Three kinds of mutation are distinguished:

(a) Soft mutation (lenition): /p, t, k/ mutate into their voiced correlatives /b, d, g/; /b, d, g/ become /f, ð, Ø/; *m → f, ll → l, rh → r*. This is by far the commonest form of mutation; Williams (1980) lists over 40 instances in which it occurs.

(b) Nasal mutation; this affects the stops only; the unvoiced become *mh, nh, ngh*, the voiced become *m, n, ng*.

(c) The spirant mutation; only the unvoiced stops are affected: → *ph, th, ch*.

For example, *pen* 'head': *ei ben e* 'his head' (lenition); *'y mhen i* 'my head' (nasal mutation); *ei phen hi* 'her head' (spirant mutation). Similarly, *gardd* 'garden': *ei ŵardd e* 'his garden'; *'y ngardd i* 'my garden'; *ei gardd hi* 'her garden'.

MORPHOLOGY AND SYNTAX

Definitive article

yr; 'r after vowel or diphthong, *y* in interconsonantal position; e.g. *yr haf* 'summer'; *yr eira* 'the snow'; *Ble mae 'r tŷ?* 'Where is the house?'; *pen y rhiw* 'the top of the hill'.

The initial of a singular feminine noun mutates after the article: e.g. *pont* 'bridge': *y bont* 'the bridge'; *torth* 'loaf': *y dorth* 'the loaf'.

The presence or absence of mutation will help to determine gender, if the initial is a mutating consonant. There is no indefinite article.

Noun

Two genders and two numbers. Certain endings of derivative nouns are gender-related; e.g. *-edd*, *-did*, *-ad*, *-iant* are masculine, *-aeth*, *-as*, *-fa* are mostly feminine. In some cases, feminine counterparts may be formed from masculine nouns by the addition of *-es*: e.g. *brenin* 'king'; *brenhines* 'queen' (with stem modification); *llew* 'lion'; *llewes* 'lioness'.

NUMBER
There are several ways of forming the plural:

(a) by vowel change: *gafr* 'goat' – pl. *geifr*;
(b) by suffix: *afal* 'apple' – *afalau*; *esgob* 'bishop' – *esgobion*; *mor* 'sea' – *moroedd*; *llwynog* 'fox' – *llwynogod*;
(c) (a) and (b) combined: *mab* 'son' – *meibion*;
(d) singular ending dropped, with or without ablaut: *eisen* 'rib' – *ais*; *meipen* 'turnip' – *maip*;
(e) many irregular formations; some nouns have more than one plural.

Plural nouns do not show mutation; there are some exceptions to this rule.

POSSESSIVE
By juxtaposition: the noun denoting the possessor does not mutate: e.g. *mab bardd* 'a poet's son'; *drws y ty* 'the door of the house'; *pen y rhiw* 'the top of the hill'. As in the Semitic languages, the possessed noun does not take the article.

Adjective

Adjective follows noun and mutates after feminine singular. Many adjectives have plural forms, and may also be marked for feminine gender. In literary Welsh, concord between noun and adjective is normal (though a singular adjective may accompany a plural noun). In the colloquial, concord is very rare. Like nouns, adjectives may be pluralized (a) by ablaut; (b) by ending; (c) by a combination of (a) and (b): e.g. *marw* 'dead': pl. *meirw* or *meirwon*.

Masculine adjectival forms with root *w* or *y* change these to *e*/*o* for feminine: e.g. *gwyn* 'white', fem. *gwen*; *hyll* 'ugly', fem. *hell*.

The adjective mutates after a feminine singular noun: e.g. *coch* 'red': *het goch* 'red hat'; *het wen* 'white hat'.

COMPARATIVE
The ending is *-ach*, which may induce vowel change: e.g. *cryf* 'strong' – comp. *cryfach*; *tlws* 'pretty' – comp. *tlysach*.

Suppletive comparatives: *da* 'good' – *gwell* (with an equative *cystal*, and a superlative *gorau*); *drwg* 'bad' – *gwaeth*.

If the adjective precedes the noun, the initial is lenited: *castell* 'castle' – *hen gastell* 'old castle'.

Pronoun

Standard literary forms:

			Independent	Prefixed	Infixed	Affixed
sing.	1		mi/fi	fy	'm	i/fi
	2		ti/di	dy	'th	di/ti
	3	masc.	ef	ei	'i/'w	ef(o)/fo/fe hi
		fem.	hi			
pl.	1		ni	ein	'n	ni
	2		chwi	eich	'ch	chwi
	3		hwy(nt)	eu	'u/'w	hwy(nt)

The columns *Independent* and *Dependent* head the table; *Dependent* covers Prefixed, Infixed, Affixed.

The accusative forms are identical to the infixed (genitive) forms, except for *'w* in the third person, which is replaced by *'s*. Examples:

Prefixed: *fy mam* 'my mother'; *fy mrawd* 'my brother' (*brawd* 'brother').
Infixed: *fy mrawd a'm chwaer* 'my brother and my sister'; *o'th gartref* 'from thy home'; *i'm gweld* 'to see me'.
Affixed: used after personal forms of verbs; e.g. the ending *-f* is sufficient to identify a verbal form as 1st person singular but *i/fi* may be added. Similarly, in the possessive formula: e.g. *'y mhen i* 'my head'.

In the colloquial language, the possessive forms are as follows:

		Singular	Plural
1		'yn...i	ein...ni
(2		dy... di)	eich...chi
3	masc.	ei + soft mutation ... e	eu...nhw
	fem.	ei + aspirate mutation ...hi	

Thus, with the noun *car* 'car': *ei gar e* 'his car'; *ei char hi* 'her car'.

In the colloquial language, the first person prefixed form *fy* is reduced to *'y*, plus nasal mutation; after a vowel, the *'y* may also be dropped: e.g. *'y nghar i* 'my car'; *Mae 0 nghar i...* 'My car is...'

The formula for transitive verb + objective pronominal complement is copula + sbj. + *yn* ('in') + possessive adjective in concord with object + sense-verb + personal marker in concord with object: e.g. *mae e yn 'yn nabod i* 'he (*e*) is (*mae*) in (*yn*) knowing (*nabod*) me (*'yn...i*)'; *rydw i yn ei nabod e* 'I know him'. *See also* **Preposition**, below.

DEMONSTRATIVE PRONOUN/ADJECTIVE
The literary series: masc. *hwn*, fem. *hon*; pl. common: *hyn*.

Colloquial Welsh has three forms for differing degree of distance: *dyma* 'this' – *dyna* 'that' – *dacw* 'that (yonder)'. The formula: article + noun + *'ma* (< *yma* 'here') may also be used: e.g. *y stafell 'ma* 'this room'.

INTERROGATIVE PRONOUN
Literary and colloquial: *pwy* 'who?'; literary *pa* 'what?'; colloquial, *beth*.

The interrogative of the copula is formed by dropping initial *r*: e.g. *rydw* 'I am': *Øydw* 'am I?'

In the literary language the relative particle is *a* + lenition for both subject and object. The negative counterpart is *na(d)*. Since *a* is singular, the verb is third person singular: e.g. *Ef yw'r dyn a ddaeth* 'This is the man who came' (*daeth* = 'came'). This relative *a* is no longer used in spoken Welsh, but its attendant lenition remains where compatible. In older literary Welsh, the verb was in concord with the antecedent.

In the colloquial language, the relative construction is marked for tense: e.g. *y ferch sy'n canu* 'the girl who is singing'; *y car oedd/fydd o flaen y tŷ* 'the car that was/will be in front of the house', where *fydd*, the mutated form of *bydd*, indicates the former presence of *a*.

Numerals

1–10: *un, dau/dwy, tri/tair, pedwar/pedair, pump, chwech, saith, wyth, naw, deg*. *Dwy, tair*, and *pedair* are feminine forms. *Dau* and *dwy* take lenition: e.g. *dau fachgen* 'two boys' (*bachgen* 'boy'). *Tri* (but not *tair*) takes aspiration: e.g. *tri chae* 'three fields' (*cae* 'field').

From 20 upwards, there is a choice between the decimal and the vigesimal systems: 11 *un deg un* (*un ar ddeg*); 12 *un deg dau* (*deuddeg*); 20 *ugain* (vig.) or *dau ddeg* (dec.); 40 *deugain* (vig.) or *pedwar deg* (dec.); 100 *cant*.

Verb

In the literary language there are three moods (indicative, subjunctive, imperative); the indicative has four tenses (present, imperfect, preterite, and pluperfect), the subjunctive has a present and an imperfect. As an example of conjugation in the literary language, here is the paradigm of *canu* 'to sing':

	Present		*Imperfect*		*Preterite*	
	Singular	*Plural*	*Singular*	*Plural*	*Singular*	*Plural*
1	canaf	canwn	canwn	canem	cenais	canasom
2	ceni	cenwch	canit	canech	cenaist	canasoch
3	can	canant	canai	canent	canodd	canasant

Impersonal: cenir   cenid   canwyd

Subjunctive mood: present sing. *canwyf, cenych, cano*; pl. *canom, canoch, canont*; impersonal: *caner*. The imperfect subjunctive is the same as the imperfect indicative.

Tenses are perfective or imperfective. Present affirmative: imperfective: the formula is copula + sbj. + *yn* + sense-verb (+ obj.); the verb does not mutate: e.g. *rydw i'n yfed coffi* 'I am drinking coffee'; *rydyn ni'n yfed coffi* 'we are drinking coffee'; *mae e'n darllen llyfr* 'he is reading a book'. Negative: the *r*-initial of the copula becomes *d*, and *ddim* follows the person marker: e.g. *dydw i ddim yn yfed coffi* 'I'm not drinking coffee'. Likewise, the *r*- initial becomes Ø for the interrogative: e.g. *Ødw i'n yfed coffi?* 'Am I drinking coffee?'

Past imperfect, affirmative: imperfective: the formula is: *roedd* + person marker + sbj. marker (if pronominal) + *yn* + sense-verb: e.g. *roedd-wn i* 'I was'; *roedd-en-ni* 'we were'; *roedd-en-ni yn gweithio* 'we were working'. Negative: *r-* → *d-*: e.g. *doedd-wn i ddim yn gweithio* 'I wasn't working'. Interrogative: *r-* → Ø: e.g. *Øoedd-wn i yn gweithio?* 'Was I working?'

Preterite affirmative: perfective: the formula is: *fe* + stem (with mutation) + personal ending + sbj. pronominal marker: e.g. *fe weles i* 'I saw' (root *gweled* 'see'); *fe brynodd hi* 'she bought' (root *prynu* 'buy'). Negative: mutation of stem initial, if possible, + *ddim*: e.g. *Ddaeth e ddim i'r dre* 'He didn't go to town.'

Perfect affirmative: perfective: *wedi 'after'* replaces *yn* in present tense forms: e.g. *mae e wedi darllen* 'he's after reading' = 'he has read'. Negative: *dydy e ddim wedi dod* 'he hasn't come' (root *dod* 'come'; irregular).

Future affirmative: imperfective: the future tense of the verb *bod* 'to be' is *bydda*: preceded by the future marker *fe*, *bydda* becomes *fydda*: e.g. *fe fydda i* 'I shall be': *fe fydda i'n chwarae* 'I'll be playing'; *fe fyddwn ni'n chwarae* 'we'll be playing'. Negative: Ø *fydda i ddim yn chwarae* 'I shan't be playing'.

A perfective plural is made with *wedi* replacing *yn*.

The impersonal forms (see the *canu* paradigm above) are used in the literary language, when the agent of an action is not specifically expressed: e.g. *nid cenir yn i capel* 'it is not sung in the chapel' = 'there is no one singing...' (*nid*, in this example, is the literary negative marker).

Passive: the literary language has no passive construction. In the colloquial, *cael* 'to have', is used as an auxiliary: e.g. *Mae'r ffilm yn cael ei dangos* 'The film is being shown.'

Preposition

In the literary language, prepositions are (a) inflected for person when governing a pronoun, or (b) uninflected. Those in (a) are further sub-divided, with a suggestion of vowel harmony, into three sets: these are classified by first person singular affix: *-af*, *-of*, *-yf*. For example, with

> *ar* 'on': *arnaf* 'on me', *arnat* 'on you', *arno/arni* 'on him/her';
> *o* 'from': *o.hon.of* 'from me', *o.hon.ot* 'from you';
> *er* 'for': *erof* 'for me', *erddo* 'for him', *erom* 'for us';
> *tros* 'over': *trosof*, *trosoch* 'over you (pl.)', *trostynt* 'over them';
> *gan* 'with': *gennyf* 'with me'.

The personal deixis *may* be reinforced by addition of the personal markers: e.g. *arnaf fi*, *arnat ti*. This addition is obligatory in the colloquial language: e.g. *arna/arno i* 'on me'; *arno fe* 'on him'; *i ni* 'for us'; *ynoch chwi* 'in you'; *ohonot ti* 'from you (sing.)'.

Word order

VSO is normal.

YN y dechreuad yr oedd y Gair, a'r Gair oedd gyd â Duw, a Duw oedd y Gair.

2 Hwn oedd yn y dechreuad gyd â Duw.

3 Trwyddo ef y gwnaethpwyd pob peth ; ac hebddo ef ni wnaethpwyd dim a'r a wnaethpwyd.

4 Ynddo ef yr oedd bywyd ; a'r bywyd oedd oleuni dynion.

5 A'r goleuni sydd yn llewyrchu yn y tywyllwch ; a'r tywyllwch nid oedd yn ei amgyffred.

6 ¶ Yr ydoedd gŵr wedi ei anfon oddi wrth Dduw, a'i enw Ioan.

7 Hwn a ddaeth yn dystiolaeth, fel y tystiolaethai am y Goleuni, fel y credai pawb trwyddo ef.

8 Nid efe oedd y Goleuni, eithr *efe a anfonasid* fel y tystiolaethai am y Goleuni.

WENLI

See **Chinese, Classical**.

WOLOF

INTRODUCTION

A member of the West Atlantic group of the Niger-Congo family, Wolof is the main language of Senegal, spoken by about 2 million people in that country, plus about 100,000 in Gambia. It is not standardized and there are many dialects; Dakar Wolof seems to be emerging as a potential standard form. The mass of the Wolof people were converted to Islam in the middle of the nineteenth century and there is a substantial body of literature in Arabic by Wolof writers. Writing in Wolof itself dates from the late nineteenth century and includes some notable poets. Radio broadcasts of Wolof oral literature are popular.

SCRIPT

Arabic or Roman.

PHONOLOGY

Consonants

    stops: p, b, t, d, k, g; pre-nasalized: ᵐb, ⁿd; palatalized: t', d'
    fricatives: f, s, x, h
    nasals: m, n, ɲ, ŋ
    lateral and flap: l, r
    semi-vowels: j, w

Medial stops are weakened to semi-vowels: /-b-/ → [-ww-], /-d'-/ → [-jj-].

    Nasalized consonants appear, for example, in the formation of nouns from verbs; thus, *ngem* = /ŋɛm/ 'faith', from *gem* 'to believe'. (*See* **Word formation**, below.) Nasalization is signalled by *m* preceding *p*, *b*; by *n* before other consonants. The nasalized reflexes of /f/, /s/ are /mp/, /nt'/: cf. *fut* 'wash' – *mput* 'detergent'; *sub* 'dye, tinge' – *nt'ub* 'dye' (noun).

Vowels

The basic inventory is

    i, e, a, o, u, ə

All, except /ə/, (notated as *ë*), have long and short values. *e* notates both /e/ and

/ɛ/; *o* notates long /o/, long or short /ɔ/. All vowels are subject to nasalization preceding *n* + velar consonant. Thus, *man* 'I, me' = /man/ but *mangi* 'as for me' = /mãŋi/.

Interchangeability of initial consonant: the liquids /l, r, m, n/ are interchangeable, as are the dentals /t, d/ with /r/, /n/: cf. *rokos/nokos* 'to stuff, pad'; *dau/rau* 'to run'.

MORPHOLOGY AND SYNTAX

Noun

There is no grammatical gender. Nouns are followed by class-defining particles, which function more or less as definite articles. They take the form CV, where V varies for degree of distancing; *-i* being proximate, *-a* remote. In the singular, eight consonants are used for this purpose: *b, g, dy, l, m, s, w, k*, reduced to *y-, ny-* in the plural. In practice, *b-* is the most frequently used, and there is a tendency for it to replace theoretically more correct determinatives. Examples: *goor gi* 'the man (here)'; *goor ga* 'the man (there)'; *gaa nyi* 'the people'; *dyigeen dyi* 'the woman'; *dyant wi* 'the sun'; *nyey wi* 'the elephant'; *ndyamala li* 'the giraffe'.

In general, nouns are not marked for number, the *y-/ny-* form of the class particle being sufficient to indicate plurality. A few nouns, however, preserve traces of an ancient Bantu-type class plural by mutation of initial: cf. *lef* 'thing', pl. *yef*; *pan* 'day', pl. *fan*; *bante* 'wood', pl. *wante*.

POSSESSION

Possessor follows, e.g. with *bunt* 'door': *bunt-u kër gi* 'the door of the house'; *bunt-i kër gi* 'the doors of the house' (where *-u/-i* are singular/plural connective markers, establishing *bunt* as definite). As a unit, the genitive phrase can be preceded by the possessive pronoun: e.g. *suma doom-u xarit* 'my (*suma*) friend's (*xarit*) son (*doom*)'.

Adjective

As attribute, the adjective is turned into a stative verb: 'the good store' becomes 'the store which is good', *butig bu baax la*. See Relative clause, below.

Pronoun

The independent forms are: sing. 1 *man*, 2 *yow*, 3 *moom*; pl. 1 *nyun*, 2 *yeen*, 3 *nyoom*; with object forms: sing. *ma – la – ko*; pl. *nyu – leen – leen*; and conjunct forms sing. *ma – nga – mu*; pl. *nyu – ngeen – nyu*. The conjunct forms function as subject pronouns with verbs, and coalesce with the focus marker *angi*: e.g. *nyungi ko-y lekk* 'they are eating it'. (*See* **Verb**, below.)

POSSESSIVE PRONOUN

In the third person singular the marker is *-am* following the noun; elsewhere the formula is pronoun + noun: e.g. *suma xarit* 'my friend', *sunyu xarit* 'our friend'; *suma-y xarit* 'my friends' (where *-y* is the pluralizing particle); *ker am* 'his/her house'.

DEMONSTRATIVE PRONOUN/ADJECTIVE

The vowels of the determinative particles are lengthened: *bi* 'the' – *bii* 'this': e.g. *mus mi* 'the cat', *mus mi*: 'this cat'.

INTERROGATIVE PRONOUN

kan 'who?'; *lan* 'what?'. These have plurals: *nyan, yan*.

Numerals

1–10: *benn, nyaar, nyett, nyent, dyuroom, dyuroom benn, dyuroom nyaar, dyuroom nyett, dyuroom nyent, fukk*. 11 *fukk ak benn*, 12 *fukk ak nyaar*; 20 *nyaar y fukk*, 30 *nyett i fukk*; 100 *teemeer*.

Verb

Wolof verbs are active or stative; the exact distinction between the two categories is not always clear in Indo-European terms. Thus, *gëm* 'to believe in something', is apparently stative, while *xalaat* 'to think about something', is active. *Nob* 'to love' is also stative.

The verb itself is not inflected. Three persons and two numbers are expressed by means of pronominal series, which vary for aspect, mode, tense, and state (absolute or conjunctive). The basic division is into perfective and imperfective aspects. To express action in progress at a given moment, the formula is conjunct pronoun + particle *angi/a* + sense-verb. The conjunct pronoun coalesces with *angi/a* as follows: sing. 1 *màngi*, 2 *yàngi*, 3 *mungi*; pl. 1 *nyungi*, 2 *yeen angi*, 3 *nyungi*: e.g. *màngi lekk* 'I am eating now'; *yàngi lekk* 'you are eating now'.

The focus marker *angi/a* cannot be used with a stative verb; *na* replaces it. This *na* marker shares a specific pronominal series with the particle *di/y*, which is an imperfective/future marker: the pronominal series is sing. *naa – nga – na*; pl. *na nyu – ngeen – na nyu*: e.g. *di naa wax* 'I'm in the habit of speaking', or 'I shall speak'.

PERFECTIVE ASPECT

With active verbs, *na* is used with its pronominal series: e.g. *wax naa* 'I have spoken'; *gis ngeen sunyu kër* 'you have seen our house'. *Woon* is a past-tense marker: e.g. *wax woon naa* 'I spoke'. *Na* with the relevant pronominal series is also used to form an optative mood. The imperative is the bare stem or stem + *-(a)l*: e.g. *dellul* 'go back!'

RELATIVE CLAUSE

The relative pronoun is formed from the class initial + *-u*: e.g. *bi → bu*, *dyi → dyu*: e.g. *xale bu baax* 'a child that is good'; *xale bu baax bi* 'the child that is good'. If the relative pronoun refers to the object of the principal predicate, the *-i* form is used: e.g. *xale bi nga indi* 'the child which you (sing.) brought'. A temporal relative is made with the particle *bu* 'when' + pronominal series; the sense-verb takes the suffix *-ee/-oon*: e.g. *bu ma waxee* 'when/if I speak'; *bu ma wax.oon* 'when/if I spoke'.

NEGATION

The marker is *-(w)ul*: e.g. *wax* 'to speak' – *waxul* 'not to speak'. There is a specific pronominal series for use with the negative form: sing. *ma – loo – Ø*; pl. *nyu – leen – nyu*. The final *-l* of the negated verb is dropped before the pronoun: e.g. *waxu ma* 'I haven't spoken'; *mungi wax* 'he is speaking' – *waxul* 'he isn't speaking'.

Prepositions

Examples: *ag* 'with', e.g. *mungi wax ag man* 'he is speaking with me'; *tyi* 'in, at', etc.: often + nominal, e.g. *tyi biir* 'inside', *tyi suuf* 'at the foot of'.

Word formation

Wolof forms nouns from verbs (a) by nasalization of initial, as noted above: cf. *fo* 'to play' – *mpo* 'game'; (b) by reduplication: *kham* 'to know' – *khamkham* 'knowledge'; (c) by affixation, e.g. *-it*: *dog* 'to cut' – *dogit* 'a piece cut off'; *-ai*: *rafet* 'to be pretty' – *rafetai* 'beauty'; *-kat*: *rab* 'to weave' – *rabekat* 'weaver'; *same* 'to graze' – *samekat* 'shepherd'.

Word order

Complicated because of the pronominal series; in the case of nominal sentences, SVO is common; VSO occurs.

1 Tă ndorté gă, Bât bă amon
nă, té Bât bă nèk'on ţă Yalla, tė
Bât bă Yalla la on.

2 Tă ndorté gă nèk'on nă ţă
Yalla.

3 Yef yă yep mou lén défar,
té amoul dara lou gnou défar,
lou moy lou mou défar.

4 Tă mom lä doundă gă nè-
k'on nă, té doundă gă lèr'ou nit
gnă la on.

5 Té lèr gă mélaḥ nă ţă lendem yă, té lendem yă nangou-
wou gnou ko.

6 Yalla ébal nă bén gour gou
toudă Yoana.

7 Mou gnaw ndaḥ sédé ak séré
ţă lèr gă, ndaḥ gnou gem yep ţi
mom.

8 Mom saḥ, nèkouwoul won
lèr gă, wandé ndig sédé ţă lèr
gă.

(Senegal dialect)

WU

INTRODUCTION

Wu is the form of Chinese that is spoken by about 80 million people in Shanghai and its surroundings, and in the Yangzi delta.

The distinguishing characteristic of the Wu dialects lies in the extension of the labial, dental, and velar initial stop series to include a voiced aspirate member. Thus, where Mandarin Chinese has /p, ph; t, th; k, kh/ notated in *pinyin* as *b*, *p*, *t*, *d*, *k*, *g*, Wu has /p, ph, bh; t, th, dh; k, kh gh/.

The palatal affricate series is also extended by the addition of /z̢h/ to /tʂ/, /tʂh/.

Aspiration of the voiced member is carried through the syllable thus initiated, whose tone and vocal pitch are always low.

Wu has two varieties of glottal fricative /h/ and /ɦ/. Possible finals are the vowels, the glottal stop and velar /ŋ/.

Vowels: thirteen, including a buzzing alveolar fricative, notated in transcription as *z*, which occurs in association with the dental affricates and fricatives.

Seven or eight tones are general in Wu, except in Shanghai, where only five are used. Citation tones are subject to a very elaborate system of tonal sandhi in connected speech.

As in the Yue dialects, the direct object precedes the indirect.

XIANG

Xiang belongs to the Sinitic family. The Xiang speech area centres on Hunan, and falls into two broad dialectal divisions. In one of these – urban or 'new' Xiang – the diachronic processes of consonantal mutation and lexical replacement have been accelerated by close contact with Modern Standard Chinese: so much so that, as Ramsey points out (1987: 97), between urban Xiang and Modern Standard Chinese there is a considerable degree of mutual intelligibility.

On the phonological plane, urban Xiang has replaced the voiced stops /b, d, g/, with the homorganic unvoiced non-aspirated, /p, t, k/. The voiced stops are retained in 'old' Xiang, the dialect form assiociated with the more backward rural communities. Thus, while the mountain peasant will talk about his *din* 'field', the Xiang trader and his Mandarin counterpart both call it *tián*.

About 50 million people speak the two forms of the Xiang language.

!XŨ

See **!Kung**.

YAGNOB

INTRODUCTION

Yagnob belongs to the Eastern branch of the Iranian family. It is spoken by about 2,000 people (all of them bilingual in Yagnob and Tadzhik) in the high mountain valleys of the Yagnob and the Varzob rivers in the north of the Tadzhik Soviet Socialist Republic. Yagnob is of particular interest in Iranian philology as it is the sole remaining representative of Sogdian (*see* **Iranian Languages**). Much of the Yagnob vocabulary is Sogdian, though structurally the language has been much influenced by Tadzhik. There are two main dialects. Yagnob is unwritten.

PHONOLOGY

The consonantal system is close to that of Tadzhik; a specific Yagnob sound is the labialized velar /x°/. In the vocalic system, the typically Iranian opposition between long and short vowels is maintained.

MORPHOLOGY AND SYNTAX

Noun

A plural marker is *-t*: e.g. *pōda* 'foot', pl. *pōdōt*. The noun has two cases, direct and oblique; e.g. from *pōda*, the oblique singular is *pōday/pōdē*, the plural oblique is *pōdōti*. The oblique form figures as direct/indirect object, and as the subject of the perfect tense of transitive verbs: e.g. *hamma ōdāmti* 'to all men'; *Rahmoni čōy uxta.x či bōzōri* 'Rahman brought tea from the bazaar.'

Adjective

The adjective is invariable.

Pronoun

The personal pronouns have full (direct and oblique) and enclitic forms: the singular set is:

	Direct	Oblique	Enclitic
1	man	man	-m
2	tu	taw	-t
3	iš/ax	īti/awi	-š

The plural direct forms are 1 *mōx*, 2 *šumōx*, 3 *īštit/axtit*.

Numerals

1–10: *ī, du, sirau, tafōr, panč, uxš, awd, ašt, naw, das.* From 20 on, Tadzhik forms are used.

Verb

A single base system is general, though a few have dual base system (e.g. *kun-/kar-* 'do'). There are indicative, imperative, and subjunctive moods.

FORMATION OF PAST AND PERFECT TENSES

(a) from the root, with augment *a-*, e.g. *wēnom* 'I see' – *awēnim* 'I saw'; + enclitic *-išt* for past habitual: e.g. *atīsim.išt* 'I was (in the habit of) going in';
(b) from the infinitive, e.g. *tirak* 'to go': *tirak.im ast* 'my going is' = 'I go'; *tirak.im ōy* 'my going was' = 'I went';
(c) perfect: from the past participle, e.g. *wēn* 'to see', pp. *wēta*: *wēta.m.x* 'by me was seen' = 'I saw him'; *wēta.t.x* 'you saw him'; *wēta.š.m* 'he saw me'.

NEGATION

Example: *na.m wēta.x* 'I didn't see him'; *na.t wēta.x* 'you didn't see him'.

YAKUT

INTRODUCTION

The Yakuts live in the Yakut Autonomous Soviet Socialist Republic, which centres on the river Lena, and covers about 2 million square miles of territory. The language, classified by Baskakov (1966) in the Uygur group of Eastern Turkic, is spoken by about 300,000 people in the ASSR, and also by groups of Yakut elsewhere, e.g. in the Taymir and Evenki National Areas. There are several dialects, the most interesting of which is the Dolgan dialect (about 5,000 speakers), which preserves some very archaic features and which has adopted many Evenki words.

Like Chuvash, Yakut deviates considerably from standard Turkic forms. Particularly interesting are the disappearance of the genitive case and the use of the locative ending to mark a partitive case. The lexicon shows Mongolian and Evenki influence, and certain features of Old Turkish are preserved.

SCRIPT

Since 1939 Cyrillic with several additional letters, including *h* for the pharyngeal fricative.

PHONOLOGY

Consonants

> stops: p, b, t, d, k, g; palatalized: d′
> affricate: tʃ
> fricatives: s, x, γ/ʁ, h
> nasals: m, n, ɲ, ŋ
> laterals and flap: l, l′, r
> semi-vowel: j

Assimilation is both progressive and regressive.

Vowels

> front: i, ε, œ, y
> back: ɪ, a, o, u

There are four diphthongs. In this article, /ε/ is notated as *ẹ*, /œ/ as *ö*; /y/ as *ü*.

VOWEL HARMONY

Vowel harmony is strictly observed: front with front, back with back, rounded with rounded. Examples will be found in words quoted below.

Stress

Stress is consistently on the final syllable.

MORPHOLOGY AND SYNTAX

Noun

The plural affix has 16 allophones: *l/d/t/n* initials + V^4; e.g. *lar*, *lör*, *lor*, *ler*. The affix may be added to an expanded base; cf. *börö.lör* 'wolves'; *kɪɪs* 'girl', pl. *kɪrgɪt.tar*; *ęr* 'man', pl. *ęręt.tęr*.

DECELENSION
Nominative = base;

accusative	-(n)ɪ
partitive	-ta, with 16 variants
dative	-ɣa, also with 16 variants
ablative	-(t)tan
instrumental	-(ɪ)nan

The comitative affix *-lɪɪn* is borrowed from Evenki; the comparative is in *-taaɣar*. The missing genitive case is replaced by the formula X (singular or plural base) – Y + third person possessive marker 'X's Y'. The possessive markers are:

	Singular	Plural
1	-m	-bit
2	-ŋ	-ɣit
3	-tę	-lęrę

Example: *d'ię.m* 'my house' (Evenki loan-word).

Adjective

The adjective is more sharply differentiated from the noun than is usual in Turkic. The Yakut adjective can, for example, take the personal possessive endings and be declined as a nominal; it is then equivalent to a relative clause whose referent may not be overtly expressed: e.g. (*kini*) *xara.tɪn* ... 'that he/it is black (acc.)'.

NEGATION
The adjective is in the third person possessive form followed by *suox*: e.g. *xara.ta* 'his/her/its black' – *xarata suox* 'not black'.

Pronoun

The base forms with their correlated predicative suffixes are:

	Singular	Plural
1	min...bin	bihigi...bit
2	ẹn...gin	ẹhigi...git
3	kini...Ø	kinilẹr...lẹr

The base forms are declined in six cases (the partitive is missing).

DEMONSTRATIVE PRONOUN
bu 'this'; *ol* 'that'. These cannot take possessive markers.

INTERROGATIVE PRONOUN
kim 'who?'; *tuox* 'what?'. These are declined both with and without the personal possessive markers.

Numerals

1–10: *biir, ikki, üs, tüört, biẹs, alta, sẹttẹ, aɣıs, toɣus, won*; 20 *süürbẹ*; 30 *otut*; 40 *tüört won*; 100 *süüs*.

Verb

There are finite and non-finite forms, with several of the latter – participial and gerundial endings – playing an important part in tense formation. The indicative mood has a present tense, eight past tenses, and a future, the general model being: stem – tense marker – predicative ending: e.g. in the present tense the marker is *-a(r)/-ı(r)*: *ıl.a.bın* 'I take'; *ıl.a.ɣın* 'you take'; *ıl.ar.Ø* 'he/she takes'. This tense is negated by *bat* + personal predicative ending: e.g. *ıl.bap.pın* 'I don't take' (*-t + b- → pp*).

Recent past: the marker is *-t-*: e.g. *diẹ.t.im* 'I spoke'; here the possessive ending is used instead of the predicative, and the negating particle is *-ma-/-ba-*: e.g. *diẹ.bẹ.t.im* 'I didn't speak'.

Another way of forming the negative is by means of the negative auxiliary *ilik*: e.g. in the imperfective past, *dii ilik ẹtim* 'I have not yet spoken'.

Future: the marker is *-ıa(x)*, the possessive marker is added: e.g. *diẹm* 'I shall say'; negative *diẹm suoɣa*.

The imperative mood has present and future forms: e.g. in the present, *ılıım* 'let me take'; negative *ılımıım* 'let me not take'. There are also necessitative, optative, potential, conditional, and presumptive moods. The conditional, for example, has the marker *-tar* with the predicative affix: e.g. *diẹ.tẹr.bin* 'if I say'; negative *diẹ.bẹ.tẹr.bin*.

Over a dozen auxiliary verbs are used to express various modal and aspectual shades of meaning affecting the action: e.g. *tüs-* 'to fall', denotes sudden and momentary action, e.g. *oloro tüs-* 'to sit down for a moment'. Other auxiliaries are *biẹr-* 'to give' (benefactive nuance), *gın-* 'to do' (intentional), *kör-* 'to look at' (suggesting some effort in performing the action).

Yakut is especially rich in alliterating verbal compounds. Reduplication, both formal and semantic, serves a three-fold purpose: the expression of collectivity in nouns, intensification in qualifiers, e.g. adjectives, and of frequency in verbs.

Postpositions

Postpositions are nominal or verbal in origin; e.g. *d'iẹ ihigẹr* 'in the house'; *d'iẹ ihittẹn* 'from/out of the house'. The Yakut liking for alliterative reduplication is found here: e.g. *d'iẹ ihigẹr-tahıgar* 'in and out of the house'. Postpositions derived from verbs take various cases – accusative, dative, ablative.

Word order

SOV.

---

1. *1.* Маңнайгытыгар Тыл бара, Тыл Таңарага бара, Тыл да Таңара бара. *2.* Тыл маңнайгытыгар Таңарага бара. *3.* Барытын Кіні айбыта; айыллыбыт ӓрӓ Кіні суогуна айыллыбатага. *4.* Тыннах гынар кініӓхӓ бара, тыннах да гынар кісілӓргӓ сырдык бара. *5.* Сырдык харанага сырдыыр, харана да кыайан Кініні ылбатага. *6.* Іоанн діӓн аттах Таңараттан ытыллыбыт кісі бара. *7.* Кініттӓн барылара ітӓгӓйдіннӓр діӓн кіні сырдык тусун кӓрӓсітті кӓлбітӓ. *8.* Кіні бӓйӓтӓ сырдык буолбатага, хата кіні сырдык тусугар туосу буолуогун ісін ытыллыбыта.

YI

INTRODUCTION

Formerly known as Lolo, Yi belongs to the Tibeto-Burman family. About 5 million Yi live in the mountains of southern Sichuan and Yunnan, where they maintained a semi-independent presence from the time of the Han Dynasty until the establishment of the People's Republic of China. Apart from the dialect complex of Yi itself, there are several related languages on Chinese territory, e.g. Lisu, Naxi (*see* **Naxi**).

The Nasu form of Yi (spoken near Kunming in Yunnan) may be taken as example.

SCRIPT

The Yi have a syllabary which appears to be very old, and which was, at least until recently, the preserve of a hereditary priestly caste. Allegedly it had a very large number of graphs, some of which look like rough versions of Chinese radicals. In the 1970s the Chinese authorities produced a standardized system of 819 graphs.

PHONOLOGY

Nasu has 44 consonants, none of which can be final except the glottal stop. The consonantal inventory shows six series of four terms: voiceless non-aspirate, voiceless aspirate, voiced non-aspirate, voiced aspirate: e.g. /p, p', b, b'; k, k', g, g'/; etc., + retroflex, dental, palatal affricate series. There are voiceless nasals and a voiceless lateral, /lh/.

Nasu has ten basic vowels, including a phoneme variously described as *z* or *r*: a kind of buzzing sound.

There are seven tones, one of which is a checked tone preceding the glottal stop.

MORPHOLOGY AND SYNTAX

The language is uninflected. Almost all Nasu words are monosyllabic, of the form CV + tone (+ glottal stop). Roots are polyfunctional; meaning depends on position. As in Chinese, classifiers proliferate, but, unlike Chinese, these *follow* the noun. All modifiers follow the words modified. The verb is invariably last. Verbal aspect, mood, tense, etc. are generated from verbal strings compounding stems, resultatives, co-verbs, auxiliaries.

YIDDISH

INTRODUCTION

Half-way through the first millennium of our era, Jewish immigrants began arriving in western Europe, and at once the bilingualism, or even trilingualism, that had been a characteristic feature of diaspora life since the Babylonian Exile, asserted itself in new surroundings. Judaeo-Latin was succeeded by Judaeo-Old French, based on a Frankish dialect, which forms the first *galut* (Hebrew *gālūṯ* 'exile') language in the West.

In this context, bilingualism operated on two planes. The Holy Language, the Hebrew of the Torah, remained the canonical written language of Jewish institutions, *vis-à-vis* the spoken Aramaic of daily life, which, in its turn, entered upon a symbiosis with the language of the host country. By the ninth and tenth centuries the Jews had moved on to the cities along the middle course of the Rhine, and the appropriation process was under way, this time as applied to Middle High German. In the transfer process, the phonological profile of Middle High German was somewhat modified, while the morphological structure was appropriated almost intact. Décsy (1981) describes Yiddish as a co-Sprache, a co-language of German. The earliest documents of the Judaeo-German language as spoken and written in Worms, Speyer, and Mainz, date from the eleventh and twelfth centuries.

Religious persecution in the late Middle Ages led first to an eastwards extension of Yiddish culture, subsequently to its near total transfer to eastern Europe, especially to Poland and Russia; and Yiddish began to assimilate a Slavonic element, which did little, however, to alter its essentially German nature. Large members of Jews settled throughout eastern Europe, spreading into Hungary, Romania, and Lithuania. Two or three hundred years later, faced with religious persecution and intolerance in the East, many Jews started out on the reverse migration to the West. But by then it was too late for Yiddish – particularly a slavicized Yiddish – to re-establish itself in western Europe. The ideas of the Aufklärung had been taken up by the Jewish Haskalah movement (Hebrew root *SXL*: *sāxal* 'to have understanding, insight') whose outstanding protagonist was Moses Mendelssohn, the prototype for Lessing's Nathan der Weise. As an exercise in cultural symbiosis, Mendelssohn translated the Pentateuch into German, using Hebrew script. Part of the price, however, for induction into the economic, political, and cultural mainstream of western Europe was the rejection of Yiddish in favour of Standard High German or other standard host language. Warnings from traditionalist circles that Haskalah spelled the destruction of Yiddish culture in western Europe were not idle. The Netherlands and north Germany became staging posts on the trek to America; those who felt they could integrate stayed. By the early twentieth century, western European Yiddish was virtually extinct, apart from a small enclave in Alsace, where it may still linger on.

In eastern Europe, Yiddish continued to thrive as the language of the *shtetl* or small-town culture. In 1908, at the Czernowitz Conference, it was agreed that Yiddish was *a* national Jewish language.

After the 1917 Revolution in Russia, Yiddish was accorded equal status with the other minority languages of the Soviet Union, and in 1934 the Ievrejskaja Autonomous Region – also known, after its principal town, as Birobidzhan – was established on the middle course of the Amur, close to Khabarovsk. This was supposed to be a 'Sovietisch Heimland' for Jews, with Yiddish as its official language. The experiment was not a great success; urbanized and educated Jews were not drawn to the Middle Amur.

In 1925 the Yiddish Scientific Institute was inaugurated in Berlin, with headquarters in Vilnius (moved subsequently to New York).

When the opportunity finally came for Jews to select a national language for the state of Israel, an updated Hebrew in its Sephardic version was the natural choice. As a co-language of German, Yiddish hardly stood a chance.

Estimates of the number of Yiddish speakers at the present time vary very considerably. Crystal (1988) gives a maximum total of 600,000. The 1970 USSR census lists 379,000 speakers of Yiddish out of a total Jewish population of just over 2 million. As for the USA, Décsy (1981) gives a figure of half a million, while Weber (1989) has the following statistics: USA 1 million, USSR slightly under 1 million, Israel 200,000. Finally Solomon Birnbaum (1979) estimates that a figure of 12 million Yiddish speakers before the First World War had been reduced by the 1980s to roughly half.

Eastern Yiddish literature centres round the 'classical triumvirate' of Mendele Mocher Sforim, Sholem Alejchem, and Yitzhak Leibush Peretz, chroniclers and visionaries of the *Shtetl* culture, of Jewish life in the Pale of Settlement (*čerta osedlost'i*, the Russian territory allotted to Jewish settlers). Sholem Ash and David Pinski were products of the Peretz circle. The translation of the Hebrew Bible into Yiddish by Yehoash should also be mentioned.

SCRIPT

Yiddish is written in the Hebrew character (*see* **Hebrew**), with many innovations due to (a) the use of a *scripta plena*, i.e. with certain consonantal signs doing duty for vowels, as inherited from the original *galut* languages; and (b) an imitation of German orthography, particularly widespread in the Haskalah period.

At present, several spelling systems are current. Steps towards a standardization are being taken at the Yiddish Scientific Institute in New York. The transliteration used here is based on Fal'kovič (1966).

Some of the more important innovations are: 'aleph with qāmeṣ is generalized as /ɔ/, long or short; 'ayin represents /ɛ/; /ej/ is represented by double yodh, /aj/ by double yodh plus paṭaḥ, /oj/ by waw plus yodh; e.g.

דער מאַן *der man*;

די פֿרוי *di froj*;

דאָס קינד *dos kind*;

beth represents /b/, i.e. the voiced stop only; the correlative fricative /v/ is represented by double waw; zayin + sin = /ʒ/; ṭeth + sin = /tʃ/; initial 'aleph before yodh, waw or a diphthong is silent.

PHONOLOGY

Consonants

stops: p, b, t, d, k, g
affricates: ts, tʃ, (dz, dʒ)
fricatives: f, v, s, z, ʃ, ʒ, x, h
nasals: m, n
lateral and flap: l, r
semi-vowel: j

The palatalized consonants /t', d', s', z', n', l'/, the affricates /dz, dʒ/, and the fricative /ʒ/ occur under Slavonic influence. /n/ and /l/ are syllabic. Voiced consonants are not devoiced in final position.

Vowels

i, e, a, o, u

e = [ɛ]; o = [ɔ]. Diphthongs: /ej, aj, oj/

Stress

Stress tends to fall on the first syllable, thus often varying from a German original: e.g. *lébedik* 'alive' < *lebéndig*

MORPHOLOGY AND SYNTAX

Noun

The original gender of German nouns is largely retained, but there are exceptions, e.g. *di shif* (< Gm. *das Schiff*).

The indefinite article is *a/an* (invariable); the definite article is marked for gender: e.g. *der man* 'the man'; *di froj* 'the woman'; *dos kind* 'the child'. The plural definite article is *di*.

DECLENSION

The genitive marker -s is retained for proper nouns and nouns denoting people: e.g. *šolem-alejxems werk* 'the works of SA'. For the oblique case of inanimate and abstract nouns, the use of the preposition *fun* (< Gm. *von*) plus article is preferred: e.g. *fun der xoxme* 'of (about) wisdom'. The article changes to *des* for masculine/neuter genitive, to *der* for the feminine.

Certain kinship terms take -*n* in the accusative/dative, adding -*s* for the genitive: e.g. *zaidy* 'grandfather', obl. *zaidn*, gen. *zaidns*.

PLURAL

Typical endings are -*s*, -*is*, -*er*, -(*i*)*n*, -*im*; often with stem mutation in Semitic roots, the original or secondary umlaut in German words: e.g. *der xusn* 'bridegroom' – *di xasanim*; *der con* 'tooth' – *di cejner* (Gm. *Zahn – Zähne*); *dos hojz* 'house' – *di hajzer* (Gm. *Haus – Häuser*); *der fojgl* 'bird' – *di fejgl* (Gm. *Vogel – Vögel*); *der barg* 'mountain' – *di berg* (Gm. *Berg – Berge*).

Adjective

The adjective has strong and weak declensions with reduced endings. Birnbaum (1979) gives the following example: *Er vil koifn a groisn suud mit alte bajmer* 'He's going to buy a big garden with old trees' (*suud* < Russ. *sad* 'garden'). In the plural the adjectival endings are reduced to -*e*.

Predictively, the adjective seems to be inflected when reference is to stable, permanent qualities, and invariable for contingent and temporary states, for example: cf. *er iz a gezunter* 'he is a healthy man', *zi iz a gezunte* 'she is a healthy person'; contrasted with *er iz gezunt* 'he's fine (today)'; *zi zajnen gezunt* 'they're fine'.

A remarkable innovation in word order occurs where an adverb modifies an adjective: e.g. *zaier a hojexer bojm* = Gm. *ein sehr hoher Baum* 'a very high tree'.

Pronoun

The personal pronominal grid is a replica of the German, with certain innovations, e.g. first person plural *mir* (< Gm. *wir*); second person plural oblique *ajx* (< *euch*); third person plural *zaj* (< *sie*); first person plural oblique *undz* (< *uns*).

It is noteworthy that the reflexive pronoun *zix* (< Gm. *sich*) has been generalized to refer to all three persons: e.g. *ix vaš zix* 'I wash myself'.

POSSESSIVE PRONOUNS

The pronoun may show concord or take -*s*, and is followed by the indefinite article in, e.g. *majner/majns a bruder* 'a brother of mine'; *majn bruder* 'my brother'. In the plural, only the form *majne brider* is possible.

DEMONSTRATIVE PRONOUNS

The definite article is used.

vejer 'who?'; *vos* 'what?'. A yes–no question is introduced by the particle *či* (Polish *czy*).

RELATIVE PRONOUN
vos, e.g. *der man, vos zict bajm tiš* 'the man who is sitting at the table'. Note here, in contrast to German word order, the verb is not in final position.

Numerals

As in German, with adjusted spellings: 1–10: (*a*)*ejns, cvej, draj, fir, finf, zeks, zibn, axt, najn, cen*; 11 *elf*; 12 *zvelf*; 13 *drajcen*; 20 *cvancik*; 40 *fercik*; 100 *hundert*.

Verb

The Yiddish verb has an inflected present tense, composite general and frequentative past tenses, a composite future, an imperative mood, participial forms, and an infinitive. The composite forms are made with the auxiliaries *hobn* 'to have', *zajn* 'to be', *veln* 'to want to'.

SPECIMEN PARADIGM
hern 'to hear':

	Singular	Plural
1	ix her	mir hern
2	du herst	ir hert
3	er, zi, es hert	zi hern

Past general: *ix hob gehert*: The present tense of *hobn* used in this tense is: sing. 1 *hob*, 2 *host*, 3 *hot*; pl. 1 *hobn*, 2 *hot*, 3 *hobn*.

Past frequentative: *ix pleg hern* (Gm. *pflegen* 'to be in the habit of').

Future: e.g. *ix vel hern, du velst hern*.

Past participle: *gehert*; gerundive *herndik*.

Imperative mood: sing. *her*; pl. *hert*.

Verbs of motion are conjugated, as in German, with *zajn*; the present tense is: sing. 1 *bin*, 2 *bist*, 3 *iz*; pl. 1 *zajnen*, 2 *zajt*, 3 *zajnen*.

German stems such as *darfen* (< *dürfen*), *weln* (< *wollen*), *zoln* (< *sollen*), *megn* (< *mögen*), etc. have not been levelled; i.e. they follow German in not taking -*t* in the third person singular: *vil*, *darf*, *zol*, etc.

German ablaut series (strong verbs) are reflected in many past participles: e.g. *visn* 'know' – *gevust*; *veln* 'want to' – *gevolt*; *brengen* 'bring' – *gebracht*.

As in German, directional prefixes are frequently used: e.g.

fanander	fanander.nemen 'to take apart' (< Gm. voneinander)
mit	mit.filen 'to sympathize with' (< mit)
(a)hin	(a)hin.ton 'to put (there)' (< hin)
anider	anider.lejgn 'to place, put down' (< nieder)
arum	arum.nemen 'to embrace' (< herum)
curik	curik.gejn 'to go back' (< zurück)
arejn	arejn.gejn 'to go in' (< herein)

NEGATION

The particle of negation is *nit/ništ*. Double negatives are used: e.g. *kain menč vajst es ništ* 'no one knows it'.

Prepositions

Both Hebrew and German roots are used: e.g. Hebrew *veroš* 'headed by'; *mixuc* 'outside, out of'. German: *kegniber* (< *gegenüber*) 'opposite'; *cvišn* (< *zwischen*) 'between, among'; *on* (< *ohne*) 'without'; *onštat* (< *anstatt*) 'instead of'.

The prepositions take the dative case, i.e. are followed by the *dem/der* form of the article, with no distinction between motion towards/rest in a place: e.g. *oyf der erd* 'on (the) earth'; *leibn dem bojm* 'beside the tree'; *in der grojser štuut* 'in(to) the big town'.

Article and preposition may fuse: e.g. *inym jam* 'in(to) the sea' (*jam* 'sea'; Hebrew noun). The preposition *fun* (< Gm. *von*) 'of, from', combines with the postposition *veijgn* to denote 'on account of, for': e.g. *fun der zixerkejt veign* 'for (in the interests of) security'.

Semitic roots are not always formally stable in Yiddish usage: e.g. the triliteral *MLX* is stable in *MejLeX* 'emperor', pl. *MeLoXim*, and in *MeLuXe* 'empire'; but *X > K* in *MaLKe* 'queen' (cf. Hebrew *MaLXah* /malka/).

Word order

SVO order is adhered to in composite tenses, where German has the non-finite part of the verb following the object; e.g. *ix vel im hajnt šrajbn a briv* = *ich will ihm heute einen Brief schreiben* 'I shall write him a letter today'.

YORUBA

INTRODUCTION

Yoruba belongs to the Kwa group of Niger-Congo languages, and is spoken by about 16 million people in Nigeria and in Dahomey. Standard Yoruba is a blend of two closely similar dialects, Ọyọ and Lagos. There are many other dialectal forms.

  Yoruba was one of the earliest west African languages to be codified in the shape of a written grammar and a vocabulary (1843–9), and the credit for this goes to Samuel Crowther, a Yoruba who was sold as a slave in 1821, freed by the British, baptised and ordained to serve as a missionary in the Yoruba country. In 1859 a Yoruba news-sheet began to appear; in 1900 a complete translation of the Bible, initiated and, in part, carried out by Crowther, was published. Original Yoruba writing in both prose and verse dates from the 1920s, when literacy in Yoruba was spreading rapidly. The period 1945–60 produced the four very popular novels by Daniel Fagunwa, and since the 1950s there has been a steady flow of fiction, drama, and verse. Mention should also be made of the Yoruba folk-opera, a genre primarily associated with religious festivals but one which readily lends itself to social criticism – e.g. in the satirical plays of Hubert Ogunde. The fertility of the Yoruba literary scene is matched by the keen critical interest taken by Yoruba scholars in both traditional and modern writing. Albert Gérard (1981) speaks of a stupendous growth in what he calls 'native scholarship'.

SCRIPT

Romanization with diacritics: tone marks (acute, grave) and subscript dot to distinguish open ẹ and ọ, and the palato-alveolar fricative ṣ.

PHONOLOGY

Consonants

  stops: b, d, t, g, k; + two labio-velars: kp, gb (non-tense)
  affricates: dʒ (j)
  fricatives: f, s, ʃ, h
  nasals: m, n, ŋ
  lateral and flap: l, r
  semi-vowels: j, w

/kp/ is notated as *p*.

Vowels

i, e, ε, a, ɔ, o, u

/ε/ and /ɔ/ are notated as ẹ, ọ.
/e/ and /o/ are not nasalized; all the others are, and nasalization is phonemic. Long vowels are written double: e.g. *déédéé* 'exactly'.

Tones

There are three stative tones – high, mid, and low level – with portamento glides between tones; a low tone following a high tone, has a pronounced downward glide. Stress is evenly distributed on all syllables. Tone is phonemic.

MORPHOLOGY AND SYNTAX

Noun

Yoruba has no grammatical gender, no class system of nouns, and no articles. Nouns share certain formal characteristics, e.g. they are never monosyllabic, and usually have an initial vowel which is never a high tone. Natural gender is distinguished lexically: e.g. *ọmọkọnrin* 'son', *ọmọbinrin* 'daughter'. The plural is not specifically marked: context decides. The word *àwọn* may be used to suggest a plurality of individuals, i.e. not a collective: e.g. *àwọn ọkùnrin* 'the men'.

POSSESSION
Possession is expressed positionally, the possessed object preceding the possessor. This is the normal order for referent plus attribute; cf. *apa òkè Afrika* 'the mountainous (*òkè*) part (*apa*) of Africa'; *ọgbà ọlọ́pa* 'police (*ọlọ́pa*) station'; *aṣọ òyìnbó* 'European clothes'.

Adjective

From stative verbs like *kéré* 'to be small', *dára* 'to be good', an adjectival form can be made by prefixing a high-tone pre-echo of the first syllable: e.g. *kékeré* 'small'; *dídára* 'good'. Reduplicative forms, not associated with any Yoruba verb, are also found; Rowlands (1969) calls these 'phonaesthetic' words: e.g. *wúruwùru* 'untidy', *ṣákiṣàki* 'rough'.

Normally, the adjective follows the noun, but may precede it for emphasis; and in many cases Yoruba prefers to use a relative clause; thus, 'a strong man' can be expressed as: *ọkùnrin alágbára, ọkùnrin t'ó alágbára, alágbára ọkùnrin*.

Pronoun

There are two sets of unstressed pronominal markers, subject and object; there is a specific set for use with the negator *ko*, and a nominal emphatic set:

		Subject	Negative	Object	Emphatic
singular	1	mo	ng	mi	èmi
	2	o	o	ọ/ẹ	ìwọ
	3	ó	Ø	repeat of verb vowel	òun
plural	1	a	a	wa	àwa
	2	ẹ	ẹ	nyin	ènyin
	3	nwọ́n	nwọn	wọn	àwọn

The possessive pronoun forms are: sing. 1 *mi*, 2 *rẹ*, *ẹ*, 3 *rẹ̀*, *ẹ̀*; pl. 1 *wa*, 2 *nyín*, 3 *wọn*: e.g. *ilé wa* 'our house'. These are phonotactically linked to the vocalic final of the preceding referent, which then shows tonal and quantitative change.

Examples of repeat of verb vowel in third person objective form: *ó rí i* 'he sees him'; *ó rà a* 'he buys it'; *mo gbé e wá fún u* 'I brought it for her' (*gbé...fún* 'lift...give' = 'bring'; *wá* 'come').

DEMONSTRATIVE PRONOUN
èyí 'this'; *nì/náà* 'that'.

INTERROGATIVE PRONOUN
tani/tali 'who?'; *kíni/kílí* 'what?'.

RELATIVE PRONOUN
tí is invariable, and requires pronominal recapitulation if the antecedent is a noun or pronoun: e.g. *ọmọkọnrin tí ó rí i → ọmọkọnrin t'ó rí i* 'the boy who saw him' (*tí + ó → t'ó*).

Numerals

The traditional system is based on the use of cowry shells as currency; and in one set of numerals the word *owó* 'money' is present, at least in residual form. There is a 'basic' set of numerals with low-tone initials, and a full set in which the basic numerals receive an initial *m-* and change initial low tone for high. The basic set is as follows: 1–10: *ení, èjì, ẹta, ẹrin, àrún, èfà, èje, èjọ, ẹsán, ẹwá*. From 10 to 20 the formula is 10 + 1, 2, 3, 4, 5: 20 − 4, 3, 2, 1; i.e. at 15, cowries began to be taken from the 20 pile instead of being added from the 10 pile. Similarly, 23 is *mẹ́tà.lé.lógún* (*ogún* '20'), 27 *mẹ́tà.dí.lógbọ̀n* (*ọgbọ̀n* '30'). From 40 upwards the even decades are made by multiplying 20 by 2, 3, etc.; the odd decades involve subtraction from an even decade. In its higher reaches the system is of extreme complexity and has been largely abandoned in favour of the decimal system.

Verb

The Yoruba verb has a consonantal initial. There are accordingly many homonyms distinguished only by tone: *dé* 'to arrive, happen' – *dè* 'to await'; *rò* 'to think, relate' – *ro* 'to till the ground'.

Many compound verbs are formed from simple verb + noun: e.g. *dáhùn* 'to answer', formed from *dá* 'to do' + *ohùn* 'voice'. Transitive verbs formed in this way are separable: e.g. *rígbà* 'to get': *mo rí owó gbà* 'I got the money'.

As the Yoruba verb is marked for neither person nor number, the personal pronouns are required throughout.

TENSE SYSTEM

The only tenses in the strict sense are the present and the future. The present consists of the bare stem: e.g. *mo gbọ́* 'I hear/understand'. This tense is negated by *kò*: *ng kò gbọ́* 'I do not hear'. The future is made with the particle *yió → ó* + stem; the *ng* series of pronominal markers is used to denote subject: e.g. *ng ó wa lọ́là* 'I'll come tomorrow'. In the spoken language, this form is usually negated by the phrase *(ng) kò ní(ì)* '(I) do not have a ...'; *ng kò ní ṣe e* 'I shan't do it'.

ASPECT

The imperfective aspect is marked by prefixed *ń-/ḿ-*; negated by *ko/ki*: e.g. *nwọn ńjó* 'they are playing'; *ó ńṣiṣẹ́* 'he is working'. The perfective, with reference to both past and future, is made with *ti*: e.g. *mo ti ṣe gbogbo iṣẹ́* 'I have done all the work'. A present perfect (i.e. action begun in the past and still going on) is made by combining the two aspectual markers: e.g. *mo ti ńṣiṣẹ lati àárọ̀* 'I've been working since morning'.

The presence of mood in Yoruba is a disputed point.

As in Chinese, many verbs require a supporting directional verb, e.g. *wá* 'come' – *mú...wá, gbé...wá*: both mean 'to bring', literally 'take...come', 'lift...come'.

Prepositions

Prepositions are primary or derived.

Word order

SVO.

LI àtetekọṣe li Ọ̀rọ wà, Ọ̀rọ si wà pẹlu Ọlọrun, Ọlọrun si li Ọ̀rọ na.

2 On na li o wà li àtetekọṣe pẹlu Ọlọrun.

3 Nipasẹ̀ rẹ̀ li a ti da ohun gbogbo; lẹhin rẹ̀ a ko si da ohun kan ninu ohun ti a da.

4 Ninu rẹ̀ ni ìye wà; ìye na si ni imọle araiye.

5 Imọlẹ na si nmọlẹ ninu òkunkun; òkunkun na kò si bori rẹ̀.

6 ¶ Ọkọnrin kan wà ti a rán lati ọdọ Ọlọrun wá, orukọ ẹniti njẹ Johannu.

7 On na li a si rán fun ẹri, ki o le ṣe ẹlẹri fun imọlẹ na, ki gbogbo enia ki o le gbagbọ́ nipasẹ rẹ̀.

8 On kì iṣe Imọlẹ na, ṣugbọn a rán a wá lati ṣe ẹlẹri fun Imọlẹ na.

YUE

INTRODUCTION

Belonging to the Sinitic branch of Sino-Tibetan family, the Yue language complex is centred in Guangdong and Guangxi. The most important form of Yue, that of Canton, has provided the umbrella term for the whole complex – Cantonese. The Yue speech area also includes Hong Kong and Macau. Altogether, about 55 million people speak a Yue dialect in the People's Republic of China and adjacent territories.

From its home ground, however, Yue speech has spread all over the world, notably to the USA and western Europe, where 'Chinese' restaurants are usually Yue. Probably between 80 and 90 per cent of all *huáqiáo* ('overseas Chinese') are from the Yue linguistic and cultural background.

SCRIPT

Standard Chinese script is used plus additional characters developed in the Yue context. Some of these denote specifically Yue concepts, others replace standard *pǔtōnghuà* graphs, including some very common ones: e.g. the Modern Standard Chinese relational particle: *de*

is written as

in Yue (pronounced /ke/³).

   di¹ is also used.

The verb 'to come', which is *lái* in Modern Standard Chinese and *lai*⁵ in Yue, is written as

in Modern Standard Chinese, as

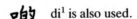

in Yue.

PHONOLOGY

Consonants

The following consonants are permissible initials in Yue words:

stops: p, p', t, t', k, k' plus the labialized velars k°, k'°
affricates: ts, ts' (> tʃ' in some dialects)
fricatives: f, j, w, s, h
nasals: m, n, ŋ
lateral: l (r is missing)

Permitted consonantal finals are: the nasals, and /p, t, k/: these stops are clipped as finals, tending to /ʔ/, the glottal stop.

The Yue inventory is remarkable for the absence of the palatal and retroflex fricatives, so characteristic of Mandarin: cf.

Modern Standard Chinese	Yue
shān 'mountain'	saan
xiān-shēng 'Mr'	seensang
jiǔ 'spirits, wine'	tsau
zhōng 'middle'	tsung

/p, t, k/ finals: cf.

Modern Standard Chinese	Yue
yuè 'moon'	yüt
fǎ 'method'	faat
chū 'go out'	choot
shí 'ten'	sup
guó 'country'	kwok

Words with these finals are pronounced in the middle level tone.

Vowels

There are seven, including /y/ and /œ/; /a/ is realized as [ɑ] or [ə], /i/ is [i] or [ɪ]. Length is phonemic.

/m/ and /ŋ/ occur as nasalized vowels: m^4 = MSC bú/bù 'not'; $ŋ^5$ = MSC wu 'five'. The indices indicate the numbers of possible variants.

Tones

Authorities differ as to the exact number of tones in Yue. Ramsey (1987) lists nine basic tones plus two 'changed tones' – a high level and a high rising tone occurring in derived words, i.e. phonemes used in a non-primary sense. Loanwords from Western languages are also usually pronounced in 'changed tone'.

MORPHOLOGY AND SYNTAX

In general, as in **Modern Standard Chinese** (*q.v.*). One cardinal difference lies in the Yue reversal of Modern Standard Chinese order where both direct and indirect objects are present: cf.

Yue: ngo pei bo sue **nei**   'I (*ngo*) give (*pei*) **you** (*nei*) a book (*sue*)'
MSC: wó géi **nĭ** yibĕn shū   (*gĕi* 'give'; *shū* 'book')

The relational particle *ke* is used to mark possession, even when inalienable relationship is involved – in cases, that is, where Modern Standard Chinese would not use *de*: cf. Yue *ngo.ke taai-taai* 'my wife' = MSC *wŏ ∅ àiren*
The Yue pronouns are:

	Singular	Plural
1	ngo⁵	ngo.tei⁶
2	nei⁵	nei.tei
3	kui⁵/köi	kui.tei

The Yue script forms for the first and second personal pronouns are as in Modern Standard Chinese; the third person form is

佢 ·

> **1** T'aai-ch'oh yau Tò, Tò t'ūng-maai
>   Sheûng-Tai, Tò tsik-hai Sheûng-Tai.
> ² Ni-kòh Tò t'aai-ch'oh t'ūng-maai Sheûng-
> Tai à. ³ Maân māt pei k'uĭ ch'òng tsò,
> taân-faān shaû tsò kè, mŏ yat yeûng m̄ hai
> yaū k'uĭ shóh tsô. ⁴ Shang-mêng hai tsoi
> Tò chung, i-ch'é kòh-ti shang-mêng hai
> yān-kè kwong. ⁵ Kòh kwong chiù tsoi hak-
> òm chi chung, taân hak-òm m̄ ying-shik k'uĭ.
> ⁶ Yaū kòh yān yaū Sheûng-Tai tá-faat₀
> kè, mêng kiù tsô Yeuk₀-hôn. ⁷ K'uĭ lai tsô
> kin-chìng, tsik-hai wai kòh Kwong tsô kin-
> chìng, ling chùng yān yan k'uĭ chì sùn.
> ⁸ K'uĭ m̄ hai kòh Kwong, tūk-hai wai kòh
> Kwong tsô kin-chìng che.

YUKAGIR

INTRODUCTION

Sometimes regarded as a Palaeo-Siberian outlier, this Siberian language is of doubtful affinity. There seem to be good grounds, however, for linking it with the Uralic languages. Two groups of Yukagir speakers, numbering altogether two or three hundred, live in the Yakut ASSR: the *wadul*, who are reindeer-breeding nomads in the tundra, and the *odul*, who live by fishing in the Kolyma area.

The language is unwritten.

PHONOLOGY

Consonants

    stops: p, b, t, d, k, g, q; palatalized t', d'
    fricatives: s, ʁ
    nasals: m, n, ɲ, ŋ
    laterals and flap: l, ʎ, r
    semi-vowels: j, w

Vowels

    i, ɛ, œ, a, o, u

/ɛ/ is represented here by *e*, /œ/ by *ö*; long vowels are marked by a macron.

MORPHOLOGY AND SYNTAX

Noun

The noun has two numbers, the plural ending being *-p/-pe/-pul*; e.g. *ile* 'reindeer', pl. *ile.pe*; *lā:me* 'dog', pl. *lā:me.pul*.

There are seven cases. A specimen declension of the singular noun *nime* 'house' follows; there is no accusative case:

nominative	nime	lateral	nimeʁan
instrumental	nimelek	aditive	nimeŋin'
locative	nimeʁa	genitive	nimen
ablative	nimaʁat		

The logical focus marker -*le* (*see* **Verb**, below) can be used predicatively: e.g. *Ten nime.le* 'This is a house.'

POSSESSION
A specific possessive construction is available for the third person only: -*gi* follows the nominative, -*d*- is infixed in oblique cases: e.g. *köde.gi* 'her husband'; *nimedeʁa* 'in his house'.

Adjective

As a separate part of speech, the adjective is absent in Yukagir. Qualitative distinctions are made by the use of stative verbs, or by adding suffixes to nouns: e.g. *nime* 'house', *nime-tege(ŋ)* 'big house', where -*tege(ŋ)* is an augmentative suffix.

Pronoun

PERSONAL INDEPENDENT
Sing. 1 *met*, 2 *tet*, 3 *tudel*; pl. 1 *mit*, 2 *tit*, 3 *tittel*. These are declined, and may be logically focused by adding -*k* to first and second persons and by dropping -*l* from third: e.g. *metek...* = 'it is/was I who...'; *tude...* 'it is/was he who...'.

DEMONSTRATIVE PRONOUN
The basic series is: *ten* 'this' – *an* 'that' – *tigin* 'that (yonder)'. These are amplified in two series – (a) without logical stress; and (b) with logical stress: cf. *Ten mine(le)* 'This is a house'; *Tuŋn'e nemeleŋ?* '*What* is this?'; *Tuŋut monul* 'He said *this*.'

INTERROGATIVE PRONOUN
kin 'who?'; *nemeŋ* 'what?'.

Numerals

There are two types of base: predicative and attributive. The predicative bases 1–5 are: *mōrqo-, kujo-, jalo-, jalakla-, imdal'd'a*; to these, the third person singular marker -*n'* is added (n' = /ɲ/): e.g. *mōrqon'* '...is one'.

The attributive bases are *mārqa-, ki-, ja-, jeluku-, imdal'd'i*: to these the singular genitive ending -*n*/-*d* is added: e.g. *kin gödek* 'two men'; *kid ilek* 'two reindeer'. The system is decimal.

Verb

TRANSITIVE/INTRANSITIVE
Marked for voice, mood, tense, person.

ACTIVE VOICE
Moods: indicative, imperative, optative, subjunctive, inferential. Markers are:

imperative -k/-ŋik; optative -bu(n')-; subjunctive -at-; inferential: -l'el: e.g. *Met moriŋ, tet ilele pull'elmeŋ* 'I heard that you killed a reindeer.'

TENSE

Past, verbal base + Ø; present, -nu-; future, -t(e)-.

As specimen, the past tense of (a) *met merūjeŋ* 'I was going'; (b) *met meraiŋ* 'I was shooting (something)'

	Intransitive		Transitive	
	Singular	*Plural*	*Singular*	*Plural*
1	met merūjeŋ	mit merūjeli	met meraiŋ	mit meraij
2	tet merūjek	tit merūjemut	tet meraimek	tit meraimk
3	tudel meruj	tittel merūŋi	tudel meraim	tittel meraiŋa

Present *met merūnujeŋ* 'I am going', etc.; future *met merūtejeŋ* 'I shall go', etc.

FOCUS

Subject, object, or verb can be promoted to stressed position, or focused: for example, the pronoun can be focused; the verb forms given above then become *metek ūl* 'I went'; *tetek ūl* 'you went', etc.; *met ai* 'I shot'; *tet ai* 'you shot'; etc.: cf. *met ai* 'I shot', *met mer.ai.ŋ* 'I was shooting'; *met ile.leŋ ai.meŋ* 'I shot *the deer*'.

NEGATION

Example: in past tense: *el* + stem + personal endings: *met el.ū.jeŋ* 'I didn't come', *tet el.ū.jek, tudel el.ū*, etc.

Participial forms in -j-, -t'e-, -d'e-, etc. are used to make relative clauses: e.g. *keluj göde* 'the man who came'; *kel.un.uj göde* 'the man who is coming'; *kel.te.j göde* 'the man who will come'.

PASSIVE VOICE

The marker is -(j)o-: e.g. from *wuek* 'to do' – *wuejon* 'done'; *tu morijol jaqtele* 'this song which has been/is heard'. Derivatory forms are available to express such notions as 'to come across something', 'to possess something over a longer period', etc. There are also inceptive, frequentative, and semelfactive modes.

Postpositions

Yukagir uses postpositions: e.g. *bure* 'above', *al* 'under', *tuduru* 'in(side)'.

Word order

SOV appears to be normal.

ZAPOTEC

INTRODUCTION

Along with Mixtec, Otomi, Mazatec, Popolac, and several other languages or language complexes, Zapotec belongs to the Otomanguean group of Mesoamerican languages. Whatever its original provenance, it seems to have been sited in Oaxaca state and the Vera Cruz area in southern Mexico for about two thousand years: the Monte Alban complex, which is associated with Zapotec culture, dates from some hundreds of years before the Christian era. The term Zapotecan denotes a large number of dialects, with an overall total of about 300,000 speakers. The form described here, following Butler (1980), is Yatzachi, one of the central group of dialects. There is some written literature.

SCRIPT

Roman with the following additional letters: ç, ə, ɟ, ḻ, ṇ, ñ, š, x̣, ž.

PHONOLOGY

Consonants

stops: p, b, t, d, k, g, ʔ; with labialized k°, g°
affricates: tʃ‘ (aspirate), tʃ (non-aspirate)
fricatives: s, z, ʃ, ʒ, ṣ, z̦, x, x°, χ, χ° (for ṣ see below)
nasals: m, n (ṇ see note below)
lateral and flap: ḻ (see note below), r, rr
semi-vowel: j

/f, ʎ, ɲ/ occur in Spanish loan-words.

In written Zapotec, /k°, g°/ are notated as *cw, gw*; /tʃ‘, tʃ/ as *ch, ch*; /ʃ, ʒ/ as š, ž; /ṣ‘, ṣ/ as x̣, x; /x/ as *j*; /χ, χ°/ as ɟ, ɟw.

Characteristically, ten Zapotec phonemes are paired: /b/p, d/t, g/k, tʃ/tʃ‘, z/s, ʒ/ʃ, ṣ‘/ṣ, g°/k°, ḻ/l, n/ṇ/, where the second member is the strong/emphatic correlative of the first. The qualitative distinction is clear in six of the ten pairs. As regards the other four, /ṣ/ is described as a sibilant palatal retroflex fricative; its strong correlative is tenser and more emphatic. The same qualitative distinction seems to distinguish /tʃ/ from /tʃ‘/. /ḻ/ is a sonant, while its weak correlative tends towards a lateral unvoiced fricative. The exact nature of the distinction between /ṇ/ and its weak correlative is unclear; /ṇ/ is described as typically sited medially preceding /b/p/.

The two series provide many examples of minimal pairs: cf.

cuat 'never'	x̱a' 'my father'	naco' 'thou art'
guat 'dead'	xa' 'my clothing'	nago' 'thy ear'
ša'a 'I go'	ṇa'a 'now'	
ža'a 'hot'	na'a 'my hand'	

Vowels

i, e, a, o, u, ə

Tones

Two- or three-tone systems have been identified in some forms of Zapotec. In this article, the orthography outlined above is followed.

MORPHOLOGY AND SYNTAX

Noun

Zapotec has no grammatical gender, and nouns are not marked for number. Plurality of a nominal subject may, of course, be inferred from verbal inflection (*see* **Verb**, below). The modifier *zan* 'many' may be used if necessary: e.g. *bia* 'animal' – *bia zan* '(many) animals'.

The numeral *to* 'one' can be used as an indefinite article. The suffixed particle *-n/-nə'* corresponds in some ways to a definite article, but it can only be used if the referent has already been mentioned in discourse; that is, if it defines an object or topic already known to the audience. Thus, *biz* 'cat': *bizən'* 'the cat (which we've been talking about)'.

POSSESSION

Possession in Zapotec is alienable or inalienable. Alienable possession is marked by *c̱he* or by the prefix *x-*: e.g. *bia c̱he Bed* 'Pedro's animal'; *bia c̱hebo'* 'his animal', where *c̱he* has taken the third person pronominal marker (*see* **Pronoun**, below): cf. *ɉeid* 'hen': *xɉeid* '…'s hen': *xɉeida'* 'my hen': *xɉeidga'aque* 'their hen'.

Nouns referring to parts of the body are always marked for inalienable possession; that is, the possessive pronominal markers are added to the noun without any additional marker: e.g. *yic̱hɉ* 'head of…'; *yic̱hɉa'* 'my head'; *yic̱hɉo'* 'thy head'; *yic̱hɉbo'* 'his/her head'.

The possessive construction has phonetic adjustment where necessary: cf. *bey* 'basket': *x.pey.a'* 'my basket'; *nis* 'water': *xis.ga'aque* 'their water'. The possessed form may be suppletive: *beco'* 'dog': *xicua'a'* 'my dog'.

Adjective

As attributive, adjective follows noun and is invariable: e.g. *beṇə' golə* 'old person'; *beṇə' yašə* 'poor person'; *nis zag* 'cold water'.

Pronoun

Pronouns in Zapotec are independent or bound. The basic independent forms together with their inseparable verbal enclitics are:

		Singular			Plural	
		Independent	*Bound*		*Independent*	*Bound*
1		nada'	-(d)a'	incl.	chio'o	-cho
				excl.	neto'	-to'
2		le'	-(do)o'		le'e	-le
3	(respectful)	le'	-(n)e'		le'	-(n)e'
	(familiar)	lebo'	-bo'		lebo'	-bo'
	(animals)	leb	-(ə)b		leb	-(ə)b
	(things)	len	-(ə)n		len	-(ə)n

The forms in parentheses are used in the *da'* conjugation (*see* **Verb**, below). The other forms are used in the *-a'* conjugation.

The indirect and direct objective pronominal series is, in general, close to or identical with the subjective series: e.g. *beco' na'anə' gwdaob nada'* 'that dog bit me'; *ble'ida' ḷebo'* 'I saw him'. However, third person plural objective pronouns have variant forms which are used when they are governed by first or second person pronominal subjects; e.g. the third person familiar objective form (plural) following a 1st person singular subject is *-ga'ac(a'a)ne'* in the *-a'* conjugation.

DEMONSTRATIVE PRONOUN

There are three degrees of removal: *nga* 'this'; *ni/na* 'that'; *ni'* 'that (remote)'. These have plural forms: *quinga, qui, ca'*. They follow the noun: e.g. *xoa' nga* 'this maize'.

INTERROGATIVE PRONOUN

¿no? 'who?'; *¿bi?* 'what?'. A sentence can be made interrogative by prefixing /ə/-, written as *E*, to the first word, whose tone appears to be heightened: e.g. *¿E.zono' žin ṇeža?* 'Did you work today?' (*žin* 'work'; *ṇeža* 'today').

RELATIVE PRONOUN

In Zapotec, relative clauses are often made by inversion of the normal indicative order: e.g. *gw.xi'ibo' yo'o nga* 'he bought this house' – *yo'o nga gw.xi'ibo'* 'the house he bought'. *De'en* 'the thing just mentioned' and its synonyms, e.g. *be'en* for persons, can also be used: e.g. *mech de'en gw.xi'e par bete'e yin'* 'the money he got for selling the pepper' (*mech* 'money'; *par* 'for' (Spanish loan); *yin'* 'pepper').

Numerals

1–10: *to*, *c̦hopə*, *šonə*, *tap*, *gueyə'*, *χop*, *gažə*, *χon'*, *ga*, *ši*; 11 *šnei̦*; 12 *šižin̦*; 13 *ši'in̦*; 14 *žda'*; 15 *šino'*; 16 *ši'into*; 17 *ši'in̦chopə*; 18 *ši'inšonə*; 19 *tguali̦*; 20 *gali̦ə*.

From 21 to 39 the numerals are based on *c̦hoa* 'forty', preceded by the forms for 1 to 19: thus, 21 *to.choa*; 22 *c̦hopəchoa* (notice that in the compound forms, the *c̦-* of *c̦hoa* 'forty' becomes *c-*); 31 is *snei̦echoa*.

Similarly, 41 to 59 are based on *gyon* 'sixty'; 61 to 79 also on *gyon* but in reverse order: cf. 51 *šnei̦eyon*; 71 *gyonšnei̦*. 80 is *taplali̦* and the numerals from 81 to 99 are based on this form.

100 is *to gueyoa* or *gueyə'əlali̦* 'five twenties'.

Verb

The Zapotec verb is heavily inflected for person, number, tense/aspect, and mood. There are progressive, stative, perfective, and potential aspects; the first three have specific markers prefixed to the root. Typical markers are: progressive *ch-*, stative *n-/b-*, perfective *b-*, *gw-*, *g-*, *i̦-*. There is no specific marker for the potential aspect, which provides the future tense-form. Cf. *ch.c̦hogue'en* 'he is cutting it now'; *n.c̦hogue'en* 'the state of affairs is that he has cut it'; *gw.c̦hogue'en* 'he cut it (at some time in the past)'; *ə.c̦hogue'en* 'he will cut/is going to cut it'.

There are two basic conjugations: verbs ending in a consonant, a diphthong, or the glottal stop, form the *-a'* conjugation; verbs ending in *-e* or *-i* form the *-da'* conjugation. The two conjugations have slightly differing pronominal subject enclitics (*see* **Pronoun**, above).

A typical Zapotec verb form is aspectual prefix – stem – pronominal marker. Extensive variation occurs depending on the phonetic structure of the root, e.g. the nature of the initial. Many verbs lack the stative aspect. As illustration, the progressive aspect of the verb *chol̦bo'* 'sing', (*-a'* conjugation): *chol̦-a'*, *-o'*, *-e'/-bo'/-əb/-ən*; *chol̦-chol/-to'*, *-le*. Special forms apply to third person plural, including a plural marker: *-əsə'ə* (with variants). Thus, *ch.sed.bo'* 'he studies' (progressive) *ch.əsə'ə.sed.bo'* 'they study'.

Directional infixes are added between the aspect prefix and the stem. Thus, *-edə-* indicates motion towards speaker, *-i̦ə/-e* motion away from: cf. *ch.edə.c̦hogue'en* 'he comes (towards me) to be cutting it' (progressive); *z.edə.c̦hogue'en* 'the state of affairs is that he has come towards me to cut ("be cutting") it'; *ch.i̦e.c̦hogue'en* 'he goes off (from here) habitually to cut it'.

IMPERATIVE

The second person singular form is the same as the perfective aspect base minus the pronominal affix: e.g. *gui'obo'* 'he buys' – *gui'o* 'buy!'.

A passive form is made by very radical and unpredictable modulation of the active stem; cf. *che'ei̦bo'on* 'to drink something' – *chdo'oi̦ən* 'to be drunk'; *cha'obo'on* 'to buy something' – *chda'on* 'to be bought'.

CAUSATIVE
All four aspects – progressive, stative, perfective, and potential – have causative
versions, marked in gender by replacement of a weak stem-initial by the strong
correlative: e.g. $b \rightarrow p$, $ž \rightarrow š$, $gw \rightarrow cw$, etc. Examples:

Neutral progressive base	Causative
ch.dabo' 'to move' (intrans.)	ch.tabo'on 'to move something'
ch.xopbo' 'to fall'	ch.xopbo'on 'to fell'
ch.ža'an 'to get warm'	ch.ša'abo'on 'to warm something'

Causatives are also made by insertion of -g-/-gw- or -z-:

ch.olbo' 'to sing'	ch.golbo'on
ch.ombo' žin 'to work'	ch.gombo'on žin
ch.enebo' 'to hear'	ch.zenebo'

There are also suppletive forms.

MODAL VERBS
Both components – auxiliary and sense-verb – are in finite form: e.g. *ch.ene'ebo'
ch.olbo'* 'he wants to sing': here, use of the progressive form suggests that he is
singing and wants to go on doing so: cf. *ch.ene'ebo' golbo'* 'he wants to sing',
where the potential aspect indicates that he is not yet singing but would like to
begin.
   'Can, able to': e.g. *chac chomb žin gual* 'it can work hard': here, the verb
forms *chac* and *chomb* show that the referent is an animal; *gual* 'hard'.

NEGATION
The general negating adverb is *bito*: e.g. *bito naca' nada' gual* 'I am not strong';
Bito goquə yejw bedo bio' mey 'No rain (*yejw*) fell during (*bedo*) May.'

Prepositions

Many Zapotec prepositions are nouns denoting parts of the body; e.g. *xni'a*
'one's foot', and hence 'at the foot of, under': *xni'a ze'enə* 'at the foot of the
wall'; *yichɨ* 'one's head, up, above': *yichɨ yež* 'above the village', e.g. *Chəse-
'əchogue' yas yichɨ yež* 'They're cutting trees above the village'; *le'e* 'in, on':
bzoje' le'e yišən 'he wrote on the paper'.
   It is particularly interesting that the prepositions can take the aspect markers;
cf. **chedo** 'during' (with reference to present time); **bedo** 'during' (with reference
to past); **yedo** 'during' (with reference to future).

Word order

Zapotec is verb-initial, and syntactically right-branching; VSO is frequent.

1 Desde principio de Guixhila-yuh nuhucá Jesús, Verbo Divino láhhbé; núhubé né Dios; né lacá labé ngá Dios.
2 Labé nabéxabé né Dios.

3 Guirá cosa por labé guca; sin que labé gastí de cani ni gúcacá ñaca.
4 Né labé nuhú vida; né vida ngá biani stid hombre.
5 Biani ruxani lu guêlacahuí; guêlacahuí que hualluniganarní.

6 Gulluhu ti hombre láhh Juan; Dios bicenda lah.
7 Ngá para gudih fé de bianicá; nessu guirá biní gacacreer por labé.

8 Cadi biani labé; xêhdabé para gudîhbé fé biani.

ZUNI

INTRODUCTION

Of uncertain affinity, this language is usually associated with Hopi as one of the Pueblo (regional) group, although there is no genetic connection between the two. Like the Hopi, the Zuni believe that their ancestors reached their present location by climbing upwards through underground chambers. Some 3,000 speakers live in western New Mexico.

PHONOLOGY

Consonants

Zuni has the voiceless stops /p, t, k/, without their voiced counterparts. /k/ has a labialized allophone [k°]. /ts/ and /tʃ/ are present. There are two nasals, /m, n/, two laterals, /l and ł/, two sibilants, /s, ʃ/, the semi-vowels /w, j/, and the glottal stop. /r/ is missing.

Vowels

   long and short: i, e, a, o, u

There are three pitch levels; stress is on the initial syllable.

MORPHOLOGY AND SYNTAX

Noun

Nouns and verbs are distinguished by specific sets of suffixes. Particles are uninflected. Nouns are marked for number. The following two examples from Newman (1965) illustrate nominal compounding, modal infix, and suffixed definite article coded for number: *he.ɫpo.nne* 'bridle bit' (*he* 'metal'; *-ɫpo-* indicates design, fashioning; *-nne* is one form of the definite article marking singularity); *he.pačči̵.we*' 'tortillas' (*he* 'metal'; *-pačči̵* to be stuck on to (something)'; *-we*' is the plural definite article).

Pronoun

There are singular, dual, and plural pronouns, which have subject, object, and possessive forms. The first and second personal forms are analogous sets, the third person form (which has no subject form except in the dual) is variant. Where first and second person forms coincide, as in dual and plural subject and object, the presence or absence of a plural indicator in the verb fixes the requisite choice: cf. Newman's examples: *to'na' ho' 'il'aˑnuwa* 'I will take you (dual) with me'; *to'na' ho' 'aw-il 'a.nuwa* 'I will take you (pl.) with me' (where the plural marker *'aw* fixes *to'na'* as plural object).

The first person forms for subject, object, and possessive are: sing. *ho'/ho.'o – hom – hom(ma)*; e.g. *hom k'ak°enne* 'my house'. Second person: *to'/to'o – tom – tom(ma)*.

Verb

The Zuni verb has present and past stems, formed in various ways from the root; verbs are classified according to these variations: e.g. the root *'iy* 'to come', has a present stem identical with the root, while the past stem is *'i-*. The root *pen* 'to speak', has *pen-* present stem and *pe-* past. In general, past stems differ from present stems only in the addition or subtraction of a vowel or consonant or both.

TENSE AND MOOD MARKERS

-*'a* (with allophones) marks present tense: e.g. *'iy.a* 'he comes';

-*'a* also marks the imperative mood: e.g. *'iton čun.'a* 'stop eating';

-*ka* (with allophones) marks past tense: e.g. *'a.ka* 'he went' (*'a.n* 'to go');

-*'anna* (with allophones) marks the future tense or conditional mood: e.g. *we'anna* 'he will be/would be sick';

'a and *'anna* are added to the present stem; *ka* to the past.

A hortative mood is marked by -*še*, and a permissive by -*tu*: e.g. *'ota'še* 'let's dance'.

Zuni has a considerable inventory of suffixes which relate principal verbs to subordinate verbs in specific functional ways. Thus, e.g., *'appa/-ppa* signals a subject switch in the subordinate clause, and -*(k)kan* the resultative sense of a subordinate verb: e.g. *hom yałašo.kkan 'ika* 'he came to visit me'.

Verb formants for number, voice, and aspect are prefixed or suffixed to the stem. The prefixes include *te(t)-*, which marks the plural subject of intransitive verbs, and *te-*, which relates an action or state to its natural setting: e.g. *te.k'ałi* 'the weather is hot'.

Aspectual and modal suffixes are sequentially ordered between stem and inflection. They include one set which specifies the locus and distribution of objects – whether they are on the ground, piled up, in something (and, if so, the nature of the container), in growth, etc. Further, there are inceptive, causative and continuative markers: -*(na).wa* marks the plural subject of a transitive verb: e.g. *hon'anikk'a.nap.ka* 'we taught him' (*hon* 'we'; -*k'a* is the causative marker; *nap* is allophone of *na.wa*; -*ka* is past tense).

The negative marker *-na'ma* always concludes the modal suffix sequence: e.g. *'an'awa.na'ma.n* 'as (he) did not remember it, (he)...' (where *-n* relates clauses with the same subject).

Attached to words of any class are various enclitics, e.g. *-ši*, interrogative; *-'te*, adversative; *-k°in*, directional; *-an*, locative: e.g. *kalapa.k°in 'a.ka* 'he went to Gallup'.

31 Jesus lesa:wanikwekkya deꞏan, an
a:suwe dap an tsitda Jesus inkwin a:wiynan,
dekꞏwanꞏan iɬuwa yuɬaknan, shemanapkya.
32 Shemana:wap akkya a:hoꞏi Jesus illabaꞏ dinan
ullapnona leꞏandikwekkya, "Hadiya:wa! Dom tsitda
dap dom a:suwe dom sheme:na.we. Dekꞏwanꞏan din
ꞏuɬaye." 33 A:hoꞏi lesandikwap, Jesus
yansewahkꞏekkya, "Kop hoꞏ inꞏona hom tsitda? Dap
kop a:hoꞏ a:winꞏona hom a:suwe?" 34 Akkya Jesus
dinan ullapnona a:wunan, leꞏkwekkya, "Lukno dinan
ullapnona hom a:tsitda dap hom a:suwe a:deꞏona.
35 Kwaꞏhoɬ God haydoshkowaꞏ dens chuhoɬ
lesne:nona, uhsonaꞏ da: hom suwe, dap hom ikina,
da: hom tsitda." Jesus lesn a:wambekya.

(Mark 3: 31–5)

APPENDIX OF SCRIPTS

ARABIC

THE ALPHABET

Transliteration	Final	Medial	Initial	Alone	Name
ā	ا			ا	ʔalif
b	ب	ـبـ	بـ	ب	bāʔ
t	ت	ـتـ	تـ	ت	tāʔ
θ	ث	ـثـ	ثـ	ث	θaʔ
ǰ	ج	ـجـ	جـ	ج	ǰīm
ħ	ح	ـحـ	حـ	ح	ħāʔ
x	خ	ـخـ	خـ	خ	xāʔ
d	د			د	dāl
ð	ذ			ذ	ðāl
r	ر			ر	rāʔ
z	ز			ز	zāy
s	س	ـسـ	سـ	س	sīn
š	ش	ـشـ	شـ	ش	šīn
ṣ	ص	ـصـ	صـ	ص	ṣād
ḍ	ض	ـضـ	ضـ	ض	ḍād
ṭ	ط	ط	ط	ط	ṭāʔ
ð̣	ظ	ظـ	ظـ	ظ	ð̣aʔ
ʕ	ع	ـعـ	عـ	ع	ʕayn
ɣ	غ	ـغـ	غـ	غ	ɣayn
f	ف	ـفـ	فـ	ف	fāʔ
q	ق	ـقـ	قـ	ق	qāf
k	ك	ـكـ	كـ	ك	kāf
l	ل	لـ	لـ	ل	lām

Transliteration	Final	Medial	Initial	Alone	Name
m	م	ـمـ	مـ	م	mīm
n	ن	ـنـ	نـ	ن	nūn
h	ه	ـهـ	هـ	ه	hā?
w	و			و	wāw
y	ى	ـيـ	يـ	ى	yā?

The vowel diacritics are: *fatḥa* ´ /a/; *ḍamma* ˀ /u/; *kasra* ˏ /i/; and *sukūn* ° for zero (no vowel). Long vowels are represented thus: /ā/ by *ʔalif* or *ʔalif madda* (initially), Ī ; /ī/ by *yāسـ*; and /ū/ by *wāw*.

Source: Kaye, A.S. (1987) 'Arabic', in B. Comrie (ed.) *The World's Major Languages*, London, Routledge.

ARMENIAN

THE ALPHABET

Capitals	Lower case	Transliteration	Cursive	
Ա	ա	a	*Ա*	*ա*
Բ	բ	b	*Բ*	*բ*
Գ	գ	g	*Գ*	*գ*
Դ	դ	d	*Դ*	*դ*
Ե	ե	e	*Ե*	*ե*
Զ	զ	z	*Զ*	*զ*
Է	է	ē	*Է*	*է*
Ը	ը	ə	*Ը*	*ը*
Թ	թ	t'	*Թ*	*թ*
Ժ	ժ	ž	*Ժ*	*ժ*
Ի	ի	i	*Ի*	*ի*
Լ	լ	l	*Լ*	*լ*
Խ	խ	x	*Խ*	*խ*
Ծ	ծ	c	*Ծ*	*ծ*
Կ	կ	k	*Կ*	*կ*
Հ	հ	h	*Հ*	*հ*
Ձ	ձ	j	*Ձ*	*ձ*
Ղ	ղ	ł	*Ղ*	*ղ*
Ճ	ճ	č	*Ճ*	*ճ*
Մ	մ	m	*Մ*	*մ*
Յ	յ	y	*Յ*	*յ*
Ն	ն	n	*Ն*	*ն*
Շ	շ	š	*Շ*	*շ*
Ո	ո	o	*Ո*	*ո*
Չ	չ	č'	*Չ*	*չ*
Պ	պ	p	*Պ*	*պ*
Ջ	ջ	ǰ	*Ջ*	*ջ*

Capitals	Lower case	Transliteration	Cursive	
Ռ	ռ	$\dot{r}$	Ր	ռ
Ս	ս	s	Ս	ս
Վ	վ	v	վ	վ
Տ	տ	t	Ս	տ
Ր	ր	r	ր	ր
Ց	ց	c'	ց	ց
Ի	ւ	w	ի	ւ
Փ	փ	p'	փ	փ
Ք	ք	k'	ք	ք

Source: Adapted from Minassian, M. (1976) *Manuel pratique d'Arménien ancien,* Paris, Librairie Klincksieck.

BATAK

THE ALPHABET

∿	*a*	⋛	*dja*
⁊	*ha*	⋋	*da*
✕	*ma*	⋖	*nga*
⌐	*na*	∽	*ba*
⇒	*ra*	⌐	*wa*
✕	*ta*	∿	*ja*
⋜	*sa*	℮	*nja*
—	*pa*	⚏	*i*
⇐	*la*	⚐	*u*
⇁	*ga*		

MEDIAL AND FINAL VOWELS

O *-i* **>** *-u* **✕** *-o* **—** *-e*

⇒O—O = *ripi* ⇒ = *pu* ∽⇁ = *bu*

∽✕ = *bo* ∽̄ = *be*

pangolat \ makes consonant mute: ⇒—\ = *rap*

hamisaran ⁻ nasalization: ∽̄ = *bang;* ∽̄O = *bing*

BENGALI

CONSONANTS

ক *k*	খ *k*	গ *g*	ঘ *gh*	ঙ *ṅ*
চ *c*	ছ *ch*	জ *j*	ঝ *jh*	ঞ *ñ*
ট *ṭ*	ঠ *ṭh*	ড *ḍ*	ঢ *ḍh*	ণ *ṇ*
ত *t*	থ *th*	দ *d*	ধ *dh*	ন *n*
প *p*	ফ *ph*	ব *b*	ভ *bh*	ম *m*
য *y*	র *r*	ল *l*	ব *v*	
শ *ś*	ষ *ṣ*	স *s*	হ *h*	য *z*	ড় *ṛ*	ঢ় *ṛh*

VOWELS

(a) independent:

অ *a*	আ *ā*	ই *i*	ঈ *ī*	উ *u*	ঊ *ū*	ঋ *ri*
এ *ē*	ঐ *ai*	ও *ō*	ঔ *au*	অং *aṅ*	অঃ *a'*	

(b) in combination with /k/:

কা *kā*	কি *ki*	কী *kī*	কু *ku*	কূ *kū*
কৃ *kri*	কে *kē*	কৈ *kai*	কো *kō*	কৌ *kau*

Conjunct graphs are formed as in Devanagari by juxtaposition, amalgamation or subscript. Cancellation of inherent base vowel (/ɔ/ in Bengali) and nasalization are indicated as in Devanagari.

NUMERALS

১	২	৩	৪	৫	৬	৭	৮	৯	০
1	2	3	4	5	6	7	8	9	0

BERBER

The Tifinagh alphabet (*tifinagh* is a plural form: 'letters'; the singular is *tafineq*), as used for certain forms of Berber, is here reproduced, in amended form, from Hanoteau 1896.

The short vowel, notated as *a, i, u*, is not normally written.

THE ALPHABET

Tar′erit	·	*a, i, u*	Iel	‖	*l*
Ieb	▥ ◐	*b*	Iem	⊐	*m*
Iet	+	*t*	Ien	I	*n*
Ied	⊓ ∧ ⊔	*d*	Iek	·:	*k*
Iej	⊐⊏	*j*	Iak′	···	*q*
Iez	♯	*z*	Ier′	⋮	*ɣ*
Iez′	X X̵	*z′*	Iech	Ɔ	*ʃ*
Ier	□ ○	*r*	Iah	⋮	*h*
Ies	⊡ ⊙	*s*	Iadh	Ǝ	*d̥, t̥*
Ieg	∴ ⵝ	*g*	Iakh	∷	*χ*
Ieg′	⋈	*g′*	Iaou	:	*ū*
Ief	ⵀ ⵊⵀ	*f*	Iéy	≤	*ī*

COMBINED LETTERS

Iebt	+⊟	*bt*	Ielt	ⱨ	*lt*
Iezt	♯	*zt*	Iemt	+Ǝ	*mt*
Iert	⊞	*rt*	Ient	†	*nt*
Iest	+⊡	*st*	Iecht	+Ɔ	*ʃt*
Iegt	ⱦ	*gt*	Ienk	⫯	*nk*
Ieg′t	+⋈	*g′t*			

Source: Hanoteau, A. (1890) *La Langue Tamachek*, Algiers

BUGINESE

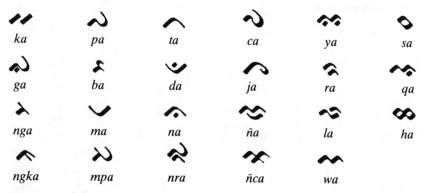

ka	pa	ta	ca	ya	sa
ga	ba	da	ja	ra	qa
nga	ma	na	ña	la	ha
ngka	mpa	nra	ñca	wa	

The letter *qa* 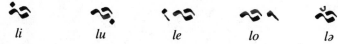 is used to notate initial 'a/a. There is no separate letter for the glottal stop. *qa* is also used as a base for the diacritics notating the other vowels i, u, e, o, ə, in initial position.

The diacritics are here shown in combination with the consonant *la* :

li	lu	le	lo	lə

In Macassarese, which does not have the vowel /ə/, the diacritic is used to indicate that the vowel so marked is followed by a nasal consonant.

1503

BURMESE

CONSONANTS

က	ခ	ဂ	ဃ	င
ka	*kha*	*ga*	*ga*	*nga*
စ	ဆ	ဇ	ဈ	ည
sa	*sa*	*za*	*za*	*nya*
ဋ	ဌ	ဍ	ဎ	ဏ
ta	*tha*	*da*	*da*	*na*
တ	ထ	ဒ	ဓ	န
ta	*tha*	*da*	*da*	*na*
ပ	ဖ	ဗ	ဘ	မ
pa	*pha*	*ba*	*ba*	*ma*

ယ	ရ	လ	ဝ	သ	ဟ	ဠ
ya	*ya(ra)*	*la*	*wa*	*sa*	*ha*	*la*

VOWELS

(a) independent:

အ	အာ	အား	ဣ(အိ)	ဤ(အီ)	ဥ(အု)
a	*ā*	*ā*	*i*	*ī*	*u*

ဦ(အူ)	အေ့	ဧ(အေ)	အဲ	ဩဝ်(အော်)
ū	*e*	*ē*	*ē*	*ō*

ဪ(အော)	အို	အံ
ō	*ō*	*an*

(b) as used with bearer consonant, represented by ◯ :

◯ *-a*   ◯ာ *-ā*   ◯ား *-ā*   ◌ိ *-i*   ◌ီ *-ī*

◌ု (◯ု) *-u*   ◌ူ (◯ူ) *-ū*   ေ◯ *-e*   ေ◯ *-ē*

◌ဲ *-ē*   ေ◯ာ် *-ō*   ေ◯ာ *-ō*   ◌ို *-ō*

Vowel length is correlated with tone as follows:

(a) short vowels with first tone: e.g. using *ka*:

　　　 က *ka*,　　 ကိ *ki*,　　 ကု *ku*,　　 ကေ့ *ke*,　　 ကဲ့ *ke*,　　 ကော့ *ko*,　　 ကို့ *ko*.

(b) long vowels with second tone (long low):

　　　 ကာ *kā*,　　 ကီ *kī*,　　 ကူ *kū*,　　 ကေ *kē*,　　 ကယ် *kē*,　　 ကော် *kō*,　　 ကို *kō*.

(c) vowels marked by ◯း , ◌ဲ , ေ◯ာ with third tone (long high):

　　　 ကား *kā*,　　 ကီး *kī*,　　 ကူး *kū*,　　 ကေး *kē*,　　 ကဲ *kē*,　　 ကော *kō*,　　 ကိုး *kō*.

CONJUNCT CONSONANTS

As a general rule, conjunct consonants retain their primary form and are written as subscripts, but four – ya, ra, wa, ha – have specific forms, shown here as applied to *ma*:

ဟ *ma*, မျ *mya*, မြ *mya*, မွ *mwa*, မှ *hma*, မျွ *mywa*, မျှ *hmya*,

မြှ *hmya*, မွှ *hmwa*, မြို *myo*.

NUMERALS

၁	၂	၃	၄	၅	၆	၇	၈	၉	၀
1	2	3	4	5	6	7	8	9	0

CAMBODIAN

CONSONANTAL PHONEMES

As in the Devanagari writing system from which it is derived, the Cambodian script arranges the consonantal phonemes of the language in five parallel series: velar, palatal, (retroflex), dental and labial; with a sixth group comprising the sibilants and liquids.

ꯀ	kɑɑ	k	ꯑ	dɑɑ	d	ꯑ	bɑɑ	b
ꯀ	khɑɑ	kh	ꯑ (ꯑ)	thɑɑ	th	ꯑ	phɑɑ	ph
ꯀ	kɔɔ	k	ꯑ	dɔɔ	d	ꯑ	pɔɔ	p
ꯀ	khɔɔ	kh	ꯑ	thɔɔ	th	ꯑ	phɔɔ	ph
ꯀ	ŋɔɔ	ŋ	ꯑ	nɑɑ	n	ꯑ	mɔɔ	m

ꯀ	cɑɑ	c	ꯀ	tɑɑ	t	ꯀ	yɔɔ	y
ꯀ	chɑɑ	ch	ꯀ	thɑɑ	th	ꯀ	rɔɔ	r
ꯀ	cɔɔ	c	ꯀ	tɔɔ	t	ꯀ	lɔɔ	l
ꯀ	chɔɔ	ch	ꯀ	thɔɔ	th	ꯀ	wɔɔ	w
ꯀ	ñɔɔ	ñ	ꯀ	nɔɔ	n	ꯀ	sɑɑ	s
						ꯀ	hɑɑ	h
						ꯀ	lɑɑ	l
						ꯀ	qɑɑ	q

Note that, as there are no retroflex sounds in Cambodian, the *daa* series, which represents the original *ʈa* series of Devanagari, coincides in point of articulation with the *taa* series of dental consonants.

The phonemic values shown in the above inventory are those of consonants preceding vowels. As first components in clusters, and as finals, the aspirate consonants are reduced to their non-aspirate values: /kh/ > /k/, etc. Consonants with inherent *aa* belong to the First Series, those with inherent *ɔɔ* to the Second. For a note on the two series of consonants, *see* **Cambodian** pp. 255–6.

VOWEL SYMBOLS

Each vowel symbol has either of two values, depending on whether it follows a First or Second Series consonant: thus

Symbol	Name	Values 1st Series	2nd Series	Symbol	Name	Values 1st Series	2nd Series
—	sraq qɑɑ	*aa*	*ɔɔ*	ʃ –	sraq qei	*ei*	*ee*
–̑	sraq qaa	*aa*	*iə*	ʔ̑–	sraq qae	*ae*	*ɛɛ*
–̑	sraq qeq	*e*	*i*	ʒ̑–	sraq qay	*ay*	*iy*
–̑	sraq qəy	*əy*	*ii*	ʃ–̑	sraq qao	*ao*	*oo*
–̑	sraq qəq	*ə*	*i*	ʃ–̑	sraq qaw	*aw*	*iw*
–̑	sraq qəɨ	*əɨ*	*ɨɨ*	–̊	sraq qom	*om*	*um*
–̑	sraq qoq	*o*	*u*	–̊	sraq qɑm	*am*	*um¹*
–̑	sraq qou	*ou*	*uu*	–̊̑	sraq qam	*am*	*oə̆m¹*
–̑	sraq quə	*uə*	*uə*	–̊	sraq qah	*ah*	*eə̆h*
ʃ–	sraq qaə	*aə*	*əə*				
ʃ–̑	sraq qɨə	*ɨə*	*ɨə*				
ʃ–̑	sraq qiə	*iə*	*iə*				

Some examples from the velar, palatal and dental series:

1st Series			2nd Series		
Symbol	Example		Symbol	Example	
ក	ក	/kɑɑ/ neck	គ	គ	/kɔɔ/ mute
ខ	ខាត់	/khat/ to polish	ឃ	ឃាត់	/khŏăt/ to prevent
ច	ចា	/caa/ to inscribe	ជ	ជា	/ciə/ be
ឆ	ឆោង	chaoŋ/ interval	ឈ	ឈោង	/chooŋ/ to reach out
ញ	ញុំ	/ñam/ to eat	ញ	ញុំ	/ñoăm/ meat salad
ដ	ដិន	/don/ elephant command	ឌ	ឌិន	/dun/alike
ត	តា	/taa/ old man	ទ	ទា	/tiə/ duck

As will be seen from the consonant chart, certain Cambodian phonemes are not paired, e.g. Second Series *mɔɔ* has no First Series correlative *maa. Where it is necessary to produce such a correlative, a consonant can be 'converted' by diacritic: ″converts a Second Class into a First Class consonant:

e.g. ម៉ = m*aa*.

Similarly, ˆ converts a First Class into a Second Class consonant.

Conjunct consonants are frequent in Cambodian. The second component is written as a subscript, which is usually a reduced version of the base form. There are, however, several irregularities.

CHEROKEE

THE SYLLABARY

Ꭰ *a*	Ꭱ *e*	Ꭲ *i*	Ꭳ *o*	Ꭴ *u*	Ꭵ *v*
Ꭶ *ga* Ꭷ *ka*	Ꭸ *ge*	Ꭹ *gi*	Ꭺ *go*	Ꭻ *gu*	Ꭼ *gv*
Ꭽ *ha*	Ꭾ *he*	Ꭿ *hi*	Ꮀ *ho*	Ꮁ *hu*	Ꮂ *hv*
Ꮃ *la*	Ꮄ *le*	Ꮅ *li*	Ꮆ *lo*	Ꮇ *lu*	Ꮈ *lv*
Ꮉ *ma*	Ꮊ *me*	Ꮋ *mi*	Ꮌ *mo*	Ꮍ *mu*	
Ꮎ *na* Ꮏ *hna* Ꮐ *nah*	Ꮑ *ne*	Ꮒ *ni*	Ꮓ *no*	Ꮔ *nu*	Ꮕ *nv*
Ꮖ *qua*	Ꮗ *que*	Ꮘ *qui*	Ꮙ *quo*	Ꮚ *quu*	Ꮛ *quv*
Ꮜ *sa* Ꮝ *s*	Ꮞ *se*	Ꮟ *si*	Ꮠ *so*	Ꮡ *su*	Ꮢ *sv*
Ꮣ *da* Ꮤ *ta*	Ꮥ *de* Ꮦ *te*	Ꮧ *di* Ꮨ *ti*	Ꮩ *do*	Ꮪ *du*	Ꮫ *dv*
Ꮬ *dla* Ꮭ *tla*	Ꮮ *tle*	Ꮯ *tli*	Ꮰ *tlo*	Ꮱ *tlu*	Ꮲ *tlv*
Ꮳ *tsa*	Ꮴ *tse*	Ꮵ *tsi*	Ꮶ *tso*	Ꮷ *tsu*	Ꮸ *tsv*
Ꮹ *wa*	Ꮺ *we*	Ꮻ *wi*	Ꮼ *wo*	Ꮽ *wu*	Ꮾ *wv*
Ꮿ *ya*	Ᏸ *ye*	Ᏹ *yi*	Ᏺ *yo*	Ᏻ *yu*	Ᏼ *yv*

Source: Holmes, R. B. and Smith, B. S. (1976) *Beginning Cherokee,* Norman, OK

CHINESE

For a general note on the Chinese script and its history, see **Chinese** (Archaic, Classical, Modern Standard) pp. 306–19. Here, the nature of the script, and one standard method of looking up characters in a Chinese dictionary, are illustrated by means of (a) eight full-form characters in bold printed form; (b) the same eight characters in standard written form (not in the so-called 'grass script', *căozi*, which is a highly personalized cursive); (c) stroke order and number; (d) the radical system; (e) search procedure in a Chinese dictionary.

(a) Eight full-form printed characters:

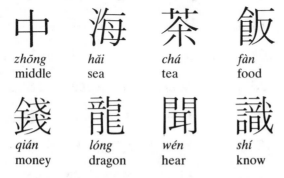

中 *zhōng* middle   海 *hăi* sea   茶 *chá* tea   飯 *fàn* food

錢 *qián* money   龍 *lóng* dragon   聞 *wén* hear   識 *shí* know

(b) The same characters in standard written form:

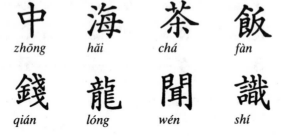

中 *zhōng*   海 *hăi*   茶 *chá*   飯 *fàn*

錢 *qián*   龍 *lóng*   聞 *wén*   識 *shí*

(c) Stroke order is illustrated here by means of four of the above characters:

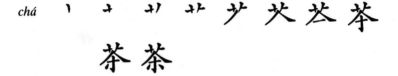

chá

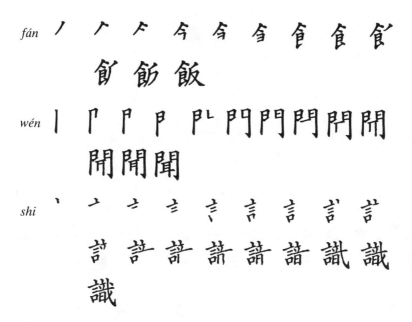

It will be seen that by writing a Chinese character in the correct *order*, we arrive at the correct *number* of component strokes. The number of components underlies both the radical system and the indexing of characters in a Chinese dictionary.

(d) The radical system is now set out (pp. 1512–13) in traditional form, as a table of 214 radicals, beginning with 1 stroke and rising to 17. This is reproduced from Matthews' Chinese–English Dictionary. The radical table is followed by a specific example – the list of all characters having the 7-stroke radical 言 (pp. 1514–15).

1 stroke

1 一
2 丨
3 丶
4 丿
5 乙
6 亅

2 strokes

7 二
8 亠
9 人、亻
10 儿
11 入
12 八
13 冂
14 冖
15 冫
16 几
17 凵

36 夕
37 大
38 女
39 子
40 宀
41 寸
42 小
43 尤兀尣
44 尸
45 屮
46 山
47 巛川巜
48 工
49 己
50 巾
51 干
52 幺
53 广
54 廴
55 廾
56 弋

74 月
75 木
76 欠
77 止
78 歹歺
79 殳
80 毋
81 比
82 毛
83 氏
84 气
85 水、氵
86 火、灬
87 爪、爫
88 父
89 爻
90 爿
91 片
92 牙

110 矛
111 矢
112 石
113 示礻
114 禸
115 禾
116 穴
117 立

6 strokes

118 竹、⺮
119 米
120 糸糹
121 缶
122 网罒罓
123 羊
124 羽
125 老
126 而

7 strokes

147 見
148 角
149 言
150 谷
151 豆
152 豕
153 豸
154 貝
155 赤
156 走
157 足
158 身
159 車
160 辛
161 辰
162 辵辶
163 邑阝
164 酉
165 釆

181 頁
182 風
183 飛
184 食
185 首
186 香

10 strokes

187 馬
188 骨
189 高
190 髟
191 鬥
192 鬯
193 鬲
194 鬼

11 strokes

195 魚

14 strokes

209 鼻
210 齊

15 strokes

211 齒

16 strokes

212 龍
213 龜

17 strokes

214 龠

18 刀,刂
19 力
20 勹
21 匕
22 匚
23 匸
24 十
25 卜
26 卩,㔾
27 厂
28 厶
29 又

3 strokes

30 口
31 囗
32 土
33 士
34 夂
35 夊

57 弓
58 彐,彑
59 彡
60 彳

4 strokes

61 心,忄,⺗
62 戈
63 戶
64 手,扌
65 支
66 攴,攵
67 文
68 斗
69 斤
70 方
71 无,旡
72 日
73 曰

93 牛,牜
94 犬,犭

5 strokes

95 玄
96 玉,玊,王
97 瓜
98 瓦
99 甘
100 生
101 用
102 田
103 疋
104 疒
105 癶
106 白
107 皮
108 皿
109 目,⺫

127 耒
128 耳
129 聿
130 肉,⺼
131 臣
132 自
133 至
134 臼
135 舌
136 舛
137 舟
138 艮
139 色
140 艸,⺾,艹
141 虍
142 虫
143 血
144 行
145 衣,⻂
146 襾,西

166 里

8 strokes

167 金
168 長,长
169 門
170 阜,阝
171 隶
172 隹
173 雨,⻗
174 靑
175 非

9 strokes

176 面
177 革
178 韋
179 韭
180 音

196 鳥
197 鹵
198 鹿
199 麥
200 麻

12 strokes

201 黃
202 黍
203 黑
204 黹

13 strokes

205 黽
206 鼎
207 鼓
208 鼠

The 214 Radicals

1513

言 (149)

護 2190	讜 903	**15**	讚 877	讀 6521	讟 279	**16**	譶 4795	讝 7364	變 5245	譽 7091	讎(讐) 1333			
聲 1166	謬 4539	讅 1074	謨 4591	講 2159	**12**	謹 4640	謾 1435	讇 416	讌 5825	讖 6563	讒 323	讙 758	譌 4789	證 357
譚 2369	譖 2357	譆 37	諷 1893	**10**	謙 885	講 645	譏 5476	詞 3364	譯 2428	謇 842	謝 2630	謫 5645	譽 4919	譯 5900
謢 2163	闇 7437	誰 5923	講 1172	誹 1833	**9**	譑 7641	誧 4621	誇 4795	諴 2667	諮 6923	誼 2874	譜 6208	讒 7374	譎 5251
譁 5004	誕 7165	誕 6051	誌 973	認 3113	誠 381	誡 628	誓 5803	諛 2338	註 3602	誦 5567	誘 7538	誚 762	言 1133	**8**
6	詭 2273	該 3191	詮 1672	詢 2813	詗 2923	誆 3599	詭 3626	詹 150	訴 3423	註 783	詿 3513	誇 3530	詫 108	詩 5783
訓 5732	訝 7220	訂 2728	訪 1816	設 5711	**5**	詛 6818	詿 1343	詐 82	詅 4055	診 306	說 1303	詞 2817	誳 1622	詔 239
149	言 7334	**2**	訂 6386	訇 2391	計 456	訃 1954	**3**	託 6461	詑 2943	訏 567	訊 2820	訊 2750	詔 3117	
覽 3804	覲 6230	觀 3575	**148**	角 1174	觔 1059	觖 1699	**5**	觜 6856	觚 6194	觚 3473				

148 見 149 角 150 谷

Radical Index Nos 147-150

(e) To sum up: looking up characters in a Chinese dictionary involves the following steps.

1. Identify the radical; with experience this becomes automatic. The correct radical is usually obvious, but there are many cases where the radical is obscure, or where there is a choice.
2. Count the strokes remaining in the character after the radical has been subtracted.
3. Find the radical in the index of characters. All characters having this radical are listed in order of number of strokes; inspection in correct section yields desired character.

As example, we take the character 識 having the 7-stroke radical 言 . After subtraction of radical 149, the character has 12 strokes. By inspection in the 12-stroke section of radical 149 we find 識 numbered 5825. Turning to 5825 in the body of the dictionary, we find the character with translation and many examples of usage.

COPTIC

Coptic was written in a version of the Greek alphabet, plus seven letters – Shai to Di inclusive – which are derived from the Demotic Egyptian script. Chai is found only in Bohairic Coptic.

THE ALPHABET

Name	Letter	Transcription	Name	Letter	Transcription
Alfa	Ⲁ ⲁ	a	Ro	Ⲣ ⲣ	r
Vida	Ⲃ ⲃ	b [b, v]	Sīma	Ⲥ ⲥ	s
Gamma	Ⲅ ⲅ	g	Dau	Ⲧ ⲧ	t
Dalda	Ⲇ ⲇ	d	He	Ⲩ ⲩ	y [i, y]
Ei	Ⲉ ⲉ	e [ĕ]	Phi	Ⲫ ⲫ	ph [p + h]
Sīta	Ⲍ ⲍ	z	Chi	Ⲭ ⲭ	kh [k + h]
Hîda	Ⲏ ⲏ	ē	Epsi	Ⲯ ⲯ	ps
Tīda	Ⲑ ⲑ	th [t + h]	O	Ⲱ ⲱ	ō
Jōda	Ⲓ ⲓ	i [i, j]	Shāi	Ϣ ϣ	š
Kappa	Ⲕ ⲕ	k	Fāi	Ϥ ϥ	f
Lōla	Ⲗ ⲗ	l	Chāi	Ϧ ϧ	ḫ [ch]
Mi	Ⲙ ⲙ	m	Hori	Ϩ ϩ	h
Ni	Ⲛ ⲛ	n	Džandža	Ϫ ϫ	dž
Exi	Ⲝ ⲝ	x [ks]	Schima	Ϭ ϭ	č
O	Ⲟ ⲟ	o [ŏ]	Di	Ϯ ϯ	ti
Bi	Ⲡ ⲡ	p			

CREE

THE SYLLABARY

	e'	i	o	a	Finals Moose (M)	Western (W)
Independent Vowel	∇	Δ	▷	◁		
p	V	∧	>	<	‹	l
t	U	∩	)	(	ᒡ	/
c	⌐	⌐	ᒍ	ᒐ	ᒡ	—
k	ᑫ	ᑭ	ᑯ	ᑲ	ᒃ	\
m	⌐	⌐	ᒍ	L	ᒻ	ᒡ
n	ᓀ	ᓂ	ᓄ	ᓇ	ᓐ	⊃
l	ᖉ	ᖆ	ᖌ	ᖊ	ᖬ	{
s	ᕂ	ᕆ	ᕊ	ᕊ	ᔅ	⌐
š	ᖚ	S	∾	ᕀ	ᔥ	
y	ᕃ	ᕆ	ᕋ	ᕊ	°	•
r	ᖊ	ᖇ	ᖉ	ᖋ	ᖋ	}

Long vowels – apart from /ē/ – are marked by a dot over the consonant. Short /e/ does not occur in Cree. Other diacritics are used, e.g. for final y (° above the syllabic), final h (" above the syllabic) and final w (° following last consonant, above the line).

CYRILLIC

THE ALPHABET

Printed		Handwritten		Transliteration
А	а	*Ꭺ*	*а*	a
Б	б	*Б*	*б*	b
В	в	*В*	*в*	v
Г	г	*Г*	*г*	g
Д	д	*Д*	*g*	d
Е	е	*Е*	*е*	e
Ё	ё	*Ё*	*ё*	ë
Ж	ж	*Ж*	*ж*	ž
З	з	*З*	*з*	z
И	и	*И*	*и*	i
Й	й	*Й*	*й*	j
К	к	*К*	*к*	k
Л	л	*Л*	*л*	l
М	м	*М*	*м*	m
Н	н	*Н*	*н*	n
О	о	*О*	*о*	o
П	п	*П*	*п*	p
Р	р	*Р*	*р*	r
С	с	*С*	*с*	s
Т	т	*Т*	*т*	t
У	у	*У*	*у*	u
Ф	ф	*Ф*	*ф*	f
Х	х	*Х*	*х*	x
Ц	ц	*Ц*	*ц*	c
Ч	ч	*Ч*	*ч*	č
Ш	ш	*Ш*	*ш*	š
Щ	щ	*Щ*	*щ*	šč
	ъ		*ъ*	"
	ы		*ы*	y
	ь		*ь*	'
Э	э	*Э*	*э*	e
Ю	ю	*Ю*	*ю*	ju
Я	я	*Я*	*я*	ja

Source: Comrie, B. (1987) 'Russian', in B. Comrie (ed.) *The World's Major Languages*, London, Routledge

DEVANĀGARĪ

VOWELS (SVARĀH)

अ	आ	इ	ई	उ	ऊ
a	*ā*	*i*	*ī*	*u*	*ū*

ऋ	ॠ	ऌ	ए	ऐ	ओ	औ
r̥	*r̥̄*	*l̥*	*e*	*ai*	*o*	*au*

CONSONANTS (VYAÑJANĀNI)

Stops (sparśāḥ)					Semi-vowels (antaḥsthāḥ)	Spirants (ūṣmāṇaḥ)	Others
क	ख	ग	घ	ङ		ह	ः
k	*kh*	*g*	*gh*	*ṅ*		h	*ḥ*
च	छ	ज	झ	ञ	य	श	
c	*ch*	*j*	*jh*	*ñ*	y	*ś*	
ट	ठ	ड	ढ	ण	र	ष	ळ
ṭ	*ṭh*	*ḍ*	*ḍh*	*ṇ*	r	*ṣ*	*ḷ*
त	थ	द	ध	न	ल	स	
t	*th*	*d*	*dh*	*n*	l	s	
प	फ	ब	भ	म	व		
p	*ph*	*b*	*bh*	*m*	v		

Source: Cardona, G. (1987) 'Sanskrit' in B. Comrie (ed.) *The World's Major Languages*, London, Routledge.

EXAMPLES OF COMBINATIONS

का	काँ	कि	की	कु	कू	कृ
kā	*kāṁ*	*ki*	*kī*	*ku*	*kū*	*kṛ*

कॄ	कॢ	क्त	क्र	क्ष	ज्ञ	त्र
kṝ	*kḷ*	*kta*	*kra*	*kṣa*	*jña*	*tra*

त्व	द्य	द्र	द्व	प्त	ब्द	र्क
tva	*dya*	*dra*	*dva*	*pta*	*bda*	*rka*

र्कं	श्च	श्र	श्व	स्त	स्य	स्र
rkaṁ	*śca*	*śra*	*śva*	*sta*	*sya*	*sra*

स्व	ह्म	ह्य	ह्र	ह्ल	ह्व	र्त्स्न्य
sva	*hma*	*hya*	*hra*	*hla*	*hva*	*rtsnya*

NUMERALS

१	२	३	४	५	६	७	८	९	०
1	2	3	4	5	6	7	8	9	0

The following additional signs are important:

1. virāma: this is a slanting stroke drawn to the bottom right of a consonant to indicate cancellation of the inherent /a/: thus,

    तत् = *tat*

2. anusvāra: a dot over a consonant or vowel indicating nasalization:

    अं = *aṁ*, कं = *kaṁ*

3. pre- and post-consonantal r: r preceding a consonant is written as ꞈ above the consonant; thus,

    र्म = *rma*, र्क = *rka*

    r following a consonant is written as a short stroke slanting to the left from the lower part of the consonant:

    क्र = *kra*, प्र = *pra*

These features are reflected more or less completely in all Indian and South-East Asian scripts based on Devanagari.

ETHIOPIC (AMHARIC)

THE SYLLABARY

	a		ū		ī		ā		ē		e		ō
ሀ	ha	ሁ	hū	ሂ	hī	ሃ	hā	ሄ	hē	ህ	he	ሆ	hō
ለ	la	ሉ	lū	ሊ	lī	ላ	lā	ሌ	lē	ል	le	ሎ	lō
ሐ	ḥa	ሑ	ḥū	ሒ	ḥī	ሓ	ḥā	ሔ	ḥē	ሕ	ḥe	ሖ	ḥō
መ	ma	ሙ	mū	ሚ	mī	ማ	mā	ሜ	mē	ም	me	ሞ	mō
ሠ	ša	ሡ	šū	ሢ	šī	ሣ	šā	ሤ	šē	ሥ	še	ሦ	šō
ረ	ra	ሩ	rū	ሪ	rī	ራ	rā	ሬ	rē	ር	re	ሮ	rō
ሰ	sa	ሱ	sū	ሲ	sī	ሳ	sā	ሴ	sē	ስ	se	ሶ	sō
ቀ	qa	ቁ	qū	ቂ	qī	ቃ	qā	ቄ	qē	ቅ	qe	ቆ	qō
በ	ba	ቡ	bū	ቢ	bī	ባ	bā	ቤ	bē	ብ	be	ቦ	bō
ተ	ta	ቱ	tū	ቲ	tī	ታ	tā	ቴ	tē	ት	te	ቶ	tō
ኀ	ḫa	ኁ	ḫū	ኂ	ḫī	ኃ	ḫā	ኄ	ḫē	ኅ	ḫe	ኆ	ḫō
ነ	na	ኑ	nū	ኒ	nī	ና	nā'	ኔ	nē	ን	ne	ኖ	nō
አ	'a	ኡ	'ū	ኢ	'ī	ኣ	ā	ኤ	'ē	እ	'e	ኦ	'ō
ከ	ka	ኩ	kū	ኪ	kī	ካ	kā	ኬ	kē	ክ	ke	ኮ	kō
ወ	wa	ዉ	wū	ዊ	wī	ዋ	wā	ዌ	wē	ው	we	ዎ	wō
ዐ	'a	ዑ	'ū	ዒ	'ī	ዓ	'ā	ዔ	'ē	ዕ	'e	ዖ	'ō
ዘ	za	ዙ	zū	ዚ	zī	ዛ	zā	ዜ	zē	ዝ	ze	ዞ	zō
የ	ja	ዩ	jū	ዪ	jī	ያ	jā	ዬ	jē	ይ	je	ዮ	jō
ደ	da	ዱ	dū	ዲ	dī	ዳ	dā	ዴ	dē	ድ	de	ዶ	dō
ገ	ga	ጉ	gū	ጊ	gī	ጋ	gā	ጌ	gē	ግ	ge	ጎ	gō
ጠ	ṭa	ጡ	ṭū	ጢ	ṭī	ጣ	ṭā	ጤ	ṭē	ጥ	ṭe	ጦ	ṭō
ጰ	pa	ጱ	pū	ጲ	pī	ጳ	pā	ጴ	pē	ጵ	pe	ጶ	pō
ጸ	ṣa	ጹ	ṣū	ጺ	ṣī	ጻ	ṣā	ጼ	ṣē	ጽ	ṣe	ጾ	ṣō
ፀ	ḍa	ፁ	ḍū	ፂ	ḍī	ፃ	ḍā	ፄ	ḍē	ፅ	ḍe	ፆ	ḍō
ፈ	fa	ፉ	fū	ፊ	fī	ፋ	fā	ፌ	fē	ፍ	fe	ፎ	fō
ፐ	pa	ፑ	pū	ፒ	pī	ፓ	pā	ፔ	pē	ፕ	pe	ፖ	pō

THE LABIALIZED VELAR SERIES

ኰ	kua	ኵ	kuī	ኵ	kue	ኳ	kuā	ኴ	kuē
ጐ	gua	ጕ	guī	ጕ	gue	ጓ	guā	ጔ	guē
ቈ	qua	ቍ	quī	ቍ	que	ቋ	quā	ቌ	quē
ኈ	ḫua	ኍ	ḫuī	ኍ	ḫue	ኋ	ḫuā	ኌ	ḫuē

GEORGIAN

Georgian is written in the Mkhedruli script, which had originally 40 letters. Seven of these are now obsolete, or very rarely used. The following 33 are in regular use.

THE ALPHABET

ა	*a*	რ	*r*
ბ	*b*	ს	*s*
გ	*g*	ტ	*ṭ*
დ	*d*	უ	*u*
ე	*e*	ფ	*ph*
ვ	*v*	ქ	*kh*
ზ	*z*	ღ	*γ*
თ	*th*	ყ	*q*
ი	*i*	შ	*ʃ*
კ	*ḳ*	ჩ	*čh*
ლ	*l*	ც	*ts*
მ	*m*	ძ	*dz*
ნ	*n*	წ	*ṭs*
ო	*o*	ჭ	*tʃ*
პ	*p*	ხ	*χ*
ჟ	*ž*	ჯ	*dž*
		ჰ	*h*

The ecclesiastical script known as Khutsuri is no longer in use.

GOTHIC

The alphabet which Bishop Wulfila (Ulfilas) created, for his translation of the Bible into Gothic, is based partly on Latin but mainly on Greek models. Two letters – those for u and o – are derived from the Old Nordic runic script,

THE ALPHABET

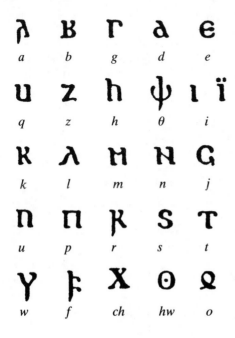

GREEK

THE ALPHABET

Capital letter	Small Letter	Ancient phonetics	Usual transliteration	Modern pronunciation	Usual transliteration
A	α	[a]	a	[a]	a
B	β	[b]	b	[v]	v
Γ	γ	[g]	g	[j] (/—i,e)	y
				[γ]	
				(elsewhere)	g(h)
Δ	δ	[d]	d	[ð]	d(h)
E	ε	[ɛ]	e	[ɛ]	e
Z	ζ	[zd]	z	[z]	z
H	η	[ɛː]	e:, ē	[i]	i
Θ	θ	[tʰ]	th	[θ]	th
I	ι	[i]	i	[i]	i
K	ϰ	[k]	k	[k]	k
Λ	λ	[l]	l	[l]	l
M	μ	[m]	m	[m]	m
N	ν	[n]	n	[n]	n
Ξ	ξ	[ks]	x	[ks]	ks, x (as in *box*)
O	ο	[o]	o	[o]	o
Π	π	[p]	p	[p]	p
P	ϱ	[r]	r	[ɾ]	r
Σ	σ (ς)	[s]	s	[s]	s
T	τ	[t]	t	[t]	t
Y	υ	[y]	y, u	[i]	i
Φ	φ	[pʰ]	ph	[f]	f
X	χ	[kʰ]	ch, kh	[χ]	h, x (IPA value)
Ψ	ψ	[ps]	ps	[ps]	ps
Ω	ω	[ɔː]	o:, ō	[o]	o

Diphthongs and clusters	Ancient phonetics	Usual transliteration	Modern pronunciation	Usual transliteration
αι	[aι̯]	ai	[ε]	e
αυ	[au̯]	au	[av] (/__ + voice) [af] (/__ − voice)	av af
ει	[eː]	ei	[i]	i
ευ	[εu̯]	eu	[ev] (/__ + voice) [ef] (/__ − voice)	ev ef
οι	[oι̯]	oi	[i]	i
ου	[oː]	ou	[u]	u
υι	[yι̯]	yi, ui	[i]	i
γ before γ χ ξ	[ŋ]	n (g, kh, ks)	[ŋ]	n (g, h, ks)
γκ	[ŋk]	nk	[(ŋ)g] (medially) [g] (initially)	(n)g g
μπ/μβ	[mp/mb]	mp/mb	[(m)b] (medially) [b] (initially)	(m)b b
ντ/νδ	[nt/nd]	nt/nd	[(n)d] (medially) [d] (initially)	(n)d d
τζ	-----	-----	[dz]	dz

Source: Joseph, B.D. (1987) 'Greek', in B. Comrie (ed.) The World's Major Languages, London, Routledge

GUJARATI

The absence of the horizontal line on top of the letters distinguishes the Gujarati script from the closely connected and very similar Devanagari.

CONSONANTS

ક	ખ	ગ	ઘ	ઙ
ka	kha	ga	gha	nga
ચ	છ	જ	ઝ	ઞ
ca	cha	ja	jha	nya
ટ	ઠ	ડ	ઢ	ણ
ṭa	ṭha	ḍa	ḍha	ṇa
ત	થ	દ	ધ	ન
ta	tha	da	dha	na
પ	ફ	બ	ભ	મ
pa	pha	ba	bha	ma
ય	૨	લ	વ	
ya	ra	la	wa, va	
શ	ષ	સ	હ	ળ
śa	ṣa	sa	ha	la

VOWELS

(a) independent:

અ	આ	ઇ	ઈ	ઉ	ઊ	ઋ
a	ā	i	ī	u	ū	ri
એ	ઐ	ઓ	ઔ			
ē	ai	ō	au			

(b) in combination with the consonant *ba*:

બા	બિ	બી	બુ	બૂ	બૃ
bā	bi	bī	bu	bū	bri
બે	બૈ	બો	બૌ		
bē	bai	bō	bau		

Conjunct consonants are formed as in Devanagari and Bengali by juxtaposition, amalgamation or subscript.

NUMERALS

૧	૨	૩	૪	૫	૬	૭	૮	૯	૦
1	2	3	4	5	6	7	8	9	0

GURMUKHI (FOR PANJABI)

Panjabi is written in the Gurmukhi script.

CONSONANTS

ਸ	ਹ			
sa	*ha*			

ਕ	ਖ	ਗ	ਘ	ਙ
ka	*kha*	*ga*	*gha*	*nga*

ਚ	ਛ	ਜ	ਝ	ਞ
ca	*cha*	*ja*	*jha*	*nya*

ਟ	ਠ	ਡ	ਢ	ਣ
ṭa	*ṭha*	*ḍa*	*ḍha*	*ṇa*

ਤ	ਥ	ਦ	ਧ	ਨ
ta	*tha*	*da*	*dha*	*na*

ਪ	ਫ	ਬ	ਭ	ਮ
pa	*pha*	*ba*	*bha*	*ma*

ਯ	ਰ	ਲ	ਵ	ੜ
ya	*ra*	*la*	*va*	*ṛa*

VOWELS

Three letters:

ੳ *ūṛā*   ਅ *āiṛā*   ੲ *īṛī*

are used to provide bases for free-standing vowels. Thus:

ੳ	ੳ	ੳ	ਅ	ਆ	ਐ	ਔ
u	*ū*	*ō*	*a*	*ā*	*ai*	*au*

ਇ	ਈ	ਏ
i	*ī*	*ē*

As illustration, here are the vowel signs in combination with *ka*:

क   का   कि   की   कु   कू
ka   *kā*   *ki*   *kī*   *ku*   *kū*

के   कै   को   कौ
kē   *kai*   *kō*   *kau*

CONJUNCT CONSONANTS

There are very few conjunct consonants in Panjabi. In general, for C_1C_2, C_1 is in base form, C_2 is attached in schematic outline. Specific subscript forms are used for *ra*, *wa*, *ha*.

Tone is indicated by *ha* or by voiced aspirate (*see* **Panjabi**).

HEBREW

CONSONANTS

Phoenician (= Old Hebrew)	Jewish Square (modern print)	Cursive (modern)	Name	Transcription
✚	א	*k*	alef	ʔ
٩	ב	*ə*	bet	B; b, b ~ v
٨	ג	*ɗ*	g'imel	G; g, ğ
△	ד	*ʔ*	d'alet	D; d, đ
ⅎ	ה	*ɒ*	he	H; h
Y	ו	*I*	vav	W; w ~ v, u, o
I	ז	*ʒ*	z'ayin	Z; z
H	ח	*n*	xet	Ḥ; ḥ ~ x
⊕	ט	*ɕ*	tet	Ṭ; ṭ ~ t
٦	י	*ı*	yod	Y; y, i,e
⅄	כ (ך)	*ɔ (ρ)*	kaf	K; k, k ~ x
l	ל	*ʃ*	l'amed	L; l
۳	מ (ם)	*N(ρ)*	mem	M; m
٧	נ (ן)	*J(ı)*	nun	N; n
‡	ס	*ο*	s'amex	S; s
O	ע	*ɤ*	'ayin	ʿ
٦	פ (ף)	*ə (ʝ)*	pe	P; p, p ~ f
⊬	צ (ץ)	*ʒ(ɣ)*	tsade	Ṣ; ṣ ~ c(=ts)
φ	ק	*ρ*	qof	Q; q ~ k
٩	ר	*ɔ*	resh	R; r
W	ש	*e*	shin	Š; š
X	ת	*ɲ*	tav	T; t, t ~ t

POINTING

A   The dot in the consonant (*dagesh*)

   (a) Spirantization

t ת t תּ p פ(ף) p פּ k כ(ך) k כּ(ךּ)

d ד d דּ g ג g גּ b ב b בּ

   (b) Gemination

   ...qq קּ   ... mm מּ   ...ww וּ   ...bb בּ

B   The letter *Š*

   $ś$ שׂ $š$ שׁ

C   The vowels (combined with various consonants)

Long		Short	Ultrashort
$ṭå$ טָ		$ṭa$ טַ	$‘ă$ עֲ
$lē^y$ לִי	$lē$ לֵ	$lɛ$ לֶ	$ʔɛ̆$ אֶ
$mō^w$ מוֹ	$rō$ רֹ	$ṣå$ צָ	$ḥă$ חֲ
$tī^y$ תִי		si סִ	$zə, z$ זְ
$nū^w$ נוּ		nu נֻ	

Source: Hetzron, R. (1987) 'Hebrew', in B. Comrie (ed.) *The World's Major Languages*, London, Routledge

JAPANESE

THE SYLLABARIES

HIRAGANA

あ	か	が	さ	ざ	た	だ	な	は	ば	ぱ	ま	ら	わ	ん
a	ka	ga	sa	za	ta	da	na	ha	ba	pa	ma	ra	wa	n
い	き	ぎ	し	じ	ち	ぢ	に	ひ	び	ぴ	み	り		
i	ki	gi	shi	ji	chi	ji	ni	hi	bi	pi	mi	ri		
う	く	ぐ	す	ず	つ	づ	ぬ	ふ	ぶ	ぷ	む	る		
u	ku	gu	su	zu	tsu	zu	nu	fu	bu	pu	mu	ru		
え	け	げ	せ	ぜ	て	で	ね	へ	べ	ぺ	め	れ		
e	ke	ge	se	ze	te	de	ne	he	be	pe	me	re		
お	こ	ご	そ	ぞ	と	ど	の	ほ	ぼ	ぽ	も	ろ		を
o	ko	go	so	zo	to	do	no	ho	bo	po	mo	ro		o
や	きゃ	ぎゃ	しゃ	じゃ	ちゃ	ぢゃ	にゃ	ひゃ	びゃ	ぴゃ	みゃ	りゃ		
ya	kya	gya	sha	ja	cha	ja	nya	hya	bya	pya	mya	rya		
ゆ	きゅ	ぎゅ	しゅ	じゅ	ちゅ	ぢゅ	にゅ	ひゅ	びゅ	ぴゅ	みゅ	りゅ		
yu	kyu	gyu	shu	ju	chu	ju	nyu	hyu	byu	pyu	myu	ryu		
よ	きょ	ぎょ	しょ	じょ	ちょ	ぢょ	にょ	ひょ	びょ	ぴょ	みょ	りょ		
yo	kyo	gyo	sho	jo	cho	jo	nyo	hyo	byo	pyo	myo	ryo		

KATAKANA

ア	カ	ガ	サ	ザ	タ	ダ	ナ	ハ	バ	パ	マ	ラ	ワ	ファ	ン
a	*ka*	*ga*	*sa*	*za*	*ta*	*da*	*na*	*ha*	*ba*	*pa*	*ma*	*ra*	*wa*	*fa*	*n*
イ	キ	ギ	シ	ジ	チ	ヂ	ニ	ヒ	ビ	ピ	ミ	リ		フィ	
i	*ki*	*gi*	*shi*	*ji*	*chi*	*ji*	*ni*	*hi*	*bi*	*pi*	*mi*	*ri*		*fi*	
ウ	ク	グ	ス	ズ	ツ	ヅ	ヌ	フ	ブ	プ	ム	ル			
u	*ku*	*gu*	*su*	*zu*	*tsu*	*zu*	*nu*	*fu*	*bu*	*pu*	*mu*	*ru*			
エ	ケ	ゲ	セ	ゼ	テ	デ	ネ	ヘ	ベ	ペ	メ	レ		フェ	
e	*ke*	*ge*	*se*	*ze*	*te*	*de*	*ne*	*he*	*be*	*pe*	*me*	*re*		*fe*	
オ	コ	ゴ	ソ	ゾ	ト	ド	ノ	ホ	ボ	ポ	モ	ロ		フォ	ヲ
o	*ko*	*go*	*so*	*zo*	*to*	*do*	*no*	*ho*	*bo*	*po*	*mo*	*ro*		*fo*	*o*
ヤ	キャ	ギャ	シャ	ジャ	チャ	ヂャ	ニャ	ヒャ	ビャ	ピャ	ミャ	リャ			
ya	*kya*	*gya*	*sha*	*ja*	*cha*	*ja*	*nya*	*hya*	*bya*	*pya*	*mya*	*rya*			
ユ	キュ	ギュ	シュ	ジュ	チュ	ヂュ	ニュ	ヒュ	ビュ	ピュ	ミュ	リュ			
yu	*kyu*	*gyu*	*shu*	*ju*	*chu*	*ju*	*nyu*	*hyu*	*byu*	*pyu*	*myu*	*ryu*			
ヨ	キョ	ギョ	ショ	ジョ	チョ	ヂョ	ニョ	ヒョ	ビョ	ピョ	ミョ	リョ			
yo	*kyo*	*gyo*	*sho*	*jo*	*cho*	*jo*	*nyo*	*hyo*	*byo*	*pyo*	*myo*	*ryo*			

Long vowels are notated in Hiragana by adding あ, う, え, or お, e.g.

おかあさん *okā-san;*

and in Katakana by adding ー, e.g.

テーブル *téburu.*

Syllabic final consonants other than /n/ are notated

by つ in Hiragama

and by ツ in Katakana, e.g.

いった *itta*, and マッチ *matchi.*

JAVANESE

Column 1 shows the *aksara legena* ('bare letters'), the base consonantal forms. Column 2 shows their *pasangan* ('decoration') secondary forms, which figure as the second components of conjuncts, i.e. C_2 in C_1C_2.

1	2	Name	Value
		hå	h (mute)
		nå	n
		cå	tʃ
		rå	r
		kå	k (as final > ?)
		då	d
		tå	t
		så	s
		wå	w
		lå	l
		på	p
		ḍå	ḍ
		jå	dʒ
		yå	j
		ñå	ɲ
		må	m
		gå	g
		bå	b
		ṭå	t
		ngå	ŋ

a > /ɔ/ is inherent in these consonants. In order to notate the vowels e, i, o, u in post-consonantal position, and other combinations, the following *sandangan* ('clothed') signs are used:

Sign		Name	Value
		pĕpĕt	ĕ
		wulu	i
		suku	u
		taling	é/è
		taling-tarung	o (circumfix)
		pangkon Kr., patĕn Ng.	cancels inherent vowel; corresponds to Devanagari virāma
		pingkal	marks palatalized consonant
		cåkrå	post-consonantal r
		kĕrĕt	rĕ following a consonant
		layar	syllabic final r
		wigūan	syllabic final h
		cĕcak	syllabic final ŋ
		pa-cĕrĕk	rĕ
		ngå-lĕlĕt	lĕ

Vowels in isolation: these occur mainly in foreign words:

a   e   i

o   u

In addition, the classical Javanese script had a series of 'large' letters for use in the names and titles of distinguished personages. Seven Arabic phonemes were represented by placing the diacritic ♣ over the Javanese equivalent; thus, Arabic (ʃ/, for example, is Javanese *så* with ♣ added.

KANNADA

CONSONANTS

ಕ	ಖ	ಗ	ಘ	ಙ
ka	*kha*	*ga*	*gha*	*nga*

ಚ	ಛ	ಜ	ಝ	ಞ
ca	*cha*	*ja*	*jha*	*nya*

ಟ	ಠ	ಡ	ಢ	ಣ
ṭa	*ṭha*	*ḍa*	*ḍha*	*ṇa*

ತ	ಥ	ದ	ಧ	ನ
ta	*tha*	*da*	*dha*	*na*

ಪ	ಫ	ಬ	ಭ	ಮ
pa	*pha*	*ba*	*bha*	*ma*

ಯ	ರ	ಲ	ವ
ya	*ra*	*la*	*va*

ಶ	ಷ	ಸ	ಹ	ಳ
śa	*ṣa*	*sa*	*ha*	*la*

VOWELS

ಅ	ಆ	ಇ	ಈ	ಉ	ಊ	ಋ
a	*ā*	*i*	*ī*	*u*	*ū*	*ru*

ಎ	ಏ	ಐ	ಒ	ಓ	ಔ
e	*ē*	*ai*	*o*	*ō*	*au*

Vowel signs: here illustrated as applied to *ka*:

ಕಾ *kā*,   ಕಿ *ki*,   ಕೀ *kī*,   ಕು *ku*,   ಕೂ *kū*,   ಕೃ *kru*,   ಕೆ *ke*,
ಕೇ *kē*,   ಕೈ *kai*,   ಕೊ *ko*,   ಕೋ *kō*,   ಕೌ *kau*

There are several irregularities in the writing of *-i* and *-u*.

Conjunct consonants in Kannada are generally formed by subscription of the second component, which may be altered in form.

KOREAN

The *Hangul* script, used to write Korean, is a syllabary, in which consonants and vowels combine in their base forms to form syllables. That is to say, vowels following consonants do not assume specific secondary forms as in Devanagari, nor are the consonants themselves amended as in Ethiopic. Pure vowels cannot be written in isolation, i.e. unsupported by a consonant: the bearer ○ must be used: thus /a/ is notated as 아

The basic forms are given in the following table.

Letter	Transcription	Letter	Transcription
Pure vowels:			
ㅣ	/i/	ㅡ	/ŭ/
ㅔ	/e/	ㅓ	/ə/
ㅐ	/æ/	ㅏ	/a/
ㅟ	/ü/	ㅜ	/u/
ㅚ	/ö/	ㅗ	/o/
Compound vowels:			
ㅑ	/ya/	ㅘ	/wa
ㅒ	/yæ/	ㅙ	/wæ/
ㅕ	/yə/	ㅝ	/wə/
ㅖ	/ye/	ㅞ	/we/
ㅛ	/yo/	ㅢ	/ŭi/
ㅠ	/yu/		
Consonants:			
ㄱ	/k/	ㅇ	/ŋ/
ㄴ	/n/	ㅈ	/c/
ㄷ	/t/	ㅊ	/cʰ/
ㄹ	/l/	ㅋ	/kʰ/
ㅁ	/m/	ㅌ	/tʰ/
ㅂ	/p/	ㅍ	/pʰ/
ㅅ	/s/	ㅎ	/h/
Double consonants:			
ㄲ	/k'/	ㅆ	/s'/
ㄸ	/t'/	ㅉ	/c'/
ㅃ	/p'/		

Source: Kim, N. – K. (1987) 'Korean', in B. Comrie (ed.) *The World's Major Languages*, London, Routledge

1539

Two sample rows follow:

(a) C + V

가	갸	거	겨	고	교	구	규	그
ka	kya	kə	kyə	ko	kyo	ku	kyu	kŭ

기	개	걔	게	계	괴	귀	긔	과
ki	kæ	kyæ	ke	kye	ko	ki	kwi	kwa

궈	괘	궤
kwə	kwæ	kwe

(b) C + V + C (phonetic realizations)

각	간	갇	갈	감	갑	갓	강
kak	kan	kat	kal	kam	kap	kat	kang

갖	갗	같	갚	갛	갉	값	갔
kat	kat	kat	kap	ka'	kak	kap	kat

LAO

CONSONANTS

ກ	ຂ	ຄ	ງ	ຈ	ຊ	ຊ
ko	*kho*	*kho*	*ngo*	*cho*	*so*	*so*
ຍ	ດ	ຕ	ຖ	ທ	ນ	ບ
nyo	*do*	*to*	*tho*	*tho*	*no*	*bo*
ປ	ຜ	ຝ	ພ	ຟ	ມ	ຍ
po	*pho*	*fo*	*pho*	*fo*	*mo*	*yo*
ຣ	ລ	ວ	ຫ	ອ	ຮ	
ro	*lo*	*wo*	*ho*	*'o*	*ho*	

VOWELS

Notation of the rich vocalic system is virtually identical with that of Thai (q.v.), using superscript, subscript, prefixed and suffixed markers, and circumfix. For example, if C represents a consonant, Cາ = Cā, C$_{u}$ = Cū, C̃ = Ci, (Ĉາ = Cau, ເCາະ = Co, ໂC = Cō.

NUMERALS

໑	໒	໓	໔	໕	໖	໗	໘	໙	໐
1	2	3	4	5	6	7	8	9	0

MALAYALAM

CONSONANTS

ക	ഖ	ഗ	ഘ	ങ
ka	kha	ga	gha	nga
ച	ഛ	ജ	ഝ	ഞ
ca	cha	ja	jha	nya
ട	ഠ	ഡ	ഢ	ണ
ṭa	ṭha	ḍa	ḍha	ṇa
ത	ഥ	ദ	ധ	ന
ta	tha	da	dha	na
പ	ഫ	ബ	ഭ	മ
pa	pha	ba	bha	ma
യ	ര	ല	വ	
ya	ra	la	va	

ശ	ഷ	സ	ഹ	ള	ഴ	റ
śa	ṣa	sa	ha	ḷa	ṛa	ṟa

VOWELS

(a) independent

അ	ആ	ഇ	ഈ	ഉ	ഊ	ഋ
a	ā	i	ī	u	ū	ṛu

എ	ഏ	ഐ	ഒ	ഓ	ഔ
e	ē	ai	o	ō	au

(b) as applied to letter ṭa:

ടാ ṭā	ടി ṭi	ടീ ṭī	ടു ṭu	ടൂ ṭū	ടൃ ṭru
ടെ ṭe	ടേ ṭē	ടൈ ṭai	ടൊ ṭo	ടോ ṭō	ടൌ ṭau

Conjunct consonants are formed by duplication (often vertical) or by fusion, which may involve substantial deformation. Cf. (6.2) gga, (15.18) lla.

NUMERALS

൧	൨	൩	൪	൫	൬	൭	൮	൯	൦
1	2	3	4	5	6	7	8	9	0

MAYA

The spurious 'alphabet' of glyphs provided by Bishop Diego de Landa (see p. 906):

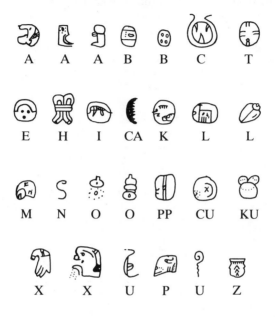

MONGOLIAN

The Classical Mongolian script – now replaced in the MPR for all ordinary purposes by Cyrillic – is written in vertical lines, from left to right. If the letters are viewed horizontally, their derivation (via an Uighur intermediary) from the Syriac Estrangelo script becomes plain.

Initial	Medial	Final		Transcription
┥	◄	┙ ┶		*a*
┙	◄	┙ ┶		*e*
ㅓ	∕	♪		*i*
┧	◁	♪		*o*
┧	◁	♪		*u*
ㅓ	я ◁	♪		*ö*
ㅓ	я ◁	♪		*ü*
·┙	·◄	┘ ┶		*n*
၅	♪	┚		*b*
┵	┧	—		*ch*
·┵	፧	—		*gh*
⌐	⌐	┛ ┷		*k*
⌐	⌐	—		*g*
ħ	ħ	◿		*m*
ฯ	ฯ	⌐		*l*
ㄳ	ㄳ	♪		*r*

Initial	Medial	Final	Transcription
			t
		—	*d*
		—	*y*
		—	*j, ds*
		—	*ts*
			s
		—	*š*
		—	*w*

As in Semitic scripts generally, letters have different forms depending on whether they are initial, medial or final.

Important ligatures are:

Initial	Medial	Final	Transcription
			ai
			oi

Final		Medial	
	ba, be	*bi*	*bo, bu*
	ke, ge	*ki, gi*	*kö, kü / gö, gü*
	ng		

OLD CHURCH SLAVONIC

THE ALPHABET

Name	Symbol		Transliteration	Name	Symbol		Transliteration
As	Ⰰ	ⰰ	a	Ch^{j}er	Х	х	kh
Buki	Б	б	b	O	Ѡ	ѡ	o
W^{j}edi	В	в	v	Tßi	Ц	ц	c
Glagol^j	Г	г	g	Tscherw^j	Ч	ч	č
Dobro	Д	д	d	Scha	Ш	ш	š
Eßt^j	Є	є	e	Schta	Щ	щ	št
Żiw^{j}ete	Ж	ж	ž	Jer	Ъ	ъ	ŭ
Z^{j}elo	Ѕ	ѕ	dſ	Jery	⎰ ЪІ ъі ⎱		y
Semlja	З	з	ſ		⎱ Ы ы ⎰		
Iže	И	и	i	Jerek	Ь	ь	ĭ
I	І	іi	i	Jet^j	Ѣ	ѣ	ě
Kako	К	к	k	Ju	Ю	ю	ju
Ljudi	Л	л	l	Ja	Ꙗ	ꙗ	ja
Myslite	М	м	m	Je	Ѥ	ѥ	je
Nasch	Н	н	n	Ęß	Ѧ	ѧ	ę
On	О	о	o	Ąß	Ѫ	ѫ	ǫ
Pokoj	П	п	p	Jęß	Ѩ	ѩ	ję
Rtßi	Р	р	r	Jąß	Ѭ	ѭ	jǫ
Sslovo	С	с	ß	Kßi	Ѯ	ѯ	kß
Twerdo	Т	т	t	Pßi	Ѱ	ѱ	ps
Uk	⎰ Ꙋ ꙋ ⎱		u	Thita	Ѳ	ѳ	f/θ
	⎱ Оу оу ⎰			Ižitßa	Ѵ	ѵ	ẏ [i]
Fert	Ф	ф	f				

1546

ORIYA

The horizontal line drawn over letters in Devanagari is replaced in Oriya by a curved line.

CONSONANTS

କ	ଖ	ଗ	ଘ	ଙ
ka	kha	ga	gha	nga

ଚ	ଛ	ଜ	ଝ	ଞ
ca	cha	ja	jha	nya

ଟ	ଠ	ଡ	ଢ	ଣ
ṭa	ṭha	ḍa	ḍha	ṇa

ତ	ଥ	ଦ	ଧ	ନ
ta	tha	da	dha	na

ପ	ଫ	ବ	ଭ	ମ
pa	pha	ba	bha	ma

ଯ	ର	ଲ	ଳ	ଵ
(ja)	ra	la	ḷa	wa

ଶ	ଷ	ସ	ହ	କ୍ଷ
śa	ṣa	sa	ha	khya

VOWELS

(a) independent:

ଅ	ଆ	ଇ	ଈ	ଉ	ଊ	ଋ	ଌ
a	ā	i	ī	u	ū	ru	rū

ଌ	ଏ	ଐ	ଓ	ଔ	ଅଂ	ଅଃ
lu	ē	ai	ō	au	aṅ	a'

(b) the secondary vowel signs, used in combination with consonants, are closely similar to the Devanagari series. As illustration, they are here shown with the consonant *ga*:

ଗା	ଗି	ଗୀ	ଗୁ	ଗୂ	ଗୃ
gā	gi	gī	gu	gū	gru

ଗେ	ଗୈ	ଗୋ	ଗୌ
gē	gai	gō	gau

There are several irregularities in the use of these signs, particularly as regards the notation of *i*, *ī*, and *u*.

Conjunct consonants in Oriya are numerous and unpredictable, individual components being substantially transformed in combination.

NUMERALS

୧	୨	୩	୪	୫	୬	୭	୮	୯	୦
1	2	3	4	5	6	7	8	9	0

SAMARITAN

Column 1: square form; Column 2: cursive; Column 3; transliteration; Column 4: phonetic value.

1	2	3	4		1	2	3	4
𐤀	𐤀	'	∅, '		𐤋	𐤋	l	l, ł
𐤁	𐤁	b	b		𐤌	𐤌	m	m
𐤂	𐤂	g	g		𐤍	𐤍	n	n
𐤃	𐤃	d	d		𐤎	𐤎	s	s
𐤄	𐤄	h	'		𐤏	𐤏	ʿ	ʿ, ', ∅
𐤅	𐤅	w	w, b, u		𐤐	𐤐	f	f
𐤆	𐤆	z	z		𐤑	𐤑	ṣ	s
𐤇	𐤇	ḥ	ʿ, ', ∅		𐤒	𐤒	q	q
𐤈	𐤈	ṭ	ł		𐤓	𐤓	r	r
𐤉	𐤉	y	j		𐤔	𐤔	š	ʃ
𐤊	𐤊	k	k		𐤕	𐤕	t	t

Certain diacritics accompanying individual words in some Samaritan manuscripts have been taken as indicating short vowels, but there is controversy as to their exact meaning.

Source: Vil'sker, L. (1974) *Samaritanskij jazyk*, Moscow

SINHALESE

CONSONANTS

ක	බ	ග	ඝ	ඞ
ka	kha	ga	gha	nga
ච	ඡ	ජ	ඣ	ඤ
ca	cha	ja	jha	nya
ට	ඨ	ඩ	ඪ	ණ
ṭa	ṭha	ḍa	ḍha	ṇa
ත	ථ	ද	ධ	න
ta	tha	da	dha	na
ප	ඵ	බ	භ	ම
pa	pha	ba	bha	ma
ය	ර	ල	ව	
ya	ra	la	va	
ශ	ෂ	ස	හ	ළ
śa	ṣa	sa	ha	la

VOWELS

(a) independent:

අ	ආ	ඇ	ඈ	ඉ	ඊ	උ	ඌ
a	ā	æ	ǣ	i	ī	u	ū
සෘ	එ	ඒ	ඔ	ඔ	ඕ	ඖ	
ri	e	ē	ai	o	ō	au	

(b) as applied to the consonant *na*:

නා	නැ	නෑ	නි	නී	නු	නූ
nā	næ	nǣ	ni	nī	nu	nū
නෘ	නෙ	නේ	නෛ	නො	නෝ	නෞ
nri	ne	nē	nai	no	nō	nau

CONJUNCT CONSONANTS

The subscript model typical of Telugu, for example, is not used in Sinhalese. Instead, there is an extensive repertory of ligatures, many of great complexity.

SYRIAC

THE ALPHABET

Separate	Joined	Name	Hebrew	English
ا		Ālaph	א	'
ڡ ۵		Beth	ב	b, bh (v)
ܓ ܓ		Gāmal	ג	g, gh
?		Dālath	ד	d, dh
ܗ		He	ה	h
۰		Vau	ו	v or w
ܙ		Zain	ז	z
ܚ ܚ ܚ		Ḥeth	ח	ḥ
ܛ ܛ		Ṭeth	ט	ṭ
ܝ ܝ ܝ		Yud	י	y in yet
ܟ ܟ ܟ		Kāph	ך כ	k, kh
ܠ ܠ		Lāmad	ל	l
ܡ ܡ		Mim	ם מ	m
ܢ ܢ		Nun	ן נ	n
ܣ ܣ		Semkath	ס	s
ܥ ܥ		'Ē	ע	'
ܦ ܦ		Pe	ף פ	p, ph
ܨ		Tsāde	ץ צ	ts
ܩ ܩ		Ḳuph	ק	ḳ
ܪ		Rish	ר	r
ܫ		Shin	ש	sh
ܬ		Thau	ת	t, th

Source: *Elements of Syriac Grammar*, London, Bagster (no date)

TAMIL

THE SYLLABARY

—		அ	*a*	ஆ	*ā*	இ	*i*	ஈ	*ī*	உ	*u*	ஊ	*ū*
க்	*k*	க	*ka*	கா	*kā*	கி	*ki*	கீ	*kī*	கு	*ku*	கூ	*kū*
ங்	*ṅ*	ங	*ṅa*	ஙா	*ṅā*	ஙி	*ṅi*	ஙீ	*ṅī*	ஙு	*ṅu*	ஙூ	*ṅū*
ச்	*ç*	ச	*ça*	சா	*çā*	சி	*çi*	சீ	*çī*	சு	*çu*	சூ	*çū*
ஞ்	*ñ*	ஞ	*ña*	ஞா	*ñā*	ஞி	*ñi*	ஞீ	*ñī*	ஞு	*ñu*	ஞூ	*ñū*
ட்	*ḍ*	ட	*ḍa*	டா	*ḍā*	டி	*ḍi*	டீ	*ḍī*	டு	*ḍu*	டூ	*ḍū*
ண்	*ṇ*	ண	*ṇa*	ணா	*ṇā*	ணி	*ṇi*	ணீ	*ṇī*	ணு	*ṇu*	ணூ	*ṇū*
த்	*t*	த	*ta*	தா	*tā*	தி	*ti*	தீ	*tī*	து	*tu*	தூ	*tū*
ந்	*n*	ந	*na*	நா	*nā*	நி	*ni*	நீ	*nī*	நு	*nu*	நூ	*nū*
ப்	*p*	ப	*pa*	பா	*pā*	பி	*pi*	பீ	*pī*	பு	*pu*	பூ	*pū*
ம்	*m*	ம	*ma*	மா	*mā*	மி	*mi*	மீ	*mī*	மு	*mu*	மூ	*mū*
ய்	*y*	ய	*ya*	யா	*yā*	யி	*yi*	யீ	*yī*	யு	*yu*	யூ	*yū*
ர்	*r*	ர	*ra*	ரா	*rā*	ரி	*ri*	ரீ	*rī*	ரு	*ru*	ரூ	*rū*
ல்	*l*	ல	*la*	லா	*lā*	லி	*li*	லீ	*lī*	லு	*lu*	லூ	*lū*
வ்	*v*	வ	*va*	வா	*vā*	வி	*vi*	வீ	*vī*	வு	*vu*	வூ	*vū*
ழ்	*ẓ*	ழ	*ẓa*	ழா	*ẓā*	ழி	*ẓi*	ழீ	*ẓī*	ழு	*ẓu*	ழூ	*ẓū*
ள்	*ḷ*	ள	*ḷa*	ளா	*ḷā*	ளி	*ḷi*	ளீ	*ḷī*	ளு	*ḷu*	ளூ	*ḷū*
ற்	*R*	ற	*Ra*	றா	*Rā*	றி	*Ri*	றீ	*Rī*	று	*Ru*	றூ	*Rū*
ன்	*N*	ன	*Na*	னா	*Nā*	னி	*Ni*	னீ	*Nī*	னு	*Nu*	னூ	*Nū*

	e		ē		ai		o		ō		au
எ	*e*	ஏ	*ē*	ஐ	*ai*	ஒ	*o*	ஓ	*ō*	ஒள	*au*
கெ	*ke*	கே	*kē*	கை	*kai*	கொ	*ko*	கோ	*kō*	கௌ	*kau*
ஙெ	*ṅe*	ஙே	*ṅē*	ஙை	*ṅai*	ஙொ	*ṅo*	ஙோ	*ṅō*	ஙௌ	*ṅau*
செ	*çe*	சே	*çē*	சை	*çai*	சொ	*ço*	சோ	*çō*	சௌ	*çau*
ஞெ	*ñe*	ஞே	*ñē*	ஞை	*ñai*	ஞொ	*ño*	ஞோ	*ñō*	ஞௌ	*ñau*
டெ	*ḍe*	டே	*ḍē*	டை	*ḍai*	டொ	*ḍo*	டோ	*ḍō*	டௌ	*ḍau*
ணெ	*ṇe*	ணே	*ṇē*	ணை	*ṇai*	ணொ	*ṇo*	ணோ	*ṇō*	ணௌ	*ṇau*
தெ	*te*	தே	*tē*	தை	*tai*	தொ	*to*	தோ	*tō*	தௌ	*tau*
நெ	*ne*	நே	*nē*	நை	*nai*	நொ	*no*	நோ	*nō*	நௌ	*nau*
பெ	*pe*	பே	*pē*	பை	*pai*	பொ	*po*	போ	*pō*	பௌ	*pau*
மெ	*me*	மே	*mē*	மை	*mai*	மொ	*mo*	மோ	*mō*	மௌ	*mau*
யெ	*ye*	யே	*yē*	யை	*yai*	யொ	*yo*	யோ	*yō*	யௌ	*yau*
ரெ	*re*	ரே	*rē*	ரை	*rai*	ரொ	*ro*	ரோ	*rō*	ரௌ	*rau*
லெ	*le*	லே	*lē*	லை	*lai*	லொ	*lo*	லோ	*lō*	லௌ	*lau*
வெ	*ve*	வே	*vē*	வை	*vai*	வொ	*vo*	வோ	*vō*	வௌ	*vau*
ழெ	*ẓe*	ழே	*ẓē*	ழை	*ẓai*	ழொ	*ẓo*	ழோ	*ẓō*	ழௌ	*ẓau*
ளெ	*ḷe*	ளே	*ḷē*	ளை	*ḷai*	ளொ	*ḷo*	ளோ	*ḷō*	ளௌ	*ḷau*
றெ	*Re*	றே	*Rē*	றை	*Rai*	றொ	*Ro*	றோ	*Rō*	றௌ	*Rau*
னெ	*Ne*	னே	*Nē*	னை	*Nai*	னொ	*No*	னோ	*Nō*	னௌ	*Nau*

Source: Steever, S.B. (1987) 'Tamil and the Dravidian Languages', in B. Comrie (ed.) *The World's Major Languages*, London, Routledge, adapted from Pope, G.U. (1979) *A Handbook of the Tamil Language*, New Delhi, Asian Education Services

TELUGU

CONSONANTS

Traditionally, the Telugu consonantal grid has 34 letters, and is set out, in Devanagari order, as follows:

క	ఖ	గ	ఘు	జ
ka	*kha*	*ga*	*gha*	*nga*
చ	ఛ	జ	ఝ	ఞ
ca	*cha*	*ja*	*jha*	*nya*
ట	ఠ	డ	ఢ	ణ
ṭa	*ṭha*	*ḍa*	*ḍha*	*ṇa*
త	థ	ద	ధ	న
ta	*tha*	*da*	*dha*	*na*
ప	ఫ	బ	భ	మ
pa	*pha*	*ba*	*bha*	*ma*
య	ర	ల	ళ	వ
ya	*ra*	*la*	*ḷa*	*va*
శ	ష	స	హ	
śa	*ṣa*	*sa*	*ha*	

However, the ten aspirated consonants occur in only a few Sanskrit borrowings, and *nga* and *nya* are also rare. The great majority of Telugu words can be written in terms of the remaining 22 letters, plus ం , the sign for nasalization.

VOWELS

(a) independent:

అ	ఆ	ఇ	ఈ	ఉ	ఊ	ఋ
a	*ā*	*i*	*ī*	*u*	*ū*	*ru*

ఎ	ఏ	ఐ	ఒ	ఓ	ఔ
e	*ē*	*ai*	*o*	*ō*	*au*

(b) as applied to the consonant *ka*:

కా	కి	కీ	కు	కూ	కృ
kā	*ki*	*kī*	*ku*	*kū*	*kru*

కె	కే	కై	కొ	కో	కౌ
ke	*kē*	*kai*	*ko*	*kō*	*kau*

There are many irregularities.

CONJUNCT CONSONANTS

Most conjunct consonants in Telugu are geminates, the second component being subscribed in primary or secondary form.

NUMERALS

౧	౨	౩	౪	౫	౬	౭	౮	౯	౦
1	2	3	4	5	6	7	8	9	0

THAI

CONSONANTS

The five positional series of the Devanagari source (transmitted to Thai via Khmer), have additional letters in the Thai inventory, which has to accommodate a tonal system. The positional grid in Thai is as follows:

Mid	Mid	High	High	Low	Low	Low	Low
ก	ข	ฃ		ค	ฅ	ฆ	ง
k	kh	kh		kh	kh	kh	ŋ
	จ	ฉ		ช	ซ	ฌ	ญ
	c	ch		ch	s	ch	y
ฎ	ฏ	ฐ		ฑ		ฒ	ณ
d	t	th		th		th	n
ด	ต	ถ		ท		ธ	น
d	t	th		th		th	n
บ	ป	ผ	ฝ	พ	ฟ	ภ	ม
b	p	ph	f	ph	f	ph	m

The sixth group in Devanagari, comprising the semi-vowels, and the spirants, is represented in Thai as follows:

(a) the semi-vowels (all low class consonants):

ย	ร	ล	ว
y	r	l	w

(b) the spirants (all high class consonants):

ศ	ษ	ส
s	s	s

(c) the mixed group ห h (high), ฬ l (low), อ ʔ (middle), ฮ h (low).

VOWELS

Thai has no forms for independent vowels. The vocalization system is shown here as applied to the low class consonant ค kh:

	Long			Short					
	With final		*Without final*	*With final*					*Without final*
	y	*Other*		*y*	*w*	*m*		*Other*	
a		คา		ไค ใค	เคา	คำ		คัน	คะ ค
ə	เคย	เคิน	เคอ						เคอะ
e		เค			เค็น				เคะ
o		โค				คน			โคะ
ua	ควน		คัว		*				คัวะ
ia		เคีย			*				เคียะ
ɨa		เคือ			*				เคือะ
ɛ		แค			แค็น				แคะ
		คอ			คอน				เคาะ
ɨ	คืน	คือ			คึ				
i		คี			คิ				
u		คู			คุ				

Source: Hudak, T.J. (1987) 'Thai', in B. Comrie (ed.) *The World's Major Languages*, London, Routledge, adapted from Brown, J.M. (1967) *A.U.A Center Thai Course*, vol. 3, Bangkok, Social Science Association Press of Thailand, pp. 211–12.

TIBETAN

The *dbu.can* (/u.ceen/) script, consisting of 30 basic letters plus 5 denoting retroflex sounds in Sanskrit words, is shown here, accompanied by a table of conjunct consonants:

ཀ	ka	ཀྱ	kya		rju		bla
ཁ	kha	ཀྲ	kra		lja		rba
ག	ga	ཀླ	kla		rña		lba
ང	ṅa	ཀྭ	kva		sña		sba
ཅ	ca	རྐ	rka		tra		sbya
ཆ	cha	རྐྱ	rkya		rta		sbra
ཇ	ja	ལྐ	lka		lta		mu
ཉ	ña	སྐ	ska		sta		mya
ཏ	ta	སྐྱ	skya		thra		mra
ཐ	tha	སྐྲ	skra		dra		rma
ད	da	ཁྱ	khya		dva		rmya
ན	na	ཁྲ	khra		rda		sma
པ	pa	ཁྭ	khva		lda		smya
ཕ	pha	གྱ	gya		sda		smra
བ	ba	གྲ	gra		sdu		tsu
མ	ma	གླ	gla		nra		rtsa
ཙ	tsa	གྭ	gva		rna		rtsva
ཚ	tsha	རྒ	rga		sna		stsa
ཛ	dsa	རྒྱ	rgya		snra		rdsa
	wa	ལྒ	lga		pu		žu
ཞ	ža	སྒ	sga		pya		zu
ཟ	za	སྒྱ	sgya		pra		zla
འ	a, *a*	སྒྲ	sgra		lpa		u
ཡ	ya		ṅu		spa		yu
ར	ra		rṅa		spya		ru
ལ	la						lu
ཤ	śa						
ས	sa						

1558

ཧ	ha	སྙ	sña	སྤྲ	spra	རླ	rla
ཨ	'a	ལྙ	lña	ཕུ	phu	ཤྲ	śra
ཊ	ṭa	ཅུ	cu	ཕྱ	phya	སུ	su
ཋ	ṭha	ལྕ	lca	ཕྲ	phra	སྲ	sra
ཌ	ḍa	ཆུ	chu	བུ	bu	སླ	sla
ཎ	ṇa	ཇུ	ju	བྱ	bya	ཧྲ	hra
ཥ	ṣa	རྗ	rja	བྲ	bra	ལྷ	lha

The Tibetan vowels i, e, o, are notated by superscript signs, the vowel *u* by a subscript. They are shown here as applied to the consonant *ka*:

ཀི	ཀུ	ཀེ	ཀོ
ki	*ku*	*ke*	*ko*

Numerals:

༡	༢	༣	༤	༥	༦	༧	༨	༩	༠
1	2	3	4	5	6	7	8	9	0

BIBLIOGRAPHY

Aaltio, M.H. (1963–75) *Finnish for Foreigners*, 3 vols, Helsinki.

Abaev, V.I. (1950) *Russko–Osetinskij Slovar'*, Moscow.

Adbulla, J.J. and E.N. McCarus (1967) *Kurdish Basic Course*, Ann Arbor, MI.

Aben, K. (1960) *Učebnik Estonskogo Jazyka*, Tallinn.

Ağralı, S., L.Y. Fotos, S.S. Demiray, and L.B. Swift (1970 *Turkish Basic Course: Reader*, Washington, DC.

Akabirov, S.F., Z.M. Magrufov, and A.T. Khodzhakhanov (1959) *Uzbeksko–Russkij Slovar'*, Moscow.

Akiner, S. (1983) *Islamic Peoples of the Soviet Union*, London.

Alavi, B. and M. Lorenz (1988) *Lehrbuch der Persischen Sprache*, Leipzig.

Amipa, S.G. (1974) *Textbook of Colloquial Tibetan*, Zürich.

Ammār ibn Sa'īd (called Bū Līfah) (1910) *Une Première Année de la langue Kabyle*, Algiers.

Andrews, J.R. (1975) *Introduction to Classical Nahuatl*, 2 vols, Austin, TX, and London.

Andronov, M.S. (1960) *Tamil'skij Jazyk*, Moscow.

Andronov, M.S. (1962) *Jazyk Kannada*, Moscow.

Andronov, M.S. (1965) *Dravidijskie Jazyki*, Moscow.

Andronov, M.S. (1966) *Grammatika Tamil'skogo Jazyka*, Moscow.

Andronov, M.S. (1971) *Jazyk Braui*, Moscow.

Antoine, R. (1954–6) *A Sanskrit Manual*, Calcutta.

Aquilina, J. (1965) *Teach Yourself Maltese*, London.

Arakin, V.D. (1963) *Mal'gasskij Jazyk*, Moscow.

Arakin, V.D. (1965) *Indonezijskie Jazyki*, Moscow.

Arakin, V.D. (1973) *Samoanskij Jazyk*, Moscow.

Arakin, V.D. (1981) *Taitjanskij Jazyk*, Moscow.

Arden, A.H. (1937) *A Progressive Grammar of the Telugu Language*, Madras.

Aronson, H.I. (1982) *Georgian: a Reading Grammar*, Columbus, OH.

Arroyo, V.M. (1972) *Lenguas indígenas costarricenses*, San José.

Aspillera, P.S. (1969) *Basic Tagalog*, Rutland, VT, and Tokyo.

Augusta, Felix José de (1916; 1989) *Diccionario Mapuche–Español*, Santiago de Chile.

Austin, W.M., G. Hangin and U. Onon (1956) *A Mongol Reader*, Washington, DC.

Avery, P.W., M.A. Jazayery and H.H. Paper (1962–3) *Modern Persian Reader*, 3 vols. Ann Arbor, MI.

Aymonier, E. (1889) *Grammaire de la langue Chame*, Saigon.

Babakaev, V.D. (1961) *Assamskij Jazyk*, Moscow.

Bachmann, A. (1936) *Mittelhochdeutsches Lesebuch*, Zürich.

Badudu, Y. (1982) *Morfologi Bahasa Gorontalo*, Jakarta.

Bakaev, Ch. K. (1957) *Kurdsko–Russkij Slovar'*, Moscow.

Bakir, A.M. (1984) *Notes on Middle Egyptian Grammar*, Warminster.

Bammesberger, A. (1982) *A Handbook of Irish*, Heidelberg.

Barlow, A.R. (1951) *Studies on Kikuyu Grammar and Idiom*, Edinburgh.

Barnes, A.S.V. (n.d.) *Afrikaanse Grammatika vir Engelssprekende Leerlinge*, Elsiesrivier, Nasou Beperk.

Basset, A. (1952) *La Langue Berbère*, Oxford.

Bayle, L. (1982) *Grammaire du Provençal moderne*, Toulon.

Beeston, A.F.L. (1970) *The Arabic Language Today*, London.

Bell, A.R. and A.A. Koski (1968) *Finnish Graded Reader*, Washington, DC.

Bell, C.R.V. (1953) *The Somali Language*, London.

Benveniste, E. (1969) *Le Vocabulaire des institutions indo-européenes*, 2 vols, Paris.

Benzing, J. (1955) *Lamutische Grammatik*, Wiesbaden.

Berckenhagen, H. (1894) *Grammar of the Miskito Language*, Bluefields, Moskito Coast.

Bergsträsser, G. (1928) *Einführung in die semitischen Sprachen*, Munich.

Berkov, V.P. and A. Böðvarssonar (1962) *Islandsko–Russkij Slovar'*, Moscow.

Bernabe, E. and E. Constantine (1971) *Ilokano Lessons*, Honolulu.

Bidwell, C.E. (1963) *Slavic Historical Phonology in Tabular Form*, The Hague.

Bills, G.D., B. Vallejo and R.C. Troike (1969) *Introduction to Spoken Bolivian Quechua*, Austin, TX, and London.

Birnbaum, S.A. (1966) *Grammatik der Jiddischen Sprache*, Hamburg.

Birnbaum, S.A. (1979) *Yiddish: a Survey and Grammar*, Toronto and Manchester.

Blakeley, L. (1964) *Old English*, London.

Blau, J. (1980) *Manuel de Kurde (dialecte Sorani)*, Paris.

Bloomfield, L. (1962) *The Menomini Language*, Yale.

Boas, F. and J.R. Swanton (1911) *Handbook of American Indian Languages*, Part 1, Washington, DC.

Bodding, P.O. (1929) *A Santali Grammar for Beginners*, Benagaria.

Bödey, J. and T. Nagypál (1963) *Bolgár Nyelvkönyv*, Budapest.

Bohatta, H. (n.d.) *Praktische Grammatik der Javanischen Sprache*, Vienna.

Borello, M. (1939) *Grammatica di lingua Galla (Oromo)*, Turin.

Borras, F.M. and R.F. Christian (1971) *Russian Syntax*, Oxford and London.

Børretzen, J. (1977) *Liten Samsk Grammatik*, Trondheim.

Bosson, J.E. (1962) *Buriat Reader*, Bloomington, IN, and The Hague.

Bosson, J.E. (1964) *Modern Mongolian*, Bloomington, IN, and The Hague.

Bowen, J.D. (1965) *Beginning Tagalog*, Berkeley and Los Angeles, CA.

Bradley, C.H. (1970) *A Linguistic Sketch of Jicaltepec Mixtec*, Norman, OK.

Brandt, J. (n.d.) *Introduction to Literary Chinese*, New York.

Braun, M. (n.d.) *Grundzüge der Slawischen Sprachen*, Göttingen.

Brauner, S. (1974) *Lehrbuch des Bambara*, Leipzig.

Brauner, S. and M. Ashiwaju (1966) *Lehrbuch der Hausa-Sprache*, Leipzig.

Brennu-Njáls Saga, ed. E.O. Sveinsson (1954), Reykjavik.

Brown, J.M. (1967–9) *Thai Course*, 3 vols, Bangkok.

Brown, W. (1984) *A Grammar of Modern Cornish*, Saltash.

Bruce, B. (1970) *Teach Yourself Cantonese*, London.

Budiņa Lazdiņa, T. (1966) *Teach Yourself Latvian*, London.

Bullock, R., ed. (n.d.) *The Story of Sinuhe*, London.

Bunye, M. and E. Yap (1971) *Cebuano for Beginners*, Hawaii.

Burgers, M.P.O. (1957) *Teach Yourself Afrikaans*, London.

Burling, R. (1961) *A Garo Grammar*, Poona.
Butler, I.M. (1980) *Gramatica Zapoteca*, Mexico City.
Byington, C. (1870) *Grammar of the Choctaw Language*, Philadelphia.
Bykova, E.M. (1966) *Bengal'skij Jazyk*, Moscow.

Calder, G. (1972) *A Gaelic Grammar*, Glasgow.
Camaj, M. (1984) *Albanian Grammar*, Wiesbaden.
Campbell, S. and Ch. Shaweevongse (1957) *The Fundamentals of the Thai Language*, Bangkok.
Cantarino, V. (1974–5) *Syntax of Modern Arabic Prose*, 3 vols, Bloomington, IN, and London.
Carter, H. and G.P. Kahari (1986) *Kuverenga Chishona*, London.
Chinesisch–Deutsches Wörterbuch (1974) Beijing.
Churchward, G.M. (1953) *A Grammar of Tongan*, Oxford and London.
Churchward, S. (1951) *A New Samoan Grammar*, Melbourne.
Clark, M. (1981) *The Ao-Naga Language*, Delhi.
Clark, S.J. and E. Siahaan (1967) *Structure Drill in Indonesian*, London.
Clarke, H.D.B. and Motoko Hamamura (1981) *Colloquial Japanese*, London.
Clayton, A.C. (1939) *Introduction to Spoken Tamil*, Madras.
Collinder, B. (1957) *Survey of the Uralic Languages*, Stockholm.
Comrie, B., ed. (1987) *The World's Major Languages*, London and Sydney.
Comrie, B., B.G. Hewitt and J.R. Payne (1981) *The Languages of the Soviet Union*, Cambridge.
Conti Rossini, C. (1941) *Grammatica elementare della lingua etiopica*, Rome.
Cortade, J-M. (1969) *Essai de grammaire Touareg*, Algiers.
Coulson, M. (1976) *Teach Yourself Sanskrit*, London.
Cowan, H.K.J. (1981) 'Outline of Achehnese', *Bulletin of the School of Oriental and African Studies*, 44.
Crapo, R.H. and P. Aitken (1986) *Bolivian Quechua Reader and Grammar-Dictionary*, Ann Arbor, MI.
Crawford, J.M., ed. (1975) *Studies in South-Eastern Indian Languages*, Athens, GA.
Cruz, M. and S.P. Ignashev (1959) *Tagal'sko–Russkij Slovar'*, Moscow.
Cruz, M. and S.P. Ignashev (1965) *Russko–Tagal'skij Slovar'*, Moscow.
Cruz, M. and L.T. Škarban (1966) *Tagal'skij Jazyk*, Moscow.
Cunha, C. and L. Cintra (1985) *Breve gramática do Português contemporâneo*, Lisbon.

Dale, C. (1972) *Shona Companion*, Gweru.
Dambriūnas, L., A. Klimas and W.R. Schmalstieg (1966) *Introduction to Modern Lithuanian*, New York.
Dardjowidjojo, S. (1978) *Sentence Patterns of Indonesian*, Honolulu.
Das Gupta, B.B. (1975) *Oriya Self-Taught*, Calcutta.
De Bray, R.G.A. (1980) *Guide to the Slavonic Languages*, 3 vols, Columbus, OH.
Décsy, G. (1965) *Einführung in die Finnisch-Ugrische Sprachwissenschaft*, Wiesbaden.
Décsy, G. (1973) *Die linguistische Struktur Europas*, Wiesbaden.
Deletant, D. (1983) *Colloquial Romanian*, London.
Desbordes, Y. *Petite grammaire du Breton moderne*, Lesneven.
Dillon, M. and D. Ó Cróinín (1961) *Irish*, London.
Dirr, A. (n.d.) *Theoretisch-praktische Grammatik der Annamitischen Sprache*, Vienna.

Dixon, R.M.W. (1980) *The Languages of Australia*, Cambridge.

Diyin God Bizaad: the New Testament, Psalms and Proverbs in Navajo, (1975) New York.

D'jakonov, I.M. (1965) *Semito-Xamitskie Jazyki*, Moscow.

Dodds, R.W. (1977) *Teach Yourself Malay*, London.

Dow, F.D.M. (1984) *The Pronunciation of Chinese*, Edinburgh.

Dresden, M.J. (1958) *Reader in Modern Persian*, New York.

Dunajevskaja, I.M. (1969) *Jazyk Xettskix Ieroglifov*, Moscow.

Dunn, C.J. and S. Yamada (1958) *Teach Yourself Japanese*, London.

Dvorjankov, N.A. (1960) *Jazyk Puštu*, Moscow.

Dyen, I. (1965) *A Sketch of Trukese Grammar*, New Haven, CT.

Dyk, A. and B. Stoudt (1965) *Vocabulario Mixteco de San Miguel el Grande*, Mexico City.

Eagling, G.G. (1951) *Elementary Thai*, Bangkok.

Edel'man, D.I. (1965) *Dardskie Jazyki*, Moscow.

Egorova, R.P. (1966) *Jazyk Sindhi*, Moscow.

Einarsson, S. (1945) *Icelandic*, Baltimore.

Elanskaja, A.I. (1964) *Koptskij Jazyk*, Moscow.

Elbert, S.H. and M.P. Pukui (1979) *Hawaiian Grammar*, Honolulu.

Elements of Syriac Grammar (n.d.), London.

Elizarenkova, T.J. and V.N. Toporov (1965) *Jazyk Pali*, Moscow.

El-Solami-Mewis, C. (1987) *Lehrbuch des Somali*, Leipzig.

Elson, B. (1960) *Mayan Studies*, Norman, OK.

England, N.C. (1983) *A Grammar of Mam*, Austin, TX.

Englert, P.S. (1938) *Idioma Rapanui*, Santiago de Chile.

Englund, R. and W. Wolf (1953) *Finnische Sprachlehre*, Heidelberg.

Estones Lasa, J. (1972) *Come aprender el vasco facilmente*, San Sebastian.

Ezkila (1963) *Méthode de Basque pour débutants*, Bayonne.

Fairbanks, G.H. and E.W. Stevick (1958) *Spoken East Armenian*, New York.

Fairbanks, G.H., J.W. Gair and M.W.S. De Silva (1968) *Colloquial Sinhalese*, Ithaca, NY.

Farmakides, A. (1983) *Manual of Modern Greek, and Modern Greek Reader*, 5 vols, New Haven and London.

Febres, S.J. and P. Andres (1884) *Gramática araucana*, Buenos Aires.

Fennell, T.G. and H. Gelsen (1980) *A Grammar of Modern Latvian*, 3 vols, The Hague, Paris, New York.

Fixman, B.S. (1975) *Jazyk Igbo*, Moscow.

Fortescue, M. (1984) *West Greenlandic*, London.

Friedrich, J. (1940) *Hethitisches Elementarbuch*, Heidelberg.

Friedrich, J. (1955) *Kurze Grammatik der alten Quiché-Sprache im Popol Vuh*, Wiesbaden.

Frolova, B.A. (1960) *Beludžskij Jazyk*, Moscow.

Gabb, W. (1891–6), *Tribusy lenguas indígines de Costa Rica*, San José.

Gagkaev, K.E. (1956) *Sintaksis Osetinskogo Jazyka*, Ordzhonikidze.

Gakken (1973) *Japanese for Today*, Tokyo.

Gamkrelidze, T.V. and V.V. Ivanov (1986) *Indoevropejskij Jazyk i Indoevropejcy*, Tbilisi.

Gankin, E.B. (1969) *Amxarsko–Russkij Slovar'*, Moscow.

Gankin, E.B. and Kebbede Desta (1965) *Russko–Amxarskij Slovar'*, Moscow.

Gardiner, A. (1957) *Egyptian Grammar*, Oxford and London.

Garibay, A.M. (1978) *Llave del Náhuatl*, Mexico City.

Garibjan, A.S. and Zh.A. Garibjan (1965) *Kratkij Kurs Armjanskogo Jazyka*, Erevan.

Geoghegan, R.H. (1944) *The Aleut Language*, Washington, DC.

Gerard, A.S. (1981) *African Language Literatures*, Harlow, Essex.

Gereno, X. (1983) *Método fácil para aprender Euskara basico*, Bilbao.

Goldstein, M.C. (1973) *Modern Literary Tibetan*, Urbana, IL.

Goldstein, M.C. (1975) *Tibetan–English Dictionary of Modern Tibetan*, Kathmandu.

Goldstein, M.C. (1984) *English–Tibetan Dictionary of Modern Tibetan*, Berkeley, Los Angeles, CA; London.

Goldstein, M.C. and Nawang Nornang (1970) *Modern Spoken Tibetan: Lhasa Dialect*, Seattle and London.

Goodenough, W.H. and H. Sugita (1980) *Trukese–English Dictionary*, Philadelphia.

Goodwin, W.W. (1924) *A Greek Grammar*, London.

Goossen, I.W. (1979) *Navajo Made Easier*, Flagstaff.

Gordon, E.V. (1944) *An Introduction to Old Norse*, Oxford.

Gorgoniev, J.A. (1961) *Khmerskij Jazyk*, Moscow.

Grammatika Kabardino-čerkesskogo literaturnogo jazyka (1957) Moscow.

Green, M.M. and G.E. Igwe (1966) *Introductory Igbo Course*, London.

Gregor, D.B. (1980) *Celtic: a Comparative Study*, Cambridge and New York.

Grondin, M. (1985) *Método de Aymara*, La Paz and Cochabamba.

Guardia Mayorga, C.A. (1973) *Gramática Kechwa*, Lima.

Guasch, A. (1956) *El Idioma Guaraní*, Asunción.

Guthrie, M. (1948) *The Classification of the Bantu Languages*, London.

Guttorm, I., J. Jernsletten and K.P. Nickel (1984) *Davvin 1: Saamen kielen peruskurssi*, Helsinki.

Haas, M. (1954) *Thai Reader*, Washington, DC.

Haas, M. (1955) *Thai Vocabulary*, Washington, DC.

Haenisch, E. (1961) *Mandschu-Grammatik*, Leipzig.

Hagman, R.S. (1977) *Nama Hottentot Grammar*, Bloomington, IN.

Hahn, M. (1971) *Lehrbuch der klassischen Tibetischen Schriftsprache*, Hamburg.

Haile, B. (1937) *A Catechism and Guide, Navaho–English*, Saint Michaels, AZ.

Hajdu, P. (1963) *The Samoyed Peoples and Languages*, Bloomington, IN, and The Hague.

Hallberg, P. (1975) *Old Icelandic Poetry, Eddic Lay and Skaldic Verse*, Lincoln, NE, and London.

Halliday, M.R.A.S. (1955) *A Mon–English Dictionary*, Rangoon.

Hammer, A.E. (1971) *German Grammar and Usage*, London.

Hangin, J.G. (1968) *Basic Course in Mongolian*, Bloomington, IN, and The Hague.

Hangin, J.G. (1970) *A Concise English–Mongolian Dictionary*, Bloomington, IN, and The Hague.

Hangin, J.G. (1973) *Intermediate Mongolian*, Bloomington, IN, and The Hague.

Hanoteau, A. (1890) *La Langue Tamachek*, Algiers.

Harries, J. (1974) *Tamazight Basic Course*, Washington, DC.

Harrison, R.K. (1955) *Biblical Hebrew*, London.

Harter, J.M., J. Chadran and A.S. Poeraatmadja (1968) *Indonesian Newspaper Reader*, Washington, DC.

Haugen, E. and K.G. Chapman (1964) *Spoken Norwegian*, New York.

Hawkesworth, C. (1986) *Colloquial Serbo-Croat*, London.

Haywood, J.A. and H.M. Nahmad (1965) *A New Arabic Grammar*, London.

Healey, J.F. (1980) *First Studies in Syriac*, Sheffield.

Hebert, R.J. and N. Poppe. *Kirghiz Manual*, Bloomington, IN, and The Hague.

Herrfurth, H. (1964) *Lehrbuch des modernen Djawanisch*, Leipzig.

Herzenberg, A.G. (1965) *Xotano-Sakskij Jazyk*, Moscow.

Hewitt, B.G. (1979) *Abkhaz*, London.

Hives, H.E. (1948) *A Cree Grammar*, Toronto.

Hoffmann, C. (1963) *A Grammar of Margi*, Oxford and London.

Hoffmann, J. (1903) *A Grammar of Mundari*, Calcutta.

Hohenwart-Gerlachstein, A. (1979) *Nubienforschungen*, Vienna.

Hojier, H., ed. (1946) *Linguistic Structures of Native America*, New York.

Holmes, N. (1954) *The Seneca Language*, Upsala and Copenhagen.

Holmes, R.B. and B.S. Smith (1976) *Beginning Cherokee*, Norman, OK.

Horden, J. (1881) *A Grammar of the Cree Language*, London.

Hoshino, T. and R. Marcus (1981) *Lao for Beginners*, Rutland, VT, and Tokyo.

Householder, F.W. and M. Lotfi (1965) *Basic Course in Azerbaijani*, Bloomington, IN, and The Hague.

Hudson, D.F. (1965) *Bengali*, London.

Huffman, F.E. (1970) *Modern Spoken Cambodian*, New Haven and London.

Huffman, F.E. (1970) *Cambodian System of Writing and Beginning Reader*, New Haven and London.

Humesky, A. (1986) *Modern Ukrainian*, Edmonton and Toronto.

Ikeda, T. (1975) *Classical Japanese Grammar Illustrated with Texts*, Tokyo.

Ingamells, L. and P. Standish (1975) *Variedades del Español actual*, London.

Innes, G. (1971) *A Practical Introduction to Mende*, London.

Issa, A.A. and J.D. Murphy (1984) *Somali Newspaper Reader*, Kensington, MD.

Ivanov, V.V. (1963) *Khettskij jazyk*, Moscow.

Ivanov, V.V. and V.N. Toporov (1960) *Sanskrit*, Moscow.

JaAA, see *Jazyki Azii i Afriki*.

Jacob, J.M. (1968) *Introduction to Cambodian*, London.

JaNSSSR, see *Jazyki Narodov SSSR*.

Jäschke, H.A. (1968) *Tibetan–English Dictionary*, London.

Jazyki Azii i Afriki (1976–9) 3 vols, Moscow.

Jazyki Narodov SSSR (1966–8) 5 vols, Moscow.

Jelinek, J. (1978) *Reader in Scientific and Technical Japanese*, Sheffield.

Jensen, H. (1969) *Grammatik der Kanaresischen Schriftsprache*, Leipzig.

Jestin, R. (1951) *Abrégé de grammaire sumérienne*, Paris.

Joest, W. (1883) *Zur Holontalo-Sprache*, Berlin.

Johns, Y. (1977–81) *Bahasa Indonesia*, 2 vols, Canberra.

Jones, P.V. and K.C. Sidwell (1978) *Reading Greek*, 2 vols, Cambridge.

Jones, P.V. and K.C. Sidwell (1986) *Reading Latin*, 2 vols, Cambridge.

Jones, R.B. (1961) *Karen Linguistic Studies*, Berkeley, CA.
Jonsson, S. (1927) *A Primer of Modern Icelandic*, London.
Jothimuththu, P. (1965) *A Guide to Tamil*, Madras.
Jover-Peralta, A. and T. Osuna (1951) *Diccionario Guaraní–Español y Español–Guaraní*, Buenos Aires.

Kachru, B.B. (1969) *A Reference Grammar of Kashmiri*, Urbana, IL.
Kardanov, B.M., ed. (1957) *Kabardinsko– Russkij Slovar'*, Moscow.
Kardanov, B.M. and A.T. Bičoev (1955) *Russko–Kabardinsko–Čerkesskij Slovar'*, Moscow.
Karpuškin, B.M. (1964) *Jazyk Oriya*, Moscow.
Kaschube, D.V. (1967) *Structural Elements of the Language of the Crow Indians of Montana*, Boulder, CO.
Katenina, T.E. (1963) *Jazyk Marathi*, Moscow.
Kebede, M. and J.D. Murphy (1984) *Amharic Newspaper Reader*, Kensington, MD.
Kennedy, B.H. (1962) *Revised Latin Primer*, London.
Kersten, J. (1948) *Balische gramatica*, The Hague.
Kintana, X. and J. Tobar (1977) *Euskal Hiztegi modernoa*, Bilbao.
Klein, H.E.M. and L.R. Stark, eds (1985) *South American Indian Languages*, Austin, TX.
Klimov, G.A. and D.I. Edel'man (1970) *Jazyk Burušaski*, Moscow.
Kneen, J.J. (1931) *A Manx Grammar*, Oxford.
Koçi, R.D., A. Kostallari and D. Skendi (1951) *Albansko–Russkij Slovar'*, Moscow.
Koefoed, H.A. (1958) *Teach Yourself Danish*, London.
Kollar, D., V. Dorotjakova, M. Filkusová and E. Vasilievová (1976) *Slovatsko–Russkij Slovar'*, Moscow and Bratislava.
Koolhoven, H. (1941) *Teach Yourself Dutch*, London.
Konstantinova, O.A. (1964) *Evenkijskij jazyk*, Moscow.
Kopecký, L.V., J. Filipec and O. Leška (1973) *Česko–Ruský Slovník*, 2 vols, Moscow and Prague.
Korigodskij, R.N., O.N. Kondraškin and B.J. Zinov'iev (1961) *Indonezijsko–Russkij Slovar'*, Moscow.
Korolev, N.I. (1965) *Jazyk Nepali*, Moscow.
Korostovtsev, M.A. (1961) *Egipetskij jazyk*, Moscow.
Kosack, W. (1974) *Lehrbuch der Koptischen Sprache*, Graz.
Kosambi, D.D. (1965) *The Culture and Civilisation of Ancient India*, London.
Koshal, S. (1979) *Ladakhi Grammar*, Delhi.
Koski, A.A. and I. Mihályfy (1962–4) *Hungarian Basic Course*, 2 vols, Washington, DC.
Kraft, C.H. and H.M. Kirk-Greene (1973) *Teach Yourself Hausa*, London.
Krahe, H. (1966) *Indogermanische Sprachwissenschaft*, 2 vols, Berlin.
Kratochvil, P. (1968) *The Chinese Language Today*, London.
Krause, W. and W. Thomas (1960–4) *Tocharisches Elementarbuch*, 2 vols, Heidelberg.
Kreemer, J. (1931) *Atjèhsch Handwoordenboek*, Leiden.
Krenn, E. (1940) *Föroyische Sprachlehre*, Heidelberg.
Krishnamurti, B.H. and J.P.L. Gwynn (1985) *A Grammar of Modern Telugu*, Delhi.
Krjukov, M.V. (1973) *Jazyk In'skix Nadpisej*, Moscow.
Krjukov, M.V. and Huan Su-yin (1978) *Drevnekitajskij jazyk*, Moscow.
Krupa, V. (1967) *Jazyk Maori*, Moscow.

Krupa, V. (1982) *The Polynesian Languages*, London.
Kuipers, A.H. (1967–9) *The Squamish Language*, 2 vols, The Hague.
Kurkjian, H. (1973) *Manuel pratique de la langue arménienne occidentale*, Beirut.

La Grasserie, R. de (1898) *Langue Auca*, Paris.
Lambert, H.M. (1971) *Gujarati Language Course*, Cambridge.
Lambertz, M. (1954–9) *Lehrgang des Albanischen*, 3 vols, Berlin and Halle.
Lambkin, T.O. (1973) *Introduction to Biblical Hebrew*, London.
Lambton, A.K.S. (1967) *Persian Grammar*, Cambridge.
Lau, S. (1972) *Intermediate Cantonese*, Hong Kong.
Lavrent'ev, B.P. and S.V. Neverov (1975) *Russko–Japonskij Razgovornik*, Moscow.
Legge, J., ed. and trans. (1893–5) *The Four Books*, Oxford (1st edn 1861).
Lemos Barbosa, A. (1956) *Curso de Tupí antigo*, Rio and São Paulo.
Leont'ev, A.A. (1974) *Papuasskie jazyki*, Moscow.
Lepsius, R. (1880) *Nubische Grammatik*, Berlin.
Leslau, W. (1941) *Documents tigrigna (éthiopien septentrional) grammaire et textes*, Paris.
Leslau, W. (1965) *An Amharic Conversation Book*, Wiesbaden.
Leslau, W. (1967) *Amharic Textbook*, Wiesbaden.
Leslau, W. (1973) *English–Amharic Context Dictionary*, Wiesbaden.
Levy, H. (1953) *Hebrew for All*, London.
Lewis, G.L. (1967) *Turkish Grammar*, Oxford and London.
Lim Hak Kheang and D. Purtle (1972) *Contemporary Cambodian*, Washington, DC.
Lipin, L.A. (1964) *Akkadskij jazyk*, Moscow.
Lisker, L. (1963) *Introduction to Spoken Telugu*, New York.
Lockwood, W.B. (1969) *Indo-European Philology*, London.
Lockwood, W.B. (1972) *A Panorama of Indo-European Languages*, London.
Lorenz, M. (1982) *Lehrbuch des Pashto (Afghanisch)*, Leipzig.
Lowie, R.H. (1941) *The Crow Language*, Berkeley and Los Angeles, CA.
Luvsandendev, A. (1957) *Mongol'sko–Russkij Slovar'*, Moscow.
Lytkin, V.I. (1952) *Drevnepermskij jazyk*, Moscow.

McCarus, E.N. and A.I. Yacoub (1962) *Newspaper Arabic*, Ann Arbor, MI.
McClain, Y.M. (1973) *Intermediate Japanese Reading Aids*, Tokyo.
McClure, H.D. and J.O. Oyewale (1967) *Yoruba Intermediate Texts*, Washington, DC.
Macdonald, J.A. (1976) *Gaidhlig Bheo*, 3 vols, Cambridge.
Macdonell, A.A. (1917) *A Vedic Reader for Students*, Oxford and London.
Macdonell, A.A. (1924) *Sanskrit Dictionary*, Oxford and London.
Macdonell, A.A. (1927) *A Sanskrit Grammar for Students*, Oxford and London.
McGregor, R.S. (1972) *Outline of Hindi Grammar*, Oxford and London.
M'ačina, E.N. (1960) *Jazyk Suahili*, Moscow.
Mackinnon, R. (1971) *Teach Yourself Gaelic*, London.
Magometov, A.A. (1970) *Agul'skij jazyk*, Tbilisi.
Makarova, H.I., L.M. Palamar and N.K. Prisjažnjuk (1975) *Learn Ukrainian*, Kiev.
Man, E.H. (1888) *A Dictionary of the Central Nicobarese Language, with Notes on Grammar*, London.
Mann, S.E. (1932) *Albanian Grammar*, London.
Maun Maun N'un, J.A. Orlova, E.V. Puzitskij and J.M. Tagunova (1963) *Birmanskij jazyk*, Moscow.

Mansurov, R.I. and I.A. Kissen (1953) *Uzbek tili*, Tashkent.

Mardin, Y. (1976) *Colloquial Turkish*, London.

Marsack, T.Y. (1962) *Teach Yourself Samoan*, London.

Martin, S.E. (1954) *Essential Japanese*, Rutland, VT.

Martin, S.E. (1975) *A Reference Grammar of Japanese*, New Haven and London.

Martinet, A. (1986) *Des Steppes aux océans*, Paris.

Matthes, B.F. (1858) *Makassarsche spraakkunst*, Amsterdam.

Matthews, D. (1984) *A Course in Nepali*, London.

Matthews, W.K. (1953) *The Structure and Development of Russian*, Cambridge.

Mayers, M.K., ed. (1966) *Languages of Guatemala*, The Hague.

Mayo, P.T. (1976) *A Grammar of Byelorussian*, Sheffield.

Mays, E. and W. Morgan (1957) *Talking Navajo before You Know It*, Window Rock, AZ.

Mazur, B.W. (1983) *Colloquial Polish*, London.

Mazur, J.N. (1960) *Korejskij jazyk*, Moscow.

Meinhof, C. (1906) *Grundzüge einer vergleichenden Grammatik der Bantusprachen*, Berlin.

Meliá Lliteras, B., A. Pérez Peñasco and L. Farré Malaquar (1960) *El Guaraní a su alcance*, Asunción.

Melikišvili, G.A. (1964) *Urartskij jazyk*, Moscow.

Middendorf, E.W. (1890) *Die einheimischen Sprachen Perus*, 6 vols, Leipzig.

Miettunen, G. (1968) *Abbes*, Pieksämäki.

Miller, R.A. (1967) *The Japanese Language*, Chicago and London.

Milne, L. (1921) *An Elementary Palaung Grammar*, Oxford and London.

Milner, G.B. (1972) *Fijian Grammar*, Suva.

Minassian, M. (1976) *Manuel pratique d'arménien ancien*, Paris.

Mintz, M.W. (1971) *Bikol Text*, Honolulu.

Mironov, S.A. (1969) *Jazyk Afrikaans*, Moscow.

Mitterrutzner, J.C. (1866) *Die Dinka-Sprache in Central-Africa*, Brixen.

Monteil, V. (1960) *L'Arabe moderne*, Paris.

Moreno, M.M. (1939) *Grammatica teorico-practica della lingua Galla*, Rome.

Morev, L.N., J.J. Plam and M.F. Fomičeva (1961) *Tajskij jazyk*, Moscow.

Morev, L.N., A.A. Moskalev and J.J. Plam (1972) *Laosskij jazyk*, Moscow.

Morvannon, F. (1975) *Le Breton sans peine*, London.

Moscati, S., A. Spitaler, E. Ullendorff and W. von Soden (1980) *Introduction to the Comparative Grammar of the Semitic Languages*, Wiesbaden.

Moshiri, L. (1988) *Colloquial Persian*, London.

Moussay, G. (1981) *La Langue Minangkebau*, Paris.

Mudra J. and J. Petr (1983) *Učebnik Verxne-Lužitskogo jazyka*, Bautzen.

Nadžip, E.N. (1960) *Sovremennyj Ujgurskij jazyk*, Moscow.

Nagaraja, K.G. (1985) *Khasi: a Descriptive Analysis*, Pune, Deccan.

Nasilov, V.M. (1963) *Drevne-Ujgurskij jazyk*, Moscow.

Nemec, J. (1947) *Grammatica della lingua slovena*, Gorizia.

New Redhouse Turkish–English Dictionary (1968), Istanbul.

Newman, S. (1965) *Zuni Grammar*, Albuquerque, NM.

Newark, L., I. Haznedari, P. Hubbard and P. Prifti (1980) *Spoken Albanian*, New York.

Nguyen Dang Liem (1971) *Intermediate Vietnamese*, South Orange, NJ.

Nguyen-Dinh-Hoa (1966) *Speak Vietnamese*, Rutland, VT, and Tokyo.

Nguyen-Dinh-Hoa (1966) *Read Vietnamese*, Rutland, VT, and Tokyo.

Nicklas, T.D. (1975) 'Choctaw Morphophonemics', in J.M. Crawford (ed.), *Studies in South-Eastern Indian Languages*, Athens, GA.

Norbait (n.d.) *Método audio-oral de Euskara básico*, San Sebastian.

Noss, R.B. (1964) *Thai Reference Grammar*, Washington, DC.

Noss, R.B. and Im Proum (1966–70) *Cambodian Basic Course*, Washington, DC.

Nussbaum, L.V., W.W. Gage and D. Varre (1970) *Dakar Wolof; Basic Course*, Washington, DC.

Nyberg, H.S. (1964–74) *A Manual of Pahlavi*, 2 vols, Wiesbaden.

Obolensky, S., D. Zelelie and M. Andualem (1964) *Amharic Basic Course*, Washington, DC.

Oinas, F.J. (1963) *Estonian General Reader*, Bloomington, IN.

Oinas, F.J. (1966) *Basic Course in Estonian*, Bloomington, IN.

Okell, J. (1969) *Reference Grammar of Colloquial Burmese*, Oxford and London.

Okhotina, I.M. (1961) *Jazyk Zulu*, Moscow.

Onatibia, J. (1973) *Método de Euskera radiofonico*, San Sebastian.

O'Neill, P.G. (1966) *Respect Language in Modern Japanese*, London.

O'Neill, P.G. (1968) *A Programmed Introduction to Literary-style Japanese*, London.

Oranskij, I.M. (1963) *Iranskie jazyki*, Moscow.

Orvidienė, E. (1968) *Lietuvių kalbos vadovėlis*, Vilnius.

Owens, J. (1985) *A Grammar of Harar Oromo*, Hamburg.

Pakhalina, T.N. (1969) *Pamirskie jazyki*, Moscow.

Panfilov, V.Z. (1962–5) *Grammatika Nivkhskogo jazyka*, 2 vols, Moscow and Leningrad.

Papp, I. (1967) *Finn Nyelvkönyv*, Budapest.

Parfinovič, J.M. (1970) *Tibetskij pis'mennyj jazyk*, Moscow.

Park, B. Nam (1968–9) *Korean Basic Course*, 2 vols, Washington, DC.

Paroz, R.A. (1946) *Elements of Southern Sotho*, Morija, Basutoland.

Paskov, B.K. (1963) *Man'čzhurskij jazyk*, Moscow.

Paterson, J.M. (1952–67) *Gaelic Made Easy*, 4 vols, Glasgow.

Patkaniowska, M. (1944) *Essentials of Polish Grammar*, Glasgow.

Pavlenko, A.P. (1965) *Sundanskij jazyk*, Moscow.

Pedersen, K.T. (1973) *Grønlandsk for Begyndere*, Copenhagen.

Penny, B. and K.T. Malinowska (1974) *Communicating in Polish*, Washington, DC.

Perevoščikov, P.N. (1956) 'Kratkij očerk grammatiki udmurtskogo jazyka', in *Udmurtsko-Russkij Slovar'*, Moscow.

Perrott, D.V. (1951) *Swahili*, London.

Perroud, C. (1961) *Gramatica Quechua*, Lima.

Petruničeva, Z.N. (1960) *Jazyk Telugu*, Moscow.

Petter, R. (1952) *Cheyenne Grammar*, Newton, KS.

Pfiffig, A.J. (1969) *Die Etruskische Sprache*, Graz.

Pharr, C. (1959) *Homeric Greek*, Norman, OK.

Pipa, F. (n.d.) *Elementary Albanian*, Rome.

Pjall', I.E. (1955) *Učebnik Estonskogo jazyka*, Tallinn.

Pjatigorskij, A.M. and S.G. Rudin (1960) *Tamil'sko-Russkij Slovar'*, Moscow.

Pokorny, J. (1969) *Altirische Grammatik*, Berlin.

Pope, G.U. (1911) *A Handbook of the Ordinary Dialect of the Tamil Language*, Oxford.

Poppe, N. (1962) *Uzbek Newspaper Reader*, Bloomington, IN.

Poppe, N. (1964) *Bashkir Manual*, Bloomington, IN.
Poppe, N. (1964) *Grammar of Written Mongolian*, Wiesbaden.
Portman, M.V. (1898) *Notes on the Languages of the South Andaman Group of Islands*, Calcutta.
Pragnell, F.A. (1984) *A Week in the Middle East*, London.
Press, I. (1986) *A Grammar of Modern Breton*, The Hague.
Průšek, J., ed. (1974) *Dictionary of Oriental Literatures*, 3 vols, London.
Puglielli, A., ed. (1981) *Studi Somali, 2: Sintassi della lingua Somali*, Rome.
Puzitskij, E.V. (1968) *Kačinskij jazyk*, Moscow.

Quin, E.G. (1975) *Old Irish Workbook*, Dublin.
Quirk, R. and C.L. Wrenn (1957) *An Old English Grammar*, London.

Rabel, L. (1961) *Khasi, a Language of Assam*, Baton Rouge, LA.
Radhakrishnan, S. (1950) *The Dhammapada*, Oxford and London.
Radovicka, L., Z. Karapici and A. Toma (1981) *Gjuha Shqipe*, vol. 3, Tirana.
Ramanujan, A.K. (1970) *The Interior Landscape*, London.
Rambaud, J.-B. (1903) *La Langue Wolof*, Paris.
Ramos, T.V. (1971) *Tagalog Structures*, Honolulu.
Ramsey, S.R. (1987) *The Languages of China*, Princeton.
Ranisch, W. (1903) *Eddalieder*, Leipzig.
Rapp, E.L. (1966) *Die Gurenne-Sprache in Nordghana*, Leipzig.
Rastorgueva, V.S. (1966) *Sredne-persidskij jazyk*, Moscow.
Raun, A. (1969) *Basic Course in Uzbek*, Bloomington, IN.
Raz, S. (1983) *Tigre Grammar and Texts*, Malibu.
Read, A.F.C. (1934) *Balti Grammar*, London.
Redden, J.E. *et al.* (1963) *Twi Basic Course*, Washington, DC.
Refsing, K. (1986) *The Ainu Language*, Aarhus.
Reichard, G.A. (1951) *Navaho Grammar*, New York.
Reif, J.A. and H. Levinson (1965) *Hebrew Basic Course*, Washington, DC.
Reynolds, C.H.B. (1980) *Sinhalese*, London.
Rhys-Jones, J.J. (1977) *Living Welsh*, London.
Richter, E. (1983) *Lehrbuch des modernen Burmesisch*, Lepizig.
Richter, R. (1987) *Lehrbuch der Amharischen Sprache*, Leipzig.
Riemschneider, K.K. (1969) *Lehrbuch des Akkadischen*, Leipzig.
Riggs, S.R. (1893, repr. 1973) *Dakota Grammar*, Minneapolis, MN.
Rinchin, A.R. (1952) *Učebnik Mongol'skogo jazyka*, Moscow.
Rasen, H.B. (1966) *A Textbook of Israeli Hebrew*, Chicago and London.
Rosenhagen, G. (1929) *Vom Mittelalter zur Neuzeit*, Leipzig and Berlin.
Rosenthal, F. (1961) *Grammar of Biblical Aramaic*, Wiesbaden.
Rowlands, E.C. (1969) *Teach Yourself Yoruba*, London.

Safioedin, A. (1977) *Kamus Bahasa Madura-Indonesia*, Jakarta.
Saguier, E. (1951) *El Idioma Guaraní*, Buenos Aires.
Saidov, M. (1967) *Avarsko–Russkij Slovar'*, Moscow.
Saltarelli, M. (1988) *Basque*, London.
Salzmann, Z. (1956, 1965) 'Arapaho: Texts'; 'Arapaho: Noun', *International Journal of American Linguistics*, 22, 31, 33.

Sansom, G.B. (1928) *An Historical Grammar of Japanese*, Oxford and London.

Sanžeev, G.D. (1964) *Staro-pis'mennyj mongol'skij jazyk*, Moscow.

Šára, M., J. Šárová and A. Bytel (1970) *Čestina pro cizince*, Prague.

Sarumpaet, J.P. and H. Hendrata (1968) *A Modern Reader in Bahasa Indonesia*, Melbourne.

Šastri, K.M. (1985) *Descriptive Grammar and Handbook of Modern Telugu*, Stuttgart.

Savel'eva, L.V. (1965) *Jazyk Gudzharati*, Moscow.

Savel'eva, V.N. and C.M. Taksani (1965) *Russko–Nivkhskij Slovar'*, Moscow.

Schmalstieg, W.R. (1983) *Introduction to Old Church Slavonic*, Columbus, OH.

Schmaus, A. (1964) *Lehrbuch der Serbokroatischen Sprache*, Munich and Belgrade.

Schmidt, W. (1952) *Die Tasmanischen Sprachen*, Utrecht and Antwerp.

Schultze, L.S. (1933–8) *Indiana*, 3 vols, Jena.

Schütz, A.J. and R.T. Komaitai (1971) *Spoken Fijian*, Honolulu.

Sedláček, K. (1972) *Tibetan Newspaper Reader*, 2 vols, Leipzig.

Segert, S. (1965) *Ugaritskij jazyk*, Moscow.

Sekhar, C. and J.J. Glazov (1961) *Jazyk Malayalam*, Moscow.

Serdjučenko, G.P. (1961) *Čžuanskij jazyk*, Moscow.

Ševoroškin, V.V. (1967) *Lidijskij jazyk*, Moscow.

Shackle, C. (1972) *Teach Yourself Punjabi*, London.

Shetter, W.Z. (1984) *Introduction to Dutch*, Leiden.

Shorto, H.L. (1971) *A Dictionary of the Mon Inscriptions from VI to XVI Century*, Oxford and London.

Šifman, I.S. (1963) *Finikijskij jazyk*, Moscow.

Simon, W. and T.C. Chao (1945) *Structure Drill in Chinese*, London.

Sirk, J.X. (1975) *Bugijskij jazyk*, Moscow.

Smirnov, J.A. (1970) *Jazyk Lendi*, Moscow.

Smirnova, M.A. (1960) *Jazyk Khausa*, Moscow.

Snell, R. and S. Weightman (1989) *Teach Yourself Hindi*, London.

Snyman, J.W. (1970) *Introduction to the !Xũ–!Kung Language*, Cape Town.

Sobol'eva, V.S. *et al.* (1988) *Russko–Laosskij i Laossko–Russkij Razgovornik*, Moscow.

Sofronov, M.V. (1968) *Grammatika Tangutskogo jazyka*, 2 vols, Moscow.

Sokolov, S.N. (1961) *Avestijskij jazyk*, Moscow.

Sommerfelt, A. (1943) *Norwegian*, London.

Soto Ruiz, C. (1979) *Quechua: Manual de enseñanza*, Lima.

Starinin, V.P. *Efiopskij jazyk*, Moscow.

Ştefănescu-Drăgăneşti, V. and M. Murrell (1970) *Teach Yourself Romanian*, London.

Stetkevych, J. (1970) *The Modern Arabic Literary Language*, Chicago and London.

Suarez, J.A. (1983) *The Mesoamerican Indian Languages*, Cambridge.

Sulaiman Budiman (1979) *Bahasa Aceh*, Jakarta.

Stokmans, W.J.E. and J.C.P. Marinissen (1880) *Handleiding tot de beoefening der Madoereesche Taal met Woordenboek*, Surabaya.

Strang, B.M. (1970) *A History of English*, London.

Subrahmanyam, P.S. (1968) *A Descriptive Grammar of Gondi*, Annamalainagar.

Sweet, H. (1891) *New English Grammar*, Oxford and London.

Swift, L.B. and S. Ağralı (1966–8) *Turkish Basic Course*, 2 vols, Washington, DC.

Sylvain, S. (1936) *Le Créole Haitien*, Wetteren and Port-au-Prince.

Syromjatnikov, N.A. (1972) *Drevnejaponskij jazyk*, Moscow.

Syromjatnikov, N.A. (1978) *Razvitie Novojaponskogo jazyka*, Moscow.

Szemerényi, O. (1980) *Einführung in die vergleichende Sprachwissenschaft*, Darmstadt.

Talibov, B.B. and M.M. Gadžiev (1966) *Lezginsko–Russkij Slovar'*, Moscow.

Taraporevala, I.J.S. (1940) *Zarathoshti Daily Prayers*, Bombay.

Taylor, F.W. (1953) *A Grammar of Fulani*, Oxford and London.

Teselkin, A.S. (1961) *Javanskij jazyk*, Moscow.

Teselkin, A.S. (1963) *Drevne-javanskij jazyk*, Moscow.

Teselkin, A.S. and N.F. Alieva (1960) *Indonezijskij jazyk*, Moscow.

Thomson, R.W. (1975) *Introduction to Classical Armenian*, New York.

Till, W.C. (1970) *Koptische Grammatik*, Leipzig.

Tims, J.W. (1889) *Grammar and Dictionary of the Blackfoot Language*, London.

Titov, E.G. (1971) *Sovremennyj Amxarskij jazyk*, Moscow.

Todaeva, B.X. (1960) *Mongol'skie jazyki i dialekty Kitaja*, Moscow.

Tolstaja, N.I. (1960) *Jazyk Pandžabi*, Moscow.

Tomulić, R. (1984) *Manuel de Tibétain, parler de Lhasa*, Paris.

Toporova, I.N. (1973) *Jazyk Lingala*, Moscow.

Toporova, I.N. (1983) *Lingala–Russkij Slovar'*, Moscow.

Topping, D.M. (1969) *Spoken Chamorro*, Honolulu.

Tozzer, A.M. (1921) *A Maya Grammar*, Cambridge, MA.

Tritton, A.S. (1943) *Teach Yourself Arabic*, London.

Tryon, D.T. (1970) *Conversational Tahitian*, Berkeley and Los Angeles, CA.

Tschenkeli, K. (1958) *Einführung in die Georgische Sprache*, 2 vols, Zürich.

Tsereteli, K.G. (1964) *Sovremennyj Assirijskij jazyk*, Moscow.

Tsereteli, K.G. (1979) *Sirijskij jazyk*, Moscow.

Tsintsius, V.I. and L.D. Rišes (1952) *Russko–Evenskij Slovar'*, Moscow.

T'ung, P.C. and D.E. Pollard (1982) *Colloquial Chinese*, London.

Uehara, T. and G.N. Kiyose (1974) *Fundamentals of Japanese*, Bloomington, IN, London and Tokyo.

Uhle, M. and A. Kelm (1968) *Vom Kondor und vom Fuchs*, Berlin.

Uhlenbeck. C.C. (1938) *Concise Grammar of Blackfoot*, Amsterdam.

Urioste-Herrero, S.I. (1955) *Gramática y vocabulario de la lengua Quechua*, La Paz and Cochabamba.

Usatov, D.M., J.N. Mazur and V.M. Mozdykov (1954) *Russko–Korejskij Slovar'*, Moscow.

Valdivia, L. de (1606, repr. 1887) *Arte y vocabulario de la lengua de Chile*, Lima.

Valfells, S. and J.E. Cathey (1981) *Old Icelandic: an Introductory Course*, Oxford and London.

Van der Tuuk, H.N. (1864–7, trans. and repr. 1971) *A Grammar of Toba-Batak*, The Hague.

Vasil'evič, G.M. (1958) *Evenkijsko–Russkij Slovar'*, Moscow.

Ventcel', T.V. (1964) *Tsyganskij jazyk (severnorusskij dialekt)*, Moscow.

Vietze, H.-P. (1963) *Deutsch–Mongolisches Gesprächsbuch*, Leipzig.

Vietze, H.-P. (1969) *Lehrbuch der Mongolischen Sprache*, Leipzig.

Vil'sker, L.H. (1974) *Samaritanskij jazyk*, Moscow.

Vyxuxolev, V.V. (1974) *Singal'skij jazyk*, Moscow.

Wallis Budge, E.A. (1978) *Egyptian Language*, London.
Wang, F.F. (1967) *Mandarin Chinese Dictionary*, South Orange, NJ.
Ward, I.C. (1933) *The Phonetic and Tonal Structure of Efik*, Cambridge.
Warder, A.K. (1984) *Introduction to Pali*, London.
Watkins, E.A. (1865, ed. R. Faries, 1938) *A Dictionary of the Cree Language*, Toronto.
Wauchope, R., ed. (1967) *Handbook of Middle American Indians*, vol. 5, Austin, TX.
Wehr, H. (1971, ed. J. Milton Cowan) *Dictionary of Modern Written Arabic*, Wiesbaden and London.
Welmers, W.E. (1968) *Efik*, Ibadan.
Westermann, D.A. (1910?) *A Short Grammar of the Shilluk Language*, Berlin.
Westermann, D.A. (1930) *A Study of the Ewe Language*, Oxford and London.
Westermann, D.A. and H.J. Melzian (1930) *The Kpelle Language in Liberia*, Berlin.
Whittaker, M. (1969) *New Testament Greek Grammar*, 2 vols, London.
Williams, S.J. (1980) *A Welsh Grammar*, Cardiff.
Willis, R.C. (1971) *An Essential Course in Modern Portuguese*, London.
Wilson, P.M. (1985) *Simplified Swahili*, London.
Witter, W.E. (1888) *Outline Grammar of the Lhota-Naga Language*, Calcutta.
Wolfart, H.C. and J.F. Carroll (1981) *Meet Cree*, Edmonton.
Woolner, A.C. (1928) *Introduction to Prakrit*, Delhi.
Wowčerk, P. (1954) *Kurzgefasste Obersorbische Grammatik*, Berlin.
Wright, J. (1954) *Grammar of the Gothic Language*, Oxford and London.

Yakovleva, I.P. (1961) *Jazyk Ganda*, Moscow.
Yakovleva, V.K. (1963) *Jazyk Yoruba*, Moscow.
Yates, A. (1975) *Teach Yourself Catalan*, London.
Yaxontov, S.E. (1965) *Drevne-Kitajskij jazyk*, Moscow.
Young, R.W. and W. Morgan (1948) *The Function and Signification of Certain Navaho Particles*, Phoenix, AZ.
Young, R.W. and W. Morgan (1976) *The Navaho Language*, Salt Lake City.
Yuan Jia-Hua (1965) *Dialekty Kitajskogo Jazyka*, Moscow.

Zavadovskij, J.N. (1967) *Berberskij jazyk*, Moscow.
Zavadovskij. J.N. and I.S. Katsnel'son (1980) *Meroitskij jazyk*, Moscow.
Zavala, M. (1896) *Gramatica maya*, Merida de Yucatan.
Zawawi, S. (1971) *Kiswahili kwa Kitendo*, New York and London.
Zaxar'in, B.A. and D.I. Edel'man (1971) *Jazyk Kašmiri*, Moscow.
Zbavitel, D. (1953) *Učebnice Bengálštiny*, Prague.
Zhirkov, L.I. (1955) *Lakskij jazyk*, Moscow.
Ziegler, F. (1920) *Practical Key to the Kanarese Language*, Mangalore.
Zograph, G.A. (1976) *Morfologiceskij stroj novyx indoarijskix jazykov*, Moscow.
Zograph, G.A. (1982) *The Languages of South Asia*, London.
Zograph, I.T. (1979) *Srednekitajskij jazyk*, Moscow.
Zurbuchen, M.S. (1976) *Introduction to Old Javanese Language and Literature*, Ann Arbor, MI.
Zyhlarz, E. (1928) *Grundzüge der nubischen Grammatik im Christlichen Frühmittelalter (Altnubisch)*, Leipzig.